You Are Not Alone

Also by Clara Claiborne Park

The Siege: The First Eight Years of an Autistic Child

You Are Not Alone

Understanding and Dealing with Mental Illness

A Guide for Patients, Families, Doctors and Other Professionals

by

Clara Claiborne Park

with

Leon N. Shapiro, M.D.

Professor of Psychiatry, Cornell University Medical College
Medical Director, New York Hospital, Westchester Division

An Atlantic Monthly Press Book

Little, Brown and Company Boston | Toronto

FIRST EDITION

T 05/76

"Requiem for Agnews State" by Richard Gardner reprinted from *Madness Network News Reader,* Sherry Hirsch, et al., San Francisco: Glide Publications, 1974.

Grateful acknowledgment is made to Richard I. Shader, M.D., who gave us access to proofs of his *Manual of Psychiatric Therapeutics: Practical Psychopharmacology and Psychiatry* (Boston: Little, Brown, 1975).

The "Dear Abby" letter signed "Princess" is reprinted with the permission of Abigail Van Buren.

The excerpt from Manfred Bleuler's article, "The Offspring of Schizophrenics," Spring 1974 issue of *Schizophrenia Bulletin,* is reprinted with the permission of the Department of Health, Education, and Welfare and the National Institute of Mental Health.

Library of Congress Cataloging in Publication Data
Park, Clara Claiborne.
You are not alone.

"An Atlantic Monthly Press book."
Bibliography: p.
Includes index.
1. Psychiatry. 2. Mental health services.
3. Mental health laws. 4. Insurance, Mental health.
5. Consumer education. I. Shapiro, Leon N., joint author. II. Title.
RC454.4.P37 362.2 76-3423
ISBN 0-316-69073-2

ATLANTIC–LITTLE, BROWN BOOKS
ARE PUBLISHED BY
LITTLE, BROWN AND COMPANY
IN ASSOCIATION WITH
THE ATLANTIC MONTHLY PRESS

Published simultaneously in Canada
by Little, Brown & Company (Canada) Limited

PRINTED IN THE UNITED STATES OF AMERICA

TO

Elizabeth Faragoh

Hattie Mandelbaum

Bernie Rimland

Lorna and John Wing

Ruth Sullivan

Chris Griffith

Rosalind Oppenheim

Margaret Dewey

Victor Winston

Denise Ribadeau-Dumas

Denise and Jean Roulet

Rosemarie Daum

John Pringle

Joan Curtis

James and Nancy Wechsler

and to the countless other indomitable ones,

known and unknown, in many lands,

who have learned to make of their pain

an instrument to help others.

Acknowledgments

This is a book that grew, not out of research alone, but out of the lived and living experience of many people. The names that follow include those of concerned citizens and dedicated state officials, of psychiatrists and other physicians, of psychologists, social workers, nurses, paraprofessionals, teachers, and of others who have contributed knowledge not professional but deeply personal. They are all mixed up together; those who read the book will see that that is as it should be. Their contributions are too various to describe or classify; they can only be gratefully acknowledged.

Thanks to:

Eve Grantham Auchincloss; Susan Bailis of New England Medical Center (Boston, Mass.); Betsy Baird of the Pioneer Valley Girl Scout Council (Springfield, Mass.); D. A. Begelman of Kirkland College; Martin Berezin of Harvard Medical School; Steven Bernstein of New England Medical Center; Charles Binger of Langley Porter Children's Service (San Francisco, Cal.); Cynthia Bishop; Rosemary Watson Blunden; David Bond of the Young Adult Institute (New York, N.Y.); Graham Bourhill of Catawba (Va.) State Hospital; Frances Bradley of NAMH; Gregg Brewer of Camphill Village (Copake, N.Y.); George W. Brooks of Vermont State Hospital; Douglas Burgoyne of St. John's Episcopal Church (Williamstown, Mass.); Dorothy Butler of the Massachusetts Department of Mental Health; Deryle Capozzi of Mount Greylock Regional High School (Williamstown, Mass.); Elizabeth Case; John M. Catlin of the Ramsay County (Minn.) Mental Health Center; Edson Chick of Williams College; Robert Claiborne; Virginia McKenney Claiborne; Ann Clark; Deborah Clark; Martin Cooperman of the Austen Riggs Center (Stockbridge, Mass.); Nicola Costa of the Disabled American Veterans and the Veterans of Foreign Wars; John Couchman of Hamm Clinic (St. Paul, Minn.); Clare Creer of the Institute of Psychiatry, London; Andrew Crider of Williams College; Richard Culley; Ida J. Davis of the Hennepin County (Minn.) Mental Health Center; Marion Garneau DeWyngaert; Golda Edinburg of McLean Hospital (Belmont, Mass.); Stephanie Engel; Doris Epstein of the Social Work Associates Program, Middlesex Community College (Bedford, Mass.); Josie Eusden of United Counseling Service (Bennington, Vt.); Elizabeth Faragoh of the Alameda County (Cal.) Mental Health Association; Meg Fardy of the Pioneer Valley Girl Scout Council; Pamela Perkins Fay; Carl Fenichel of the League School (Brooklyn, N.Y.); James Fenn; Joan Fenn of WBZ Call for Action; Thomas E. Foster; Shervert H. Frazier of McLean Hospital; Carolyn Gallant of the Pioneer Valley Girl Scout Council; Joan Gazzaniga of the Williamstown (Mass.) Elementary Schools; Mary Gerry; George Gibeau of the Massachusetts Rehabilitation Commission; Mary Stewart

Goodwin; Leonard Goveia of Rehabilitation Mental Health Services (San José, Cal.); Frances Groves; Mary Hagamen of Sagamore Children's Center (New York, N.Y.); Leo Hanvik of the Washburn Child Guidance Center (Minneapolis, Minn.); Barbara Herlitz of United Counseling Service; Fred Hollander of Napa (Cal.) State Hospital; William Huddleston of Boston Area Associates for Learning Therapies; John Hughes of the Lenox (Mass.) Public Schools; Robert Hyde of Vermont State Hospital; Elizabeth E. Irvine; Matthew Israel of the Behavior Research Institute (Providence, R.I.); Rosalie Israel of the Model Cities Program (Fall River, Mass.); Elizabeth Johnston; Lothar Kalinowsky of New York Medical College; Miriam Karlins of the Minnesota Department of Public Welfare; Ann Keck; Seymour Kety of Massachusetts General Hospital; Frederick Kiel of the Center for Behavior Modification (Minneapolis, Minn.); Miriam Alburn Kimball; Emily Kirby of Central YMCA Community College (Chicago, Ill.); R. Kummer of Napa State Hospital; Rosanne Labree of the Countway Library, Harvard Medical School; Paul Lapuc of the Veterans' Administration Hospital (Northampton, Mass.); H. Peter Laqueur of Vermont State Hospital; Thomas Leamon of the First Congregational Church (Williamstown, Mass.); Marilynn Lee of the Wilder Foundation (St. Paul, Minn.); Irwin Lehrhoff of the Psychological Professional Corporation (Beverly Hills, Cal.); Lorie Leininger; Amy Lettick of Benhaven School (New Haven, Conn.); Carolynne Lines of Kalihi-Palama Mental Health Center (Honolulu, Hawaii); Joseph Lo Piccolo of United Counseling Service; Valerie Lynn of Chestnut Lodge (Rockville, Md.); John Mack of Cambridge (Mass.) City Hospital; Clare Marshall of Vermont State Hospital; Linda Foley Martino; Paul Messplay of NAMH; Sue Mettsitti of Uptown House (Washington, D.C.); Pamela Toombs Michell; Rudolph Moz of United Counseling Service; Nancy Nally of the Community Mental Health Training Program (Northampton, Mass.); Martha Needleman of the Nathan W. Ackerman Family Institute (Lee, Mass.); Ralph Nemir of the American Psychological Association; William B. Ober of Beth Israel Medical Center (New York, N.Y.); Roger Ochs of the Pittsfield (Mass.) Help Line; Brian O'Connell of NAMH; Mary O'Connell; Patricia O'Connell of the Massachusetts Department of Public Welfare; Jill Hays O'Connor; John Osberg; Humphry Osmond of Bryce Hospital (Tuscaloosa, Ala.); David Park; Katharine Park; Paul Park; Rachel Park; Deborah Peck of the Program for Severe Communications Disorders (Hallowell, Me.); William Perry, Jr., of NAMH; Valerie Pinsky; Claude Price; Helen Reardon of the Minnesota Department of Public Welfare; Alice Redmond of the Area D Community Mental Health Center (Washington, D.C.); Shirley Reece of Langley Porter Children's Service; Harold E. Resteiner of the Genesee County (Mich.) Probate Court; Luther D. Robinson of St. Elizabeths Hospital (Washington, D.C.); Andrea Rock; John Rock of the Massachusetts State Advisory Council for Chapter 766; Herbert Rooney of NIMH; Susan Rothenberg of Massachusetts Mental Health Center (Boston, Mass.); Arthur E. Rubin of the Los Angeles (Cal.) County 4-H Youth Program; Megan Rutherford; Anna Saldo; Diana Saldo; Barbara Schaechter of the League School (Boston, Mass.); Moselio Schaechter of Tufts University; James Scharosch of Napa State Hospital; Lida Schneider of Langley Porter Children's Service; Eric Schopler of the University of North Carolina School of Medicine; Rena Schulman of the Child Development Center of the Jewish Board of Guardians (New York, N.Y.); Edward Shapiro of McLean Hospital; Rose Shapiro of the Eliot-Pearson Child Study Center of Tufts University; Denise Sheahan of United Counseling Service; Miriam Siegler; Jurgen and

Louise Sierau of Berkshire Village, Inc. (South Egremont, Mass.); Dale A. Simonson of the Hennepin County Mental Health–Mental Retardation Area Program; David L. Singer of Williamstown Psychological Consultants; Susan Spalder of The Creative Community (Berkeley, Cal.); Julia Stacy; Marjorie Stark of the Pittsfield Help Line; Zigfrids T. Stelmachers of the Hennepin County General Hospital Crisis Center; Meredith Johnston Stevens; Katharine Stokes; Uwe Stuecher of the University of Minnesota; Thomas Sturm of the Center for Behavior Modification; Ruth Christ Sullivan of the Information and Referral Service of the National Society for Autistic Children; James R. Suttle; Eugene Talbot of the South Berkshire Free Counseling Service (Stockbridge, Mass.); Norman Tallent of the Veterans' Administration Hospital (Northampton, Mass.); Esther Moss Tauber; Gail Thibadeau of the Nathan W. Ackerman Family Institute; Lawrence Thompson of Vermont State Hospital; James M. Toolan of United Counseling Service; E. Fuller Torrey of NIMH; John Vorenberg of The Springfield (Mass.) Hospital; Elaine Vosit of Recovery, Inc.; Gregg Wahlstrom of Hamm Clinic; Marcie Wallace of Hamm Clinic; Muriel Weckstein of the Mystic Valley Mental Health Center (Lexington, Mass.); Frederick Whitham of Berkshire Home Care (Pittsfield, Mass.); Daniel Wiener of the University of Minnesota; Charlee Wilbur; Landry Wildwind of the Berkeley (Cal.) Day Treatment Program; Otto Will, Jr., of the Austen Riggs Center; Gloria Williamson of St. Elizabeths Hospital; John Wing of the Institute of Psychiatry, London; Howard Wishnie of Cambridge City Hospital; Raymond Yerkes of Greater Lawrence (Mass.) Mental Health Center; Philip Youderian; Peter S. Yozell of Massachusetts Mutual Life Insurance Company (Boston, Mass.); Barbara Zinken of Northampton State Hospital.

The assistance of Jane Maslow Cohen of Snyder, Tepper, and Berlin, Boston, requires its own acknowledgment; this book is deeply indebted to the extensive materials she provided, and even more to the range and precision of her knowledge of the law and the human sensitivity which informs it.

More than thanks are due to Esther Shiverick Yntema of the Atlantic Monthly Press, who conceived the book, partook of a labor both painful and protracted, and shares the relief of a safe delivery. Natalie Greenberg and Hedy Landry of the Press assisted far beyond the call of duty. We share our editor's gratitude for the early advice and encouragement of Fred Belliveau, William Decker, Arthur H. Thornhill and J. Randall Williams of Little, Brown and Company; Norman R. Bernstein, Robert Coles and Henry U. Grunebaum of Harvard Medical School; Alvin S. Hochberg of Broude & Hochberg, Boston; Harvey L. P. Resnik of NIMH; and, at the Atlantic Monthly Company, Upton B. Brady, Peter Davison, Barbara Gale, and Robert J. Manning.

Finally, heartfelt appreciation to our patient families, not least to David Park of Williams College, who helped with the index.

Foreword

Very few people get through life without some personal or family crisis. Fortunately, most crises are self-limiting or resolve themselves in time, but others may require professional help. If you live in the United States in the second half of the twentieth century, it is practically certain that you or a member of your family will have occasion to use the services of one or more of a variety of mental health professionals. Some of their help can be enormously useful, some of it worthless, and some of it harmful. You had better know the difference.

In the pages that follow we have tried to tell you what you need to know about the mental illnesses and problems in living that usually bring people to mental health services; to mention the kinds of services that are available; and to describe the kinds of people who provide these services. We have tried to provide a guide to the mental health field that will be useful not only to the layman but to the professional, young or old, who may be familiar only with his piece of the puzzle. This book is a collaborative effort — Mrs. Park's effort and my collaboration.

Clara Park is an angry woman. Fortunately, she is angry for all of us: for parents who can't find services for their disturbed children; for children who don't know what to do with aging and failing parents; for the brothers and sisters, aunts and uncles and friends who struggle to find help for their relatives and themselves. She is also angry for and sometimes at the psychiatrists and other mental health workers who have confusing methods, conflicting ideas, blind spots and dumb spots, and who still have far to go in their efforts to be helpful.

Her preparation for this book required visits to numerous mental health facilities, discussions with dozens of teachers, researchers, and workers in the field, and the review, digestion, and translation into ordinary language of a mass of mental health literature. I tried to make sure that she was aware of every current issue, controversy, and advance in the field. We discussed and often disagreed on the merits of various methods and points of view. Most of our disagreements were resolved but none were simply smoothed over. Some issues are unresolvable and must remain matters of opinion – in those instances (for example, on the value of orthomolecular psychiatry) we simply present both sides.

On the practical side we had few problems, since we both felt that what you need to know is fairly straightforward. Obviously the answers to your questions will differ depending on whether you live in Manhattan or Mississippi, but every area has some services, and we try to show you how to get them, how to be reasonably sure you're getting proper treatment, and what to do if you are not.

What you can do especially when you realize that you are not alone is a central theme of this book. The mental health field has no sharp boundaries. On one side it merges with the general problems of medical care; on the other, it extends into the province of the general welfare. Issues of poverty, race, morality, drugs, and general social philosophy have profound effects on the forms of human misery described here. There is no group, professional or otherwise, to whom we can delegate responsibility for these things. If this book helps you to grasp the nature of the problems, maybe we can help each other.

L. N. S.

Introduction

SOMEBODY ATE A PIECE OF THE SALAD
ONLY 399 THINGS IN A BOWL
I HAVE A COLD
$7256425570 = 5\frac{2}{7} \times 1372837270$
I CRIED WHEN SOMEBODY ATE A PIECE OF THE SALAD

Sixteen years ago my youngest child was born, the child who twelve years later wrote the words you have just read. Strange words – printed in capitals, almost the first written communication she had ever made. Every statement, with the exception of the second, was literally true, yet to us, as to you, they did not make sense. They made sense, though, to Elly.* That sense could make her shriek with eerie anguish and (inside a few minutes) laugh with delight. There are words to describe Elly, of course, technical terms, terms I'm going, among other things, to try to explain in this book. But no one who knows Elly makes the mistake of thinking those words *explain* Elly, or her disorder, illness, impairment, or perhaps best, her condition, her strange, human condition.

It is because of Elly that I wanted to write this book. But more important, it is because of Elly, and the understanding she has given our family, that I have been *able* to write it. For sixteen years ago I knew nothing of what I was going to need to learn.

No one whose own life has been profoundly altered by the mental illness of a loved family member can hand out easy assurances. In some places there's no help, for some journeys no safe haven. I came to write this book because I'd looked for help myself, and failed to find it, and

*** For a glimpse of that sense, see the article by David Park, Elly's father, and Philip Youderian, the young mathematics student who worked with her, titled "Light and Number: Ordering Principles in the World of an Autistic Child,"** ***Journal of Autism and Childhood Schizophrenia,*** **4 (Dec. 1974).**

found it from unexpected people in unexpected places, and learned that for some things there is no help, only acceptance. Elly taught me that, but she taught me much more.

Elly's first gift to us was that understanding, terrible and precious, that the mind has many mansions, that the way we see the world is not the only way it can be seen. We all know this, but families of the mentally ill are reminded continually of their knowledge.

Pain too is a gift, if one can learn to use it. Elly gave us pain, as sharp, as aching as any that human beings can suffer, the pain of knowing that the child whose growth should carry with it so much joy and hope is growing inexplicably wrong. Through Elly, too, came other pain, though others than she bestowed it. This pain, like the first, turned out to be something one could make use of. That there were people who could convince themselves and almost a whole profession that who we were and what we had done as parents had had the power to distort and cripple our daughter's mind and spirit was a kind of pain that only those can understand who have lived it, an assault on the most fundamental of animal instincts, the desire to benefit the young creatures one has brought into the world. Out of the first pain came a longing for understanding; out of the second, anger; out of both, a slow discovery: we were not alone.

First over years, then faster, families of the mentally ill have found each other, have worked together, have built organizations, have discovered for the searching a growing host of friends among professionals, friends who were ready to respect our pain and our anger, even, some of them, to share it. In the not yet ten years since I first wrote Elly's story, I — we — have watched a whole profession opening up, a growing reluctance to point so readily to families as prime causers of harms whose causes nobody can yet know. We have seen the growth of a new confidence in the possibilities of fundamental research into the biology that underlies the mysteries of the brain and the emotions, and into the efficacy of the treatments offered when the mind and the emotions go wrong. We have seen the rise of new treatments — not panaceas, but workable ways to teach and restore, and we have seen the improvement of old ones. We have seen the growth of an idea unheard of when Elly and our family began our lifelong journey together, the idea that families can share in the treatment of their ill member as true co-therapists, the necessary accompaniment to another new idea, that the mentally ill can live and be helped and often get well in their own communities. We have seen a new recognition of the rights of the mentally ill, and a new recognition that society bears a responsibility for the quality of their lives. We have learned how to get things done now, and begun to work for the future. We have had the happiness of discovering new friends where trouble was deepest, and of finding that even more often than anger, we share laughter. We have shared the pride of knowing that our work was making new things happen.

It has been exhilarating and exhausting learning together, searching, reading, teaching each other, writing, talking, wearing ourselves out in communication. Caught up in enthusiasm, we might almost find ourselves saying that using pain can make you forget it, except that it can't and doesn't. But it can help us toward what we – what I – need most of all. The faith at the base of all faiths – as of so many therapies – is the conviction that we do not suffer at random, but that what happens to us has meaning. For me, the strength of that faith is Elly's gift.

Contents

Contents

PART ONE

Mental "Illness"

How It Feels, What It's Called, How It's Treated, What Caused It

»» CHAPTER I ««

Getting Started

SOMETHING HAPPENS

PERHAPS IT HAPPENS SUDDENLY. The telephone call is from an unknown doctor; your son, who when you last heard from him had just got engaged to a lovely girl, is in the university hospital, hallucinating and incoherent. Or it happens slowly. Your wife's eccentricities have increased so gradually that you are scarcely aware of how far you must go out of your way, these days, to get along with her, or of the exhaustion that is leading you to the agonized recognition that something you've been trying not even to think about has got to be done. Perhaps it was always there: you begin to realize your strange, remote baby was never like other babies. However it comes, it throws up walls around you, as all your neighbors, it seems, go about their business of living with an ordinariness which seems suddenly enviable. There may be a hundred people with a similar experience of trouble living within a mile of you — indeed, if you live in a city, there certainly are — but the families of the mentally ill have a low visibility. Exhaustion and misery, if not shame and a conviction of guilt, may keep the knowledge of their plight even from their close friends. A mother's personality changes after the birth of her fourth child; her rages and suicidal depressions terrify her adolescent children less than their speculations about the nameless condition no one will explain to them, as they wonder alternately whether their misbehavior has caused it and if it will rub off onto them. A couple of their school friends know about it; the neighbors don't. Another family's life is shadowed by an uncle, whose paranoid schizophrenia is not incompatible with a certain charm. Intermittently he finds a way out of the hospital where he's confined and shows up on his elderly sister's doorstep, or his niece's. Her children are asleep upstairs; last time he had a gun. A middle-aged man drifts in and out of jobs and relationships until one day he blacks out and murders a young woman who has befriended him while her children nap in the next room. He has a father, a wife, adolescent children. A brilliant young man is killing himself with alcohol and drugs; he takes a melancholy satisfaction in telling his friends about it. His father still owes thousands of dollars for the hospital treatment that didn't make him well.

Every community can provide counterparts to these stories. And the overwhelming majority of these people have relatives whose lives are involved in their condition, morally, legally, emotionally. In a recent poll just under one person in four answered that someone close to them had suffered from mental illness or breakdown. How many more were unwilling to share their pain? Imprisoned in their own unique experience, cut off not only from each other but too often from the people whose profession it is to help them, they try to accommodate the inescapable demands of "normal" life to those other desperate demands that so many know and so few can share. It is to these individuals and families, in their lonely millions, that this book is addressed, to whom it seeks to say, out of the experience of many – You Are Not Alone.

QUESTIONS

Anxious, uncertain, yet with a working mind that cannot help trying to cope with its experience, you search for some understanding of what has happened to your relative. What can he be feeling – what, perhaps, can he be hearing and seeing – that makes him act so strangely? Is he frightened? Hostile? Hopeless? Confused? Perverse? (Is some of his behavior a put-on?) And what about yourself and those around you? What did you do wrong, if anything? What had you better get ready for? What kind of treatment is he having? What should you know about it? Have you a place in it? Should you have? As a responsible person you must deal with your relative's practical needs, and your family's, and your community's, needs that generate further sets of questions, as various as the web of life itself. Some are in the center of your attention, some on the fringes, perhaps scarcely realized. Some are relentlessly practical. Some seek deeper understanding. Most try to bring understanding and practice together, so that you can decide what to do next. Of course there can be no one place where you can find answers to all your questions, but you can learn whom to ask or where and how to find answers for yourself. The practical services that make so much difference if, for instance, your mentally ill relative lives with you, exist in some places – where they do not, your insistent, informed demands can help bring them into being. Above all, everywhere, helpful people exist. The purpose of this book is to provide a bridge which the solitary family can cross to find others with whom they can work toward understanding and effective action.

Who are those others? Some are skilled professionals, experienced in helping where minds and emotions are troubled. Some work in your community – the clergymen, teachers, lawyers, probation officers, policemen who, besides their ordinary duties, are often a front-line resource against mental illness. Some are citizens like ourselves. They too can help, not because it is their job but because they have lived with the same problems you face and have banded together to do something about them. These three groups, and the help they offer, weave in and out of this book. Community resources and citizens' groups will have their own chapters. But we must introduce the mental health professionals at the beginning.

INTRODUCING THE MENTAL HEALTH PROFESSIONALS

The mental health professionals

Psychiatrist, psychoanalyst, psychologist – many people use the words interchangeably, especially since all three are usually addressed as "Doctor." But they have arrived at that title by different routes. Psychiatric social workers and psychiatric nurses too have different kinds of training. Since you may find yourself talking to any one of these professionals, here is a brief introduction to what are often called "the helping professions."

Psychiatrist

The *psychiatrist* is a medical doctor, a specialist in the treatment of mental and emotional disturbances. "Psyche" means "soul" in Greek, and "iatros" means "healer." Though any M.D. can call himself a psychiatrist on the basis of interest or experience, to qualify for membership in the American Psychiatric Association a doctor must follow his basic medical course with three more years of training. This *psychiatric residency* is spent in a hospital, approved for training by the American Board of Psychiatry and Neurology, where he works under the supervision of experienced psychiatrists to acquire familiarity with a full variety of psychiatric problems. His training combines three important perspectives. From a biological or medical perspective, he studies the ways in which our psychic behavior is influenced by what is going on in our bodies (and vice versa) and the medical means of treating psychiatric symptoms. Modern psychiatric training adds a second perspective, in which the resident is taught to consider the patient's social environment – how his mental and emotional state are affected by what goes on in the world around him. Such things as where a troubled person can live or whether he can get a job and hold it may be more relevant than biological understanding to how sick he gets or whether he can stay out of the hospital. This is important background for the third perspective, which may be called experiential, as the doctor explores the experience of the individual sufferer – which is, by the way, what the word *patient* means – to try to experience its development for himself. So at least half the psychiatric resident's time is spent talking to patients, under the supervision of someone who has learned this difficult art.

His training combines biological, socioeconomic, and experiential perspectives.

After his residency the new psychiatrist is ready to practice. He needs two years of documented experience before he may take the examinations of the American Board of Psychiatry and Neurology, to become *board-certified* or a *diplomate.* This certification is not to be confused with the licensing your state requires before any M.D. can practice. You can be sure that the forty percent* of psychiatrists who are board-certified have met the rigorous standards set by their own professional organizations, but the examinations are entirely voluntary, and many psychiatrists who do not take them are nevertheless competent practitioners.

Board certification

These cool qualifications seem to have little to do with the common picture of a psychiatrist. The beard of that benign personage is neatly clipped, his accent faintly Viennese; his sharp eyes look beneath the surface to uncover unconscious meanings. He has his own vocabulary and his own equipment: a couch. In fact, this is the cartoon image of a *psychoanalyst,* drawn from the features of Sigmund Freud, whose revolutionary psychology – some would call it a philosophy – spread from its obscure beginnings in pre–World War I Vienna to become in the forties and fifties the dominant theory of human psychology in the Western world.

The stereotype of a psychiatrist is drawn from psychoanalysis.

In America, a psychoanalyst is usually a psychiatrist, though relatively few psychiatrists are psychoanalysts.† Our most influential psychiatrists, however, including most heads of teaching hospitals, are almost all analysts, and psychoanalysis is one of the most important influences in psychiatric training. It contributes heavily to that experiential perspective mentioned earlier, teaching doctors to consider how a patient's problems take on new meaning when understood in the light of the experiences of his childhood.

Psychoanalysis and psychiatry

Most psychoanalysts are doctors

Yet Freud, though himself a doctor, came to believe that a medical background was not necessary to psychoanalytic understanding, and some of the best known and most influential psychoanalysts are not physicians‡ (as indeed the psychoanalyst's typical patient is not what most people would call sick). People with advanced training in many fields study in psychoanalytic institutes, where candidates learn psychoanalytic theory and methods, reinforced by a *training analysis.* In this the candidate is himself analyzed by an experienced analyst, so that before he comes to explore with a patient the nature of his trouble he knows the ways in which his own mind and emotions work, and understands the problems which might make it difficult for him to respond to some of his patients.

but not all.

Psychoanalytic training

* Report of 1970 American Psychiatric Association survey, *Psychiatric News* (Aug. 15, 1975). The percentage is likely to increase as new professional review organizations (see Chapter XI) put a new emphasis on certification and the maintenance of physicians' qualifications.

† In 1970 there were 26,000 psychiatrists in the United States, fewer than 2,500 of whom called themselves psychoanalysts.

‡ Among them Erik Erikson, Bruno Bettelheim, and Erich Fromm, whose *Art of Loving* is a perennial best-seller.

In the forty years since the rise of Hitler scattered the pioneers of the psychoanalytic movement, most of them to this country, psychoanalysis has profoundly influenced not only the ways psychiatrists treat the mentally disturbed and their families but also the ways Americans think about themselves and their fellow men and women. Today the "inferiority complex" is not the new concept that Alfred Adler introduced before the First World War to modify Freud's emphasis on the primary importance of sexuality, but a phrase you may hear from the ten-year-old next door. The "introverts," "extroverts," "Oedipus complexes" have grown familiar. We hear about "ego-satisfactions" on TV. We've learned to note when a friend responds "defensively" to our well-meant suggestions. We understand the difficulties of our neighbor's son, if not our own, as he goes through an "identity crisis." We deplore the dangers of "repression." Even slips of the tongue are recognized as "Freudian." How would we manage if a time machine swept us back to the time of our great-grandmothers, to stammer out our comments on our neighbors and ourselves without what was once the specialized vocabulary of psychoanalysis?

We refer to psychoanalytic ideas every day.

Clinical psychologist

Training

The *clinical psychologist* follows a third road to the mental health professions. He may have studied in a psychoanalytic institute, but he is not an M.D. When he's called "Doctor," it indicates the Ph.D. degree in psychology. As the psychiatrist, in medical school, studies much about medical illness that the psychologist does not learn, so the clinical psychologist, in a training which lasts as long as the medical student's, studies aspects of psychology that most psychiatrists are not concerned with. He studies many kinds of behavior, human and animal, normal and abnormal, and many different ways of explaining it. Other names are added to those of the giants of psychoanalysis: Pavlov, Skinner, Piaget, and many more. The psychologist studies how personalities are formed and function; how people develop from infancy to old age; how people (and animals) perceive, learn, and behave. He learns to give and interpret psychological tests and to conduct research. In addition to academic work, the clinical psychologist must have at least a year of internship in a mental hospital, mental health clinic, or similar facility. The American Board of Professional Psychology certifies individual practitioners, and psychologists are also licensed by states, most of which require roughly these qualifications. However, psychologists with fewer years of study (the M.A., for instance) offer counseling or psychotherapy too.

in personality theory, developmental psychology, learning theory, testing, research methods

Certification

Much more often than not, psychiatrists, psychoanalysts, and psychologists are male, so (regretfully) we're speaking of them as "he." Now we switch: the *psychiatric social worker* is more often female. She generally takes a two-year course after college for the degree of M.S.W. – Master of Social Work – though the Bachelor of Social Work is

Psychiatric social worker

becoming more common. Much of her study parallels that of the psychologist, though with an emphasis on working with people rather than on testing or research. (Many social workers, too, have psychoanalytic training.) A typical *psychiatric team* consists of a psychiatrist to see the patient, a psychologist to test him, and a psychiatric social worker to talk to his family and help with practical problems at home and in the community. But like psychologists, social workers today offer psychotherapy, though they often call it "counseling" (and the patient a "client"). Though most psychiatric social workers work in community agencies and hospitals, there are now many in private practice. For certification by the American Academy of Social Workers, candidates must work for two years under the supervision of a certified social worker and pass the academy's examination. They may then put A.C.S.W. (Academy of Certified Social Workers) after their names. Many are also licensed by their own states.

The psychiatric team

Psychotherapy or counseling

Certification

The *psychiatric nurse* is an R.N. who has had special training and experience with disturbed people, usually in a mental hospital, where she is the professional closest to the patients' daily lives. Unlike the psychologist or social worker, she (too rarely he) can give medical treatment, and although she cannot prescribe it, her recommendation often guides the doctor. She may also work in a community agency or move out to give treatment anywhere she is needed, alone or as a member of a mobile mental health team, visiting patients in their homes, guiding therapy for them and their families, and reporting on the progress of treatment. Nurses today often lead group therapy sessions, and some give individual therapy too.

Psychiatric nurse

Therapy, in fact, can come from many hands. And that's lucky, when 125,000 people a year are hospitalized for depression alone, when half the hospital beds in this country are occupied by mental patients and it is impossible to count the people needing help who have not (thank heaven!) had to be hospitalized. These figures do a lot to explain the rise of a new kind of mental health worker, the *paraprofessional,* who works alongside the professional.*

Paraprofessional

It was in the early sixties that some professionals, realizing that the need for personal contact in state hospitals was greater than existing staff could ever meet, experimented with bringing in completely untrained people to help — housewives and students whose only qualifications were their own warmth, compassion, and common sense. It worked better than anyone had expected. Patients who hadn't had a visitor in years began to respond to the enthusiasm of the volunteers. Controlled studies showed that amateur therapists could have a measurable effect on recovery rates. The idea spread to the new community

* We are now seeing the spread of paraprofessionals to assist doctors in regular medical care as well.

mental health centers; in some of these, much of the clinical work is done by paraprofessionals – local people, some still volunteers, many now trained and paid. Many paraprofessionals take courses leading to special degrees. They do a great deal of helping with practical problems like budgeting and housing, but they may be involved in individual and group therapy as well, working under professional supervision.

Other doctors

Before we leave the mental health professions, we must return to medicine, for *doctors who are not psychiatrists* do a lot of front-line psychiatry. In fact, the majority of psychological complaints are probably taken care of by internists (specialists in internal medicine), gynecologists, pediatricians, and general practitioners. With the rise of effective drug treatment, the G.P. or internist who has kept up in his field may be able to give effective treatment even for a recognized psychiatric condition like depression. Many count chronic schizophrenics among their patients, and they are a major resource for the psychiatric problems of old age. A good doctor will know when symptoms need more specialized consultation and refer you to a mental health professional as needed.

Neurologist

The *neurologist,* or specialist in diseases of the nervous system, joins the mental health professions when he assesses the role of neurological impairment and suggests treatment. Epilepsy and stroke are examples of neurological conditions that can cause mental and emotional symptoms, and the neurologist will be consulted in the more serious psychological disorders of childhood. The neurologist's three-year residency usually includes at least six months of psychiatry.

What is the relationship between members of "the helping professions"? It would be a pleasure to write that they invariably work together in harmony for the welfare of the patient and his family, all fully aware of one anothers' strengths and special skills, readily referring the patient to another kind of practitioner if his or her expertise is more appropriate to the condition and the circumstances. And it is sometimes so – most commonly, again, in the good mental health center, where the team of psychiatrist/psychologist/social worker/nurse – now often joined by the paraprofessional – is the common model. Unfortunately, however, Utopia is not found around every corner, particularly since the different kinds of professionals may have very good reasons for considering their own expertise particularly suited to the treatment of emotional disorders. Many psychiatrists will defend the principle that those who conduct psychotherapy should have medical training or work under a physician's direct supervision, since (as one Harvard Medical School psychiatrist says) "emotional and physical distress are inextricably intertwined."[1] Many clinical psychologists, however (like many psychiatrists), consider that most of the "mentally ill" are not ill in any medical sense, and that a medical setting and medical assumptions may miss the point of their condition and even make it worse. To the "talking cure" they may add behavior therapy, which they developed, and note that medical science contributed little to either. They may speak of "breaking the physician monopoly" and complain that since they are not defined as independent practitioners under Medicare, the government itself discriminates among professionals. Even among physicians there may be tensions. Psychiatrists themselves have different philosophies of illness and treatment; psychiatrists and neurologists sometimes tread on each others' toes. There are rival professional associations of psychoanalysts; members often confine their referrals to their own group. Highly trained professionals do not always accept that others with different training may suit the case as well or better. They are human beings like the rest of us, and many of them retain the age-old human interest in protecting their own turf.

Do they know about each other?

Ideally, you should be able to depend on any professional to refer you to another as needed. The psychologist should stand ever ready to call in the physician; the psychiatrist should be continually aware of the kinds of therapy which the psychologist or social worker is able to give. In practice, however, the ideal is rarely reached. The psychiatrist may refer you to a clinical psychologist skilled in behavior modification techniques, if such methods have been found helpful in cases like your relative's. However, he may not believe in them; he may not know about them; he may simply not know where to get that kind of help. The effect for you is the same. The psychologist will call in a doctor readily enough if he sees the necessity, but he has not been trained to recognize the signs of physical disease (though efforts are being made to include this in his training) and may underestimate the applicability of medical therapies or the relevance of medical training. Many psychologists – and psychiatrists too, for that matter – are leery of even such a well-established medical therapy as electroshock treatment; though they do not administer it themselves, they will be reluctant to refer you to someone who does. It is obvious, of course, that no one practitioner can be universally trained in all techniques, and no one person universally gifted to help all who come to him. Professionals, like the rest of us, should have the wit to know their limitations – but like the rest of us, they don't always. This book would be quite unnecessary if every professional you consulted were guaranteed to tell you everything you need to know. Sometimes he won't; more often he can't, because he doesn't know himself. Your best insurance is in information, so you can make an informed choice of what's available. It is tempting to dream of handing over one's troubles to some superauthority who will wisely make every necessary decision. Even in physical illness, however, this is more often dream than reality. In mental illness, which is so much less understood, the perfect authority is even less likely to be found. The ultimate responsibility for all health care belongs to the individual seeking it — or, if that individual is too young or too incapacitated to seek it for himself, to you, his responsible relative.

Psychotherapist?

You'll have noticed that mental health professionals, for all their differences of training, seem to spend a lot of their time doing the same thing. Whether they call it therapy or counseling, they talk to patients and try to find ways to help them. Dr. Leon Salzman has called for an end to notions of hierarchy, in which the psychiatrist must direct and supervise the work of the other professions, and for a new profession of *psychotherapy*.[2] In the meantime, Dr. Jerome Frank's 1960 prediction, that "the very same patient might be treated by a psychiatrist, a psychologist, a psychiatric social worker, or even a clergyman, depending on where his feet carry him,"[3] is in many places the fact.

HELP FROM BOOKS

Help from books

Reading

and cost effectiveness.

In the mental health professions as in other fields there are a few outstanding practitioners, mostly concentrated in a few cities and university centers, mostly very busy, and thus mostly out of reach of most patients and their families. There is, however, a way in which any of us, anywhere, can consult one of these first-class professionals. Almost all of them write books and articles. Usually these are addressed to other professionals; you can learn a lot from them if you read carefully and selectively. But when a great practitioner writes directly for the general public, like the pediatrician (and psychoanalyst) Dr. Spock, you're in luck. A book could be written about your relative's condition — but no professional could pack the material of a book into a consultation, and if he did you couldn't absorb it. For clear explanation and patient repetition, for information and wisdom available whenever you need it, there's nothing like a book. We'll be mentioning some of these books for the general reader; you'll find them listed in the Reading List (Appendix A). (More specialized works cited are listed in the Bibliography.) Order from the publisher if your library can't oblige; a top-flight professional's book will cost you a small fraction of a visit to his office.*

* And if you *can* visit his office, reading something he's written is a good preparation.

HOW TO USE THIS BOOK

Using this book

This book is long and heavy, but you don't have to read it all at once. If you're looking for a particular subject, check the list of topics at the beginning of each chapter.* Headings and running summaries are printed in the margins to help you skim; you can keep track of where you are while dipping in and out of the text. Skip the notes at the bottom of the page unless you're particularly interested. (Numbered references will be found at the back of the book.) We've tried to explain medical and psychological terms as needed; when we do, we put them in italics. The Index marks the page where they're explained by bold-face type. Fuller definitions, authoritative yet clear, may be found in the inexpensive 800-term mini-dictionary put out by the American Psychiatric Association.†

"MENTALLY ILL"?

"For families of the mentally ill"

Words, words, words‡

This book is "a guide for families of the mentally ill." But who and what are they? "Mental illness" is such a slippery term that we find ourselves substituting others – "mentally (or emotionally) disturbed" (sometimes "severely disturbed") or "troubled" or "disordered" or "distressed." They turn out to be just as slippery. Terms once medical – "neurotic," "psychotic," "paranoid," even "schizoid" and "schizophrenic" – have become familiar, but familiarity hasn't made their meanings less cloudy. We may feel a little nostalgia for simpler days, when people were crazy or sane, and being disturbed or troubled wasn't at all the same thing as being sick.§

In fact, though we're all aware there are many gradations between illness and what we somewhat uncomfortably call normality, professionals and ordinary people alike sense a difference in what we feel are "really crazy" people – the people professionals call psychotic. Others – also troubled, sometimes even more troubled – may be called neurotic,|| but increasingly they're seen, and treated, as people with prob-

* Check the Index if you don't find it.

† *A Psychiatric Glossary: The Meaning of Terms Frequently Used in Psychiatry*, 4th ed. Order from A.P.A. Publication Services Division, 1700 18th Street N.W., Washington, DC 20009.

‡ As Hamlet replied to Polonius while feigning madness.

§ Often this word is used even more loosely. Consider this definition, from an article on "Surviving Psychotherapy": "Oh yes, I was sick. I was unable to view myself as I was." To say the least, this is a very widespread illness. James Coleman, in *Motive*, 32, No. 2 (1972).

|| Especially if they have disabling symptoms. See Chapter III.

lems — problems in living. It's a sensible phrase, for the words "mentally ill" are not to be used lightly. You will be seeing it a lot in this book.

"The myth of mental illness"?

When that phrase was first created, however, by the very articulate psychiatrist and psychoanalyst Thomas Szasz, he was not applying it to neurosis but to psychosis. Calling mental illness a myth, he argued that unless mental disturbances are known to be physically caused diseases* they should be recognized as "problems in living." "Mental illness," he believes, is not illness but a label psychiatrists and the rest of us apply to people who deviate from what we agree to be normal behavior. "The belief in mental illness, other than man's trouble in getting along with his fellow man, is the heir to demonology and witchcraft."[4]

Illness?

Yet every language has a word for "crazy," and even animals go mad. Insanity has been treated as a medical illness since the time of the Greeks; at no time before our own has madness been regarded as anything but a real and terrible scourge. Dr. Szasz is right to caution us not to put the heavy stigma of mental illness on behavior that society finds troublesome. Indiscriminate thinking about "illness" opens the door to indiscriminate application of medical treatment to people whose illness is to have chosen to live and believe differently from their fellows. Soviet psychiatrists diagnosed the dissenting physicist Zhorez Medvedev as schizophrenic and shut him up in a hospital, and it was only recently that the American Psychiatric Association decided, against strong opposition, that homosexuality was not a psychiatric disorder. Yet most of us feel we, at least, could have seen the difference between Medvedev and someone who was "really crazy." Those who have returned from what Dr. R. D. Laing calls the "inner journey" to the altered world of madness are usually the first to feel that they have been ill, and most psychiatrists would agree with Dr. Joel Parris that "the quickest way to condemn a patient to the back ward is to treat his illness as a metaphor."[5]

Or choice?

"Inner journey?"

Our relatives' problems in living, in different circumstances and times, may be mild or severe, neurotic or psychotic. However we define mental illness, this book is for the families of people who are troubled, disturbed, disordered, or sick enough to need a responsible relative behind them. There are plenty of them and of us. We'll distinguish some of the forms their psychiatric problems take when we get to Chapter III. But before we are ready to explore the various psychiatric diagnoses — *or* labels — we'll turn to the experience of the "mentally ill" themselves. They, after all, are the real experts.

* In which case he believes the neurologist, not the psychiatrist, should treat them.

⋙ CHAPTER II ⋘

The Sufferer's World

For I will consider my cat Jeoffrey.
For he is the servant of the Living God duly and daily serving him.
For at the first glance of the glory of God in the East he worships in his way.
For this is done by wreathing his body seven times round with elegant quickness. . . .
For he keeps the Lord's watch in the night against the adversary.
For he counteracts the powers of darkness by his electrical skin and glaring eyes.
For he counteracts the Devil, who is death, by brisking about the life. . . .
For he purrs in thankfulness, when God tells him he's a good Cat.
For the English cats are the best in Europe. . . .
For he knows that God is his Savior.
For there is nothing sweeter than his peace when at rest.
For there is nothing brisker than his life when in motion. . . .
For he can spraggle upon waggle at the word of command. . . .
For I am possessed of a cat, surpassing in beauty, from whom I take occasion to bless Almighty God.

CHRISTOPHER SMART, *Rejoice in the Lamb*

CHRISTOPHER SMART wrote these words more than two hundred years ago, in a mental hospital, maybe in Bedlam itself. He never wrote anything half so lovely when he was sane. In the thousands of lines he produced during the seven years he was confined, he wrote that the Trumpet of God is a blessed intelligence and so are all the instruments in heaven; that flowers are the poetry of Christ, their warp and woof worked by perpetual moving spirits; that each letter of the alphabet is a spirit, "and therefore he is God." It is easy to see how someone who actually saw God's glory everywhere might have attracted attention by compelling people to fall to their knees in inappropriate places, and that is what he did, and why, his friend Dr. Johnson told us, he was locked up. Let Kit Smart remind us that the world is more beautiful than we give it credit for and that sensible people may have something to learn from looking through the eyes of the insane.

For our mentally ill relatives experience a different world from ourselves. Yet it is not totally different. We say they are "not themselves," but even at their strangest, parts of them remain unchanged. They have still so much in common with the rest of us that if we are sensitive we can recognize in them our own thoughts and emotions, intensified and transformed.

We are all familiar with the milder transformations; we see them in ourselves and all around us. No one calls them illness. A friend flares up and we're not surprised; we know he's under stress this week. Some people get tense before a menstrual period; others cave in when they don't get enough sleep. Some people get high on Coke or coffee, or just the stimulation of a party. Alcohol, marijuana, amphetamines, LSD can make us act and feel in the same ways some people do without them. They are called mentally ill and we're not. Yet the world they experience is one we can recognize and partly share.

CASE HISTORIES (BY THE "CASES")

We can share it more fully and understand it better for a very encouraging reason: most mentally ill people recover. When they do, a surprising number of them write down what they've been through and what it was like, to help others, and because those who've visited a strange country almost always learn something worth the telling. There are literally hundreds of these accounts; our Reading List has room for only a few. Our relatives and friends may also have things to tell us, once they know that we really want to listen. In this chapter we'll try to find out a little of what it was like, from people who have been there.

ANXIETY NEUROSIS

We'll start with the milder disturbances, the ones closest to our own daily condition. Problems of living we all have, and many people are "nervous." How much further it gets us to change a few of the letters in that word and come up with "neurotic" is open to question. Those of our relatives whose problems of living have temporarily swamped them are probably reacting enough like us so that we can muster the ordinary sympathy, listen, talk, and if we can't help, suggest someone who can. There are, however, neurotic conditions which are much more severe than this. These people are not psychotic, they're in touch with the same reality we are, but for some reason they're hurting more. What we can shake off, they can't seem to. We sympathize for a bit, but we soon lose patience. Why don't they just pull themselves together, stop thinking about themselves so much, worry about someone else for a change?

Neurotic? (see pp. 32–38)

Well, they don't do these sensible things, maybe, because they feel like this:

Anxiety Neurosis *(see p. 35)*

> It is almost impossible to describe this kind of anxiety to someone who has never felt it. At the extreme, it confuses perception itself, and there is that sinking sensation . . . of being on the edge of a dead faint. Or the commonplace street suddenly seemed angled and awry as if reflected in the mirrors of a fun house and you clutch at a wall for support. On an errand of no importance, a motor races or someone jostles you slightly and the day goes to pieces. . . . I would walk into the post office and the mere fact that I was going to have to stand in line for a minute or two would seem so outrageous that I would flee in panic.[1]

One man's nervous breakdown

Michael Harrington, who gives us these "Notes on My Nervous Breakdown," *couldn't* pull himself together. His mind wasn't out of touch, but his emotions were. He'd been making a speech when his anxiety attack came on. Before his breakdown he'd made hundreds of speeches, but it took four years of psychotherapy before he again "could casually accept an invitation to give a speech and make it without careful calculations and a drink. And to this day, every time I approach a podium I rehearse the excuse I had prepared during 1965 and 1966."

PHOBIA

Phobia *(see p. 36)*

William Ellery Leonard's mind was also quite in touch. But he so feared locomotives that he was virtually a prisoner in the university town where he taught. Let him describe his emotions:

> I am walking down University Drive by the Lake. I am a normal man for the first quarter of a mile; for the next hundred yards I am in a mild state of dread, controllable and controlled; for the next twenty yards in an acute state of dread, yet controlled; for the next ten, in an anguish of terror that hasn't reached the crisis of explosion; and in a half dozen steps more I am in as fierce a panic of isolation from help and home and of immediate death as a man overboard in mid-Atlantic or on a window-ledge far up in a sky-scraper with flames lapping his shoulders.

He ought to pull himself together?

> The reader who can't understand why I have not merely whistled or laughed or ordered the phobias off my psychic premises, or who thinks that I must be grossly exaggerating a mere normal discomfort . . . is not the reader for whom I am writing. . . . It is as scientific a fact as any I know that my phobic seizures at their worst approach any limits of terror that the human mind is capable of in the actual presence of death. . . . That I have never fainted away or died under them is due to two factors: first, my physical vitality; and, second, my skill in devising escapes – psychic surrogates, deflections of attention, or actual retreats to

> safety. . . . The fools say nothing ever happened from one of these seizures — so why worry. Nothing ever happened? Well, here is what happens always. First, the seizure happens — as well say, nothing happens, if a red-hot iron is run down the throat, even though it should miraculously leave no after-effects. The seizure happens; the acutest agony of the conscious brain happens. Second, the seizure leaves me always far more exposed to phobic seizures for weeks or months; increases my fear of the Fear . . . robs me of a goodly part of what little freedom of movement . . . I have. "Nothing ever happened." This means simply that to date I've lived through the seizures and continued for fifteen years to teach school, write books, and make jokes at the University Club across the street.[2]

Leonard thought psychoanalysis might have helped, but there was none available at that time in Madison, Wisconsin; in any event, he worked out a routine of rest and exercise which allowed him the strength to cope with his terror even though he couldn't get rid of it. But across the years, even through the printed page, we can feel the outrage he felt against people — like us — who pursued him with empty reassurances and wouldn't try to understand.

We've said that our mentally ill relatives experience a different world from ourselves. We must underline that. They really do experience it, feel it, sometimes even see and hear it; they don't just think they do. When their emotions surface in physical symptoms, these are as real as tears are, or the stitch in our sides when we've laughed too much. (Leonard's hair grew gray in the summer of his first attack.) In helping them, we start by recognizing that what they experience is not mere imagination.

PSYCHEDELIC DRUGS

Psychedelic drugs

In recent years this has become easier to do. Whatever we think of the psychedelic or "mind-altering" drugs — marijuana, amphetamines, LSD, mescaline, and the rest — we must acknowledge that they've dissolved some of the barriers between the sane (us) and the crazy (them). They have shown us that psychotic symptoms can be experienced by anybody. Whether we've taken these drugs ourselves or heard about it from others, we know that in the space of minutes a person's perceptions of the world can be utterly transformed. Accounts of drug experiences are just about impossible to tell from accounts of recovered mental patients.

> The first thing I became aware of was an extreme paranoia: I continually was turning around or looking over my shoulder. My senses became acute, and the flood of sensory inputs was more than my mind could handle. Disorientation in time and space became so complete that I

began talking out loud to myself to try to maintain some sort of link with the real world. In spite of my talking to myself, the idea that I was dead drifted around in my head. . . . The separation from body was complete. Separation from the "real" world was complete. There was only nothingness. . . . When I entered the bathroom to ready myself for bed, I stood in front of the sink for what seemed like hours before telling myself, out loud, to squirt some toothpaste on the toothbrush and move my hand back and forth and up and down. . . . I began thinking "Where am I? Who am I? What am I?" . . . With no associations to build on, . . . with much effort – I had to fight the continuing barrage of sensory input and the wild oscillations of my mind – I was finally able to define myself as the son of Mr. and Mrs. Dryer; roommate of Scott, Dave, and Hal; and a student at Williams College.*

There are many more flamboyant accounts than this one, which describes an unusually intense reaction to a relatively mild drug by a person who found his brief journey into mental illness revealing, but frightening. We can use these tales of trips – if not the trips themselves – to help us believe in the reality of our relative's experience.

But let's not think it's the same. For no matter how bad the trip, the drug user knows in one part of his mind that a chemical is causing his transformation, that he chose to introduce it into his body, and that in a while its effects will go away. Our relatives are not so lucky. An essential part of what they undergo is the feeling of being trapped inside their experience, powerless to emerge.

DEPRESSION

Depression *(pp. 35, 44–45)*

Depression, like neurosis, seems close to our normal experience, for doesn't everybody get depressed sometimes? But listen to Percy Knauth describing the depression which "robbed me of the very tool with which I could save myself." "If you break an arm," he told a meeting of the National Association for Mental Health, "or cripple a leg, or lose your sight or your speech, it's bad enough, but when you feel your mind beginning to go, the essence of anything you can use to fight back is going with it."[3]

Another nervous breakdown

Knauth was a successful and respected journalist when it hit him, a man who "never in my life thought I would have a nervous breakdown." For months he'd been having trouble sleeping, but one particular early morning he woke up and all the fears and regrets of his fifty-seven years came at him "one after the other, mercilessly, in a dreadful parade of real and imagined shortcomings."

Somehow, some part of my mind that was still rational knew that this was nonsense, that my imaginings were wildly distorted, exaggerated and un-

* John Dryer, unpublished paper (Fall 1973); the drug in question is marijuana.

> real. But I could not bring myself to recognize this fact. I knew of only one thing that could help me and at the thought of it I felt a momentarily warming rush of deliverance: the pills. They were there in a small bottle beside me, enough of them to . . . still my dread forever. The thought was so persuasive, so logical, so comforting, that it broke down all the barriers I tried to build against it and left me sobbing helplessly.[4]

His sobs woke his sleeping wife. "Without a word, she took my head into her arms and rocked it on her breast while the tears flowed on and on. . . . That was the moment I have to thank for the fact that I am still alive: that moment when I was rocked and loved and comforted like the baby I had become."

Mrs. Knauth got him to a doctor that morning. The antidepressant drugs prescribed took time to act; in the meantime –

> The smallest decision . . . floored me. I could not make up my mind about anything. Every morning I lay helpless, debating the pros and cons of arising, until at last my wife brought me coffee and got me out of bed herself.

A child asks him if he'd like some lemonade:

> Did I or didn't I? I could taste the sweet-sour lemonade in my mouth, feel it slaking my thirst; but did I want a child to go to the trouble of making it and bringing it to me? I would debate this until someone made up my mind for me.

Colonel "Buzz" Aldrin, one of the original Apollo 11 moon-walkers (and now, like Knauth, a board member of the National Association for Mental Health), also describes this commonest of depressive symptoms: "I was unable to make the simplest decisions . . . could see no hope, no possibility of controlling anything in my life."[5]

Depression, or melancholia, is one of the oldest of recognized psychiatric conditions. Albrecht Dürer represented it as a huge, powerful woman sitting immobilized, the tools of productive thinking and working lying unused on the ground around her. Hamlet, "the melancholy Dane," could not bring himself to the point of action and debated suicide. Lincoln's law partner considered him "a hopeless victim of melancholy"; his future in-laws thought him "insane."[6] Leo Tolstoy describes his

"Why?"

> strange state of mind-torpor . . . of a stoppage, as it were, of life. . . . The same questions always presented themselves to me: "Why?" and "What after?" . . . If I wished for anything, I knew beforehand that, were I to satisfy the wish, nothing would come of it. . . . Such was the condition I had come to, at the time when all the circumstances of my life were preeminently happy ones, and when I had not reached my fiftieth year. . . .[7]

Even in the days before shock treatment and antidepressant drugs, people recovered from depressive illnesses. Lincoln and Tolstoy did, and most other people did too if they waited long enough, and if they didn't kill themselves first. "This was the feeling," writes Tolstoy, "that, above all, drew me to think of suicide." Dr. William Bunney, Jr., of the National Institute of Mental Health, says that most of America's 30,000 suicides a year are victims of depression.[8] Knauth's doctor told his wife to watch him constantly until the antidepressants could take effect.* He knew what he was doing. Depression is often quite literally a fatal illness.

Suicide

SUICIDE

The will to suicide of the severely depressed† person is quite different from the threats and halfhearted attempts that may be made in some other kinds of emotional disturbance. None of these should be ignored, of course, because even a perennial threatener may be successful this time. But it's not the depressed person who's out to scare you half to death, manipulating your emotions and his own, imagining how sorry you'll be when he's dead and gone. He's more likely to hide his store of pills, as Knauth did. Understanding your depressed relative's world means understanding that for the time being life is literally not worth living and that the possibility of suicide must be taken absolutely seriously. We must believe in the emptiness of that tremendous "why?"

MANIC-DEPRESSIVE PSYCHOSIS

Another nervous breakdown: depression, paranoia *(see p. 43)*

In June, 1900, Clifford Beers fell into a depression so deep that, unlike Knauth's, it was a truly psychotic state. He stopped talking. He did not recognize his brother but believed he was a detective, that he himself was under indictment for an unknown crime, that only by suicide could he escape the disgrace and shame of public trial. His

* Knauth's case provides families with a model of effective modern treatment. Mrs. Knauth got him to a doctor as soon as she was aware of his condition; the doctor (not himself a psychiatrist) prescribed appropriate medical treatment and supportive psychotherapy; his family provided conditions as stress-free as possible, including making up his mind for him when he couldn't. Within five months he was well enough to start the research on his illness that led to his article.

† Or schizophrenic. It's been estimated that a schizophrenic is twenty times as likely to commit suicide as a normal person. *The Schizophrenias — Yours and Mine,* prepared by the Professional Committee of the American Schizophrenia Foundation (New York: Pyramid Books, 1970), p. 61.

book, *A Mind That Found Itself,* is the classic account of a manic-depressive psychosis (see pp. 45–46).*

Beers counted the seven hundred and ninety-eight days of his depression and estimated the minutes: over one million, in which he suffered "what was in reality a hell." On August 30, 1902, his depression ended, as he felt "a sensation not unlike that of a menthol pencil rubbed ever so gently over a fevered brow . . . so delicate, crisp, and exhilarating that words fail me in my attempt to describe it." For a few hours he felt and appeared quite normal; his brother, whom he had recognized for the first time in two years, thought he'd soon be home. But the cool sensation in fact announced the manic phase. "Medically speaking, I was as disordered as before – yet I was happy!" Silent so long, he now wanted "to utter as many thousand words a day as possible." Those who know the effects of "speed" will be reminded of them. "For several weeks I did not sleep more than two or three hours a night . . . however . . . all signs of fatigue were entirely absent. . . ."

followed by a period of normality

followed by manic elation

After his long suffering, Beers now enjoyed himself. "Though based on fancy, the delights of some forms of mental disorder are real," though "few, if any, sane persons would care to test the matter at so great a price." And searching the past for experiences like his own, he quotes the essayist Charles Lamb, who wrote Coleridge that he looked back upon his illness "at times with a gloomy kind of envy; for while it lasted I had many, many hours of pure happiness. . . . All now seems to me vapid, comparatively so!"

While depressed, Beers had found "a sinister significance to everything said or done in my presence." Now he interpreted the most trifling incidents as messages from God. "Vast but vague humanitarian projects began joyously to shape themselves in my mind." In church, he heard the words of the Forty-fifth Psalm, "My heart is inditing a good matter . . . my tongue is the pen of a ready writer." They seemed directed right at him.

Ideas of reference *(see p. 43)*

But there is much more to Clifford Beers's story than a vivid account of a psychotic experience, complete with paranoid delusions, ideas of reference, and other textbook symptoms. Dr. Ronald Fieve of the New York Psychiatric Institute speaks of the manic phase as a "high-energy state," and considers it an element in the success of many creative people.† Beers, at any rate, emerged from his long confinement "a ready writer" and a far more effective person than he went in.

* First published in 1908 by Longmans, Green (later taken over by Doubleday), *A Mind That Found Itself* has been reprinted more than thirty times, most recently in 1971. Beers assigned all profits from it to the mental hygiene movement, "absolutely and forever." The quotations in this account are found on pp. 87–94.

† Presentation to the American Medical Association, reported in *New York Times* (June 25, 1973). He recommends lithium treatment because it stabilizes without stifling creativity. One of his patients, the theatrical director Joshua Logan, appeared with him on the program to tell of his own cure.

> Since that August 30th, which I regard as my second birthday . . . my mind has exhibited qualities which, prior to that time, were so latent as to be scarcely distinguishable. As a result, I find myself able to do desirable things I never before dreamed of doing — the writing of this book is one of them.

Charged with his new energy, the "vast but vague humanitarian projects" became practical and real. *A Mind That Found Itself* appeared in 1908. In 1909, Beers inaugurated the mental hygiene movement in America, founding the National Committee for Mental Hygiene, now the National Association for Mental Health. Its aims reflected his own suffering: to bring mental illness out of the shadow of shame and disgrace, to counter the widespread belief that it was incurable, and to improve the terrible conditions in mental hospitals. All of us who have mentally ill relatives are in debt to Clifford Beers, and to the remarkable energies released by his psychosis.

SCHIZOPHRENIA

Schizophrenia *(see pp. 41-47)*

The list of famous schizophrenics is long. The novelist Virginia Woolf was intermittently ill throughout her life; doctors called it "neurasthenia" in those days, but during her worst attack she heard the sparrows sing in Greek outside her window and put it in her novel *Mrs. Dalloway;* the experiences she describes would make an easy diagnosis of schizophrenia today.

Beautiful

> . . . They are signalling to me. . . . He could not read the language yet; but it was plain enough, this . . . exquisite beauty . . . they beckoned; leaves were alive; trees were alive. And the leaves being connected by millions of fibres with his own body . . . fanned it up and down; when the branch stretched he, too, made that statement. . . . Sounds made harmonies with premeditation; the spaces between them were as significant as the sounds. . . . A child cried. Rightly far away a horn sounded. All taken together meant the birth of a new religion.[9]

And the roses on the wallpaper were alive too. The so-called florid symptoms of schizophrenia have never been better described.

"I gather from others that during their attacks they have also heard strange sounds and voices as I did, and that in their eyes too things seemed to be changing." So wrote van Gogh, and in some of his paintings we can see the trees twist and writhe. The lamp above the billiard table, the stars in the sky quiver, surrounded by unquiet waves of light. Perspectives are distorted. Not in all his pictures, only in some. It seems likely that a great artist has made visible to our eyes the changing vision of the schizophrenic.

and terrible

Van Gogh's diary conveys the horror of sensations he can no longer trust. It comforts him to learn that these distortions are "part of the disease" and that others experience them.

> That lessens the horror that I retained at first of the attack I have had, and which when it comes on you unawares, cannot but frighten you without measure. Once you know it is part of the disease, you take it like anything else. If I had not seen other lunatics close up, I should not have been able to free myself from dwelling on it constantly. For the anguish and suffering are no joke once you are caught in an attack. . . . Rey told me that he had seen a case where someone had mutilated his own ear, as I did. . . . I really think that once you know what it is, once you are conscious of your condition and of being subject to attack, then you can do something yourself to prevent your being taken unawares by the suffering or the terror.[10]

Yet taken unawares by the suffering and the terror, van Gogh killed himself not long after writing this. Virginia Woolf lived and worked for twenty-five years after she heard the birds sing in Greek. There were no antipsychotic drugs then, and she was acutely psychotic for two full years, with brief intermissions. But upon her recovery her husband's dogged insistence on rest and quiet had an effect, and the florid symptoms did not recur. It was in an attack of depression that she finally weighted her pockets with stones and walked into the river.

OVERLAPPING CONDITIONS

Overlapping conditions

This should remind us of what we already know: that the varied experiences of mental illness can't be understood by means of the neat categories the next chapter will describe. Depression was a stage in Beers's psychosis, and in Virginia Woolf's too; she describes the same early-morning guilt and misery as Knauth, as "all the other crimes raised their heads and shook their fingers and jeered and sneered over the rail of the bed in the early hours of morning at the prostrate body which lay realizing its degradation. . . ."[11] Manic elation may be felt by schizophrenics. Paranoia cuts across diagnostic categories. Obsessive thoughts and rituals get called obsessive-compulsive neurosis (see p. 36), but they occur in psychotic states as well.* As for anxiety, it is everywhere.

* "The ingredients of the cake began to have a special meaning. The process became a ritual. At certain stages the stirring must be counter-clockwise; at another time it was necessary to stand up and beat the batter toward the east; the egg whites must be folded in from left to right; for each thing that had to be done there were complicated reasons." Patient's narrative, from Josef A. Kindwall and Elaine F. Kinder, "Postscript on a Benign Psychosis," *Psychiatry*, 3 (1940): 527–534; reprinted in Kaplan, *op. cit.*

ILLNESS AND ROMANTICIZING

As in ordinary life, joy is less common than distress. Mental patients can pull misery out of the air:

> I picked up my children's edition of Peter Rabbit because the pictures comforted me, but I wept at the end because I had never given my children camomile tea – even a rabbit had been a better mother than I had been.[12]

Romanticizing illness

They can also cling to it, like the gifted young man, diagnosed schizophrenic, who asked, "What if I'm cured and wake up and find I'm just a shoe salesman?" Schizophrenics can look down on those (often including their doctors and their relatives) who lack "the imagination to go mad."[13] Some patients romanticize their illness. Some therapists do too, and even some relatives.* There's a lot of pain to be borne (and inconvenience, and annoyance, and deprivation, and fear); it makes the bearing easier if you can see beauty and fascination along with it.

It's hard to balance things: in the midst of the pain, to give the beauty and the fascination their due. Perhaps we can't do it, we whose commitment must be to something we call sanity, to thinking and acting not too differently from other people, in a life where responsiveness and responsibility must be combined. If we try we can appreciate the experience of the mad, but we can't afford to romanticize it, unless we're content to give up our part in bringing our relatives into the everyday world we live in. It may not be much of a world, but it's all we've got, and we want them to share it.

In his book *The Mind Game,* Dr. E. Fuller Torrey quotes a story of Harvard's Dr. Alexander Leighton. He tells of an interview with a Nigerian healer, a "witch doctor." "This man," said the healer, pointing to a patient, "came here three months ago full of delusions and hallucinations: now he is free of them." Thinking how cultures differ, and that in his own country the methods the healer had used in the cure would themselves be thought of as delusions, Dr. Leighton asked, "What do these words 'hallucination' and 'delusion' mean, I don't understand?" The native healer scratched his head and looked puzzled; it seemed a strange question to hear from another doctor. Then he said: "Well, when this man came here he was standing right where you

* See Mary Barnes and Joseph Berke, M.D., *Mary Barnes: Two Accounts of a Journey Through Madness* (New York: Harcourt Brace Jovanovich, 1971), and works by R. D. Laing and other "radical therapists"; see also Paul West's beautiful celebration of his deaf and psychotic child's aberrations in *Words for a Deaf Daughter* (New York: Harper and Row, 1970).

see him now and he thought he was in Abeokuta [which is about thirty miles away], he thought I was his uncle and he thought God was speaking to him from the clouds. Now I don't know what you call that in the United States, but here we consider that these are hallucinations and delusions!"[14] Indeed we do. Here and in Africa, therapists, witch doctors, and families, we do the best we can to help get rid of them. We can be encouraged by those returned travelers, the mentally ill who've recovered, yet kept the insight they gained in that other country. The poet William Blake could see the sun both ways, "a round disc somewhat like a guinea," but also "an innumerable company of the heavenly host crying 'Holy, holy, holy is the Lord God Almighty.' " But most schizophrenics don't have the choice. "Schizophrenics," wrote one who got well, "are mystics who don't have the luxury of vacations."[15]

⋙ CHAPTER III ⋘

Diagnoses: Labeling Illness

MEDICAL TERMS AND THE MEDICAL MODEL

Diagnosis

THE IDEA OF ILLNESS implies diagnosis. To diagnose, in Greek, is to distinguish. Doctors have used the word since the time of Hippocrates, "the Father of Medicine," who gave us so many of the words doctors use to talk about diseases. Long before they could accurately explain any illnesses, doctors distinguished them, named them, and attempted to understand their causes. Until less than two hundred years ago they rarely succeeded, because they didn't yet know enough. Still, the words they used allowed them to make sense of the things they noted when they saw suffering people — the fact that their noses ran, or they shivered or burned, or came out in spots, or coughed blood, or jerked involuntarily, or did other things that people have been observed to do from the beginning of time. Noting these things, doctors could often predict whether they'd get worse or better, and what would help them.

Symptoms

Today, doctors can do better: they can explain most of the physical diseases which plagued our ancestors through the centuries. When a patient is called diabetic, for instance, that name sums up a great deal of medical knowledge. He has acquired that label because he presents *symptoms,* recognized as usually occurring together, for reasons which may be understood and can guide treatment. In medical terms, diabetes presents a recognizable *syndrome* of symptoms which are *pathological* (the result of disease), and a known *etiology* (an account of causes). Its *prognosis,* or probable course, is favorable, because there is an effective *therapy,* or treatment. Before that the disease, in time, was *terminal,* or fatal: because it doesn't clear up by itself and there is no known *cure,* it is now *chronic.* All these terms, and many more, are applied to psychological as well as physical conditions, for mental and emotional symptoms too have been considered from the beginning of medicine as the result of disease, and a proper concern of the physician.

and other medical terms

If we're talking about problems in living, of course, these terms are much less appropriate. If mental illness is a myth, this *medical model,* or medical way of thinking about a problem, is irrelevant at best; at worst, misleading or harmful. Dr. Szasz believes that people undergoing the kinds of experiences described in Chapter II are hurt, not helped, by being diagnosed as psychiatric cases. He feels that medicine cannot help them, that the things that can help them are not medical; that, in short, the medical model only adds to their problems in living. Many other highly qualified people agree.[1] Most psychiatrists don't.[2]

The medical model

Disadvantages

But the argument has been healthy. It has contributed to the spread of an important idea, that disturbed people can often be helped, not in hospitals, but in their own community. And it has posed a basic question: What use *is* the medical model?

Advantages general

Even in the centuries when the causes of disease were still unknown and treatments had no sure foundation, this traditional way of thinking had immense advantages. First, it was compassionate, since it did not fear the disorder or blame it or attribute it to supernatural causes, but tried to treat and cure it. Secondly, it was rational. It worked by the collection and careful interpretation of evidence. This scientific method has borne its fruit in the past two hundred years, which have brought us understanding, hope, and cure for diseases that have tormented mankind since the beginning of its history.*

and specific

But these are very general advantages. More to the point is this question: What, if anything, can the medical model do for the person-in-trouble it calls the patient? Being labeled as mentally ill can stigmatize him and separate him from family, friends, and community. What *good* can it do?

Of course the greatest good it can do is to lead to effective treatment. But even when this doesn't happen, a medical diagnosis can serve the patient and his family. Many patients — and families — are relieved to have a doctor confirm the strangeness of what they are going through by a medical diagnosis.† It gives the sufferer an accepted status in society: he's sick. Mentally ill people may do foolish or brutal or disgusting things, things they may be bitterly ashamed of. A person who has been fighting a losing battle with impulses he cannot control may hear even a word like schizophrenia not with horror but relief. "So that's it! I'm not bad, I'm sick — I never used to act like that when I was well. What's more, a lot of other people are sick in the same way I am." The sick role conferred by a formal diagnosis may also make it easier for us to accept our relative's strange behavior.

Diagnosis is reassuring to some;

to others not.

Some patients, however, may repudiate any lessening of responsibility for their actions. Some families regard a diagnosis of mental illness as a matter for shame. Some therapists feel that the sick role weakens a patient's feeling that he can control his life and work his way out of his symptoms. (Defenders of the medical model reply that the patient must accept the responsibility to cooperate with treatment.) Where feelings are so very individual, responses to diagnosis are individual too.

The medical model has limitations. There are many conditions that

* A powerful brief for the medical model will be found in Miriam Siegler's and Humphry Osmond's *Models of Madness, Models of Medicine* (New York: Macmillan, 1974).

† Van Gogh felt that way: "Once you know it is part of the disease, you take it like anything else."

doctors can as yet only diagnose and describe and that must be served as best they can by other means and other people. There are others that most doctors would be content not to diagnose, but to leave as problems in living.* But in more and more of the major psychiatric disorders, treatment according to the medical model can alleviate or cure. When diagnosis points to a single effective treatment, a *treatment of choice,* this ancient way of putting scattered impressions in order finds a justification all can recognize.

PROBLEMS OF DIAGNOSIS

Diagnosis is a very tricky business. Symptoms overlap. Patients act differently at different times. They look different in the office from what they do at home. They look different to different physicians. There are as yet no objective methods – no Schick test or Wassermann – for assessing what ails mental patients. As was true in general medicine 100 years ago, the psychiatrist is dependent on what he can learn in the diagnostic interview, and this depends on skill, luck, the co-operation of the patient, and a host of other variables. It is not rare but common for the same patient to be diagnosed differently by different practitioners. There are even national styles in diagnosis;†[3] if your relative were to be hospitalized in England with mental symptoms he would be much more likely to be diagnosed as suffering from depression (or mania) and much less likely to be diagnosed schizophrenic. A diagnosis is all too often a precise term applied to a condition of which our knowledge is anything but precise.

Remember this as you read the rest of this chapter. We shall describe the major diagnoses, following the classification of the American Psychiatric Association's *Diagnostic and Statistical Manual.*[4] Our descriptions will be brief and superficial, and deliberately so.‡ Our purpose is

* They may have to diagnose anyway: for insurance purposes, a diagnostic label is a formal requirement. (See Chapter XI, on money.)

† J. K. Wing and Janice Nixon, "Discriminating Symptoms in Schizophrenia: A Report from the International Pilot Study of Schizophrenia," *Archives of General Psychiatry* (accepted for publication: probably in 1976), describes a nine-nation study of diagnoses of more than one thousand patients in Colombia, Czechoslovakia, Denmark, India, Nigeria, Taiwan, Britain, the U.S., and the USSR. American and Russian psychiatrists were found to use a broader concept of schizophrenia than psychiatrists in the seven other countries. This has "important implications for treatment and prognosis, and explains to some extent the range of very different types of aetiological hypotheses in vogue at the moment." "The Functional Psychoses; A Review," in (British) *Medical Research Council Annual Report* (London: Her Majesty's Stationery Office, 1974).

‡ If you want to learn more, ask the head of the psychology department of the college nearest you to recommend a text in abnormal psychology. Be sure to check the publication date, and don't waste your time with books more than ten years old. What you read will be confusing enough without being out of date as well.

not to tempt you into diagnosing your relative (or yourself) ; diagnosis is even trickier for amateurs than for professionals. Your best guide to diagnosis should be the qualified professional you have chosen to consult. It is his job to give an informative explanation of the diagnosis and its application to this particular case – in terms you can understand. If he (or she) rejects the idea of diagnosis he should make that clear, and tell you why.

THE MAJOR PSYCHIATRIC DIAGNOSES

Neurosis

This is the most common of psychiatric diagnoses and the hardest to pin down. Although the word "neurotic" is in everybody's mouth, it tells you very little about the person it is applied to, even if the person who applies it is a competent and imaginative professional.* (In point of fact, he is more likely to be your golf partner or your next door neighbor.) A neurosis may first be defined in terms of what it isn't. It isn't a psychosis; the sufferer is in touch – perhaps too much in touch – with the real circumstances of his life. It isn't an organic disorder; if the neurotic's symptoms were thought to have a physical basis he wouldn't be considered neurotic. Neuroses may be viewed as expressions of conflict – conflict between impulse and reality, between one impulse and another, between desire and duties that are irreconcilable. We can observe these conflicts in ourselves and in others, for conflict is normal. We are angry with people we love, or we feel guilty about our avarice, or we find ourselves having sexual fantasies that conflict with our love for our families. Conflicts may be conscious or unconscious, or somewhere between. We may manage them maturely, or childishly. If they are really unconscious, we may not manage them at all: they may manage us.

A conflict view of neurosis

Most of us can accept conflicts as an inevitable part of life. They may cause temporary upsets, but we expect these to pass, and they generally do. Some upsets, however, are not temporary, and some responses are markedly out of proportion to the actual situation in which they seem to arise. The people who have difficulty in adapting to living with conflicts, who overreact to their continuing life circumstances, are those who may be called neurotic.

It is at moments of crisis that conflicts are most likely to break out in symptoms. A change in job or status, a move, the death of a loved one may precipitate neurotic responses. The individual is particularly vulnerable at *points of developmental transition* – when first going to school, during the changes of puberty, when a child is born, when gray

* One competent and imaginative professional, who works mainly with neurotics, says, "A diagnosis is a term you apply to someone you don't know very well."

hair first appears or sexual responsiveness begins to decrease, when children leave home and the nest is empty.

in childhood

For example, a child may return to wetting or soiling at the birth of a new baby. In response to changes in circumstances or family relationships, he may resist going to school, refuse food (or overeat), develop involuntary movements (tics) or night terrors. In most cases these effects are minor and *self-limiting;* that is, they go away by themselves, although a good pediatrician, or family doctor — or teacher, or friend — may help ease the process. In childhood it is rather unusual for such self-defeating behavior patterns to become self-perpetuating, as they do in the adult neurotic; when they do, more specialized help is indicated.

in adolescence

In adolescence, problems tend to cluster around such predictable trouble spots as separation from the family, the development of independence, sexual experimentation, and choice of life-style and career. The famous *identity crisis* — a term of Erik Erikson's — comes in here, as the growing person tries to figure out who he is, where she's going, what values they should be loyal to. The adolescent is trying to put a lot of things together; she or he may be under a lot of stress without much experience in handling it. Depression is common in adolescence, usually mild, but occasionally deepening to the point of threats or even actual attempts of suicide. The personnel of college mental health services are expert in the understanding of adolescent neuroses.*

in adulthood

The adult who fails to adapt to the stresses of his conflicts may express his maladaptation in various ways — through depression, anxiety, sleeping or eating disturbances, infidelity or sexual difficulties, excessive drinking, for a sample. All these are responses which we recognize in ourselves or the normal people around us, but the neurotic's responses are more severe and long-lasting. Neurotics repeat the same self-defeating behavior patterns over and over. The problems in living thus caused may sometimes be more severe than those of the psychotic, who often has fewer such problems than those who are close to him.

Another view

A learning theory

of neurotic behavior

Not everyone sees conflicts as the products of inward or unconscious forces. *Behaviorists,* so called from their emphasis on *observable behavior,* believe that behavior, normal and abnormal, does not arise from within the psyche but is *learned.* Psychologists have produced so-called experimental neuroses in animals by manipulating their environments. If a laboratory rat is placed in a position in which it can obtain food only at the cost of an electric shock — creating, of course, a conflict — its behavior may change in such a way as to suggest the anxiety or depression that characterizes human neurotic behavior. Behaviorism, too, is critical of the medical model. It is largely an American school; its most famous exponent is B. F. Skinner. In recent

* The special problems of the delicate relationship between the disturbed adolescent, his family, and his therapist are discussed in Chapter VII, pp. 182–183.

years, behaviorists have become active in the treatment of mental and emotional disorders; we will be saying more about them in Chapter IV.

The major neuroses

What are the major types of neurosis? If you were to look up neurosis in the most authoritative psychiatric dictionary[5] you would find what seems like a triumph of the medical model; thirty-four different neuroses, some in common use, more that few but specialists have ever heard of.* But the neuroses are no longer subdivided as enthusiastically as they once were. A diagnosis of a neurotic that ignores his actual life-situation tells us nothing about how to help him, even when it's accurate. Most *clinicians* — professionals who actually work with patients — feel that neuroses are not diseases and that the medical model here is not much help.

Symptoms or labels?

Many feel it makes better sense to think in terms of neurotic personalities rather than of neurotic symptoms. Patients have symptoms; personalities have character traits and form habits. "Often," write Frederick Redlich and Daniel Freedman in one of the most authoritative textbooks of psychiatry, "it is impossible to state clearly whether we are dealing with symptoms or habits. Is a patient's life-long anxiety a symptom or a habit?" Is the self-defeating response pattern with which the patient repeatedly meets losses or opportunities a symptom or a character trait?[6]

Anxiety neurosis

According to the diagnostic manual of the American Psychiatric Association, "Anxiety is the chief characteristic of the neuroses."[7] Most of us, in one situation or another, have felt our hearts pound, noticed our palms begin to sweat, lost our appetites, had trouble sleeping. We know what it's like to have our thoughts cover the same fruitless ground over and over. Most of the time, our anxiety passes with the situation that evoked it. In an anxiety neurosis, it doesn't, yet there doesn't seem to be any adequate reason for the hovering feelings of apprehension. (Michael Harrington, after all, was quite used to making speeches.) There may be problems at home, at the plant, or in the office — aren't there always? — but even so, the anxiety-neurotic's response seems disproportionate to what's actually going on.

Depressive neurosis

Neurotic, or reactive, depressions usually start as natural reactions to situations and events that are depressing in themselves. (More serious depressions like Percy Knauth's will be discussed later in this chapter.) It's not neurotic to be depressed or saddened by the loss of someone you love or an unwilling move to a strange city. Such feelings usually lighten after a few weeks or months. A neurotic depression is one in which they persist, and seem too extreme for the situation which provoked them.

Obsessive-compulsive neurosis

We all know what obsessions are, and the word "compulsive" has

* "Housewife's neurosis" is "characterized by a constant preoccupation with cleaning, washing, and dusting the house."

recently moved out of the vocabulary of psychology into common speech – another reminder that most neurotic responses are intensifications of states of mind we readily recognize in our friends and ourselves.* "Obsessive" refers to *thoughts,* those recurring thoughts that we can't seem to get out of our minds. "Compulsive" refers to *acts,* sometimes a complicated series of acts, that the compulsive person feels compelled to perform again and again. Compulsives may wash their hands over and over, count the clothes in their closets (one patient did this twelve times morning and evening),[8] lay out their shirts thirty days in advance, check their cars several times a day to see that the tools in the trunk are properly arranged. We may speak of someone as "compulsively neat," but we can recognize a difference between compulsiveness and scrupulous neatness. It lies in the sense of freedom of choice. The true compulsive *cannot* skip his rituals. If he does he feels so anxious that in severe cases he may organize his whole life around them.

Phobias

Phobias are less common. They too are reactions of irrational anxiety, but the phobic reaction is not vague or ritualized, but extremely specific. What Professor Leonard feared was locomotives; his phobia kept him virtually a prisoner in the university town where he taught.†

Many normal people are uncomfortable around cats or heights, or prefer to avoid air travel if they have the choice. But the woman who fears to leave the house to shop, or the man whose fear of dirt absorbs a large part of his attention, suffer disabilities which are no less crippling for being "all in their heads."

Overlap

All these conditions can overlap. A phobia like those just described may seem a very specific, limited difficulty, but it may arise out of complicated circumstances in the sufferer's life, and the complications it can give rise to may be worse yet. The father of a family who gives up his job because he is afraid to drive to work may have not only the distress of his phobia but the anxiety and depression that goes with joblessness and inadequacy. Neuroses are human conditions, not neatly defined diseases.

* As Redlich and Freedman observe, "The obsessive character is obstinate, orderly, perfectionistic, and overly punctual and meticulous" – like a lot of people we know. *Op cit.,* p. 376.

† Early psychiatrists produced a dazzling variety of labels for the various phobias, something which is not hard to do, since all that is necessary to produce an impressive-sounding medical term is to look up the Greek word for the feared object or situation and attach it to the suffix *-phobia* (fear). *Claustrophobia* (fear of enclosed places) and *xenophobia* (fear of strangers) have entered the common vocabulary, but there are plenty more where those came from, for example, *agoraphobia* (fear of open places, fear of going outside), *cynophobia* (fear of dogs), *ailurophobia* (fear of cats), *zoophobia* (fear of animals), *mysophobia* (fear of dirt and germs), and *acrophobia* (fear of heights). Few of these are much used today, reflecting the growing disenchantment with elaborate labels which contribute neither to understanding nor treatment.

Hysterical or conversion neurosis

The *hysterical neurosis* is traditionally included among the major neuroses, although you are more likely to come across it in fiction than in real life. It's a movie staple; a beautiful young girl loses her voice or the use of her limbs, to be cured by hypnosis or a shock. The term *hysteria* goes back to Hippocrates, who took it from the Greek word for womb. The symptoms called hysterical have changed over the centuries, but physicians have followed the Father of Medicine in attributing hysterical states primarily to women, and hysteria is still a frequent diagnosis in young girls. Here too we should distinguish hysterical character traits from hysterical *symptoms*. Redlich and Freedman describe the personalities that clinicians call hysterical. They dramatize their conflicts, romanticize their lives. They have "a flair for dramatic, exhibitionistic behavior, a certain infantile eccentricity," are emotional, changeable, suggestible, gullible.[9]

Evidently, the world is full of hysterical personalities, male and female. But it is no longer full of the *hysterical symptoms* or *states* which were apparently an important part of nineteenth-century medical practice. Much of Freud's thinking was based on his work with hysterical young women,* and the hysteric remained Freud's archetypal patient.[10] Yet hysterical states are now so rare that students of abnormal psychology find themselves reading about the same cases over and over. The classic cases are those of Freud and his colleague Joseph Breuer, but another case that keeps turning up is that of the young man who, having married reluctantly with the understanding that he wanted no children, lost his sight after a trivial accident on the way to the hospital to see his wife and new baby, later remarking that his duty to his wife now was to divorce her, since he could not tie her down to a blind man.[11] When no physical explanation can be found, symptoms like these are called *conversion symptoms,* since they appear to convert emotions into physical states. Hysteria today takes less dramatic forms, and may appear as frigidity or impotence.

Hysterical states or conversion symptoms

The rarity of what was once an important medical syndrome may remind us how deeply human psychology, normal and abnormal, is influenced by its social setting, by the institutions and values that to a large extent determine how people feel and act and what they expect of themselves. One of the reasons that the manifestations of neuroses shift over time is that our sense of what is right and acceptable about our wishes — what the layman calls his conscience and the psychoanalyst his *superego* — is influenced by cultural change. The hysterical symptoms of the women who consulted the psychiatrists of three generations ago were explainable as their personal responses to particular events and conflicts in their very private lives. Those private lives, however,

* For some second thoughts on Freud's most famous hysteric see Salvatore R. Maddi, "The Victimization of Dora," *Psychology Today* (Sept. 1974).

were lived in a social context that has changed almost beyond recognition. The near-disappearance of classical hysterical symptoms shows how even the most personal responses of our minds and bodies can be affected by the society we live in.

Psychosomatic disorders

To the layman hysterical neurosis seems such a perfect example of what is meant by a "psychosomatic disorder" that it's a surprise to find that nowhere is it so classified. When your wife suggests that your mother's symptoms are psychosomatic, she probably means she thinks they have no physical basis, or not much of one; if not simply that it's "all in her head," that certainly that's where it started. When the practicing physician, whether internist, psychiatrist, or family doctor, speaks of a psychosomatic disorder, he is much more cautious. Ulcers, asthma, colitis (to name only the most common psychosomatic illnesses) are by no means all in the patient's head, but rather in his stomach, chest, bowels, and other organs. When the doctor speaks of them as psychosomatic illnesses, he does not mean that he knows they were caused by emotional factors; he means he knows that emotional factors often contribute heavily to these types of illness. Psychosomatic illnesses are not mental but physical illnesses (and thus will not take up much space in this book). They are illnesses, say Redlich and Freedman, "of unknown etiology in which psychological factors play a variably important role and one that is supposed to be greater than in diseases in general."[12]

A greater role than in other diseases – but there are many diseases in which psychological factors play a part. Any doctor, and most people with experience of illness, know the contribution such intangibles as "the will to live" make to the progress even of diseases such as polio and cancer that nobody would think of calling psychosomatic. Most of us have felt how much harder it is to recover, even from the common cold, when we are overburdened and worried. It is because our bodies and our minds are so mysteriously linked that doctors estimate that more than half the ailments seen in an ordinary doctor's daily practice have a significant psychological component. Everybody knows someone with a "nervous stomach" or who responds to a threatening situation with overeating or a "sick headache." Usually these problems are not severe enough to bring in a doctor, but when they take on more extreme forms they turn up as some of the commonest diagnoses of medical practice – ulcer, obesity, high blood pressure. It is not that the ulcer is not real – a barium meal will locate it, a bland diet will bring it under control, surgery can remove it. Yet psychosomatic factors may be evident too, so that the doctor diagnoses it as "duodenal ulcer with episodes of pain and vomiting associated with work deadlines." The patient is probably vulnerable to stomach trouble (babies can be born with ulcers, and nervous stomachs can run in families); tension and worry make it worse.* Asthma is another illness that can have significant psychological components. Where in one person it is the digestive system that is vulnerable, in another it is the respiratory system, and threat or anxiety may bring on choking fits. Psychosomatic illnesses are in fact somatic illnesses and are normally treated by the internist, not the psychiatrist, but a good doctor will try to understand the psychological factors and take them into account, knowing that unless the patient is encouraged to modify his life to suit his symptoms, they are likely to recur.

Psychosomatic symptoms

A psychosomatic *disorder* is one thing; a psychosomatic *symptom* is another. After listening to your mother, observing her, and giving her medical tests, the doctor may conclude that her symptoms are caused by emotional factors, and will agree with your wife that they are psychosomatic – in the usual sense. He will probably be able to treat them adequately himself, with reassurance and understanding and perhaps an appropriate pill. Nine times out of ten these will do the job.[13]

"Functional?"

Or not?

But not always. Deciding whether a persistent symptom is the result of physical or psychological processes is one of the greatest challenges to a doctor's diagnostic skill. The important concept of a *functional disorder* is, in fact, still defined by our ignorance rather than our knowledge; it's a disorder which has no known physical cause, and which is therefore provisionally assumed to have no physical cause at all.

The words "psychosomatic" and "functional" can cloak medical ignorance. It can happen as the neurosurgeon I. S. Cooper describes: "He didn't have a clue so he said it must be emotional." In this case the misdiagnosis of a young girl's crippling muscular disease as "conversion symptoms" was very nearly fatal. As treatment, she was queried about her sexual feelings; later, she was locked in an empty room, fed on the floor, and told she could come out as soon as she would walk. Her parents removed her against medical advice; the organic causes of her crippling condition were later relieved by brain surgery. On the other hand, Dr. Cooper points out that "many times operations have been performed upon persons whose real trouble was actually emotional distress.†

* Of course stress contributes to mental disorders too. It can trigger depression or even a schizophrenic reaction – which is why Leonard Woolf took Virginia to live quietly in the country. The word *decompensate,* borrowed from the vocabulary of heart disease (where it describes what happens when the heart is overloaded), is often used in such cases. One psychiatrist defined decompensation as "the condition of the camel between the time the last straw hits his back and the time his knee hits the ground."

† *The Victim Is Always the Same* (New York: Harper and Row, 1973), p. 84. The "he" was an orthopedist; in this case symptoms were misdiagnosed by a pediatrician, a neurologist, a neurosurgeon, and a psychologist; their physical nature was finally recognized by a psychiatrist. "In some cases a psychiatric diagnosis is being made for the benefit of doctors who can't stand to say 'I don't know.' " *Ibid.,* p. 111.

Character disorders

Somewhere between the neuroses and the psychoses fall the *character* or *personality disorders,* the neutral term for what is also sometimes called *psychopathic* or *sociopathic personality*. A neutral term is needed. We expect diagnostic terms to be objective and avoid moral judgments, but even the cool textbook descriptions do not succeed in avoiding moral overtones when describing people with "character disorders." Such words as "destructive," "immature," "irresponsible," "shallow," abound. People with character disorders are impulsive and manipulative; they generally disregard the needs and feelings of others. Their behavior ranges from continually distressing to grossly criminal. They are said to suffer from defects of conscience and judgment, but it's pointed out that it's usually other people who do the suffering. One of the many deficiencies attributed to them is a deficiency in the capacity to feel guilt or shame. It is the neurotic who reproaches himself for what he does or fails to do, not the person with a character disorder. Their lack of self-control may make them physically dangerous. Often their families, and sometimes even their therapists, are afraid of them. There are degrees of character disorder, as of most other conditions; the con man, the cheerful rogue who gambles away his family's livelihood, the habitual criminal are often given as examples of people with character disorders. No one would spot them as "crazy." Their day-to-day behavior and their contact with reality are no worse than most people's. Yet they do not seem to take into account the consequences of their actions; they get into the same kinds of trouble again and again. And they are very difficult to help. Distrustful, deceitful, courting rebuff with their insatiable wishes, blaming the world for their disappointments and unable to examine themselves, they flee – or even bite – your outstretched hand.[14]

and some more problems of diagnosis

Are such people mentally or emotionally disordered? Should they be given a psychiatric label? Should they be treated for their problems in living, rather than being punished, or imprisoned, or avoided? Suppose they don't want treatment? They often don't, and treatment seldom does them much good. How socially deviant does a person have to be, how unreliable, how dangerous, how much of a scourge to his children and a grief to his parents before it makes sense to label him "character disordered"? Have we any right to judge him by society's norms and suggest that his failure to measure up is a sign of illness? Is his misconduct really beyond his control? As between calling him a bad man and calling him a sick man – which is preferable? For him? For society? Which is more accurate?

More than any other psychiatric diagnosis, "character disorder" brings up the troublesome problem of the individual's freedom, of his responsibility for what he does. These are questions we cannot dodge, but neither can we attempt to answer them in a practical guide. They have too many possible answers, depending upon whom you ask. Psychology, since it deals with how people think and feel and act, is always shading into ethics; questions of fact and questions of value merge. So we return to questions of fact: character disorder (or some equivalent phrase) is an increasingly common diagnosis, which accounts for a significant proportion of patients in treatment. As to the social meaning of the diagnosis, each of us must sort that out for himself.

Psychosis

The mark of a *psychosis* is that the patient is out of contact with the reality accepted by those around him. He may actually hear or see what they cannot. He may withdraw and fail to respond to ordinary social overtures. He may laugh or cry, talk when he should be silent or be silent when he should talk, say strange things. He "acts crazy." Subtle as the finer discriminations of psychosis may be, people who are psychotic are pretty easy to spot. They have a strange quality which is unnerving to people who aren't used to it; even the way they move or stand or sit may be different from normal people, in ways we don't analyze but feel. These are the severest mental disorders; these are the people who in the past were put into institutions because they were so disruptive and because they were often unable to care for themselves, and who more often than not never came out again. Yet it is exactly with these most severely disordered people that in recent years most progress has been made. Neurotics, or those with character disorders, recover, or change, or fail to do so, much as they did a generation ago. The prognosis for the psychotic who has just become ill is today more hopeful than it has ever been. With proper medication and a supportive environment, he or she may not even need to be hospitalized. If they are hospitalized it is often in a general, not a mental, hospital, and they'll probably be out soon. Fewer than 15 percent of cases now require prolonged hospitalization, and the average length of stay is less than three weeks.*

and a great achievement of modern medicine

Schizophrenia

For years the diagnosis of schizophrenia accounted for about a quarter of first admissions to state and county mental hospitals and up to half the total of resident patients. Between 1963 and 1969, with new treatment methods and philosophies of community care (and perhaps changed diagnostic practice), the figure for first admissions fell to about 15 percent, and the number of schizophrenic residents also fell markedly. At the same time, however, the number of young persons admitted — those under twenty-five — rose by almost 20 percent. They don't stay nearly as long as they used to, but in place of the long, hopeless hospitalizations is a troubling development: something that doctors and administrators call "the revolving door syndrome," as patients

* In 1962, the median length of stay (in state and county mental hospitals in twenty-three selected states) was 8 *years.* Morton Kramer *et al., Mental Disorder/Suicide* (Cambridge, Mass.: Harvard University Press, 1972), p. 27.

move in and out of the hospital – and in and out again. The tendency of schizophrenia to recur remains unchecked, says Dr. Loren Mosher of the National Institute of Mental Health, in his 1972 report on schizophrenia.[15] According to Harvard's Dr. Leon Eisenberg, 30 to 50 percent of schizophrenic patients will be readmitted within one year; 60 to 70 percent within five years.[16] If we look at the number of separate episodes of schizophrenia requiring patient care we get some idea of the dimensions of the problem. It is enormous – some 840,000.[17] Schizophrenia remains one of our most formidable health problems, and research into its causes, prevention, and cure should be one of our first health priorities. It causes untold personal and social havoc – in spite of the fact that there is no generally accepted definition of what schizophrenia is. Is it a disease? A group of diseases? A severe maladjustment? A meaningful response to an overwhelming situation that would make sense if we understood the situation fully? A label?* Is it the result of pathological processes within the patient, or within the family and society that surround him, or of both?

More questions we can record but not answer. These questions, however, suggest the elusiveness of the condition. They also suggest the difficulties that beset research on the causes of a condition so hard to define, and the likelihood that any cause that is discovered will turn out to be a cause of some cases now diagnosed as schizophrenia and not of others. It is the variousness of these cases that lead some experts to speak, not of schizophrenia, but of the *schizophrenias* or of *schizophrenic reactions.*

"The schizophrenias?"

One thing schizophrenia is *not;* it is not a "split personality."† Dr. Jekyll/Mr. Hyde or Eve and her three faces do not represent the schizophrenic. The cases in which one body appears to be inhabited by two or more independent personalities make good material for novelists and movie-makers, but they are in fact so extremely rare that they need not concern us. The Greek root *schizo-* does mean "split," but

* "There's no condition called schizophrenia – it's a term of personal and social invalidation." Joseph Berke, in *Going Crazy: The Radical Therapy of R. D. Laing and Others,* ed. Hendrik A. Ruitenbeck (New York: Bantam Books, 1972), p. 54.

† You should also distinguish two words which are easily confused, "schizoid" and "schizophrenic." If your relative is called schizoid it does not mean that he is on the road to schizophrenia. A withdrawn and isolated person who is emotionally detached from people and events may be said to have a *schizoid personality.* ("Schizoid personality" is classified as a personality disorder.) Though his isolation may resemble the withdrawal seen in the early stages of chronic schizophrenia, the "schizoid personality" (in plain English, the loner) does not ordinarily disintegrate into psychosis but continues to function in the same way throughout life. He may even adapt better to the aging process than a "normal" person, since his personality style insulates him against loss. Robert N. Butler and Myrna I. Lewis, *Aging and Mental Health* (St. Louis: C. V. Mosby Co., 1973).

when Eugen Bleuler coined the term *schizophrenia* in 1911* he was thinking of less dramatic splits – between perception and reality, between aspects of the patient's own experience which are normally connected. In Redlich and Freedman's words, he was calling attention to "the lack of unity and coherence of the patient's personality."[18]

Hallucinations, visual and auditory

The schizophrenic's fundamental perceptions of reality are fragmented and distorted. She may look at a telephone and see a pointed gun; he may look at his therapist and see the President. They may hear voices, as ideas seem to split off and take on a life of their own. They may feel that their will is controlled by outside forces. In *paranoid* schizophrenia, a person may think that everyone is talking about him, that newspaper stories or TV programs are referring to him. Those are called *ideas of reference;* Clifford Beers had them.

Ideas of reference

Symptoms like these are the *core symptoms* of schizophrenia. Most American psychiatrists follow Bleuler in considering them secondary to a basic personality disturbance. However, many European psychiatrists do not make this assumption. On the whole, this is for practical rather than theoretical reasons. The core symptoms are relatively easy to recognize, and the effects of treatment can therefore be directly assessed. The wider the concept of schizophrenia, the more disagreement between psychiatrists and the less certainty about causes, treatment, and outcome.[19]

Primary or secondary symptoms?

The variety of schizophrenic behavior

Schizophrenics may be torpid or agitated, their minds may seem empty or a well of rich fantasies. Their insights may be poetic, or their speech may fracture into nonsense, "word salad." They may laugh or for months on end be silent. They may be apathetic, or cruelly upset. And we should remember that much of the time, all but the most regressed may act a good deal like the rest of us. The variety of schizophrenic symptoms is very great. Some are mild, some severe; some spread to the whole personality and cause complete inability to function, some spontaneously disappear.

Naturally schizophrenia has not escaped the human yen to classify. The older subdivisions, which classified patients according to their symptoms, *simple, paranoid, catatonic,* and *hebephrenic,* may be found in any abnormal psychology text. In modern American practice, they have been largely replaced by two newer ones, which refer to the patient's history: *acute* and *process* schizophrenia.

Acute schizophrenia

Acute (or *reactive*) schizophrenia comes on suddenly and hits hard. It attacks someone who has previously been functioning well (Virginia Woolf, for instance) and is usually precipitated by some kind of

* To replace the older term "dementia praecox." "Praecox" (precocious) called attention to the frequency with which the illness attacks young people.

identifiable stress. The patient may be depressed; he is usually confused and highly emotional. Severe as the onset is, in a benign environment and with modern drug treatment, the prognosis for complete recovery is very good.

Process schizophrenia

"Flatness of affect"

Process schizophrenia* develops slowly and insidiously, with no apparent precipitating factors. The patient has probably always been somewhat withdrawn and socially inadequate. He or she is not notably anxious or depressed; rather, their feelings seem to be dulled and out of touch with what is going on. Although the condition is less acute, the prognosis for real recovery, even with drugs, is much less favorable. Formerly, such patients usually became chronic inmates of mental hospitals; now we know that in an understanding environment with medication and adequate social services, many, perhaps most of them, can continue to function in the community.

Many people regard schizophrenia as a kind of diagnostic catchall, hardly better than a synonym for "crazy" (and indeed, you'll have noted that the descriptions we've given of "psychosis" and "schizophrenia" are much the same).† The other psychoses are in fact much less crazy. They are primarily disturbances of mood, emotion, and judgment rather than of fundamental ways of perceiving the world. In American classification, these are grouped together as *affective disorders* – roughly, disorders of feeling, *affect* being the technical word philosophers and psychologists have traditionally used for emotion. The most common of the affective disorders is *depression.*

Affective disorders; disturbances of mood

Depression

To be considered a psychosis, a depression has to be more severe and more persistent than normal, justified sadness or even the out-of-proportion neurotic depressions described on p. 35. Depressions which have some reasonable connection with events in the environment are labeled *exogenous* (or *reactive*) depressions, because they are thought to originate outside the patient. *Endogenous* depressions are those that seem to "come out of nowhere." In fact, they probably come from within the patient as a result of bodily processes not yet fully understood.[20] (We know that some diseases like mononucleosis and infectious hepatitis are regularly accompanied by mild depression, and that more severe depressions may accompany arteriosclerosis – "hardening of the arteries.")

The diagnosis of depression is a matter of degree. The psychotically depressed person feels like the neurotically depressed person, only worse and longer – tired, hopeless, powerless, perhaps apathetic, per-

* So-called because it suggests the existence of a disease process which is not likely to be reversed.

† Dr. Altschule remarks of schizophrenia: "The word, I'm sorry to say, will probably last forever for two reasons, one is that it's meaningless and the other is that it's euphonious. The combination of euphony and lack of meaning is unbeatable." *The Schizophrenic Reactions,* ed. R. Cancro (New York: Brunner/Mazel, 1970), p. 86.

haps suicidal. One kind that is often referred to is *involutional psychosis* (or involutional *melancholia*), a kind of depression that comes on in middle age and is often accompanied by agitation and hypochondria.

Although the boundary between psychotic and neurotic depression is blurred, most (not all) doctors believe that there is an underlying biological basis for severe depressions like Percy Knauth's. Many depressions lift surprisingly rapidly after treatment with electroshock or antidepressant drugs. These drugs are chemically quite different from those that are effective in schizophrenia, which suggests that medical diagnosis, while often deceptive, is still worthwhile, and that the major kinds of mental illnesses have distinct biological differences which require different kinds of treatment.

The rate of admission to state hospitals of people with affective disorders is about a third of that of schizophrenics.[21] Affective disorders, however, are more common than that figure indicates; since depressed and even manic people are less disorganized than schizophrenics, they are more often treated outside hospitals. In the United States, 125,000 people are hospitalized each year for depressive symptoms, and another 200,000 are treated as outpatients.[22] With antidepressant drugs, even severe depressions are now well handled by competent general practitioners or internists, and most of them probably never come to the attention of a psychiatrist.

Manic-depressive psychosis

Much less common than severe depression is *manic-depressive psychosis,* that strange condition in which emotional highs and lows alternate, often with intervals of full normality in between. In contrast to most neurotics and many psychotics, in his manic phase the manic-depressive is not suffering. Like Clifford Beers, he or she feels marvelous, his energy never flags, there's nothing she can't do. This high may last for months, to be succeeded by a deep depression — or a period of normality. Even when manic-depressives are riding high their memory and intelligence are usually intact (for an example of this see Chapter X, p. 292) though they may be oblivious to social consequences. In a manic phase, the leader of a federation of women's clubs appeared at a formal party in a bathing suit — and brought it off, so great was her poise and self-confidence. Whereas even the inexperienced observer may sense something queer about a schizophrenic, manic behavior often goes unrecognized, since it may seem only an intensification of normal optimism.

If we have made manic-depressive psychosis sound rather cheerful, it isn't, not only because of the depression, but because even the manic phase can cruelly disrupt personal and family life. Formerly responsible people, in the grip of a manic interval, spend money they don't have and start in on other people's. They undertake grandiose projects they can't carry out and neglect their humdrum responsibilities. Manic episodes eventually end by themselves (the average length of first attacks, untreated, is six months), but may often leave havoc in their wake. They usually recur, sometimes after months, sometimes years; a few people have a predictable cycle. Recently a specific chemical, lithium carbonate, has been found to be remarkably effective in bringing manic symptoms under control without sedation.

Overlap, gray areas

If you have had actual experience of mentally ill people, you should by now be feeling somewhat uneasy. The people you know – relatives, friends, acquaintances – probably don't seem to fit neatly into clear, well-defined categories. It's true; typical textbook cases of mental illness are found chiefly in textbooks – and we have not yet seen a textbook which does not contain a prominently featured section on the weaknesses of current systems of psychiatric classification. Process and reactive schizophrenia certainly seem entirely different, so different, in fact, that many psychiatrists question whether the acute psychotic reactions should be called schizophrenia at all. Yet even so, Drs. Mosher and Gunderson remind us that "the majority of schizophrenic patients fall midway along the process-reactive continuum."[23] Schizophrenia is clearly distinguished from mania and depression – on paper. But what does the doctor call a person whose thoughts are disordered and who is *also* elated – or deeply depressed?

Process-reactive continuum?

"Schizo-affective?"

> The prevailing concept of schizophrenia is much broader in the United States than in Britain, embracing substantial parts of what British psychiatrists would regard as depressive illness, neurotic illness or personality disorder, and almost the whole of what they would call mania.[24]

We may feel safe in thinking that a diagnosis of schizophrenia means the patient is out of touch with reality. The books say so. But sometimes it is applied to people (particularly young people) who are unusually withdrawn and unrealistic, even when their speech and perceptions are well in order.* One of the chief specialists in schizophrenia, Dr. Robert Cancro, sums it up: "In a very real sense, the

What is schizophrenia?

* "Lena . . . is hard . . . to understand as 'crazy.' She is the type of schizophrenic person whose symptoms are not especially bizarre: preoccupation with herself, withdrawal, somatic preoccupations, an active fantasy life, and hypochondriasis (a fear of heart attacks). The delusional system is not too well elaborated, although she gets paranoid at times – erupting with anger and aggression, threatening to kill people, and fearing that other people might kill her in turn. It's a not uncommon pattern. . . ." Ross Speck and Carolyn Attneave, *Family Networks* (New York: Pantheon, 1973), p. 129.

"Susan arrived with the diagnostic label 'schizophrenic,' despite the fact that she was coherent, logical, did not display hallucinations or delusions, inappropriate affect, or even terribly unrealistic notions or odd behavior. Had I been further along in my training, I would have realized that 'Pseudoneurotic schizophrenia' has a peculiar prevalence at Columbia Presbyterian Hospital." Marc Hertzman, "The Tale of a Pseudoneurotic: or, a Little Knowledge May Be a Good Thing," *Psychiatric Opinion,* 11 (Aug. 1974).

schizophrenic syndrome is anything we wish it to be. The unfortunate thing is that psychiatrists in fact differ sharply in what they wish it to be."[25]

Addiction

Addiction to alcohol and narcotics probably causes more suffering than all other psychiatric problems put together. It contributes to some, it makes others worse. Some it quite simply causes. It cuts across diagnostic categories. Neurotic conflicts may cause people to escape into alcohol or drugs; alcohol and drugs may make character disorders insupportable; prolonged alcoholism can cause psychotic symptoms and brain deterioration. It is exactly because addiction is so common, and so serious, that we are omitting it from this book. If that is your relative's major problem, much of what you read here will still be useful. But for specific information on this most devastating of mental health problems you will need to look further.*

Organic brain disorders

The *organic brain disorders* are mental disturbances or deterioration which, in the words of the American Psychiatric Association's classification, are "caused by or associated with impairment of brain tissue function."[26] In these cases, the patient is acting the way he is for a physical reason, which, as in other medical conditions, can be inferred from his symptoms, his history, and perhaps from medical tests as well. They account for a significant proportion of all psychiatric diagnoses and an even larger proportion of the population of mental hospitals, since so many of them are chronic. Organic brain syndromes account for at least 10 percent of psychiatric patients and almost 30 percent of first admissions to state and county mental hospitals.† The vast majority of these are the sad and familiar confusions of old age, caused by deterioration of brain tissue and hardening of the arteries supplying blood to the brain, and classified as *senile dementia.*

Senile dementia

Syphilitic and alcoholic disorders

Other organic brain disorders result from syphilis and alcoholism: from syphilis, *general paresis,* a mental and emotional deterioration which may involve delusions of grandeur, from alcoholism, *delirium tremens.* Injuries to the brain account for a small number of first admissions, but for a larger number of hospital patients, since once they are in the hospital they tend to remain. An injury to the brain can affect personality and mood as well as the mind and body, as those of us who have known victims of stroke‡ or brain tumor are aware.

Brain injuries

* For a start, there are useful chapters on alcoholics and narcotics addicts in Claire Burch's *Stranger in the Family: A Guide to Living with the Emotionally Disturbed* (New York: Bobbs-Merrill, 1972).

† Redlich and Freedman, *op. cit.,* p. 564; Morton Kramer *et al., Mental Disorders/ Suicide* (Cambridge, Mass.: Harvard University Press, 1972), p. 39. The figures are for the period 1959–1961.

‡ In *Episode: A Report on the Accident inside My Skull* (New York: Atheneum, 1964; Simon and Schuster paperback, 1971), Eric Hodgins gives an informative and readable account of his recovery from a stroke, including his psychiatric hospitalization for depression.

Diseases, drugs, deficiencies

Postpartum depression

Disturbances of menopause

Disorders resulting from alcoholism

Mental deficiency

And anything that inflames or otherwise affects the brain can lead to psychotic symptoms, like the delirium and hallucinations that can be caused by high fever or drugs.* Such symptoms can also be caused by disorders of the endocrine glands, by nutritional deficiencies, and by many other organic conditions. Changes in the balance of hormones in the body can cause emotional symptoms, often severe, as sometimes happens after the birth of a baby (*postpartum depression*, even *psychosis*) or at menopause. Such effects are usually, though not always, temporary. Permanent damage, however, can result from prolonged alcoholism, and alcoholics account for more than a fifth of first admissions to mental hospitals. Mental deficiency is, of course, an organic brain disorder. It is often accompanied by emotional disturbance, and although in theory we distinguish retardation sharply from mental illness, in practice it is often hard to tell where one begins and the other leaves off.

Epilepsy (or "the epilepsies")

Epilepsy is the oldest of all psychiatric diagnoses: the word, and a recognizable description, go back to Hippocrates. For thousands of years the "falling sickness" was among the most frightening and mysterious of mental disorders. The "Idiot" in Dostoevsky's novel of that title was not an idiot but an epileptic whose condition deteriorated as a result of terrible stress, and Dostoevsky knew what he was talking about, since he was an epileptic himself. Now that it is better understood, epilepsy is no longer considered a mental illness, but it is still common. The Epilepsy Foundation of America estimates that 4,000,000 Americans suffer from it, and medical and welfare costs for epileptics run to some one billion dollars a year.

The word "epilepsy" suggests a single disorder. It would be more accurate to say "the epilepsies," for *epilepsy* simply means seizure – what used to be called a fit. Seizures can be caused by head injuries (at birth or after), scars in brain tissue, malformations, and certain chemical disorders. Sometimes the cause is unknown. Epileptic seizures are marked by sudden massive discharges of electrical energy in the brain; even between seizures brainwave patterns are somewhat abnormal in 85 percent of epileptics. (Electrical activity in the brain is recorded in the *electroencephalogram* [EEG]; it is abnormal in many severe mental conditions, though by no means in all.)

* Dr. Mark Altschule of Harvard Medical School points out that schizophrenic symptoms "may be produced not only by brain diseases, *e.g.*, encephalitis and tumors, but by a variety of other organic conditions such as acute mercury or atropine intoxication."[27] More than twenty such conditions are listed in Richard I. Shader, ed., *Manual of Psychiatric Therapeutics: Practical Psychopharmacology* (Boston: Little, Brown, 1975), p. 69. High doses of amphetamines produce a condition indistinguishable from paranoid schizophrenia. Such illnesses as hepatitis and mononucleosis can cause affective disorders; severe influenza has been known to produce "a prolonged manic psychosis indistinguishable from a functional disorder."[28]

Today, medicine can control this ancient disorder, though not cure it. Drugs completely control the seizures of the majority of epileptics; for another 25 percent control is partial. For 20 percent it is still not possible. As with retardation, there is a good deal of overlap with other mental disorders. Epileptics are found in mental hospitals, halfway houses, wherever there are mental patients. In some cases the symptoms of epilepsy are hard to distinguish from those of schizophrenia.*

Accepting the diagnosis

Once an organic brain disorder has been diagnosed, the patient's family can usually be sure that they know the cause of the condition, and the limitations, sometimes minimal, sometimes cruel, which it sets upon the patient's future. This kind of certainty, which is rarely found in other severe psychiatric conditions, has two faces, one extremely painful, one reassuring. Unlike the acute psychoses, in which recovery is often complete, the patient must live his life with his damaged brain and nervous system, and his family can only learn to live with them too. Yet "organic" need not mean "hopeless." Not only is medicine finding a growing number of effective ways to intervene, but the idea of a handicap or impairment can encourage constructive thinking where the idea of a chronic disease may merely make one feel helpless. A handicap suggests that something can be done to overcome it, or at least to compensate for it. This is not always true, but it often is, and it is always true in children. There are many stories, which are both inspiring and true, which tell how courageous families of brain-damaged people have helped them learn, or re-learn, to live in the world. Since the feeling of helplessness is one of the things that hurts families most, when an organic diagnosis is followed by constructive suggestions, it can bring bittersweet comfort. It is too bad – it is far worse than too bad – that this happens so much less often than it could, and that the love and energy of the patient's family go unused for lack of encouragement and guidance.

The burden of guilt

An organic diagnosis can also bring another kind of comfort, relief from guilt. No one believes that the way a person is treated by his family causes epilepsy or retardation, whereas many people believe it causes neurosis or schizophrenia. Cases in which an organic condition is first diagnosed as neurosis or functional psychosis can be extremely painful for families, and these are by no means uncommon. An organic diagnosis seems certain only after it has been made, when all the evidence has finally been put together. Organic disorders are not easier to recognize than other psychiatric conditions; they may be harder.

* For a review of references on this, see Silvano Arieti, *Interpretation of Schizophrenia,* 2nd ed. (New York: Basic Books, 1974). Lesions in the temporal lobe of the brain result chiefly in disturbances of thought and behavior; lesions elsewhere may cause abnormal muscular movements, loss of consciousness, or other symptoms. The best source of information on epilepsy is the Epilepsy Foundation of America (see Chapter XIV).

Organically caused disruptive and bewildering behavior may be labeled as anything from delinquency to schizophrenia, and it may go on for years before its causes become clear. When this happens, there is tension and guilt to spare for all concerned, and an organic diagnosis comes as a relief.[29]

Medical triumphs

In the last seventy-five years, the establishing of organic causes has moved many illnesses once thought "mental" out of the category of "functional disorders" to become the province of neurology or other medical specialties. The delusions of general paresis and pellagra, the strange "aura" of the epileptic seizure, were once attributed to mental illness; the asylums of the last century were full of patients called insane, whose symptoms, as mysterious to the psychiatrists of that day as any others, are now understood as the results of syphilis, vitamin deficiency, and lesions of the brain and no longer called mental illness.

Families whose relative suffers from an organic brain disorder can still use this book, since such patients share the community services, the hospitals, the legal and financial problems – and even some of the treatments – that we will be discussing. *All* families should take to heart one caution: *Before you act upon a diagnosis of mental illness, make as sure as you can of your relative's physical condition.** Neither doctors nor mental health professionals know as much as they should about the complex interaction between the body and the mind.† Be skeptical, be well-informed, and be persistent. And while you take to heart good people's distrust of substituting diagnoses for human problems, remember the continuing progress in medical science. Give diagnosis its due, if you give it no more. We have left behind the days when the psychiatric diagnoses could be dismissed as mere labels, and are moving into an era when reliable diagnosis is the essential first step to effective treatment.

A major caution

* At the spring, 1974, meeting of the American Psychiatric Association, Dr. John Greden of Washington's Walter Reed Hospital, in "Anxiety or Caffeinism: A Diagnostic Dilemma," reported on several cases of "anxiety neurosis" that cleared up when rediagnosed as the result of too much coffee.

† "Psychiatrists professing a somatic-organic therapeutic orientation are scarce; there are simply far fewer than we thought. . . . One index of their rarity is the difficulty our informants, all highly knowledgeable of their respective mental health scenes, had in suggesting prospective interviewees who would fit this category." William E. Henry, John H. Sims, and S. Lee Spray, *Public and Private Lives of Psychotherapists* (San Francisco: Jossey-Bass Publishers, 1973), p. 236. The authors note that both psychoanalysts and psychiatrists, as youths, were much more likely to be interested in the humanities than in the sciences (p. 211). On the other hand: "Unfortunately, denial of both depression and anxiety by the young physician is supported by systematic preoccupation with physical structure and mechanism in medical education and by the gallows humor of medical culture." L. N. Shapiro, "The Influence of Psychiatry in Medical Education," *Seminars in Psychiatry,* 2, No. 2 (May 1970).

CHAPTER IV

Treatments

THE MAJOR CONCERN of families, of course, is not diagnosis but treatment. In this chapter we will outline some of the different versions of the three major types of treatment which might be recommended for your relative: *psychotherapy, behavioral therapy,* and *somatic* (that is, organically based medical) *therapy*. Though this will be a long chapter, we can do none of them justice. It would take an encyclopedia to describe every important treatment method, and no encyclopedia could keep up with the media in reporting new ones, many of which, in any case, are here today and gone tomorrow. If you want to know more about particular methods, consult the reading list in the back of this book.

Each treatment described in the pages to follow was developed by highly qualified and reputable professionals; for each treatment, there are grateful patients and their families who enthusiastically endorse it and highly qualified and reputable professionals who recommend and administer it. That is the most we can say, for modern psychiatry is not a unified field, and there is no treatment, even the best established, that some highly qualified and reputable professionals do not question or bitterly oppose.

Whenever there are many options, the range of choices can be felt as an opportunity or a frightening burden. Yet we believe that the possibility of choice brings, on balance, more hope than discouragement.

1. PSYCHOTHERAPY 1: VERBAL OR INSIGHT THERAPY

> Have I wasted my time by taking stock of myself so carefully? For those who go over themselves only in their minds and occasionally in speech do not penetrate to essentials in their examination as does a man who makes that his study. . . .
> MICHEL DE MONTAIGNE

> The heart has reasons which reason does not know.
> BLAISE PASCAL

Verbal therapy, insight therapy, psychodynamic therapy —

"Listening is the most important technical tool possessed by the psychiatrist,"[1] wrote Dr. Karl Menninger. The doctor listens while the patient talks; the doctor talks (much less) while the patient listens. The talking *is* the treatment. The doctor's skill is to know how to listen, how to encourage and guide the patient's talking, how to help him use what is said. For of course, talking is only a means to an end

— a deeper understanding of the patient's inner life. In Freud's pioneer therapy the talking was expected to go on for years. Its goal was *insight* into the hidden sources of the patient's symptoms. To bring these into awareness out of the deeps of the unconscious would be no easy task. But if it could be done, not only would the symptoms disappear, but the patient, no longer at the mercy of unremembered experiences, unrealized conflicts, and blind drives, would at the end of treatment be ready to live with strength and fullness. No longer "ill," he would be "cured."

three terms for the same approach

Time and experience have tempered early confidence; today therapists of every kind are leery of the word "cure." As Dr. John Romano of the University of Rochester Medical School has remarked, "The evangelical hopes of many of us in the psychotherapy of neurosis have not been adequately fulfilled,"[2] and relatively few psychiatrists ever had any evangelical hopes for the psychotherapy of psychosis. Besides, "cure" implies the idea of a disease, and with it the medical model. Some psychotherapists are still comfortable with this model. But others are increasingly uncomfortable. Many effective psychotherapists are not physicians, and more and more, psychotherapists think of what they do in terms of what we might call an *educational model*. Instead of speaking of cure, with its implication of a doubtful ideal of perfect health to which treatment should bring the patient, they think of therapy as a process which helps a person learn and change, toward new insights about himself and others, toward better ways of handling problems in living, perhaps both. Seen this way, psychotherapy is closer to teaching than medicine.* No wonder so many of our modern gurus are psychotherapists.

An educational model

Dr. Menninger has spoken of a psychiatry that "passes from being a science of classifying and name-calling into a discipline of counsel for the maximizing of the potentialities of the individual and the improvement of social happiness."[3] But counselors and teachers do not teach the sick, but rather all those who want to learn. Insight is a widely sought-after goal. Many seek psychotherapy today not because of illnesses or even problems but because they feel something lacking in their lives. Dr. Leslie Farber speaks of "office practice . . . with people who are complaining that they are not successful enough in this world."[4] Washington psychiatrist Paul Chodoff speaks of patients who seek through psychotherapy the spiritual insight which in an earlier age they might have sought through religion.[5] For better or worse, vast areas of contemporary psychiatry have developed in such a way as to have little or nothing to do with our relatives' problems. "The debate

For whom?

* Dr. E. Fuller Torrey, in *The Death of Psychiatry* (Radnor, Pa.: Chilton, 1974), recommends a medical model for mental illness and an educational model for problems in living; he sees psychotherapists as behavioral "tutors."

ranges," says Dr. Bertram Brown, Director of the National Institute of Mental Health, "between what our priorities should be, the severely mentally ill, or the prevention of all unhappiness."[6] At present, the prevention of unhappiness seems to be in the lead; from Freud to *I'm OK—You're OK* the bulk of what is written about psychotherapy is concerned not with mental illness but with personal and social discomfort.*

Nevertheless, we need to know about psychotherapy. Though our relatives are often too sick for insight or for talking, they aren't always. The prevention of all unhappiness seems a somewhat ambitious goal. But psychotherapy to help our very vulnerable relatives deal with their own unhappiness may be both desirable and possible.

Insight into personal meanings

All verbal or insight therapies have grown out of psychoanalysis, which is at its core a theory of human development. Each of us has developed, over time, his own system of personal meanings – because of them, the way we feel and understand one event is different, sometimes very different, from the way someone else understands it. As one analyst puts it, everybody drags around a variety of excess baggage from childhood experience. Those personal meanings can get us into difficulty when they conflict with one another, or with the meanings other people bring to a situation. When these meanings and the way we handle them are restricting our freedom, becoming aware of the ways they have developed and the ways they distort and disrupt our more adult intentions can allow us to act more freely. The fundamental commitment of psychoanalysis is to increasing the patient's control over his life – his autonomy. At its most ambitious, it speaks of reconstructing a patient's personality. We may distinguish this from *supportive* psychotherapy, whose goal is simply to support the person as needed, without attempting basic changes.

and their development

The criteria of "analyzability"

Analysts consider a certain level of intelligence and verbal sophistication necessary in order to benefit from psychoanalysis. The patient's life should be in reasonable order; psychoanalysis is not a treatment for people who are already overwhelmed by their problems. For all its influence, it is not a common treatment. Of the vast number of Americans who are receiving psychotherapy today, very few are actually "in analysis"; the criteria of "analyzability" and the length and high cost

and cost

* "The results of this study [of one class of Harvard alumni] confirm evidence well summarized by Kadushin, *Why People Go to Psychiatrists* [New York: Atherton Press, 1969], that the rich, the educated, and the comparatively healthy seek and obtain a disproportionate share of psychotherapists' time. There is not adequate psychiatric manpower to offer the adult population of the United States the degree of psychiatric care obtained by these relatively healthy men." George E. Vaillant, "Why Men Seek Psychotherapy: I. Results of a Survey of College Graduates," *American Journal of Psychiatry*, 129 (Dec. 1972).

of a personal analysis* guarantee this, even apart from a growing tendency to challenge psychoanalytic theory and practice.† The chief contribution of psychoanalysis today is to provide therapeutic-educational experience for professionals in the field and for others who wish to pursue that age-old goal, to "know thyself."

limit the use of psychoanalysis.

Yet although you and your relative will probably never be psychoanalyzed, you need to know something of its theory and specialized vocabulary, for it would be hard to find a mental health professional (or indeed any American who can read) completely untouched by its ideas.

Classical psychoanalysis

He (or she) lies on a couch. The analyst is out of sight behind him. The purpose of this position, and of everything else in the analysis, is to make it possible for the patient to re-experience, in the analytic hour, the major developmental influences in his life. It is these the patient is to focus on, not the analyst himself. For this reason, classical psychoanalysts consider it important that the patient not form too clear an idea of what the analyst is really like. This is why they sit out of the patient's line of vision, why they do not treat people they know, why they evade patient's questions about their personal lives or even their nonprofessional interests. This is not professional reserve, or even mistrust of the strong emotions that can arise in so prolonged and intense a relationship. One aspect of psychoanalysis is an exploration into the past, into forgotten scenes and long-repressed fears and anxieties. The more neutral the analyst, the easier it is for the patient to identify him with figures who were important to him, so he can relive these experiences. It's not easy; the more crucial they are, the more likely the patient is to repress them. And it's not enough merely to recall them; with the analyst's guidance, they must be *refelt,* over and over again, if they are to move from unconscious to conscious and lose their power to disturb.

Repression

Bruno Bettelheim describes what he calls "the protocols of psychoanalysis."

> The couch, the supine position, the silence that is essentially broken only by the patient, the encouragement . . . to follow one's fantasy rather than suppress it, all of which induce regression to earlier forms of experience and make it safe to do so. In short, the *setting* encourages re-experiencing in fantasy, but nevertheless with very strong emotions, ma-

Regression

* Assuming several sessions per week for a year or more at forty dollars per hour, several thousand dollars.

† In 1973 analyst Dr. Allen Enelow told a meeting of his colleagues that psychoanalysis was "a dead science and belief system" leaning on questionable "articles of faith" and protected by a training process that amounts to "a long process of indoctrination." *Psychiatric News* (July 18, 1973).

terial that had been traumatic [wounding] when experienced in reality. . . . What was so emotionally destructive in reality can now be safely worked through.[7]

Free association

Other techniques also serve this end. Freud introduced *free association,* in which the patient, relaxed, eyes closed, responds to a word suggested by the analyst with other words he associates with it, often revealing connections that surprise them both. Dreams are a clue to the unconscious; Freud made dream analysis intellectually respectable for the first time since Biblical days.* But these were merely techniques of investigation. The most powerful therapeutic tool, Freud discovered, was the patient's relationship with the analyst.

The interpretation of dreams

A prolonged affectionate relationship with an admired person who cares enough about you to devote large chunks of his or her time to trying to help you can make you feel, and even act, very much better. Many therapists after Freud have thought that therapy works by love; some have gone farther and maintained that this was all the therapeutic benefit consisted of. If Freud had had anything as simple as this in mind, however, he would not have coined the term *transference,* which is a very awkward word for love. According to Freud, it isn't the analyst the patient loves. He doesn't *know* the analyst well enough to love him, and if he did, reasoned Freud (with more modesty than common sense), why should he love this balding, middle-aged man? The analyst's position out of sight of the patient, his brief and noncommittal answers, the studied neutrality of the furnishings of his office, are intended to insure that the patient's feelings, though the analyst attracts them as a lightning rod attracts lightning, are not actually rooted in this relationship at all. Those emotions have been *transferred* from their original objects – father, mother, sister, friend, lover – who were close to the patient long ago. So Freud called the patient's feeling for him transference, and noting his own liking for his patients (which he found equally surprising), he called that *counter-transference.*† He thought psychotics untreatable by psychoanalysis; one of his reasons was that they seemed too absorbed in their strange mental processes to form a transference. The neurotic, however, by shifting onto the analyst the conflicts he first experienced with others, learns to understand both the conflicts themselves and his own characteristic way of living.

Transference

Counter-transference

The therapeutic alliance

Naturally, however, he is aware that the analyst is not in fact his father or mother, but his therapist. The progress of the analysis depends on *the therapeutic alliance* – the phrase therapists use to de-

* Cf. Joseph's interpretation of Pharaoh's dream in Genesis 40–41.

† Though Freud originally noted his patients' tendency to fall in love with him, analysts distinguish *positive* and *negative* transference (and counter-transference). Patients (and analysts) can feel hostility as well as affection.

scribe that sense of a common task which therapist and patient must share. They have work to do together, problems to consider, attitudes to understand. Trust is the basis of the therapeutic alliance. If the alliance is firmly established, the patient can accept, for example, the analyst's apparent unresponsiveness as part of his effort to help him. Without an effective therapeutic alliance, the analysis becomes a futile tug-of-war.

Interpretations

As the analysis progresses, instead of the "hm's" with which he (or she) encouraged recall in the initial stages, they now offer *interpretations,* suggesting why the patient did or felt what he has just reported. Often the patient accepts these, but if they seem implausible, or touch an especially sore area, the therapeutic alliance may falter as the analyst encounters *resistance.* Resistance is more or less present in every stage of the analysis. Expecting it, the analyst tries to understand its meaning, as with anything else the patient does (an analyst would say, "any other production of the patient"). In time the analytic relationship becomes the single most intense relationship in the patient's life. These intensities must be *worked through* too, and the patient brought at length to the point where he is ready, however reluctantly, to *terminate* this relationship which has absorbed so much of his time and energy. The analysis has given him *insight* into the *dynamics* of his responses to life.* The patient understands the meanings which lie beneath his behavior, then, and can recognize for himself the ways in which his past experiences permeate his present ones. Is he "cured"? The modern analyst will probably ask, "Of what?" If he can think, act, and feel more freely, that is enough.

Resistance

Termination, insight

Ego, superego, id

In Freud's three-way division of the psyche, the *superego* tends to represent the values of society, as first experienced in the authority of the parents, particularly the father. It checks, restrains; it is the locus of guilt. The *ego,* the "I," is the more or less conscious awareness and will of the person himself. It is conceived as having major unconscious elements, unspoken assumptions, self-defeating aspects. All the defenses are unconscious ego-mechanisms. The *id* (the undifferentiated "that" of Latin) represents what is repressed, unknown, unconscious — a source of power, perhaps, of creativity in some, but often a source of trouble. The aim of therapy is not to unleash the unknown powers (as some modern schools of thought would wish), but to know them and control them in the interests of the conscious personality. This is the force of Freud's famous formulation: "Where id was, there shall ego be."

* Freud thought in terms of unconscious forces or drives which determined the way the patient met the world. This is why the traditional verbal therapies are called psycho*dynamic* — from the Greek word for force, which also gives us dynamo. The word "psychodynamic" is still current, but the idea of forces has come to sound a little old-fashioned.

Infantile sexuality

Freud shocked his contemporaries by his emphasis on unconscious forces, particularly by his insistence that small children had sexual feelings and experiences, and that these, forgotten and repressed, lay at the root of adult neurosis. It was unpleasant to be told that the baby at the breast was receiving *oral* satisfaction, and that this was sexual in nature. It was worse yet to be told that the next stage was *anal,* that the innocent toddler invested all sorts of emotions in his own excrement, and that the way he was toilet trained might affect him years later. Compulsive smokers (Freud was one) could be seen as having failed to get over the oral stage; collectors and misers were anal. The *Oedipus complex,* which Freud named for the Greek hero who unknowingly murdered his father and married his mother, draws attention to the complex feelings the small boy may feel for his mother and father – for mother, possessive love; jealousy and hostility for father. (Freud called the corresponding relationship in girls the *Electra complex.*) Freud considered that these were universal stages of human development. Normal children passed through them to identify with the parent of the same sex. If for one reason or another this failed to happen, the child was in for trouble. Arrested in the oral, anal, or Oedipal stage, a person would not reach the goal of full *genitality.* A boy might fail to identify with his father, remain attached to his mother, and become homosexual; too masculine a girl would have difficulty adjusting to her biological tasks of sexual receptivity and motherhood. Though Freud abandoned biological research, he was trained as a medical scientist, and biology permeated his view of human personality. Oral, anal, oedipal stages (followed by *latency,* a brief period between six and eleven in which sexual urges lay low) reflected universal biological drives. They were not occasional phenomena, nor were they the result of a particular kind of family or social system. When Freud wrote that "biology is destiny," he was talking about women, but he would have said the same of men. Man's phallic drive determines his life, as woman's receptive uterus determines hers. The *libido,* the basic sexual drive, underlies all creation and achievement. It may perhaps be *sublimated* to produce, not babies, but empires, works of art, and psychoanalytic theories. Beneath all human achievement is nature's biological drive toward self-perpetuation.

The stages of psychosexual development

Genitality

Latency

Sublimation

Psychoanalysis, with its poetic mix of dreams, hidden conflicts, and dark instincts, so caught the popular imagination that it has become, for many people, almost completely identified with psychotherapy. And indeed a person who had just been told her son needed *psychoanalytic psychotherapy* might be excused for thinking that what had been recommended was psychoanalysis, complete with couch. Not at all. Psychoanalytic psychotherapy is merely one broad term for a

Psychoanalytic psychotherapy

therapy that makes use of psychoanalytic assumptions but modifies the psychoanalytic method. It is a term most likely to be used by analysts (to describe what they do when they aren't doing psychoanalysis) and is roughly equivalent to psychodynamic therapy – helpful talking about the conflicts within.

Differences from psychoanalysis:

Psychotherapy in this broad sense (unlike psychoanalysis) is very widely obtainable. You may get it from an analyst (for relatively few analysts today confine their practice to classical psychoanalysis), a psychiatrist, a psychologist, or a social worker. You may get it in a community mental health center or a luxurious private office. It may cost a little or a lot. But wherever you find it, the patient (or *client,* as he may be called if he's not consulting an M.D.) won't lie on a couch; he or she will sit on a chair facing the therapist, usually with a desk between them. Instead of listening and waiting for hidden feelings to emerge in dreams and fantasy, the therapist talks more and is much more active. He asks more questions, interprets more freely, even gives advice. There is more give and take, since the participants can see each other. The sitting position itself encourages conscious rather than unconscious processes. Position carries a lot of meaning, as modern students of "body language" attest. One psychiatrist titles her account of her methods *Beyond the Couch;* abandoning the desk, she sits close enough to her patients to touch, to push, to hold hands. The new position alone suggests what she is recommending: a move beyond insight to "a new therapy of contact, risk, and involvement."[8]

A different position,

more focus on specifics, shorter

Psychotherapy tends to focus on specific problems rather than on thorough exploration of what's within; it's therefore shorter than psychoanalysis.* It shares the basic psychoanalytic assumption: that the patient's trouble probably did not arise yesterday, but is only the latest example of a way of dealing with things which has developed over time. Unlike psychoanalysis, however, it rarely pushes back into infancy and early childhood; it finds plenty to work on in later childhood and adolescence.

Assumptions shared with psychoanalysis: problems go back to childhood and are best treated by personal interaction.

A second shared assumption is that problems are best worked through in the personal interaction of patient (or client) and therapist. "Transference" occurs in psychotherapy too. The insight the client develops in the office, it is hoped, will carry over into the way he handles his daily life.

Who gets psychotherapy?

Psychotherapy, like psychoanalysis, is largely consumed by people who are not mentally ill. Few clinicians would treat a chronic schizophrenic with traditional psychotherapy, although most would accept a

* It need not therefore be less effective. Professor Peter Sifneos of Harvard Medical School reported to the Honolulu meeting of the American Psychiatric Association in May, 1973, that patients improved more in a weekly treatment program averaging four months than under more prolonged traditional treatment.

young person already recovering from an acute schizophrenic reaction. Psychotherapy will often be recommended for depression, however, alone or in combination with other treatments, depending on severity. In general, the more normal your relative's behavior and conversation, the more likely he is to obtain verbal psychotherapy – and to benefit from it.

You shouldn't conclude from the foregoing highly generalized descriptions that all psychotherapy shares pretty much the same assumptions and proceeds in the same way. Descriptions like these average out many differences in theory and practice. These may be exactly the differences you or your relative would find most significant.

> Psychotherapy does not consist of a definite set of operations and the essence of the procedure is still a matter of personal preference, bias, and lively controversy. . . . The procedures subsumed under the "psychotherapy" label include the classical psychoanalytic procedure, those based upon it, and those emphasizing only understanding or affect-expression or modification of observable behaviors by operant techniques – to name only a few of the occupants of this psychosocial Tower of Babel.[9]

Tower of Babel?

This guide can identify some of the louder and more persistent voices (not all, though); it cannot attempt to guess which ones have something to tell you about your particular problem.

Psychotherapy no sooner began than it began changing. Freud changed both his theory and his practice in the course of his long lifetime,* and his disciples altered them still more. Alfred Adler, who gave us the phrase "inferiority complex," emphasized sex less and power more; he traced the adult's troubles to the sense of inferiority he thought necessarily present in every child. Wilhelm Reich, on the other hand, intensified Freud's sexual emphasis, founding a therapy on the liberation of the drives Freud had wished to recognize but control. Otto Rank emphasized the role of the will and insisted that therapies could be brief long before the idea became common. Carl Jung was the most intellectually influential analyst next to Freud himself; the two of them should have shared a Nobel Prize for literature, for their ideas have shaped the literature of the twentieth century more than the work of any single novelist or poet. Jung interested himself in basic personality types and originated the terms "extrovert" and "introvert." More optimistic than Freud, for him the unconscious was even more important – a deep reservoir of energy and potential creativity, a repository of collective experience and basic patterns of human life. He called these *archetypes,* and saw them repeated in myths and fairy tales from all over the world. Differences like these

Adler

Reich

Rank

Jung

* For example, he abandoned hypnotism (early) and introduced the idea of Eros and Thanatos – Love and Death (late).

guaranteed that even in Freud's lifetime, it would not have been enough to say you were being analyzed; you would have had to say with whom. Representatives of all these approaches (and more) exist among present-day psychotherapists.

The interpersonal approach

However Jung, Rank, Reich, and the rest differed from Freud and from one another, they retained Freud's emphasis on inner conflicts, unconscious drives – what the trade calls *intrapsychic processes.* The great psychiatrist Adolf Meyer, a contemporary of Freud's who practiced all his life in America, saw things differently. He considered that man's outer life was no less important than his inner life to his mental balance. It was necessary to take into account the actual facts of how a patient lived, the people and situations that faced him daily in family and community. This common-sense view led Meyer out of hospital and office, into mental health work with policemen, ministers, schoolteachers. Dr. Leston Havens of Harvard Medical School calls him "the principal moving force in the community hygiene movement."[10] (Chapter VI, "What the Community Can Offer," will give an account of the fruits of this concept of community psychiatry.)

Adolf Meyer

Harry Stack Sullivan, a great "neo-Freudian"

In the next generation, Harry Stack Sullivan, whom Havens calls "the most original figure in American psychiatry," elaborated and deepened this interpersonal point of view. When the same imaginative attention was paid to events outside the patient as had been paid to events inside, all sorts of subtle interactions might be detected. Transference, for instance, wasn't limited to the patient and his doctors, "it occurs every day with everyone. . . ."*[11] The patient's everyday present turned out to be as rich and complex as the classical psychoanalysts had found his past, and as worthy of therapeutic attention.

Today there is a significant group of interpersonal psychotherapists centered in the Washington School of Psychiatry that Sullivan helped found and in the William Alanson White Institute of Psychiatry, Psychoanalysis, and Psychology in New York. But Sullivan's emphasis on interpersonal relations in the here-and-now has influenced the practice of psychotherapy of all kinds. Some analytic purists still concentrate on inner responses to events long past, but most psychotherapists today, however orthodox their credentials, deal willingly with present problems and relationships, suggesting new ways of handling them. Some even give practical advice, as the classical analyst never did. Many work in family and community psychiatry to modify the interpersonal environment that makes it hard for people to keep their emotional balance. What was heresy in the thirties and forties is now taken for granted.

* This account of the interpersonal, or social, approach leans heavily on Dr. Havens's account. His evaluation of Meyer and Sullivan makes fascinating reading, though directed more to professionals than to the general reader.

Who gets interpersonal psychotherapy?

Unlike most orthodox psychoanalysts, Sullivan worked with psychotic patients. He himself had experienced psychotic episodes, and he talked to his psychotic patients with legendary adroitness, combining delicacy, firmness, surprise, and human respect in a potent mix. He is said to have remarked, "No one is schizophrenic when he talks to me"[12] — which, true or not, can remind us that the great clinicians have extraordinary effects on patients others have found unreachable. Other gifted therapists who reported remarkable success with schizophrenics are Frieda Fromm-Reichmann, John Rosen, and Silvano Arieti,* as well as R. D. Laing, Abraham Esterson, and the young psychiatrists who have been influenced by their work. From your practical point of view, however, you should consider that even their successes are fragile and uncertain (even Sullivan's patients could not be talking to him all the time) and that the services of a master clinician are difficult to come by.

Another who saw social and cultural influences as more important than biologically determined intrapsychic drives was Dr. Karen Horney. Excluded from teaching at the New York Psychoanalytic Institute, she founded an institute of her own. Freud's view of feminine psychology was to her plain cultural prejudice masquerading as biology. Anatomy was not destiny. It was not instinctual sexual drives, repressed in childhood, which caused neurosis, but the insecurity a child felt when his or her family did not adequately meet the need to develop a sense of confidence and strength.

Family therapy

Family therapy is such a natural outgrowth of the concern with interpersonal relations that it is surprising it did not come on the scene until the fifties. If a person's problems are rooted in his relationships with others, family therapists feel that therapy should bring those others into the treatment. Most people live in families, and family conflicts and alliances are among the most potent shapers of our lives. This realization, of course, is not limited to the interpersonal school. What else, after all, is the Oedipus complex about? Individual therapy also hopes to influence the client's relationship with others, but it expects to do this indirectly, through changes in the person undergoing therapy. Traditionally, psychoanalytic psychotherapy avoided contact with others close to the patient, usually refusing to treat other members of the family. It was (and is) thought important to the therapeutic process that the patient should feel he could say anything. The intimacy and trust between patient and therapist could not be compromised by the possibility that the therapist had an equally intimate relationship with mother, father, or sister. The advantages of such a

* Dr. Arieti's *Interpretation of Schizophrenia* (2nd, revised ed.; New York: Basic Books, 1974) gives a fine account of a lifetime's work in the psychotherapy of schizophrenia, with sympathetic accounts of many patients.

confidential relationship are obvious, and when psychoanalytic psychotherapy focuses on the past (especially if the patient has grown up and left home) it may be strongly argued that what actually happened between family members is less important than what the patient thinks happened and how he or she feels about it. But what about therapy that focuses on present problems? Many therapists are remarkably shrewd listeners, adept at assessing the real situation which may lie beneath the exaggerations or evasions of a troubled client, whether he insists that his home life is perfect or blames it for all his troubles. Family therapists, however, take a more direct approach; they get the family into the office – or better yet, see them at home – and check the situation out.* When they do this, they often find a situation more complex than they ever could have predicted, and one which may be contributing to the troubled person's problems in ways neither he nor his family suspect. The therapist's work is to show these people what they are doing to each other, and to teach them to do better. Since actions speak louder than words, the talking treatment is supplemented by many ingenious techniques. The therapist may help family members to appreciate one another's viewpoints by assigning them to take over one another's roles, so that a son takes his father's customary chair and says the kind of thing he usually hears his father saying, while the father answers like his son. The universal difficulty in seeing ourselves as others see us may be attacked with videotapes and recordings, in which families can see and study the discrepancies between what they mean (or think they mean) to do and what they do do.

New techniques –

Role playing

Videotapes

Although the bulk of their work is still with problems of living that might be diagnosed neurotic, family therapists work with psychotics as well. In this kind of therapy, however, it is important to understand that the *family,* not the individual, is the unit being treated. One member of that family happens to have come to professional attention. He might be diagnosed as neurotic, or character disordered, or psychotic (or brain-damaged or retarded) by a clinician who was interested in diagnosis. To family therapists, however, this troubled person is merely the *index patient;* his troubles, his deviant behavior, his delusions, no matter how severe, must be seen as an index to what is really significant: trouble in the whole family. Though no one has labeled them patients, the rest of the family may be sicker than the member who has come to professional attention. Family therapists in general do not accept the medical model of *individual* psychosis, though they talk freely about sick or pathological *families.* They are

Who gets it?

The index patient and *his family*

* The layman is likely to see this as simple common sense, but it is considerably less obvious to the clinician trained (as most are) in individual therapy. Dr. Lewis Wolberg, an analyst widely respected for his knowledge and flexibility, writes of a well-known family therapist with surprise that is almost audible: "Speck even makes home visits." In Adelaide Bry, *Inside Psychotherapy* (New York: Basic Books, 1973).

very reluctant to believe that other members of a family can be healthy if one member is mentally ill. Most accept the natural implication of the interpersonal approach, that emotional problems, including psychosis, are caused not by inner frustrations or by biological processes, but by faulty interpersonal relationships. Sullivan, and many after him, emphasized the evasive and ambiguous ways of communicating which can grow up within a family. These, it is held, may confuse and mystify a person to the point where he or she is unsure even of what is being heard or seen, leading in time to symptoms which are diagnosed as schizophrenia.* Family therapy aims to substitute clearer and more open communication for these unhealthy interactions, in the hope that the family can change the ways of living that have brought them such distress.

Faulty patterns of communication

Mystification: one theory of the cause of schizophrenia.

Scapegoating

The communication theory of schizophrenia, like other theories, has its own vocabulary. Central to the theory are *scapegoating* and the *double bind.* In scapegoating, the family is thought to choose unconsciously one member to bear the burden of the family pathology, or disease process. He or she is the scapegoat, the one who is called "mentally ill." What she says isn't taken seriously; her communications, and she, are *invalidated.* Seeing her as ill enables the others to function so that the family, instead of welcoming the recovery of the "ill" member, often resists it.

Invalidation

The double bind

The *double bind* describes the familiar human predicament summed up in the phrase "heads I win, tails you lose." A typical double bind: a hostile and anxious mother who withdraws when her child approaches her affectionately, but because she doesn't recognize her hostility still encourages his affection and also withdraws if he *doesn't* approach her. The child can't afford to see through the inconsistency; he's safer if he remains confused, since he'll suffer if he perceives his mother's hostility, and if he doesn't. Enough of this sort of thing and "the victim has learned to perceive his universe in double-bind patterns." The stage is set for the development of schizophrenia.†

You should be aware that from the point of view of family therapy the book you are reading is open to serious challenge. The very idea of a guide for families of the mentally ill reinforces "the notion that families can be conceptually separated from the events called The Psychiatric Illness of a Family Member," an "archaic" and "clinically very damaging" point of view, "because it perpetuates the scapegoating

* The most influential modern spokesman for this point of view, which was developed by the anthropologist Gregory Bateson and others in the late fifties, is R. D. Laing.

† This is the double bind as described in the original paper by G. Bateson, Don D. Jackson, Jay Haley, and J. H. Weakland, "Toward a Theory of Schizophrenia," *Behavioral Science,* 1 (1956):251–64. It has since been broadened and popularized, notably by Laing.

of that person the family identifies as the index patient."[13] Family therapy is obviously of intense interest to relatives of the mentally ill. Its theory and practice raise painful questions, questions that are so important that a later chapter of this book will consider them at length.

For further discussion see Chapter V

Another school of psychotherapy is that which calls itself Existentialist. Its roots in the philosophy of Martin Heidegger and Jean-Paul Sartre are outside the scope of this practical guide, but in general, existential therapists strive for an authenticity and closeness that go far beyond the usual attachment between therapist and patient. Existential therapists, unlike orthodox psychoanalytic or interpersonal therapists, are not after an objective view of the patient so that they can help him. They do not believe such a view is possible. In the existential therapeutic encounter, the therapist as well as the patient expects to be changed and welcomes it; "Nothing happens," one wrote, "until the doctor is touched by the patient."[14] The goal, for doctor and patient, is no predetermined idea of health, but contact, togetherness, true emotional sharing of experience. The therapist risks himself to reach out for the patient, in the hope that the best way to reach someone else is not as a doctor (or other professional) but as a vulnerable and imperfect human being.*

Existential therapy: not "transference" but the human encounter

Existential psychiatry was developed first with psychotic patients, but existential psychotherapists today usually treat the same kind of patient as other private psychoanalytic practitioners.

Who gets it?

Unlike most other major schools of therapy, non-directive, or "client-centered," therapy originated not with a psychiatrist but a clinical psychologist, Carl Rogers at the University of Chicago, in the thirties and forties. (Hence the word "client" rather than the doctor's word "patient.") The non-directive therapist feels that his (or her) function is not to probe the depths of past or present emotion, but to support and encourage the constructive impulses and values they are sure exist within the client. Like classical psychoanalysts, non-directive therapists talk relatively little, but for a different reason. As Professor Daniel Wiener of the University of Minnesota puts it, "they feel that the desired ingredients for feeling better already lie within the client, and need only to be freed, expressed, and used."[15] The forces for change are already present; they need only sympathetic reinforcement. Therapist and client have a warm relationship, but "transference" is not particularly important.

Non-directive therapy: client-centered, optimistic counseling

supportive, not probing

Like psychoanalytic and existential therapy, non-directive therapy is relatively uninterested in altering the patient's social milieu. With

* Efforts to explain existential philosophy briefly are notoriously futile, and this seems to extend to efforts to explain existential psychotherapy as well. Havens calls it "a clinical method still little understood" but considers it one of the four major schools of psychiatry.

help client or patient can learn to live better in the world as he finds it; the potentiality for change lies within him.

You are less likely to come across non-directive (or existential) therapists than those whose orientation is interpersonal or Freudian; Rogerians (rarely explicitly identified as such) are found mostly around universities and in large cities. The non-directive method, however, has had a strong influence on other kinds of therapy, especially in that important area where "therapy" shades into "counseling."* Since it concentrates on what the client wants for himself and intervenes less in profound psychic processes, the non-directive approach is often used by guidance counselors, teachers, social workers, ministers, and others, who understand that analytic probing can be profoundly disturbing even in the hands of a highly trained practitioner. Sympathetic support of a troubled person's best impulses should help him, they feel, and can't possibly hurt.

Who gets non-directive therapy?

In private practice, non-directive therapists, too, see mostly those who seek a happier life rather than those we'd call ill. Since most counseling, however, goes on in public settings such as schools, clinics, and mental health centers, your mentally ill relative may well encounter this approach in one of these.

Sociotherapy

Sociotherapy is a fancy word for the kind of active counseling that tries to help a client (or patient) by improving the circumstances he has to cope with and his ability to cope with them. It is more likely to be given by social workers and paraprofessionals than psychiatrists. They may locate a suitable job for a recovering patient, coach him for the interview, talk to his employer, find him an apartment, find him another when he's evicted, visit him there. It is one of the most important kinds of aid for the mentally ill and will be described at greater length in Chapters VI and IX.

One of the most important kinds of therapy for the mentally ill

"Radical therapy"

"Radical therapy," a creation of the troubled sixties, derives ultimately from the interpersonal approach. It finds the causes of mental illness in society itself. R. D. Laing finds schizophrenia a reasonable reaction to an unreasonable society. "Both Szasz and Laing see the individual's state of mind from the viewpoint of the failure of the world."[16] Everybody's out of step but Johnny.

Radical therapists challenge the assumptions of psychoanalysis as bitterly as they do the idea of a biological basis for mental illness. The sources of our troubles lie outside us, not within the psyche or the body. Society not only defines normal behavior, and thus the deviation from normal that we call mental illness, it deprives us of basic needs. It

* Of psychotherapy, Dr. Henry A. Davidson writes, "You cannot distinguish it from counseling or casework unless you relate it to the concept of illness," which many clinicians refuse to do. "The Semantics of Psychotherapy," *American Journal of Psychiatry,* 115 (Nov. 1958).

crowds people into cities, teaches them an ethic of competition, expects its young men to kill in wartime and abroad but refrain in peacetime and at home, suppresses the spontaneity of its children by a conformist educational system. It throws up special roadblocks in the way of those who are female, or homosexual, or poor, or black. In short, society oppresses the individual, and it is no wonder he and she go mad — a term radical therapists use rather freely. When this occurs, little relief can be expected from psychotherapy, since most therapists are members of the establishment. They impose an oppressive society's definition of illness and consider that the goal of treatment is to enable the troubled person to adjust to society, rather than working to adjust society to her or him.* Radical therapists recommend, not psychiatry, but "antipsychiatry." They regard psychiatry as all too often a brutal assault on vulnerable minds, and by this they do not mean only the use of behavior therapy, drugs, and surgery (which they uniformly oppose), but much of psychotherapy as well. True health is not a matter of adjustment, but of finding yourself. The schizophrenic may see more clearly than his family or his doctor; the social deviant may be healthier than the policeman who jails him.

Antipsychiatry

The radical patient may have recourse to a growing number of radical therapists, especially if he lives in New York, Boston, Los Angeles, or the Bay Area. Most have been trained in traditional therapies, either psychoanalytic or interpersonal, and become disillusioned. The therapies they practice are versions of these therapies, modified to fit their social emphasis. They represent a small but significant current in psychotherapy. R. D. Laing's books are useful but incomplete introductions to their point of view. A fuller overview may be found in *Going Crazy: The Radical Therapy of R. D. Laing and Others.*

Radical therapists are committed to treat everybody who needs it, psychotics not excluded. In practice, like everybody else, they treat mostly articulate neurotics. Some, like Laing and his colleagues, Abraham Esterson, and David Cooper, have done remarkable work in setting up humane halfway houses (see Chapter VI) where "sane" and "crazy" mingle without much attention paid to who is which. In this insistence that therapist and patient are both human beings on a common journey, radical therapy and existential therapy have something in common.

Group therapy

Except for family therapy, everything we have said assumes that the special kind of personal interaction we call psychotherapy takes place

* The publisher's blurb for *Going Crazy: The Radical Therapy of R. D. Laing and Others* describes them as ("by and large") "power-hungry, money-grubbing apologists for the existing order, male chauvinists and bourgeois rationalists who have lacked all respect for the awesome depth and complexity of the human experience."

between two people only. In the early psychoanalytic days, this *dyadic* relationship, based on the ancient doctor-patient twosome, seemed essential. But in the depression years, some classical psychoanalysts, looking for ways to reach more people at lower cost, began to experiment with treating patients in groups. They were soon joined by other clinicians, as it began to be seen that patients could learn from each other as well as from the therapist and that there were certain kinds of learning which took place better in a social situation. (We may see here the educational model supplanting the medical model. Education has traditionally taken place in groups, since individual tutoring has always been expensive.)

Psychoanalytic, interpersonal, Rogerian, radical, and other approaches are all represented in group therapy, in various combinations. Membership in the American Group Psychotherapy Association is steadily increasing, and Beverly Hills analyst Dr. Martin Grotjahn envisages a future in which "almost all therapy will take place in groups."[17] Not all clinicians would be ready to go that far. Psychiatric training still emphasizes individual treatment and gives little training in group work. But most therapists, whatever their own practice, recognize that group therapy is the most practical way of offering psychotherapy to the hosts of people who want it, and they are willing at least to contemplate Dr. Grotjahn's picture of a future in which "it will never be a question of a group or no group, but of *which* group."

Lay groups

There are groups for children, for parents, for couples, for adolescents, for alcoholics, for people with assorted problems in living. Some of the most effective groups are run by laymen and cost nothing; examples are Alcoholics Anonymous and Recovery, Inc., an organization for former mental patients. Such groups will be described further in Chapter XIV, "The Lord Helps Those Who Help Themselves."

Who gets group therapy?

Private group therapy serves the same clientele as individual psychotherapy. In mental hospitals and community mental health centers, however (see Chapter VI and Chapter IX), group therapy serves all who are thought to be able to benefit from it, including the severely ill. Group therapies offered the mentally ill are likely to be less verbal and focus less on the patients' inner lives and conflicts. The goal is to increase their contact with the actual world. Many nonverbal techniques are used, which may shade imperceptibly into occupational therapy, art therapy, dance therapy, psychodrama, and others. These will be described briefly at the end of this section.

Group therapy for the mentally ill

Since psychiatrists rarely work more than part-time in community facilities (their time is too expensive), group leaders in public facilities are more often psychologists or social workers. Increasingly, they are paraprofessionals. In hospitals it is very often the psychiatric nurse who undertakes the difficult task of keeping patients in contact with a world that contains other people, instead of sinking into isolation, despair, or indifference. Since group therapy is the major kind of psychotherapy available to the mentally ill, more will be said about it in Chapter IX.

Therapy groups and encounter groups

A distinction should be made between therapy groups, and *encounter groups* (or "sensitivity training"), where essentially well people meet, frequently with a trained therapist (but sometimes with practitioners whose enthusiasm for new methods outruns their experience or common sense), in search of intimacy, genuineness, openness, self-realization, and other good things. Recent research suggests that emotional stability is an important quality to take with you into an encounter group, and that it is a mistake to enter one in search of it.

Encounter groups are not for sick people.

In a controlled and careful study of seventeen encounter groups led by experienced professionals, Morton Lieberman, Matthew Miles, and Irvin Yalom (two professors of psychology and a psychiatrist) reported a "casualty rate" of almost 10 percent – among ordinary students at Stanford University who volunteered for the study. The rate is particularly disturbing, since Dr. Lieberman and his colleagues suspect that the full extent of psychological damage was even greater.

> We were conservative when it came to defining casualties. We put persons in this category only if we found evidence of serious psychological harm six to eight months after the group ended and if we felt that their psychological difficulties could reasonably be attributed to the group experiences. We were also disturbed to find that a leader's judgments about casualties in his group were unreliable. The co-participants' perceptions of who got hurt were much more reliable.[18]

Who enters an encounter group?

Many encounter groups make no attempt to screen applicants, so mentally ill people may enter them. Considering their effect upon a significant proportion of college students who were apparently well, it seems prudent to advise people who have any influence over the therapy of emotionally unstable relatives to use it to steer them away from encounter groups.

"Transactional analysis"

Transactional analysis is a therapy that usually (though not always) takes place in groups. Founded by a psychoanalyst, Dr. Eric Berne, author of the famous *Games People Play*,[19] it combines psychoanalytic and interpersonal insights, presented with a kind of brisk common sense. It concentrates on people's interactions ("transactions," sometimes "games") with each other, shrewdly analyzed in terms of an inner trio of Parent-Adult-Child strongly reminiscent of Freud's Superego-Ego-Id. Dr. Thomas Harris's best selling *I'm OK – You're OK* (New York: Harper and Row, 1967) gives a clear presentation of theory and practice.

Transactional analysis is an example of a growing tendency to approach psychological problems directly and pragmatically, without prolonged inner exploration. Many "T.A. analysts" focus on specific changes in behavior, using such methods of achieving them as renewable contracts with the patient. In this their practice is close to the "Reality Therapy" which Dr. William Glasser has practiced successfully with delinquents, prisoners, and just plain people.[20] This emphasis on here-and-now change, and concrete ways of achieving it, is similar to that of the therapies to be discussed in the next section, Psychotherapy 2: Behavior Therapy, particularly in the active part taken by the therapist, since many of the newer therapies are anything but non-directive.

Other therapies

Psychodrama

Developed by Dr. J. L. Moreno in the 1930's, *psychodrama* was one of the first of the therapies to supplement talking with doing, encouraging troubled people to act out the conflicts which were bothering them. Its assumption is the same one which underlies most verbal psychotherapies, that *catharsis,* the free expression of emotions – even (perhaps especially) those which are negative and hostile – in a safe and accepting setting is itself therapeutic. Role playing can allow us to let off steam; it also can be used to increase our insight into a total situation. Group therapy sessions can easily become little dramas, and psychodrama has been widely adapted by many kinds of therapists.

Movement therapy

Art therapy

Music therapy

A derivative of psychodrama is *dance* or *movement therapy.* In this technique, feelings and conflicts are expressed without words, by body movements alone. *Art therapy* also encourages nonverbal expression. *Music therapy* has a long history; the Bible mentions it,[21] and King Lear's doctor used music with rest and sedatives to bring him to his senses. Today, combined with dance, it may be used imaginatively with very disturbed patients, including psychotic and retarded children.

Occupational therapy and others

Occupational therapy goes back to what pioneer directors of nineteenth-century mental hospitals called the "moral treatment." (See Chapter IX, p. 224n.) That the mentally ill should be occupied and not idle, that if possible they should practice the skills they have and acquire others, has seemed self-evident to most clinicians since the mentally ill were first liberated from chains and prisons.*

Who gets them?

Since it is possible for a skilled and imaginative person to do almost anything therapeutically, the number of therapies of this kind is almost unlimited. (Recreational therapy is another one.) Sometimes given by specially trained professionals, often not, they are extremely important aspects of the treatment of the mentally ill. Moreno developed psychodrama in a public mental hospital, and although these approaches

* In the humane and imaginative "retreats" and asylums founded in the early years of the nineteenth century by such giants of psychiatry as William Tuke and Samuel Woodward, the recovery rates of mental patients were almost as high as they are today, and far higher than they were a hundred years later, when these hopeful early hospitals had become huge, impersonal human warehouses.

have obviously influenced group therapy and the encounter movement, they are especially important for mentally ill patients, many of whom are difficult or impossible to reach through conventional verbal means. As in King Lear's treatment, however, music therapy, art therapy, and the rest are usually adjuncts to other types of therapy, usually somatic. They are generally given in institutional and community, rather than private, settings.

The mentally ill, mostly

A thought you may find reassuring amid the confusion: the various psychotherapies sound a great deal more different than they are. This seems to be true whether they are called therapy or counseling, whether they are directive or non-directive, existential or interpersonal or psychoanalytic, Freudian or Jungian, Sullivanian or Gestalt (to throw in one we haven't even mentioned).

A reassuring thought: most psychotherapies are more different in theory than in practice.

Dr. Jerome Frank, Professor of Psychiatry at Johns Hopkins, tells of two remarkable studies:

> One experimental study found that therapists of different schools agreed highly as to the nature of the therapeutic relationship, and that experienced practitioners of different schools agreed more highly than did junior and senior members of the same persuasion. Furthermore, study of taped interviews showed that experts of different schools created relationships more similar to each other than experts and novices of the same school. Apparently experience in actual practice overcomes doctrinaire differences. This finding was confirmed from the standpoint of the patient, in that patients treated by therapists of different schools attributed their improvement to different therapeutic methods, but described their relationship with the therapist similarly.[22]

Psychotherapies are given by people who have devoted their lives to learning good ways to help — and while there are very great differences in how such people are trained and what they believe, there is surprisingly and hopefully very much less difference in what they actually do.*

2. PSYCHOTHERAPY 2: BEHAVIOR THERAPY

> I concluded, at length, that the mere speculative conviction that it was our interest to be completely virtuous, was not sufficient to prevent our slipping; and that the contrary habits must be broken, and good ones acquired and established. . . . I therefore contriv'd the following method. . . . I made a little book, in which I allowed a page for each of the virtues. I rul'd each page with red ink, so as to have seven columns, one for each day of the week. . . . I cross'd these columns with thirteen red lines, marking the beginning of each line with the first letter of one of the virtues [temperance, silence, order, resolution, frugality, industry,

* For guidance in locating the particular types of therapy described in this chapter, see Appendix B, 2, Guide to Locating Types of Treatment.

> sincerity, justice, moderation, cleanliness, tranquility, chastity, and humility], on which line, and in its proper column, I might mark, by a little black spot, every fault I found upon examination to have been committed respecting that virtue upon that day. . . . I was surpris'd to find myself so much fuller of faults than I had imagined; but I had the satisfaction of seeing them diminish. . . . After a while I went thro' one course only in a year [having begun with four thirteen-week courses, one week for each virtue], and afterward only one in several years . . . but I always carried my little book with me. . . . On the whole, tho' I never arrived at the perfection I had been so ambitious of obtaining . . . yet I was, by the endeavour, a better and a happier man than I otherwise should have been if I had not attempted it. . . . It may be well my posterity should be informed that to this little artifice, with the blessing of God, their ancestor ow'd the constant felicity of his life, down to his 79th year, in which this is written.

Behavior therapy seeks to change behavior

That ancestor was Benjamin Franklin, who more than two hundred and fifty years ago successfully applied the principles of the newest of the major approaches to psychotherapy – behavior therapy. Behavior therapy did not develop until the late fifties. It is also called *behavior change* or *behavior modification* therapy – which invites a question. Don't all psychotherapies seek to change behavior? Redlich and Freedman, both psychoanalysts, describe psychotherapy as "geared to an attempt to 'unlearn' neurotic behavior and acquire adaptive behavior patterns,"[23] words which describe behavior therapy to perfection. Yet when they were writing (in the early sixties), behavior therapy was still a collection of little-known experimental techniques. They were defining the kind of psychodynamic, verbal treatments described in "Psychotherapy 1."

like other psychotherapies

but by different methods.

Behavior therapy and traditional psychotherapy do share common goals, but they work toward them in different ways. When Freud, as a doctor, saw patients who complained of various kinds of discomfort in their daily lives, it was natural for him to think of these in terms of his medical training, as *symptoms*. He hoped to make these disappear as a doctor would, not by treating them specifically, giving temporary relief, but by curing the disease he assumed lay beneath them. Behavior therapists, however, view "symptoms" quite differently, as specific, troublesome *behavior* – or behavior*s*, as psychologists call them to emphasize their separateness. They are things that patients *do;* by applying the principles of learning theory, behavior therapists hope to teach them to do other, better things instead.

Symptoms – or behaviors?

Learning theory

Behavioral psychologists are by no means sure of all the ways in which behavior is actually learned. But they have been deeply influenced by the Russian physiologist I. P. Pavlov and the great Harvard psychologist B. F. Skinner, whose painstaking research taught us much about learning. Pavlov's experiments demonstrated that animals can

Skinner's work

learn new and unusual behavior by what he called *conditioning*. He taught dogs to salivate at the sound of a bell by pairing the sound with the sight of food, which he later withdrew. Building on Pavlov's work, B. F. Skinner in the thirties found that by application of the principles of conditioning he could teach pigeons complex tasks no pigeon had ever performed before. The task must be broken up into easily performed separate steps and the pigeon rewarded for each step until the task is mastered. In behavioral terms, the task is analyzed into a series of separate behaviors, each manageable in itself, which are then systematically *reinforced*. Quite difficult goals can thus be attained. Benjamin Franklin started with a goal that was initially unmanageable – it was no less, he tells us, than "moral perfection" – but by analyzing it into thirteen parts and continually measuring his progress, a process he evidently found reinforcing, he was able to achieve, if not perfection, at least "constant felicity." Most of us would settle for that.

Learning through task analysis and reinforcement

"Any man," writes the behavioral therapist Daniel L. Wiener, Professor of Psychology at the University of Minnesota, "through carefully spaced rewards and punishments, can be trained during his lifetime to act in certain ways, even if he is not aware of the rewards and punishments."[24] Unlike the pigeon, Benjamin Franklin could set his own goal, analyze it, and devise a systematic way to work on it. Less gifted people may need some assistance in acquiring new ways of behaving – though considerably less than a pigeon. This is the assistance the behavior therapist proposes to give. Believing that behavior is maintained by its consequences, he believes also that, in the words of Dr. W. Stewart Agras of the University of Mississippi School of Medicine, "to change behavior it is necessary to change these consequences so that deviant behavior will disappear, and to arrange an environment in which appropriate new behavior can be learned" by building up desired behaviors in "small progressive steps in a specially designed program."[25]

since behavior is maintained by its consequences

Whereas dynamic or insight therapy works to change behavior from the inside out, behavior therapists, finding the results of this approach slow and uncertain, work from the outside in. They doubt that insight and understanding into the sources of psychological problems in themselves have power to change them.* Professor E. Lakin Phillips defines the position of the behavior therapist: he "works primarily to change

Changing behavior from the outside in

* Their doubts are shared even by psychodynamic psychotherapists. The psychoanalyst Allen Wheelis writes that "the most common illusion of patients and strangely, even of experienced therapists, is that insight produces change; and the most common disappointment of therapy is that it does not. . . . The most comprehensive and penetrating interpretation – true, relevant, well-expressed, perfectly timed – may lie inert in the patient's mind; for he may always if he be so inclined, say 'Yes, but it doesn't help.' " *How People Change* (New York: Harper and Row, 1973). Dr. Wiener puts it more strongly: "Self-knowledge is no guarantee whatever of effective problem solving, and may not even be necessary to it."[26]

external behavior directly (through the patient's assertions and actions) rather than to change internalized feelings and attitudes in the hope that external behavior would then change automatically."[27] His assumption is just the opposite: as the patient, aided by his therapy, begins to act differently, "feelings and attitudes will change, following changes in . . . actual behavior. The rewards [the patient] will obtain by obtaining [his] goals, however small the steps, will continually provide [him] with what [he] needs to continue with more effective activity."[28]

The behavior therapist sees himself as a technician; rather than reconstructing a personality, he devises techniques (to be described later) to help set realistic goals and develop the habits necessary to reach them. Behavior-change therapy, in Professor Wiener's words, is "essentially *goal-centered* rather than *relationship-centered*."[29] Behavioral therapists are as likely as psychodynamic therapists to be warm, emphatic, genuine people, and the personal qualities of the therapist are never unimportant. Yet behavior therapists believe that the success of the therapy depends less on those qualities than on what they and the patient do.

What they do is of particular interest to families of the mentally ill — even though behavioral therapists are even more likely than other therapists to challenge the idea of mental illness. Many of them reject diagnostic labels altogether: all of them try to think in terms of what a patient does rather than what he's called.* For these reasons, and because behavioral techniques depend less than other kinds of psychotherapy on the patient's talking and understanding, behavioral therapy is the least exclusive of the psychotherapies. William Schofield, in *Psychotherapy: The Purchase of Friendship,* described the ideal patient for insight therapy as Young, Attractive, Verbal, Intelligent, and Successful ("the YAVIS Syndrome").[31] Behavior therapy has no ideal patient; some of its most spectacular results have been with back-ward chronic patients who were Middle-Aged or Old, Unattractive, Nonverbal, Unintelligent, and Poor. Because they are based on fundamental principles of learning, behavioral techniques are supposed to work for everybody — for the chronically insane, for the brain-damaged and retarded, for the character-disordered and delinquent, for neurotics and normal people who want to handle their lives better. (Like Benjamin Franklin, behavioral therapists use their methods on themselves). Not all these people are capable of forming a productive verbal relationship with a therapist, but learning goals can be set for them

Who gets behavioral therapy?

All kinds of people including the mentally ill

* "Why should a concept such as 'schizoid personality' be injected into the situation when a person's problem is that of feeling alienated from people, and not knowing how to make personal friends and perform daily tasks which will keep him constantly in touch with his environment and away from daydreaming?"[30]

all. If learning is particularly difficult, the program must be particularly gradual, the goals set with particular realism, the rewards chosen with particular care. As Professor Frank Hewett of the University of California at Los Angeles told an audience of parents of gravely impaired mentally ill children, "Everybody is ready to learn something."[32] The business of the behavior therapist is to determine what, and to find techniques to help him do it.

Behavioral techniques:

Reinforcement therapies

Professor Wiener tells the story of a college psychology class who decided to condition their teacher by the use of reinforcement techniques. When he moved toward the edge of the lecture platform, they nodded approval; they yawned and looked bored when he moved away. They soon had him teetering on the edge while they nodded enthusiastically. The principles of reinforcement therapy, or *operant conditioning,* are not difficult to grasp. People tend to do things if they are *positively reinforced;* if *negatively reinforced,* they tend not to do them.* There are all sorts of reinforcements – M and M's, smiles and embraces, gold stars, high grades, money, promotions, a Bigelow on the floor. They are in continual use in our society and all others; the use of reward and punishment in shaping human behavior was not invented by B. F. Skinner. The subtleties of reinforcement therapy lie not in the simple principle, but in the practice. Analyzing a remote goal into a linked series of achievable behaviors requires skill and experience, enough empathy to know what reinforces the person being worked with, and imagination to see where this particular person might be ready to go next. (One man's meat, after all, is another man's negative reinforcement.) All of us, say behavior therapists, use reinforcement techniques to some degree. They would like to show us how to use them more effectively.

Positive and negative reinforcement

Parents, teachers, employers, psychotherapists, and other people often reinforce exactly the behavior they wish to discourage, because they don't realize that attention – even unfavorable attention – may be reinforcing, especially if behavior we approve is merely taken for granted. Ignoring behavior can be negative reinforcement of a very effective kind, and behavior therapists often use it to eliminate – they say *extinguish* – a behavior. But to change behavior, you first have to define exactly what the behavior consists of, when it occurs, how often, for how long.

Extinction by negative reinforcement

* Dr. Agras puts it scientifically – and modestly: "The probability of a behavior occurring is increased when the behavior is followed by a rewarding event. It now appears that much animal behavior, normal human behavior, and deviant human behavior follows the same laws, although the demonstrations have been most numerous in the case of animal behavior and least in the case of human behavior."[33] Purists' note: though many behavioral theorists, like Dr. Agras, use "negative reinforcement" as we will here to mean "unpleasant consequences," in strict usage the term is reserved for cases in which previous positive reinforcement is withdrawn, while what we are calling negative reinforcement is termed "punishment."

Measuring behavior in order to change it

Measurement is the first step in setting up a program of reinforcement. Benjamin Franklin began his program by taking what behavior therapists call a *baseline measurement,* and was "surpris'd to find himself fuller of faults than he had imagined." It's important to know where you start from. Progress may be slow, but imperceptible progress becomes perceptible if you keep track of daily (sometimes hourly) changes. This gives the patient and his therapist *feedback,* and this feedback is reinforcing in itself.

Feedback

Because behavior modification is less familiar than other kinds of psychotherapy, let's consider an actual case.[34]

The Story of Fay

Fay was almost five, an alert and friendly child. When her mother brought her to the University of Washington Developmental Psychology Laboratory she had been scratching herself for a year. She had large open sores on her body and all over her face, and it looked as if she might be permanently disfigured. Her mother, who was expecting another baby, was almost beside herself with worry and irritation. She had consulted a psychiatrist and a pediatrician, but the scratching hadn't stopped. She was reluctant to try the latest suggestion, to keep Fay's arms in an expensive pair of metal splints, but she didn't know what to do. At home, she said, they'd tried everything. She had scolded, father spanked; they quarreled continually about how to handle the child. Fay's mother could hardly bear to look at her; she thought it might be better to put her in a foster home.

Observation

The therapist observed Fay and her mother for half an hour, directly and through one-way glass. She noted that Fay was a capable, well-mannered youngster who played normally and reacted appropriately – and that her mother spoke to her only to criticize, give directions, or explain why she should behave differently. Instead of pointing this out, however, she asked Fay's mother to keep a one-week record of the child's behavior – and her own and her husband's. How often did Fay scratch? How often did she do other things her mother disapproved of? How often was she spanked, isolated, scolded? How often did she do things her mother approved of? What happened then?

Baseline measurement recorded

The record, when it came in, was sketchy, but it yielded interesting information. Sometimes Fay didn't scratch at all, usually when she was engrossed in constructive play. Father spanked her frequently and mother scolded constantly, but father spanked only for scratching, whereas mother scolded for everything. When father saw Fay's face bloody he lost his temper, but often Fay and her father had fun together.

On the basis of this, a program was begun. The therapist made no attempt to explore why the family acted as they did. Instead, she gave Fay's mother extremely specific instructions; to stop correcting all Fay's misbehavior and concentrate on the scratching – by ignoring it, even if Fay's face was covered with blood. But, said Fay's mother, they'd tried that already – for a whole month. It didn't do a bit of good. They'd told Fay they just weren't going to talk about her scratching. When Fay came to them to show them that she hadn't scratched herself, she'd been told, "We don't care whether you scratch or not. You're a big girl now and it's up to you. I don't want to hear any more about it."

A specific program for a specific goal: Extinction by withdrawing the reinforcing stimulus — attention —

The therapist pointed out that this amounted to *negative* reinforcement. They had ignored, even punished, the behavior they wished to strengthen. So while she was to pay absolutely no attention to scratching, Fay's mother was instructed to reinforce all other appropriate behavior. When Fay played with her dolls, looked at books, set the table, *didn't scratch,* she was to be given approval and attention.

And reinforcing appropriate behavior by social approval

In an ordinary situation this might have been enough, for adult approval means a lot to small children. But the therapist had observed that this mother found it really hard to respond positively to her child. So further instructions were given: every twenty or thirty minutes, if Fay hadn't scratched, her mother was to go to her, approve whatever she was doing as warmly as she could, and give her a gold star to paste in a special booklet. (Because gold stars are not a natural result of good behavior they are considered external, or *extrinsic,* reinforcers). Twice a day the stars were to be counted, approved as an achievement, and reinforced by a small trinket (a *material* reinforcer).

and extrinsic reinforcers

exchanged for material reinforcers

Reporting after a week, Fay's mother was still discouraged; it was working pretty well by day, but at night Fay was still scratching her sores open. What now? Careful questioning revealed something Fay really liked: new items for her Barbie doll. So Fay and her mother were to go shopping each afternoon of a scratch-free day. Fay could choose a new Barbie item, to be given in the morning – if there was no evidence of scratching. The gold stars and approval were to be continued.

A more powerful reinforcer added and the schedule of reinforcements adjusted

On the fifth day of this program, Fay's mother spontaneously telephoned to report four scratch-free days and nights. At the next session she was exuberant. Some of the sores were beginning to heal. She pointed these out proudly, and – for the first time – mentioned something nice that Fay had done. Not only Fay's behavior was being modified; her mother's was too. The therapist reinforced her warmly, of course – but Fay's improved appearance and the pleasanter relationship between them was the best reinforcement of all.

New behaviors

Reinforcement for everybody

But the next week the whole program fell apart. One night Fay opened all her newly healed sores. Father spanked her so hard he left

Reinstatement of nearly extinguished behavior

marks. Mother screamed at Fay and father. Both parents were disgusted and wanted to give up the whole thing.

when the maintaining consequence was suddenly withdrawn

Careful questioning showed no mystery in what had happened. On the afternoon shopping trip, Fay, with a five-year-old's disregard of what things cost, had chosen an expensive Barbie item. Mother hadn't that much money with her and got something cheaper. Fay sulked — and scratched. It made sense. As Fay's mother responded to the therapist's guiding questions, she herself suggested the probable explanation of Fay's relapse. The next week, father telephoned to ask for suggestions on controlling his anger.

Behavior changes self-reinforcing

At the end of the program, which lasted six weeks, Fay's face was completely healed, though her scars were still red. Toward the end of the program, trinkets and Barbie accessories were spaced farther and farther apart until they were being given only occasionally. The gold stars were kept, because Fay liked them — and to remind her mother how often Fay did something nice. But the new warmth and relaxation in the family might well have been enough to maintain the new behaviors — for the whole family. Four months later, at a checkup visit, even the red scars were barely visible.

You'll note that in this therapy a lot of things are missing that most people expect to find. Although the therapist was obviously keenly aware of the mother's hostility toward her daughter and of severe marital tensions, she did not explore the inner experiences that might explain the family's maladaptive behavior; she concentrated on the behavior itself. If Fay's mother obtained any insight from the therapy it was the result of her activity in modifying her behavior and her daughter's, not the cause. In short, although the therapist was evidently a sympathetic and perceptive person, she used these qualities not in order to understand the family's dynamics, but to teach specific techniques of social interaction. For of course the family learned a great deal besides how to control scratching.

The family's role in behavior therapy

Behavior therapists pioneered in making families participants in their relatives' treatment. Their lack of interest in the inner sources of behavior made it easier for them to do this. Most psychodynamic approaches work by opening up intensely personal concerns, matters that the patient is not likely to wish to share with his family. Consequently, most traditional psychotherapists scrupulously respect the patient's privacy, and don't discuss his or her therapy with their families, particularly if working with young people who feel oppressed by family expectations and demands.[35] For years this was true even when the patient was a small child.[36]

With the rise of family therapy this picture began to change. But though families were accepted as *co-patients* in family therapy, they were not encouraged to learn treatment methods themselves and become *co-therapists.* Behavior therapists, however, are positively enthusiastic about sharing their techniques. They have no particular opinions on the origins of family pathology, and they learn relatively little about their patients' secret places. And because behavioral, particularly reinforcement, methods can be made so specific, they are much easier to communicate than the subtle techniques of psychodynamic psychotherapy. Nurses, nursery-school teachers, paraprofessionals — and families — can be taught quite quickly to become effective participants in treatment, and behavioral therapists, knowing their time is limited, want to teach them. Today, families are taught ways of working with family members whose behavior is far more disordered than Fay's — or her mother's.

Who gets reinforcement therapy?

Both Fay and her mother were normal individuals with bad problems. A psychiatrist, if he labeled them at all, would probably have classified them as neurotic. They are typical of many people who receive psychodynamic psychotherapy, although their problems were more dramatic than most. But they were also extremely specific — Fay's family, her therapist, and very possibly Fay herself had no difficulty in defining the behavior they wanted changed. For people who come into the office complaining of more general distress — alienation, anxiety, depression, existential despair — it's not so simple, since they don't present easily definable behaviors to work on. The behavior therapist, in these (very common) cases, has either to deny this, maintaining that generalized complaints if closely analyzed turn out to be the results of specific unsatisfactory behaviors* — or to do what we hope all good therapists do: recognize the limitations of their methods and refer the patient whom they cannot help elsewhere.

People with problems — neurotics —

and the mentally ill

But of more concern to the readers of this book is that fact that behavior therapists work with the mentally ill. It's harder work than it was with bright little Fay and her family. The objectives may have to be limited. Progress may be slow, toward unspectacular results, but the principles are the same. The techniques can be used anywhere — in offices, homes, schools, hospitals — to extinguish unwanted behavior

* Which some do. John Marquis, Chief Psychologist at the Mental Hygiene Clinic at the Palo Alto (California) Veterans' Hospital, maintains that "usually a few minutes of careful questioning of a person who claims no specific areas of anxiety, but generalized depression or philosophical ennui, will suffice to reveal a number of very discrete and specific problems, often of considerable severity. . . . A careful behavior analysis often reveals dozens of specific subjective fears. . . . When those persons who are seeking philosophical solutions to difficulties construed in overgeneralized terms have found basic solutions to their specific problems such as fear of criticism, rejection, disapproval; fear of being the center of attention; inability to reinforce others, or to accept affection or kindness without anxiety; and when they have become relaxed and effective in dealing with other people through . . . acquiring necessary interpersonal skills, then one can look in vain for the existential problems which brought them to the consulting room."[37]

and (much more difficult) to establish new behavior in its place. They are increasingly used with the kind of severely disordered children who are often diagnosed as autistic or schizophrenic, as well as with chronic schizophrenics and the retarded.

The place of negative reinforcement in therapy

What about negative reinforcement? Therapists, of course, prefer to see what they can accomplish with positive means. Most use little or no negative reinforcement as such – although any program of positive reinforcement necessarily implies some negative reinforcement, since it's negatively reinforcing not to get gold stars. Frowns, a sharpened voice, a sigh, even a therapist's failure to come forth with an encouraging "hm" – all may be negatively reinforcing. Part of the psychoanalyst's skill lies in knowing how to mold the content of his patient's preoccupations by responding to them selectively – positively and negatively. Nobody objects to this sort of thing, and most people accept the next steps beyond it – fines, loss of privileges, or brief "time outs" in an isolation room, methods which are often used with children. *Aversion therapy,* however – the programmed use of strong physical measures as negative reinforcement – is one of the most controversial kinds of psychotherapy.

Aversion therapy

There are various aversive procedures. An unpleasant (aversive) stimulus may be paired with a stimulus which usually elicits the problem behavior; for an alcoholic the sight of a drink might be paired with an uncomfortable (but not devastating) electric shock.* Or the aversive stimulus might follow the actual behavior; reach for the drink or the cigarette, and the shock is automatic. In *avoidance training* the shock may be avoided altogether; just push away the glass, the cigarette, the dirty picture. Nauseating drugs may also be used.

A partial treatment

Aversive techniques may extinguish problem behaviors quickly, but the improvement is not likely to last unless they are part of a fuller program. Building up new behaviors to take the place of the old is more important – and harder. The effectiveness of aversive conditioning is much exaggerated: the alcoholic will return to alcohol unless he can develop satisfying ways of behaving without it; the child molester needs not to avoid children but to develop a normal sex life. For this reason, aversive therapy is usually combined with other types of therapy – other behavioral methods, sociotherapy, dynamic psychotherapy.[38] Best of all is when the patient's new avoidance behavior is backed up by newly possible and satisfying experiences in his daily life.

Who gets it?

This is a crucial question. Those who get aversion therapy should be those who themselves seek powerful measures to help them control their behavior. It has been used with repeated rapists, child molesters, and others whose sexual deviations get them into bad trouble, as well as with alcoholics, compulsive smokers, and people dissatisfied with their sexual orientation.

* Not to be confused with electroshock treatment. (See pp. 99–102.)

Obviously, aversive therapy is strong medicine. Misused, it can have serious and lasting side effects — fear, hostility, mistrust. It must be fully discussed and understood beforehand. As Professor David Barlow of the University of Mississippi points out, it is important, even for the success of the therapy itself, that *the person receiving it do so of his own free will.*[39] In general, strong aversive measures should not be used on involuntary patients. Yet in extreme cases, responsible therapists do make exceptions to this rule. Aversive measures can be justified when a brief, temporary use can extinguish the habits of physically self-destructive behavior sometimes found in severely retarded or psychotic patients.* And many who have worked with autistic or psychotic children would argue that aversive methods, carefully supervised and evaluated, are justified when necessary to eliminate behavior so intolerable for those around the child that he is in danger of exclusion from school or of institutionalization.† The best safeguards against the abuse of aversive methods on involuntary patients are the skill and decency of the therapist and the close involvement of a concerned family.

Who should *get it?*

No responsible therapist will institute aversion therapy without the consent of the patient (or in the case of a child, the parents). And this must be *informed consent.* Dr. Agras emphasizes the importance of a full explanation of the aversive stimulus, how it is used and how long, any possible side effects, the chance of success, and how the results are evaluated.[40]

The importance of informed consent

But the real ethical problems arise, not in the office, to which the patient can't be made to return, but with "captive populations" — in mental hospitals or prisons. Even if they consent to treatment, how free — or informed — is their consent? If criminal or psychotic behavior could be permanently eliminated by behavior therapy (and this is very doubtful), should it be? Many people are concerned at the idea of a "Clockwork Orange" society where behavior is managed not only by

Ethical problems with captive populations

A conditioned society?

* In June, 1970, Dr. Ivar Lovaas told a meeting of the National Society for Autistic Children, "I have not an autistic child myself, but I care for your children, with a kind of caring which is itself reason enough to live. . . . I try to frame useful questions. What can we give to these kids to help them? A child bites himself so badly that he has already mutilated himself for life. We ask, not what in his past makes him do it, but what we can do about it right now. This boy has actually bitten off a good deal of his right shoulder. Another is spreadeagled on his bed, restrained hand and foot to prevent such behavior. This would be a meaningful direction to human work, wouldn't it? — just to get him out of restraint. What is the natural response of any human being? It is, of course, to love, to comfort, to cherish. But what is the effect if we follow this response? *The days we do this the child gets worse.*" "Strengths and Weaknesses of Operant Conditioning Techniques in the Treatment of Autism," in *Research and Education: Proceedings of the Second Annual Meeting and Conference of the National Society for Autistic Children,* ed. C. C. Park (NIMH Publication No. 2164, 1971).

† Dr. Eric Schopler gives a vivid example: urinating in the school heat vents. (Personal communication, May 1975.) Dr. Schopler, whose imaginative and flexible treatment methods have kept many children in their families and out of institutions, is not a behaviorist, but uses behavioral techniques among others.

conditioning but by surgery and drugs to produce a numbered, conforming population no longer fully human. These very serious issues will be examined together in the section on manipulation at the end of this chapter.

Other behavioral procedures: Systematic desensitization

Who gets it?

People with phobias and other neurotic disorders

Systematic desensitization was developed by Dr. Joseph Wolpe of Temple University specifically for phobias. It is one of the most widely used behavior therapies, its effectiveness accepted even by dynamic psychiatrists. Like other behavioral methods, it depends on a very commonplace principle: you get rid of fears by getting used to the things that scare you. You can't do this, however, unless you encounter them frequently – which most phobic patients make sure they never do. Systematic desensitization accustoms the patient to what he fears, by introducing it gradually, first in imagination, at length in reality. To desensitize the patient to heights, or going outside, or driving, a *hierarchy* is constructed of stimuli which approach closer and closer to the feared situation. There is no exploration of the possible sources of the problem. The patient is taught ways of relaxing deeply (sometimes with the aid of drugs) while imagining what he fears as vividly as he can. The unfortunate Professor Leonard, for instance, might have tackled his fear of locomotives by imagining himself far down the street leading to the railroad, in summer, with trees obscuring the station. Next he might have imagined a winter scene with the station in full view. He would move closer and closer, with no train in sight, then with a small engine standing still. Finally he would imagine himself onto the train. This process (which can be varied in many ways) has made it possible for many patients to master their fears in reality. Of course the situation may be more complicated than this; for example, the patient's family may be reinforcing his helplessness by sympathy and special arrangements. If so, this too will come in for the therapist's attention. Like competent therapists of all sorts, competent behavioral therapists have a variety of techniques, and much of their skill lies in knowing when to use them.

A desensitization hierarchy

Mixing procedures

Desensitization and relaxation therapy are also used with anxiety neuroses, obsessive-compulsive disorders, and frigidity. There is evidence that the method does *not* help phobic patients who are also schizophrenic.[41]

Flooding (Implosion)

Implosion therapy, or flooding, is another form of "getting used to it." The difference between this method and desensitization is one of degree.[42] In flooding, the patient is also exposed to what makes him anxious, but much less gradually, and rather than relaxing he is encouraged to experience his terror as vividly as he can. Flooding methods vary; therapy can be given individually or in groups, it can minimize anxiety or intensify it, it can be given in imagination or in real life (*in vivo*). As in the other behavioral therapies, systematic measurement enhances the effect and keeps the patient conscious of progress. Behavior therapists like to quote Freud himself on the need for *in vivo* treatment: "One can hardly ever master a phobia if one waits till the patient lets the analysis influence him enough to give it up. . . . One succeeds only when one can induce them through the influence of the analysis . . . to go about alone and struggle with the anxiety while they make the attempt."[43]

Modeling, behavior rehearsal, assertive training

These techniques are commonsensical too. *Modeling,* in Dr. Agras's words, is simply "showing people how to do things."[44] Behaviors are easier to acquire if you watch someone else do them. Withdrawn children, for example, can be shown films; they watch two children their own age sharing a book and talking about it, a child walking up to a group and joining it, a group playing in the sandbox. Imitation is the most natural way to learn, and recent research shows that in most people it works better and faster than elaborate reinforcement procedures.[45] Sometimes, however, as with autistic children and some of the chronically mentally ill, imitative behavior itself is impaired, and reinforcement techniques are necessary to teach them to imitate.

Modeling, of course, is not confined to behavior therapy. Behavior therapists and some psychoanalysts consider it an important factor in the success of verbal psychotherapies, as patients model their behavior on the therapist's suggestions – or even try to be like him.

In *behavior rehearsal* and *assertive training,* new behavioral skills are acquired by supervised practice – as they have been from time immemorial. They even *call* it coaching.[46] People who aren't able to do things – to ask a girl for a date, to speak up for themselves, to converse comfortably, get a therapist's help in *rehearsing* the behaviors in realistic situations. As in other types of behavior therapy, it's important to analyze the desired behavior into its component parts. Refusing an unreasonable request, for example, is a pretty specific behavior which can be practiced on its own; getting along with your wife, however, is a complex of many different behaviors, some of which will need to be worked on one at a time. Assertive training is a particular kind of behavior rehearsal aimed at showing people how to assert themselves.

Behavior rehearsal has some similarities with psychodrama; a talented therapist can make the sessions exciting and realistic. But whereas the role-playing of psychodrama aims primarily at insight and understanding (and the relief given by expressing feelings), behavior rehearsal aims directly at behavior change: "role-playing permits the patient to simulate problem situations and practice new modes of responding without concern for the immediate, real-life consequences of his experimental behavior."[47] He can get good at them before he goes out to practice them where it matters.

Who gets behavior rehearsal?

These therapies sound pretty talky, and indeed, they are used most often with the same kinds of patients who get verbal psychotherapy.

Modeling and behavior rehearsal, however, can also be used to teach behaviors to the mentally ill; they are especially useful in preparing long-term patients for the new social demands which will be made on them once they are released.

People with problems and the mentally ill

Simple as they are, behavior modification techniques have their own drawbacks. In the hands of inexperienced or unimaginative people they may degenerate into rigid and mechanical routines, no longer responsive to the needs of those they are meant to serve. In the hands of insensitive or stupid or cruel people they can obviously do very serious harm – as can any other therapy. The personal qualities of the therapist may no longer be central to treatment, but they remain important. In this field, too, there is art as well as technique, and human qualities count. Of the famous Ivar Lovaas of the University of California at Los Angeles, who pioneered in the behavioral treatment of severely autistic children, one grateful parent noted that the children responded to him as to no one else: "His students are stiff and derivative compared to him."[48] So if you and your relative do come in contact with behavior therapy, take advantage of its openness to look carefully at what is going on in the therapeutic situation. In this kind of psychotherapy as in others, correct applications of plausible theory are no substitute for warmth, flexibility, and common sense.

A caution: human qualities count here too.

But regardless of personal qualities, isn't it asking for trouble to work for superficial changes while ignoring what's beneath? Users of the medical model see those phobias, compulsions, and problem behaviors as *symptoms* of something deeper. Biologically oriented psychiatrists talk of organic causes; psychoanalytically oriented psychiatrists speak of intrapsychic processes. Both consider that the way to get rid of symptoms is to find the cause – to discover the illness and cure that. The symptom isn't just something to get rid of; it's a valuable clue to what's really wrong. Without it, the patient might be worse off than he was before. The famous children's analyst Bruno Bettelheim puts the psychodynamic case as strongly as he knows how:

Behaviors or symptoms?

> The mental patient's symptoms, as distressing as they may be to him, as upsetting and even dangerous as they may be to his surroundings, are nevertheless his highest achievement. They need to be recognized and respected as such by his psychiatrist [and] by the whole institution. . . . The techniques of conditioned-reflex psychology (under the name of behavior modification) show utter disrespect for the symptoms and with it for the patient.[49]

If, as Freud taught, symptoms are the surfacing of unconscious conflicts and thwarted instinctual drives, when one symptom is eradicated another will take its place; the fundamental condition will find another way to express itself. This danger is often cited. Bettelheim believes that not only behavior therapy, but also somatic treatments such as shock therapy or drugs, work to "drive symptoms underground

Symptom substitution?

. . . [and] convince the patient only that his environment wishes to shape him as it seems best, and not as he in a strenuous and tortuous process of self-discovery may wish to do."[50] Fay's scratching, according to this view, was only a symptom of deeper psychic disturbances in her family and herself. It was a cry for help which should not be neglected.

Behavior therapists would agree as to that. But as in other things, they move the discussion from philosophy to fact: their follow-up studies show that symptom substitution doesn't occur.* After she stopped scratching, Fay didn't start to bite her nails or wake up screaming. The outside-in approach worked for the symptom — and improved the family situation too. Behavior therapists, applying reinforcement principles, also question whether paying the kind of respectful attention to symptoms recommended by Bettelheim won't make them worse.

"Illness" again

Nevertheless, behavior therapists are softening toward the medical model. Behavior therapists once avoided any mention of "illness" — they theorized that the maladaptive behavior that attracted psychiatric labels was not the result of interior processes, physical or psychic, but learned. If so, it could be unlearned; their new and efficient techniques, working on behavior after behavior, should be able at length to bring clients to full normality. That hasn't happened. In behavior therapy too, time and experience have tempered early enthusiasm with therapeutic realism. Behavioral techniques can accomplish much with mentally ill people, including chronic schizophrenics and autistic children who once seemed hopeless. But there have been no miracles. These crippling illnesses, it seems, are far more than a collection of deviant behaviors.† While we await a better understanding of medical causes,

and no miracles

* "As several recent papers have cogently argued, there is no empiric evidence for the notion of symptom substitution in the context of behavior therapy. The more likely form of failure is relapse of the old symptoms rather than the development of new ones." Agras, *op. cit.*, p. 52. The papers cited are D. D. Cahoon, "Symptom Substitution and the Behavior Therapies," *Psychological Bulletin*, 69 (1968):149; A. J. Yates, "Symptoms and Symptom Substitution," *Psychological Review*, 65 (1958):371. Dr. Judd Marmor, an internationally known psychoanalyst, restates this in his own language: "The myth of symptom substitution is based on the closed system psychodynamic 'hydraulic' model that we inherited from Freud. If, however, personality dynamics are more accurately perceived within an open-system frame of reference, [symptom substitution] is not inevitable. Removal of an ego-dystonic symptom may, on the contrary, produce such positive feedback from the environment as to result in major constructive shifts in the original conflictual pattern. Removal of a symptom may also lead to changes in self-perception with resultant ego-syntonic internal feedbacks and heightening of self-esteem, thus also contributing to positive restructuring of internal psychodynamics."[51]

† Travis Thompson, "Behavior Therapy in Treating Acute Major Psychoses," *Center for Behavior Modification Newsletter*, 1 (May 1974). "First, it must be recognized that the major psychoses exist in reality, and were not a figment of Kraepelin's imagination. Many of our colleagues trained in the behaviorist tradition would like to believe that no such categories exist (or even if they do, that such categories are behaviorally meaningless). In the more obvious limiting cases, the behavior of a manic-depressive is as distinctively different from that of a schizophrenic as is the behavior of a rat and a pigeon." See also William J. DiScipio, ed., *The Behavioral Treatment of Psychotic Illness* (New York: Behavioral Publications, 1974).

however, behavior therapy, like psychodynamic therapy, has plenty of work to do helping people learn new ways to behave and be.

Comparing behavior therapy and insight therapy

It is tempting to try to compare their results, but it isn't really possible. Behavior therapy and psychodynamic therapy represent two familiar and valuable types of education. You can't compare the effectiveness of a year of accounting or secretarial training with the effectiveness of a year at Harvard. Harvard offers a liberal education, or tries to. It doesn't always succeed, for liberal education, like dynamic psychotherapy, has diffuse and ambitious goals – understanding, self-realization, the development of a better, freer person. The noted journalist Pete Hamill said of his analytic therapy, "My own experience was the most profoundly human of my life. The doctor was a kind, intelligent man, and he led me into areas of my life that I was always too afraid to examine. I began to understand my rages, my jealousies, my self-destructiveness; but I also understood my strengths, my generosity, my capacity to love."[52] Patients treated by behavior therapy seldom if ever say anything like that. The goals of vocational education are specific and modest, to teach a desired set of behaviors; it produces acceptable stenographers, motor mechanics, engineers, doctors. Like behavior therapy, vocational education has developed specific methods for reaching its goals. For this reason it is generally successful; most people who are accepted into the course and complete it can function as intended. But how "effective" is a liberal education? Does it make you a better person? Smarter? Wiser? Does it help you solve problems in living? Does it help you make more money? Even if we could agree on how to judge effectiveness, how many years would it take to find out? As we search for effective education – or treatment – we must always ask, "effective for what?"

Vocational and liberal education

Effectiveness

Evaluation

and cost effectiveness

Interest in determining the effectiveness of different kinds of therapy, a long time in developing, is now spurred by the growing public expenditures for mental health. Public agencies want to spend taxpayers' money where it will do the most good. How to evaluate is now a major question.* The work is still in its early stages, and it's not easy, whether therapy is publicly or privately paid for. Therapists have not been in the habit of keeping statistics on what proportion of their patients or clients improve, or how much. Nor do they follow them up once they have left treatment. Patient, family, and therapist may evaluate "improvement" differently. Therapists disagree. A further difficulty is that, happily for the human race, neurotic "problems in living" tend to get better by themselves.† (This is, of course, much less true of psychoses, but most consumers of psychotherapy are not psychotic.)

Difficulties

* The Department of Health, Education and Welfare now publishes *Evaluation,* a magazine concerned with just that.

† So do most physical illnesses as well. All physicians are taught to respect the *vis medicatrix naturae,* "the healing power of nature."

When a large proportion of people who feel bad enough to seek professional help get better anyway, it is impossible to show conclusively that those who improve get better because of their treatment. In the fifties and sixties Professor H. E. Eysenck of London University studied all the reports of the outcomes of treated patients that he could find. His conclusions shocked many:

Eysenck's challenge

> On the whole it seemed that about two out of three neurotic patients got better after two years of treatment. This looked pretty good, but it had to be compared with the spontaneous remission rate, i.e., the rate at which patients recover who have not had any kind of psychiatric treatment. It turned out that they too recovered at the rate of about two out of three in two year's time.*

A reconsideration of these figures, however, finds the two-thirds figures deceptive. People treated with psychotherapy showed more substantial changes than untreated people, who tended to improve, but slightly. However, of the treated patients, some got substantially better while others got substantially worse, so that the statistics cancelled.[53]

and a response

Why did they get better? A recent Menninger Foundation report on a fifteen-year follow-up of the results of both psychoanalysis and psychotherapy has some interesting suggestions. At the beginning of the project, the researchers had thought that patients who achieved insight into psychodynamic issues would do better — in therapist's parlance, have a more stable outcome. But though the findings aren't conclusive, it looks as if supportive therapy is more important than the clarification of dynamics. "Transference cures" used not to be taken too seriously in orthodox circles, it seemed too simple to say that people got better for the sake of the therapist. The Menninger study suggests it happens, and that the results can last.[54] Professor Arnold Lazarus (a behavior therapist) summarizes the qualities of a successful therapist: "accurate empathy, non-possessive warmth, and authenticity or genuineness."[55] The "Truax triad"[56] is good news for you, for while in many places it will be impossible to locate a specific brand of therapy, you can hope to find a therapist who is empathetic, genuine, and warm — with enough experience for his empathy to be accurate and enough self-knowledge for his warmth to be nonpossessive. Psychoanalytic, Interpersonal, Existential, Non-Directive? or Behavioral? Professor Lazarus, who is one of the few therapists to do follow-up studies on his patients, believes: "Therapists are too intent to attach a label to their activities instead of spelling out precisely what operations they perform with various patients."[57] He would like to "persuade psychotherapists

The "Truax triad"

* *Psychology Is About People* (New York: Library Press, 1972), pp. 113–114. A thorough (and discouraging) summary of outcome studies from 1946 to 1965 can be found on pp. 52–54 of Dr. Lewis Wolberg's *The Technique of Psychotherapy*, 2nd ed. (New York: Grune and Stratton, 1967).

to separate what they do from why they think it works." Until they do, questions about the effectiveness of different kinds of psychotherapy will remain difficult to answer — and well worth asking.

3. SOMATIC TREATMENTS

CORDELIA: What can man's wisdom
In the restoring his bereaved sense?
He that helps him take all my outward worth.
DOCTOR: There is means, Madam. . . .

King Lear

The means were rest and drugs — somatic treatments, which reach the mind by way of the body, the *soma*. Somatic treatments have been from the beginning the physician's primary means for treating severe mental illness — seconded always by that ancient form of psychotherapy that combines gentleness and authority in the "bedside manner."

Who gets somatic treatment? Almost everybody gets some — rest, diet, sedatives, minor tranquilizers

Who gets somatic treatment for their psychological malaises? Almost everybody who consults a doctor, for the family doctor's pill, the diets, rest, regular hours, and change of air that he prescribes are all somatic treatments. The old remedies decline, however, as the pills proliferate — the Miltown, Equanil, Librium, Valium, and the others that are prescribed (and overprescribed) to tide us through temporary stress and calm our neurotic anxiety. Some people seem to suffer more than others, for whatever reason. The psychological factors are legion, and as for biology, Redlich and Freedman note that " 'more or less' aspects in neurosis, 'thresholds' for conflict, and the like, may well have important biological if not genetic components."[58] Freud was prepared to believe that "toxins," as well as conflicts, played a part in neurosis, and Redlich and Freedman envisage a future in which "the biological roots of neurotic behavior will become more relevant to clinical psychiatry."[59] As yet, however, science has little to add to the common observation that some people just naturally seem to be more high-strung than others. For them (for us?) psychotherapy (aided, perhaps, by the minor tranquilizers) is the treatment of choice — unless we choose to bet on the "healing power of nature" and make it through without either. All clinicians would agree that "neurotic problems, at present at least, cannot be dissolved or resolved chemically," and that "organic therapies such as lobotomy and electronconvulsive treatment have no place in the treatment of most neuroses."[60] This is also true of character disorders, which are much closer to neuroses than psychoses. The somatic therapies we are about to describe were developed in hospitals for the mentally ill, and it is primarily the mentally ill who get these treatments — which more than anything else are responsible for getting them out of hospitals.

But organic therapies are primarily for the mentally ill.

Today, the physician has powerful new agents to add to the sedatives, warm baths, wet sheets, and physical restraints of the past. One of the most distinguished of American psychiatrists, Dr. John Romano of the University of Rochester Medical School, says that "at no time in the history of psychiatry have there been effective instruments like our new drugs. . . . I believe we may be entering a period in which psychosis rather than neurosis will be a major theme. Suddenly we can do something for psychotics."[61] And doing something for psychotics includes doing something, not only for those with acute reactions, but for the chronically ill, who, as Dr. Romano points out, have been chronically neglected by doctors, and everybody else.

Psychoactive or psychotropic drugs

The new drugs work. But before we get pegged as pill-pushers, let us admit right here what everybody knows, that we indeed are an overdrugged nation, prone to pill popping. In a study of a representative small American city, it was found that 17 percent of *all* prescriptions were for mood-altering drugs.[62] Most of these were probably for the *minor tranquilizers,* which have joined aspirin in so many medicine chests, and it was not the mentally ill who consumed them but ourselves. But the mentally ill get their share, and many get much more; there are plenty of hospitals where drugs do what straitjackets and isolation used to, and people sit groggy and dim from powerful chemicals, which have been given routinely without determining the actual requirements of the individual. These people could certainly benefit from less *pharmacotherapy** (pharmaco- = drug) and more sympathy, understanding, and help in learning (or relearning) the skills of social behavior. All useful tools can be misused, and often are.† We should take this melancholy fact for granted – but we should also take for granted what the vast majority of psychiatrists will corroborate: that properly used, drugs can do more for the psychotic patient than any other single therapy.

The minor tranquilizers

The major tranquilizers

The best known of the *psychotropic* drugs (also called *neuroleptics,* from the Greek roots for "nerve" and "seize") is chlorpromazine, sold in this country under the trade name Thorazine. Chlorpromazine was developed in France in the early fifties. It was soon joined by reserpine, from the Rauwolfia plant, long used in India for its calming effect on manic states.‡ Unlike the varieties of psychotherapy, drug therapy is international. Psychoanalysis migrated from the German-speaking countries to America; it has never been as influential elsewhere. Behavior therapy is hardly known outside the United States. China, Japan, and Russia have their own approaches, which are not necessarily for export.

Chlorpromazine, the first of the neuroleptics

* Also, *chemotherapy.*

† See Henry L. Lennard, L. S. Epstein, *et al., Mystification and Drug Misuse: Hazards in Using Psychoactive Drugs* (New York: Harper and Row, 1971).

‡ Reserpine has largely lost its importance in psychiatry, having been replaced by newer drugs.

The somatic therapies, however, have come from many nations; our body chemistry is less sensitive than our psyches to national styles.

The phenothiazine derivatives

Chlorpromazine belongs to a family of drugs, the phenothiazines, all derived from the single chemical molecule of phenothiazine. There are at least eighteen phenothiazine derivatives sold under brand names here and in Europe, as well as derivatives of other chemicals. New drugs are constantly being developed. Most doctors become familiar with the effects of a few drugs and stick to them, and this seems to work well enough; as Dr. Sidney Malitz of Columbia told an audience of physicians:

> Multi-hospital control studies . . . have borne out that there's really not much difference; after about six weeks or so, it doesn't matter which major tranquilizer you give. If the patient is agitated, I would tend to use something like chlorpromazine . . . an aliphatic, whereas if he is retarded, perhaps a piperazine phenothiazine might be of value. But that is only initially. Later on, the major antipsychotic effect is much the same.[63]

Readers who want to know more about their various effects can consult the detailed descriptions in the advertisements in their family doctor's *Journal of the American Medical Association;* if they *really* want to know, they can consult Dr. Solomon Snyder's *Madness and the Brain.*[64] Psychoactive drugs most commonly prescribed are listed in the chart on p. 92. Even psychiatrists have a hard time keeping up with the new drugs; many don't even try. They seem to help people act less crazy and be more accessible to other people; we'll let it go at that.

Acute reactions

Although the antipsychotic drugs help both acute and process schizophrenia, they help these very different conditions in different ways. Often, drugs fix up acute cases pretty fast — as clear a cure as anything in medicine. Your relative may be hallucinating or accusing people of trying to poison him; she may be taking off her clothes or calling her friends with wild projects in the middle of the night. It's terrifying to see someone you know transformed into a stranger. But the very suddenness of the change suggests a good outcome. After the acute phase is over, drugs can be reduced, then withdrawn. In this stage, psychotherapy may help, especially when he or she is anxious over what happened, or about continuing problems of living. When the patient, through drugs, has been brought to his usual level of function — normal, neurotic, or whatever — the possibility of psychotherapy should be considered as anyone else in trouble might consider it, though intensive psychotherapy is rarely indicated.[65] Unlike those who are still psychotic, patients like these are readily accepted by psychotherapists to be treated, like other people, in the office. Many consider that one of the greatest advantages of drugs is that they make psychotherapy possible for people who otherwise would remain inaccessible.

Antipsychotic drugs can be combined with psychotherapy

Process or chronic

With the "process" type of patient, whose condition has come on over years, the situation is quite different. Antipsychotic drugs can help them, sometimes dramatically, but they cannot cure them. They can stabilize and normalize erratic behavior, they can reduce bizarre thought processes and make them less distressing to the patient and others. Because of them classical types of schizophrenia familiar from two generations of textbooks have become a rarity. The *catatonic schizophrenic,* inactive to the point where he seems paralyzed or agitated in bizarre or stereotyped motion, the silly, giggling *hebephrenic,* are now seldom seen, even in back wards. Patients just don't deteriorate that much today. It is common now for chronic patients to leave the hospital. When they do, however, they rarely have a functioning life to go back to – a set of skills, a school, a job. So they need all the social therapy and support they can get. Insight therapy is rarely useful for them, but humane and friendly contact, behavioral therapy, and the whole range of sociotherapy may make the difference between a life of productiveness and dignity and a back-bedroom existence different from the hospital only in that it's lonelier.

Drugs and social therapy

Patients vary widely in their responses to drugs; laboratory tests have shown as much as a fortyfold difference in the levels of drug found in the blood of patients receiving identical dosages. Thus there can be no fixed or "correct" dosage. You should report at once to the doctor if you notice changes you think may be due to your relative's medication. According to the Food and Drug Administration, dosages markedly above the usual range should be considered experimental – which means the patient's consent should be gotten, as for any experimental treatment.

Dosages vary widely and

It is tempting, for both doctor and patient, to reduce the dosage as soon as possible; no one wants to continue giving strong drugs when they're not necessary, and many patients give up their drugs as soon as they feel better.* That, in fact, is one of the main things the patient's family has to watch for. Chronic schizophrenics need their drugs, just as a diabetic needs insulin – even though they are at home and functioning well. One careful study found that twice as many released patients had to be rehospitalized in the course of a year if they did not continue on drugs.† Injectable, long-acting drugs have been developed

medication may need to be continued indefinitely.

* "Studies have been conducted that show that 30 to 70 percent of patients being treated with medications on an outpatient basis do not follow their prescribed drug regimen . . . a person may have an inordinate fear of being controlled by a pill." Dr. Ronald Fieve, quoted in B. F. Benziger's *Speaking Out: Therapists and Patients – How They Cure and Cope with Mental Illness Today* (New York: Walker, 1976).

† Gerald Hogarty and Dr. Solomon Goldberg of the National Institute of Mental Health followed up 374 chronic schizophrenic patients released to the community. They divided them into four groups: one treated with chlorpromazine alone, one with chlorpromazine and social therapy, one with social therapy and placebo (a deliberately ineffective pill), one with placebo only. After a year, 72.5 percent of the placebo-alone group had been rehospitalized, but only 32.6 percent of the drugs-alone group. The social therapy reduced relapse still further – about 10 percent for the placebo group, 7 percent for those on chlorpromazine. "Drug and Sociotherapy in the Aftercare of Schizophrenic Patients: One-Year Relapse Rates," *Archives of General Psychiatry,* 28 (Jan. 1973).

PSYCHOACTIVE (OR PSYCHOTROPIC) DRUGS

SEDATIVES AND MINOR TRANQUILIZERS*

(sedative, sleep-producing, and/or anti-anxiety effects)

GENERIC NAME		BRAND NAME
secobarbital	short-acting	Seconal
pentobarbital	short-acting	Nembutal
amobarbital	intermediate	Amytal
butabarbital	intermediate	Butisol
phenobarbital	long-acting	Luminal
		(and many others)
meprobamate		Equanil, Miltown
tybamate		Solocen, Tybatran
chlordiazepoxide		Librium
diazepam		Valium
oxazepam		Serax
clorazepate		Tranxene
hydroxyzine		Atarax, Vistaril
methaqualone		Quāālude,
		Somnafac
		(many others)

MAJOR TRANQUILIZERS ANTIPSYCHOTIC (OR NEUROLEPTIC) DRUGS

(antipsychotic and anti-anxiety effects)

GENERIC NAME	BRAND NAME
Phenothiazines	
Aliphatic series:	
chlorpromazine	Thorazine
promazine	Sparine
triflupromazine	Vesprin
Piperidine series:	
thioridazine	Mellaril
mesoridazine	Serentil
piperacetazine	Quide
Piperazine series:	
prochlorperazine	Compazine
trifluoperazine	Stelazine
butaperazine	Repoise
perphenazine	Trilafon
fluphenazine	Permitil, Prolixin
acetophenazine	Tindal
carphenazine	Proketazine
Butyrophenones	
haloperidol	Haldol
droperidol	Inapsine
Thioxanthenes	
thioxanthixene	Taractan
thiothixene	Navane
Dihydroindolones	
molindone	Moban
Dibenzoxazepines	
loxapine	Loxinate

TRICYCLIC ANTIDEPRESSANTS*

GENERIC NAME	BRAND NAME
imipramine	Tofrānil, Imavate, SK-Pramine, Presamine
desipramine	Norpramin, Pertofrane
amitriptyline	Elavil
nortriptyline	Aventyl
protriptyline	Vivactil
doxepin	Sinequan, Adapin

* Partial listing; for further information see R. I. Shader, M.D., ed., *Manual of Psychiatric Therapeutics: Practical Psychopharmacology and Psychiatry* (Boston: Little, Brown, 1975), from which this table is adapted. The minor tranquilizers may produce some degree of addiction; the major tranquilizers do not. For side effects of individual drugs, see the fine print of drug advertisements in medical journals. Drugs can be bought much more cheaply when prescribed under their generic names.

which can be given at intervals of two or three weeks. This goes far to eliminate relapses, as well as family wrangles over medicine ignored or forgotten.

Side effects

The neuroleptic drugs have significant side effects – one reason patients may fail to take them. These are particularly important when medication must go on for years. Most of these are motor disturbances, affecting the patient's ability to move normally. The most frequent is Parkinsonism, a syndrome which occurs naturally in Parkinson's disease. Patients suffer from a rhythmic tremor when at rest, although it subsides when they move voluntarily; muscles may be stiff, the face expressionless, movements slow. Less common are spasmodic movements and difficulties in swallowing and speech (*dyskinesia*) and a peculiar "itchiness" in the muscles that makes the patient unable to sit still (*akathisia*). Other drugs are generally given to control these symptoms, which are usually not serious – not as serious, at least, as schizophrenia. In some patients, however, particularly older women who have been on drugs for years, a more severe dyskinesia may appear (called *tardive*, or late-appearing). Because of this possibility, long-term dosages are kept as low as possible (maintenance doses). Sometimes "drug holidays" are recommended.

Parkinsonism

Dyskinesia

Akathisia

Maintenance doses

There are other less predictable side effects – *idiosyncratic* – which vary with the individual,* since people differ widely in their sensitivity to drugs.

Side effects cannot be shrugged off. But if a patient deteriorates without a drug, the risk has to be prayerfully balanced – by doctor, patient, and family – against the advantages of the drug. The choice between evils is never easy, or sure.

A penetrating question

But radical therapists – and others not so radical – ask a question we cannot ignore. Isn't the drug revolution an excuse for therapy on the cheap, for leaving therapy of the severely ill to social workers and paraprofessionals; for substituting a chemical reaction for the skilled deep human contact that alone can heal? Isn't it still another way of shortchanging the poor – since all studies show that the upper socioeconomic groups are far more likely to get intensive psychotherapy, while the lower socioeconomic groups get mostly somatic treatments?† Is it really true that insight therapy isn't much use for chronic schizophrenics? What about Harry Stack Sullivan and those other devoted

* Weight gain and disturbances in menstruation are among them.

† Studies also show that neurosis is more common in the upper socioeconomic groups, psychosis in the lower. Diagnosis may be tied to class levels, as the radical therapists say, and the incidence of psychosis among the poor is indeed a judgment on our society. Most psychiatrists will maintain, however, that when a poor man gets somatic treatment while a rich man gets psychotherapy, the type of treatment is chosen not according to money, but therapeutic appropriateness. Dr. Milton Greenblatt points out that lower-class patients accept drugs better than purely verbal treatment, since they perceive them as treatment for "bad nerves."[66]

clinicians, who poured all those years of sensitivity, imagination, and love into their relationships with psychotic people?

Fortunately, treatments are not necessarily second-rate because the poor get them – in spite of what radical therapists maintain. And unfortunately, deep human contact, though it may help a patient feel and act better, rarely heals severe mental illness – any more than it heals severe physical illness. (On the rare occasions when it does, we have a word for it – a miracle.) Nor is it true that more drug treatment means less psychotherapy – rather, it's the reverse. Drugs relieve the mental hospital staff from the sheer burdens of managing disturbed or inert patients, making other therapies possible. From 1963 to 1965, for example, the percentage of patients at Boston State Hospital receiving *no* therapy was cut in half – from 36.8 percent to 18 percent. At the same time the use of verbal therapies *rose,* from 18.2 percent to 27.7 percent.[67]

There is, however, a real question as to how much good these verbal therapies did the patients. Careful and thorough studies have been done to discover what types of treatment, in what combinations, make schizophrenic patients get better. Their results are increasingly difficult (but not impossible) * to challenge.

Dr. Greenblatt sums them up thus:

> These studies showed that psychotherapy was not the treatment of choice for chronic schizophrenia, although its addition to drugs alone might yield improved behavior in a few relatively minor respects, and, to an extent, might facilitate insight. . . . It may come as a shock . . . to learn that psychotherapy of chronic schizophrenics seemed to add little of significance to clinical improvement unless associated with drug intake. Drugs apparently are the patient's best friends, and the removal of drugs with substitution of placebo . . . results so regularly in behavioral regression as to leave little doubt in anybody's mind of the efficacy of the drug factor. . . . What then of the report of so many individual therapists as to their clinical achievements in chronic schizophrenic patients by psychotherapy alone? We leave an opening for the validity of such claims when they suggest that the inspired psychotherapist, working with just the right case, may accomplish much.†

We could put it this way. If your relative, rich or poor, has been reliably diagnosed as schizophrenic – if he or she is chronically ill, or

* See "Controversies About the Psychotherapy of Schizophrenia," by John Gunderson, *American Journal of Psychiatry,* 130 (June 1973), in which the only controversy is about what kind of psychotherapy should be given. See also the review article by David Feinsilver and Dr. Gunderson, "Psychotherapy for Schizophrenics," *Schizophrenia Bulletin,* 6 (Fall 1972), which concludes that the five studies reviewed "have neither proved psychotherapy ineffective nor provided any strong evidence of its helpfulness."

† Grinspoon *et al., op. cit.,* pp. ix–x. Fuller accounts of these studies may be found in D. Feinsilver and J. Gunderson, "Psychotherapy for Schizophrenics," *Schizophrenia Bulletin,* 6 (Fall 1972); see also P. R. A. May in "Psychotherapy Research on Schizophrenia: Another View of Present Reality," *Schizophrenia Bulletin,* 9 (Summer 1974).

is in the first phases of an acute psychotic reaction — and is getting no therapy beyond drugs and a rest in a reasonably decent place, don't assume he is being shortchanged. He is being treated according to what are generally believed to be the best methods at present known for his condition. If, however, he is getting psychotherapy but not drug therapy, you should wonder why, and ask.

How do drugs work?

We don't know yet, but we're beginning to find out. Dr. Seymour Kety, one of the leading researchers into the biological causes of mental illness, remarked in 1972 that "what we have learned about behavior and the brain in the last few decades is more than man learned in all the time before."[68] Some hard facts seem to underlie the success of pharmacotherapy, both with phenothiazines and with the mood-altering drugs to be discussed in the next section. We have learned that the brain is indeed a complex of hard-working chemicals; we have learned that abnormal amounts of these may be at work in the brains (and analyzable in the urine) of psychotic individuals. Some of these chemicals, the *neurotransmitters,* help carry nerve impulses from cell to cell. Among these, dopamine, serotonin, and norepinephrine are affected by drugs, which can raise or lower their amounts, causing marked psychological changes, and raising the question whether some mental illnesses may not be caused by excesses and deficiencies of brain chemicals. A readable and authoritative guide to these and other organic explanations of psychotic conditions is Dr. Solomon H. Snyder's *Madness and the Brain.**

Chemicals and the brain:

a clue to causes?

Mood-altering drugs

Mood-altering drugs are prescribed for those who suffer from affective disorders, who get too depressed or, more rarely, too elated, to go on without help. Mild depressions are treated with psychotherapy and — or — the minor tranquilizers (occasionally with stimulant drugs like amphetamines). More severe conditions get stronger medicine. The function of antidepressant drugs is indicated by their name. Here the phenothiazines don't help; they may clear up a depressed schizophrenic's psychotic symptoms, but they won't make him any less sad. Conversely, antidepressants won't make him any less crazy; they may even make him worse. Psychiatry has at length progressed beyond the days of general sedatives, prescribed without regard for diagnoses, to the point where it can offer different medications that work for different disorders in reasonably predictable ways.

Anti-depressants

It is hard to judge whether a depression is "justified" by what's going on in someone's life, in which case it's called reactive, or *exogenous* (coming from outside), or whether it seems to "come up out of nowhere" (in which case it's assumed to come from inside and called *endogenous*). Exogenous depressions are more like neuroses and are

* See also the excellent brief explanation in Dr. Paul Wender's *The Hyperactive Child* (New York: Crown Publishers, 1973), p. 33.

treated with psychotherapy; endogenous depressions are more like psychoses, and are more likely to respond to drugs.*

For both kinds, the outlook is hopeful. "How many other diseases are there," asks Dr. Bertram Brown, head of the National Institute for Mental Health, "where, with accurate diagnosis and really effective care, you've got a 95 percent chance of getting back to totally full functioning?"[69]

The two major types of antidepressants, the *tricyclic antidepressants* and the *monoamine oxidase inhibitors,* were discovered in the late fifties, as the success of the phenothiazines sparked new interest in drug chemistry. The first tricyclic antidepressant, *imipramine,* like chlorpromazine, gave rise to a whole new family of drugs. Under the trade name Tofrānil, it is still the most commonly prescribed of the dozen or so tricyclic antidepressants; the other most generally used is *amitriptyline* (Elavil). Imipramine increases initiative and drive and is useful in *retarded depressions,* where the patient's activity is slowed down by the way he feels; in *agitated depressions* the calming effect of amitriptyline may be more appropriate.

Tricyclic antidepressants

The effects of antidepressants may not show for some weeks. Dosages vary – of course. High dosages can produce in some people a psychotic state with visual illusions. Side effects also vary, from patient to patient and drug to drug; patients may complain of dry mouth, blurred vision, dizziness, constipation, frequent urination, weight gain, drowsiness (or insomnia), and psychological effects such as anxiety and nightmares. When these persist, a change to another tricyclic antidepressant will often obtain the therapeutic effect without the side effects.

Side effects

Nothing certain is yet known about how the tricyclics work. It's suspected they affect the neurotransmitter chemicals in the brain, but since it's also suspected that the phenothiazines do this, that doesn't tell us very much. What's more certain is that they make a lot of the people who take them – somewhere between 60 percent and 80 percent[70] – feel very much better.

The very name of the next class of antidepressants, *monoamine oxidase inhibitors,* suggests that something more is known about what they do inside the body. They were developed from a drug used for the treatment of tuberculosis, which astute clinicians had noticed made their patients unusually cheerful. This drug (iproniazid, no longer used in America as an antidepressant because of its toxic effects) is known to inhibit the production of *monoamine oxidase.* Monoamine oxidase is a brain enzyme; it counteracts the chemicals known as *amines,* among which are the neurotransmitters previously mentioned, serotonin and norepinephrine. Not enough is known about what triggers this action, but one of the drugs that can do it is reserpine, and it

Monoamine oxidase inhibitors (MAO's)

* Dr. Nathan Kline recommends drugs for both kinds. *From Sad to Glad: Kline on Depression* (New York: Putnam, 1974), chapter 6.

was soon observed in reserpine therapy that low levels of brain amines and depression go together. Drugs such as iproniazid seemed to block the monoamine oxidase, preventing it from breaking down the amines chemically. When iproniazid was given before the reserpine, the patients became excited rather than depressed.[71] But we should not conclude that these impressive-sounding terms add up to a full explanation. Does the effect take place through serotonin, or norepinephrine, or both? And how? And what are those amines doing in the first place? Drugs can alter their concentration; can't emotions do that too? How? The neuropharmacologists are hard at work. They may have some answers by the time you read this book — and some new questions.

Side effects

Although they hold great promise for the study of depression, the MAO's are used less than the tricyclic antidepressants, since they are more likely to have toxic side effects.* The rule is usually to try the tricyclics first. The effect of MAO's, however, can seem — as author Percy Knauth reported of his own bout with depression — "little short of miraculous." His account of his "season in hell" shows that "feeling better" is an inadequate phrase for expressing what drugs can do for the utter hopelessness that is severe depression. He did feel better, though, so much better that he reduced his dose — only to wake up one morning "with the familiar clammy feelings of despair."[72] For depressed patients, too, continued medication may sometimes be necessary, either alone or combined with psychotherapy — which the patient can make better use of in his or her new frame of mind.

Lithium salts for manic-depressive psychosis

Until the seventies, the manic states, the states of excited elation that are at the other extreme of affective disorders, were treated with phenothiazines, shock, and psychotherapy, with variable success, usually temporary, while the depressive states of manic-depressive psychosis were treated with antidepressants. But in the late sixties, American doctors and patients began hearing about a new treatment with an old drug, lithium carbonate, a treatment that works so well that it has become the treatment of choice for manic-depressive psychosis.

The drug companies don't bother to advertise lithium. It's cheap, it has no exotic chemistry, and it's been around for more than a hundred years. Lithium salts were used in the nineteenth century for gout and rheumatism and were a fairly common constituent of the mineral waters that were then such an important part of medical practice. J. F. J. Cade, an Australian psychiatrist, reported using lithium for mania in 1949, but the treatment took twenty years to reach America. Then it caught on fast: lithium, in the judgment of Columbia's Dr. Malitz, is "one of the major breakthroughs since the advent of the era of psychopharmacology."[73]

* Foods containing amines — most commonly cheese — may bring on a dangerous crisis in patients taking MAO's. The list, which includes chocolate, raisins, sauerkraut, pickled herring, chicken livers, and lox, should be discussed carefully with the patient and his family.

Lithium treats manic episodes

Lithium brings people down from a manic high without any sedating effect. It does this so well that it's hard to compare it with other drugs. In "blind studies" comparing lithium with chlorpromazine, the lithium patients were so much more alert that the doctors recognized the treatment without being told.[74] But even more important than its effect on mania is its success in preventing the recurring manic episodes whose mysterious, cyclic reappearances give to manic-depressive psychosis what one analyst calls "a relentless organic feel." (If it is organic, nobody knows how lithium works on the malfunctioning organism, although you won't be surprised to learn that it's thought it may affect the action of neurotransmitters in the brain.) It prevents recurrent depressions to a lesser degree; Dr. Malitz estimates a 75 percent of patients "whose manic states are controlled but whose depressions are not."* For these patients, tricyclics may be added to lithium treatment. And since the effects of lithium take weeks to build up, phenothiazines may be used in the early stages, if it's important to bring the patient down from his acute state. These drug combinations, like all others, should be watched carefully, for drugs can do things in combination that they don't do separately.

and largely prevents recurring episodes of mania

as well as some depressions.

It's sometimes used with other drugs.

Two levels of dosage

There are two levels of dosage for lithium, one for prevention, one for treatment. The preventive, or *prophylactic,* maintenance dose is lower than the *therapeutic* dose, which is given to bring the actual attack under control.

Lithium is less effective than antidepressants for severe depressions, and it makes schizophrenic disorders worse. This may be encouraging evidence for those who think the best hope for treating disordered mental states is to establish them as distinct diseases, but we are still far from being able to make full use of it. Dr. Malitz emphasizes the importance of careful diagnosis, made with close attention to the patient's history, genetics (has someone else in the family had a similar condition?), symptoms – especially the lack of schizophrenic signs. But especially in the United States, where the diagnosis of schizophrenia has been so loosely applied, doctors are giving lithium to patients with whom other drug treatments have been unsuccessful and finding that some of them respond. It's a backwards process, when the effectiveness of the treatment helps us decide what the illness is, but it underlies how much we still have to learn.

Problems of diagnosis

Lithium's narrow margin of safety requires careful physical

Lithium is a potent drug, and the margin between the amount that is therapeutic and the amount that poisons is much narrower than in the phenothiazines and antidepressants. The prescription of lithium cannot be made from a routine calculation of average doses. The patient must be carefully tested for evidence of kidney or heart disease.

* Dr. Malcolm Lader quotes a patient: "Okay, Doc, I don't go up any more, but I can still go down quite a bit." Both Dr. Malitz and Dr. Lader are quoted in "Recent Advances in Psychotherapeutic Drugs," *Psychiatric Annals,* 3 (July 1973).

His blood serum levels must be regularly checked; the amount of lithium in the blood serum is a reliable guide to whether the dose is too high or too low. Once the dosage is established, the patient must not vary it; the patient who "has a habit of taking an extra pill or two when he isn't feeling well or wishes to sleep" may get into bad trouble on lithium.[75] Salt intake is important. It shouldn't vary much; too little salt (or defective kidneys) may result in too much lithium remaining in the body. High doses of phenothiazines may or may not be good for your relative, but he can die from too much lithium. Used carefully, however, lithium is safe; it "can be administered indefinitely without fear of serious complications. Lithium appears to have no significant effect on normal mental functions. There has been no report of habituation or altered tolerance even after years of continuous intake."[76] And continuous intake is necessary: "Failure to take medication, even after a number of years, may result in relapse." This caution is particularly important, since manic depressives are quite normal between episodes and may easily conclude that people who aren't sick don't need medicine.

examination, frequent blood checks, and exact doses

which must be continued indefinitely to prevent recurrences.

Side effects

Side effects are in general less marked than with other psychoactive drugs. In the early weeks of treatment there may be some gastrointestinal irritations (diarrhea, nausea); these are not severe, and usually disappear. A fine hand tremor and frequent urination may persist. Like many drugs, lithium in pregnancy may harm the unborn baby. Lithium is remarkably free of "psychiatric" side effects; the patient feels truly "himself," his emotional and intellectual functioning unchanged.

Shock treatments

Shock treatments were the first spectacularly effective treatments for mental illness, and they should have come first in this discussion of somatic therapies. But shock therapy — or more properly, *electroconvulsive treatment,* or ECT — has become highly controversial. Patients are more likely to object to it than to any other form of treatment;* distrust, even contempt for psychiatrists who administer it is widespread. If it had come first among the somatic treatments, you might have laid this book down in disgust. You still may, for we are about to say that for many patients shock therapy is a rapid, effective, and humane treatment. Nobody likes the idea. But in an emergency it works faster than anything else. Even analysts who don't use shock themselves may recommend it. Be critical, of course. If your doctor recommends shock treatment for an adolescent or young adult, insist on a consultation with another physician; shock has been overused with young people. But if he or she does *not* recommend shock treatment for a delusional, severely depressed, suicidal fifty-five-year-old, insist on a consultation. Severe suicidal depression isn't something you

When speed counts

* See Sylvia Plath's widely read *The Bell Jar,* for example; see also Bruce Ennis and Loren Siegel's American Civil Liberties Union Handbook, *The Rights of Mental Patients* (New York: Richard W. Baron, 1973), pp. 69–71, which doubts that shock therapy is *ever* "really helpful" and tells lawyers how to enable patients to avoid it.

fool around with, least of all on humanitarian grounds. There's time for psychotherapy or preventive drug therapy when the danger is over.

Trouble with words

It's too bad that the convulsive treatments so soon picked up the name "shock treatment"; the word alone accounts for much of the fear and horror in which they're held. The different meanings of "shock" don't help a bit. People imagine the shock is psychological, which it isn't. Nor does the "shock" to the system have anything to do with the electric shock which is most commonly used to bring it about. The first "shock" treatments made no use of electricity, but achieved their results by drugs. In 1933, in Vienna, Manfred Sakel used insulin to bring on a state of deep hypoglycemic coma (low blood sugar) which was soon referred to as insulin shock, though it is more exactly described as *insulin coma treatment.* It helped schizophrenics as nothing had up to that time, and is still used in a few hospitals here, although because of the elaborateness of the treatment and the need for specially trained staff, ECT and drugs have largely taken its place.* Less than two years later the Hungarian psychiatrist L. V. von Meduna used camphor injections to bring on convulsions — having observed schizophrenic symptoms disappear after spontaneous convulsions or seizures. In 1937 two Italian psychiatrists, Ugo Cerletti and Lucio Bini, first induced convulsions electrically. The effects were remarkable. Psychoses and depressions cleared up, patients went home. The doors of the mental hospital began to open.

Insulin coma treatment

Electro-convulsive or electroshock treatment (ECT or EST)

It was a violent treatment then. Many of the horrifying descriptions of it date from the past, when assistants held down the patient's arms and legs and the convulsion sometimes broke bones. Even then, however, the patient lost consciousness instantly.

How it's given

In modern ECT, anesthesia and muscle relaxants are given. Two metal disks, the electrodes, are applied to the temples; current (100 or so volts at 200 to 1600 milliamps) passes through the brain for about a second. The patient's toes twitch only slightly; it is in his head that the changes take place. What they are we don't know, although we know that electrical impulses the brain gives off change during seizures. Forty years have seen many theories come, most of which have gone. By now you'll automatically think of those brain amines, and indeed studies on animals have shown that convulsions do produce changes in them.[77] What changes, and how, remain a mystery.

Who gets ECT?

Many, many people. ECT works with a greater variety of conditions than lithium and the psychoactive drugs. United States Senator Thomas Eagleton got it, as everybody knows. He recovered completely. It's more than possible you know people who've had shock, but they'd have to

* It is still widely used abroad. Psychiatrists experienced in insulin treatment, like Dr. Lothar Kalinowsky and Dr. H. Peter Laqueur (known also for his work in family therapy), feel it has been too readily abandoned for drugs, since it can achieve complete remission of symptoms without side effects or continued maintenance doses. Kalinowsky, *op. cit.*, and personal interview with Dr. Laqueur, March 1974.

tell you – you couldn't guess. Severe depression is the major indication; for that, ECT is still the fastest and most reliable treatment known. It may be used, too, in acute psychotic episodes, while waiting for the slow-acting phenothiazines or the slower lithium to act. It's less effective when depression shades into symptoms that recall schizophrenia and in the paranoid delusions that sometime afflict people in middle age (involutional psychosis). Whereas depressed patients usually respond after a few treatments, paranoid and schizophrenic patients require many before any improvement is noted, so that many doctors are reluctant to recommend them, especially now that drugs are available. Some very experienced doctors, however, still consider ECT a valuable treatment in schizophrenia.[78] For neurosis, or problems in living, ECT is obviously not the treatment of choice.

People who are severely depressed or acutely psychotic

Its use in chronic schizophrenia is controversial

and it's not for neurotics.

Unfortunately, that doesn't prevent it from being given for them. There are psychiatrists who make it almost the only type of treatment, prescribing it for troubled adolescents, drug addicts, housewives depressed by empty or harassed lives – people skilled psychotherapy might help more surely if more slowly. ECT is one of the most effective treatments in psychiatry, but it's also the quickest and easiest. Quickness can be an advantage, of course. The average course of treatments is over inside two weeks, making it a convenient treatment for someone who can't get time off for lengthy psychotherapy – or afford it – and is uncomfortable with the side effects of drugs. But quick and easy treatment methods tempt doctors to use them routinely, casually. In his book *The Making of a Psychiatrist,* Dr. David Viscott writes sourly, "Finding that the patient has insurance seemed like the most common indication for giving shock; the second is depression."* Health insurance, which often doesn't cover psychotherapy, usually pays for ECT without question. The cost of treatment is comparable to an hour of psychotherapy, and a doctor can treat a lot of patients in a day.† In Boston, reporters found one woman who had had nearly two hundred treatments – after which she attempted suicide.[80]

Too many people get it

too routinely.

Dr. Leo Alexander, President of the American Electroshock Society and a leading proponent of the treatment, writes of patients "whose sustained recovery depends on the administration of forty to forty-

* (New York: Arbor House, 1972), p. 352. In his first months of practice Dr. Viscott found shock routinely given to patients whose physical problems (low serum potassium, brain tumor) had been misdiagnosed as psychiatric as well as for problems in living, which called for psychotherapy.

† "In Canada, and especially in Quebec where the amount of money paid the psychiatrist for giving ECT has dropped to somewhere between $5 and $10 a treatment as opposed to the $40 or $50 here, the use of ECT has dropped precipitously. It is no secret that psychiatrists who heavily use ECT and medications for that matter, treatments that can be exploited for maximum earnings per hour, frequently have income in excess of $100,000 to $200,000 per year. On the other hand, psychiatrists who restrict their practices to mild to moderate use of medication, avoidance of hospitalization and little or no use of ECT rarely have incomes in excess of $60,000. . . ."[79]

eight treatments"; but he notes that he encounters such patients rarely – perhaps one or two a year.[81] ECT is a useful treatment which is all too easily abused.

You should not conclude that there is an ECT epidemic, however. The psychoactive drugs have greatly reduced reliance on shock. Some hospitals have never used it. Others, under public pressure, have abandoned a treatment which has become controversial and for which there are now substitutes – even though these may not always do the job as well.

Memory loss: a significant side effect

The patient wakes up in a half hour or so, groggy and confused. He or she has forgotten a good deal, particularly about recent events. Usually, past memories come back gradually, over a few weeks, though many patients never recover memory of the time immediately surrounding the treatment. Typically, a patient will feel and function much better after ECT; the world seems itself again if they've been depressed; if delusional, the delusions have subsided.* The number of treatments varies – it's estimated that 80 percent of all depressives recover after six to eight. But patients have had many times this number without any lingering harmful effects. Permanent, disabling memory loss can happen, however,† reminding us that *no major medical treatment is without risk.*

In some states, like Massachusetts and California, who can get ECT and how often is regulated by law. Anywhere, you can block shock treatment for a relative for whom you are responsible by withholding your consent. If your relative is a voluntary patient, he or she can refuse it, and in some states if he is an involuntary patient as well.

Questions

If a doctor recommends shock treatment for your relative, you have questions to ask him and yourself. How severe is the emergency? Is there a serious risk of suicide? Above all, what are the alternatives to the treatment?‡

Psychosurgery

He's a young man, twenty-two – in and out of mental hospitals since

* Good, readable accounts of how it feels before and after shock treatment can be found in Barbara Benziger's *The Prison of My Mind* (New York: Walker, 1969) and Ellen Wolfe's *Aftershock: The Story of a Psychotic Episode* (New York: Putnam, 1969).

Both Mrs. Benziger and Mrs. Wolfe recovered speedily after shock, though they found the memory loss distressing; both had had psychotherapy before and continued it afterward. ECT is often combined with other treatments.

† Berton Roueché, in "As Empty as Eve," *The New Yorker* (September 9, 1974), describes the case of a government economist treated for severe depression with ECT. It improved the depression, but she found not only that she had lost essential professional knowledge, but that her impaired memory did not allow her to relearn it. She was forced to retire on a disability pension before she was fifty. Astonishingly, there seem to be no reliable studies of the frequency of significant memory loss after ECT.

‡ In his guide for families of depressed patients, *Up from Depression* (New York: Simon and Schuster, 1969), Dr. Leonard Cammer describes the major alternative for the suicidal person: *"Someone should stay with him at all times or find a means of protecting him so long as he retains the desire to die"* (p. 29). He gives detailed suggestions on how to recognize suicidal tendencies, and recommends that you remove all interior locks from doors.

he was eighteen. Unless he's watched constantly he burns himself with cigarettes, smashes his head against the wall. He has already blinded one eye and injured the other. A brain operation should succeed in controlling his self-destructive violence, maybe even let him come home. Dr. Donald Becker, of the Medical College of Virginia, thinks so. The young man has consented, and so have his parents. His mother says, "We couldn't stand to see him tear himself apart piece by piece." But before the operation can be performed, somebody calls the state attorney general's office and the Washington *Post*. He doesn't say who he is; maybe he's a fellow patient. But he raises ethical and legal questions. They are the same questions that are asked in relation to behavior modification, drugs, and ECT, but here they are even more intensely felt. Does anyone have the right to tamper with another person's brain, even if the intention is to help him? Is it possible for a patient like this to give "informed" consent? Is he — or his family — in a position to evaluate risks and possible benefits?

This operation was canceled.[82] Many similar operations have been canceled, postponed indefinitely, or rejected even as a possibility by doctors who believe that such operations can help patients who can be helped no other way — but who draw back from the angry controversy that surrounds psychosurgery. For many other doctors believe that psychosurgery is a violation of the fundamental precept of their Hippocratic oath: *primum non nocere* — first of all, to do no harm.

The last resort

Psychosurgery is surgery performed on an intact brain, in order to bring about psychological changes: to change behavior or relieve tensions and anxieties. Intact — there is no way of demonstrating it is diseased. Psychosurgery should be distinguished from plain brain surgery, which also may alleviate psychological symptoms, but which is undertaken to correct a known organic condition such as a tumor. Psychosurgery ought to be the last resort in mental illness, and it is. In the entire United States, an estimated five hundred operations are performed each year; only fifteen operations were performed in Veterans' Administration hospitals in the twelve years before 1972.[83] It is a very rare treatment, and our watchdogs in the press, the law, and in psychiatry want to be sure it remains so. They have reason to be uneasy, remembering the early days of psychosurgery, in the forties and early fifties, when there were 50,000 operations in a single year. Dr. Karl Pribram of Stanford, the eminent specialist in brain function,* recalls that

The bad old days

> heyday of psychosurgery, when frontal lobotomy was an accepted routine procedure. Psychiatrists would certify a patient for surgery. The surgeon would, frequently sight unseen, deploy the leucotome; a long dull knife blade, an egg beater, or an ice pick, depending on his preference. Often surgeon and patient did not become acquainted until after the operation when dressings had to be changed.[84]

*** His four-volume compilation, *Brain and Behavior,* is a full review of what was known in that field up to 1969, its date of publication (Penguin Books).**

This is the vision that sticks in the minds of those who sound the alarm lest psychosurgery (seconded by behavior modification and drugs) be used to silence our dissenters and rob us of our humanity.

It is a vision that is obsolete. Much more is known now about the various parts of the brain and how they affect our emotions and behavior (much of it due to those early, crude lobotomies). Surgical techniques, too, are far more precise now, and much less brain tissue is destroyed. Surgeons today may not cut at all, but pass weak electric currents through electrodes left in place in the brain. The effects are temporary, but how they affect the patient's mood and behavior is a guide to exactly where the psychosurgeon should operate. An increase in the current, carefully controlled, will destroy only the cells around the top of the electrode, minimizing the risk of changes in personality.

More precise techniques affect less brain tissue.

In the bad old days, even when the operation was successful and a more normal and satisfying life became possible for the patient and those close to him,* this change was often at the price of a dulling of the emotions – one of the reasons for recommending the operation was unbearable anxiety. Psychosurgeons say that with today's more limited operations such personality changes are less common; when they do occur, they are slighter. Though the casualties are rarer than they used to be, no one denies that they exist. Statistics may be misleading; any type of treatment which is tried only on the severest cases will have a relatively high proportion of treatment failures. Dr. Orlando Andy of the University of Mississippi Medical School, who has done thirty to forty operations since the late fifties, reports a quarter unimproved, with the rest showing fair to good results with minimal adverse effects; the figure of one-quarter unimproved recurs in other doctors' statistics.[85]

Personality changes?

Casualties?

Results?

Who gets psychosurgery?

In the past, psychosurgery has been used with drug addicts, chronic alcoholics, and those troubled people doctors call character-disordered or psychopathic. But, in spite of what you've heard, the typical psychosurgery patient isn't poor or friendless; he's probably a member of the upper middle class who's tried everything else and is desperate for relief.† Brain surgery is not cheap.

* In the forties, when the word "lobotomy" was just becoming known, I went to college with a girl who'd had one. It was only a year before, and you could still see the scar under her bangs. She said she'd put on weight since the operation. I don't know what else had changed, or what continuing misery could have induced doctors to operate on a nineteen-year-old girl. However, at the time I knew her she was not a vegetable but the editor of the college newspaper. C.C.P.

† Dr. Alan Stone, Professor of Law and Psychiatry at Harvard Law School and also a psychoanalyst, calls the furor over psychosurgery "a wave of hysteria that has come about over the claim it's being used against minority groups, a claim which is totally untrue and unrealistic. In fact, it is . . . actually performed on middle and upper-class people who don't like psychiatrists, who don't like talking, who don't want to explore their problems, and who, when shock treatment fails, go get themselves lobotomized."[86]

Neurotics with crippling symptoms,

Unlike the other major somatic therapies, psychosurgery is sometimes recommended for neuroses by responsible physicians. But you shouldn't assume that this means a drastic remedy is being recommended for a mild condition. Some neuroses are more incapacitating than many psychoses. One woman's fear that she can't swallow dominates her life; she's afraid to eat except at home, afraid to meet anyone; she has spent twenty years going from one psychotherapist to another. One man's obsessive preoccupation with germs obliges him to spend most of his time in the bathroom.[87] Dr. Kalinowsky considers that "the best results of psychosurgery are obtained in severe intractable psychoneuroses"; psychosurgery can enable such patients, who are often highly intelligent, to return to a productive life, and they are less likely than others to suffer personality changes. Dr. Kalinowsky emphasizes that "no patient should be considered for surgical procedures who has not been tried adequately on all other forms of treatment"; "intensive psychotherapy and pharmacotherapy must be tried prior to brain surgery in all types of neurosis."[88]

some epileptics

Some of psychosurgery's most dramatic successes have been with epileptic patients. Let's repeat: with drugs, the majority of epileptics can lead normal lives; they suffer from prejudice more than epilepsy. But a few experience overwhelming moods of depression or terror, often accompanied by distorted perceptions and violent or self-destructive behavior which makes life unlivable for them and those around them. Dr. Vernon Mark of Harvard Medical School is a pioneer in psychosurgery on epileptics.*

Other conditions?

The effectiveness of drugs and ECT insures that psychosurgery is not used for affective disorders. It has no application in chronic schizophrenia except where intense emotional states make a bad situation very much worse. Psychosurgery rarely eliminates schizophrenic delusions (though they may bother the patient less), and it cannot sharpen a deteriorating mind.

Guidelines

The National Association for Mental Health suggests a guideline:

> Psychosurgery should not be used except in those instances where the patient is in such great personal distress due to his mental disorder that he would prefer such psychosurgery rather than to remain with his existing condition, and where all alternatives have been considered or have been given an adequate trial as defined by consensus of the patient, his family, and at least two reputable physicians, at least one of whom should be a psychiatrist.†

* An informative report of his work is to be found in the *Boston Globe,* January 21, 1971.

† *NAMH Reporter* (Summer 1973). Full text available from NAMH. (For address, see Appendix.)

Psychosurgery cannot be undertaken without the consent of the patient and his family.

Nutritional treatments:

The mildest of all somatic treatments, nutritional treatments seek to affect mental and emotional functioning by diet. Unquestionably this can be done. Some babies are born with phenylketonuria, a chemical abnormality that turns good food into poisons that cause inevitable brain damage. Blood tests for the newborn, followed by a strict diet, prevent retardation and psychosis. The mental and physical symptoms of pellagra, which once accounted for 10 percent of admissions to southern state hospitals, are now known to be the result of a deficiency of niacin – vitamin B_3. The understanding and prevention of these diseases is a medical triumph, and scientists, some psychiatrists among them, continue to be interested in the possibility that diet contributes to other mental illness. The extreme vegetarian diets now frequent among young people (often compounded with drug use) are drawing increasing attention as casualties begin to show up in psychiatrists' offices.* Some doctors report that cereal grains and milk make schizophrenic symptoms worse.[90] Others implicate food and other allergies in psychiatric disorders.† A number of physicians consider that hypoglycemia (low blood sugar) can cause or intensify a wide variety of psychiatric problems.‡ None of these theories is solidly established. Doctors are generally suspicious of nutritional treatments, conscious that special diets attract a special breed of fanatic, and loath to believe that complex mental symptoms can be caused by something so simple as faulty nutrition.

Some doctors think nutrition or allergies contribute to mental symptoms.

Most doctors don't.

Megavitamin therapy

Most controversial of nutritional treatments is *megavitamin therapy,*

* Norman Cousins, editor and columnist, reports on a girl whose schizophrenic symptoms were treated for five years with shock, drugs, and whatever else an expensive mental hospital can offer, before they were at length diagnosed as resulting from combined amphetamine abuse and malnutrition. Treated with vitamins and diet, she recovered.[89]

† Dr. Ben F. Feingold, chief emeritus in the department of allergy at Kaiser-Permanente Medical Center in San Francisco, treating hyperactive schoolchildren with a diet free of artificial flavorings and colorings, reports marked improvement in learning and behavior (at 122nd Annual Convention of the American Medical Association, reported in Honolulu *Star-Bulletin,* June 26, 1973). Dr. Feingold has written a book for parents, *Why Your Child Is Hyperactive* (New York: Random House, 1975). Dr. Richard Mackarness, writing in *Mind Out,* the magazine of the British Association for Mental Health, estimates that a third of all mental illness may be the result of unrecognized allergies. The New York psychiatrist Allen Cott, though a psychoanalyst, now works mainly through controlling diet, including fasting (a therapy used also in Russia for some severe psychoses). See UPI report, *Berkshire Eagle,* December 20, 1974, and *Village Voice,* August 22, 1974.

‡ Among them are Dr. Leonard Klyston, an endocrinologist at Hahnemann Medical College, Philadelphia; psychiatrist Jack L. Ward of Mercer Hospital in Trenton, N.J.; and Dr. James Field of the University of Pittsburgh School of Medicine, quoted in Joan Arehart-Treichel, "The Great Medical Debate Over Low Blood Sugar," *Science News,* 103 (March 17, 1973).

or *orthomolecular psychiatry,* as Nobel prizewinner Linus Pauling has renamed it for theoretical reasons too complex to go into here. In the early fifties, impressed with the power of the newly discovered LSD to produce psychotic symptoms, Dr. Humphry Osmond speculated that this might be a key to the distorted perceptions of schizophrenics. The phenothiazine drugs had not yet come into use when he and the Canadian psychiatrist Abram Hoffer began to experiment with a cheap and readily available B vitamin, niacin, which they hoped would affect the chemical disturbance they believed caused the disease. Niacin is the same vitamin used in small doses for pellagra. Osmond and Hoffer used much larger doses – three to six grams a day, sometimes higher. Their own *double-blind** studies confirmed their clinical impression that the vitamins reduced or even eliminated the symptoms.[91] (Like everyone else, they found that acute schizophrenic reactions responded better than chronic conditions.) The treatment drew little attention at the time, when phenothiazine drugs were revolutionizing the therapy of schizophrenia. It was not until the mid-sixties, when vitamins and nutrition (and LSD) † became popular, that it began to attract notice. Some doctors began to experiment with it, adding other vitamins to the mix, and sometimes special diets as well, notably a diet for hypoglycemia.

Acute and chronic again

A highly controversial treatment

Because vitamins can be bought without prescription, this therapy appeals to people who question established medical treatments and like to doctor themselves. Physicians naturally discourage self-medication (megavitamin psychiatrists also strongly recommend medical supervision). But the controversy is not over unsupervised medication. Those who oppose vitamin therapy do not claim it does harm. Side effects can occur, but they are uncommon and less severe than those considered routine in drug therapy. They contend it does no good.

As with other treatments, there are enthusiastic patients‡ and grateful families who are sure it has helped, and even cured: the number seems large and the enthusiasm unusually lasting. There is a growing number of psychiatrists who prescribe the treatment and have formed their own institute (see Chapter XIV). But though these doctors and their patients tell many encouraging stories (*anecdotal reports,* these are called in the literature), reliable clinical results are hard to get, especially since vitamin therapy, which its practitioners say takes months to show effects, is usually supplemented by phenothiazines and

* Studies in which neither the patient nor the researcher knows whether the patient is getting the treatment under investigation or a placebo.

† Many LSD users report that niacin speeds return trips.

‡ Mark Vonnegut, whose book *The Eden Express* describes his experience with schizophrenia, remarks, "I haven't run across any other therapy that *patients* are enthusiastic about." Personal interview, July, 1975.

often by psychotherapy or ECT as well.* A special task force of the American Psychiatric Association, reporting on megavitamin therapy in July, 1973, complained that "it is virtually impossible to replicate studies in which each patient receives a highly individualized therapeutic program with from one to seven vitamins, plus hormones, special diets, other drugs, and ECT."[92]

Unsuccessful attempts to confirm results

Nevertheless, attempts to replicate (that is, to duplicate) Osmond and Hoffer's early results were made. They have been unsuccessful. In 1973 the A.P.A. task force concluded that the theoretical basis of orthomolecular psychiatry had been "found wanting," and that the results of careful evaluations of the treatment were "uniformly negative."[93] Doctors who have had success with megavitamin therapy maintain that the studies did not in fact duplicate Osmond and Hoffer's conditions.† Besides, no two groups are alike, says Dr. Nina Toll, a board-certified psychiatrist practicing in Connecticut. She is convinced of the value of the therapy and intends to go on prescribing it, in combination with psychotherapy and phenothiazines. (She finds it especially useful, however, with young people whose problems have been complicated by narcotics; they will often accept vitamins while refusing psychoactive drugs.) Side effects, she contends, are few and rare if the vitamins (which are acid) are taken with milk and after meals.[95]

Favorable clinical impressions

So there you have it. Many psychiatrists are sure it doesn't work. Some are convinced it does.‡ But nobody can be sure as long as impressions are based only on individual recoveries. Acute schizophrenic reactions, after all, often get better by themselves. Still, vitamins are cheap, and the ones used in orthomolecular psychiatry don't seem to hurt you. (*Don't* conclude that all vitamins are safe in large doses;

* For the best overview of the present theory and practice of megavitamin therapy — from the viewpoint of its defenders — see David Hawkins and Linus Pauling, eds., *Orthomolecular Psychiatry: Treatment of Schizophrenia* (San Francisco: W. H. Freeman, 1972). The book is addressed to the medical profession, but a number of the articles are nontechnical and can be understood by anyone. See especially the articles by Dr. Hawkins, which are based on work with over five thousand patients at the Nassau County (L.I.) Mental Health Center, which he directs. Accounts (by a mother and a patient) of striking recoveries after years of unsuccessful conventional treatments are Jessie Foy's *Gone Is Shadow's Child* (New York: Pyramid Books, 1971) and Gregor Stefan's *In Search of Sanity* (Hyde Park, N.Y.: University Books, n.d.).

† For example, the study of Dr. Thomas Ban of McGill University, who has been studying megavitamin therapy since 1966, found no difference between the effect of nicotinic acid and the effect of inactive placebo on schizophrenic symptoms in unselected patients; it is challenged because patients were given only three grams of nicotinic acid.[94]

‡ For a readable review of all somatic treatments from a strongly biological point of view, see *The Schizophrenias: Yours and Mine,* prepared by the Professional Advisory Committee of the American Schizophrenia Foundation, Carl M. Pfeiffer, Chairman. Extremely informative on drugs and their side effects, it recommends vitamins, but only as "supportive treatment."

vitamins A and D, which aren't used in megavitamin treatment, can cause serious damage.) The internationally known specialist Dr. Silvano Arieti notes that "in my personal experience I have never seen good results in patients treated exclusively with this method." He then quotes with approval the conclusions of Dr. H. E. Lehmann:

A temperate conclusion

> There does not seem to be sufficient evidence at this time to initiate megavitamin therapy on clinical grounds alone, but its possible negative effects are probably not serious enough to refuse treating a patient with megavitamins – in addition to the generally accepted physical therapeutic approaches to schizophrenia, e.g. pharmacotherapy – if the patient and his family insist on it.[96]

4. THINKING ABOUT THEM

Considering therapies

Of course there are many therapies we haven't mentioned. By the time you read this book there will be more. Some will be flexible new approaches to old problems; others will apply a single technique to all comers. (There are well-trained therapists today who propose to tickle people out of their hangups in eight-hour sessions.) Looking for a practical test, we ask, "Do they work?" only to get an answer both hopeful and frustrating: Many things work – well or fairly well – and different things work for different people.

Do they work?

Be aware of the role of missionary fervor as you investigate new treatments. It can signal quackery, but it has also accompanied every established treatment in its early years. Believing in any treatment helps – for both patient and therapist. That's why so many patients – from a third up to 70 percent in some studies – improve on *placebo,* a dummy pill.*

The role of faith and hope

Both technical and popular accounts of new therapies always describe successful cases. Don't be swept away; never forget that while one case – like Fay's – can *show* a great deal, it can *prove* nothing. No matter how extraordinary the recovery, it might have happened without the therapy – or because of some element in the therapy the therapist didn't think important enough to mention. Only a large number of cases, followed up over time, can prove the effectiveness of a treatment – and then only if these cases are compared with *controls,* similar people with similar problems who receive different treatments or no treatments at all. This is regularly done for drugs, which is why we could sound so sure about them. Behavior therapists too are pretty good at measuring what they're doing. Studies of comparative methods of dynamic psychotherapy are only now beginning; reports of earlier

Reliable outcome studies require a large number of cases with controls.

* Chapter 4 of Jerome Frank's *Persuasion and Healing* is entirely devoted to the placebo effect.

therapies, from Freud to Erikson, are based almost entirely upon case histories, and (since analytic therapies took so long) not many of those. We can expect an increasing number of careful studies of different types of treatment in the future. Right now they're not available for many therapies – which doesn't mean these might not help your relative.

A clue:

Ask who gets them.

As you read about a new therapy, note the kind of people who are getting it. Do they recall the person you are worried about? Do they seem to be disoriented or out of touch with reality? Or are they people taking full responsibility for themselves and their treatment, seeking relief from anxiety or alienation, better ways to deal with conflicts, or simply a better version of themselves? Notice where the new therapy is offered. Is it in use in a community mental health center, university clinics, a mental hospital? Or is it available through private consultation only? The answers to these questions will not, of course, tell you if it's a good therapy but they should simplify your search for help by allowing you to ignore much of what you read (unless, of course, you are interested in therapy for yourself).

Mysteries still . . .

"We are treating empirically disorders whose etiology is unknown, with methods whose action is also shrouded in mystery." Dr. Kalinowsky closed his book with these words in 1946; interviewed in 1973, he could find no reason to change them.* In the absence of certain knowledge, work proceeds empirically – by trial, and sometimes by error. When in the missionary mood, philosophies wrangle. Behaviorists challenge psychoanalysis and drugs, analysts challenge behavior therapy and psychosurgery, somatic therapists challenge dynamic psychotherapy, family therapists and radical therapists challenge everybody. Most practicing clinicians, however, realize that many things contribute to an individual's or a family's agony, and are ready to combine types of treatment according to need.

Trial and error

Theories divide;

practice brings together.

Somatic treatments and the types of psychotherapy – insight, supportive, behavioral – are regularly combined. And time is tempering the opposition between behavioral and psychodynamic therapies. In 1973, a task force of the American Psychiatric Assocation concluded that "behavior therapy and behavioral principles have reached a stage of development where they now unquestionably have much to offer informed clinicians" and recommended that they be incorporated into psychiatric training.[97] On their side, behavior therapists are recognizing that thinking and feeling are important kinds of behavior and are calling for more attention to inner experience.† Says Professor Arnold Lazarus, "A person riddled with self-doubt and self-defeating attitudes

* These are the words of the first edition, written with the late, much respected psychiatrist Paul Hoch; the 1969 edition still closes with them.

† See the discussion of "thought behaviors" and "cognitive habits" by R. E. Cronin, O. F. Kiel, and Rosemary C. Molitor in *Center for Behavior Modification Newsletter,* 2 (Jan. 1975).

is unlikely to derive much benefit from any therapy which ignores introspective material."[98] "Durable outcomes usually require philosophical as well as behavioral changes."[99] The year these words appeared, Dr. Birk, the chairman of the Psychiatric Association's task force, reported his own careful study of a treatment combining aversion therapy and prolonged psychodynamic therapy.[100] The year before, Professor Lazarus described a case where behavioral methods failed miserably until they were combined with an exploration of the patient's inner experience.[101]

Combining methods

Michael Harrington's account of the treatment of his anxiety neurosis shows how one analyst back in 1966 was combining dynamic and behavioral techniques before anybody was discussing it, beginning therapy not with childhood but with the immediate problem of "how to give a speech or just walk down the street without being attacked by anxiety," teaching him to rehearse every detail of the speaking trips that so distressed him, "including the cab ride or the question of whether or not I would have dinner with the organizers of the meeting." She helped him talk his way to understanding himself better. And though she wasn't a doctor, she prescribed a well-known drug: one martini as indicated.[102] Where the welfare of their patients is concerned, few experienced clinicians set a very high priority on maintaining theoretical purity.

Ethical and social considerations

Most families must consider treatment methods not on grounds of philosophical preference or public policy but on grounds of what will best help their relative and themselves. Yet we are citizens as well as troubled family members, and private and public considerations merge. The four years spent preparing this book have seen a flood of books and articles on mental health care in America, most of it bitterly critical. The criticism reflects the divisions and soul-searching within the profession itself.* In a practical guide we can only brush these larger questions; you yourself know what they mean to you, and how much.

An adjustment ethic?

Psychoanalysis and its influence has been coming under increasing attack. The criticisms are too various to attempt to survey, but one of the most common is that psychoanalytic therapies have not in fact sought to free the patient, but to teach him to adjust to circumstances which he – or she – ought to challenge. Women, like homosexuals, have had a great deal to put up with from traditional psychotherapeutic theory and practice; their protests are joined by others whose values or life-styles are at odds with prevailing values.

Other protests are made on behalf of the nonverbal and nonaffluent.

* For instance, from outside the profession, Anthony Brandt's *Reality Police* (New York: William Morrow, 1975) and Philip Hilts's *Behavior Mod* (New York: Harper's Magazine Press, 1974). Professional soul-searching appears in every professional journal; for the general reader, see the books of R. D. Laing and E. Fuller Torrey for a start.

They have had little to put up with but neglect, but they have had a great deal of that, as the fascinations of psychoanalysis diverted the energies of two generations of our finest psychiatric intelligences to exploring the problems of those least in need of psychiatric care and best able to pay for it.* Taxpayers subsidize the training of mental health professionals, of doctors in particular; what they do with their training and who benefits from it are questions more and more people are asking.

Elitism?

The prestige and influence of psychoanalytic thinking, say critics, have obscured the narrowness of its scope. A 1970 survey of four thousand members of the "fifth profession," psychotherapy, including psychoanalysts, psychiatrists, psychologists, and psychiatric social workers, found them astonishingly like each other, not only in professional point of view but in social, cultural, and even religious and national background. Few were from small town or rural backgrounds. Very few were black, of course. Few were Republicans. Few were religious. Very few were Catholic. The patients and clients who used their services, by and large, had similar characteristics. The picture given of psychodynamic psychotherapy was of people with shared values talking to each other.[104] The survey was taken in urban areas, before the new emphasis on community psychiatry; it is not entirely representative. Still, there's more than a suspicion that the values of many Americans get left out. The rise of community psychiatry has spurred a new sympathy for the values and problems of the very poor; we may expect that a responsiveness to the values and problems of those who are called Middle Americans may follow along.† In the meantime, too many of us, if we do consult a mental health professional, find ourselves talking to a stranger (see Chapter VII, "Fit," pp. 193–194).

Undue influence?

When values differ significantly, the therapist's influence comes into question; it may come into question anyway. Dynamic psychotherapy is a shared enterprise, often a shared quest. Many therapists are scrupulous in pursuing the pure goal of psychoanalysis, the patient's fuller freedom. Many others try to be and aren't; the continuing influence of an intensely admired guide is likely to be greater than he intends. Others don't even try. If we feel the influence is good, we are grateful. If not . . .

Manipulation?

Therapists of all kinds influence their patients.‡ And what is

* In the late sixties, Dr. Garfield Tourney wrote acidly that Freud had earned a unique position in the history of medicine "by introducing a treatment modality that, as it developed, became lengthier, more expensive, and applicable to fewer and fewer patients."[103]

† If there is to be such a development, its harbinger is Dr. Robert Coles. His sympathy and respect for all kinds of Americans pervades all his books; see especially *The Middle Americans* (Boston: Atlantic–Little, Brown, 1971).

‡ Dr. Leonard Cammer defines "the psychotherapeutic method": it "consists of techniques used by the individual to influence the thinking, feeling, and behavior of another."[105]

manipulation but the combination of influence with lack of candor? All therapists – analytic, behavioral, somatic – manipulate their patients sometimes. We do the same, for the same reasons. After all, if our relatives were to be depended upon to make free, rational, trustworthy decisions in their best interests and those of others, would we be consulting mental health professionals in their behalf?

Yes,

The nightmare of manipulation, however, goes far beyond these common strategies. "In another century it will undoubtedly be clear that psychosurgery and psychopharmacology, while being technical advances, were used simply as means of torture and persecution of our unfortunate fringe souls."[106] Behavioral and somatic treatments are seen as brutal assaults on man's free will, enabling us to condition, drug, and lobotomize dissenters into conformity. Dr. Peter Breggin, a psychoanalyst who devotes much of his time to crusading against psychosurgery, believes that "if America ever falls to totalitarianism, the dictator will be a behavioral scientist, and the secret police will be armed with lobotomy and psychosurgery."*

but . . .

Perhaps. But in our nightmare vision of a totalitarian America, we might reflect that the tyrants of the future will still be armed with guns and prisons, traditional if less sensational means for modifying behavior, weapons that are far easier to hand than psychosurgery and conditioning and that offer no possible benefit to sick people today. Drugs, psychosurgery, and behavior therapy are certainly not without risks, both individual and social. The only treatment which carries no risk of harmful effects, however, is one that has no effects at all. After visions of a lobotomized society, the risks of psychotherapy may seem unexciting, but individuals and families are beginning to testify to their importance. Patients have been injured, families have been driven apart and their resources exhausted as side effects of psychotherapy practiced with the best of intentions. Patients have been led into morbid self-absorption or overdependence. And intentions are not always of the best; patients may be exploited emotionally, even sexually. Since the bulk of psychotherapy goes on behind doors closed even to colleagues, the incompetent or the suspect therapist may practice unchecked.

Risks in all treatment,

even psychotherapy

The charge of manipulation can be brought against all therapy. Sometimes it can be brought justly. But responsible therapists of all kinds want not to manipulate the people who come to them for help, but to aid them to learn better ways of acting on their own.

This is not to minimize the dehumanizing effects of mass medication, or to maintain that we can trust that behavioral and surgical proce-

* "The Second Wave," *MH* (Winter 1973). Dr. Breggin's position is stated in the *Congressional Record* for February 24 and March 30, 1972, and in his books *The Crazy from the Sane* (New York: Lyle Stuart, 1971) and *After the Good War* (New York: Stein and Day, 1972).

dures will not be abused. We must be grateful for watchdogs like Dr. Breggin. Though the effectiveness of aversive conditioning, like the prevalence of psychosurgery, is generally overestimated, that doesn't license us to be complacent. The professionals who best understand the techniques are working with members of the public on detailed guidelines* to insure that they are used to help disordered people lead lives that are more rather than less human. Those who do not trust professional goodwill and responsibility will opt for eternal vigilance — the traditional price of liberty.

The price of liberty

Vigilance

Families of the mentally ill who have had a long, rough time of it (see the next chapter) sometimes feel ready to fall in with any criticism that comes along. But as the attacks on psychiatry and psychology proliferate, we may remember the traditional sign in the western saloon: "Don't shoot the piano player, he's doing his best." Not only is he the only one we've got, but the bullets whistling past his ears are even inspiring him to learn some new tunes. In short, blanket distrust and uncritical anger can't help us or our relatives. Whether we espouse a medical or an educational model, or both together, trust and faith are therapeutic. It was the Father of Medicine himself, Hippocrates, who noted that "some patients, though conscious that their situation is perilous, recover their health simply through their contentment with the goodness of the physician." So with all your other challenges, here's one more: to believe enough — but not too much, for the placebo effect does not work forever. Useless treatments can cut you off from useful ones, and it's a thin line that separates faith from gullibility. It's encouraging, at any rate, that today therapists of all kinds are learning to learn from each other. And therapists of all kinds can agree on the credo of the nineteenth-century internist cited by psychiatrist George Vaillant: "To cure sometimes, to relieve often, to comfort always."[108]

and trust

* In 1974 the Board of Directors of the American Psychological Association appointed a Commission on Behavior Modification to develop guidelines for the use of behavior modification in various settings. Commission members include psychologists Sidney Bijou of the University of Illinois, Nicholas Hobbs of Vanderbilt University, James Holland of the University of Pittsburgh, and G. Terence Wilson of Rutgers; psychiatrist Jerome Frank of Johns Hopkins Hospital; attorneys Paul Friedman of the Mental Health Law Project and David Wexler of the University of Arizona Law School; and philosopher Hugh Lacey of Swarthmore College.[107]

⋙ CHAPTER V ⋘

Thinking about Causes

Something terrible happens, and nobody is to blame.
ROBERT FROST'S DEFINITION OF TRAGEDY

DISAGREEMENT

When doctors disagree

WHAT CAUSES MENTAL ILLNESS? When something terrible happens, we want to know why. Yet "psychiatry," says Dr. Kalinowsky, "differs from other fields of medicine in a deplorable lack of facts on which all psychiatrists can agree. There is no generally accepted etiology of most mental diseases, and the entire foundation of the specialty of psychiatry is based on theories believed by some and opposed by others."[1]

Many causes have already been mentioned in the previous chapter, for most treatment approaches have an etiology to match. We return to these theories "believed by some and opposed by others," not because we hope to give a full account of them (that would take another book), but for practical reasons: what professionals believe about the causes of mental illness is of crucial importance to the mentally ill and their families now, and what they are able to learn about them through research will be crucial to us in the future. The main division comes between those who have placed their bets on biological causes and those who opt for causes that are psychological or social. What is the *genesis* of the problem, where does it begin? In the biology of the organism? If so, the point of view will be called *biogenic* or *organicist*. In the psyche itself, or as it is acted upon by the environmental factors of family and society? If so, it will be called psychodynamic or *psychogenic* – and perhaps we should add the word *sociogenic* to take care of those who see individual disorders arising out of society's pressures.

Psychogenesis vs. biogenesis

In this argument, both sides can call on Freud, who in 1914 wrote that "all our psychological ideas are, as it were, provisional, and will have, therefore, at some future time, to be based on an organic foundation."[2] Freud's successors, however, did not share his confidence in an ultimate biological explanation. They were far more impressed with his clinical work; his accounts of his patients seemed to show that not biology but repressed and unacknowledged conflicts, rooted in early childhood experience, were the source of our discontents. Over the years the conflict theory was elaborated into a fascinating variety of possible etiologies. Neurosis might be due to the failure to move beyond Oedipal fixations (Freud), to the child's experience of inferiority (Adler), to the birth trauma (Rank), to impacted sexuality (Reich), to the child's frustrated need for security (Horney). Psychosis might be due to more primitive conflicts experienced earlier and thus less

Psychodynamic etiologies

amenable to conscious process (Freud); it might be due to the unreasonable expectations and ambiguous communications of a pathological family (Sullivan, Bateson, Laing). These theories, and many others, were the foundation for a bewildering variety of dynamic therapies.

BIOLOGICAL ETIOLOGIES

For some patients — nobody knew how many — the therapies worked, tempting the conclusion that the success of the therapy demonstrated the truth of the theory. If success can establish etiology, however, the biogenic theorists were coming out ahead. With biological methods, they were treating more serious conditions, with more evident success. They had results for large numbers of patients, not just individual cases, and their studies included controls. These showed that shock treatments really were lifting depressions psychotherapy had left untouched, drugs really were clearing up the disorientations of schizophrenia so patients could go home. If chemical or electrical intervention could make sick brains better, even well, wouldn't an understanding of how these treatments worked explain why the brains got sick in the first place?

Biological etiologies

Or would it? It is always possible to turn the explanation backwards. Changes in brain or body chemistry might be a result of psychological experience, not a cause. After all, a telephone call from your brother-in-law can give you a sick headache, curable with aspirin.

can be reversed.

It is important to realize that the effectiveness of a therapy is not sufficient to establish what causes the discomfort it alleviates. Aspirin brings down various kinds of fevers; it works for both headache and menstrual pain, without telling us what causes either. Clearly organic conditions like mongolism or the aftermath of stroke may be helped by educational therapies although they are beyond the reach of present medical techniques, while conditions originating in psychological stress may be effectively treated with a pill. When complex phenomena are involved, it's hard to be sure whether the chicken or the egg came first.

You can't determine causes from treatment results.

INHERITANCE

This objection is less applicable to another focus of biological research: whether a tendency to mental illness can be inherited. Both schizophrenia and affective disorders seem to run in families. Identical twins, who share the same biological makeup, are much more likely to suffer from the same mental illness than fraternal twins or ordinary siblings. Psychodynamic theorists, however, particularly family thera-

Genetic factors

Twins

pists, have argued that the evidence for the inheritance of mental illness was inconclusive, since families – and particularly identical twins – usually share their social environment as well as their biology.[3] In response to such objections, a research team directed by Harvard's Dr. Seymour Kety has spent years testing out the effects of heredity and environment, locating schizophrenics who grew up in families other than their own, and comparing the incidence of schizophrenic and related disorders* in their biological families, from whom they were separated in infancy, with the incidence in the biological families of a control group of adopted children who did not develop schizophrenia.[4] It is very much higher. Since the publication of the careful work of Dr. Kety's research team, a significant genetic factor is now accepted by all but the most die-hard defenders of psychogenesis. (Studies of families of manic-depressive patients point the same way.) As Dr. Sarnoff Mednick sums it up, "Schizophrenia, like piano-playing, takes an inborn aptitude as well as training."[5]†

Adoption studies

Is schizophrenia inherited?

Schizophrenia

and "superphrenia"

Schizophrenia is not the only thing which runs in the families of schizophrenics. Studies have shown that creativity and imagination do too. Over the generations, families of psychotic patients in Iceland included an unusual number of scholars, political and financial leaders, and generally gifted people – "superphrenics," the researcher called them. A relative of a psychotic patient was twice as likely to be listed in Who's Who in Iceland as an ordinary member of the population. The saying that "great wit is sure to madness close allied" seems to be genetically true.[6]

"Genetic" does not mean inevitable.

Of course this is no revelation. People have always noticed that mental illness (and creativity) ran in families. We can guess, if we don't already know, how the presence of more than one emotionally unstable person intensifies what many families suffer. The realization that a hereditary factor is now confirmed is one of the many painful realizations that families of the mentally ill must face. Yet it is important to realize that "genetic" does not mean "inevitable" – or even "probable." Dr. Manfred Bleuler, Eugen Bleuler's son, grew up in his father's psychiatric hospital; his sympathy for schizophrenics and their families comes from a lifetime spent among them. Summing up a twenty-year study, he finds that psychoses in the children of schizophrenics develop similarly to those of their parents in symptoms and severity; "the conclusion of previous investigators that 8–10 percent of the children of schizophrenics are themselves doomed to schizophrenia is one that I, alas, cannot challenge."[7] Nevertheless, the very large majority will *not* become schizophrenic. Though it is much more likely that schizophrenia will appear in the children of schizophrenics than

A genetic possibility

* Dr. Kety speaks of "schizophreniform" conditions and a "schizophrenia spectrum." In addition, he found more cases of character disorder, delinquency, and suicide.

† For a clear, readable account of the issues, and of Dr. Kety's study, see Dr. Solomon Snyder's *Madness and the Brain*, pp. 91–98.

in the general population (in which the rate is about 1 percent), it is still not likely. It is still less likely for brothers and sisters. And Dr. Bleuler reports that his cases show that the grandchildren of schizophrenics have no higher incidence of the disease than anybody else. (We should also remember that nine out of ten schizophrenics do *not* have a schizophrenic parent.[8]) Dr. Bleuler feels his findings (which are further described in Chapter VIII) "should be helpful to many who are depressed because a relative is schizophrenic."

not a certainty or even a likelihood

> In particular, these findings offer hope to the children of schizophrenics who, tortured by doubt, seek medical advice as to whether they should have children. If they themselves have remained normal up to age 25 and beyond, and for this reason the danger that they may become ill has diminished, the risk that their children will become schizophrenic is probably little or no greater than that of the general public.[9]

The figures are for chronic not acute schizophrenia.

There is further reassurance if we remember that in Europe, where Dr. Kety's and Dr. Bleuler's research was done, the definition of schizophrenia is much narrower than in America. The schizophrenics of Kety's study were all reliably diagnosed "process" (chronic) schizophrenics. He found *acute* schizophrenia no more common among their relatives than in the general population, confirming his conviction that the two conditions are fundamentally different. So if your relative is one of the many who acquired the diagnosis of schizophrenia through a sudden psychotic episode from which he recovered, that discouraging 10 percent doesn't apply.

What identical twins can tell us

Even an identical (monozygotic) twin, who developed from the same egg and shares an identical genetic makeup with his schizophrenic brother, has a better than even chance of not becoming schizophrenic. He's much more likely to than ordinary siblings or even fraternal (dizygotic) twins (those who shared the womb but developed from different eggs). Yet recent studies show that fewer than 40 percent of identical twins are what is called "concordant" for schizophrenia (a much lower figure than that given by earlier studies based on institutionalized populations). As Dr. Leston Havens points out, genetics is not "a modern form of predestination."[10] If genes and chromosomes were everything, that 38 percent would quite simply be 100 percent.

CONSTITUTIONAL VULNERABILITY

What converts possibility into illness?

Given the genetic possibility, what determines whether or not a given person develops the disease? In children already vulnerable because of a psychotic parent, low birth weight, a light body build, and general physical frailness seem to increase the risk of later psychosis.*

* "The summation of birth weight, birth size, body build, and body strength data is already suggestive of constitutional differences between the prepsychotic child and his siblings."[11]

A real birth trauma

Dr. Sarnoff Mednick, studying children of schizophrenic mothers, finds that those with psychiatric problems are much more likely to have had difficult births than those who are developing normally.* His studies also confirm what other investigators have found: a kind of "hyper-responsiveness" of the nervous system which shows up in tests which record the response of heart rates, breathing, skin responses, and brain waves to laboratory stimuli. (This is trustworthy data, since the investigators made sure that the testers did not know whether the children they were testing had psychiatric problems or not.) These children's teachers often reported that they were "easily upset." Apparently they had good physiological reasons for it. Dr. Mednick thinks that people may "learn" to be schizophrenic; hyperresponsive children may adapt by developing a pattern of withdrawal.[12]

Hyperarousal

Heredity and environment

We are used to contrasting heredity and environment. When we do, we usually think of the social environment – the home, the school, the community, society. But work like this reminds us that the environment is biological too. It includes deprivation, illness, and injury not only after birth but during birth and before it.† A virus infection or malnutrition in the pregnant mother, the lack of oxygen or the use of instruments during a difficult delivery are as much part of a child's environment as the poor housing he lives in or his parent's irrationality. None of these factors, of course, has anything to do with his genetic endowment; his genes know nothing about them and cannot pass them on.

The environment is biological as well as social.

PSYCHOSOCIAL FACTORS

Psychosocial factors in psychosis

But of course the environment is primarily social, and volumes have been written about psychosocial causes. People have always known that deprivation, stress, misery, emotional shock can bring on mental illness. Vulnerable people can crack under strain. Though psychotic symptoms do sometimes begin when everything is going smoothly, more often they follow close upon some experience that at that particular time was just too much to bear. Your relative's experiences, both recent and long past, clearly have a lot to do with his illness, since they provide the content of his disturbance. What he's lived through is what he will be disturbed about. He's who he is, sick or well, and if he's elated or

Precipitating factors?

* Dr. Mednick's studies, like Dr. Kety's, are long-term, so-called longitudinal studies of populations in which the risk of schizophrenia may be assumed to be greatest, whether for biological or psychological reasons. All are still in their preliminary stages; the children under observation are still young. We can expect important information to emerge over the next thirty years; be watching!

† Of twenty-six pairs of monozygotic twins of which only one was schizophrenic, in nineteen cases the schizophrenic twin had been the lighter of the two in birth weight. Biology? Or the family? (The researchers suggest that mothers may treat the lighter twin differently.) [13]

depressed or deluded, it must be about the people, events, and ideas that are significant to him.* There's no doubt that what's going on in his life, inside and outside the family, contributes to his mental illness, can make him worse or better. (That's the subject of Chapter VIII of this book.) Whether bad experiences, however, are in themselves enough to *cause* mental illness, nobody knows. Until the attempts to establish a solid link between body chemistry, or genetic inheritance, and particular cases of psychosis are more successful than they have been to date, the way remains open to consider that the primary cause is psychosocial; particularly since we can be certain that much disordered and maladaptive behavior *is* caused by psychosocial factors. For everybody knows that stress, misery, bad luck, poverty, affluence, and a host of other things can cause problems in living.†

Or causes?

There's no doubt they cause problems in living.

That "social" in "psychosocial" deserves at least a paragraph. (In fact, it deserves much more, and if we don't give it, it's because this is a practical guide and few relatives of the mentally ill have surplus energy to go to work on social conditions.) It can be argued that the key factor in mental illness isn't what goes on inside the individual's body, or psyche, or family, but what goes on in his society. The sociologist M. Harvey Brenner finds a close correlation between the number of admissions to mental hospitals and the state of the economy; when times are bad admissions rise.[16] It is a well-known and disturbing fact that severity of mental disorders in the United States is linked to income; psychosis is much more commonly found among the poor. Here is evidence for both psychogenic and biogenic arguments. The poor suffer more psychological stress, especially in bad times; they have worse prenatal care and poorer nutrition as well.

Social causes of mental illness?

Social conditions affect psychological and biological conditions.

But the social approach isn't all gloom. What to do, for instance, with the widely reported figures showing that new cases of schizophrenia diminished markedly during World War II, both in Europe and in Asia? Shall we call it a vote for social causes and lay it to full employment and a booming economy? Or psychological causes and guess that people who have plenty to do and a good reason for doing it are less likely to get sick? Or biological causes and point out that schizophrenic first admissions were "highly correlated . . . with marked changes in wheat and rye consumption and were unrelated to war status"?[17] Or shall we hold off and say it all depends?

As Dr. Kety wrote in 1972, "The relative roles of genetic and environmental variables in schizophrenia have not been clearly eluci-

* Dr. David Hawkins: "Family interaction studies and other formulations help to explain the particular manifestations of the illness in a given patient."[14] Psychologist Bernard Rimland, in a comprehensive challenge of psychogenic etiology, puts it more cynically: "If a person raised in a French home becomes psychotic, his bizarre speech is ordinarily in French."[15]

† If we call these "character disorders" and "neuroses," many researchers consider biological factors to be important here too.

dated." He added with some sourness, "It is for this reason that schools of thought have been developed to take the place of evidence."[18] In the same year he told the National Association for Mental Health, assembled to honor him for his research, in words very like Dr. Kalinowsky's:

> For none of the major mental illnesses do we as yet know the cause or understand the pathogenesis, nor can we cite specific prophylactic or therapeutic measures.[19]

You may, therefore, be skeptical the next time a plausible etiology of schizophrenia hits the media, whether it is psychogenic or biogenic — unless it's accompanied by the kind of scrupulous reservations made by careful researchers such as Dr. Arnold J. Mandell and David S. Segal of the University of California at San Diego. They speculate that "if Freud were alive today he would be looking for the loci of his theories in neurochemical systems rather than on the couch." But they nevertheless add something we do well to ponder:

A single cause is unlikely.

> Major mental illnesses such as schizophrenia or manic depressive psychosis are complex psychobiological phenomena made up of genetic, developmental, and psychosocial parameters. They are no more likely to have a single cause than do such traits as height, weight, personality, and intelligence. For this reason, claims that some laboratory has found a "cause" or a "cure" for these mental diseases are highly suspect and at times may even damage the serious work by the thousands of researchers who are taking the myriad, small steps which are necessary before we can understand these illnesses.[20]

FAMILY "PATHOLOGY"

The family

We'll say it again, then; we don't know. For an awful lot of people talk — and act — as if we do. "It Comes in Two Kinds" is the headline for an article in *Psychology Today*. "Process Schizophrenia: the mother is dominant, carping, punitive, generally unpleasant. The father is weak, ineffectual and submissive. . . . Reactive Schizophrenia: The father is harsh, aggressive and demanding. The mother is weak, vacillating and submissive."[21] If that's a sample of how people see families of the mentally ill, it's small wonder that families feel that mental illness is something to be ashamed of, to keep hidden, even to deny. True, it's only an article in a popular magazine. But how many times have you come across the same descriptions or worse? It's journalism, but it's journalism that's solidly based in the convictions of many — until recently, most — of the most imaginative and most articulate members of the American psychiatric community. Families of the mentally ill are used to unpleasantness — noises, smells, fear in the night, remarks from storekeepers, objections from neighbors, visits from the police. We have to be pretty tough to keep going. We get accustomed to feeling hurt, and disappointed, and ashamed, and embarrassed; that's part of our relative's condition, that's the way things are. The edge wears off these feelings after a while; as our grandmothers used to say, "You can get used to anything except hanging." Still, there's a kind of pain we don't get used to, although Lord knows we've had time: the pain of knowing that people think our relative's condition is our fault.

Families have to face this point of view, because it's everywhere. Sometimes it's stated roughly ("Well, what do you expect with that family?"), sometimes compassionately ("That mother needs help."). You get it from mental health professionals, teachers, relatives, friends, bare acquaintances, people who don't even know you. Just about everyone who can read is aware of one of psychotherapy's most common assumptions: that mental illness is caused, primarily or solely, by pathological family interactions.

as a cause of mental illness.

It was Dr. Frieda Fromm-Reichmann, who worked so long and lovingly with schizophrenics, who originated the term "schizophrenogenic [schizophrenia-causing] mother,"[22] soon extended to "the schizogenic family." Here are some more statements. There are thousands to choose from. They were made, not by magazine writers, but by superbly gifted psychotherapists, many with international reputations.

> If the parents were not difficult or peculiar, it is unlikely that the patient would be schizophrenic.[23]

"If the parents were not difficult or peculiar . . ."

> The precipitating factor in infantile autism is the parent's wish that his child should not exist.[24]
>
> Along with the fairly well established finding that some kind of inherited predisposition is necessary for the development of schizophrenia, there can be little doubt that another necessary condition – and indeed the one with the greater legitimate claim on our interest – is the special form of personal hell which the psychotic experiences in the family.[25]
>
> There has never been a schizophrenic who came from a stable family.[26]
>
> Often we find that a person who is labeled "insane" is the sanest member of his or her family.[27]
>
> The system needs a certain number of persons to scapegoat – to define as sick – in order to define itself.[28]
>
> In psychotic or schizophrenic families, one socially useful function of the scapegoating is so that the other members in the family can function. That's a pretty big price for one person to pay.[29]
>
> The patient is . . . only externalizing through his symptoms an illness which is inherent in the family itself. He is a symptomatic organ of a diseased organism.[30]

What do you think when you read statements like these? Better yet, here's the place for the psychotherapist's question: How do you *feel*?

How do you feel now?

If you're like most families, you feel awful. You feel personally attacked, just where you're most vulnerable, in your pride in your home and the wish and need to believe that you've done the best you could for those you love. No wonder your neighbors are unfriendly. No wonder the doctor doesn't explain things to you, no wonder the social worker doesn't seem to take anything you say at face value. If these things are true, how could they? How do you feel? You feel angry if you're lucky, guilty if you're not. If you feel both together you're really unlucky, and so is everyone around you. In any case, the turmoil of emotions distracts you from the task at hand – the dogged, sensible, responsible daily task of doing the best you can.

You feel even worse if your relative's therapist has encouraged him to believe that you are the cause of his or her distress. Your relative is apt to want to believe this anyway. "The therapist's knowledge that the patient transforms his experiences drastically is very important in psychotherapy," says Dr. Silvano Arieti.

> Until recently the therapist and the patient established a so-called therapeutic alliance based mainly on recrimination for what the parents had allegedly done in engendering the patient's misery. Certainly the parents have played a role, but to magnify that role is also to alter the truth and to hinder the progress of psychotherapy beyond the initial stages.[31]

The blame game

Why did it happen? Whose fault is it? This is a question which leads nowhere but to more pain. The therapists who developed the family interaction theory of mental illness, knowing this, thought up a matching phrase, "the blame game." Blaming's no good, they tell us, whether in families who blame one member – the "scapegoat" – or themselves. Therapists emphasize strongly that they're "not in the blame game." However "pathological" or harmful they believe the family interactions to be, there's no blame attached. Instead, there's compassion:

and compassion

> It serves no good purpose to make the parents feel guilty as having caused the disturbance. . . . They did as they did because they could not help themselves to do otherwise. They suffer more than enough in having such a child. . . . To make them guilty will only add to the misery and help no one.[32]*

* This passage of Bruno Bettelheim's is quoted with approval by Drs. S. A. Szurek and I. N. Berlin ("The Problem of Blame in Therapy with Parents and Their Children," in *Clinical Studies in Childhood Psychoses* [New York: Brunner/Mazel, 1973]). It is a continuing theme in therapists' discussions of blame. Now and then an especially sympathetic therapist is able to communicate his vision of universal compassion to the patient: "Occasionally, the patient gains sufficient independence, rationality, and perspective to appreciate that his parents had been so deprived in their own childhoods, so caught up in a net created by their parents' difficulties, that they could not have been different than they were . . . and that [he can] break the pathological chain that has extended from generation to generation. Then, the ambivalent animosities toward his parents and his fears of them can dissolve into compassion for them."[33]

Mothers, fathers, families, however schizogenic, have only done what they had to do. You are what your experience has made you. Your childhood was no bed of roses either. If what you did harmed your relative, you couldn't help it.

Feel better now? No? You've got company. A lot of families would rather shoulder the blame and try to do better than be sympathized with because they couldn't have done any differently. Responsible people expect to be responsible for the harm they do. A pioneer family therapist understands the blame game better than most of his colleagues. For all the sympathy and understanding, blame is blame.

> Blame is handled in a paradoxical way [in family therapy]. . . . The parents are told they are not to blame for the child's difficulties, because they cannot help themselves, and yet it is indicated that they should behave differently so the child will not have difficulties.[34]

Jay Haley helped develop the faulty-communications theory of schizophrenia (see Chapter III, p. 64); he knows a double bind when he sees one.

When people accept responsibility for harming others they feel guilt and misery, however kindly they're treated. So another question becomes important: not only are you willing to accept the responsibility, but do you need to? Because of course we shouldn't choose among etiologies on the basis of what hurts us, but according to the evidence.

EVIDENCE AND INTERPRETATION

Evidence for family pathology

Nobody can doubt that what parents do with their children, and the way they think about them, influences how they grow up. And, clearly, there's evidence for what so many experienced people believe; if there weren't, family etiologies of mental illness would never have become so widespread. For years therapists have listened to patients tell their distress; for years they have noted that conflicts, pressures, peculiarities exist in their families. It's true that few families containing mentally ill members live just like other people. It's true that therapists see families doing terrible things to each other.* Noting all this, it was natural for therapists accustomed to tracing their patients' conflicts back to early childhood to explain psychoses by what had gone on and was going on in their families, and to treat them accordingly.

At first, they were treated by individual psychoanalytic therapy; later, according to the theories of family therapy, whole families were

* Transcripts of conversations between schizophrenic young women and their families are quoted at length by R. D. Laing and Abraham Esterson in *Sanity, Madness, and the Family* (New York: Basic Books, 1964). Families reading them will realize how easy it is to devalue the experience of a family member once she's seen as schizophrenic, in a good demonstration of how not to communicate with a troubled daughter.

taken into treatment. As with other therapies, the results were sometimes good, sometimes not.* What carried conviction was not treatment results, but the descriptions of the families themselves.† Not only therapists' impressions but extensive research on many families showed a picture of parents not only troubled but irrational, unable to communicate with their offspring or each other, themselves suffering from severe personality disorders[35] and significant disorders of thought.[36]

To mental health professionals who saw troubled families every day the evidence was compelling. Yet there were always doubts, and recently there have been challenges from both families and professionals. Today the theory that mental illness is caused by pathological family interactions is a prime example of those Dr. Kalinowsky speaks of, "believed by some and opposed by others."

Difficulties with evidence

Although the facts of biology can eventually be established so as to command general agreement, the facts of human behavior go on looking different according to what researchers hope and expect to find.

When do researchers look for deviant behavior? When they expect to find it

Dr. Manfred Bleuler has pointed out that psychiatrists who were seeking evidence for the hereditary nature of schizophrenia found much more deviant behavior in the children of schizophrenics than he did. (See p. 220.) Psychiatrists committed to an explanation in terms of family dynamics are also able to find what they look for. It's easy to project pathology back into the past to explain it in the present. When some psychology reseachers, all under the impression they were as healthy as the next man, got themselves admitted to mental hospitals by claiming they heard voices, one of them discovered how readily his family history could be interpreted to suit his nonexistent symptoms:

A 39-year-old male pseudopatient with family problems

> This white 39-year-old male . . . manifests a long history of considerable ambivalence in close relationships, which begins in early childhood. A warm relationship with his mother cools during his adolescence. A distant relationship to his father is described as becoming very intense. Affective stability is absent. His attempts to control emotionality with his wife and children are punctuated by angry outbursts and, in the case of the children, spankings. And while he says that he has several good

* "Hannah Green's" novel *I Never Promised You a Rose Garden* (New York: Holt, Rinehart, and Winston, 1964) describes the treatment of a schizophrenic young girl by a psychoanalyst modeled on Dr. Frieda Fromm-Reichmann; the heroine got well. Two who got worse are described (by their mothers) in Louise Wilson's *This Stranger, My Son* (New York: Putnam, 1968) and Sara Lorenz's *Our Son Ken,* which describes the hospitalization of a whole family in the early days of family therapy (New York: Dell Publishing Co., 1969). For a recent account of family hospitalization, see Gene M. Abroms, Carl H. Fellner, and Carl A. Whitaker, "The Family Enters the Hospital," *American Journal of Psychiatry,* 127 (April 1971). Treatment "relies heavily on psychoactive drugs, behavior modification techniques, psychodrama videotape playback, programmed learning and social engineering, as well as traditional forms of individual and group psychotherapy."

† Compelling accounts can be found in any of the sources quoted on p. 123; the most extensive evidence is presented in the publications of Dr. Theodore Lidz and his research team at Yale.

friends, one senses the considerable ambivalence embedded in those relationships also.*

In other words, if you think someone is crazy, you can easily arrange a family to match. "Diagnoses were in no way affected by the relative health of a pseudopatient's life. Rather, the reverse occurred: the perceptions of his circumstances were shaped entirely by his diagnosis."

There are other difficulties. Because nobody can go back into the past and replay those early days when future psychosis was being prepared (or wasn't), the evidence has to come either from recollection – the family's, the patient's – or from looking at the family as it is today. Nobody can be sure how much to believe of whose recollections, how much to discount, how much to interpret differently.† Looking at the family as it is today also has drawbacks. Therapists go by their impressions, and they often don't agree on what they see. Dr. Alfred Scheflen describes his research group's "reservations about the objectivity of subjective reports."

Recollection

and impressions

> We were never certain that various subjects and raters attributed similar meaning to the items. We could obtain a statistically significant consensus only among raters who had been trained in psychoanalysis by the same training analyst. And a broader doubt always hung in the background. Suppose various subjects did agree. Consensus in a belief system may mean only that members of culture [sic] share the same myth. . . . A group of experienced psychoanalysts, psychologists, and social scientists watched sessions of Dr. John Rosen's method of direct analysis every day for three years and discussed the observations in great detail. . . . Each of the observers noticed different facets of the complex processes of psychotherapy. Consequently the various researchers disagreed strongly, and each published his own report. . . . Not only did we disagree about conclusions, but we disagreed as well about what actually took place.[39]‡

are unreliable.

And even if there is agreement on the existence and kind of patho-

* Comments the author of the study, which will be further described in Chapter IX: "The facts of the case were unintentionally distorted by the staff to achieve consistency with a popular theory of the dynamics of a schizophrenic reaction. . . . An entirely different meaning would have been ascribed if it were known that the man was 'normal' "[37] Professor Robert Rosenthal has spent years studying how the expectations and behavior of experimenters influence their results. He describes his work in the well-known *Pygmalion in the Classroom* (New York: Holt, Rinehart and Winston, 1968) and in *Experimenter Effect in Behavioral Research* (New York: Appleton-Century-Crofts, 1966).

† Freud's error with his hysterical patients is famous; it was years before he became suspicious of their recollections of incestuous relations with their relatives. Recalling this, Dr. Silvano Arieti, while still convinced that family pathology is "a necessary condition" for the development of schizophrenia, calls attention to the unreliability of schizophrenic patients' descriptions of their families.[38] "They talk about their mothers," says another experienced analyst, "about these wicked witches, whose breasts ooze poisonous milk – and then I'll make an appointment with one of them, and this nice ordinary lady walks in. . . ."

‡ A film made under Dr. Scheflen's direction shows the contrasting styles of the pioneer family therapists Nathan Ackerman, Murray Bowen, and Don Jackson in interviewing the same family. The therapists' interpretations differ markedly.

Chicken or egg:

Is abnormal family life

a cause or a result?

logical family interactions (bad things going on), who can be sure whether these represent the kind of thing that in fact made the "index patient" what he is, or whether they are the result of the strains of living with him? Dr. J. G. Howells, a convinced family therapist who nevertheless does not believe in a family-interaction theory for schizophrenia, notes that although "it can be argued that the family psychopathology has causal significance for schizophrenia, it can also be held that the schizophrenia causes family psychopathology. It would be strange if such a severe and perplexing disorder did not have some effect on the family state."*

Pathology without illness?

Lack of controls

Or is this pathology just the kind of thing that goes on in many families anyway, without leading to mental illness? This is a real possibility, since there has been no comparison with control families.† Experience and common sense suggest that there is a lot more family pathology than there is psychosis. Or neurosis either, for that matter. A remarkable study of the family histories of one hundred men selected particularly for their normality – which included above-average functioning in home, job, and community as well as excellent physical health – surprised its authors:

100 normal childhoods

> The reported childhood histories of these men were laden with events of a kind ordinarily considered productive of later mental disturbance. Included in abundance were overt parental discord as seen in divorce or separation; covert parental discord as manifest in lengthy periods of withdrawal, seclusiveness, or lack of mutuality; excessively rigid or overindulgent patterns of discipline, or both; resolution of Oedipal anxieties through overidentification with one parent to the exclusion of the other; unresolved sibling rivalries; repressive and unrealistic approaches to sexual information and sexual practises; frequent maternal physical complaints of a type recognized today as related to tension and conflict. In short, these data abound with material such as we are accustomed to encounter in the histories of psychiatric patients.[41]

Other studies also show family "pathology" is widespread. Dr. Howells estimates that "approximately a third of the population are significantly emotionally disturbed. Should schizophrenics come from a representative group of families of the population at large, then in a third of families of schizophrenics family psychopathology will be found by chance alone." He also notes that "the double bind situation . . . is very common in everyday life," and that there are many more

* "Family Psychopathology and Schizophrenia," in *Modern Perspectives in World Psychiatry,* ed. J. G. Howells (New York: Brunner/Mazel, 1972), p. 414. This long review article presents a complete survey of theories of the family genesis of schizophrenia, with extensive summaries of the views of the major theorists – Murray Bowen, Nathan Ackerman, L. C. Wynne, Theodore Lidz, Bateson, Haley and Jackson, Laing, and others. Its nine-page, 207-item bibliography is a complete guide to the literature of family therapy up to 1971.

† "We do not believe that a true controls series can be established in this type of study."[40]

likely ways of adjusting to it than to develop the symptoms of schizophrenia.[42]

New studies

Faulty family communications and parental thought disorders, too, are being reconsidered; researchers attempting to repeat the previous studies get quite different results.* Even the "schizophrenogenic mother" is now in question. Dr. Arieti finds himself "inclined to say that only 20 percent correspond to this image," although he'll concede "a maximum of 25 percent," including doubtful cases.†

MOTHERS

Dominant mothers

Some schizophrenogenic mothers are passive, but many more are dominant. The child of a dominant mother, until recently, has been considered out of luck. Schizophrenia is not the only hazard. Redlich and Freedman's authoritative textbook notes that "dominant mothers have been credited with an etiological role in bronchial asthma, the allergies, peptic ulcer, and also in schizophrenia and depressions."[47] Dr. David Abrahamsen, a prominent New York psychiatrist and author of *The Murdering Mind,* points out that Arthur Bremer, James Earl Ray, Sirhan Sirhan, and Lee Harvey Oswald "grew up without a father or a strong father-figure and the mother was sometimes dominating."[48] Another psychiatrist describes a schizophrenic patient's family as "skewed, with the mother dominating the family transactions, preempting roles usually filled by the husband."[49] Sociologists and government policy-makers note the difficulties of boys growing up in black families where mothers and grandmothers often assume a dominant role.

* S. Hirsch and J. Leff reported in 1971 that they were unable to replicate Wynne and Singer's findings concerning communications deviance in the parents of schizophrenic patients.[43] Another failure to replicate the Yale studies implicates the climate of anxiety in which they took place. "It appears that the research situation itself may have had a differential effect on normal and schizophrenic families; situational anxiety may have been greater for schizophrenic sons and their parents. In spite of that fact [in the current study] parents of schizophrenic offspring did as well as and sometimes better than normal parents in their communicator and respondent roles."[44] As early as 1969, Eric Schopler and J. Loftin reported that parents who showed "thought disorders" when tested in a context of psychodynamic exploration of the problems of a psychotic child lost their "pathology" when examined in a reassuring context involving their normal children.[45]

† The image, as summarized by Dr. Arieti: "overprotective, hostile, overtly or subtly rejecting, overanxious, cold, distant, and so forth. Because of these characteristics she was unable to give herself to the child and was unfit for motherhood. Sometimes she tried, but she did not know how. . . . In the writings of a large number of authors she was described as a malevolent creature and was portrayed in an intensely negative, judgmental way. . . . She has been called a monstrous human being." Dr. Arieti concludes: "Therapists, including myself, have believed what the patients told us. Inasmuch as a considerable percentage of mothers have proved to be just as they were described by the patient, we have considered this percentage as typical and have made an unwarranted generalization that includes all the mothers of schizophrenics."[46]

It's a pervasive problem. Dr. Edgar Levenson notes the pattern for college dropouts, and "the same constellation is described by Theodore Lidz, Stephen Fleck et al. for families of schizophrenics, Kenneth Keniston for his uncommitted students, Irving Bieber for homosexuals and Erik Erikson for identity crisis."[50] There is obviously much to be said about the dominant mother; you might get some interesting ideas from the National Organization for Women. Dr. Levenson sums up:

> In a word, it is the ultimate psychoanalytic banality explaining everything from schizophrenia to ingrown toenails. . . . It is said that this family constellation – that is, an aggressive, domineering, seductive mother and a weak, passive, undermining father – is characteristic for the alcoholic. But this is also the classic Jewish family structure. So, it is asked, why are there so few Jewish alcoholics? The answer is – of course – their mothers won't let them!

INTERACTING FACTORS

Many factors working together

So don't jump to conclusions. Many factors work together. If we are to believe recent research, a person might combine a genetic predisposition to mental illness with a constitutional susceptibility which could make him vulnerable to psychosocial stresses which another person might take in his stride. As Harvard's Dr. Leon Eisenberg sees it, "Psychobiological stress acts on an individual with a genetic predisposition to psychosis and eventually leads to abnormal metabolic processes that cause disorders of mood and thought."[51] Most clinicians today agree with Dr. John Romano when he says that "in my experience, I know of no case which had exclusively single-cause determinants, whether they be solely biologic, or genetic, psychological, or social."[52] Dr. Leston Havens shows how what are at first called "causes" are "gradually ordered into sequences of events and interacting factors." "As sequences are discovered bit by bit, each bit has its moment of etiological glory. . . . Instead of one, we have now two, three, or more causes." We should be glad, for "they provide that many more points of intervention,"[53] that many more ways to treat, and hope to prevent.

PREMATURE CERTAINTY

Suspend judgment on etiology.

So a review of the facts suggests that you, and your relative, and the professionals you are consulting can save controversy by suspending judgment on the causes of mental illness until more of the facts come in. The assumption of a family etiology causes such pain and harm that one would think it would be arrived at only after a careful study of all the facts of the individual case, and only if there were a consensus within the profession. There is no such consensus. Yet many therapists seem to make this assumption as a matter of routine, before they have even fully informed themselves about the case. (How often does the average social worker, or even psychiatrist, inquire as to a patient's birth weight or his mother's prenatal health?) If you are being made to feel that the source of your relative's disorder lies in what has gone on inside your family, ask the therapist to discuss with you the following quotations:

> The theory according to which schizophrenic irrationality is transmitted directly from the parents is aesthetically elegant. . . . Unfortunately, at the present state of our knowledge this theory has all the aspects of being a reductionistic and invalid one.[54]

> Much has been written recently concerning family dynamics, their internal and external systems of communication, decision-making processes, and the "scapegoating" of one family member. Some of these theoretical concepts have taken hold temporarily but careful empirical research has negated the application of most of them. The findings, however interesting, have yet to demonstrate the precise causal link to the changes we have described.[55]

> A striking quality of most of the literature on this subject . . . is the lack of clear concepts. Experts on communication, it seems, find it difficult to communicate. Intellectualization, based on a modicum of fact, flourishes. The danger of such vagueness is that it may be interpreted as a cloak for ignorance. . . . An even greater danger is that we may assume knowledge where there is none. . . .[56]

"The danger of such vagueness . . ."

> Family therapy, however, has spread more as a messianic movement and not because of convincing evidence from well-designed therapeutic trials.[57]

> It seems facile to say that schizophrenia is an option available to all . . . it is doubtful that we all could become schizophrenic even growing up in a characteristically disturbed family.[58]

> Because of the constant talk about schizophrenogenic mothers and double binds, many mindlessly believed that these were indeed the etiology of the dysfunction.[59]

The authors of these comments are some of the most eminent psychiatrists in the world; their statements are a good balance for the quotations at the midpoint of this chapter. Any therapist should be glad to discuss them with you. The air should be clearer for all of you after that.

THE NEED FOR RESEARCH INTO CAUSES

Do causes matter?

Do causes matter? When thinking about them brings so little agreement — and so much pain — it's a temptation to fall in with those who tell us that behavior matters and causes don't. If time – and money – are limited, why not concentrate on therapy and social services, and stop asking why things happen?

Yes.

Unless you believe that mental illness is indeed a myth, causes matter. Medical science, like other science, progresses, through errors, false starts, and hard, slow work, from uncertainties to findings on which all can agree. There was no agreement when Ignaz Semmelweiss announced to the medical profession that childbed fever was an infection spread by the dirty hands of doctors. Semmelweiss was contradicted and vilified, but doctors started washing their hands, and childbed fever became a rarity. The discovery of the etiology of mental disorders matters a great deal to us all. The search for causes is the foundation of science. The discovery of the causes of mental disorders is what will make it possible to prevent or cure them. If defective mothering, or faulty genes, or malfunctioning body chemistry, or the double bind, can really be shown to cause mental illness, that information can help us. There's nothing wrong with searching for causes. The trouble is not in searching, but in finding them prematurely. As Mark Twain remarked, the trouble with human beings is that they know so many things that ain't so.

The need for research

and for avoiding premature certainty

Families are more directly concerned with treatment, but we must never forget the importance of basic research. For a generation, research into mental illness (causes *and* treatment) has been strongly supported by state and federal government. In that generation, by Dr. Seymour Kety's estimate, we bought, at a cost of "about twenty cents a year for each American . . . a greater understanding of brain and behavior than civilized man had achieved in fifty centuries."[60] He is deeply concerned about recent cutbacks in this support. You should be too. Biological research now promises excitement to match that which psychodynamic ideas have held for psychology and psychiatry. Together they offer the hope that at length our groping therapies will be based on true knowledge. Today, when so many issues seem to reduce to what we can afford, let's say this: We cannot afford not to press on with basic research into the causes of mental illness.

Research brings hope of prevention and cure;

support it.

PART TWO

Practical Matters

»» CHAPTER VI ««

What the Community Can Offer

WHAT THE COMMUNITY CAN OFFER

> I did not think he ought to be shut up. His infirmities were not noxious to society. He insisted on people praying with him, and I'd as lief pray with Kit Smart as anyone else. SAMUEL JOHNSON, IN 1763

De-institutionalization, helping the mentally ill in their own community,

"MADNESS," remarked Dr. Johnson, "frequently discovers itself by unnecessary deviation from the usual modes of the world. My poor friend Smart showed the disturbance of his mind by falling upon his knees and saying his prayers in the street, or in any unusual place. Now although rationally speaking, it is greater madness not to pray at all, than to pray as Smart did, I am afraid there are so many who do not pray, that their understanding is not called in question." It has taken more than two hundred years for our attitudes to catch up to Dr. Johnson's. But over the last twenty years – with the help of the new drug treatments for deviant behavior – people have come to see that most of those people who are classified "mentally ill" need not leave their own communities – *if* social services are available for them there.

requires services

This, of course, is the big if. There is no automatic magic in home and community to help disoriented people who got to the hospital in the first place because they couldn't cope with themselves or their responsibilities. People often get worse in hospitals, especially when they stay for years, but simply letting them out doesn't make them get better. The mentally ill continue to need help, wherever they find themselves, and help continues to cost money. The family's services are free, but many mentally ill people don't have families, and when they do, family living is not always the best thing either for the disturbed person or for the family. People for whom there is serious question of hospitalization are usually those whose families already feel they cannot go on any longer without help. The severely disturbed share their problems in living with everyone around them. The community can only become the preferred place of treatment for mental disturbance if society – that same society that built and staffed the mental hospitals because the mentally ill were better off there than on the streets and in the jails – is willing to spend money to back up the efforts of the people who live in daily contact with those problems: the neighbors, the landladies, the employers – and the families – of those we call mentally ill.

and services require money.

Communities differ widely in their consciousness of mental illness, and in the degree of responsibility they are willing to assume for the welfare of the sick and troubled in their midst, from the publicly financed network of comprehensive services provided by a state like Minnesota, to the heart-sickening vacuum of service that, it may be, seems to be all there is near you.

What's available in your area?

Yet, even so, there may be sources of help you haven't thought of. There are all sorts of organizations and agencies, public and private, formal and informal. There are all sorts of individuals, professional and nonprofessional. Sometimes they know about each other, and one can refer you to another. All too often the overburdened family must find its own way to help. What follows, we hope, will make your task a little easier.

SOMEONE TO TALK TO

First resorts

The film star Melina Mercouri has said that in Greece, where people are poor, they don't talk to psychiatrists, they talk to their friends. Even in New York City, where a significant proportion of the nation's psychiatrists practice,* a survey showed that when most people were asked whom they'd consult if there was emotional trouble in the family, they answered that they'd talk to relatives, or friends, or to the minister or the priest, or to the family doctor. Less than a third said that their first thought would be to consult a psychiatrist.[2]

Nor is their instinct naive or wrong. Yet in America today it is not as easy as in Melina Mercouri's Greece to get help by talking to your friends, your favorite aunt, or the priest or teacher who has known you since you were a girl. And you may have problems that no ordinary talking can solve. The natural instinct of millions of people is to consult a doctor – not the highly specialized psychiatrist, though he is a doctor too, but some M.D. they know and trust.

Doctor

It is estimated that a huge proportion, perhaps the majority, of psychological complaints are taken care of by the kind of professional you mean when you say "our doctor" – the general practitioner, or the internist, or the pediatrician. Even for such a serious condition as severe depression, the general practitioner or internist who has kept up in his field and knows his patients may be able to treat your relative with the new psychotropic drugs so it isn't necessary to see a psychia-

* Judging from a 1970 survey by the American Psychiatric Association, there's about one psychiatrist for every 8,000 people in the nation, but in West Virginia, there's only one for 33,000. Washington, D.C., tops the nation with one per 1,700 (just as well, considering what goes on there), and though New York must make do with one per 3,000, more than one-quarter of all the psychiatrists in the country live in the New York area. "Fuller Torrey recently pointed out that there are more psychiatrists in two buildings in New York City than there are in 17 of our states."[1]

trist at all. Or he may find that the depression, like many other psychological symptoms, is an aspect of a treatable physical disease. He may even provide some brief counseling himself to supplement his purely medical treatment. A good doctor, however, will know when the symptoms need more specialized consultation and be ready to refer you further.

Clergyman

In time of personal turmoil, however, many people turn naturally to the clergy. Counseling people in trouble is part of the job of the minister, priest, or rabbi, who often has been drawn to the ministry exactly because he was deeply interested in helping others to deal with their perplexities. In modern religious seminaries, natural gifts of compassion and insight are deepened by courses in pastoral counseling. So the estimated 42 percent of Americans who take their personal problems first to religious leaders may well find the help they need; another study found that of those who did seek help from a clergyman when trouble struck their family, over half were satisfied. Like the doctor, your minister is a professional, and his profession brings him in contact with many of the resources available in your community. An active clergyman has a real liaison with social services and private practitioners. In some large cities churches cooperate to provide skilled counseling even to people who walk in off the street. In any case, a local clergyman will help you to the best of his ability — and it may be an important consideration that he will help you fast and that, unlike other professionals, his help is free.† For many families he is the natural first step and the best, a thoughtful person whose concern is people and how they live their lives, who knows your family (or will get to know them if you ask), and whose interest may continue through this crisis and after it.

BACK TO THE COMMUNITY

Your community, however, has many people and agencies that can help you, and you don't need a doctor or clergyman to put you in touch with them. You do need a lot of persistence.* You may call any

* We speak of the ordinary pastor, priest, or rabbi of a local congregation. Particularly in large cities, there may also be clergymen, often with degrees in pastoral counseling, who practice psychotherapy professionally and offer psychotherapy on a fee-for-service basis.

† One state mental health official describes the situation in his state in terms which probably apply to yours:

"Each community or neighborhood has a system of human services which is available for solving problems or nurturing growth. These services, however, in no way resemble a system. They might more aptly be described as a non-system, for their outstanding characteristics are duplication, isolation, competition and lack of coordination. The services exist, however, and despite their fragmented form provided

one of these agencies and be told that your problem isn't the kind they can help with. In fact, if a single phone call does bring you the help you need, consider yourself unusually lucky. But if you are turned away, don't be discouraged, and don't be apologetic. *Ask for a referral and expect to get one.* Feel no shame when you make your relative's and your family's needs known to your community. If we want to think dollars and cents instead of human misery, you are saving them money in the long run. Unless you are rich enough to pay the enormous cost of indefinite private hospitalization, it will be the community that ends up paying for your relative anyway, in the state hospital. The alternative – helping him and you at home – is not only more humane, but cheaper. One reason it's cheaper is that you, the patient's family, are bearing much of the economic, social, and emotional cost. By trying to help your relative, you are helping your community. You have a right to expect your community to help you.

Don't take "No" for an answer.

In keeping your relative at home you are doing society's work

and have a right to society's assistance.

THE TELEPHONE BOOK AS GUIDE TO COMMUNITY SERVICES

Your first resource is the simplest: the telephone book. It is the easiest way to survey what services are available in your area, and who offers them. You are making a survey, of course, not a choice. Before you make your decision you will need to know more than the telephone book can tell you. But the only way of knowing what to choose is to know what's there.

The telephone book as guide to community services

To consult the telephone books of neighboring cities, visit the telephone company's local office; the directory of your state capital should also be there and is important for surveying state services. The local Chamber of Commerce often has telephone books of major cities all over the country, which bring many other resources within reach of your phone.

Out-of-town directories

Turn to the Yellow Pages. You'll find the quickest summary of what's available under *Social Service Organizations.* It's full of good leads.

Yellow Pages

a wider base of resources than most of us recognize. They encompass roughly three dimensions: state human services, community caregivers, and community citizens. . . . Approximately 30 state human service personnel are available to deliver services in each community of 10,000. However, few of these personnel ever enter the community. They deliver their specialty services in area or regional facilities. In this same community of 10,000 there are between 300 and 400 persons paid by the community . . . or private organizations to deliver human services. These community caregivers include teachers, school counselors, special education personnel, school administrators, clergy, social agency personnel, privately supported mental health workers, police, recreation agency personnel, court personnel, the staff of nursing and rest homes, hospital personnel, physicians, public health nurses, etc. Like state human service personnel, most community care-givers are primarily interested in their own specialty and are seldom encouraged to relate their specialty service to a community human service network."[3]

Under that heading you ought to find a community mental health center — offering a full range of services, with a phone number that you can call twenty-four hours a day. You ought to, but like as not you won't. There may not be one in your area. Even if there is, it may be listed separately. Or it may be there under Social Service, but under a name that does not reveal that it *is* a community mental health center. (One of the best comprehensive centers we know of is called United Counseling Services.) Alternately, something which calls itself a Mental Health Center may offer only a few scattered services. So while you're scanning Social Service Organizations, be alert for other possibilities.

Most communities have a *Family and Children's Service.* Many (but not enough) have halfway houses for people who cannot live entirely on their own; these too will be described later in the chapter. These are often listed under Social Service — but again, unless *"Halfway House"* is part of the name you may not recognize them. (Most services are overburdened; they don't go out of their way to make it easy for you to find them.) If your problem involves mental retardation as well as mental illness — and there is a great deal of overlap, especially in the chronically ill — look for organizations with *"Retarded"* in their titles. They can give information, and sometimes help. Similarly for *Epilepsy* and *Cerebral Palsy. Suicide Prevention* — usually a twenty-four-hour service — may be listed. Some cities (San Francisco and Honolulu are among them) have *information and referral services* which try to keep abreast of social services of all sorts. These, too, will be listed under Social Service Organizations. It's possible that you will spot a title that shows a concern with *aging* or with *"exceptional" children.* If you see the letters FISH, write down the number; this is an organization of church people who offer various sorts of temporary help to families in trouble. (If you don't find it, try the main directory under "F.") *Homemaker services* may also be listed, an important service when someone is hospitalized or incapacitated. Social Service listings vary in comprehensiveness from city to city, and there are always important omissions — services that exist, that you'd think would be listed but aren't. But there are more than you'd think, and it's the place to begin.

Volunteer telephone services

The informal telephone services that are springing up all over the country deserve a paragraph of their own. They are an impressive attempt by ordinary citizens, often students, to show that however lost we feel, we are not alone. They bear names like Help, Emergency Trips, Call for Action. They should be listed under Social Service Organizations too, but the number is usually well publicized through radio and television. The volunteers who staff them are usually knowledgeable about services and where to find them. (These are by no means limited to mental health or illness.) As well as information, they may offer a sympathetic ear when you need it most. They answer in the evening as well as by day, and often round the clock.

Social workers

If it's a good-sized directory, you'll probably find *Social Workers* right after *Social Service Organizations.* Social workers list their names because they want you to know they do counseling and therapy. Sometimes after a name you'll see M.S.W. (Master of Social Work), or A.C.S.W. (Academy of Certified Social Workers) – the highest level of qualification. "Licensed," which also appears often in the listings, means that the standards your state sets for this profession have been met.

Psychologists

Psychologists will be listed too. They too note the fact that they are licensed and give their professional degree, if they have one. They may also note what kind of therapy they give.

Psychiatrists (under Physicians and Surgeons)

Psychiatrists* are to be found under *Physicians and Surgeons,* classified together in large cities, by name in small ones. The listing may also have some such notation as "practice limited to children." In large cities, however, the best-known (and busiest) psychiatrists may not be listed.

Nurses, nursing homes, hospitals

Nurses, too, can be found through the Yellow Pages; usually agencies rather than the names of individuals are listed, and you will have to ask whether they can supply someone with psychiatric experience. *Nursing Homes* and *Hospitals* are also listed.

Family counselors, speech therapists

You may be tempted to look under *Family;* don't bother. The listing is *Marriage and Family Counselors.*

Speech Therapists are especially helpful in severe childhood disorders which affect communication. They are listed in some cities (and others may be located through the public schools). Before you consult one, however, make sure that she/he understands more by speech therapy than correct pronunciation and voice production. Ask if he or she has experience with *language pathology.*

Churches

You'll find nothing under *Priests, Clergymen,* or *Pastoral Counseling,* but all *Churches* are listed. A call to one should bring at least a sympathetic ear, and possibly much more.

Professional organizations

In large cities, *Professional Organizations* are listed, the local medical society among them, and perhaps a psychological society as well. The medical society should be able to tell you if a local psychiatrist is board-certified, and where he did his training. (If you can't find the number, get it from a local doctor.)

The regular directory

Other sources of help must be sought in the regular directory. Look

* An aside – if you seek a private practitioner, try your local medical school, teaching hospital, or MHC if there are any nearby.

first under *Psy-,* if you live in a big city. (Also try the city name + Psy-.) You'll probably find a couple of leads – a Psychological Counseling Center (as in Philadelphia), a Psychiatric Emergency number (as in Wilmington), even a referral service (as in New York and Los Angeles). Nonprofessional self-help groups, such as *Alcoholics Anonymous, Synanon, Recovery,* may be a help to your relative and a source of strength to you. (See Chapter XIV, "The Lord Helps Those Who Help Themselves.") Looking under *Catholic* or *Jewish* is a quick way to locate reliable and experienced social service organizations in huge cities like New York where the Social Service listings are overwhelming. (Looking under Protestant will get you nowhere.) These agencies do not limit their services to members of their own religion.

Visiting Nurses are listed in most cities. Looking under the name of your state is worth doing: there'll be a *Rehabilitation Service* for those whose ability to work is impaired. If there is a state listing under *Welfare,* don't assume it doesn't apply to you; it may be that branch of your state government which deals with general social services to which all citizens are entitled. (Try *Human Services,* too, and scan for the words *Children* or *Elderly.*) *Mental Health* (or *Hygiene,* as it's listed in many states) speaks for itself – though the state department is often pretty remote from actual services. Ask for the office serving your region. *City welfare offices* are also knowledgeable. In some areas, *county* programs are important.

Offices and organizations concerned with *Veterans* will be helpful if you or your relative has been in the service. They may be under "V," or under the name of your town or state.

NAMH AND OTHER NATIONAL ORGANIZATIONS

A shortcut: Call your local branch of NAMH.

By now you have some sense of the kinds of help that may be available. Yet how much can you guess about them from their names? A call to your local branch of the National Association for Mental Health may save a lot of time and discouragement. NAMH makes it its business to know what's available both publicly and privately; they can put you on to clinics and services you're not likely to know about. They will supply the names of private psychiatrists if you ask, though they make no recommendations. (One California branch can even connect you with therapists speaking Korean or Portuguese.)

The National Association for Mental Health is a nationwide organization, not of mental health professionals, but of citizens and consumers of mental health services. More will be said about it in Chapter XIV. If your area has a branch, in it you'll probably find the most knowledgeable people around. Most large cities have branches, listed under "M," or the name of the city or county. Many not only run information and referral services, but publish directories of resources. You never know who's going to publish a directory – the state, perhaps, the city, the local United Way. In any case, the MHA and the United Way will know if there is one. Besides names and numbers, they may show services, fee scales, staff, and eligibility. They are used mainly by professionals, since few consumers know about them, but you can use them too.

Directories of services in your area

There are a number of other national organizations which represent the interests of people and families with special mental and emotional problems – the Epilepsy Foundation of America, the National Society for Autistic Children, and many more. Some of these will be described in Chapter XIV; addresses of these and others are listed in Appendix B. Local branches will put you in touch with people who've traveled the same road you're on, and who know better than most professionals where help is – and isn't – to be found. They may be your best sources of information on what your locality can offer. And being in touch with other people who know what it's like to have an epileptic – or schizophrenic, or alcoholic, or retarded – relative is "therapeutic" for you.

Other national organizations

COMMUNITY MENTAL HEALTH CENTERS

Community Mental Health Centers

In 1973, your chances of living within the area served by a comprehensive community mental health center (the *catchment area*) were about one in three. They should be better now; by 1980, CCMHC's are supposed to cover the whole country. The first Community Mental Health Centers Act, passed in 1963, envisaged that federal funding would start the centers, but that it would eventually be up to the states and to local communities – to us and our neighbors – to support them. Whether they – we – can, or will, and whether the federal government will continue to contribute if we can't or won't, is still an open question. Some 485 were in operation in 1975 with 591 funded – not bad, since the program didn't get going until 1965. You might keep an eye on progress toward the figure of 1,500, the number that NIMH Director Bertram Brown says would be necessary "to bring comprehensive, coordinated mental health services within the reach of every man, woman, and child in the nation." Ask your congressman from time to time how many new ones have been added. If he doesn't know, he ought to, and he can find out.

Money

and the future

To receive federal support a CMHC has to provide at least five "essential services." They are as follows: (1) inpatient services, either within the center itself or, more often, by arrangement with a general

The five essential services:

hospital nearby; (2) outpatient services; (3) emergency service; (4) partial hospitalization, consisting of at least day care;* and (5) consultation and education.†

Do the words "Mental Health Center" guarantee these services? No, even if you add "comprehensive." "Community" is a more reliable indication, but you can't go by the name. The center near you may be privately funded by a medical school or university, or supported by city or state money and patients' fees and fund appeals, or by a combination of these. Unless it's federally funded it doesn't have to give all five services, although of course it may do so. There are even private facilities, run at a profit, which use the words.‡ To find out if a mental health center is a comprehensive community center under the 1963 Act, offering the five essential services, call and ask.

Even if the center near you isn't a CCMHC, it may still provide valuable services, most commonly outpatient psychotherapy, diagnostic services, psychological testing, and prescription and adjustment of medication. Use them. But if your relative is really disoriented, behaving erratically, unequal to everyday stresses and responsibilities so that you must take over (see how hard it is to avoid those words "mentally ill"), those five essential services have a special importance for you. For the majority, the community mental health center offers needed help with problems in living. For you it offers more.

(1) Inpatient services

Hospitalization may be necessary. When the mental health center offers this service, those who need it need not leave their community. Their friends and relatives can keep in contact with them, usually in a local general hospital, and when they are ready to come home, the stigma of the state hospital has been avoided.

(2) Outpatient services

Outpatient services are important, too. Individual therapy, or meeting with a group, may be just what your relative needs to keep on course (and maybe you too can use some help). If there are also "outreach" services, which come directly into his home — hers, yours — they may help a lot, especially if the center is hard to get to.

(3) Emergency services

Emergency services have a special importance: crises have a way of arising after five, when family life is at its most complex, and holidays and weekends may be worst of all.

(4) Partial hospitalization

From the point of view of many families, no service is more essential than partial hospitalization, or day treatment. Many more of us could

* Night hospitalization, for those who can work during the day, is rare in practice.

† In 1975, Congress (over presidential veto) passed a health services authorization bill containing a major redrafting of the Community Mental Health Center program. The bill mandates additional "essential services" for populations that have been underserved: specialized services for children and the elderly, follow-up and halfway-house services for discharged mental patients, and assistance to courts and other agencies in screening people being considered for referral to mental hospitals.

‡ "The Human Resource Institute of Boston is a private, comprehensive mental health center," according to its promotional brochure, directed to doctors.

manage if the responsibility for our sister, father, daughter, husband could be shared, at least for a few hours a day. Many people have grown old in state hospitals, not because their relatives "rejected" them, but because the hard requirements of jobs, children, and health made it impossible to keep them at home any longer. Day treatment services, more than any others, can spare many families this most agonizing of decisions.

(5) Education and consultation

Education and consultation, the fifth essential service, may look like a frill. It isn't. Of course it helps you and your relative if your community has a better general understanding of disordered behavior. But more than that, this is the service that can make a difference to your relative where he lives, goes to school, works. It may, in fact, be what makes it possible for him to live, go to school, or work in the community. That educational and consulting responsibility should mean that the staff of the comprehensive community mental health center stands ready to work with your relative's landlady, or his employer, or his teacher, to help them understand, accept, contribute – which, when they have overcome their fear and bewilderment, is what most people want to do.

Whom will you see at work in a CCMHC?

Primarily nonmedical staff

Whom will you or your relative see when you go to a community mental health center? If you don't see a psychiatrist, don't be surprised. The bulk of therapy is done by nonmedical staff – social workers, psychologists, nurses, and paraprofessionals. Psychiatric residents will be available to work with patients if there is a medical school or teaching hospital nearby, since this is an important part of the training of student psychiatrists. But few experienced psychiatrists devote their full time to CMHC's, although they consult with staff and supervise therapy. Psychologists are active in psychotherapy, as well as testing and evaluation. So are social workers; in addition, it's their particular business to help solve problems about jobs, housing, and transportation; to find homemaker services when needed; to serve as the link with other services in the community. Paraprofessionals and volunteers also help with these problems, and they may give psychotherapy too. For some of us, these may be the most effective workers we see, if they know the same problems we do and can talk to us in our own language.* Psychiatric nurses are important in the CMHC, to give medication, conduct therapy, supervise day treatment.

What will it cost?

Are services free? Not unless you're very poor. Fees are graded according to ability to pay; the center will therefore need to know your financial resources. Even the top of the range is below the fees of private practitioners (which averaged about $40 an hour in 1975). If you can afford private therapy, the CMHC may well offer its diagnostic

* "My doctor was a nice enough guy, but I never knew what the hell he was talking about. . . . He didn't make no sense at all."[4]

services and then refer you elsewhere, very likely to a staff member who also practices privately. If you can't, fees will be adjusted. Whether or not you or your relative has money, services like day treatment should be available.

What they do

What goes on in a CCMHC? Individual therapy. Group therapy. Sociotherapy, vocational counseling, rehabilitation. Psychodynamic psychotherapy. Psychodrama. Reality therapy. Behavioral therapy. Counseling, help with practical problems. A few centers have a unified treatment philosophy (behavior therapy, for evample, in Huntsville, Alabama).[5] But most reflect the variations and disagreements in the mental health field as a whole – although it may not be quite true that (as one therapist remarked of his own center) there are as many treatment philosophies as there are staff members. This variety can be a good thing for you and your relative, if it gives you some of the choices you'd have if you were consulting a private practitioner.

CMHC staff understandably do not go out of their way to emphasize choice. Writes Professor Wiener in his *Practical Guide to Psychotherapy:*

> Almost all applicants at an agency or clinic are herded through a standard intake procedure, at the end of which they are assigned to a therapist according to who has free time, what student needs cases for training purposes, whose "team" happens to get the case, who happens to like this kind of patient. Practically never does an applicant investigate the competence of the different staff therapists and then ask for a particular person. Some clinics would probably bridle at any effort by a patient to interfere with their usual procedures; others will welcome the well-informed applicant, and the therapist he asks for may well be flattered and help arrange for the requested assignment.[6]

Try asking, anyway, says Wiener, and he further suggests that even if you know nothing about particular therapists, you can ask to be seen by an experienced staff member rather than by a student. And you can ask about types of treatment, just as you can with a private practitioner. A well-run CMHC will not insist that you work with a therapist you're not in sympathy with, and lack of sympathy can extend to approach as well as personality.

Can you change therapists?

Although there are good reasons for sticking with a therapist and getting the most out of that relationship and approach, you should be able to change therapists in a mental health center, and you usually can. (This is obviously subject to practical considerations; in a small center, choice will be limited.) If no one who offers the kind of treatment you want is available, they may well suggest that another kind will serve you as well or better, but they should also be able to tell you if that treatment is available elsewhere, and from whom. An alert community mental health center serves as a link with other services, both public and private.

Good and bad

An alert mental health center. The words go down easily, and to talk about what you should expect is easy too. From these citizen-funded centers, you should expect the best for your relative and yourself, work for it,* complain when you don't get it.† For it's all too likely that you won't. First, there's that better than even chance that there's no community health center serving you at all. Second, those that do exist vary from excellent to grossly inadequate. We can go down the list, essential service by essential service. In some centers, the hospital treatment the community mental health centers are supposed to offer may be unavailable except to private patients of center psychiatrists.[7] Outpatient therapy of any sort can be good, bad, indifferent, or unavailable when you need it. Therapists and counselors may be knowledgeable and resourceful about other community services — or not. Emergency services may range from a twenty-four-hour walk-in clinic[8] to an inefficient telephone response that subjects the night caller to a discouraging "game of pass-the-patient."[9] There are day treatment centers which are little more than baby-sitting services. (Let's not knock them; even that helps.) The center may reach out effectively to educate and consult outside its walls, or it may wait for an indifferent community to come to it.

What a good day hospital can do

Considering the importance of partial hospitalization to families of the mentally ill, let's talk about it at more length. A good day treatment center is an inspiring sight. With skilled guidance, people may paint out the things that bother them or the dreams they hope for. Dance therapy may help them move and relate to others in ways they can't at home alone. Group therapy helps them share problems, and solve them. Books, carpentry, crafts, sports may help inadequate people to adequacy: call the process bibliotherapy, occupational therapy, recreational therapy, if that is necessary to underline their importance, and honor the resourceful, hard-working people who help others through simple things.

The ordinary tasks of daily life — shopping, handling money, planning lunch and making it, going on trips — are therapeutic for people who have never done, or can no longer do, these things. More ambitious training may focus on the skills and attitudes necessary for getting and keeping a job. People can learn, or relearn, to dress appropriately, take buses, get to places on time, control bizarre behavior or obsessive talk. Do these goals seem elementary? More suited to children or the retarded? Not to those of us who have actual experience of mentally ill people. There's a wide overlap between mental retardation and mental illness. Some of the retarded are mentally ill too, and prolonged mental illness can rob a person of mental and social skills he once possessed. Counselors, therapists, friends, teachers, those who find

*** Join your local Mental Health Association.**
† For hints on how to complain publicly and effectively, see Chapter XIV.

ways to improve an impaired person's functioning are among the most constructively occupied members of our society.

Too old? Too young?

Two important groups have been neglected by the CMHC's. Though the situation is improving, you may find little help for your relative if he or she is old,* or a young child.[11] This reflects the priorities of our society all too well (see Chapters XII and XIII, "Children" and "When Your Relative Is Old"); if there's nothing for your relative because he's too old or too young, you should tell the world.

Or too sick?

You should also be ready to protest if you're told he's too sick. He may be, of course; no community center or general hospital can handle long-term hospitalization. But the combination of outpatient therapy (probably including drug maintenance treatment), short-term hospitalization, and day treatment should make referral to a psychiatric hospital uncommon. Comprehensive community mental health centers were intended to replace long-term hospitalization for most of the mentally ill. They've done pretty well – a 1970 report indicated that state mental hospitals in areas that are served by well-established community mental health centers have less than half the admission rate of the national average.[12] But here too some centers fail; one, located on the grounds of a state hospital and largely run by its personnel, has actually increased admissions.[13] No matter how sick your son or mother is, if you want to keep them at home, you have a right to expect the center's help.

Advantages of public facilities

Community mental health centers have advantages and disadvantages, like everything else. You'll save money there – not an awful lot, if you're prosperous,† but a great deal if you're not. They provide easier access to a range of varied services and professionals than private practitioners can. They offer more different types of treatment, they're there in emergencies, they're oriented to the community, they're subject to supervision and criticism from professional organizations. In public facilities, as Professor Daniel Wiener points out, "therapeutic brilliance is not as likely to be rewarded as in private practice," but "neither is incompetence as likely to be overlooked."‡

Mixed blessings

Since the centers, like other public facilities, are used as training grounds in each of the mental health professions, the M.D., the psy-

* "Community mental health services have not traditionally serviced the needs of the aging."[10]

† Most mental health centers assess fairly – i.e., according to ability to pay – and a comfortable middle-class family will usually end up paying not more than $10 below the average private rate for the area. The fees of private practitioners range between $25 and $40 per hour (in some places more), with psychiatrists and clinical psychologists toward the top of the scale and psychiatric social workers toward the bottom. (See also Chapter VII, p. 170.)

‡ Professor Wiener's *Practical Guide to Psychotherapy* underlies many of the suggestions in this chapter and the next. It's out of print, but it's well worth getting from Interlibrary Loan at your library, especially if you seek psychotherapy for yourself.

chologist, or the social worker you are assigned to may be an inexperienced student. Although he or she is being supervised by a qualified professional, lack of experience is an obvious disadvantage. (If you're lucky, your relative and you may benefit from someone who's talented and young and willing to try new things. If not . . .) Students also finish their training and leave; staff leave too, in search of greener pastures, for there is always somebody to outbid public facilities for skilled and qualified people. Thus you may have to change therapists whether you want to or not. Instead of your therapist, it may be the center which arranges appointments, cancels them, handles your personal emergencies. The therapist may be flexible, but the center's procedures may not. "Your therapist is less likely to take full responsibility for your treatment and maintain contact with you than would a private practitioner."[14]

Inclusion in research

You may also be used in experimental research, especially if university personnel are involved in the center. This is not necessarily a disadvantage. What you may get are effective new methods of therapy you couldn't get elsewhere. They may also be duds, or even do more harm than good. For participation in research your permission should be asked, but it may not be; Professor Wiener recommends that you ask specifically about inclusion in research, how the research is designed, and what it's supposed to accomplish, both in general *and* for the patient.[15]

Who gets to see records?

Two more cautions have to do with records of tests, diagnoses, and treatment. You want them to be confidential, yet available where needed. You might take it for granted, for example, that your family doctor would get full reports on a patient of his whom he referred to a center. Don't. If you want him to be kept informed, make that clear, and check with him to make sure he is. You may have brought your child to the center because you're worried about him in school, and you may assume that information about his tests and his problems will automatically be put into the hands of your child's teacher, the school psychologist, the principal. It won't, unless you ask for this to be done. Most agencies will require you specifically to authorize it in writing. This is for your protection. Community mental health centers try to safeguard your privacy, but no agency where records are available to a large number of staff, clerical personnel, and students can be as close-mouthed as a private practitioner. Further dangers to confidentiality are implied in the growing computerization of records. One state already has plans for any mental health facility it licenses, approves, or funds to forward to a central record-keeping system information on the treatment of all individual patients.[16] Safeguards as to who could retrieve such information should be ironclad; many people doubt they can be, or that such central data banks should exist. At any rate, they're one more thing to watch out for.

Those you authorize — if you request it,

and nobody else, you hope

Though we are most concerned with what mental health centers do for the mentally ill, let's make clear that they were conceived as mental *health* centers, and that most of the people who go there are not mentally ill in any sense. "Problems in living" account for the greatest part of the centers' work. They have still been bitterly criticized for not concerning themselves enough over the social problems that affect mental health, especially the health of the poor, who have the most problems in living and the worst ones.* Work on broad social problems will bear fruits in the future; our relatives need services right now. There are two social problems, however, that we must recognize as of crucial importance, even though they are outside the scope of this book. Alcohol and narcotics cause some of the cruelest problems in living. They can both cause mental illness and make it worse. A great deal of the energy of community mental health center staff must go into alcohol- and drug-related problems.

Social problems and mental health

Alcohol, narcotics

Mental retardation, too, is beyond our scope here, but under the terms of the original Act (which, passed in 1963, reflected President Kennedy's family concern with retardation), community mental health centers must provide services to the retarded. So if your relative's problems are complicated by alcohol, drugs, or retardation, your claim upon the community mental health center is not less but greater.

FINDING A PRIVATE PRACTITIONER

Retardation

When you are looking for a private practitioner, the community mental health center is very well placed to suggest a good one. A call to the director or the chief psychiatric social worker may be enough, if he or she will listen to your problem over the phone. Or you could ask to come in and talk it over, making clear that you don't want to begin therapy but are looking for a private therapist. Very likely you'll get a recommendation to a staff member who also practices privately, but small city mental health centers know who's good in the locality, whether or not they're affiliated with the center.†

Private practitioner: Ask your CMHC or teaching hospital or medical school.

If there is a medical school or teaching hospital in your area, you

* This is the main thrust of the 1972 report, by Ralph Nader's study group. Franklin Chu and Sharland Trotter, *The Mental Health Complex; Part I: Community Mental Health Centers* (Washington, D.C.: Center for the Study of Responsive Law, 1972).

† Dr. Herbert Lazarus suggests some of the tact you'll need to get a helpful answer — for you don't want to put your consultant in the position of saying that one practitioner is better than another. Lazarus suggests you begin by saying, " 'I don't want you to give me any names yet. I want to tell you a little about the problem first; then you can tell me which of the many qualified psychiatrists in this town will be best able to handle it.' In this way you are giving him lots of leeway, but also plenty of reason to give you a specific name."[17]

could try to get an appointment with the chairman of the psychiatric department — failing that, a member of the department — for an evaluation and a referral to a private practitioner. A good evaluation, by the most experienced professional you can find, is crucial.

For diagnosis and general assessment of really disturbing behavior a general psychiatrist (the psychiatric equivalent of a G.P.) is probably your best bet, preferably associated with a hospital where he sees a variety of cases, rather than someone with an office practice consisting mainly of neurotic problems. Yet office therapists are common, and general psychiatrists are hard to find.[18] (See Appendix B, 2., "Finding Types of Treatment.")

Professional associations

You can get three names of psychiatrists from your city or county medical society, as well as the MHA. The medical society can also tell you the qualifications of member psychiatrists — their medical school, where they did their psychiatric residency, whether they are board-certified. Hospitals, too, may provide this information about their own doctors. You can get a list of board-certified psychiatrists from the American Psychiatric Association. Your state Psychological Association will supply a list of psychologists within a given geographical area and specialty.*

To check a psychiatrist's credentials, you can refer to the three-volume *American Medical Directory,* which lists every licensed M.D. in the United States, or the *Directory of Medical Specialists.* Biographical directories also give professional histories with useful information. (See Appendix A.) However, these aren't always available in libraries, they don't all get published regularly, and they're often out of date. You'll need more than paper and print to guide you to a competent private practitioner.

Liaison with other community resources is not the private practitioner's strong point.

It's the unusual private practitioner who is expert on what other community resources can contribute to his patient's well-being. Even if he knows about them, you can't expect him to coordinate their efforts. Yet families often do expect their doctor to be a kind of miracle man, an all-round ombudsman who knows everything we need and can tell us where to find it. We'd avoid much disappointment and resentment if we realized this isn't so. In general, when you go to a private practitioner, he'll help you all he can, but the job of locating other needed services will be up to you. If you think you need broader services than he or she is providing, you can go to Family Service or the mental health center as well. Any of the community services described here will be glad to consult with a private practitioner.

* Write or call the association secretary, but don't rely on the phone book unless you already know where your state association is located; ask the American Psychological Association (Appendix B) for their list of state secretaries. The secretary of your state board of examiners has a list of psychologists licensed or certified under the laws of your state.

COMMUNITY INSTITUTIONS

Even if there's no community mental health center — and often in addition to it — there are many other agencies that offer services geared to ability to pay. They generally share in local fund drives; often they have their own endowments. They are privately run but may get public money; states, for instance, often contract and pay for services that they do not themselves offer. One of the most widespread of these is Family and Children's Service, which exists all over the country, sometimes under slightly different names.

Family and Children's Service Agencies

Usually (but not always) they belong to the Family Service Association, and often to the Child Welfare League as well, national organizations that set standards for services.*

Staffed by social workers, Family Service offers supportive counseling and help with practical problems. If more than that seems indicated, they'll probably refer you to the mental health center or a private practitioner. But if you and your mentally ill relative share a problem of living, they will help. If, for instance, your daughter or wife is ill and needs relief from the care of children, Family Service knows about homemakers. They know about foster homes, if it's as bad as that. If your brother has been released from the state hospital and your spare room is where he'll live until he finds a job, a good Family Service agency will counsel for the homecoming and the first difficult weeks, and later help locate a place for him to live. Most of a Family Service agency's work, of course, does not involve mental illness. The whole range of family problems is their concern. They do marriage counseling, help unmarried mothers, handle adoptions, supervise foster care. Family Service won't be able to help you with all the problems of mental illness, but they can ease some of the worst ones. And — like other agencies, public and private — if they can't help they'll do their best to refer you to someone who can.

And other private agencies, clinics

There are hundreds of privately run agencies and clinics. Most of these offer therapy of various sorts in addition to practical counseling. Mental health services may be provided by religious groups: Catholics, Jews, Episcopalians, Presbyterians, Mennonites — the list goes on. Universities may provide them; departments of special education may run therapeutic classes; medical schools have clinics where their students train and their professors supervise and do some therapy. Associations for the retarded run activity centers and sheltered workshops. Public-spirited citizens have endowed some outstanding clinics; these usually bear the founder's name but now are often maintained by a combina-

* Some good agencies don't belong, but most do. If you're doubtful you can write to the national organization in New York to see if your local agency is a member.

tion of public and private funds. Agencies like these are generally limited to outpatient treatment, and their telephones rarely answer after five or on weekends. Their advantages (and disadvantages) are similar to those listed for CMHC's. They often serve specialized groups — children, families, addicts, (rarely) the aging. Even a clinic with a general clientèle is not bound to accept every kind of patient; one facility will exclude the alcoholic, another the suicidal, another the chronic schizophrenic, another the senile patient. (Community mental health centers make similar exclusions, but probably fewer of them. And if a public facility excludes your relative, as a citizen you're in a better position to get indignant about it.) Like CMHC's, private agencies, if they can't help you, should be expected to refer you to someone who can. Be alert for the names of private agencies in your community and learn what they do. Often their services are of a very high quality.

Exclusions

Community institutions we take for granted may be a significant source of help. Most schools have school psychologists and guidance counselors. Above all, they have teachers. All these can help an emotionally disturbed child where it counts most, in his daily environment. Increasingly, public schools offer classes for emotionally disturbed children and those with learning disabilities, as well as the retarded — three conditions that in children overlap a great deal. More than anything else, the acceptance of mentally ill children in schools makes it possible for them to live at home rather than in institutions.

Schools

All school personnel who come in contact with a troubled child are ready to consult with any mental health professionals you authorize. The school should also be able to put you in touch with a Big Brother or Sister, a volunteer who will offer companionship to a socially isolated child. The local college, too, is a resource. Every college has students who want to help. If the school can't locate a companion, you can approach the college directly; the college chaplain is a good person to call, and a notice on the psychology department bulletin board may bring results. Sometimes such companions offer far more than companionship; many a freshman has enviable therapeutic resources of patience and ingenuity.

Colleges

YMCA's, Scout troops, church and youth groups, service clubs, senior citizens' groups are also valuable resources. With persistence, many families can develop their own corps of devoted paraprofessionals, for your neighbors are ready, and able, to help more than you realize.

Community groups

Court probation officers are some of our most important mental health workers.* Many states offer additional mental health services. In Massachusetts, court clinics provide evaluation and treatment for defendants and train correctional officers and guards in counseling

Courts

* For an enthralling account of what they do, see Dan Sakall and Alan Harrington, *Love and Evil* (Boston: Little, Brown, 1974).

techniques; psychiatric and counseling services are provided in all Massachusetts state prisons. Probate courts in Michigan, through their Juvenile Division, offer various mental health services for children that would be handled in other areas by state or private agencies.[19] Two thousand district courts in the United States have a program of Volunteers in Probation who work with people referred to them by court probation officers, providing a one-to-one relationship which can make a real difference to a disturbed person already in trouble with the law. Ask the local judge what help is available in your area.

Police

Don't forget the local police station. Introduce your relative to the policeman on the beat in a calm, friendly atmosphere. It may bear fruit later, if he gets lost or into trouble. Says one psychiatrist, known for his work in the development of police training programs, "in general psychiatry, the usefulness and absolute necessity of the police are proved every day of the week." Good police departments give training in how to handle psychiatric patients, and will help you if you must get your relative to a hospital. "It's very reassuring, for the family and for the patient, when a couple of husky guys appear to take him where he can't hurt himself or anybody else."

Services for veterans

If your relative is a veteran, or you are, this opens a number of special possibilities for help. If there is a Veterans' Administration Hospital near you, it provides free inpatient and outpatient services for service-connected disorders. Members of a disabled veteran's family may be eligible for certain kinds of help. There may be a Veterans' Service Office listed under the name of your town or state government. The quickest way, however, is to call one of the veterans' organizations found in almost every town. Ask for the service officer; it's his business to know what's available, how to get it, whether you qualify, and how to use the celebrated veterans' clout in your behalf.

Unions

Help may be available through your union. Some unions finance clinics. Others have good insurance programs. AFL Community Service Committees in 150 cities, staffed by people from within the labor movement, offer counseling on family problems and will refer to professionals. Their services are available to everyone, not just union members. (For the AFL Community Service Representative nearest you, write AFL-CIO Community Services, 815 16th Street N.W., Washington, DC 20006.)

INFORMAL MENTAL HEALTH SERVICES

Informal and volunteer services

Now that there are so many more mental patients in the community, informal organizations have sprung up in some cities to help them.

Where mental health centers are nonexistent or inadequate, or simply where a need has been felt for alternative approaches, dedicated people have got together to provide somewhere to go, something to do, someone to talk to. Some are professionals who want to fill a need, and never mind the money. Some are just good people. There are all gradations of training, skill, and experience in between. These setups are usually no bigger than can fit into a run-down old house. The paid staff, if there is one, isn't paid much, and sometimes the rent comes out of their own pockets. Most of the work is done by volunteers.

Out of this spontaneous, grass-roots movement have come crisis centers, drop-in centers, full-fledged day treatment programs. Operating on a shoestring (often with the backup of interested professionals), always on the lookout for secure funding, seldom getting it, they are an extraordinary development in mental health care. The bulletin board of one such program lists a day's activities: Hatha Yoga, Individual Counseling, Lunch (including shopping, cooking, eating, and cleaning up, therapies all), Musical Fantasy, Gestalt. Others offer group therapy, crafts, painting, poetry, depending on who can do what. They help with practical adjustment too; in Berkeley, California (where the phasing out of state hospitals makes community problems especially acute), the Advocacy Collective, sharing space with a day treatment program, helps former hospital patients with housing, money, jobs, and social contacts. One staff member gets some city money. The rest are volunteers, many of them students or ex-students; a big university town is a likely place for such services to grow.

No two centers are alike, but they tend to be both radical and strongly idealistic. They emphasize authenticity of communication, freedom, shared experience, and responsibility. R. D. Laing and Thomas Szasz are strong influences. Medications are de-emphasized as much as possible and probably a little bit more.* At their best, these services provide a directness, genuineness, and rapidity of response that more professionalized services can hardly match; in one of these your relative stands perhaps the best chance anywhere of being treated not as a sick person or a child, but as another human being. There are drawbacks to this unbuttoned approach, of course; whether you think they outweigh the advantages depends on your point of view, on whether there are more professional services available, and on how good these are.

* In the San Francisco area, the remarkable *Madness Network News* ("All the fits that's news to print — garnered from a schizophrenic love-chain wound out of Chestnut Lodge") alternates articles on local services, poetry by the perplexed, and such articles as "Thomas Szasz, Freedom Fighter" and "R. D. Laing, Superstar." "Dr. Caligari," a regular columnist, strongly opposes drugs and ECT.

HOSPITAL SERVICES

Local hospitals

Local hospitals are a major resource for keeping mentally ill people in the community. (See Chapter IX, p. 226.) In addition to complete hospitalization, some run their own day treatment centers. More common are outpatient psychiatric units, especially in large cities. (There are at least twelve in Manhattan alone.) Such clinics offer after-care for released patients, but are also open to the general public.

Hospital outpatient units

Crisis centers

Crisis centers are just what they sound like. They are becoming common in large cities; there may be a new one in yours. Usually connected with a hospital, they are a twenty-four-hour emergency service. If a telephone call isn't enough, the crisis center is open all night to ease situations as they happen. Most of the crises they serve are one-shot affairs, "transient situational difficulties," "acute emotional storms,"[20] often involving alcohol or drugs. They frequently offer overnight or brief hospitalization, still in the emergency ward, with release as easy as intake and no psychiatric stigma. The crisis center is especially helpful if violence threatens and something must be done fast.

Nursing homes

Nursing homes may help keep your relative nearby, if he or she is not acutely ill. Few offer more than sympathetic care, and many offer less. Some good mental health centers provide supervision and outreach services for nursing homes in their region. If there's no CMHC, consult Family Service or your local welfare office. (For what to look for, see Chapter XIII, pp. 397–398.)

Visiting nurses

There is probably a Visiting Nurse Association near you. If they can provide maintenance psychiatric medication, it will save a weekly trip to the psychiatrist's office. They may be able to do more; in some states, departments of mental health are beginning to train nurses to work with families of patients who have been discharged to the community. Fees are charged according to income. Ask the association what help they can give, or go to your city or county department of public health. In rural areas, the Public Health nurse may be the major health resource and the guide to other services.

Public health nurses

HOMEMAKER SERVICES

Homemaker services

Homemaker services seem humbler than they are. Providing help in the home is one of the most effective ways of keeping people out of hospitals and nursing homes, and when a mentally ill parent has children, a homemaker may keep a family together when nothing else can. Local social service agencies and welfare offices should be able to locate a person to help out. Your relative's doctor or social worker, and you yourself, should stand ready to give guidance for home aides who are not used to working with the emotionally disturbed. The National Council of Homemaker-Health Aides sets standards for homemaker services; in 1972 there were approximately thirty thousand trained aides available throughout the country through some two thousand public and private social agencies. Such homemakers are able to work with mental health professionals as members of a team, providing not only practical help, but emotional support for the ill person and the family. If you can't get information on homemakers from local organizations in your area, write the council. (See Appendix B for the address.)

HALFWAY HOUSES AND GROUP HOMES

Halfway houses

Of course it is not always possible — or desirable — for your relative to live in your home, or in his or hers, even with the support of community agencies. When a mentally disordered person is not able, or not yet able, to live independently, halfway houses provide an encouraging alternative to hospitalization or institutionalization.* In 1961 there were only seven halfway houses for psychiatric patients in the whole country.[21] Today there are hundreds, although they are by no means evenly spread. (In 1973, 70 percent of them were in eastern states, and sixteen states had none at all.)[22] In typical halfway houses, a small group of people live together as a family. Unlike the hospital ward, the halfway house is a home, where residents can have their own possessions, cook, entertain friends and family, share a common social life and common obligations. It's not assumed that these desirable things will happen of themselves; halfway houses have houseparents or a housemanager who help them happen. Usually they live in the house; in large houses they have a staff to assist them. Their qualifications are personal rather than academic. Warmth, stability, tolerance, firmness are more important than degrees, although the usual M.S.W.'s and psychology M.A.'s are often found. If they aren't, professionally trained people may be available as consultants.

The house does not exist to provide therapy, except insofar as any supportive contact is therapeutic. The halfway house is not a mini-hospital. Those who live there are carefully called "residents" or "members," not "patients," and they get medical treatment or psychotherapy elsewhere. Most of the activity takes place evenings and weekends. In most houses, residents are expected to have somewhere to

* For information about alternatives to institutional care, write: Administrator, Social and Rehabilitation Service, U.S. Department of Health, Education and Welfare, Washington, DC 20201.

go by day — school, a job, volunteer work, a sheltered workshop, a day hospital. Helping residents meet the demands of regular responsibilities is one of the most important functions of a good halfway house. Dressing appropriately, getting places on time, behaving reasonably in a work setting, budgeting, shopping, planning and cooking meals are necessary skills, and the halfway house is a natural place to teach them. Many houses limit how long a resident can stay to six months or less, and many residents can resume independent living after this period, especially if the house remains a place they can come back to in a pinch. Others can "graduate" to community apartments which provide knowledgeable and sympathetic supervision.*

Community apartments

Can everybody graduate? Of course not. Yet few halfway houses accept people who may be expected to spend their lives there. The need for permanent, small group homes is only beginning to be recognized. (See Chapter XIV.) In most places chronic patients who can't live alone or with their families are supported (usually by public funds) in foster homes.

Group homes

Quality varies.

Some halfway houses — responsibly supported by states, communities, or private sources; supervised by hospitals, mental health centers, or boards of private citizens — can offer well-thought-out and well-staffed programs. Others may be run (often for profit) by a single individual, on whose resourcefulness and integrity everything depends. The possibilities for abuse are obvious. Mental patients today are not destitute; most draw payments from welfare, Social Security, vocational rehabilitation programs, which may cover the $250 to $500 per month fees in halfway houses. (See Chapter XI, on money.) Some can handle money, especially if they're taught. Many can't. It's natural that some of these funds stick to the fingers of unscrupulous landlords and landladies, whose "group home" is no more than a run-down lodging house whose owner is willing to put up with odd behavior.

So do philosophies.

Halfway houses vary in philosophy as well as quality. Most successful ones combine sympathetic understanding with firm expectations. "Some things are not negotiable," says Leonard Goveia, who directs Rehabilitation Mental Health Services in San José, California, an impressive and growing network of houses and related services.

> We're working with people, helping them to learn how to manage their lives in the community — vocationally, financially, socially, and emotionally. We certainly don't cure anyone, and many of our most successful outcomes have been clients in whom the symptomatology remained perfectly apparent, yet they managed themselves better. . . . We may say to a client, We're not sure what sick behavior is or what sickness is, or whether you have a disease; but in terms of how society will see you,

* Among the finest of these are the community residences run by New York City's Young Adult Institute.

> your behavior is sick, and if you keep it up, someone is going to decide that you have to be locked up. Our message is that society can stand certain kinds of behavior in certain contexts, and if you behave outside these boundaries you're in trouble.[23]

Yet Mr. Goveia bears the title of Chief Research Investigator for a halfway house with a quite different philosophy. A few blocks away is Soteria House, which like Rehabilitation Mental Health Services also got its start with NIMH funding. Patterned after R. D. Laing's famous Kingsley Hall, the staff and residents of Soteria House see schizophrenia as an experience of death and rebirth, of integration through disintegration. Though residents are young and acutely disturbed, medication is frowned upon as "closing a wound which should be allowed to drain." Activities are spontaneous, not structured in advance, and everything is negotiable. "Our people wouldn't be allowed to break all the dishes," remarks Mr. Goveia; at Soteria House they are allowed to and sometimes do. Feelings are to be expressed, and if the expression is violent or bizarre, that is acceptable too. Residents and staff are close to each other; visitors don't always find it easy to distinguish between them. People get better at Soteria House; some return to help others on their "inner journey." Though Mr. Goveia himself runs a tighter ship, he's watching Soteria House. He thinks they've got something. "There's something to the idea that people ought to ride out their difficulties."[24]

Most communities don't have one halfway house, let alone a choice of philosophies. It isn't easy to start one, even when funding is secure. If residents are to relate to the real world, halfway houses and group houses cannot be mini-institutions located in inconspicuous, isolated areas. They must be near shopping, transportation, neighbors. But, according to many local ordinances, any group of more than five unrelated people living together makes a home a lodging house and brings to bear restrictive zoning laws and building codes. These can be used when fear and misunderstanding cause a neighborhood to reject a halfway house with the familiar excuse: "It's a fine idea, but not on my block." Still, every year sees the establishment of more halfway houses. You should be able to get an up-to-date listing of halfway homes from your state department of mental health or social services. A local mental health association can tell you even quicker.

"Group homes and halfway houses are as hard to find as snow in Miami," says one de-institutionalization specialist.[25] As always, it is the chronic patients who are least well served, particularly those who are getting old. It is satisfying work helping a young student or a previously stable breadwinner get over an acute reaction and return to independent work. Working with chronic, deteriorated schizophrenics is far less rewarding. In that same San José where Leonard Goveia has worked since 1958 to build a model group of services serving some hundreds of people (a good proportion of whom are chronically impaired), two thousand former state hospital patients[26] live in one small neighborhood of old homes now turned into boardinghouses, without social programs or work programs, without therapy of any kind except maintenance drugs. Many of them have dropped out of sight and don't get even that. They have "returned to the community," a community in which the back bedroom has replaced the back ward. In New York City, Fountain House offers extensive rehabilitative services that go far beyond the simple living arrangement of a halfway house.[27] But for every mentally disturbed person lucky enough to be associated with Fountain House, there are hundreds spending their lives in cheap hotels, Bowery flophouses, or on the streets. In 1973, Dr. Robert Reich and Dr. Lloyd Siegel, two psychiatrists with the New York City Department of Social Services, described a situation as horrifying as any state hospital snake pit. "In rooming houses, foster homes, nursing homes, and run-down hotels," patients are clustered "unsupervised, unmedicated, uncared for, frequently the prey of unscrupulous and criminal elements. The mass transfer of patients from state care to diverse city and private accommodations has been without benefit, and often with detriment, to the patients themselves."[28] When patients have been returned to the community without adequate services, "tremendous hardship has been sustained by the families of discharged patients, and where families do not exist, by the community in general."

The back-to-the-community movement is no cheap panacea.

As we who love our mentally ill relatives welcome the humane aims of the back-to-the-community movement, we should realize that if hospitals are emptied while community services are not provided, it is we who will suffer most. Halfway houses and group homes must be one of our top priorities. (They won't just happen. Chapter XIV discusses some of the problems of zoning laws and tells how "the Lord helps those who help themselves," meaning us.)

FOSTER HOMES

Foster homes, good and bad

Foster homes are for adults too. They can be bleak and dangerous vacuums of needed care, as Drs. Siegel and Reich point out. Or they can be warm, good places where residents dig in gardens, help around the house, and share in the life of a stable family. In good community programs, patients in foster placements are in touch with a social worker, and homes are regularly evaluated. Vermont does an unusual job on foster placements; there are high standards and good follow-up

in Honolulu, Philadelphia, Seattle,* and many other places. Before you consider a foster home, investigate carefully with the help of your local mental health center, family service organization, or welfare department. Who else is in the home? All day, or only part? How much supervision does your relative need? In a crisis, can the foster family get professional help fast? Psychoactive drugs are powerful, but they have not entirely eliminated irresponsibility or violence. People can still get hurt, houses can still burn. Unless community residences – both foster homes and halfway houses – have adequate backup services, enthusiasm for treating the mentally ill in the community is bound to cool.

Ask questions.

VOCATIONAL REHABILITATION SERVICES

Vocational rehabilitation services

Vocational rehabilitation services concern themselves not so much with where your mentally disabled relative lives or the quality of his life there, but with how he or she can be helped to join or rejoin the world of work. Notice we have shifted the term from "ill" or "disturbed" to "disabled." Vocational rehabilitation agencies think in terms of *handicap* and *disability* rather than illness. Most people know that they assist the blind, the deaf, the crippled to train for jobs, get them, and keep them. Fewer realize that they assist the emotionally handicapped as well. In fact, mental illness is the most common of all disabling conditions.† If there's any chance your relative might be able to work, your state agency must help.

A major national resource for the mentally and emotionally handicapped

In partnership with the Rehabilitation Services Administration of the Department of Health, Education and Welfare, there is a vocational rehabilitation agency in every state plus the Virgin Islands, Puerto Rico, Guam, and the District of Columbia, with offices in most cities. Your local welfare department, or any social service agency, will give you the number of the nearest office.

Eligibility

To be eligible for vocational rehabilitation, your relative must have a degree of disability "which interferes with the ability to pursue a gainful occupation or function as a homemaker, or which threatens his or her continued employment," and he or she must have "a reason-

* There is a useful description of the Washington State program by Edward Chouinard, "Family Homes for Adults," *The Social and Rehabilitation Record* (HEW) 2 (Feb./March 1975).

† In 1969 the federal government listed mental illness as the most common disabling condition among both rehabilitated and nonrehabilitated clients, accounting for 23 percent of successful and 39 percent of unsuccessful rehabilitations.[29] In 1972, 33 percent of the Massachusetts Rehabilitation Commission's clientèle suffered from assorted mental disabilities. This did not include mental retardation (13 percent) or epilepsy and other nervous disorders (3 percent).[30]

able chance of being able to engage in a suitable occupation after necessary rehabilitation services are provided."[31] The Rehabilitation Amendments of 1973 mandate a generous interpretation of "reasonable chance," by directing state rehabilitation agencies to give priority to "those individuals with the severest handicaps."[32] Every disabled person has a right to be evaluated for eligibility, and reevaluated *annually,* since his condition may improve. This costs nothing, whether the evaluation is medical, psychiatric, psychological, social, or all together. Guidance and counseling are free too. The 1973 legislation requires a written individualized treatment plan, with specific intermediate and long-term goals, to be developed by the rehabilitation counselor and the client (or, if necessary, his parents or guardian).* Counseling is not narrowly vocational. "The vocational counselor helps the person to understand himself as much as possible so that he can work in a job which is suitable for him,"[34] realistically assessing what he can and cannot expect of himself and the world.

Priority for severe handicaps

Free evaluation

and counseling

Job training, too, is broadly understood. It may take place on the job, in a trade or commercial school, a rehabilitation center, or at home. Rehabilitation services even support students in college, if education seems the appropriate way to prepare a troubled young person for work in line with his capacities. Rehabilitation services may also pay for psychiatric treatment, in whole or part, if mental status affects a person's capacity for employment (or homemaking), and if psychiatric treatment "may be expected to reduce the impairment within a reasonable length of time."[35] The same holds for necessary drugs, psychotherapy, occupational therapy — in short, any services needed for rehabilitation. For these, the client pays according to his means; the rehabilitation service contributes as needed. When he or she is ready to start working, the vocational counselor helps find a suitable job, and follows up to see that it works out all right for employee and employer.

Job training,

education,

and other services supported according to financial need

SHELTERED WORKSHOPS

It doesn't always, as you know well enough. Chronic schizophrenics, particularly, have trouble keeping jobs. If your relative needs a more

* If services are unsatisfactory, knowing the provisions of the law (P.L. 93–112, Section 102) will help you be your relative's advocate. The law requires written long-range and intermediate rehabilitation goals, statement of specific services to be provided and timelines for providing them, and objective criteria for evaluating the program. It also "sets forth requirements for annual review and modification, and specifies procedural guidelines for terminating service and a strict standard for finding ineligibility for service," imposing "a new degree of accountability for counselor action and agency decisions."[33]

Sheltered workshops

protected environment, rehabilitation services will know about sheltered workshops in your area. They don't usually operate them, since their commitment is to competitive employment, but they use them continually; one rehabilitation expert has described them as "serving the rehabilitation counselor as the hospital serves the doctor."[36] Sheltered workshops can function as a stage in full rehabilitation, or they can be the place your relative begins and stays. Most sheltered workshops are run by private voluntary agencies. Goodwill Industries is the best known; there are also those run by the National Association for Retarded Citizens, Easter Seal Societies, the Jewish Occupational Council, and many others. State, county, and municipal agencies may also operate workshops. Work goes far beyond hooking rugs and making ashtrays, although handicrafts play their part. Work is obtained on contract from local industries and may range from simple packaging to skilled electronics assembly. Wages, though not high, are subject to the Fair Labor Standards Act floor.[37]

TRANSPORTATION

Help with transportation

If the workshop is not near your relative's home, it is not necessarily out of reach. Some states are beginning to provide or support transportation to sheltered workshops and other services. (In 1973, New Jersey, Alabama, Missouri, and Iowa were among them.) It's worth asking about.

In emergencies, or for necessary appointments when you or your relative has no car, local service organizations might help. Try your local United Way or Family Service for suggestions.

"GET TO THE REAL PEOPLE"

Getting the most out of a community agency:

Only you know if you're getting the kind of help you need. A specialist in social service delivery systems lays it on the line: "If you're not satisfied, say so. 'I want to talk to somebody else.' The person you're talking to is bound to refer you." What he says applies to all the community agencies described in this chapter, for he's thought long and knows plenty about "what behaviors are involved in negotiating the social service system." "Don't be afraid to go over someone's head. Keep asking. Open a closed door. Talk to one of his/her colleagues. Tell your problem." Agency recommendations are just that — recommendations. You can consult on them, just as with a doctor. "Where can I get another opinion?" You can dip in and out of the community system. "Talk to a private doctor and use him as an intermediary. Go to a different agency. Go to another town. *Never accept no for an answer."*

"Get to the real people."

A professional mystique can be used to avoid facing you. "Search for the real people. Get past those people who are not real. Get to those who are interested in helping you *in your terms."*[38]

Do you ever get fed up with constructive suggestions? Perhaps the most therapeutic thing we can do at this point is to recognize that there's no guarantee that these suggestions, or any others, will bring you what you need. The right help is hard to find; you can look and look and fail to find it – and find it in unexpected places. In his story of his son Checkers, *Be Not Afraid,*[39] novelist Robin White tells how hard it can be even when you are young, attractive, verbal, intelligent, and know what you want, to assemble the varied skills and people needed to help one troubled human being and his family.

Checkers

Checkers wasn't classified "mentally ill," but as the years went on, that hardly seemed to matter. He was seven when he had his first epileptic seizure, a sequel to a blow on the head. He was unlucky; though most epileptic conditions are controllable with medication, his was not. For fourteen years his family lived with him the slow agony of his mental and emotional deterioration. School, where he had been bright and popular, got harder and harder for him. As his behavior became more erratic, he was resented and bullied, increasing his emotional disturbance and even his seizures. He began to have queer, obsessive ideas; the Whites did not yet suspect that they were side effects of the various drugs necessary for his disorder.

The Whites wanted to consult a psychiatrist when they noticed the early signs of psychiatric disturbance. Checkers was getting the most competent neurological treatment available. His doctors, however, "discouraged any reference to psychologists or psychiatrists, on the premise that all Checkers's problems were physical. That was our first encounter with the fact that in the world of specialists there can be a reluctance to concert efforts in the interests of the whole patient. . . . The disparity between people working in various aspects of brain dysfunction was a status we had to accept."

As he grew older, Checkers was agonizingly conscious of his own deterioration. At school he was stigmatized as a "retard." At home, though his family included him in their own activities in every possible way, he spent more and more time alone, obsessively concerned with obscure religious questions, washing his hands compulsively, suspecting poison. Worst of all, he was responding to imagined slights by violent physical assaults.

> Under the circumstances we decided to seek psychiatric counsel for Checkers – neurology notwithstanding. We did not know then of the excellent County Services available to us, and so we looked about on the private level, surprised to find that there were specialties within the specialty. Some psychiatrists seem to deal exclusively with marriage counseling, some with delinquency, some with court cases, some with menopause and impotence, some with touch-and-scold sessions [this was California], some with whatever trip or scene was perceived as groovy, and some only with those superficial problems that fitted the ego-ideal of the psychiatrist. . . . We could find no one who had even the slightest knowledge of Checker's disability and how to handle an injury-related mental difficulty as opposed to an emotionally-oriented one. After several hundreds of dollars expended in an effort with one gentleman, who informed us beneficently that what we really needed was just to "let it all hang out" . . . I asked Checkers what he thought, and he said, "Well, Dad, every time I'd try to talk to him about how I felt, he'd interrupt to tell me, 'Peace and love, man.' "

These are bitter words, but no account that censors bitterness can be true to the facts of many families' experience. We families of what we tend to think of as *really* sick people know that neurotic problems – problems we inevitably think of as mild – are painful and widespread, but it's hard to suppress our irritation when we see those problems getting careful psychiatric attention while ours are neglected. At any rate, the Whites tried again and again to find a suitable psychiatrist, but "references were hard to come by, and no one in private practice, or at the Medical Center, suggested County Services."

The psychiatrist Checkers ended up with had no more interest than the neurologists in the psychological side effects of Checkers's drugs and maintained no liaison with Checkers's family or his other doctors. Checkers was by now clinically schizophrenic. He spent hours lying in bed, laughing. He thought the clusters forming on his grapevines were a loathsome disease. Once he came at his father with a gun.

> What the psychiatrist was accomplishing I could not determine, for he had given us no prognosis, and when I called him to try to find out, I was astonished to have him accuse me in belligerent tones of pushing him. I told him that the situation was only getting worse, that the impact on the family was critical, that we could not hold out much longer, and that this was the first time I had called a doctor for help and been told it was a pushy thing to do. He ceased being belligerent but said it was too early for him to form an opinion.

When the crisis came, Checkers was beyond the help of his neurologists or his psychiatrist; the police came (called by Checkers because he thought his family was trying to kill him by watering his plants) and took him to the maximum security ward of the state hospital.

Checkers had had fourteen years of expert medical attention, including weeks of hospitalization for exploratory brain surgery. The Whites had no more money. For them, County Services seemed the end of the road. But it wasn't. At the state hospital, under round-the-clock psychiatric observation for the first time, Checkers's medication was rationalized. The psychotic symptoms subsided, and his condition stabilized. He is now neither paranoid nor violent. With the help of the County Mental Health Services, he can live at home and work in a sheltered workshop.

Checkers's problems and his family's called for medical, psychotherapeutic, educational, and rehabilitative expertise, and for close cooperation between those who possessed these skills. No skills could have solved the problem. Such problems are not solved. But the pain could have been eased, the damage lessened. His story has no simple moral — certainly not that public care is better than private care, because there are too many stories, also true, which show just the opposite. It does tell us that finding help can be very, very hard, even when you live where there are plenty of well-trained professionals to choose from. We hope this book will make it easier, but we know better than to assume it can make it easy.

CHAPTER VII

How to Consult a Mental Health Professional

YOU'VE WORKED HARD. Few who haven't tried it realize how hard. But perceptive professionals know the effort and persistence it takes to search out the information, make the telephone calls and appointments, secure transportation, and finally "survive the intake process that many psychiatric services place between the patient and the therapist at the end of the road."*

PRACTICAL ARRANGEMENTS

We are assuming that you have already investigated your relative's physical health as carefully as you can, since so often psychological symptoms – depression, for example – can be aspects of a treatable physical disease. It is a good idea to prepare a medical history before you first consult a mental health professional.†

Talking to a stranger about mental disturbance is hard in itself, and the most sympathetic professional is a stranger to start with. Nor is talking to a mental health professional like talking to other kinds of professionals you may have consulted – accountants, for instance, lawyers, or even doctors who treat primarily physical ailments. These transactions usually start with a reasonably matter-of-fact exchange of information and explanations, leading to suggestions and prescriptions and ending in a practical plan for action, probably all within the first consultation hour.

Getting things straight

It's not likely to happen this easily in a consultation about mental or

* Milton Mazer, "Two Ways of Expressing Psychiatric Disorder," *American Journal of Psychiatry,* 128 (Feb. 1972). Dr. Mazer is Director of the Martha's Vineyard Mental Health Center. Daniel Wiener's *Practical Guide to Psychotherapy* (Harper and Row, 1968) has a four-page discussion, "Handling the Intake Process," which is invaluable for anyone planning to consult a clinic, public or private.

† Include all major illnesses and operations, with dates if possible. (If it's a child, include developmental milestones – the ages he began to walk, talk, play with others, etc.) Mention any handicap, what's been done for it, and how that affected him. Note any habits or recent changes in life-style which could affect his health, like heavy use of alcohol or narcotics, or extreme or unusual diets. Make sure the doctor knows *all* medicines your relative takes, including those prescribed by another doctor and those he gets over the counter. Many drugs have effects in combination that they don't have separately. Birth-control pills, aspirin, or antihistamines may seem routine to you; they are drugs, nevertheless, and may contain substances which combine badly with psychoactive drugs. If you write it down beforehand you can be sure it all gets in, but if you'd rather talk, a checklist will help you remember what's important.

emotional problems. You arrive with your belly full of anxiety and your mind full of questions. Different practitioners have very different attitudes toward these questions, and when, how, and if they are to be answered. Some are frank and straightforward, others evasive and oracular, with all gradations in between. Professor Wiener recommends that you write down your questions in a notebook and bring it to your interviews; he's one of the first kind. (The second kind might well ask you, "Why do you feel you ought to do that?") Don't be surprised, then, or disappointed, or upset, if you discover that in the first interview, or interviews, it's the professional who gets to ask most of the questions. He'll get to your questions eventually. If he doesn't — most people would agree — something is wrong.*

How forthcoming the practitioner is in the first interviews is related to theoretical orientation and training as well as to personal style. Psychoanalytic psychotherapists, whose motto might well be "There's more in this than meets the eye," are likely to require a longer exploratory period (take longer to "get down to business") than behavior therapists or psychiatrists who specialize in somatic treatments. (See sections later in this chapter on "listening with the third ear" and "fit.")

Some professionals may seem to be giving you no response at all. Nobody's as orthodox as they used to be, but you may still come across the neutral "yeses" and "hm's" of traditional analytic technique. Don't be disconcerted; ask why you're getting so little response and see what happens. If you sense your consultant doesn't welcome a particular line of questioning, you may be right.†

Arrangements for paying

There are some questions, however, that any professional will answer immediately. If fees are important to you, you should ask about them right away. Don't be embarrassed about it. The therapist is not a priest or (yet) a friend, but a professional who bills you for services ren-

* For an in-depth discussion of what you might ask a therapist (and what might happen if you did, and why), see Professor Wiener's chapter on "The Opening Interviews."

† "A typical demeanor is used in this initial stage of psychotherapy. In strict applications the body is held immobile, and the face is set in an impassive, deadpan expression. This kind of expressive control is believed to minimize cues which may influence the patient's selection of topics and viewpoint. . . . A therapist can exercise a great deal of influence from this position. . . . Whitaker selectively attended her when she spoke about problems in the family and ignored her other comments. . . . Since the therapist is generally impassive, the few cues he does furnish may be doubly influential. . . . Selective listening steers the direction of a speaker's topic. One can act bored when he takes certain directions and interested when he takes others. . . . Thus the patient can be conditioned to operate along certain lines of behavior." Albert E. Scheflen, *Communicational Structure: Analysis of a Psychotherapy Transaction* (Bloomington, Ind.: Indiana University Press, 1973), pp. 239–244.

dered. You and he (or she) can be perfectly matter-of-fact about money.* What you or your relative can afford, after all, will determine what kind of treatment he or she gets, who gives it, where, and how long it lasts.

Just ask the therapist what the costs will be. If you're curious about the average rate for your area and feel uncomfortable asking the therapist, you can find out from a mental health center or clinic.

Ask him, too, about arrangements for payment. If there are to be regular visits, he'll probably send a monthly bill. Get straight the various ways your relative or your family has of paying it – private insurance, Blue Cross, state or government programs. (See Chapter XI, which is entirely devoted to this subject.)

Missed appointments

He'll charge for missed appointments unless there's adequate notice or a real emergency, so get clear what he thinks adequate notice is.†

Sliding scales

He probably has a sliding scale, though it's uncommon for it to slide much more than $10 below his usual rate. Says Professor Wiener:

> If you think you deserve special consideration, you had better gird yourself to ask for it right away. Once you start at a rate you cannot afford, you are both under more pressure to continue, regardless of cost, and your request may be treated as a sign of resistance to the therapist. It will be much more difficult to change the rate after the first session.[1]

How long will treatment take? (if treatment is indicated)

Often the practitioner can tell you pretty well at the outset how long the treatment will take (and thus how much it will cost), but often he can't. It's a fair question, but realize it can't always have a definite answer. Be prepared, too, to hear that no treatment is necessary, and treat it as good news, well worth the price.

Your money's worth: what services can you expect?

There are other matters you may want to get clear at the beginning. Can you call the practitioner at night in an emergency? Will he or she furnish records, test materials, diagnoses, reports of therapy and progress to your family physician? To institutions who can use them

* Fees vary according to region and reflect demand rather than supply. Psychiatrists cluster where demand is high, in and around major cities. There fees start at $40 a visit (1975), and are often much higher. In a small town in a poor area, they will be less. Short checkup visits and routine adjustment of medication should cost less than the regular fifty-minute psychotherapy hour. Some practitioners also offer shorter sessions if you can't afford the full hour. A full diagnostic workup from a psychologist runs upward from $100; it's a good thing to get from a clinic. Medical diagnostic tests are expensive, too. Usually they are given by a neurologist or other practitioner, even if the therapist you are consulting is a doctor. Their cost will be in addition to his fee.

† The committee on Ethics of the American Psychiatric Association, in its annotations to the Code of Ethics of the American Medical Association, states that "it is ethical for a psychiatrist to make a charge for a missed appointment when this falls within the terms of the specific contractual agreement with the patient," but requires that the arrangement be "explicitly established." *Psychiatric News* (July 4, 1973).

— schools, hospitals, social agencies? Promptly? Fully? Repeatedly? Will he furnish them to the patient? To you?* Will he act as interpreter to you and to others concerned with your relative, or do his functions cease with the therapy hour?

Obviously, these questions aren't important for everybody. In general, the more severe the case and the more responsibility you must assume for your relative, the more you need to get these matters clear at the outset.

Training, certification

There are other questions to which you can expect direct, factual answers. If you want to know where this practitioner trained and the major stages in his professional experience, he (or she) should be ready to tell you. If you are interested in whether she's board-certified, or what professional standards he's met, you can ask, though you may prefer to find out less directly. (If he is board-certified he certainly won't mind telling you, but if he isn't it may get the interview off on the wrong foot.) See Chapter I on qualifications.

OTHER QUESTIONS

"Where did you train?" slides naturally into "Where do you come from?" and the related questions that people ask when they're getting to know each other. You don't usually ask personal questions of a lawyer or a doctor, of course, but consulting a therapeutic professional may feel very different, especially when you've begun to talk in a way that seems intimate. You may find yourself wanting to ask questions considerably more personal than you'd expect to ask a lawyer. Some therapists will answer them, feeling that an exchange of intimacy is important to the development of the therapeutic relationship. Others won't, feeling that a degree of professional distance is essential. (See Chapter IV, Existential Therapy, The Interpersonal Approach, Nondirective Therapy, Classical Analysis, etc.) Is it important to know a practitioner's personal background? Will it make any difference whether he or she is married, divorced, Jewish, Catholic, liberal, conservative; whether he or she got their accents in Atlanta, Vienna, or Brooklyn?

Etc.

It may, if he practices the talking treatment — verbal or insight therapy. Though all mental health professionals will try to empathize with patients from different backgrounds, some very successfully,

* The Family Educational Rights and Privacy Act of 1974 guarantees the right of parents to consult *and copy* medical and psychological records contained in a child's school file. Agencies and private practitioners have traditionally been unwilling to share much information with relatives (or patients for that matter), but things are changing. If you feel you need this information, talk about it at the outset.

shared experience can make a difference.* If his orientation is primarily medical it will matter less; few people require personal information about their internist or neurologist. Similarly, though it might be interesting to know whether the behavioral technician came from the slums or the suburbs, it probably won't affect the treatment. But traditional psychotherapy is a more personal process, and such questions — and others — may legitimately enter into assessing how well the patient/client and the therapist are going to get along. This matter is so important that it will have a section to itself later on in this chapter. (See "Fit," pp. 193–194.)

If you do wonder things about the therapist which go beyond the public facts of his or her experience and training, you had better ask at the beginning what he thinks about such questions. Otherwise you may find yourself involved in a dance of which you don't know the steps. One woman, after several intimate interviews with an extremely sympathetic therapist who conducted her practice in her own home, was met at the door one day by the therapist's husband, a pleasant man in a bathrobe who seemed to have a bad cold. When she asked the therapist what he did for a living, a question which seemed natural enough, she was met with another question, "What do *you* think he does?" Yet this was a good therapist, who later explained her reasons for this rebuff, grounded in her (classical analytical) training. The important thing for you to know is that different practitioners react to questions very differently.

Theoretical orientation?

Does it matter?

You may want to ask the practitioner's orientation, especially if you're fresh from Chapter IV of this book. Only *may,* mind you: there are good reasons for not caring. You may feel that talking to anybody sympathetic and sensible will help. You may be aware that theoretical orientations differ, but that all the schools are borrowing from each other and that what experienced psychotherapists actually do with their patients differs much less. (See Chapter IV, p. 71.) You may put personal qualities before schools of thought. On the other hand, you may care very much whether treatment is based on Freudian, or Sullivanian, or Rogerian principles, whether the therapist has theoretical reasons for excluding a patient's family from his treatment, or conversely, for insisting that you be treated along with him. You may feel strongly about behavioral, or biological, therapy.

If the professional you are consulting is seeking to understand your relative's problem rather than simply to offer support and practical

* "Optimal conditions prevail when the therapist and patient belong to the same social class. All too often, psychotherapy runs into difficulties when the therapist and patient belong to different classes. In these instances, the values of the therapist are too divergent from those of the patient and communication becomes difficult between them." August B. Hollingshead and Fredrick C. Redlich, *Social Class and Mental Illness* (New York: John Wiley and Sons, Inc., 1958), pp. 344–357.

help, his theoretical orientation will have a lot to do with how he understands it, and consequently with how your relative, and probably you, come to understand it. Professor Albert Bandura of Stanford University describes a study by R. W. Heine:[2] "Clients who were treated by client-centered, Adlerian, and psychoanalytic therapists tended to account for changes in their behavior in terms of the explanations favored by their respective interviewers" — as anybody knows who has ever listened to a friend telling about his successful therapy. Bandura adds:

> Even a casual survey of interview protocols would reveal that psychotherapists of different theoretical affiliations tend to find evidence for their own preferred psychodynamic agents rather than those cited by other schools. Thus, Freudians are likely to unearth Oedipus complexes and castration anxieties, Adlerians discover inferiority feelings and compensatory power strivings, Rogerians find compelling evidence for inappropriate self-concepts, and existentialists are likely to diagnose existential crises and anxieties. It is equally true that Skinnerians, predictably, will discern defective conditions of reinforcement as important determinants of deviant behavior.* [Professor Bandura is a behaviorist.]

When you choose a psychotherapist you are choosing an influence; you may even be choosing a philosophy.

If you do ask the mental health professional about his or her orientation, however, it is important to remember the purpose of your question: to help your relative. What suits you may not suit him. However clear it seems to you that he needs to relive his childhood conflicts or modify his behavior, he may think differently. If he believes you are delivering him kicking and screaming into the hands of B. F. Skinner or Sigmund Freud, he will be an uncooperative patient, so remember who's getting the treatment.

Picking up clues

If a therapist is vague about his orientation, you can still learn a good deal about it by the way he responds to questions. If, when you ask, he asks you, "Why is it important for you to know?" you've still learned something: when he starts to explore what your questions mean he's doing what he's been trained to do as a psychodynamically

* *Principles of Behavior Modification* (New York: Holt, Rinehart and Winston, 1969), p. 9. Patients may even unconsciously suit their experience to the therapist's assumptions, as he encourages certain communications and discourages others. Dr. Sanford M. Unger tells of the different responses of patients of Freudian and Jungian therapists while using mind-altering drugs. "The patients of the [Freudians] report childhood memories while the patients of the [Jungians] have 'transcendental experiences.' In addition, for Jungian patients, the transcendental state is associated with 'spectacular' therapeutic results, while for Freudians, should such a state incidentally occur, no such spectacular consequence is observed." "Mescaline, LSD, Psilocybin and Personality Change" (originally in *Psychiatry*, 26 [1963]:111–125), in James O. Palmer and Michael Goldstein, eds., *Perspectives in Psychopathology* (New York: Oxford University Press, 1966), p. 284.

oriented psychotherapist. Questions about your psychotic relative's diagnosis can lead to a sensitive and eloquent discussion of how little labels can tell you about the suffering of an individual human being. This is a good time to ask (if you care) if the therapist leans toward an existential or radical point of view. If he explains that diagnostic labels are useless or meaningless, you can ask if he's a behavior therapist. (He'll tell you; behavior therapists are nothing if not matter-of-fact.) If he actually *does* discuss the diagnosis, he's at home with the medical model.*

Expectations

What do you – and your relative – expect from this consultation? Encouraging support? Deep exploration? Practical help? A thorough assessment of physical factors and treatment according to the medical model? Good therapists do combine approaches, but few are equally interested, or equally competent, in all these things,† so if you haven't done your asking beforehand while you were locating the practitioner, now's the time to ask or decide it doesn't matter. Types of treatment differ, and many are effective, but experts do agree that it makes a difference whether the patient's expectations and the therapist's are similar. "An area that has been shown to be consistently related to the success of psychotherapeutic process is the congruence of patient-therapist expectations."[3] Not that you always can (or should) get what you expect. But if there's a real gap between what you expect to get when you go to a mental health professional, and what he or she expects to give you (which is, of course, what he or she believes you ought to have), the helping process is going to be an uncomfortable

* "The spirit of diagnosis [is] not one of mere labeling but rather one of suggesting causation, therapeutic action, and outcome. . . . If the diagnostic term is imperfect, it must be explained to the extent of the psychiatrist's knowledge; for example, 'The schizophrenia is such that a relapse may occur within two years and the following symptoms should be watched for.' . . . Perhaps out of an unwillingness to deemphasize the uniqueness of the individual and to view him statistically, psychiatrists collect little practical data of this kind. . . . Psychiatrists in American universities . . . do not tend to think that the schizophrenia of a 19-year-old with a good premorbid personality has 'X' number of chances of recurring in five years, ten years, or never, and is subject to influence by 'Y' number of means." William S. Appleton, "The Importance of Psychiatrists' Telling Patients the Truth," *American Journal of Psychiatry,* 129 (Dec. 1972).

† "I must point out that there were many people who used electroshock and drugs, but it was unusual to find someone who relied very heavily on drugs who was really able to use other forms of treatment." David Viscott, M.D., *The Making of a Psychiatrist* (New York: Arbor House, 1972), p. 360. "I *never* prescribe drugs for my patients." Thomas Szasz, M.D., Reply to Letter to the Editor by J. W. Goppett, *American Journal of Psychiatry,* 128 (June 1972), p. 1588. Studies at Massachusetts Mental Health Center showed that psychoanalytically oriented residents learned less about drug side effects but prescribed drugs just as often. Ching Piao Chien and William S. Appleton, "The Need for Extensive Reform in Psychiatric Teaching," in *Changing Patterns in Psychiatric Care,* Theodore Rothman, ed. (Los Angeles: Rush Research Foundation; New York: Crown, 1970.)

one – unless and until you find a purpose to the consultation you can both agree on.

Setting treatment goals

Spurred by behavior therapists,* there is a lot of talk today about setting treatment goals. The purposes of treatment can vary so widely, from the self-actualization or "being-in-the-world" of Rogerian or existential therapy to the specific behavioral goals of behavior therapy, that there's no point in trying to talk about them here. What you, your relative, and the therapist think the goals are, however, may well be something you want to get straight.

Asking about diagnosis

If the situation is bad, uppermost in most people's mind is the question "What's the matter?" When you ask, "What's wrong with my wife (son, sister, father)?" of a person whose expertise you are paying for, you have a right to an answer. (Remember, the social worker can only transmit to you the diagnosis made by another professional; if you want to discuss it you should go to him. The clinical psychologist is qualified to diagnose most mental and emotional disorders, but medical diagnosis is the recognized function of the physician.) The answer the practitioner gives should include the diagnostic terms he uses in thinking about the disorder himself, plus a careful explanation of what these mean in ordinary English and what it is about your relative which causes him to apply that diagnosis and not another. If he (or she) believes that diagnostic labels are misleading in general or inapplicable here, he should say so, and tell you why. (See in Chapter III, How Useful Are Labels?)

What is the prognosis for this kind of disorder? *Is* there a prognosis? Should you look for results of treatment in days or weeks? What kind of results? What should you do until they appear? When they appear? What possible side effects (in case of drugs) should you watch for? What are the chances of relapse or recurrence? What should you worry about? What *shouldn't* you worry about?

Differential diagnosis

Families are often worried about *differential diagnosis,* especially in serious cases when they have consulted several practitioners. Differential diagnosis is the medical term for the process of distinguishing conditions which are enough alike so that doctors find them hard to tell apart. In Huntington's chorea, for example, early symptoms are poor judgment, assaultiveness, destructiveness, sexual promiscuity, vagabondism, alcoholism.[4] Differential diagnosis would be between this disease and "character disorder" or "psychopathic personality." Differential diagnosis is extremely important when it indicates the

* "The client usually has decision-making primacy in setting the goals of therapy and the therapist makes his personal value-system quite explicit." *Annual Review of Behavior Therapy,* ed. C. M. Franks and G. T. Wilson (New York: Brunner/Mazel, 1973), p. 4. See also Wiener, *op. cit.:* "What Makes Therapy Progress?" "Defining Progress," "Judging Results."

choice of treatment, as in distinguishing manic-depressive psychosis from schizophrenia, or schizophrenia from conditions, like temporal lobe epilepsy, which may have similar symptoms.

Difficulties of communication

Traditionally, doctors are expected to provide diagnosis when they can. What's expected, however, doesn't always happen. Medical training, unfortunately, doesn't necessarily confer the ability to give clear and usable explanations.* The diagnosis of Robin White's eight-year-old son was given in a single word.

> We were given a number to call. It was in a phone booth that we finally received the pronouncement; epilepsy. Just that. Nothing more. The specialist was satisfied with clinical accuracy. He might just as well have told us that Checkers was dead, so shattering was the effect of that word. We had no idea of what to do, where to go, what was in store for us.[5]

Less clinically exact, but as painful and even more frustrating, was the answer given to another parent who got up her courage to ask her nine-year-old son's psychiatrist, "What is wrong with my child?" "Mrs. Smith," he answered, "when you know what is wrong with your son, he will be well." Trained, skilled professionals can do better than this. If they don't, take your questions elsewhere.

Your doctor will certainly tell you all he thinks you need to know. But reflect that he's a very busy man, and that many doctors are better at treating patients than at communicating. The art of explanation is so special that one doctor even gives it the name of therapy – "Explanatory Therapy."

"Explanatory therapy"

> Although patients do not always grasp every technical detail, their fears are lessened by the knowledge that explanations *do* exist. Patients want to hear such explanations, because these indicate that the illness is not an enigma, peculiar to them alone; rather, that it can be dealt with and cleared up just as any other illness. Precise explanations, then, not only provide information but restore confidence.[6]

Of course this goes for families as well as for patients: our confidence in and understanding of the treatment is a strong support for our relatives.

Reading

The first thing Robin White did, of course, was to find out all he could of what the doctor hadn't told him. (Mrs. Smith would have liked to, but she had nowhere to begin.) White had to start with the encyclopedia and the dictionary and find his own way to other sources; today he knows more about epilepsy than most physicians. The first

* See the frighteningly uncommunicative transcript of an exchange between a clinic doctor and the mother of a child with a heart murmur in Barbara A. Kersch and Vida Francis Negreto, "Doctor-Patient Communication," *Scientific American*, 227 (Aug. 1972).

thing most Americans have been educated to do when faced with a problem is to look for a book on the subject, or several.

Unfortunately many professionals distrust this natural reaction; few of them are much help in locating books or articles that might supplement the explanations they are prepared to give, and often they actively discourage reading. One young psychiatrist says that he'd probably try to find out why the patient wanted to read about the problem, why it was important to him. Himself, he thinks that abstract discussions and diagnostic terms intrude into the personal encounter between two people, and hinder the establishment of the therapeutic alliance. The expert often fears the family will misunderstand or misuse what they read, or become confused when they discover the variety of ways of explaining their relative's disorder. More simply still, professionals often don't know what books or articles to suggest, which seems surprising but is natural enough if they don't consider this part of their function. (In these cases you can probably get more information from the organizations concerned with particular disorders, most of which publish reading lists. See Appendix B.)

Feel your way at first and don't jump to conclusions. Plenty of relatives, like the Whites, have become experts themselves. If you're at all handy at ferreting out references, you may well be able to find out more than the doctor knows about a particular disorder, especially if it's an uncommon one and you've lived with it a long time. What's hard to know (unless you're a doctor yourself) * is how the information and ideas you come up with fit into the total picture of what is known, how reliable their sources are, how relevant they are to this particular case. A first-class professional should be able to give you this perspective. Professionals today are telling each other to respect the reading relative:

> We need to be aware that these days consumers read: they read professional literature as assiduously or more assiduously than most of us do ourselves. They are well informed. We may keep them out of professional conferences (some people say they cannot speak freely about mental retardation if parents are present). But we can't keep them out of our journals.[7]

Be aware, though, that the desire to learn about a disorder is sometimes seen as "intellectualizing," a word that professionals often seem

* As of course you may be. Two of the most interesting (and angriest) accounts by parents of mentally ill children were written by doctors; Jacques May's *A Physician Looks at Psychiatry* (New York: John Day, 1950) and John Kyzar's "The Two Camps in Child Psychiatry: A Report from a Psychiatrist Father of an Autistic and Retarded Child," *American Journal of Psychiatry,* 125 (July 1968). Doctors' families don't seem to fare a whole lot better than the rest of us.

to use for "thinking," especially when you and not they are doing it. (The rules of the therapeutic encounter now and then seem to be just the opposite of the real world: you can *feel* as freely as you like, it's *thinking* that will get you into trouble.) Go slowly and hopefully; how he responds to a well-informed and thoughtful client is a real test of a professional.

The professional you consult has seen many more irrational relatives and malfunctioning families than stable ones. (The better a family is managing, the less often it comes to professional attention.) We would all like to be treated as if our intelligence and common sense could be taken for granted. In the real world, that's not likely to happen. The professional's first allegiance is to his patient. The professional's trust is something that relatives have to earn.

Earning a professional's trust

How can you earn it, then? You don't do it as you might elsewhere, by sounding knowledgeable, even if you are. Mental health professionals are more interested in who you are than in what you know. If you establish that you're open, reasonable, and not too full of yourself, they'll be more ready to accept you on their turf. Avoid fancy psychiatric terms, at least at first, even if you've read them in this book. It's surprising how well you can make out in plain English. Though psychiatric professionals use those words continually, they don't seem to like them nearly as well when they hear them from us. You may be put down severely for using words a professional thinks too heavy for you, like "autistic" or "schizophrenic," even when you're merely repeating another professional's diagnosis. Psychological interpretations may be even less welcome. It's easy to get lost in symbols and abstractions (professionals do it all the time), and an idea that seems insightful when it comes from a professional may seem too clever by half if it comes from you.*

Take it easy while you're trying to establish communication: you don't want to get on the receiving end of their vocabulary. "Obsessive-compulsive character structure" is a handy mouthful to describe the kind of relative who's read a lot and is insistent in his questions; "hostile," "defensive," and "resistant" are labels you can do without. But if he does so label you, consider honestly whether he may be right, even when that's unpleasant. You *may* be intellectualizing, using your intelligence to block off realization of important human realities about you and your relative that the therapist can lead you to see if you only let him. You may be substituting thinking for the daily doing and

Are *you intellectualizing?*

* "In mental hospitals we find the engaging phenomenon of the staff using stereotyped psychiatric terminology in talking to each other or to patients but chiding patients for being 'intellectualistic' and for avoiding the issues when they use this language too." Erving Goffman, *Asylums: Essays on the Social Situation of Mental Patients and Other Inmates* (Garden City, N.Y.: Doubleday Anchor Books, 1961), p. 97.

sympathetic feeling that is needed. Though understanding helps, your big question isn't "What am I to understand?" but "What am I to do with the human reality I live with?" Part of that human reality may be that your relationship to your relative needs to be different from what it's been, in ways you need somebody else's help to see. It's easy to see how true that can be if you look at somebody else's family.

But don't sell yourself short. In most situations it helps to use your head, ask questions, inform yourself, try out ideas and methods. Don't be too ready to accept that this situation is different. What sociologists call "Aesculapian authority" is an ancient force; it goes back at least as far as the Greek god of medicine. Doctors are used to it, and all things considered, it's cured a lot more people than it's killed, especially in the past hundred years. The success of placebo treatments tells us that Aesculapian authority can be therapeutic in itself, and doctors are right to hang onto it.

Or thinking the best you know how to?

But consider also that in the light of modern knowledge the 2,500-year history of medicine is a record of placebo treatments over centuries when doctors knew little or nothing of what caused illness or how to cure it. In the field of knowledge that concerns you and your relative, doctors and psychologists still don't know a great deal, though they are learning more all the time. There's plenty of room for us to learn from each other.

What you need is attention and respect, that respect that disadvantaged groups like blacks and poor people and mental patients and families of mental patients like so much better than sympathy. It's much harder to give. Will you get it? Let's hope. Be humble and receptive when you report your observations, when you ask for practical suggestions, when you talk about how you and your relative live together and what goes badly and what goes well. It's realistic, and it's good strategy. You're in no position to one-up the professional; don't try to. But you yourself have a right to be suspicious of a professional who is "defensive" or "hostile" or "resistant." Something's the matter if he puts you down. You want people sure enough of their own expertise so that they can afford to be receptive to ideas which come from patients — (remember, they think of you as a patient out of pure habit). You have a right to ask about new treatments, about the controversies in psychiatry, about new theories, about the different ways of explaining your relative's problems and yours. You have the right to questions, even to interpretations. (How can you avoid thinking about what you observe?) There's little certainty in psychiatry. Good therapists don't need to deny this, though they'll rightly fight you if they think you're putting an intellectual smoke screen between yourself and what you need to realize.

Respectful attention not sympathy

Don't forget to be appreciative; if they're helping you, let them know it. Professionals need positive reinforcement just like the rest of us. It is written, you'll catch more flies with honey than with vinegar.

CONFIDENTIALITY

You and your relative will be providing the mental health professional with a lot of information. Can you be sure it will be kept confidential?*

Therapist-patient privilege

Not entirely. You cannot assume that the confidentiality of conversations with a psychotherapist is protected by law, as it is with priests and lawyers. The common law of most, if not all, states does contain a "privilege," which protects communications between physicians (thus, psychiatrists) and their patients from disclosure unless the patient knowingly and explicitly waives the privilege. But even this may have exceptions.† An increasing number of states (though still not many) have laws guaranteeing such a privileged status to communications with a "psychotherapist." Note, however, that even then the legislature's definition of who is a psychotherapist will almost surely be less broad than the one used in this book. If you have reason to worry about this, ask the practitioner. He should know, but if he doesn't, consult the law library at your county courthouse, or call the state attorney general's office.

Just plain confidentiality

For most families, however, the possibility that a court will subpoena their therapist need not loom large. More important is the care with which confidentiality is maintained in ordinary circumstances.

Private practice

Your privacy is certainly greater with a private practitioner, since only he and his secretary have access to his records. This security is one of the things you buy when you pay his fee. Some doctors may be sloppy about confidentiality, as Dr. Jonas Rappaport, Chief Medical Officer of the Supreme Bench of Baltimore, points out. "There's too

* For an eye-opening conversation about the limits of confidentiality, see "Silence Is Golden — or Is It?," *MH,* 56 (Winter 1972), a discussion between Dr. Harvey Ruben, psychiatric consultant to the Surgeon General of the U.S. Army; Dr. Jonas Rappaport, Chief Medical Officer of the Supreme Bench of Baltimore; Dr. Thomas Szasz; and Richard Allen, Director of the George Washington University Institute of Law, Psychiatry, and Criminology.

† For example, confidentiality is often not protected when the patient sues for damages due to mental and emotional stress, since he himself has placed his mental and emotional condition at issue. In California, one doctor risked jail by refusing to testify in an accident case involving a patient. *Psychiatric News* (March 7, 1973). Therapists may also be called upon to testify in child custody cases (see Chapter X, p. 296).

much talk at cocktail parties, at the golf course, in the locker room. Even to other patients there's too much carelessness about what is left in the typewriter when the secretary goes out of the room, or what files are left on a person's desk."[8] But they try to be careful.

and public settings

So do mental health centers and clinics, as far as that goes. That's why they will release nothing to schools or other agencies (even other doctors) without your permission. But privacy is inevitably diluted when several people consult on a case (in other respects a great advantage), when a case is used for teaching purposes, when records are available to many people within the agency. There is also the threat to privacy posed by state and federal computerized data banks. When governments pay for treatment programs, in whole or in part, they must be interested in gathering statistics on types of disorder and treatment, treatment outcomes, and effectiveness in relation to cost — statistics which, as we have seen, have been largely lacking. So far so good; statistical information poses no threat to anyone's privacy. But some states want to simplify their record-keeping by feeding into their computers not only information on an individual's diagnosis and treatment, but coded data which would make the information retrievable. It wouldn't matter that his name was not recorded; it could always be found out. An individual's record of depression, epilepsy, addiction, "character disorder," recorded in state and federal data systems, could follow him for the rest of his life.

Data banks?

It's a terrifying possibility. Watch for it, ask about it, protest against it. But don't worry about it — yet.

Confidentiality and relatives: should it ever be breached?

All mental health practitioners are trained to protect a patient's privacy as much as possible. In many cases, this will mean that he or she will protect it against *you*. You can probably think of a lot of situations in which you believe this shouldn't happen; if you are honest and put yourself in your relative's position, you can probably think of a lot in which it should. Therapists vary a great deal on this. Dr. Szasz, for example, would protect a patient's communications absolutely.

> Mr. or Mrs. Jones goes to the psychiatrist . . . and confides to the psychiatrist — in a sense, incriminates himself. I think a great deal of psychotherapy is self-incrimination. And then, the next thing that happens is that the psychiatrist talks to this patient's husband or wife, or daughter, and informs these people that the patient is very depressed and ought to be hospitalized, and then they take steps to hospitalize the person against his will.[9]

Dr. Szasz thinks the doctor should not paternalistically impose his own judgment of the situation, and certainly not the judgment of the relatives, but act as a "hired hand." He has a contract (implied, not written, of course) with his patient and no one else: to help him, "and not to do anything to him the patient doesn't want done," even if it involves concealing a threat to himself or others.

Few physicians would go that far. But most therapists would insist that the traditional therapeutic alliance of psychotherapy can only be possible when the patient feels sure that his confidences will not be communicated without his consent, even – perhaps especially – to close family members. This is as true of adolescents as of adults. "For therapy to have promise of success, the adolescent must see the therapist as a helping person rather than simply as an agent used by the parents to lever him into line."[10] A large proportion of people seeking psychotherapy *are* late adolescents or young adults who are struggling with the challenge of separating themselves from their families and establishing independent lives. Often they don't even want their parents to know they are getting treatment – although they can't very well conceal this if the parents are paying the bill. In general, you should respect your son's or daughter's wish for privacy – unless you feel his or her judgment is so impaired that you have to intervene. (The situation may be different for younger children. See Chapter XII.)

Confidentiality in student health services

Many students get psychotherapy from the student health services of their college or university, or from private practitioners recommended by the college. Mostly the disturbance that brings them in is mild or temporary and therapy is brief. Occasionally, however, there's the awful surprise – the sudden notification that your son or daughter has had to be hospitalized. It may come from a hospital doctor, even from the police. You may think that you should have been warned beforehand, that there must have been signs of this, that the therapist should have told you. Few therapists agree. You should realize that if you expect a therapist to discuss a student's psychological state with you before the situation has become critical, you will almost certainly be disappointed.*

is very carefully maintained.

Problems of confidentiality

Should absolute confidentiality be maintained when your relative – adolescent or adult – is clearly seriously disturbed? Suicidal? Threatening violence? It's a sticky problem. (How clear is "clearly"? How serious are the threats?) Many therapists would say that all bets are off and everyone had better get involved. Terrible things have happened because of what Dr. Joseph Brenner (Associate Psychiatrist in Chief at MIT's Psychiatric Service) calls "the awful silence of noncommunica-

* Student health services are not always so close-mouthed with other institutions; there have been instances where students have complained that their way into professional schools was barred by information which could only have come from student health records. Under the Family Educational Rights and Privacy Act of 1974 students may inspect their own files and remove such data.

tion between therapist and family."* But others would maintain that no one should force a patient to share his pain or anger against his will, whatever the risks. If your relative is seriously disturbed maybe you should ask your consultant what he thinks about this.

Confidentiality in newer kinds of therapy: Group and family therapy

The traditional model of individual psychotherapy, based on the ancient, confidential doctor-patient relationship, obviously undergoes changes when it is stretched to include group and family therapy. In these therapies you should be aware before you begin that complete privacy cannot be maintained.

Behavior therapy

In another direction, behavior therapy, confidentiality is less central. Behavior therapists do not set out to explore their patients' secret places: they have less to keep quiet about. Behavioral methods deal with behaviors rather than feelings and thoughts, and problem behaviors are usually no longer private. If you or your relative consults a behavior therapist you should expect a frank discussion with whatever family members and others are involved in the problem behaviors. In group, family, and behavior therapy the therapist is still expected to maintain the usual level of confidentiality in relation to the community in general.

Therapists' attitudes vary, as in everything else.

The change from an individual model of therapy is affecting the attitude of some traditional therapists. Dr. Herbert Lazarus, author of a readable book, *How to Get Your Money's Worth out of Psychiatry,* is neither a family nor a behavioral therapist, but he considers that "to exclude the patient's family from the treatment, as if the patient could be isolated from his family in any real sense," is one of the traditions of psychoanalysis which "has outlived its usefulness."[11] Dr. Lazarus writes that a psychiatrist should not only "respond properly to the questions of key relatives," but goes even farther:

> Patients . . . in some cases, lie so compulsively that the psychiatrist will never be able to get a straight story without outside assistance. . . . If you are a friend or relative who is vitally concerned about the patient's welfare, feel free to call the therapist to discuss either the background of the patient's illness or his current functioning. If the illness is a severe one, prepsychotic or psychotic, you should not hesitate to ask the psychiatrist about any problems affecting your relationship. . . . The patient usually benefits from the discussion.[12]

Many psychiatrists, as Dr. Lazarus remarks, "will shrink from the

* For an account of what can happen, see *In a Darkness,* the book James Wechsler wrote with his wife and daughter about his son Michael's years of therapy and final suicide. Dr. Brenner's words are taken from his review (*Saturday Review,* July 1, 1972) of this restrained and moving record, by one of our foremost journalists, of the "absurd, abysmal failures of communication that marred our relationships with most of the therapists we encountered" (New York: W. W. Norton and Co., 1972, p. 159).

open invitation I have extended to all concerned friends and relatives." Indeed they will, as an open invitation to the nosy. In this, as in much else, you can only make yourself aware of how much therapists differ. If you feel strongly that you must be responsible for your relative's well-being (if he or she is an adult) or development (if a child), be sure to ask what your consultant thinks about these matters. Patients may also want to inform themselves about their therapist's practice. More will be said about the range of family participation in Chapter VIII, "In the Family: Day by Day," and in Chapter XII, on children.

HOW TO TALK TO A PRO

How to talk

So far, we've been concerned with getting things straight – asking the specific questions that allow you to find out, as far as possible, where you, your relative, and the therapist stand and where you may be going. But there are many questions that aren't specific, that may not yet be definite enough in your mind so that you know what to ask or how to ask it. For you these may be more important than any of the straightforward ones.

on the surface – and under it

You are entitled to expect help from the therapist here. This is what his skill and experience is for – helping people to bring to words what they need to say. "Most often," says one analyst, "the framing of a proper question means helping the relative to ask what he really wants to know. For example, parents of suicide attempts can rarely ask any question besides 'what did I do wrong?' "

This is why your questions often lead to more questions, rather than to straightforward answers. It looks like evasion, and in anybody else it would be. Here, however, it may be part of his technique for making sure that the things that are really bothering you aren't displaced by questions he suspects are superficial. Or it may be that he is addressing himself to other issues that his experience tells him are probably significant, though unspoken. He has been trained to "listen with the third ear," to pick up the emotions that lie beneath words. He has learned ways of encouraging you to talk. A textbook for psychiatric nurses summarizes the most common techniques: "such phrases as 'yes,' 'I see,' 'uh-huh,' or . . . nodding the head and leaning forward. If these techniques are not useful . . . we suggest repeating the last word of the patient's statement or saying: 'I'd like to hear more about that' or 'and then what happened?' "[13]

Listening with the third ear

The therapist's own questions may be direct or indirect. His answers to your questions may be straightforward, or he may try to explore with you what those questions mean for you. Sometimes your idea of a question and his are so different that misunderstanding and irritation arise. "To attempt to treat all dialogue as containing significant psychological messages is not being therapeutic,"[14] warns the nurses' textbook just quoted. If you feel that in diving beneath the surface he's left your real concerns behind, let him know that. You'll understand each other better, and understanding is part of your mutual goal.

Try not to be hypersensitive. It is his business to feel you out—including some sore places. If he asks you, for example, about your relations with your father when the problem that has brought you in concerns your son, do not at once assume the questions are irrelevant. Assume that you've come to a psychoanalytic psychotherapist, and that his major effort during the diagnostic interviews will be directed at understanding the way you—or your relative, or both of you—dealt with the important people in your life, and how you deal with them now. He's trying to predict how the relationship with the therapist will develop, since in verbal, insight therapy the relationship is the primary tool.* The therapist has been trained to look for subtle parallels, hidden meanings.

Are they there? Often. Can you depend upon the person you're consulting to recognize it when they aren't? Unfortunately, not always. Robert Coles, one of the most sensitive psychiatrists alive, appeals to his colleagues in the mental health professions to think about the problem:

> Why is it that so many of us, who are so concerned about the "true feelings" of others . . . simply cannot accept at face value some of the things we hear? And why is it so hard for us to believe that sometimes people don't say things, or believe things, simply because they don't—and not because they have some "problem" or are "defensive" about this or that? . . . Do we get very far by turning every coin over and saying that "really" this is that, and that what seems to be one thing is "secretly" or "deep down" something else?[15]

If mental health professionals would post these words underneath their diplomas, they'd encounter less "resistance" and "hostility" than they do, and more gratitude.

Evasions?

So it can be hard to tell the difference between an evasion and an effective interviewing technique. If you think he is evading your questions, better come right out and say so. He may be, for good reasons or bad. And even if he isn't, you'll be irritated and resentful (maybe even "hostile") if you think he is, and that had better be talked about.

Talk about it.

Consider this: however well trained he is, however sensitive, how-

* In general, people who have had the experience of solid, dependable relationships in childhood tend to use psychotherapy well no matter what the severity of their present symptoms.

Don't expect the therapist to be a mind reader.

ever sympathetic, he cannot read your mind. He may make his guesses from your tone of voice or your silence, but he can't really know what you're thinking unless you tell him.

So if you think he's evading a question about prognosis (the future course of a disorder) because he thinks you can't stand the truth, don't take his cue. Don't swallow down the question, drop your eyes (even if he's dropped his), and pass on to something else. *Ask* him if he thinks you can't stand it. Maybe he does think so; your question may make him change his mind, or help you talk about what goes into standing things. Maybe he doesn't, but is vague because he simply doesn't know the answer and feels that to say so will seem threatening to you. There *are* people who want to believe that a professional knows everything – especially the kind of professional you call "Doctor." Your question should allow him to tell you he doesn't know. That may not be what you paid to hear. But families who have consulted many experts know this: the more respected the expert, the wider and deeper his experience, the more readily he can say the simple words "I don't know." If you are wise you will respect him even more because he doesn't pretend to knowledge he hasn't got, in this field which is still so full of uncertainties. With luck and goodwill, you and he and your relative may even pool your ignorance and your knowledge and work toward understanding and improvement that none of you could make without the others' help.

Don't be too polite

Say what's on your mind. It sounds easy, but most of us don't like to say unpleasant things, and most people have been trained to be polite, especially to people who are providing them a service. But a mental health professional deals in feelings. She or he therefore wants and expects you to show your feelings, for they are an important part of the total situation. The therapist won't mind if you get angry – or weepy. She's more likely to wonder why you don't. Politeness, control, reserve, the characteristics of ordinary intercourse with people you don't know very well, can work against the purposes of the consultation.

if you can help it.

If this is hard for you, you might try letting the professional know it. As Dr. Coles has pointed out, there are people whose personal style is likely to be at war with that of many helping professionals. Coles describes a social worker, dedicated to helping the proud, reserved people who have come from the southern mountains to live in northern cities. They don't make it easy for her to help them. "She finds herself uncomfortable with people who prefer to keep silent, watch rather than pour out ideas and feelings." She'd rather have them demonstrate sadness and dependence; can they really be as proud and self-sufficient as they seem? "They are quite inhibited by their culture," she told Coles, "so they don't feel free to express their resentments."

Sometimes she'd like to "consign all the Appalachian families I know in this city to one big group therapy meeting." "Those proud and set faces" seem hostile and resentful. But then she wonders "if it's not *me* who's hostile and resentful, because the 'poor' don't come running to me for everything they can get."*

How does this affect you? Only in that you may find you'll have better luck if you are open rather than reserved, emotional rather than intellectual. How many of us have tried to obtain or communicate important facts only to be told severely that what's at issue isn't facts but how we feel about them? How many of us have choked down our anger, not realizing that the person talking to us is waiting for us to "transfer" our anger from others, as he thinks, to him, and to interpret it as resistance if we don't? Of course it may be resistance in that specialized psychoanalytic sense – personal, irrational, unconscious. But it may also be the deep-seated social resistance of those who have been trained from childhood *not* to transfer their anger onto others. Some social and ethnic groups encourage the ready expression of emotion; others don't. There's nothing to show that one of these kinds of social habit is healthier than the other or leads to a more satisfying or constructive life, though expressing your emotions may make you feel better.

If reserve is natural to you, so be it.

It's ironic, but the better you feel about yourself the more trouble you may have. If you feel shaky and inadequate you'll be glad to find somebody to help you bring out what's on your mind. But what if beneath your distress and worry you feel much as usual, like a responsible and competent person who's shouldering a heavy burden and could use some expert assistance? It is very threatening to be treated as weak when you feel strong, groping and incompetent when you feel independent, uninformed when you know a lot – when you feel healthy, to be treated as if you were sick. When this happens it is destructive, and it happens more often than it ought to.

Can you accept the role of a patient?

Some gifted individuals can be depended on always to relate to people as people. But for many professionals there's a difference between the way they treat patients and the way they treat colleagues, healthy people, people they respect for their capabilities. Since most of the people who come to consult them *are* patients, professionals get used to this relationship. With some irony, two psychiatrists and a psychologist describe the "syndrome of psychiatric culture-shock" among psychiatrists working with community leaders on common tasks. Psychiatrists, they report, have difficulty in relating to others in situations where the others perceive themselves as "well," "people who

If you're a competent character in good shape?

* *The South Goes North,* pp. 385–394. Though most families of the mentally ill are neither Appalachians, migrants, nor blacks, they will find that again and again Dr. Coles speaks to their condition.

are peers and not patients," and this brings on "increasing alienation" in these others, "who do not see themselves as exhibiting 'pathology.' "[16] These words describe many families very well.* It can happen anywhere. In Australia, the mother of a severely ill child expresses her feelings in a letter to professionals:

> You're dealing with a woman who's managing despite enormous pressure to adapt herself and her methods to a way of life most people refuse to ever think about. She's learned where lie her strengths and weaknesses and what she must do to maintain sanity and stability. This knowledge is hard won and she's proud of it.[17]

If an interview leaves you feeling less adequate than when you went into it, there's something wrong. When others fail to recognize your strength it makes you question it yourself, and that's something you can ill afford. If you're *not* in pieces, if you *are* functioning, let the professional know that your competence is as important a part of the picture as your need.

If you're miserable yourself?

But what if you *are* doing wrong, sense it, but can't change: will the professional give you the therapy, the advice, the support you need so badly? A mother writes:

> Dr. Y. saw our 9-year-old daughter once a week; my husband and me, separately, every other month. It was a good and strengthening experience. Dr. Y. is a well-read, courteous, sunny person, I guess about ten years younger than I, and we talked like affectionate cousins — and still do when we meet, since now he is a social friend. It is difficult for me to emote; I felt no pressure to do so; and yet, eventually, I told him about problems so "severe" and issues so "shameful" that I had never been able to say a word about them to anyone else. The very telling was a comfort; and in perspective these matters came to seem quite manageable. (The way to make a mountain out of a molehill is sometimes to repress it!) More than this: admiring his kindly calm and good sense, I learned to emulate them, at least enough to lighten and sweeten the air in our house — for I am that psychiatric cliché, impatient, proud and bossy, a "dominant mother." Not such a bad thing to be, if you know how — and Dr. Y's influence made me discover how. Seven years later our daughter is doing fine, and as a family we are happier than almost any people I know. Neither my husband nor I had any sense, at the time, of "being treated"; what Dr. Y *did,* we can't say. We can only be grateful.

This couple, who had agreed to consultation at long intervals as part of their child's therapy, seem to have found their own therapy without having sought it. What if you do seek it for yourself?

*** Therapists who use the family interaction explanation of mental illness would say they *should* see themselves as exhibiting pathology, but that's another story.**

HELP FOR YOURSELF?

It may seem natural to you to go to your relative's therapist or counselor: you know where he's to be found; he or she already knows the situation and there won't be so much spadework necessary. Dr. Leonard Cammer, in his book *Up from Depression,* considers it natural for the family to consult the patient's psychiatrist. Many other professionals disagree; for a long time it was out of the question for an analytic psychiatrist to treat members of the same family. It's one of the many things you'll have to ask.

Will your relative's therapist treat you?

Recognize your own distress. Or your feelings of guilt. *If you have them.* They are so common (and so natural) that it's easy to conclude that you do. But it can be terribly destructive when authoritative professionals treat you for guilt or neurotic needs merely because they expect to find them, no matter how sympathetic they are. An experienced social worker tells it like it oughtn't to be:

And for what?

> A young nurse who had done group therapy and learned worse than nothing answered the telephone when a mother was wanting to enquire how her son was in a children's psychiatric unit. The mother expressed much anxiety about his health and his safety. The young nurse, who never met the mother but had heard the "case" discussed in the unit, said, "You really hate your son. You wish he was dead."
>
> A welfare officer visited the elderly mother of a retarded man who had episodic psychiatric illness. The old lady had sacrificed her life to keep her son at home whenever it was possible. They lived a very isolated existence. The welfare officer said, "You really resent Bill and you feel very guilty about it." The old lady was conscious of no guilt whatsoever. She felt that anyone who examined the sacrifices she had made would have to conclude that she was totally devoted. She thought the welfare officer was insane and wouldn't let her visit her again.*

The ability of the mental health professionals you consult to perceive your real needs will determine whether their psychotherapeutic expertise is something for which you'll be eternally grateful, or a time-consuming and upsetting distraction.†

* Millie Mills, "You in Partnership with Your Client," *Breakthrough,* Newsletter of the Autistic Children's Society of New South Wales (Oct./Nov./Dec. 1973). You may take such comfort as you can from the fact that these incidents happened some thousands of miles from you, in Australia.

† "Weekly sessions with a trained, skilled, and experienced person should be a rich opportunity for parents to get the kind of advice, reassurance, and support they want and need so badly. Too often the social worker seems to use these sessions as a breeding ground for the guilt and uncertainty that he should be helping the parent to overcome. Almost every parent I have ever discussed this with has felt, as I do, that these loosely structured, pseudo-psychoanalytical, non-practical sessions have been at best, a waste of time and, at worst, an encouragement of self-pity and paralyzing guilt." Molly Finn, "The Unhelpful Social Worker," *Mental Hygiene,* 51 (April 1967).

IF THINGS ARE GOING BADLY: SHOULD YOU CHANGE AND HOW?

It can happen. Sometimes you try your best, your consultant tries his best, and it just doesn't seem to be working. What can you do?

Let's assume your child is seeing a psychiatrist and you're unhappy with the treatment. The boy seems disturbed and upset after each treatment session, or a year has gone by and all you can find out is that the two of them are still silently playing chess.* Your first step: call and ask to see the therapist.

If he refuses to see you *and won't explain why,* terminate treatment with no regrets.

If he refuses to see you, explaining that he can't jeopardize his relationship with the patient, ask him: "If you can't talk to me about it, can somebody else?" Some psychiatrists employ social workers for this purpose. If he doesn't, or if he has talked with you, and you're still uneasy: "Can you recommend someone else with whom I can have a consultation?" That's courteous and tactful. But he should be ready to consult with any doctor you request.

Getting a second opinion

There is no need to feel embarrassed about this. *No reputable physician will refuse such a request.* Consultation at any time is a traditional part of medical practice, and you should be suspicious of any physician who balks at it.

He may balk all the same. Therapists are human. Professor Wiener says, "It is almost always difficult for a therapist to accept failure, especially when you want to consult someone else. He will often think he has done as well or better than anyone else could do, and it will be hard for him not to blame you." Wiener recommends asking a therapist about his attitude toward consultation and change in the first interview, and asking for a trial period if you're considering a long course of therapy. He cites a psychotherapist who told a patient that quitting him would be like quitting an antibiotic when he was dying of an infection.[18] That's a good example of the kind of therapist you might want to change.

How to change practitioners

Because you can always take your problem elsewhere. If you're consulting privately you can change doctors (whether they're M.D.'s or Ph.D.'s); you can change social workers. Even in mental health centers or clinics there's still some leeway. (See Chapter VI.) The only time you can't change – or consult – is if there's nobody to consult with, or change to.

If you're in an area where there is no alternative therapist, and are

* See Louise Wilson, *This Stranger, My Son: A Mother's Story* (New York: Putnam, 1967).

deeply dissatisfied, *discontinue therapy*. No therapy is better than bad therapy. It is estimated that not until the 1920's did a patient consulting a physician for a physical illness have more than a 50-50 chance of benefiting. The treatment of mental illness is as uncertain now as the treatment of physical illness was then. And as in conventional medicine, too much treatment can be as destructive as too little.

No therapy is better than bad therapy.

Special circumstances

Like the rest of us, therapists go on vacations, get sick, suffer breakdowns and family catastrophes, lose their grip, get old, die. If your relative is involved in intensive psychotherapy, he may form a deep tie or "transference" and really suffer when his therapy is interrupted, even when he knows it is unavoidable. For this reason a responsible psychotherapist makes provision for eventualities he can foresee. Even in cases of sudden death, colleagues often stand ready to help patients in their distress. If you wish, you should ask how a therapist arranges to cover his appointments when he can't meet them. If you or your relative suspects a real personality change (unusual, but it can happen), this is a time to ask him to recommend someone to consult with. A tactful colleague can find a way to allow him to withdraw without loss of face.

When you can't change

Is it really this easy? Not always. Sometimes it's impossible, as anguished families can testify. These procedures work well enough when your relative is a child, or an adult who depends on your judgment or is in general agreement with your assessment of the treatment. Otherwise – if your relative is of age, he is legally able to choose his own treatment, however irrational, misguided, or irresponsible you think him. If you cannot persuade him, you cannot force him to change his doctor, even when you have good reason to believe the doctor is incompetent and the treatment dangerous, even if you feel it coming between you and your relative, even when other doctors confirm your fears. The *New York Times* in 1973 reported the case of a successful entertainer who during twenty years of treatment from Dr. J., a New York psychiatrist well known for treating celebrities with amphetamines, deteriorated psychologically to the point where he was living in a charity dormitory and sometimes sleeping in doorways. His brothers, well-to-do and influential people, did everything they could. It turned out to be nothing. Dr. J. himself refused all contact with them. Other physicians, though dubious about the treatment, were unable to persuade the patient to consider any other doctor. The brothers consulted lawyers, the state medical society, even the attorney general's office. "They kept asking me, 'Will your brother testify against Dr. J?' The answer was clearly, 'No.' " The patient himself insisted that Dr. J. "saved my life," was "more than a friend," "I believe in him."[19]

Sometimes there's no way out. In the last analysis, the mind, emotions, and body of an adult are his own. As long as he is not legally committed (see Chapter X, The Law), treatment decisions require his concurrence. If he's young and you're still paying for his treatment, you can, of course, end it by notifying the practitioner you're not paying the bill. Will this make things worse or better? Will he thank you later? Or fix on it as one more bitter grievance? Reflections on the individual's freedom, or blanket reassurances about professional ethics and medical tradition, can only seem impertinent to families who must stand as "horrified but inert spectators watching someone . . . loved falter blindly toward the edge of a cliff."[20]

Reasons for changing: emotional distress, deterioration, unmet needs,

Let's leave this subject; it hurts too much. Assume you *can* change the practitioner. When *should* you?* When your relative is consistently disturbed after therapy. When he seems to you, *and to other reliable observers,* to be getting worse, not better. When after careful thought you're convinced he isn't getting what he needs – or that the total situation isn't being properly understood. People need different things at different times for different problems – sympathetic understanding and support, deep exploration, scrupulous diagnosis, medical treatment, useful referrals, practical training, advice. When you need one good thing, another good thing is no substitute.

unethical sexual conduct,

A specific warning:

You've heard, with one ear, that psychotherapy requires a certain objectivity on the part of the therapist; with the other, you've heard with surprise that some therapists, even qualified ones, have sexual relations with patients. Once virtually unheard of, this is happening more often, occasionally out of genuine conviction (the logical extension of a belief in love and involvement), often for less lofty reasons.[21] You should be aware of the American Psychiatric Association's position, binding upon its members. It notes "the unique position of power afforded . . . by the psychotherapeutic situation" and warns the psychiatrist not to use it "to influence the patient in any way not directly relevant to the treatment goals." Sexual activity with a patient is unethical, it declares flatly. Most other professionals would agree. If you suspect your son's or daughter's therapist wouldn't and are worried about what's going on, most therapists would say you should intervene. Professional organizations will give you support.†

* For an extensive and very useful discussion, see Otto and Miriam Ehrenburg, "How, When, and Why to Fire Your Shrink," *New York* (May 12, 1975).

† In the direct therapy of problems of sexual performance, such as that introduced by Masters and Johnson, the use of "sexual surrogates" *is* directly related to treatment goals. Even so, the primary therapist does not undertake personally this aspect of treatment. (*Psychiatric News,* January 16, 1974, contains the complete Code of Ethics.) At the May, 1975, Annual Meeting of the American Psychiatric Association, Dr. Masters told colleagues that malpractice charges are too mild a response to sexual intercourse between therapist and patient: "We are encouraging lawyers to sue for rape." UPI report, *Berkshire Eagle* (May 7, 1975).

professional insecurity and vulnerability

A middle-aged, highly competent social worker angrily closes a discussion with a mother: "I know my I.Q. isn't as high as yours, but there are some things I know better than you." A well-qualified psychiatrist informs a patient's father, who has just published a book, that he too could write books if circumstances didn't prevent him.* The first response of the bewildered relatives is not to believe their ears. Ordinary people may react as if they're threatened, but not mental health professionals.

It's not true. We've said it before: they're human. But if they're human enough so that your particular combination of characteristics makes them feel defensive, or hostile, or overwhelmed, you're in for trouble. Discussion and disagreement can be constructive, but a wrangle will only wear you out. Change if you can. If you can't – if this is the only professional within twenty miles, or if he or she controls access to something your relative needs, like day treatment or a school program – summon all your tact and self-control. Plenty of relatives have learned to play dumb and keep a low profile. You can too if you have to. You shouldn't have to, but never mind that. Do it, and just hope that it's enough.

"FIT" AND MISFIT

This brings us to a last reason for changing a therapist, a reason particularly important in the traditional kind of psychotherapy based on a therapeutic alliance. You and he (or more importantly, your relative and he) just don't suit each other. You hear it often: "We couldn't seem to get anywhere with Dr. (or Mr. or Ms.) X. But Dr. Y. . . ." Yet Dr. Y. may practice at the same institution, guiding his work by the same assumptions. And, of course, other people will swear by Dr. X., whose quiet passivity (or aggressive confidence) seems to fit their needs exactly.

"By the time most psychiatrists have finished their long apprenticeship they do indeed tend to know what kind of patient they work well with, what kind of patient they ought to avoid, and most important, what their vulnerabilities are."[22] Psychotherapists select their patients. You do the same. If you really don't like this person, if you don't trust him or her enough really to say what's on your mind, go elsewhere. If you can't seem to get to what's on his mind, go elsewhere. But try to be fair; some people move from therapist to therapist and never find a perfect fit. If you have consulted a therapist because you perceive that something needs changing, you cannot expect that the therapist's

* Wechsler, *op. cit.*, p. 42. For a fuller portrait of an insecure psychiatrist, see also pp. 114–118.

perceptions will mirror your own. It is in the difference between the way he or she sees things, the way you see them, the way your relative sees them, that the possibility of change is found.

"Mis-fits"

A doctor who regards homosexuality as an illness won't do much for someone who regards it as a valid choice. A woman feeling her way toward independence won't get far with a therapist who believes her problem is that she has difficulty accepting her feminine role.* A deeply mystical person will resist a behavior therapist; a person with a strong commitment to the scientific method will resist the inner journeyings of R. D. Laing. Shared value systems can be important, which is why the United States government funded a program for training Navaho medicine men.[23]

And if you're poor? Black? Catholic, Jewish, unbeliever? How close a fit do you demand? Backgrounds make a difference, and it's no good pretending otherwise. But be realistic (in 1972 there were only 400 black psychiatrists in the country,[24] and darned few Catholics[25]) and be open-minded. Someone from a different background may understand you better than someone from your own. It's actually true that one Jewish analyst asked a patient in her first interview, "What's a nice Jewish girl like you doing, living away from home?"

Fit. Fitting the patient to the therapist, the problem to the type of treatment; fitting the patient and the problem and the type of treatment to the unyielding practical factors of place, time, and cost. A wide choice of possibilities should mean better help for your relative, but you can wear yourself and him out choosing, being disappointed, choosing again. You need to shop around, for you're making an important purchase — to say the least. Yet shopping for the right fit is expensive; and though it may save money in the long run, you can't be sure. It may also be frustrating and confusing, as you experience for yourself the many ways in which experts can disagree.†

We'll hope it goes well — that you find flexible help from the professional you consult, frank discussion, a familiarity with relevant types of treatment, the ability to discover and sympathize with what's on your mind, knowledgeable and willing referral to other kinds of services. If not — recheck your community resources, call up your psychological reserves, and try again.

* See Appendix B for how to find therapists acceptable to feminists and "gays."

† It's frustrating for professionals too, and some discourage it. "Some psychiatric clinics even have a blackball system whereby they will not give you treatment in their setting once you admit that you have been to another system even for a preliminary intake." The Boston Women's Health Book Collective, *Our Bodies, Ourselves: A Book by and for Women* (New York: Simon and Schuster, 1971), p. 246.

»» CHAPTER VIII ««

In the Family: Day by Day

He who would do good to another must do it in
Minute Particulars. WILLIAM BLAKE

"WHAT AM I to do *now?*" That desperate question we all ask sometimes is the way out of desperation, if we can only recognize it. For it tells us that each day is composed of actions, most of them quite simple and often repeated, and that doing one small thing rather than another is what's going to get us through today a little better than yesterday, with a little more hope for tomorrow.

What are we to do?

What are we to do? This should not be a desperate question but a practical one. We should ask it daily, and ask it as if we expected it to have an answer. Families aren't used to asking this question of the professionals who serve them, and helping professionals aren't used to finding answers. Many of them, as we said in the preceding chapter, will help you to express and if necessary change your feelings and attitudes, but few of them have much experience with the practical problems of daily living with someone who is severely disturbed. They are going to have to learn more about it, and you, the relatives, are going to have to do some of the teaching.

Ideas adjust slowly to new models of practice. We've just got through a couple of hundred years in which the treatment not just of mental illness but of *all* serious illness was moved almost entirely from home to hospital. Those families who did keep their severely disturbed member at home received few if any social or psychiatric services. The kind of outpatient seen by the average psychiatrist or clinical psychologist was the neurotic sufferer. Such patients sought — and still seek — help on their own, and left the therapist's office to spend the day on their own, just like people who weren't in therapy. Their families weren't that much involved. There was usually no reason to involve them, and often there were excellent reasons not to.

A NEW IDEA: THE HOME AS "THERAPEUTIC MILIEU"

Moving emotional illness back to the community

The back-to-the-community movement is changing all that (see Chapter VI). Now many patients are home from the hospitals, stabilized with drugs, perhaps, but still not acting just like other people. Because of new treatment methods, many others will never go to a hospital, or go only for brief periods. The need for what we might call rehabilitative psychiatry is acute. Rehabilitation cannot take place in a therapist's office, but only where the patient lives. That is where there must be a "therapeutic milieu."

What, in fact, are we to do now here, at home? You'll probably have to work hard to get your consultant to see what you're really asking. Though the professionals may train aides and paraprofessionals to work with disturbed people, they are not used to training relatives in how to make a home a "therapeutic milieu."*

requires a new kind of professional guidance in making the home a therapeutic milieu.

Many relatives of the mentally ill have recorded their frustration at the kind of help they're offered and the kind of help they've been refused: plenty of help with their own emotions, individual therapy, family therapy, marriage counseling, but little or no thoughtful attention to helping them fill the day the best they can with experiences that help nourish and restore.† Two British specialists in schizophrenia point out the problem:

> Left to themselves, some relatives do eventually work out, by a method of trial and error, how to react to a patient in such a way that his impairments are minimized and his assets fully exploited. They do not, however, usually obtain much help in this process from professional people, and it is therefore inevitably haphazard and painful and all too often something goes irremediably wrong. Our first main conclusion is that *insufficient recognition is given to the fact that relatives are the real 'primary care' agents.*[2] [Italics mine.]

Leonard Woolf bought a printing press to give relaxing manual work to Virginia as she recovered; the publishing house that grew out

* Claire Burch points out that though the need is recognized for training auxiliary mental health manpower in sparsely populated states like Alaska, "every family is like an Alaskan family, remote, caught in a frozen sweep of ice, when emotional illness strikes.

"Help may exist thirty miles from your house, but that thirty miles is enough to take that member who is ill out of your life and into a new one from which he may eventually be ejected, his manner stiff and rigid, not sure anymore what is his world. Help may exist five minutes away but you may be unable to afford it. Help in the form of trained psychiatric personnel may simply not be available at all. There is only one answer to the agonizing doctor shortage and that is training families. You are motivated to learn, just like the Alaskans, for your stake is great; the sick people are your own."[1]

† See Molly Finn, "The Unhelpful Social Worker," *Mental Hygiene,* 51 (April 1967); Frances Eberhardy, "The View from the Couch," *Journal of Child Psychology and Psychiatry,* 8 (1967), pp. 257–263; Louise Wilson, *This Stranger, My Son* (New York: G. P. Putnam, 1968); Clara Park, *The Siege* (New York: Harcourt, Brace and World, 1967); Josh Greenfeld, *A Child Called Noah* (Holt, Rinehart and Winston, 1972). See also social worker John Boyle's "A Learning Experience in Helping Parents Get What They Want," *Children,* 17 (July–Aug. 1970): "It became clear that these parents did not need group counseling to define their problem. They all had the same problem and they knew what it was — to find a school where their child could learn something. Until this was accomplished, no other problem seemed worth tackling. . . . These overburdened parents apparently felt they could not take time to attend a meeting they still seemed to feel would not have tangible results."

of that occupational therapy still exists. Woolf's careful, intelligent campaign, which for twenty-five years provided a therapeutic milieu for a chronic invalid who at one time or another displayed virtually every major mental symptom, is more typical than we generally realize; few families of the mentally ill have been writers and could tell their stories. Plenty of families have done, and are doing, a good job; they can do an even better one when they get the right kind of help.

A wife needs specific guidance for the weeks when her husband wakes before dawn unable to face a day in which every activity has lost its meaning. A daughter-in-law needs guidance on how much to demand of the elderly ex-patient who won't change his clothes or take a bath. A father needs guidance on how to meet the conflicting needs for privacy and company of a schizophrenic daughter. A mother who must daily get a psychotic four-year-old across town to her special school via public transportation needs specific techniques to eliminate the screams which are making the journey impossible. Patients like these are now at home, when once they were in hospitals and institutions. Psychiatric practice must adapt itself to the need to treat them where they are, using those unsung, long-time paraprofessionals, the patient's family.

Be clear about this: *any* traditionally trained psychotherapist is imbued with the concept of "family pathology" (and, if he is an adherent to the new school of family therapy, he places a special emphasis on it). But he works in a pragmatic here-and-now. To him, if your relative lives at home, while you may indeed *seem* part of the problem, you *are,* inevitably, part of the solution. He and you both want to see changes in your family's situation. Try to relax. It will help you earn his trust.

> The current interest in the rehabilitation of chronic mentally ill patients, in discharging them from mental hospitals, and in finding some way for them to live in the community, has focused renewed interest in, and placed new significance upon, the patient's family. It has also meant a different approach to the family on the part of those who are responsible for the care and treatment of the patient, including the social worker. Traditionally, the social worker has been described as the link between the patient, the hospital, the family, and the community. There is something that is much more promising and challenging about using this intermediate position to find the positives in the family and the community and to make them available to the patient and the hospital, than there was when it appeared that the only, or major, use of the social worker was to make detailed studies in how the family had caused or contributed to the patient's illness.[3]

This was written in 1961, and even now, it is not always honored in practice.

FAMILIES AS CO-THERAPISTS

The word "co-therapist" was first applied to relatives of the mentally ill by clinical psychologist Eric Schopler and psychiatrist Robert Reichler,* who began to train parents to work with their own psychotic children in the late sixties after becoming discouraged at the results of traditional individual therapy.[4] Psychologists Ivar Lovaas† at UCLA and Ogden Lindsley at the University of Kansas also pioneered in training parents, using the techniques of reinforcement therapy. Training, not counseling; in these programs "it is assumed that parents of emotionally disturbed . . . children are not themselves sick and do not need help in dealing with their own problems before they are able to help their children."‡ A California team notes one of the strengths of this approach:

> Many parents cannot accept therapeutic intervention if they themselves must be the identified patient. On the other hand, they can take a certain degree of pride in being therapists themselves. They seem to enjoy being taught how to treat their child, as opposed to turning the treatment over to somebody else, as with traditional therapy. Consequently, much of the guilt and resistance we expected did not appear.[5]

Families are at liberty to be surprised at the kinds of discoveries that surprise professionals.

Extending co-therapy from children to adults

There are now numerous programs involving parents of younger children. So far, however, few but the behavior therapists have trained families to work with their disturbed adolescents and adults. Dr. Thomas Sturm, a clinical psychologist at the Minneapolis Center for Behavior Modification, specializes in rehabilitation, developing "behavior that people want for themselves or need from others in order to care for them."[6] His therapeutic team will consult in the office, make home visits, and write a program for better living with a mentally ill parent, a wife, a son or daughter. In Alabama, the behaviorally ori-

Behavior therapy

* Schopler's and Reichler's work at the University of North Carolina Medical School has become the nucleus of a comprehensive state program; in 1972 they received a gold award for achievement in community psychiatry from the American Psychiatric Association.

† "Instead of blaming the parents, excluding them from treatment, and alienating them from their children, we bring the parents in on the treatment process. We show the parents how to reward appropriate behavior, how to punish inappropriate behavior, how to shape up speech, and so on. The parents become the principal therapists and we become consultants to the parents." Ivar Lovaas, in an interview with Paul Chance, *Psychology Today* (Jan. 1974).

‡ Iris Fodor, "The Parent as a Therapist," *MH* (Spring 1972). Professor Fodor is an educational psychologist at New York University.

ented Huntsville–Madison County community mental health center teaches families of patients of all ages techniques "to maintain adaptive behavior in the home."[7] As yet, however, psychodynamic psychotherapists have not rushed to imitate them. Reasonably enough, from their point of view. You *can't* share in the highly personal process of individual insight therapy; that therapeutic relationship is rightly posted "Keep Out." Your relative has a right to call his psyche his own; that's what his growth toward independence is all about. But even individual psychotherapy shouldn't rule out consultation with you on the ways you can best support the goals of therapy, much as in good hospital treatment psychiatrists guide the actions of the staff.

Problems and possibilities

Will family therapy help you here? It sounds as if it ought to. And it just might; it's a new field, and its practitioners are a feisty, innovative bunch. There are even some behavior therapists among them.[8] More typical, however, is the psychodynamic approach of Dr. Ross Speck and psychologist Carolyn Attneave in their book *Family Networks*.[9] That could change your life; they've developed a kind of marathon therapy session which goes beyond the immediate family to pull in a good hunk of the troubled person's community. It's a family network – aunts and cousins, neighbors, friends, doctors, employers, forty or more people in one living room, mobilizing their resources to see what can be done. A good many of these people get caught up in the professional therapists' enthusiasm and begin to function as co-therapists (though that's not Speck's term), coming up with their own ideas for recreation, activities, jobs, and living arrangements in a process which is expected to continue after the professional-led sessions are over. But family therapists tend to be leery of close family members, especially father and mother. Speck and Attneave's emphasis is on the network and its bright ideas and unexpected resources, not on training the immediate family to provide a therapeutic milieu for an ill or recovering person. In fact, most family therapists would object to that way of looking at the situation. They think your relative's emotional problems are inseparable from your own. Though they are keenly alive to the actual processes of family life (they are among the few therapists who'll come to your home and try to understand your family in its daily context), they are far more interested in how you relate to each other than in helping you solve practical problems. They see the whole family as sick – caught in a web of personal interactions which are nobody's fault but which are hurting you all. They assume that if you were a healthy family you wouldn't need their help. They can be extremely useful, therefore, in the (many) cases where families can't seem to stop hurting each other. But realize before you consult them that their goals for changing your family life will prob-

Family therapy?

Network therapy?

Would you rather be a co-therapist or a co-patient?

ably cut a lot deeper than simply helping you do a better job of living with your relative.*

Not everybody can be a co-therapist,

And of course they're often right. Not all of us can provide milieu therapy for a relative. Not all of us want to. Not all of us should. Some of us do use our relatives to fill our own neurotic needs, even maintaining their symptoms without knowing it (though there should be ways of teaching us not to, as Fay's parents were taught in Chapter IV). Some of us — let's face it — are too close to our relative's problems anyway and must learn that we can contribute best by accepting his independence. Some of us are in poor health, some have a houseful of children, some have jobs. For some of us it simply hurts too much.† But if you do take on the responsibility, you have a right to demand more help than you've been getting.

of course.

WHAT HELPS; WHAT HINDERS

What makes for success?

What makes for success in keeping a mental patient at home? In one study, Dr. J. E. Barrett and his co-workers describe what happened when a hospital strike forced the emergency discharge of a number of mental patients. In spite of the unexpectedness of their return home, more than a quarter were still with their families six months later. Dr. Barrett's group studied who stayed out and who went back to the hospital. They found that the two sets of patients didn't differ significantly in the acuteness of their symptoms; it was their family circumstances that seemed to make the difference. A patient seemed to have a much better chance of staying out if he helped at home. Sixty-nine percent of those who helped with household chores stayed out of the hospital (and 92 percent of those who helped with children; maybe they are the best co-therapists!). Income level made a difference, but not in the way you'd think. Poor people did better than people in comfortable circumstances in keeping their relatives with them, and much better than those classified "very comfortable." And they were more likely to express pleasure at having them back.[10]

Involve him in family activities.

There's food for thought here. The effort it takes to get your relative involved in family activities is worth making. It does him good to be occupied, and it does him good to feel he is a contributing member of

* "We are continually causing upheavals by intervening in ways that will produce unstable situations which require change and restructuring of family organization." Salvador Minuchin and Avner Barcai, "Therapeutically Induced Family Crisis," in Sager and Kaplan, *Progress in Group and Family Therapy.*

† One mother, whose son is making slow progress in Lovaas's UCLA program, says, "Some parents just can't do it. Every time I tried it I just hurt." *Newsweek* (April 8, 1974).

the family. It does you all good; the whole family feels more positively toward a member who contributes a needed service, however simple. There's lots of work to be done around a poor home, mostly the kind of work that occupies a vulnerable person without demanding too much of him. The "very comfortable" home may not need his services, and the mental patient in a well-to-do family may not be able to keep busy in the pressured, demanding ways expected of normal people in his environment, where standards of success aren't easily relaxed. He may not be ready to go back to college, get a job, keep his checkbook, even read the newspaper. Yet that is not to say he can or should do nothing.

So, if your relative shares your home, for a short time or a long one, help him to be useful. Consult the mental health professionals who know him on what can reasonably be expected of him. (Remember that for a woman, the vocational rehabilitation service will provide training in homemaking skills.) * Take the initiative yourself when your relative can't, and be patient when things don't get done as fast or as well as you're used to. The best home therapy is not to be the focus of too much attention, but to be part of the family. Maybe this is another area where the "very comfortable" can learn from the poor, who've already learned not to expect too much and to be thankful for small blessings.†

The how-to book on providing a therapeutic milieu for the mentally ill hasn't yet been written; it certainly can't be squeezed into this chapter. The nearest to it is Dr. Leonard Cammer's *Up from Depression,* which gives hundreds of practical suggestions of what to do about depressed people when they sleep too much (or too little), when they lose contact with their surroundings, when their despair makes suicide a continuing danger, and much more. While Dr. Cammer talks about

* "I've been amazed," writes the mother of an autistic adolescent, "at how differently I feel about Elly now. She cheerily and proudly answers the phone, shovels snow, empties the garbage, vacuums the whole house. For all those years I thought we were doing fine together, yet I used to wonder if the burden would ever end, and dream about eventually finding the perfect residential placement. This may still be the right thing, since we must die sometime — but now I can actually imagine her — sweet thing that she is — as company in our old age, the prop of my declining years. Her transformation from a total taker to a partial giver has made a difference I never could have predicted. Of course one must work hard to bring that transformation about and sustain it."

† "It has been suggested that lower class families are better able to encapsulate an extremely disturbed person for longer periods of time, whereas the middle class family tends to call on outside help more rapidly when a major psychotic decompensation occurs." Norman Garmezy, "Children at Risk: The Search for the Antecedents of Schizophrenia, Part I," *Schizophrenia Bulletin,* 8 (Spring 1973). The reference is to H. Sampson, S. L. Messinger, and R. D. Towne, "Family Processes and Becoming a Mental Patient," in E. D. Sampson, ed., *Approaches, Contexts, and Problems of Social Psychology* (Englewood Cliffs, N.J.: Prentice-Hall, Inc., 1965), pp. 515–522.

depression, these symptoms, and many more, are common to many mental conditions, from extreme anxiety to schizophrenia.*

Families often deny there's a problem.

A child is in continual trouble in school; in the neighborhood, parents of other children call and complain about him. Do you react defensively and give the neighbor a piece of your mind, or do you recognize your child's call for help and get in touch with his teachers, school guidance people, the mental health center?

A man whose whole life has been geared to achievement sinks into apathy and begins to spend days in bed. Do you tell him to snap out of it, or wait and see if it will go away, or do you see that he gets help? A young woman has virtually stopped talking; each time she goes through a doorway she turns around three times. Do you accept the doctor's message that she is seriously ill, or do you go on insisting that the problem is shyness and poor diet? In *Return to Earth,* Colonel Aldrin reports that his father still has trouble admitting that his astronaut son had to be treated for psychiatric depression. The "not in our family" attitude can come from shame and pride, or from the best of motives. Nobody wants to make a fuss about a temporary letdown, and loving families can accept behavior that others find disturbing. But if we find ourselves denying deep trouble, we should ask ourselves whether we are defending our relative or our own peace of mind. If it's the latter, that kind of peace won't last long. The first way we can make a bad situation worse is to refuse to recognize it.

Families are often too involved in the problem.

A young man has recently been released from the hospital; his hardworking father is bitterly disappointed in his son's failure to achieve. His tension spills over into constant criticism, of his son, his wife, their teenage daughter. A mother "does everything" for her daughter; she worries about whether her alarm clock will go off, what she eats, even answers her telephone calls. Another mother complacently tells a visitor, "I could go out if I wanted to. I don't because I'm looking after Johnny."

We can't help being involved with our relatives. And love can be good therapy, but only if we learn what therapists have had to learn; that it must be tempered with objectivity and detachment. Love — the very word sounds too involving; the best thing we may be able to do for our relative is to cool it and call it affection.

* Here, from the table of contents of *Up from Depression,* is the outline of only *one* of its eighteen packed chapters: "General Symptoms and What You Do About Them: Sadness, Sleep Difficulties, Poor Appetite, Loss of Interest in the Surroundings and Loss of Pleasure Drive, Loss of Self-Confidence, Loss of Self-Esteem: Its Variations, Preoccupation with Body Function, Lack of Concentration, Memory Troubles, Inability to Make Decisions or Use Will Power, Poor Judgment, Agitation, Crying and Tearfulness, Anticipatory Anxiety, Fear of Being Alone, Fear of Death, Rising Tension with Loss of Hope: A Warning Sign." There are chapters on "Your Role in Drug Treatment," "in Psychotherapy," and "in Psychiatric Hospitalization," and much more.

The noted British specialist in schizophrenia Dr. John Wing has made careful studies of the progress of schizophrenic patients living with their families, and of what kind of environment best keeps them from relapse. He sees "two kinds of danger: environmental overstimulation on the one hand, and environmental understimulation on the other." You can expect too much — and too little.

Overstimulation and understimulation

> If the patient is forced to interact socially, by an overinvolved relative or a crash rehabilitation program, his cognitive abnormalities are bound to become manifest, and as his anxiety mounts, may well be secondarily elaborated as delusions, hallucinations and odd behavior. Left to his own devices, the patient will prefer to withdraw to a level of interaction at which he can cope with the environment. Without appropriate social stimulation this protective withdrawal may go too far.[11]

Warmth

If professionals have their doubts about families, more than anything else they doubt our capacity for the steady, unexcitable, therapeutic warmth our relatives need. It's a kind of caring they know themselves isn't easy to learn, the kind that's there when called on, but that doesn't suck a vulnerable person into its own emotional intensity. Again and again they've seen it happen: demands, hopes, anxiety, hostility, love itself just come over too strong.

but not too much emotion

For years Dr. Wing and his group have studied family behavior, even tried to measure it. Their research has convinced them that how well schizophrenics do at home is directly related to what they call "the level of expressed emotion" in the household.[12] The emotion may be negative or positive. The schizophrenic, with his "high level of arousal,"[13] reacts more intensely to family excitement, irritation, or concern, even if it's not directed at him.

But isn't it good to express your emotions? It is; you should have friends, counselors, perhaps your own therapist to tell about the things that seem too much to bear. Even with your relative you don't have to be a zombie; natural warmth is therapeutic. But you haven't lived with your relative this long without guessing that "being yourself" is a luxury that doesn't always fit into the therapeutic milieu. When your relative can cope fully with people being themselves he won't need a therapeutic milieu anymore. Dr. Wing's team describes the optimal social environment as providing: "structure, with clear cut rules, only as much complexity as any given individual can cope with, and emotionally neutral but active supervision to keep up standards of appearance, work and behavior."[14]

Emotionally neutral? This is not an invitation to coldness. But it *is* a reminder that an atmosphere of strong emotion is hard on hypersensitive nerves, even if it's loving emotion. Even things your relative used to enjoy may be too much for him at this time. A cheerful gathering with your brother's family, for example, may exhaust him, and no one should be hurt if he needs to withdraw. (Let's hope you can provide what's obviously necessary: your relative's own room.) But expecting nothing won't help either; it will just produce a back ward emptiness in your own home.

What makes the problem worse?

Finding the perfect balance isn't easy. The family problems that follow have been noticed again and again by all sorts of professionals, with all sorts of ideas about mental illness; they can't be dismissed as the product of a particular theory. You've noticed them yourself in other people's families, maybe even in your own.

Overinvolvement

You can be warm without burdening your relative with your overinvolvement. Lots of families manage this; Brown and Wing found that "only half of those rated as markedly warm also showed marked overinvolvement." That, however, leaves the other half. And that overinvolvement, according to their studies, is directly related to the return of schizophrenic symptoms. In families with a high level of expressed emotion, Brown and Wing found a direct relationship between relapse and the amount of time the patient spent in close contact with the family, especially with those most highly involved with him. "Fifteen hours or more a week of face-to-face contact between a schizophrenic patient and a highly-involved relative carries a very strong risk of further breakdown."[15] Withdrawal is a good thing sometimes. Both patient and family need time to themselves. Here's another underlining of the importance of a private room, a job, a recreation program, a day hospital – somewhere to go.

Overprotectiveness

Overprotectiveness is the most common problem as families adjust to the presence of a member who is or has been mentally ill. Everybody agrees on that, family therapists, old-fashioned pull-your-socks-up psychiatrists, specialists in somatic treatments.* In extreme cases parent and child can be so mutually dependent that the relationship is called *symbiotic* (from the Greek words for "life" and "together"); destructively bound together, they live at each other's expense. Some parents even react to a child's improvement by getting sick themselves. So guard against that sickroom softening of the voice. Encourage a sense of strength, not weakness.

may foster dependence.

The "child" may be past forty, but the parent *needs* his total dependence, may even resist the efforts of therapists and rehabilitation workers to build independent behavior. (This problem is not limited to mental illness; it is also common with parents of retarded and

* References are hardly necessary, but see Laqueur, "Multiple Family Therapy and General Systems Theory," in Sager and Kaplan, eds., *Progress in Group and Family Therapy;* Abraham Low, *Lectures to Relatives of Former Patients* (Boston: Christopher Publishing House, 1943); David Hawkins, in *Orthomolecular Psychiatry,* sums it up: "The most difficult obstacle to overcome has been the interaction of the dependent patient and the overprotective family" (p. 586).

physically handicapped people.) Parents who *are* working for independence may be angry when they come across professionals who assume that they aren't — but you should recognize that that assumption is based on wide experience, and that professionals are as prone to stereotype as the rest of us. As you assess your own situation, too, you should always be aware that people change and grow, and be ready to realize that a degree of protection that may have been absolutely necessary five years ago may be holding your son or daughter back today. Don't build a life around your relative if there's any alternative. Get all the help you can — not only the all-important outsider's view, but help from other relatives, neighbors, homemakers or regular sitters, sheltered workshops, day hospitals, everything the community can offer so you can have a life and interests of your own. And if you too feel that you could go out if you wanted to go out but you don't because you're looking after Johnny — it's great to feel needed, but consider getting therapy for yourself.

Families are often insensitive to needs

Yet the line between overprotection and accurate sensitivity to your relative's need isn't always easy to draw. Protection sometimes may be needed. It's Dr. Wing's fine line between an understimulating and an overstimulating environment — an environment with you in it. In *I Never Promised You a Rose Garden,* Hannah Green movingly describes the tension and pressure of the first visit home after two years in the hospital. The young girl is surrounded with love, served her favorite foods, welcomed by parents and grandparents, aunts and uncles, best-loved friends. "The whole family is doing everything it can," says the girl's mother. Her father says, "It's nice here, isn't it? It's where you belong." But all this just adds up to an impossible demand.

> Deborah tried to eat the holiday food and speak to the people who came to see her, but exhaustion would claim her where she sat. The hospital relationships had been brief and fleeting and never complicated by more than two or three people at a time. . . . Now there was chatter and threads of talk that wove in and out like a complicated cat's cradle. It was not possible to tell how immense she found the distance between herself and the rest of the human race.[16]

and expect too much

Demands can be felt, even when you don't put them into words. If your relative is sensitive, he can feel the weight of your hopes and expectations; particularly is this true between parents and adolescent or young adult children. This is why a less involved relative, or the people in a halfway house — or his therapist — may be able to help him more than all your love.

or too little,

But you can also expect too little. Though parents tend to have high hopes for their young people, they may give up all hope of change for older sons and daughters, especially if they are chronically impaired. Those are the understimulating homes, where parents live alone and no one is invited. The effort of teaching and coaxing an impaired person to do things for himself (and of worrying about the trouble he can get into when he does) often seems too much, especially for parents who are getting old. Nor is it easy to maintain reasonable expectations when abandoning them buys an escape from the tears or rage some patients use to enforce irrational demands. One family ate only one kind of meat for five years; the father couldn't even put a magazine down on the immaculate coffee table without a tantrum from his mentally unstable daughter. A husband may be helping to maintain his wife's fear of leaving the house alone by his willingness to take her shopping. (Even sympathy and concern isn't always what the doctor ordered.) * The story of Fay in Chapter IV is a classic example of how family interactions can maintain a problem behavior.

or they don't listen

Even in normal family life, we take members of our family for granted and don't always really hear what they're saying. If a family member is mentally ill and lives at home, the family gets used to irrational and disconnected talk. They tune it out; they may stop expecting *anything* Grandma says to make sense. And schizophrenics often alternate between normal talking and a kind of "inner language"; family therapist Dr. Peter Laqueur of Vermont State Hospital speaks of young patients who, "like a good boxer . . . can keep the parent constantly off balance, leaving him in doubt whether they should be reacted to as 'normal' or 'sick.'" Then, he says, love and compassion are not enough; it's terribly difficult to "sustain a dialogue with a mentally ill person without sooner or later succumbing to feelings of annoyance because of the patient's apparent misuse of words and syntax." In Dr. Laqueur's multiple groups schizophrenic patients often show an "uncanny understanding" of each other's language and may even "translate" for each other, reminding us "normals" that crazy talk may mean more than it seems to.[17]

or understand.

Dr. Laqueur looks on the bright side; he assumes families want to understand and can learn. R. D. Laing and Abraham Esterson show a darker picture, of families incapable of responding to the patient as she† is, denying and invalidating her own experience in an effort to force her into their own molds. In one of their cases, a girl who complains that everyone is talking about her seems to have "ideas of reference": when the psychiatrists take the trouble to talk to the family, they find out that the neighbors *do* talk about her but that the family

* For some good examples of this, see Robert Paul Liberman, "Behavioral Approaches to Family and Couple Therapy," in Sager and Kaplan, eds., *Progress in Group and Family Therapy.*

† For some reason, all Laing's and Esterson's cases are young women.

tells her they don't. Surrounded by such denials and mystifications, they feel, it's no wonder that a person becomes unsure of the reality that surrounds her and gets labeled schizophrenic. Again and again, Laing and Esterson find that "crazy" talk and behavior make sense as an understandable response to what's really going on in the family. They find this *every* time they investigate the family of a woman labeled schizophrenic,[18] and that may make you angry (and suspicious). Nevertheless, they taped those family interviews; they're there in *Sanity, Madness, and the Family.* You'll need a high boiling point to read Laing and Esterson, but it's possible to learn from these lessons in how families can fail to accept their daughter as a person in her own right.

Families often lock a person into a role.

Families often take a member's actions and personality so much for granted that he or she takes on a special role. One person is the baby, one's the clown, one's the rock in time of trouble. One may even be the scapegoat.* Often the person plays up to this type-casting; people may notice that he's quite different away from home. Normal people can suffer from this, but it weighs especially on the mentally ill, who are more defenseless than the rest of us, especially those who (like most of Laing's and Esterson's cases) became ill so young that they had not yet developed a secure personality of their own or worked out an independent role outside the home. Locking a person into a role may set cruel limits on his ability to grow and change.

So do some therapists.

It is curious that the very therapists who are most aware of the noxious effect, within a family, of scapegoating and role enforcement should be so quick to scapegoat you or cast you in a role, the "dominant mother" being their favorite archetype. Perhaps because they overidentify with the patient and his hostilities, perhaps simply because they're unpleasant people — and there are some in every field — some mental health professionals can be downright sadistic in their treatment of patients' families.† As conducted by professionals like these, family therapy is an especially powerful instrument for making the whole lot of you feel guilty and miserable.

Therapy as opportunity

It need not be, however. Among the many therapies described in this book you may hope to find some that are rich with opportunity, especially when the professionals treat you as collaborators. You can

* Speck's and Attneave's *Family Networks* is a good place to read about scapegoating; see also Laing and Esterson.

† See William S. Appleton, "Mistreatment of Patients' Families by Psychiatrists," *American Journal of Psychiatry,* 131 (June 1974). Dr. Appleton, however, is not describing sadism, but what he regards as common practice. See Andrew Ferber and Jules Planz, "How to Succeed in Family Therapy: Set Reachable Goals — Give Workable Tasks," *Progress in Group and Family Therapy,* for a fine account of a family therapy which interests itself, not in scapegoating, but in solving problems of family living.

use the help, the wisdom, the objectivity, the experience of people who can see your family situation with new eyes. Inside it, how hard it is to know what's too much to expect or too little, how hard it is to recognize ingrained habits, how hard to know what can be changed, or what ought to be.

COOPERATING WITH THE DOCTOR

To work with the doctor (or other therapist) you must know what you're doing. Don't be afraid to ask what and why. In psychiatry no treatment is absolutely uncontroversial (see Chapter IV), and if the family (or the patient) has unanswered questions or lingering doubts, these can cause trouble.

Cooperating in somatic treatment

Following doctors' orders is easiest when they concern the various somatic treatments, since these are the most straightforward. But if they haven't already talked it out with the doctor, families who mistrust drugs may be tempted to go along with their relative if he complains about his medication and wants to give it up before he's ready.* Or you may be a pill-popper yourself, likely to overlook it if your relative takes an extra pill or two "to sleep better." You wouldn't do that if you knew what was in the bottle. So talk it over thoroughly with the doctor. The same is true of other somatic treatments, particularly shock, about which there is so much fear and misinformation. You cannot give support and reassurance if you yourself are unsure about what and why and what to expect afterwards. Because electroconvulsive therapy is quickly and easily given, it can become routine for a doctor; he may skimp the important job of explanation unless you ask for it. Dr. Lothar Kalinowsky shows us the kind of talk relatives need but don't always get, as he discusses "ambulatory" shock treatment, the kind your relative gets in a doctor's office.†

> We warn the relatives most carefully to keep the patient away not only from friends (who seeing him in this confused state might draw the wrong conclusions as to his mental capacities) but from his business, where he might do much harm without realizing it. . . . The patients

* For chronic schizophrenics, study after study shows that terminating medication is associated with relapse and rehospitalization. One study found that while nearly 70 percent of chronic schizophrenics living in the community believed medication helped their adjustment, only 36 percent actually took it. The authors cite this as an example of the "clinical phenomenon of incongruence between intention and action on the part of the schizophrenic patient" — a fact of life you probably don't have to be reminded of. So act accordingly. George Serban and Alexander Thomas, "Attitudes and Behaviors of Acute and Chronic Schizophrenic Patients Regarding Ambulatory Treatment," *American Journal of Psychiatry,* 131 (Sept. 1974).

† Though we quote this sound advice, we would caution you that a patient sick enough to need shock treatment should, probably, be in a hospital.

> rarely have any insight into their shortcomings during the treatment, and as soon as their condition has improved they are eager to take up their usual activities. It is the task of the responsible relatives to prevent this; they should also be warned against the patient's driving a car or taking up other activities where quick reactions are necessary.[19]

Information should flow both ways.

So if your relative lives with you, ask the doctor to discuss these questions. Expect him to tell you what you need to know. But also expect him to make it easy for you to tell him what *he* needs to know. If he doesn't make it easy, tell him anyway. The sharing of information is a two-way process. In some very real ways, you know more about your relative than the doctor can. If your relative is very young, or very depressed, or very disoriented, you are likely to go with him for the first visit. Bring a medical history, as we suggested before — and, in future, keep a log.

Keeping a record:

During the years of her illness, Virginia Woolf's husband kept a daily record of "whether she could work, how she slept, whether she had sensations of headache . . . whether she had had to take aspirin or veronal at night, and of similar facts about her health."[20] It was just the kind of record that Dr. Cammer recommends you keep: "a *factual* résumé of the patient's activities . . . but not your *opinions.* Report only what your relative said or how he or she behaved, slept, socialized, and so on. Do not attempt to interpret any of this or to reel off a list of comments that are, in fact, a summary of your own worries. Let the doctor evaluate the information for himself."[21]

facts not opinions

If the doctor seems unenthusiastic about inspecting your log, keep it anyway. You'll learn something by keeping track of your relative's actions and reactions, and your record could take on unexpected significance if his condition changes suddenly. Besides, another doctor might be able to use the information later.

Helpful hints

We could give you all sorts of good advice. Respect and encourage your relative's independence, and don't be overprotective (except in depression, where for a while you may have to treat him like a baby). Have firm expectations (but don't set them too high or too low). Give a schizophrenic a place to withdraw to and don't force him into social gatherings (but if he's really depressed it may be dangerous to leave him alone). Give sympathy freely (but don't let him wallow in his misery). Don't be drawn into his crazy ideas (though some therapists work by "communicating with the patient in his delusional system"). Don't argue with the patient (but it may help to test his reality with facts he can recognize). Which to do? When? How? No advice is good if you aren't shown how to apply it.

need fleshing out.

We hope that some of the books listed in Appendix A will speak directly to your individual case. We hope you have found a wise and supportive therapist. But we know it's not easy.

It's hard,

For all the drugs, shock, insight, transference, reinforcement, and tender loving care, trouble is real and no words can make it go away. Living with our relatives is *hard.* Even the most skilled and gifted professional therapists don't find it easy to work with the mentally ill, even though, unlike us, they are in contact with them only a few hours a day. "Despair," writes Dr. Leslie Farber, chairman of the Association of Existential Psychiatry and Psychoanalysis, "is more or less intrinsic to the therapeutic life with schizophrenia."[22] "Grinding," he calls it, "frustrating," "defeating." "I myself have abdicated such work because it is simply too much for me. A friend of mine described the work with schizophrenics as rather similar to pro football. You have a few good years and then you have to get out of the game."[23] Unless they can afford someone to take over for them, however, most families are in the game for good. In fact, if you've been playing it for years you may be tempted to reassure the doctor. It can't be all that bad if so many of us are doing it.

It can't? Consider these words from the English psychologist George Brown:

> We had the impression that relatives understated their problem. . . . The most important factor . . . was probably that many relatives who lived with disabled patients subtly adapted their level of expectations so that, after a period of years, they no longer reacted according to their earlier hopes and ideals and perhaps had even forgotten them. . . . Relatives are not in a strong position to complain. . . .[24]

but we survive.

And indeed, Dr. E. James Anthony, who for years has studied mental illness in the family, notes that families seem to be able to live with psychosis, not only better than professionals expect, but better than professionals themselves can.

> As investigators intermittently in contact with psychosis, we are becoming increasingly aware that our response to the irrational and the unrealistic is not quite the same as that of individuals living at home with a close psychotic relative. We seem to lack, or to possess in short measure, certain adaptive capacities that develop only with exposure to the vicissitudes of everyday psychotic functioning.[25]

In short, we survive.* We have to. If it helps to feel heroic about it, the professionals' words certainly give us leave. (Herewith parent

* One government-supported researcher solemnly set out to test the hypothesis that "schizopresent" families differ from normal families in "integrative experiences"—that is, in "how much time family members spend in talking to each other, laughing together, or just 'having a good time.'" A member of a schizopresent family could almost get bitter, reading those words. Don't. Instead, let's share an integrative experience, laughing together. MH 15973, "A Study *in vivo* of Disturbed and Normal Family Milieux," reported in NIMH's *Special Report: Schizophrenia,* Publication No. (HSM) 72-90007 (1971), p. 23.

Clarence Griffith's epitome of life with an autistic child: what the monkey said after making love to the skunk. "I enjoyed about as much of it as I could stand.") We have to be superhuman not to be affected by the same qualities that irritate, provoke, frustrate, discourage therapists like Dr. Farber. "Emotional disturbance" is itself disturbing. A disturbed woman, convinced she is to bear the Messiah, leaves her husband and goes searching for someone to make her pregnant. A disturbed man drops in on his brother, who throws him out when he finds him masturbating with feces while his three-year-old watches. The young man can't go home; his twelve-year-old sister is afraid of him – for good reason. Life with the mentally ill isn't usually like this; most of the time their behavior is no threat to themselves or to others. It's good to have Dr. Anthony's reminder that "even the most psychotically-dominated families do many of the things that ordinary families do, such as shopping in supermarkets, attending church, taking a drive or spending an evening at a movie or restaurant."[26] But the daily grind can wear you down as much as the occasional crisis. You're likely to get help with the crises (most psychiatrists would immediately hospitalize the above young people). But there's less help with the less flamboyant symptoms – the unresponsiveness, the self-absorption and self-pity, the hypochondria, the unwillingness (or is it inability?) to perform the simplest household task, assume the slightest responsibility. Your relative may be hostile to you, sometimes justly, often not. Clifford Beers was convinced for two years that all his relatives were spies. At one stage in her illness Virginia Woolf would not speak to her husband or allow him in her room.[27] Disturbed people may avoid their relatives, accuse them, plead with them, manipulate them, play them off against each other, suck them into their own symptoms. The only mentally ill people who're easy to live with are some of the chronically ill who function near the retarded level but whose condition is stabilized and offers no dramatic crises – or hope of improvement. Even that depends on what you think is easy; this may be the hardest of all, especially if you can remember a time when they were different.

Whatever our relatives do – and don't do – hurts us all the more because we love them, or feel we ought to, or remember that we once did. That mixture of love and responsibility is all we've got, sometimes, to keep us going in the therapeutic enterprise, which can be, as Dr. Farber says, "so damned horrible,"[28] even when we know our relatives are sick, not themselves, strangers against their will.

"Co-therapy" is not a duty.

The stories just told should remind us that sometimes "co-therapy" may simply be beyond us. If psychiatric hospitalization becomes necessary, you shouldn't feel guilty about it, or that your resourcefulness, strength, or love have failed. More likely the failure has been in the provision of adequate backup services. And even these can't solve all problems. Remember, few acute illnesses of any kind are adequately treated at home.

Living with your emotions

But when your relative's acute phase is over and he *is* with you, what are you to do about your own feelings? Love and responsibility are easy to talk about, but what about resentment, when you're tied down by a relative who can't be left alone? What about envy, when your mind tells you that he's suffering too, but your exhausted body and spirit tell you that *he* has it easy? What about hurt, when someone you love turns against you, when someone you've done your best for accuses you of making her ill? What about fear, when he threatens you, or actually comes at you with a knife?* What about jealousy, when she's closer to her therapist than to you? What about anger, when the therapist seems to take sides with him against his family?† What about those thoughts you scarcely dare acknowledge, which come into your mind when you don't think you can take any more? Do you wish he were dead, or that you were?

Recognize your feelings.

Plenty of people do. It's important to recognize these feelings, if you have them, and to know you're not alone. Maybe that will help you get past them. Maybe you can talk it out with other family members; maybe they'll be shocked, but maybe they feel the same way and need to talk about it. Maybe you'll want therapy or counseling for yourself.

You and yours

You want to do the best you can for your sick relative. Yet you have to be fair to the other people who're living in your house — old people, perhaps, or children, each with their own vulnerabilities, problems, and strengths. You may be willing to sacrifice your own time and energy; it's yours. But what about them?

> Reactions of brothers and sisters may differ widely and their resentment may be deep if the sick one is not handled according to the ideas of

* Burch (p. 130) has some good advice for this situation (don't panic, be sympathetic, try to get him to substitute talk for action, remind him that this is the way to get back into the hospital), but there's no pretending it will always do the trick.

† Dr. Theodore Lidz remarks on how parents may remove a son or daughter from therapy "when as part of his improvement the patient displays hostility to the parents." "The Influence of Family Studies on the Treatment of Schizophrenia," in *Progress in Group and Family Therapy*. Dr. David Hawkins notes that "intensive psychotherapy . . . often results in alienation of the patient from the family, which is in itself a very serious side-effect." In David Hawkins, ed., *Orthomolecular Psychiatry* (San Francisco: W. H. Freeman and Co., 1973), p. 654. "Marge . . . had been seen frequently by another psychoanalytically oriented research physician and she seemed to be well acquainted with the current concepts of the etiology of schizophrenia. This was evident in her many statements implying maternal deprivation, which seemed calculated to draw the psychiatrists' attention to her mother's shortcomings." Experienced psychiatrists like Albert Scheflen, whose description this is, maintain perspective on such accusations, but you can't always count on it. *Communicational Structure: Analysis of a Psychotherapy Transaction* (Bloomington, Ind.: Indiana University Press, 1973), p. 12.

each: affectionate concern; or, alternatively, jealousy over the attention he is getting; irritation at the sufferer's "laziness" or "selfishness"; rejection; guilt for past teasing or bullying (shadowing the omnipresent and inescapable parental guilts); refusal to accept that he is ill at all, but only "being himself," "doing his own thing," that it is not he or she but "society" which is "all wrong." Do not be surprised, therefore, if your family, with the abnormalities of its home-life, shrinks from introducing too many fresh outsiders into the home. To be thereupon typecast by the investigator with the clipboard as: "introverted family which finds social contacts difficult."

Some members of your family may never accept the diagnosis and will quarrel with the parent who tries to implement it. You then have a divided and part alienated family on your hands, if you haven't one already – to say nothing of the cases where once happily married parents are themselves driven apart because one rejects or partially rejects, which the other cannot forgive.

The sheer disruptive power of schizophrenia over a family is fully intelligible only to those who have been through it.[29]

THE FAMILY BURDEN

The burden on your family is no light one. Some experts are trying to measure it – if that makes you feel better. Dr. Julius Hoenig of Memorial University in Newfoundland is one. In cool, objective language he tells his colleagues what you know in your bones:

> We assessed "burden" on the family of schizophrenics living at home by recording concrete effects such as loss of earnings, changes in the lives of other members of the household because of the illness, separation from children, etc. We also recorded the presence of certain abnormal, disturbing traits, such as noisiness, wandering, sexual abnormalities, etc. provided they occurred with some frequency – assuming that in such a case they must have had adverse effects on the life of the household.
>
> If all these effects and traits are charted and computed, we obtain a characteristic which we call "combined objective burden." The characteristic is, of course, only a crude measure. . . . The effects listed do not take into account a good many difficulties caused, for instance, by stigma attached to the illness. Such effects, although less tangible and much more difficult to assess, can be very serious indeed.
>
> Combined objective burden . . . was recorded in 84% of all cases. Only 16 percent of households did not seem affected in any of the 30 odd ways on our inquiry list.*

When is a burden not a burden?

But Dr. Hoenig also points out something just as important: what is a burden may not always be felt as one. Dr. Hoenig found he had to

* Paper on a follow-up study of the symptomatology of schizophrenic patients living at home and their families' attitudes four years after hospitalization; delivered to the Canadian Psychiatric Society and reported in *Psychiatric News* (Aug. 15, 1973). See also G. W. Brown, "Measuring the Impact of Mental Illness on the Family," *Proceedings of the Royal Society of Medicine,* vol. 59 (1966), pp. 18–20.

distinguish between "objective" and "subjective" burden; he recorded this latter only if the family "sensed it as such and complained about it." In another follow-up report, Eva Deykin, a social worker at the Massachusetts Mental Health Center, concludes that "the family's and the community's tolerance for the ex-mental patient is one of the central factors influencing the success of the discharge." She found the families' and communities' tolerance "unexpectedly high" and their expectations of patients "unexpectedly low," particularly "in cases where the informant was related to the patient and had a strong emotional investment in him."[30]

From where you sit the responses Ms. Deykin cites as typical may not seem all that unexpected.

> In spite of Mr. H.'s unsatisfactory adjustment [he was "grossly unkempt," showed "total lack of judgment," had minimal social functioning, "assumed no responsibility for himself or others"] his sister seemed pleased to have him home and did not indicate he was too sick to be put out of the hospital. . . . Mrs. K. was extremely pleased to have the patient home and seemed to feel her daughter was improving all the time. She said she did not think her daughter would ever be able to hold a job, but she felt that this was not particularly important so long as her daughter was home and happy. . . .

"It is not known," writes Ms. Deykin, "what caused such high tolerance in the families of these patients. It is hypothesized that the families' tolerance is dependent both on the deep love and interest the families had for their patients and on the guilt feelings the families had regarding their patients' 'illness.' " Everybody believes in love, of course; families will be glad to read that guilt feelings can have such positive results.

Children in the family

But what about the children in the family? If a grandfather, an aunt, a sibling, worst of all, a parent is mentally ill, how will the burden fall on them?* And what can you do to keep it manageable?

WHAT TO TELL THE CHILDREN

We ask the experts, we ask ourselves. Perhaps we should ask the children, too. A college student tells how it was in the years when her mother was ill. She speaks for many:

> Because I felt guilty and because people have tender feelings for their parents, I wanted to find out what was the matter with mother and what I could do. I used to sneak around outside rooms where people were talk-

* "The shifting patterns of health delivery services in which hospitals are being closed down and mentally ill parents returned to the community may also accentuate the problems of child care if aftercare services prove inadequate."[31]

> ing about what was wrong. I asked people who should know. I was even convinced by one of my friends to go to the psychiatrist and ask what was going on. The investigation was a failure. The psychiatrist was evasive. My father, aunts, friends wouldn't or couldn't tell me anything. The fact that I couldn't begin to understand what was going on around me was unbearable. Eventually, of course, I pieced together enough information from teachers, articles, and books to get an idea of the situation. The searching took a long time and was extremely frustrating; I'm not sure, either, that I really understood it all. If a child is old enough to be aware that something is wrong, I think he is old enough to be given the best explanation the adults in his family are capable of giving. If he doesn't understand the meaning of scientific words, explain it in other words — the child deserves to know what is wrong with his parent. It is commonly accepted that when a mother is pregnant she should explain the phenomenon to the children. Why are mentally ill parents not explained to the children too?*

need honest explanations.

Why indeed? Because, of course, it's just so hard. It will be much easier to deal frankly with a child if others have dealt frankly with you; you can't convey information you haven't got, nor dispel fears born of ignorance when you share them. But even when you are informed, it can be hard to find the words to talk about what hurts so much. Fortunately, there's a good pamphlet to help with just this problem. Helene Arnstein's *When a Parent Is Mentally Ill; What to Say to Your Child*† describes common worries and questions of children of various ages and how to respond to them. Your relative's psychiatrist should also have suggestions for you; perhaps he'll talk to the worried child directly. Dr. Herbert Lazarus finds that often "the children require as much individual help as the patient."[32]

Of course we worry that our relative's irrationality will rub off on our children (and ourselves). And we have reason; Dr. Farber has seen this happen even between patient and therapist, and Dr. Anthony writes on "The Contagious Sub-Culture of Psychosis."[33] But what health shows in that girl's letter! We can see in it what sanity is, even if emotional illness remains a mystery. The sane mind, in child or adult, seeks understanding, assumes responsibility, and if it gets no help searches on alone as best it can.

The medical model makes explanations easier.

Here you can be grateful for the trusty old medical model. Whether or not you think it's always appropriate, it makes it a lot easier for a child to accept a relative's strange behavior if you can explain that he or she is sick. A child can be terrified and deeply hurt when his usually gentle father suddenly turns on him, or his mother doesn't recognize him after shock treatment. Careful explanations, repeated as often as

* These words are taken from a long, thoughtful letter, the contribution of a friend. She wrote it when I asked her what she thought ought to go into this book. C.C.P.

† Available from Child Study Association–Well-Met, Inc., 50 Madison Avenue, New York, NY 10010 (212) 899-3450.

necessary, can take away some of the hurt and most of the bewilderment and fear.*

Assume children have questions; make it easy for them to ask.

Questions, even unhappy questions, are no cause for worry. There's more reason for worry if children seem to have no questions. For their minds will be full of them. Isn't yours? Not only the obvious questions, but other, scarier ones: Is it my fault? Was it because of something I did — or, worse yet, something I thought or wished? Is mental illness hereditary? If I have children will they get it? These questions need to be talked about. You can be sure that children notice more than they let on. The horrors imagined in ignorance are harder to bear than even the saddest knowledge.

What to worry about:

You try to be alert to signs of strain in your child, but at this time it's a good idea to talk to other people who know him. Teachers and friends may have picked up more than you've been able to. (He may be trying not to add to your worries, or he may feel that talking just makes it worse.) Occasional strain and nervousness are probably inevitable and no real cause for concern. What should worry you is any new tendency to withdraw from people and activity — to hole up in his room, or stop inviting friends over. In general it will help to involve children in the therapeutic life with your relative. They're part of the milieu, after all. Children can be the best co-therapists going for a younger sibling; a withdrawn uncle may talk to his nephew when he won't to anyone else. Don't try to "spare him" his share in the common responsibility; for a normal child, consider whether sparing him isn't depriving him of his right to participate in a significant family experience. "When something is amiss in their parents' lives," writes our young friend,

withdrawal, isolation.

It helps children to know they're helping,

> the children see that they can no longer seriously engage their parents' attention, let alone make them happy and cheerful. They feel deposed from their place in the family and they feel that they have failed. The adults in the family must give serious thought to making the children feel that they are needed and are helping to make their parent well. The parents [and let's add, the professionals] must face up to the fact that their problem is each child's problem too, and that children need and want to help.

But don't overdo it. An afternoon with Grandma while you get some respite will do you all good, but don't take advantage of a child's good nature. The more helpful and understanding a child is, the more he and she need a life of their own. Overnight visits should be encouraged; vacations out of town may be arranged. At home it's important to have a place where the relative doesn't intrude, with a

but keep it a small part of their lives.

* For a striking portrayal of the strains put on a child who receives *no* explanations, see Robert Pirsig's account of a schizophrenic father and his son, *Zen and the Art of Motorcycle Maintenance* (New York: William Morrow, 1974).

lock on it if necessary. Children should feel their possessions and their privacy are secure from a disruptive younger brother or a prowling grandmother. A room where they won't be bothered will make it easier to invite friends.

Talking to your children's friends

Will they invite friends? You can make it easier by being open. The medical model is also a great antidote for shame. Be frank with your child's friends as well as with your child. They are probably bewildered, maybe scared too. If your relative is likely to speak or act peculiarly, let them know what to expect. It won't bother them nearly as much as it does you. Don't overlook your great ally, curiosity. Teenagers, especially, are fascinated by psychology. They may be taking a course in it in high school; they come across all sorts of psychological ideas in newspapers and magazines. If you talk to them frankly and sympathetically, they will probably be interested in meeting your relative. You may even pick up a new co-therapist.

is easier than you think.

Another ally is youthful resilience and open-mindedness. Queerness, caprice, irrationality are painful and embarrassing for the family; your children's friends may find them fascinating. It's not children who are embarrassed if your relative is unkempt or laughs when nobody is talking to him. What seem to you distressing symptoms may to them be charming eccentricity. One mother who was working hard to teach more normal behavior to her nearly speechless but weirdly lovely daughter was taken aback by a teenager's query, "Why do you want to change her?" – until she realized how lucky they all were to live in a time when the young can teach us tolerance and even appreciation of those who can't be just like ourselves.

What you don't need to worry about

Children also read.

Remember that children read, too. Younger children may respond strongly to stories of children with sick or peculiar relatives. (Check with your children's librarian; some titles are listed in Appendix A. Reading one of these aloud with your child might lead to a good conversation.) Teenagers can get help from the books that help you – as you might test by leaving this book around.

The fear of serious mental disturbance

Worries like these are bad enough. But what about the agonizing fear they all add up to? Can living with mental illness affect a child seriously, permanently – not just make him unhappy from time to time, like any of life's inevitable stresses, but make him mentally abnormal himself? Need we think of mental illness as contagious?

You probably worry about this more than you need to. If there is a mentally ill person in your home, of course do your best to keep it as warm, as active, as outgoing as you can. But there's some reassurance for you, even if it's no rose garden. We can guess that a parent's mental illness is the most stressful of all for a child, yet the many studies which have been done of children of parents suffering from major mental illnesses show that the vast majority even of these "children at risk" do not themselves become mentally ill. Living with any prolonged ill-

in "children at risk"

ness is stressful. There *is* more delinquency and maladjustment among children of severely ill parents. But this isn't peculiar to *mental* illness. In fact when Dr. Anthony studied the children of both mentally and physically ill parents, he found *more* maladjustment when the parent was physically ill.[34] What's really encouraging is the large group — Dr. Anthony calls them "the invulnerables" — who grow up perfectly normal. More encouraging still is the group — as high as 10 percent of the total — whom Dr. Anthony calls "supernormal." Strong and creative, "their response to the terrible challenges life has offered them," says Dr. Anthony, "has not only been adequate, it has been extraordinary."[35]

It doesn't seem to make much difference to the child's adjustment what kind of diagnosis the parent bears, or even how severe his illness is.* What does affect a child is not so much the symptoms themselves, but how closely they involve the child.[36] A withdrawn process schizophrenic who ignores a child is less disturbing than an acutely ill parent who approaches the child aggressively or a neurotic parent who won't allow him a life of his own, even though the process schizophrenic is the sickest of the three. Spouses, grandparents, and other relatives should try especially hard to protect children from this kind of close and intense involvement, with the help of friends, teachers, and older children, and if necessary a children's therapist. Your local Family Service organization can advise. This may be one of the situations where hospitalization becomes essential.

Children should be protected from over-involvement.

How maladjusted is "maladjusted"? Dr. Manfred Bleuler has some encouraging things to say about even that group of children of mentally ill parents who were not invulnerable, who did not grow up unscarred, get off scot-free. Dr. Bleuler is the son of Eugen Bleuler, the great Swiss psychiatrist who named "schizophrenia." Growing up in his father's hospital, he took over his work there; he has literally spent his life with schizophrenics and their families. Long and loving experience has convinced him that many of those children of schizophrenics whom other investigators classified as deviant or maladjusted were not so deviant after all. They might have seemed eccentric, even "psychopathic," to someone who didn't know them as he did. To him, who knew what they'd been through, they showed "the normal responses of a healthy individual caught in trying family circumstances."[37]

> Perhaps because of my long-term personal contact with these children, my evaluation of their personalities was different than it might have been had I met them on only a few occasions and purely for the purpose of

* Drs. A. D. Beisser, N. Glasser, and M. Grant found no significant differences between the adjustment of children of schizophrenic and psychoneurotic mothers ("Psychosocial Adjustment in Children of Schizophrenic Mothers," *Journal of Nervous and Mental Disease,* 145 (1967), 429–440.

> scientific investigation. . . . Because Hoffmann (1921), Oppler (1932) and Kallman (1938) [authors of previous extremely pessimistic outcome studies] were interested in genetic aspects of schizophrenia, they searched specifically for deviant personality characteristics in the children of their schizophrenic subjects. I searched for these qualities, too, but I was also especially aware of the good and normal aspects of the children's behavior. I saw how they worried about their parents, how they struggled when their parents were to be transferred to other clinics which would be more difficult to visit. I saw how many of these children made economic sacrifices or interrupted their professional training in order to help their parents, or how they undertook to manage the family household and care for younger siblings in place of a hospitalized parent. . . . In short, it was inevitable that I found considerably more normals and fewer psychopaths than I would have if I had seen my subject children only in a single interview and only for scientific inquiry. . . . Even long-term upbringing by two schizophrenic parents does not foredoom a child to become schizophrenic, or even abnormal. . . . Normal development can take place in the face of total neglect, copious "teaching of irrationality," and the total degeneration of the imaginative world of the parents. . . . Despite the miserable childhoods described above, and despite their presumably "tainted" genes, most offspring of schizophrenics manage to lead normal productive lives. Indeed, after studying a number of family histories, one is left with the impression that pain and suffering can have a steeling — a hardening — effect on some children, rendering them capable of mastering life with all its obstacles. . . . Perhaps it would be instructive for future investigators to keep as careful watch on the favorable development of the majority of these children as they do on the progressive deterioration of the sick minority.

Of course you will worry. But don't worry more than you have to (and *don't worry out loud,* or the children will start worrying too). Human beings are more adaptive than maladaptive; that's how families of the mentally ill (and the physically ill, and the poor, and those whose lives are devastated by war and disaster) still manage to survive and grow.

Take heart.

So do the best you can. Your relative is part of the family; you don't have to apologize for his existence, to the children or to anybody else. Involve him in family work and play; seek help on how to do it. Introduce him to your community; your neighbors' willingness to help may surprise you. Here's what not to be, any more often than you can help: excitable, intrusive, overprotective, nosy, suspicious, easily offended. Here's what to be, as much of the time as you can manage: affectionate, aware, patient, a good listener. Take heart from what two prominent professionals, a psychiatrist and a nurse, tell their students in psychiatric nursing. Even the beginner, they say, has therapeutic skills. She should "trust her natural behavioral style. . . . Unless she has absolutely no friends and her relatives avoid her, she does have natural talents."[38] So have you.

»» CHAPTER IX ««

In the Mental Hospital—And Out Again

A MEMORIAL TO THE LEGISLATURE OF MASSACHUSETTS

I proceed, Gentlemen, briefly to call your attention to the *present* state of Insane Persons confined within this Commonwealth, in *cages, closets, cellars, stalls, pens! Chained, naked, beaten with rods, and lashed into obedience!* DOROTHEA DIX, BOSTON, JANUARY 1843

They're closing Agnews State
Where we hid empty wine bottles
In laundry baskets.
They're closing Agnews State
Where old men passed out flowers
In the canteen.
They're closing Agnews State
Where volunteers from the Red Cross
Cared enough to dance with you.
They're closing Agnews State
Where the gophers pop their heads out of lawns
And say "hi" to you.
They're closing Agnews State
Where Billy Hamilton broke a window
After every shock treatment.
They're closing Agnews State
And opening up lonely hearts' clubs.
RICHARD W. GARDNER*

ONE OF AMERICA's most famous mental hospitals has a ten-foot wall around it. The bricks were laid more than a hundred years ago. That wall tells the story of community fear and community horror, of a place where "inside" and "outside" were as separate as they are in any jail, a place where crazy people were locked away.

Times have changed,

Today the words "Abandon all hope, ye who enter here" may still be written over the gates of hell, but they are no longer visible over the entrance to the mental hospital.

1. THINKING AND CHOOSING

You read terrible things about mental hospitals. Not only about brutality (which is now unusual) and neglect (which is not), but about depersonalization, lack of respect for individuals, about people

* "Requiem for Agnews State," *Madness Network News,* 1 (May 1973). (It was at Agnews State that Robin White's son Checkers received the best psychiatric care he had ever had in his life.)

reduced to things, stripped of possessions and social status, deprived of the most elementary things we take for granted, like privacy when we go to the bathroom, and having people pay attention when we speak to them.

There's a rich literature on this subject; Clifford Beers's isn't the first account of life in the hospital, or the last. Some descriptions are objective and judicious, others exaggerated and overwrought.* All are upsetting.

but most mental hospitals are not enjoyable places,

You probably needn't read any more than the description of Professor D. L. Rosenhan, whose research group became "pseudopatients" so they could learn about mental hospitals from the inside. (See Chapter V, pp. 126–127.) The hospitals they entered were not the crowded snake pits of old, but the quiet, orderly hospitals of the seventies. Yet nothing, writes Rosenhan,

> can convey the overwhelming sense of powerlessness which invades the individual as he is continually exposed to the depersonalization of the psychiatric hospital. It hardly matters *which* psychiatric hospital — the excellent public ones and the very plush private hospital were better than the rural and shabby ones in this regard, but, again, the features that psychiatric hospitals had in common overwhelmed by far their apparent differences. . . . The patient is deprived of many of his legal rights by dint of his psychiatric commitment. He is shorn of credibility by virtue of his psychiatric label. His freedom of movement is restricted. He cannot initiate contact with the staff, but may only respond to such overtures as they make. . . . Patient quarters and possessions can be entered and examined by any staff member. . . . His personal history and anguish is available to any staff member (often including the "grey lady" and "candy striper" volunteer) who chooses to read his folder, regardless of their therapeutic relationship to him. His personal hygiene and waste evacuation are often monitored. The water closets may have no doors.[1]

As pseudopatients, Rosenhan and his researchers kept records of how, and how often, the staff responded to their calm and courteous questions about their treatment and release. (Between them, they made more than 1,400 attempts to discuss these matters.) Psychiatrists, they found, walked on, head averted, 71 percent of the time; nurses and attendants, 88 percent. Psychiatrists made eye-contact with the patient 23 percent of the time, nurses and attendants 10 percent. Psychiatrists stopped and talked 6 percent of the time, nurses and attendants less than 3 percent.

> The encounter frequently took the following bizarre form: (pseudopatient) "Pardon me, Dr. X. Could you tell me when I am eligible for grounds privileges?" (physician) "Good morning, Dave. How are you today?" (Moves off without waiting for a response.)

* Ken Kesey's best-selling *One Flew over the Cuckoo's Nest* gives us a tyrannical and sadistic Big Nurse, the dominant, castrating female we've all learned to hate, who uses shock and lobotomy to maintain her absolute control of a ward in which the patients are saner than the staff.

Powerlessness is an aspect of all hospitalization, whether for physical or mental causes, as you may remember from the last time you were in a hospital bed. It is also possible to argue that a patient who's really sick is less sensitive to hospital indignities than an alert and vigorous pseudopatient. Psychologists Dorothea and Benjamin Braginski, studying chronic patients in open wards, found that many long-term patients enjoy the hospital and its facilities, which in a good hospital may be superior to what they have access to at home. They see the hospital as a familiar neighborhood. Many have no desire to leave and find ways of making sure they don't.* It may even be argued that a hospital *shouldn't* be pleasant; in *I Never Promised You a Rose Garden* the analyst asks her patient, who has reported an instance of brutal treatment, why, if the hospital is so bad, she isn't working as hard as she can to get out of it. Still, our hearts sink at the idea of someone we love in a mental hospital. Talk about "scapegoating" or "extruding" a family member,† not to mention "the myth of mental illness," encourages the guilt you are likely to feel anyway. The back-to-the-community movement reinforces the belief that hospitalization is something to be avoided at all costs. And you will try to avoid it. Nevertheless, hospitals are not prisons. They are places for sick people to get well, or if that's not possible, at least to get better.

especially if you're sane.

There are times when the best therapy, for the mentally ill as for all of us, is to get away. There are treatments that cannot be given in an office or clinic, or supervised at home. There are times when you and yours can no longer cope. There are times when your relative is dangerous to himself or to others. There are, in short, times when the advantages of hospitalization outweigh the disadvantages. "Asylum" doesn't mean booby hatch. It never did.‡ It means a refuge. If your relative needs a refuge — from a situation his mind and emotions can no longer cope with, from his suicidal or violent impulses, from the terrifying distortions of a world turned suddenly unfamiliar — he

"Asylum" means refuge

* "Mental Hospitals as Resorts," *Psychology Today* (March 1973). Responding to such attitudes, programs like PUSH at Northampton (Mass.) State Hospital (Patients Under Supervised Hassling) are designed to get reluctant patients back into the community.

† "The emergency is a specific point in time when a family or a social network manifest the need to extrude a particular person to another social sub-system." Harold Goldberg, "Home Treatment," *Psychiatric Annals*, 3 (June 1973).

‡ Even in the old days, people did recover in mental hospitals. Christopher Smart got better in his, where he dug in the garden and friends came to visit. The "moral treatment" introduced by pioneers like William Tuke and Samuel Woodward, the first superintendent of Massachusetts's Worcester State Hospital, consisted of a combination of wholesome exhortation, sympathetic respect, pleasant surroundings, a healthy routine of life and diet, and a program of constructive activity. Later in the century it was largely abandoned, under pressure of numbers. But while it lasted, recovery rates reached a height they were not to reach again for more than a hundred years.

or she needs a hospital. They need a good one if possible, but there are times when even a bad hospital may be better than no hospital at all.

when community services are lacking.

The back-to-the-community movement is humane and reasonable. But "community" has no meaning for the mental patient who has spent twenty years in a state hospital and is now, under the new philosophy, "released" from the only community he knows to return to a community that no longer knows him. And the simple, manageable community of the ward may be reassuring to the acutely ill patient, even when it falls far short of what it ought to be. But you need some reassurance in your doubts. You have to believe that this hospitalization is necessary if you're to be as calm and firm as you must.* Easier said than done; we can say that again. But facts and figures have a steadying effect. Your relative won't care, but it will help your calm and determination to know that when more than four hundred patients from Washington state mental hospitals were surveyed a year after admission, 84 percent of those released felt their hospitalization had helped them, and only 13.5 percent thought it had harmed. (Even of those still hospitalized, more than 75 percent thought the experience had been helpful.) [2] Many of those people probably entered the hospital protesting bitterly. The hospital that Clifford Beers entered in 1902 was worse than any that your relative is likely to experience, but the words he wrote in 1906 can still bring strength to wavering families: "Though at the time I dreaded commitment, it was the best possible thing that could befall me.". . . And later: "Had I suspected a recommitment was imminent, I should have fled to a neighboring state during the preceding night. Fortunately, however, the right thing was done in the right way at the right time." We can only hope we too can do the right thing in the right way at the right time,† and live, as Beers's father and brothers did, to hear our relative tell his gratitude.

What ex-patients think

Unless you live in a large city, there is probably no mental hospital, public or private, near you.‡ For most people, hospitalization in a specialized psychiatric hospital — what used to be called a sanatorium — means hospitalization at a distance. If your area is served — as many are coming to be — by a community mental health center with an

What are the choices?

* The chapter on "Your Role in Psychiatric Hospitalization" in Dr. Cammer's *Up from Depression* is extremely helpful, whether or not depression is your relative's problem. Claire Burch's *Stranger in the Family* will also be useful.

† We might note that in Beers's case "the right way" included outright deception.

‡ In 1972 there were only 158 private psychiatric hospitals in the entire United States, averaging about three per state. In fact, a few states have many more than that, and some have none. NIMH, *Staffing of Mental Health Facilities in the United States,* 1972, Series B., No. 6.

inpatient unit, you're lucky. If not, you have questions. The first one: Does the nearest general hospital have a psychiatric ward? Ten years ago the answer was probably "no"; it may be "yes" today.* If not: Where is the state hospital that serves your relative's locality? What is its reputation? Is there a better one elsewhere in the state, and is there a way to wangle him into it? Where is the nearest private hospital? Does it take patients like your relative? Can the family afford it? Is it enough better than the state hospital to justify the expense? Supposing there's enough money to send your relative anywhere, what are the pros and cons of treatment far from home? In short, what *are* the choices? Don't assume a doctor will know them all, even if he *is* a psychiatrist. Except for the most famous hospitals or those right in his backyard, he probably knows no more about private hospitals than the ads he reads in his medical journals; about public hospitals, less than you can find out from a visit.

"It is impossible," writes Claire Burch, "to exaggerate the difficulties as you ask agencies and information sources for help. Painfully you see that the average doctor has only the sketchiest idea of facilities that may be suitable, and that information given even by social service agencies may be dated and inaccurate."[3]

General Hospitals

About mental hospitals in your area, as about many other things, the best source of information is your state chapter of the National Association for Mental Health. (If your relative is a child, the Information and Referral Service of the National Society for Autistic Children has information about schools and hospitals all over the country. See Chapter XII.) But you yourself can find out about psychiatric divisions of general hospitals in your area. A phone call should inform you about the number of beds, the types of treatment, costs, and limitations on length of stay. Local doctors and social service organizations should be able to comment on the quality of care; if they're reluctant, at least they should tell you whether the ward is understaffed or crowded. You yourself may know someone who's been there as a patient, a visitor, or a volunteer. (If you don't, contact the hospital director of volunteers, or ask your local mental health association.) A general hospital can't exist in isolation from the community.

Psychiatric services in the general hospital,

If there is a bed for him in a general hospital, your relative will

* There were 770 general hospital psychiatric units in 1971 and there are more today. In 1973, almost a quarter of psychiatrists worked in such units. Z. J. Lipowski, "Consultation-Liaison Psychiatry: An Overview," *American Journal of Psychiatry,* 131 (June 1974).

probably not have to enter a mental hospital at all, for today's treatments are geared to getting the patient home quickly; limitations on length of stay range from two weeks to three months, and most patients are released within the sixty-day period written into many insurance policies. If he or she is still too sick, at least you have been given time to look into alternatives, and the hospital itself will give some help with the next step.

Hospitalization seems easier to accept emotionally in the patient's own community, where friends and family can visit easily, in a building they don't associate with mental illness. As your relative gets better, he can test himself in familiar surroundings, returning to the security of the hospital at need. When he's released, a good hospital after-care service (see pp. 261–262) will know the local situation and can put him in touch with social clubs, halfway houses, vocational programs. Knowing the patient is returning to his old surroundings, they expect to involve families in planning for his release. Hospital social workers discuss problems with the family; many programs require family participation. Counseling eases the practical and emotional problems of the return home.

If it's available, and unless you have an extremely good alternative, the general hospital is probably your best bet. The number of patients admitted to general hospitals for mental illness far exceeds the number of first admissions to state hospitals. Many general hospitals provide the inpatient service of community mental health centers, making it easier to coordinate services when the patient is released.

good

The quality varies, of course. Teaching hospitals associated with medical schools are usually among the best. Programs are innovative, sophisticated medical evaluation is available, and everybody, from chief psychiatrist to attendant, has reason to be interested in your relative's symptoms and state of mind.* Most of the doctors are young residents, supervised by experienced psychiatrists. You should remember, though, that in all hospitals – mental hospitals, general hospitals, public hospitals, private hospitals – most of the actual work with patients is done not by doctors but by nurses and attendants (now usually called psychiatric aides). How they are chosen and trained may make a lot more difference to your relative than the professional qualifications of the chief of staff. In good hospitals today, aides (and of course nurses) are trained to be active and sensitive participants in the therapeutic process; the old-time attendant, whose qualifications were often all too similar to those of the barroom bouncer, is giving

* Maybe *too* interested; there are some disadvantages in providing teaching material for students. Burgess's and Lazare's nursing text (p. 87) tells the student how to handle a training interview, in which the "therapeutic contact" may be a one-shot affair. (The patient may refuse if he wishes.) The passage suggests the question, when is a service not a service?

way to a new breed. The aide who firmly calms the manic patient, or gently persuades the depressed patient to walk to the shower, may well be a student working his way through college who has chosen this job because he likes and respects people and wants to learn more about helping them.

In most general hospital psychiatric units, your relative will talk with a psychiatrist from time to time, but you can't count on his having regular individual psychotherapy. (If he already has a therapist, it may be possible to arrange to continue seeing him in the hospital.) As in most psychiatric programs today, the major treatments are drugs, group therapy, and occupational therapies of various kinds. (See Chapter IV.)

Attractive curtains and fresh colors can certainly make people feel better, including you. But don't judge a hospital by its interior decoration; it may merely reflect an active ladies' auxiliary. Some of the best-run hospitals are pretty bleak; when funds are limited, it's better to put them into people than buildings. It's the quality of the staff that makes the difference – and whether there are enough of them to allow them to do the job they'd like to do. County and municipal general hospitals are funded from taxes. Some are excellent – usually those affiliated with medical schools. Many are overpopulated and understaffed, with treatment largely limited to drugs dispensed by overworked personnel and after-care and follow-up largely nonexistent.

and bad

Private Psychiatric Hospitals

Treatment in a general hospital is very expensive, as you know if you've broken a leg recently. Rates at a private psychiatric hospital may actually be lower, since few of these maintain elaborate medical facilities.

Private psychiatric hospitals vary in cost,

It is impossible to generalize about private hospitals. Some are good, and some are terrible. Some are run to make money,* others are nonprofit. Some are cheaper than anything but the state hospital; many are so expensive that a year's stay will wipe out a well-to-do family's reserves and send them into debt. Nonprofit status has little to do with cost to patients; it has more to do with quality of care. The most expensive private hospitals may still not take in enough to pay for their high-quality staff and programs; some of the cheapest can still make

quality,

* "Recently [as of 1972] Purolator, Inc., a maker of automotive oil and air filters, acquired Carrier Clinic, a large private psychiatric hospital. . . . The president of Purolator stated that he had been influenced by a recent study of investment-banking firm Dillon Read and Co. which concluded that the psychiatric hospital industry showed signs of exceptional growth." Robert L. Taylor and E. Fuller Torrey, "Mental Health Coverage Under a National Health Insurance Plan," *World Journal of Psychosynthesis,* 6, No. 5 (1974):22–27.

money when they provide little more than a bed, a locked door, drugs, and ECT.

and the type of patient they accept.

Private hospitals differ in their clientele too. Unlike state hospitals, very few take all kinds of psychiatric patients. In some hospitals, older people are excluded; in others, chronic patients; in others, those with organic conditions; in others, children under eighteen,* in others, assaultive or suicidal people. They accept, they'll tell you, only those they feel they can help; that may not include your relative.

Good places

It's an encouraging experience to visit some private hospitals; you probably wouldn't mind spending some time there yourself. The rooms, the facilities, the beautiful grounds recall a good college. The sophisticated and intelligent staff take time to talk to you, and they talk well. The same can be said of a lot of the patients, who often don't seem very sick. There are plenty of highly trained psychiatrists, psychologists, social workers, and nurses (who probably wear street clothes). Aides are carefully recruited and trained. There are facilities for arts and crafts, drama, perhaps a gym, maybe tennis courts or a greenhouse. With them go skilled and sympathetic people who know how to get patients using them, alone if need be, together when they're ready. Group therapy is more than morose people sitting in a circle every morning at ten; the therapeutic community is a twenty-four-hour enterprise where patients are helped to assume responsibility for themselves, each other, and their common life. The staff is acutely conscious of the criticism that hospitals breed powerlessness.

Therapeutic milieu

Psychotherapy

In these élite institutions, as exclusive as Harvard, individual therapy, often with gifted psychoanalysts, is an established part of treatment. Somatic treatments are less in evidence. "The human transaction — in a one-to-one relationship and in larger groups — is the . . . basis of therapy."[4] In these hospitals, the educational model of treatment is seen at its best.

At Chestnut Lodge, where psychoanalysis is the foundation of treatment, somatic treatments are used reluctantly; in 1973, only 20 percent of patients were on psychotropic drugs, according to social worker Valerie Lynn.[5] Although McLean, in suburban Boston, takes a wider variety of patients and has a more eclectic treatment philosophy, in 1972 only 5 percent of patients had ECT.[6]

The human transaction is expensive. How expensive? Rarely less than $3,000 a month, often more. Sometimes individual therapy is included in the basic charge; family therapy, school tuition (if the patient is a child), and various extras will add to the cost. As we've seen, general hospital rates are as high or higher, but there the stay is usually measured in days, not months — or years. So the question becomes, how many months — especially, how many months after the

How many months?

* Many state hospitals do not have facilities for children, either. See Chapter XII.

insurance runs out?* Not merely how many months can the patient or his family afford, but a deeper question: in the best interests of the patient how many should they want to afford? How *desirable* is long-term treatment?

Long-term hospital care for chronic patients is obviously necessary if the patient is incapacitated and has nowhere else to live. For the few families who can afford years, perhaps a lifetime, of care in a fine hospital, the peace of mind is certainly worth the money.†

But cheer up if your relative can't afford the best:

> In the small psychiatric hospitals (Chestnut Lodge and the Yale Psychiatric Institute) described by Stanton and Schwartz and Caudill, problems of a different sort seem to arise. Indeed, the presence of so many nurses, aides, junior and senior physicians is almost an "embarras de richesse" because they are bound to get in each other's way and to argue and disagree over the patient's administrative and therapeutic program. Thus a whole series of problems . . . are related to this particular type of mental hospital social system, such as the split in functions between the administrative and the therapeutic psychiatrist. Such problems are essentially nonexistent in the state hospital system where the services of either an administrative or a therapeutic psychiatrist are more of a dream than a reality.[7]

A split in the profession: long-term vs. short-term hospitalization for acute conditions

If your relative has been acutely ill and can be expected to get better, there's a deep split in the psychiatric profession over the value of long-term hospitalization. The young girl of *I Never Promised You a Rose Garden* recovered after three years of psychoanalytic treatment (the hospital portrayed is Chestnut Lodge). That treatment today would cost over $100,000 – a fact that is itself a considerable emotional burden on a recovering, or indeed a recovered, patient.‡

The case for long-term treatment

Those who support long-term treatment believe that significant change must come from the deepest levels of the personality and cannot be hurried. Even regression may be progress. A patient may take to his bed, stop talking, stop feeding himself, smear his bowel movements like a baby. The staff can wait; when the time seems ripe, they will help him reintegrate slowly. Of regression, Dr. Leon Cooperman of the Austen Riggs Center says, "We neither promote it or try to stop it. We accept it, like any other product of the patient."[8] Dr. Loren Mosher of NIMH, applying some of the ideas of Dr. R. D. Laing, believes that "the inner voyage of the schizophrenic person . . . has

The "inner voyage"

* There are a few insurance programs, notably those that cover government workers and members of the armed forces, that do provide long-term benefits. See Chapter XI.

† Some chronic mental patients may find places in privately run sheltered villages. These serve mainly the adult retarded, and there are not nearly enough of them. The National Association for Retarded Citizens can give you names.

‡ The Dutch psychiatrist Jan Foudraine, though deeply committed to the idea of a therapeutic community, describes his disenchantment with the effects of one famous hospital's prolonged treatment in *Not Made of Wood: A Psychiatrist Discovers His Profession* (New York: Macmillan, 1974).

great potential for natural healing and growth, and we therefore do not attempt to abort, rechannel, or quell it before it has run its natural course."* Philosophies differ: not all advocates of long-term treatment would endorse these statements. But they would agree on the goal of this long-term, intensely personal treatment: to produce a basic change in how the patient meets the world. It's an ambitious goal, not likely to be reached in sixty days.

The case for short-term hospitalization: Quicker is better.

Those who challenge long-term treatment — and they include many psychoanalysts† — find no evidence that this approach is more effective than quicker methods.‡ Minimum hospitalization with massive medication, aimed at getting the patient home or to work as soon as possible is, they believe, the treatment of choice, not only cheaper, but *better*. Intensive psychotherapy isn't automatically what your relative needs; bringing unconscious conflicts to consciousness may be deeply disturbing. Accepting his bizarre behavior may reinforce it; regression to smearing feces is not exactly a therapeutic victory. Sick patients can help each other get worse as well as better; they can learn crazy behavior from each other. The hospital may satisfy too many needs; the patient may lose his desire to leave and thus be deprived of an important spur to recovery. (For a patient whose series of acute psychotic reactions cause repeated rehospitalizations, however, it might be wise to try for deeper therapy and more ambitious treatment goals during a longer stay.)

Bad places

The average private hospital does not offer the intensive personal treatment of the élite institutions. Most offer milieu therapy, group therapy, occupational therapy, and somatic therapies in various proportions, with individual psychotherapy occasional or optional. Some offer such perfunctory care that they can charge half the prices we've been talking about and still make money. These too may have attractive furnishings and beautiful grounds, but ask to see the facilities for occupational therapy or recreation and it's another story. The real difference, however, is in the staff. Attendants are important everywhere, but here they do almost all the work. Overworked nurses do little more than distribute medication and check physical symptoms; some hospitals are so understaffed that at times there are wards, even buildings, with no nurse on duty. Aides are untrained, and it's not

* L. Mosher, L. Goveia, and A. Menn, "The Treatment of Schizophrenia as a Developmental Crisis," presented to the Detroit meeting of the American Orthopsychiatric Association, April, 1972. Dr. Mosher, it should be pointed out, was talking not about a hospital program but a halfway house.

† (Like myself. L.N.S.)

‡ The proponents of long-term psychoanalytic and milieu treatment themselves make few claims for effectiveness, and no promises. (Dr. Leon Cooperman of Austen Riggs Center envisages two or more years of hospital treatment, with "no guarantee that you'll be a bit better.") They don't make many follow-up studies and are likely to question their significance, pointing out that the changes they're working for aren't the kind you can measure.

surprising that "chemical restraints" – drugs – and even old-fashioned straitjackets substitute for firmness and tact. Some hospitals are known as "shock shops" or "buzz farms," places where, in the words of Dr. Leo Alexander (himself no enemy of ECT), "they figure that if twenty treatments are good, then two hundred are better."[9] Naturally there is no psychotherapy of any kind, and the main characteristics of the therapeutic milieu are TV, old magazines, and boredom.

But patients get better, it must be remembered, even in these hospitals. At least there is no temptation to stay long. Working people who can't afford the time or money for lengthy psychotherapy often seek out ECT, which is routinely covered by most health insurance. With or without shock, they can get a few days' rest, and someone who's only staying a short time can do without therapy groups, occupational programs, even sympathetic attendants. A more important lack is the want of careful preparation for the return home; patients have been released still confused from ECT having forgotten why they went to the hospital. There is little room in the budget of such hospitals for social workers, or the liaison with the patient's family that a good hospital provides.

The private hospital and the family:

Liaison with the patient's family? Many families, veterans of the best hospital treatment of the sixties, will greet those words with a bitter laugh. Barbara Benziger describes her stay in a plush private hospital; she was allowed no telephone calls home, her letters were censored (one she wrote in French was returned to her). Her husband was not allowed to visit her for several *weeks*.[10] And Dr. Joseph Brenner, reviewing that tragic story of Michael Wechsler which has led to so much professional soul-searching, speaks of the "mystification" involved in "policies and practices that are a part of our best private mental hospitals."

> There can be special kinds of torture for families who are rich enough or well-insured enough to use these small, exclusive, heavily staffed mental hospitals. In such hospitals the lives and minds and feelings of the family are often explored and analyzed and picked to help establish "formulations" for an assumed "psychodynamic" etiology of the patient's illness. It is not always clear whether this is done out of belief, or habit, or for tidiness, or for the establishment of a basis for treatment, or for training purposes. Here again is the fundamental difference between physical and mental illness; families of the mentally ill suffer agonies of self-doubt, guilt, and shame. If it is easy to speculate why this should be so, it is harder to understand why professional staffs in mental hospitals find it necessary to drag the families ever deeper into the quicksands of guilt, while protesting – and no doubt sometimes believing – that they are doing just the opposite.[11]

Things are getting better.

Though change is slow, you are less likely to suffer from this kind of mystification today. The hospital where Michael Wechsler's parents felt so cruelly excluded today makes his story required reading for its social workers and recommends it to families. Families who could once hear about treatment only from a social worker now discuss it with the doctor in charge. In many states, the patients' right to mail and phone communication is now guaranteed by law.

Credentials

The Association of Private Psychiatric Hospitals* publishes a directory of its members, who must meet certain standards. Your relative's psychiatrist should have this directory; if you are doubtful about hospitals, ask him to look over it with you. Some very good hospitals, however, choose not to be listed. A better criterion is accreditation by the Joint Commission on Accreditation of Hospitals. You may see the certificate of accreditation in the lobby when you visit; if not, ask.

State Hospitals

Progress

The number of patients in state hospitals is half what it was in 1955. The average length of hospitalization, once measured in years, has decreased to under a month at this writing, and is still decreasing.

with a catch: chronic patients may be excluded.

These are encouraging statistics; they mean less crowded wards, less hurried staff, more possibility of active treatment programs. But they also mean that in many states (usually the richest and most progressive) you can no longer be sure that the state hospital will admit your relative. In New York, for instance, local city hospitals, "originally designed to treat acutely psychotic patients, have been increasingly obliged to provide long-term shelter to chronic patients" that state hospitals, under the new philosophy, will not accept, or have released.[12] As state hospitals move to become active treatment centers for the acutely ill (or temporarily troubled), the "less desirable" patients, the chronic, the aged, those with organic brain syndromes, are excluded. Not that you won't find them in state hospitals – in 1972, they still made up more than half the patient population.[13] But many hospitals aren't accepting new patients of these types. This is particularly devastating to desperate families, since these are also the patients least likely to be accepted by private hospitals. If you can't give a home to your relative, there's no guarantee that the nursing homes, foster homes, halfway houses that are "the new back wards of the community"[14] will be as good as the state hospital, let alone better. The run-down hotels in high-crime districts certainly aren't; some patients are "free" to roam the streets, while others, fearful of assault and robbery, are imprisoned as surely as in any locked ward.† Progress which substitutes "neighborhood snakepits"[15] for hospitals is not progress.

* 353 Broad Ave., Leonia, NJ 07605.

† "Patients . . . are still thrust into the community to enjoy its allegedly therapeutic qualities, only . . . to find their freedom has been dearly bought. Living in a single room, sleeping on a park bench, or enjoying the benefits of an overcrowded prison are poor substitutes for a well-run asylum." Humphry Osmond, "Psychiatry under Siege: The Crisis Within," *Psychiatric Annals*, 3 (Nov. 1973).

The future of the state hospital is uncertain.

What will happen to state hospitals isn't yet clear, but there is less and less talk about closing them down altogether. Agnews State is gone, but the policy that in the early seventies put California on the road to being what Dr. Nathan Kline called "the nation's first open-air mental institution" has been reconsidered, and California's eleven other state hospitals will remain.

Costs

Unless there's lots of money in your family, or the community facilities available are first rate, you and your relative are vitally interested in whether state hospitals continue to exist, and in how good they are. If your relative needs hospitalization, your family can afford it in the state hospital. But that doesn't mean you should think of it as free.* Your family won't be assessed the full cost of your relative's treatment, but you'll be expected to pay what you can.

Open doors

The best state hospitals (usually those connected with medical schools) give as good (not as luxurious) care as you can find anywhere. Even the bad ones are probably better than your nightmares. Brutality and filth are largely things of the past. State hospitals have become surprisingly open institutions, not only because most wards are not locked, but because (unlike a private hospital) any citizen can visit. They are, after all, public institutions. Not only can families visit (in a state hospital there should be no question of your not being permitted to see your relative) ; so can any taxpayer who wants to see what his money goes for. Most state hospitals are served by local volunteers; they go into any back ward they have the heart to. In many states citizen visiting committees check on conditions. You can contact the committee through the hospital or the state department of mental health. A telephone call to the hospital will locate the coordinator of volunteers, who is usually a paid member of the staff. You can also ask if the hospital is accredited by the Joint Commission on Accreditation of Hospitals.

A big public hospital is a community. Many have wide lawns, flowering shrubs, fine old trees. The trees at St. Elizabeths were planted in the 1850's; rare varieties were brought from all over the world. It is comforting to imagine the poet Ezra Pound (see Chapter X, p. 283) sitting under one, as many patients do. Most of them aren't locked up, and many leave the hospital on passes when they have somewhere to go.

What you'll find:

Facilities and amenities

You'll find: extensive buildings, sometimes new, more often old and shabby, but often with fine Victorian architectural details that make you realize that even then, somebody cared; canteens where patients can buy snacks and socialize; art materials, sewing materials, wood-

* It's free if needed, but services cost somebody's money wherever they're given, and good services cost a lot of it. In 1971 the National Institute for Mental Health reported the average daily cost per patient in state hospitals was something over $20 (ranging from Mississippi's $8 to Alaska's $62) ; the figure is higher today. Where it isn't, be sure you won't like what you'll find.

working tools; places for movies and shows; places to play music, to bowl, to grow flowers. (There's at least one hospital with a swimming pool.)[16] A school, if the hospital takes children; stores where patients can select used clothing (and get practice in buying and selling); workshops for vocational training; newspapers written and produced by patients; patients' governments with elected representatives. And even understaffed, dingy hospitals whose care is merely custodial have patients' libraries, pleasant places to sit, where librarians take a personal interest and books and newspapers affirm the existence of life outside.

You're more likely than not to find most of these facilities. Sometimes they're flourishing, often not. None seems crowded; hospital populations are down, of course, but clearly most of the patients don't use them; they're too old, too sick, or the staff is lacking to break through inertia and indifference. People who need no assistance in making use of the resources of their environment rarely spend much time in mental hospitals.

So much for the amenities; as the Braginskis point out, a good hospital has many of the aspects of a resort.[17]* But what about the less visible aspects of the milieu? Facilities may be elegant or scruffy; they're not what makes a place a hospital. People these days are talking about a right to treatment, and courts are upholding it (see Chapter X, The Law). What about *therapy* in the public hospital?

What Therapies Are Available? Many Are Not

The basis of therapy in the state hospital — as in most other mental hospitals — is drugs. In poor hospitals it may be the *only* therapy for patients who don't take part in occupational programs. The average drug dosage in state hospitals is higher than in private hospitals; the quiet, orderly wards are largely the result of drugs, whether used for therapy, or for "chemical restraint." Patients who are with it enough to object often complain about the level of drugs they're given, and there's plenty of reason to think they might be right. Understaffing leads to overprescription; it also makes possible the remedy found by many patients: flushing the pills down the toilet.

Somatic treatment: drugs aplenty

Don't assume that because your relative is in a mental hospital all somatic treatments, or even all drug treatments, are available. For example, the sophisticated chemotherapy of lithium treatment requires sophisticated medical technology and experienced staff. Very few hospitals, private or public, now give insulin coma therapy. More and

but maybe not much else

Lithium?

* Studying attitudes of patients in a first-class state hospital, the Braginskis found that many patients, even quite well-integrated ones, treated it as one. They didn't want treatment and avoided it, but used the hospital facilities.

ECT?

more public hospitals are giving up ECT; it's troublesome, a lot of people object to it, drugs are cheaper and easier.

Should you feel reassured? When an accepted treatment is never given — or given routinely — you know there's reason to feel uneasy. Inflexible policies are easy to apply. What takes intelligence and skill is to give *appropriate* treatment.

Does a mental hospital need psychiatrists?

Shocking as it may seem in a place where somatic treatments are often the only treatments, what you won't find in most state hospitals is a lot of psychiatrists. You won't even find a lot of doctors. One state hospital in a wealthy and progressive state has two psychiatrists for 850 patients, both in administrative positions. The twelve doctors who actually care for patients aren't psychiatrists; what they know about psychotropic drugs, they are likely to have found out from the nurses and patients. Considering how few of them there are to provide twenty-four-hour service, they're doing well if they can check medication and keep up with physical ailments (state hospital patients are not known for their robust general health). These twelve doctors are all foreign. Some of them have trouble understanding the patients' routine complaints; there's no question of any "talking treatment."

Or doctors

who are at home in English?

Foreign doctors

This is typical of the situation in many public hospitals.* The prestigious *New England Journal of Medicine* has called the thousands of underqualified foreign doctors working in state hospitals a "medical underground" threatening the quality of health care.[18]† State hospitals are not places where American doctors like to work; today they are staffed with graduates of the medical schools of Korea, India, the Philippines, South America — poor countries where conditions are hard and the standard of living is low. Not that these countries don't need their own medical graduates‡ — but they can make more money here. Massachusetts mental hospitals pay doctors $18,000 to $30,000 a year and still can't fill their positions. (The median yearly income for a psychiatrist in private practice in the early seventies was $37,000, which means that half of psychiatrists made more; Dr. John Nardini, in a pamphlet addressed to psychiatric residents, assures them that a general psychiatrist in the Washington area can expect to earn $75,000 a

* From a decision by Federal Judge David Bazelon in 1973: "On June 30, 1970, there were 6118 patients 'on the rolls' (i.e. in the hospital or on convalescent leave) at St. Elizabeths and 4363 total applications for admission. To contend with this volume there were only 97 physicians, aided by 18 psychologists and 39 social workers employed by the hospital." *In re John Ballay,* 482 F. 2d 648 (1973).

† In 1973, Dr. Charles Goodman, Director of the Rhode Island Department of Mental Health, stated that 95 percent of the doctors in Rhode Island state hospitals were foreign-born and -trained, and that many had significant difficulty in communicating with patients and with other staff.

‡ "Eighty-five percent of our imported medical manpower comes from countries that are least able to sustain the loss. Korea, for example, has lost over 23 percent of its medical school graduates over the past twenty years, and only 3 percent have returned." Dr. E. Fuller Torrey, Interview, *Frontiers of Psychiatry,* Roche Report, 3 (February 15, 1973).

year.) [19] Under the American system, few of us work for less than we can get in places we don't like and don't have to be. Doctors don't either.

Some foreign doctors, of course, are fully qualified and speak English well enough to be in tune with patients' needs. Unfortunately those are just the ones who follow their American colleagues to greener fields outside the state hospital. Many foreign doctors working in state hospitals aren't licensed to practice outside them;* states lower requirements because they see no other way to fill the need with the money they've got. State medical exams are the gateway to private practice, but there's a test especially for foreign doctors, designed to make sure they can speak English well enough to communicate with patients and have the equivalent of a minimal American medical education. If you want to borrow trouble, you could inquire at your state hospital what the proportion of foreign medical graduates is and how many have passed the Educational Council for Foreign Medical Graduates exam. Many have failed it more than once.

are often underqualified.

Some states, like Massachusetts, have passed laws establishing stricter standards. But getting rid of unqualified doctors won't help, except by drawing attention to the problem; it will probably substitute nothing for something. Even with more money than they see in their dreams, state hospitals can't compete with the private sector for doctors. To a sick mental patient an underqualified doctor is better than no doctor. The problem of how to get doctors to work where the need is isn't confined to state hospitals, it's a root problem of the American system.† It affects your relative and it affects you. It's also outside the scope of this book.

Gloomy reflections. Two thoughts occur to lighten them. First, though psychotropic drugs work much better when supervised by qualified physicians, they still work quite well. A patient can stay sick in the therapeutic intimacy of a private hospital and get well under the impersonal care of the state. Dr. Henry Pinsker of New York's Beth Israel Medical Center remarks that

Luckily, drugs work

> people accept the fact that they can be guided along the highways by traffic policemen who do not know their ultimate destination or motives for traveling, that they can be given money by bank clerks who do not know how they will spend it; but they hate to come up against the fact

* "In New York and Ohio, for example, 40 percent of the physicians in state mental hospitals are unlicenced. If this figure is representative for the United States as a whole, then there would be approximately 3,100 unlicenced foreign doctors staffing state medical facilities in this country." E. Fuller Torrey, Interview, *Frontiers of Psychiatry,* Roche Report, 3 (February 15, 1973).

† "The best psychiatrists do not work with the sickest patients. One of the most bitter truths about our current system is that as one's psychological condition deteriorates he is likely to lose access to the best facilities and . . . be treated by a progressively inferior system of health care." Seymour L. Halleck, "Future Trends in the Mental Health Professions," *Psychiatric Opinion,* 11 (April 1974).

> that in a modern psychiatric hospital they are likely to recover from a psychotic illness without ever telling a psychiatrist about their fears and hopes.[20]

and there can be good programs without doctors.

Second, the dearth of physicians in state hospitals has shown that hopeful, effective programs can operate without them. It's not doctors, usually, but psychologists, social workers, and particularly nurses, aides, paraprofessionals, and volunteers who provide the therapeutic milieu in the typical public hospital. There, the medical model has come close to pricing itself out of existence.

Psychotherapy

With the exception of long-term individual analytic therapy, you can find any of the major therapeutic methods in the public hospital. In well-supported teaching hospitals near good medical schools, you'll find a rich combination, complete with real doctors; Braginski and Braginski noted that "a patient, if he chose, could easily spend eight to ten hours a day in the great variety of therapy programs offered by the hospital."[21] Individual psychotherapy exists. Michael Wechsler had individual therapy three times a week in one highly rated state hospital, reminding us that in state hospitals as in clinics and mental health centers, it's the educated, verbal, "interesting" patients who tend to get chosen for individual psychotherapy. If your psychotic relative *isn't* receiving individual therapy, you may be somewhat reassured to recall Dr. Milton Greenblatt's doubts about its value in psychosis (p. 94).

Individual therapy

Dr. Greenblatt notes, even more surprisingly, that with chronic schizophrenics, active milieu therapy did not seem to be more effective than drugs alone, and makes an interesting observation: can such patients receive too much attention?

> The small ward in the Massachusetts Mental Health Center study with its high ratio of staff-to-patients, the intensive social interaction, plus the high hopes and expectations of the staff for therapeutic progress, may have threatened patients to the point of exaggerating or hardening their pathological defenses. The patients actually may have done better at Boston State, on drugs alone, with a competent staff but where "open spaces" and less intense expectations of staff concerning patient progress seemed to prevail.[22]*

We remember Dr. Wing's recognition of the schizophrenic's need to withdraw.

Milieu therapy

But not all state hospital patients are chronic schizophrenics. There are plenty of depressed people, suicidal people, people recovering from

* See also P. R. A. May: "In a five-year follow-up by Litemandia, Harris, and Willems, no striking changes in mental state were found to accompany either the introduction of an open-ward policy or of treatment in a 'therapeutic community.'" "Changing Perspectives in Research and the Treatment of the Schizophrenic Patient," in *Changing Patterns in Psychiatric Care,* ed. Theodore Rothman (New York: Crown Publishers, 1970).

acute psychotic reactions who can respond to individual psychotherapy and an active therapeutic milieu. Group therapy is often offered. Sometimes it's good, sometimes not; getting people talking takes considerable skill, let alone the kind of talking that accomplishes something. Family and couple therapy may be available. Psychodrama was developed in a public hospital. Videotapes were pioneered there. Art therapy, music therapy, dance therapy may be offered by the regular staff or by volunteers. Occupational therapy is much more reliably found; it's discouraging if there's no group therapy in a hospital, but if there's no occupational therapy it's a scandal.

Group therapy

Family therapy

Psychodrama, art, music, dance

Occupational therapy

So far these types of treatment aren't different in kind from what you'd find in private settings, though they may be very different in quality. Behavioral treatments, however, still rare in private settings,* are becoming common in public ones. Particularly important is the kind of systematic, ward-wide reinforcement program called the token economy.

Behavior therapy

An Innovation: "Token Economies"

The token economy works with patients whom traditional therapies don't reach. Much of the pioneering work on reinforcement therapy was done in state hospitals with chronically regressed patients whom the rest of the staff had long since given up on, the ones showing the "social breakdown syndrome" of apathy, dependency, and loss of basic skills that social scientists see as a result of institutionalization. These were the true back ward inhabitants, the "vegetables." Some hadn't said a word for months or years. Some didn't dress or feed themselves. Some rocked incessantly. Unreachable by any of the techniques of dynamic psychiatry, unresponsive to group or occupational programs, these patients were monumentally "uninteresting." Behavioral treatments were little known in the early sixties and what was known was distrusted.[23] But nobody objected to the behavioral psychologists' working with *them*.†

They began in the back wards with "hopeless" patients

A hospital ward is a controlled environment by its very nature. Where all the conditions of life can be controlled, it's not hard to arrange to reinforce desired behavior and discourage undesirable behavior. Patients were studied to see what behaviors they might be ready to acquire and what they might find rewarding. Desired behaviors were rewarded by tokens which could be exchanged for things people want,

* Private, prestigious McLean hired its first behavior therapist in 1974.

† "But few psychiatrists have chosen to work with the chronically sick, just as few physicians in other specialties have taken time with these persons. As a result, clinical psychologists have grown in number and authority to fill this deficit in state hospitals and elsewhere . . . a phenomenon unique to America." Dr. John Romano, interviewed in *Medical Opinion* (Jan. 1973).

for even the most apathetic patient wants something. In some token economies patients who wanted nothing more even had to earn meals and beds. Room dividers, a personal chair, a visit with a social worker, a walk on the grounds, a locked cabinet in which to keep possessions previously stuffed under a mattress, soft-boiled eggs instead of the usual hard-boiled – different things reinforce different people. Today private rooms (available now hospitals are emptying out) are often used as reinforcers.

To make a long story short, it worked. People who'd been fed for years ate by themselves, people who rocked all day began to do things. Coherent speech increased when staff paid attention to it and ignored crazy talk. Patients who'd ignored each other learned to work together if cooperation was necessary to earn their tokens.[24] Was it manipulative? Indeed it was. Did it work by making privileges of things which patients ought to have as a matter of right? The token economists' answer is more realistic than pleasant: the patients didn't have most of these things, anyway, and they were being manipulated into a more human life.*

and have spread to more capable patients.

Today, token economies aren't limited to the back wards; the principles that brought some degree of functioning to "hopeless" patients can be applied to building the complex behaviors needed for living in the outside world. Instead of responding to a totally controlled environment patients participate in setting their own goals and planning the ward program. Not only do specific behaviors improve, but patients' ability to plan their lives does too, and their self-image along with it.[25] In the "incentive ward" at one state hospital patients have to apply for admission, and there's not room enough for all who want to get in.

Cautions

It's easy to see how a token economy could be abused. It's easy, too, to see how it could be used mechanically without regard to real needs of patients. Though reinforcement principles are much easier to learn than the subtle interactions of dynamic psychotherapy, behavioral treatments still require good, smart people who care about what they're trying to accomplish.

> Partially trained and partially educated individuals are specialists in techniques only. Too often their inadequate training results in their

* For an overview, see Teodoro Ayllon and Nathan Azrin, *The Token Economy: A Motivational System for Therapy and Rehabilitation* (New York: Appleton-Century-Crofts, 1968).

> using only a single treatment technique and thus misusing it. Persons with limited training should be supervised by comprehensively trained therapists who decide on the kind of treatment, the duration of treatment and when it should be applied, only after considering the possible consequences for the patient, his family, and his associates.[26]

Professor Teodoro Ayllon (one of the originators of the token economy) warns of easy misconceptions:

> The token economy . . . is *not* the distribution of tokens. . . . It is *not* a closed economic system. . . . It is *not* an inflexible system. It cannot be "set up" *a priori.* It must be subject to constant adjustment in order to maximize motivation, learning, and growth. It is *not* designed to facilitate passive participation. . . . It *is* a system that recognizes the individuality of those involved, designed to strengthen behaviors useful to the *individual,* not merely those that will benefit the staff or the therapist.[27]

If there's an incentive ward in your state hospital and you're doubtful about it, talk to the person who develops and supervises the program and decide for yourself how close what it *is* is to what it ought to be.*

Work in the hospital

Token economies involve tasks performed for tokens earned; as patients progress, these often involve work of use to the hospital community — on the grounds, for instance, or in the laundry or canteen. The token economy is only the most recent and most systematic example of incorporating work into a therapeutic program; from the time of Pinel, in both private and public hospitals, the work patients did for the institution, unpaid or paid at nominal rates,† has been justified as beneficial not only to the institution but to the patients themselves.‡ But that depends on the individual case. It is not very therapeutic to have to do the same monotonous small task day in and day out, without rotation at least to other small tasks or, in case of improvement, "promotion" to something more interesting and responsible. Ideally, the work, if any, that is demanded of your relative

paid and unpaid

* The Guidelines for Behavior Modification Techniques in State Hospitals drawn up by the Minnesota Department of Public Welfare are a good guide to possible abuses.

† In one state, as low as 3.9 cents an hour (*Behavior Today* [December 24, 1973]). At McLean, where charges run upward of $50,000 a year, patients work in the canteen for fifty cents an hour.

‡ "New Jersey has demonstrated what can be done. In the 1950's the state began a program of hiring institution residents as aides. They were paid $100 a month, given room and board, privileges in the employee dining room and weekends in the community. The work program was accompanied by adult training and social education courses. The worker's progress and needs were continually evaluated. New Jersey's program has led to the eventual release of thousands of employable residents. Each released resident represented a personal success story, a savings of future tax dollars, and a vindication of the right to liberty."[28] As of January, 1975, however, New Jersey's work programs were in serious jeopardy from underfunding.

should be planned with him in mind, to supplement and further his treatment.

Now a 1973 court decision on "peonage," upholding the right of patients to be paid for labor at the prevailing minimum wage (or portion of it geared to productivity)[29] threatens hospital work programs. It is true that the system could be abused, and was; patients sometimes worked long hours without compensation, and some, it is charged, were even kept in the hospital as a source of free labor.[30] (See Chapter X, pp. 274, 301.) But today, when the trend is to discharge anybody who is capable of working outside (and many who aren't), this danger seems less serious than the likelihood that hospitals will simply eliminate jobs they cannot pay for.* Tokens will be out, of course, but so will money unless it's up to the minimum wage. Particularly in token economies, the right to be paid the minimum wage may run afoul of another right — the right to treatment.† At any rate, it looks as if the beautiful grounds might not look so beautiful anymore.

Hopeful and innovative programs

State hospitals offer all sorts of excellent programs: homelike cottage living, innovative family therapy, incentive wards, careful after-care and follow-up. However these differ they have one thing in common; they all cost money. Often they're research projects funded by a federal grant; when it expires the program expires too, unless the state finds the money. They're usually sparked by some live-wire professional; the more successful the program, the more likely he or she is to be offered a better job in a nicer place — and take it. The program may not survive his departure. The top-flight professionals who, like Dr. Peter Laqueur, choose to make a career in state hospitals deserve our special honor. There aren't a lot of them.

may be here today and gone tomorrow.

Be realistic. But don't be discouraged; your state hospital may be a model institution. If it isn't, it may still have some model programs. Don't blame the director, in any case, or the harassed and overworked staff. They know what good care is and what *could* be done. The best way you can help them — and everybody's relatives — is to know the situation, inform your legislators, and push for more money for better services.

What to do

in the long run

But if it's your relative in the hospital, and the time is now?

* In a state-by-state follow-up of the effects of the peonage decision, *Behavior Today* found more than 30 states markedly reducing or eliminating patient work. Of those which hoped to continue it, only one (Connecticut) was sure of funding. "From Peonage to Pay," a six-part review (Dec. 16, 23, 30, 1974; Jan. 6, 20, 27, 1975).

† "If the law's general direction in the patient-rights area proceeds uninterrupted, token economies may well become legally unavailable even if they are therapeutically *superior* to other approaches." David B. Wexler, Professor of Law, University of Arizona, "Token and Taboo: Behavior Modification, Token Economies, and the Law," *California Law Review,* 61 (1973):81–109. This is an excellent review of token economies in general and the legal and moral problems they raise. The mental patient's right *not* to be treated raises questions which are not limited to behavior modification but extend to every kind of therapy.

2. SPECIFICS

Practical Questions

in the short run

Find out what kinds of therapy the hospital gives, and who gets them. Are there any research programs that sound as if they could help your relative, and how can he be included? High morale on these usually guarantees active, if not always effective, therapy. (Remember that your relative's permission is necessary for any experimental therapy — or yours, if he is an involuntary patient.)

What kinds of therapy?

Find out what the *best* conditions are in the hospital, and what is expected of patients there. Most mental hospitals operate by a system of graded living arrangements: as described with bitterness by the sociologist Erving Goffman:

What kinds of wards?

> The "worst" level involves nothing but wooden benches to sit on, some quite indifferent food, and a small piece of room to sleep in. The "best" level may involve a room of one's own, ground and town privileges, contacts with staff that are relatively undamaging, and what is seen as good food and ample recreational facilities. For disobeying the pervasive house rules, the inmate will receive stringent punishments expressed in terms of loss of privileges; for obedience he will eventually be allowed to reacquire some of the minor satisfactions he took for granted on the outside.[31]

(Notice that it's not behavior therapy that's described, where rewards and penalties are intended to serve specific therapeutic purposes, but the ordinary working of an ordinary hospital. The date: 1956.) Patients can move up within the system — or down. One family left their chronically ill daughter in a "good" ward and returned the next week to find her in the back ward, where she remained four years, drugged, fed, sheltered, and nothing more.* No attempt was made to alter the behavior that barred her from the "good" ward — angry outbursts (not surprising from a woman who'd never been in a state hospital before), bizarre whining, turning on lights in the middle of the night. (She was at length released, not because she had improved, but because circumstances had changed to allow her family to bring her home, where she now cleans house, makes jewelry, gardens, embroiders, and takes the bus alone.)

And what determines who lives where?

A new system, originated by the internist Dr. Lawrence Weed to record and monitor general medical care, is now being adopted in many mental hospitals. The "problem-oriented record" should further

The "problem-oriented record"

* On one visit, the nurse in charge told her mother she'd been to a wonderful workshop on motivating chronic patients, and lamented that she was too busy checking medications to use what she'd learned.

the development of individual treatment plans. The system consists simply of listing problems in the order of their concern and developing a treatment plan for monitoring each of these problems. One of the requirements is that each of the initial problems either be terminated as a problem or continually referred to in subsequent annotations as the patient is followed over time. The problem list can be revised periodically – some problems drop out, newer ones may appear. The treatment designed for each is formulated, and some statement as to the patient's current condition in relation to the problem list is recorded. Another important aspect of the problem-oriented record is that it's no longer necessary for the physician to do all of the medical record keeping. Now nurses, paraprofessionals, and so forth enter their observations, their treatments, whatever, into the record at appropriate times – each of these related to the current problem list.

and individual treatment plans

Miriam Karlins, Director of Education and Manpower Development for the Minnesota Department of Public Welfare (which is in charge of state hospitals), has some advice for you if your relative is in a state hospital. Ask, she says, "Is there an individualized treatment program set up for my relative?"[32] (As you ask, she suggests, try to sound like the kind of person who might sue.) The "right to treatment" now being upheld by the courts (see Chapter X) is not a right to mass medication and a bed, or even a casual series of things to do. Says Ms. Karlins, "a schedule, a succession of activities, is *not* a plan. A plan should set specific behavioral goals, with a time projected for accomplishing them, and the patient should know the goals." The woman who flicked on lights and whined needed, not the heavy doses of drugs which brought quiet nights and stopped her noise – and her speech – but specific work on the behaviors that disturbed the "good" ward. Most staff, says Ms. Karlins, do not know how to set *measurable* goals. If a patient is alcoholic or retarded, it doesn't help to set "sobriety" or "optimum development" as a goal. That's too vague to guide treatment. The individual treatment plans now required in Minnesota must be reviewed at least quarterly and modified as necessary, if possible with the patient's participation.

With specific goals?

You couldn't have a better guide to what hospitals are and might be than the form the Minnesota Department of Public Welfare requires ward staff to fill out yearly. The forms are guides for state inspectors; they can guide your inspection too. Here are a few questions from the form's fourteen pages:[33]

Questions

> How many residents [not "patients"; they know in Minnesota that the words we use determine how we think about a person] participated in regularly scheduled group or work activities this past week?
>
> How many residents have a written individual treatment plan, including goals, in their charts?

Have you read the record of each resident you supervise?
Have you re-read any of the records in the past month?
Is the resident informed of his treatment plan and goals?
Are [residents] informed about significant changes that affect them — staff changes, transfers, policy changes?
Are relatives routinely invited and encouraged to participate in the ongoing planning for residents?
Are they notified of the planning sessions sufficiently in advance so that they can arrange to attend?
Are families routinely notified in case of sickness? Accident? Death? Transfer to another ward? Discharge?
When a resident is transferred from one area to another are the reasons always explained to him in advance?
How many instances of seclusion were there involving residents from your area? What was the maximum amount of time a resident was in continuous seclusion during the past month? Is the resident told why he is being secluded?*
Is any meal or part of it ever withheld for disciplinary reasons? If so, explain.
Are residents in your area permitted to visit other residents in other areas within the facility?
Is freedom of the grounds a privilege which is sometimes withheld? If so, are the reasons discussed with the resident?
Do residents choose their own hair styles? Do they have ready access to their own toilet articles? If not, why?†
Are residents occasionally taken on trips outside the facility?
Are residents taught how to use money, how to protect it, and to know its value? Can they work in the community for pay? In the institution?
Is most of the staff time spent in direct contact with residents?
Do residents have an opportunity to start activities themselves?
Are residents encouraged to make changes in the ward which they think will increase its attractiveness or convenience?

The patients — residents, that is — have their own questionnaire, with most of the same questions. Trained volunteers, not staff, help them fill them out; for the state inspectors who follow the forms, these provide a check on the replies of the staff.

Before you pack up to move to Minnesota, however, reflect that what you've just read doesn't announce the millennium. It's only a blueprint for it. Asking a question doesn't guarantee a satisfactory answer, it only locates a problem. Solving it depends on money and will. What those questions tell you, among other things, is that in Minnesota — and elsewhere — patients and their families *haven't* been routinely involved in treatment decisions, patients *haven't* had individualized treatment plans, that it *has* been possible for patients to be transferred or dis-

* Most hospitals have special small rooms, usually containing only a mattress, where troublesome patients are put to calm down.
† In some state hospitals, patients are not even allowed to keep their own toothbrushes.

charged, to be sick or injured or even to die, without their families being notified. But at least in Minnesota the people in charge of mental hospitals know what behaviors — of administrators and staff — need to be modified.

Why is my relative throwing a ball?

Ask, says Ms. Karlins, "*Why* is my relative throwing a ball?" That question, she says, can tell you a lot about your state hospital. Is it just "ball-throwing therapy," or part of a serious treatment plan? Or is this a hospital where you have to be grateful that your relative *is* throwing a ball instead of sitting inside staring at nothing?*

There's hope in the state hospital. Five years after a wrist-slashing episode had landed a young man there, he wrote this, which suggests that the bitter observations of Rosenhan and Goffman are not always the last word:

> Most helpful was the last doctor I met at the state hospital, who in six short weeks allowed me to become his friend and his equal. At no time was he easy on me. He made me work hard to earn his respect as well as my own. He was direct with me at all times and demanded the same of me. He told me that I must begin to make some decisions about my life. For the first time I felt confidence in myself, and in the doctor's caring about me. I no longer felt I was facing the unknown, but truly something definite that I could fight against.[34]

If your relative is hospitalized in another state

By 1974, at least forty-two of the states had agreed to participate in the Interstate Compact on Mental Health, a reciprocal agreement to provide care and treatment regardless of legal residence. It provides that a patient who is not a legal resident of a state where he has to be hospitalized *may* be transferred to another Compact state. Families or patients may request transfer; if it is granted, transportation is at the expense of the sending state.

Veterans' Hospitals:

The Veterans' Administration runs both psychiatric hospitals and psychiatric divisions in its general hospitals. Expenditures per patient per day are considerably greater than in most state and county hospitals ($65 to $70 in 1973), and VA hospitals tend to be better staffed and equipped. In addition to the usual somatic treatments, VA hos-

A pool table and a kitten

* I know of a hospital so understaffed and underfunded that it can offer little to most of its patients but sympathetic custodial care and calming drugs. It's old and shabby, and the only chance many patients get to throw a ball is when a volunteer appears to take them outside. In one ward there's a pool table, but nobody uses it — it's a women's ward. The social worker says she's asked and asked for it to be moved up the stairs into the men's ward. Six patients could do it, but she can't get permission. The table might fall apart. Somebody might get hurt. They can't take the risk. The weight of institutional inertia is heavier than the pool table.

But the picture isn't all black. In the small incentive ward of the same hospital, the only active therapy program except those provided by volunteers, a tiny kitten appears from under a bed. Surprised, I asked a question that's not on the Minnesota questionnaire: "Are the patients allowed to have pets?" "No," says the social worker, smiling, "but they do." Does a kitten come under the heading of changes made in the ward to improve its attractiveness? Or a very special incentive? C. C. P.

pitals offer a wide variety of psychological treatments — extensive alcoholism programs, family and couple therapy, group and individual therapy, behavioral therapy, videotape techniques. Clinical psychologists are particularly active in VA hospitals, where the profession got its start after World War II. Almost all admissions are voluntary, and services are free. Follow-up care, using both VA and community resources, is emphasized. Admissions follow strict priorities. First come veterans needing treatment for a service-connected psychiatric condition, then veterans with service-connected nonpsychiatric disabilities who need psychiatric treatment, then, if beds are available, nondisabled veterans who are unable to pay for psychiatric treatment elsewhere. For details of eligibility, consult your local veterans' representative or any VA office. Applications can be made there as well as at a VA hospital.

a bargain if your relative is eligible.

Admission

General, private, public — how do people get to the hospital?

Many people know they need help and enter the hospital under their own power. In Informal Admission, now legal in several states, the patient admits himself to a mental hospital as to any other and can leave at any time. You're lucky if your relative is one of these. Of course if a doctor — in some states, more than one — recommends it, you can commit him even against his will (see Chapter X, The Law, p. 273). You probably regard this as a last resort, however, and you should. Most families — and doctors — do their best to persuade the patient to sign himself into the hospital voluntarily. (Most voluntary admission forms contain an agreement to stay a specified number of days, and discharge must be requested in advance, in writing.)

Informal

Involuntary

Voluntary

How to persuade? Firmness and tact can do a lot — and an understanding of how your relative feels. He may feel worse at certain times of day, and so be more willing to take refuge in the hospital. Dr. Cammer even suggests ways of using his symptoms to persuade him. For example, to a depressed person who blames himself for upsetting the household you can admit that having him in the hospital for a while *will* make things easier. A person who's convinced the neighbors are spying might be persuaded to see the hospital as a refuge from prying eyes. It's manipulation, again. But you and the doctor agree that this hospitalization is necessary. If you don't agree, don't do it, but if you do, you can't be halfhearted.* There are worse things than persuasion, even devious persuasion; diplomacy is better than threatening committal. Above all, don't promise that your relative won't have

Persuasion

* Dr. Cammer's suggestions are particularly useful here: see *Up from Depression*, pp. 217–219.

to go to the hospital. If you must break your promise, he has reason to feel betrayed; if you keep it, you may be risking his health and perhaps his life.*

But you can't count on accompanying your relative to the hospital. What if you pick up the phone and a voice simply tells you he's there?

Emergency admission

by police

The voice may be a doctor's, but it's often a policeman's. In most states, the police are authorized by law to take someone to the hospital if they think he needs it. (But some states require that he appear dangerous, and others require authorization by a physician.) They avoid doing this if they possibly can, contrary to what some people think. Still, "more than one fifth of all referrals to the receiving psychiatric service of the public hospital come from this source."[35]

The police will try to notify you, but there are slipups. Plenty of families of adult patients, especially of those who look less disabled than they are, have been terrified when their relative didn't come home, then outraged to find, sometimes after days, that he or she had been hospitalized without notification. If you are worried about this possibility and you live in a small town or city, it's worth while introducing your relative to your police department, who'll probably surprise you by their sympathy and understanding. In big cities, contact the Missing Persons Bureau right away, and hope the police keep efficient records.

and with police assistance

If your relative is violent or suicidal, the police will help you get him to the hospital. Whether correctly or not, an attempt at suicide is taken as reason enough for hospitalization.†

When there is no threat of violence, the police won't help you hospitalize your relative unless they themselves can see that he's acting strangely and that he can't be cared for at home. This is a necessary safeguard; you wouldn't want them to hospitalize on hearsay evidence – yours or anybody else's. If his symptoms are not obvious (if he merely seems depressed, for instance) and you still need police help in getting him to the hospital, you'll need a doctor's authorization.

* "Tell your relative quietly and firmly what you have arranged to do, and do it. Be calm and determined; show him you have made up your mind that he is to go where he can have care and treatment, that none of his antics and pleadings will swerve you from your decision. This is easier said than done, but if you can manage to keep yourself under control, you will save both yourself and him much unnecessary and harmful stress and strain. . . . Make your farewell as casual as you can . . . ask him to write often and promise 'I'll write too.'" This good advice is from Edith Stern's *Mental Illness: A Guide for the Family* (New York: Commonwealth Fund, 1944; revised ed., 1968), pp. 63, 65. This short book (120 pages) is still the best guide to the details of hospitalization; you can get it from your state mental health association, or order it directly from NAMH, 1800 N. Kent St., Rosslyn, VA 22209.

† "Not only is it not necessary for the victim to exhibit other signs of a mental disorder but there is no way in which a person can demonstrate that he is not in need of psychiatric attention. . . . Both the most playful and the most rationally considered suicide attempts are treated as suggesting serious morbidity." Bittner, *op. cit.*, p. 55.

Admission at leisure

Of course emergency admission is to be avoided if possible.* It's much, much better when you look over the hospital beforehand. Go there ahead of time to talk. Go again with your relative, if he's willing. Look over the grounds. Speak to the director or chief psychiatrist if you can. Talk to the social worker who deals with families. Ask to see the kind of surroundings your relative would be in.

Visit beforehand

and ask questions;

Ask about treatment, in calm and leisure. What is the place of drugs in therapy? Does this hospital give ECT? Psychotherapy? What kinds? How often? Does it cost extra? What are the charges, and the arrangements for payment? Will your relative need money here? (Minnesota questionnaire: "When a resident is admitted, is he permitted to keep a certain amount of his money with him, with the rest put in safekeeping?") Can you see the occupational therapy facilities? What is the therapeutic milieu? Can your relative go outside? How soon? What, in short, is going to be the shape of his day if he comes here?

it's your right.

Make a list of the questions that are important to you. They may think you a pretty pesky relative, but you're a lot more likely to get answers in advance than if you delay until the actual admission, when you're upset and they're in a hurry to get your relative settled.

Practical questions on admission

Most people, though, don't visit ahead of time. If you haven't, there are things you must know right away. The background questions can wait.

Get the hospital brochure.

Most hospitals publish some sort of brochure for patients and families. Make sure you're given it, in case somebody forgets. It will give the names of the chief administrators. It will give information about religious services, clothing, laundry. Most important, it will give information about visiting hours, and mail and telephone calls from and to your relative. (Minnesota questionnaire: "Is there a free phone on the area which patients can use? Are they informed of this? Is there a pay phone? Are residents [or staff on their behalf] allowed to use the hospital WATS line for long distance calls within the state? Do residents have ready access to stationery, pens and pencils, stamps? Is outgoing or incoming mail read by staff?") The brochure will also contain a brief statement (sometimes overoptimistic) of the kinds of therapy offered. Read the brochure carefully; this will save the staff's time and guide your questions.

Is There Someone You Can Call Regularly?

Don't leave without being absolutely certain whom you call to find out about your relative and what's the best time to do it so nobody's time is wasted. (Be quietly persistent when you do call; hospital secretaries, like other secretaries, are trained to protect their bosses.) Choose one family member to do the calling and give news to the

* Avoid weekends if you possibly can; mental hospitals are most understaffed then.

others; you can't expect overburdened staff to answer the same questions over and over.

Can you talk to the doctor?

Will you be able to talk to the doctor who treats your relative? Not automatically. The doctor probably doesn't see much of your relative anyway. You'll probably learn more about how he's doing from day to day from nurses, psychiatric aides, or the social worker assigned to handle his case. If you have questions about drugs or other medical treatments, she's the one who should make it possible for you to discuss them with the doctor who prescribes for your relative. The nurse may know more about it in hospitals with much drug therapy and few doctors. Nevertheless, you have the right to discuss medical treatments with a doctor. Remember that electroconvulsive treatment requires your relative's consent, or yours if he has been committed. So does psychosurgery, aversive conditioning, or any experimental treatment. Make sure the doctor, and nurse, in charge of the ward know you know this and that you expect to be consulted well in advance of treatment.* Give them your phone number. If necessary, try again to look like the sort of person who might sue.

Physical illness

If your relative has a physical illness or a disability which needs special attention, make sure the staff knows about it on admission. Is he diabetic? Deaf?† (Think what would happen if he lost his hearing aid!) Follow up on this when you visit, especially in big public hospitals. (Minnesota: "Does your area have programs and services to meet the needs of the deaf, blind, or physically handicapped?")

Problems with Records

Delays and difficulties in getting records

For all physical conditions, the hospital should have your relative's medical records. It should have his psychiatric history as well, including records of all previous examinations and treatments. You probably haven't got these and must depend on previous consultants and hospitals to send them.‡ Never underestimate the power of bureaucracy:

* In 1974, this happened in a hospital of good reputation in a state that specifically guarantees patients the right to refuse shock treatment: a vigilant husband, making his daily phone call to the ward staff, found his wife had been placed on the list for shock treatment. Neither of them had been consulted. It was a mistake, apparently, and easily reversed, but it's lucky he called then, as the ward attendant routinely rounded up those on the list without checking to see if the required authorizations had been obtained.

† A few hospitals have special programs for deaf mental patients; Dr. Luther Robinson, former superintendent of St. Elizabeths in Washington, the only federal mental hospital, even learned sign language to bring psychotherapy to the deaf.

‡ The Hospitalization of the Mentally Ill Act of 1964, a statute applying only to the District of Columbia, provides "that the administrator of each public hospital shall keep records detailing all medical and psychiatric care and treatment received by a person hospitalized for a mental illness and the records shall be made available, upon that person's written authorization, to his attorney or personal physician."

they may not come for weeks, while you wait desperately for admission. They may not come at all. Don't *assume* they've come; check.

and in getting them read

The records may come, and the staff may not consult them. Sometimes this is a matter of policy: one mother, distressed that the doctors seemed unaware of important facts concerning her child, was told that it was the hospital's practice to make their own evaluation first and look at the history afterward. Sometimes it's just plain inefficiency. "It is a common occurrence . . . for a patient to have had extensive diagnostic studies and . . . an enormously expensive and careful history and work-up by a conscientious private psychiatrist who is not even contacted when the patient enters the hospital, nor are the extensive data that he has available on the patient requested."[36] *Never* assume that a given doctor, nurse, aide, or social worker knows an important fact about your relative because it's in his records.

Access to medical records: by relatives (no)

It would certainly make it easier, when your relative is entering a hospital or transferring to another one, if you had his records in your possession and could provide copies as needed. For reasons of confidentiality, however, you can rarely obtain access to your relative's medical records, even if you are his legal guardian. The patient can't usually see them either.* In Massachusetts, for instance, patients in public mental hospitals are specifically prohibited by statute from any access to their records except through an attorney. (A sympathetic attorney may be willing to show them to him, or you.) This prohibition has been challenged in court and upheld. (Private hospitals vary in their practice.)

by the patient (no)

by his lawyer (yes)

Tell them yourself what they need to know;

So be ready to tell as much as you know about your relative's medical and psychiatric history. If you know a lot, get it down in writing and hope they won't think you too peculiar. (Keep a copy — you might want to give one to another staff member.)

If you do all this, will everything go smoothly? Who knows? Some hospitals are well run, and what you've been told is what actually happens. In others, confusion reigns. One staff member may have told you one thing — and you and your relative may have counted on it — only to have another reverse it. You're in no position to argue. You told your daughter she could go right in with the other teenagers, but the nurse says that the doctor who said that made a mistake; the child goes into the general admissions ward, weeping and betrayed. In some hospitals you can accompany her to the ward (if you're reasonably in command of yourself) and help her settle; in others you may turn to

* Note, however, this statement from the twelve-point "Bill of Rights" adopted by the American Hospital Association in 1973: "The patient has the right to obtain from his physician complete current information concerning his diagnosis, treatment and prognosis in terms the patient can reasonably be expected to understand." *Berkshire Eagle* (Sept. 9, 1973). This right is far from being universally respected even in cases of physical illness. To apply it in mental hospitals would require the modification of some very deeply ingrained professional behavior. However, it never hurts to quote.

sign a paper and she's led away before you have a chance to say goodbye. Whether this is a good idea (and the staff can probably make out a case for it), or further feeds her feelings of abandonment, it's out of your hands. Powerlessness is not limited to patients. In any hospital, you do things their way. The hospital probably has to be an authoritarian institution to do its job. You can try to be reasonable and flexible, and hope to be met with reasonableness and flexibility in return. Expect the best; good expectations bring out the best in people and hope is free. But be prepared for very much less.

and lots of luck.

Visiting

What about visits? Where the hospital is, of course, determines whether you can visit, and how often. Don't hesitate to ask the hospital to adjust its visiting hours if you really can't come at the scheduled times (if you work days, for instance) or must come from a distance. Many hospitals are hard to reach without a car. Visits are so important to most patients that some mental health associations even provide transportation for families who need it. (This is another reason for getting together with other families from your area; see Chapter XIV, "The Lord Helps Those Who Help Themselves.") If it's hard for you to visit, be realistic and clear in what you tell your relative, so he won't expect you and be disappointed.

Getting there

What you've read so far should prepare you for what you'll see. Try to prepare yourself for what you'll *feel* and what your relative is feeling. Some of that old horror of the asylum still lurks in the corners of our minds, making even ordinary sights seem strange, strange sights seem frightening. In fact, there are no sights here that should frighten you, although there is plenty to break your heart. At least you won't see a chronic ward on your first visit—those featureless rooms, that empty inactivity. Some families can't bear to see their relatives there, especially if they can't do anything about it, and just stay away. But with today's treatments and philosophy, fewer and fewer of our relatives will end up *there*. What you will see, however, is chronic *patients,* and a good thing too; it means they're out and around, in an institution that's as open as it can be. But they do take a little getting used to. It may sometimes be true, as the radical therapists claim, that you can't tell the patients from the staff, especially when they exhibit the YAVIS syndrome (young, attractive, verbal, intelligent, suburban). Some patients will surprise you by seeming perfectly well, and you'll wonder why they're here. (You can't see the suicide attempt, now ten days in the past; the depression, perhaps temporarily responding to the interest of a visitor; the obsession which you haven't happened to hit.) But most chronic patients are all too easy to spot. Because of medica-

Sick people

tion, you'll probably not see acutely upset patients; nobody will be screaming, or throwing furniture. But you will see people who sit and stare, or say the same thing over and over, or mumble incoherently, or address you with inappropriate and touching friendliness. Even the postures of the severely ill can look strange, as they sit rigid, head perhaps bizarrely tilted, or shuffle stiffly or jerkily along. It may be the effect of the illness or of drugs, or of long-time institutionalization,* or of all together. Whatever it is, be ready for it and don't be disconcerted. At least, don't show it. Smile at the man who's staring at the air, answer the woman who keeps asking you about the weather. Above all, don't lament to your relative that he has to be with "people like these." He's probably already used to them, maybe even getting a little boost out of knowing that at his worst he's not that bad and determining that he isn't going to be. If they bother him, your comment will just make it worse. In short, how you feel about the other patients has only passing importance — unless you let it affect your visit with your relative. Don't.

who are still people

You may see your relative in bed (if he's sick), on the ward, in a "day room" (where patients spend the day).† (Minnesota questionnaire: "Is privacy provided for residents and their visitors?") She may look worse than when you last saw her, especially if she hasn't been in the hospital long. Don't be upset. It's common for patients to regress on admission; the hospital, after all, is a place to be sick. Your relative may feel relief that here he can act the way he really feels and have his "craziness" accepted. This may be a stage on the road to recovery — as one patient put it, you may have to go down before you can go up.[37] If he stays that way visit after visit, however, you have reason to be worried, and questions to ask.

Seeing your relative

who may not be looking too good,

He probably acts more normally when you aren't there. The closer his family is to his emotions, the more likely he is to act out resentment or loss or guilt. If she's still sore over being hospitalized or he's feeling sorry for himself anyway, it's likely to come out during a visit. The flowers you brought may be thrown on the floor. You may be accused of having put him away, of never coming to see him, of not caring how miserable she is. Don't try to defend yourself; Never Argue with a Mental Patient. It's hard not to be hurt, even though you realize it's part of the illness. *Realize it again,* in the true meaning of the word: make it *real* to yourself. A mentally ill person is trapped inside himself; one brilliant woman envisaged her illness as a bell jar set down

or acting too good, either.

Realize how s/he feels.

* As Dr. Philippe Pinel asked more than 160 years ago, "How are we to distinguish between the exasperation caused by the chains and the symptoms peculiar to the illness?"

† Minnesota questionnaire: "Are residents allowed to take naps in their own beds during the day?" Sleeping quarters are often locked; in some state hospitals you can see patients napping on the floor.

over her.[38] Your relative *can't* respond as he used to; that's what his illness *is*.

It's bad when he's hostile; it's worse when he doesn't seem to know you're there. It may be the treatment, it may be the illness, it may be both; anyway, it's lacerating. Keep coming, though. Inside his anger or suspicion or apathetic remoteness, your relative needs to know you care that much. Your presence can say it, sometimes better than your words. A woman who recovered tells how her "indifference" really felt:

There . . . and not there

> The people you love and have been close to may be there in reality, and yet they are not there. No one can help you, no one, and you no longer can help yourself. Yet if and when the people close to you stop trying to get through to you, if you feel they have stopped caring or loving you . . . then whatever glimmer of hope you still retained of finding your way back to those you have loved and lost is shattered.[39]

Often, of course, your relative will seem much better than this, almost his or her old self again. That's just the time, another ex-patient reminds us, not to overstay your visit. (Dr. Cammer has good suggestions for how to leave gracefully.) That new self-control is encouraging to see, but it still costs something. "It's just so hard to hold yourself together," she says, "and it's embarrassing to lose control." A short, good visit is better than one that ends in exhaustion or tears — hers or yours.

Quit while everybody's winning.

Try to keep your emotions warm rather than intense. Talk about what's going on at home, so your relative can still feel part of it. But try to feel along with him; don't make the good times seem so good he feels more excluded. And if there's trouble, ease over it. If Louise is sick or George lost his job, there's nothing your relative can do. Nor can he advise about business or family affairs. (Not only is it a strain, but his judgment is not now at its best.) Telling him things are going badly will worry him to no purpose and emphasize his feeling of powerlessness. Those worries will seem even more threatening when you have left. (The same guidelines apply to letters.)

Do's and Don'ts

Dr. Cammer is worth a special consultation on how to visit. He has good, specific advice on how to fortify a relative to cooperate with treatment, how to encourage, how to respond to complaints about the hospital, how to be sympathetic without sabotaging therapy. "When you greet your relative your first thought should be: what is best for him? You are not there to express your anxieties, turn on a sacrificial martyrdom, or start crying about the illness. If you think you might do this, better stay away."[40]

Be cautious in your relations with other patients.

Be friendly to other patients, but don't encourage them to recite long tales of woe or involve yourself in situations you can't know the whole of. Some patients may try to make you a go-between — for the delivery of unauthorized packages, for instance. Narcotics and weapons find their way into hospitals as well as prisons. Mailing letters is another thing — Edith Stern says don't do it, but Clifford Beers had to smuggle out his letter to the governor of Connecticut, and progressive states now guarantee patients the right to uncensored communication. You'll make up your own mind.

Don't question them

Don't ask other patients for inside reports on how your relative acts when you're not there. If your relative finds out about it he won't like the feeling of being watched — and the mentally ill aren't always the most reliable sources. Ask your questions of aides, nurses, doctors. If they're evasive, however, patients may be the only sources you've got beyond your relative himself. Don't resort to questioning patients, however, unless your information from the staff is hopelessly unsatisfactory, and restrict your questions to matters of fact. If another patient has something to say about your relative, he'll volunteer it.

except as a last resort.

Think what you say.

Don't discuss your relative casually with other visitors. Though the thoughtful sharing of experience may be valuable (as in organizations of relatives — see Chapter XIV — and in multiple family therapy), consider that, as Dr. Cammer says, a hospital is a rumor mill. What you say "may bounce back to the patient in distorted form and arouse a storm of agitation that may take hours to quiet."[41]

How to Use a Visit

What you can do besides talk

A state hospital may cover many acres. You're in a better position to get an overall view than your relative. He got the patient brochure when he came in, or should have, but he was probably confused then — ten to one he hasn't got it now. Familiarize yourself with the recreational and occupational possibilities. If your relative can read a map, see that he has one. (If the hospital can't furnish one, try making one yourself.) You may be able to encourage him to some activities that he resists with the staff. If you take him bowling or show him the crafts room he may be more willing to go on his own. If she's on an open ward, have her take you to the canteen; something's the matter if she doesn't know the way. If he's in the locked ward he may not even be able to go outside (let alone throw a ball), except during your visits. (Minnesota questionnaire: "For residents who require supervision, is there an enclosed area outside which permits them to be out of doors? Does it offer shade and appropriate equipment?") If you come by car, take her for a ride (but make clear from the beginning that she'll be coming back). If religion is important to him, find out the hours of services and get him into contact with the hospital chaplain.* If books

Help him to use the hospital:

Activities, recreation

Religion

* Most state hospitals have Protestant, Catholic, and Jewish services. Ward A. Knight, Jr.'s *My Church Was a Mental Hospital* (Philadelphia: United Church Press, 1974) describes the chaplain's role in a mental hospital.

Reading

play a part in her life, find out the library hours and go there with her. If she can't go alone, ask about the book carts that serve the closed wards. Some librarians run reading and poetry groups – "bibliotherapy."[42] (I've never seen a crowded hospital library. C. C. P.)

Use your visit to check conditions

Use your ears and eyes from the minute you enter the doors of the hospital. (That will cut down on the temptation to quiz patients.) Are staff warm and friendly, or indifferent? The Minnesota questionnaire asks: "Is most of staff time spent in direct contact with patients?" More likely, it's spent keeping the ward clean, checking medication, filling out forms. Is the place bleaker than even age and economy make necessary? Minnesota asks: "Are there pictures on the walls, curtains in the windows? A record player, TV, radio, games, play equipment?" If not, you could talk to the hospital volunteer organization about it.

What can you bring?

Can you help your relative to brighten his own living quarters? Know the rules; one girl, hospitalized several weeks in a good private hospital, was deeply distressed when she wasn't allowed to put up the posters her family brought her. Minnesota asks: "May residents put up pictures? Do residents have a place to put personal possessions? If it is locked, do they have a key?" The answers to other Minnesota questions will give hints as to presents which would be welcome, and how much pocket money your relative could use. (Can he earn any in the hospital?) "Is there cool drinking water readily accessible on the ward? Coffee? Snacks? Free or to be paid for? A stove or hotplate? Refrigerator? A clock? Is there a current daily newspaper available for residents on the area?" If not, you might subscribe for your relative, or bring back issues when you visit. Hospital conditions don't always support the hospital's aim – to keep patients in touch with the real world.

Though most state hospitals today allow patients to wear their own clothes, Minnesota's questions suggest some of the problems. If you're upset to find your daughter in drawers down to her knees when you know she came in with a set of bikinis, don't make a scene, ask the Minnesota question: "Are residents given or taught responsibility for maintaining their own clothing?" Keeping personal track of the garments of long-term chronic patients is often more than overworked nurses can manage, and it's easier to dress them like babies than to teach them to dress themselves. Should this, perhaps, be part of your relative's individualized treatment plan? Other Minnesota questions suggest some of the equipment necessary to foster independence: Are there irons and ironing boards available? A washer? A dryer? Is there a full length mirror in the ward? The ordinary conditions of daily life should be educational – or "therapeutic" – and the state can afford an ironing board when it can't afford a psychiatrist.

What can you expect?

Other questions guide your awareness of conditions: "Is the temperature in living and sleeping areas reasonably comfortable in extreme weather?" (Seclusion rooms in one state hospital — *not* in Minnesota — got so hot in summer that a patient died.) [43] "How many toilets have partitions? Doors? Is there privacy in bathing?"

What can you do about it?

Conditions that justify such questions exist in all too many state hospitals. If they do in yours, take your complaints to the ward personnel, to your social worker, then to the hospital higher-ups. The superintendent's name is there in the brochure; he wants to do the best he can for your relative, once he knows he's alive. If you have to (and if you've got the strength), you can go further. Specific descriptions (giving dates, ward numbers) are what give force to a letter to the superintendent, to the hospital board of visitors, to your state representative, to the chairman of the state legislative committee on institutions, to the newspapers, and (if the worse comes to the worst) to the court case you bring, alone or with other citizens. (See Chapter X, "The Law and Your Relative," and Chapter XIV, "The Lord Helps Those Who Help Themselves.")

Your relative's complaints

Such careful observations will help you evaluate your relative's complaints. Don't jump to conclusions if he says the food is terrible or he hasn't been outside in a month. He may not be seeing things just the way they are; he may be lying. But his complaints may also be justified. Don't ignore them and make him feel like a nonperson — but don't go overboard in sympathy before you know the situation. Even when you do, if nothing can be done, it may be better to encourage stoicism than anger. Do what you can, without involving your relative's emotions any more than you have to. Claire Burch tells it like it is:

> It cannot be stressed too strongly that often your role in helping long-term hospitalized relatives is to serve as some sort of battering ram between the hospital and the administration. After your relative has been admitted, you should try to maintain contact with a particular doctor . . . so that he gets to know the patient's name. . . . Simply your presence and persistence . . . can often be sufficient to bring pressure on a slow-moving administration, clogged by red tape, and bring about improvement.[44]

A last way to use your visit: be alert for signs of *physical* illness and follow up on treatment. In a questionnaire circulated among patients and families six months after leaving the hospital, denial or neglect of *physical* illness led the list of complaints.* This is especially important

* By now you can use a bit of reassurance: even that represented only 14 percent of those returning the questionnaire. Other common complaints concerned money problems (pensions, Social Security, etc.), gross neglect, poor conduct of staff, lack of therapy or counseling — none higher than 12 percent. Two percent complained because they were refused readmittance. Don Spiegel and Jenny B. Younger, "Life Outside the Hospital: A View from the Patients and Relatives," *Mental Hygiene* (Spring 1972).

where doctors are few and underqualified. Remember, consultation on request is a part of medical ethics. The hospital is not a world apart. You can ask an outside consultant to examine your relative if you are doubtful about a medical diagnosis or treatment.

Forbidden visits:

Last and most painful, what if you're not allowed to visit? "Hardest of all for a relative to accept," wrote Edith Stern, "is a doctor's order that he or she . . . must not go see the patient. Loving mothers or husbands, especially if their behavior has been faultless, cannot see

reasons

how their calls at the hospital can possibly be harmful. But the physician, through his understanding of the profound emotions underlying or causing the mental disorder, has come to the conclusion that visits from one or more particular family members tend to stir these up and to cause setbacks."[45] It used to be very common to discourage or forbid family visits, often for long periods. This was especially likely to happen in hospitals that emphasized psychoanalytic insight, where therapy was often a prolonged exploration of childhood memories and highly charged emotions. During the earlier stages of treatment, visits by the real actors in the childhood drama might focus resentments not yet "worked through" and be profoundly disturbing. When, in addition, families were considered the cause of disturbance, the hospital's commitment to treatment by separation could be even stronger.

and changes

Today there's much less of this. What remains mostly concerns children. (Dr. Eric Schopler calls it "parentectomy.") It's less and less common, though the eminent director of at least one state hospital children's unit prohibits parental visits, sometimes for months.* But family exclusion just doesn't fit in with the new emphasis on briefer treatment and quick return to the community; the emphasis is now on helping families and patients together rather than treating the patient in isolation.

In 1948 Edith Stern wrote, "If you are told by the physician that your visits are detrimental, stay away without protest no matter how hurt you feel."[46] Today you should be suspicious if you're forbidden to visit for any extended period. You can question the treatment philosophy. You can certainly ask for guidance in how to act so that

* The activity of Professor Louis Frydman of the University of Kansas in helping parents get their children out of the children's unit at Topeka State Hospital is described in the report of the Second National Conference on Human Rights and Psychiatric Oppression, held in Topeka in September, 1974. *Madness Network News,* 2 (Dec. 1974). However, the director of the unit, Dr. Donald Rinsley, also a staff member of the Menninger Foundation, is suing Frydman, charging he has "disrupted . . . [and] irreparably damaged the patient-physician and client-therapist relationships." Dr. Rinsley thinks that up to a year of "resistance" from parent and/or child is to be expected. Visiting restrictions, if any, for this and most other children's facilities, are clearly stated in the NIMH directory to children's hospitals (see Chapter XII, pp. 362n, 371n).

your visits *wouldn't* be detrimental. Times have changed: you might even protest.*

The most tragic cases of family exclusion concerned children. Adults are another matter (though you may have some doubts — and so do doctors — now that "adulthood" begins at eighteen). If your relative is an adult, he can choose not to see you and you will have to respect his choice, even if it's irrational, even if it hurts. As he gets better he'll probably change his mind. Today his therapist is likely to be on your side, at least to the extent of thinking that managing to get along with one's family is worth learning to do.

The adult patient's choice

Discharge

As we've seen, the trend is all toward early discharge. If your relative wants out, and he's a voluntary patient, he can leave by requesting discharge in advance, whether or not the doctor (or you) thinks he's ready. If he's an involuntary patient he will usually be released *if* his family insists — something you'll do only after careful thought and with good reason. You and he will then sign a paper stating the patient has been removed or has left A.M.A. — against medical advice.

Getting out: requesting discharge

A.M.A.

It is unusual for matters to go this far, but legally, a patient, like any other citizen, may get a writ of habeas corpus for a hearing before a judge, who will take testimony from one or more psychiatrists and decide on release himself, taking into account the experts' opinion and the family's. The writ, however, may be denied — that is, the clerk of the court may refuse a hearing — and you are well advised to secure counsel before filing such a writ. Note that the patient has a constitutional right to representation in habeas corpus proceedings. (See p. 280.) In some states, recent legislation insures that even involuntary patients, unless they have been judicially committed, can leave if they request discharge three days in advance. This is called a three-day notice.

habeas corpus

Three out of four released mental patients will live with relatives.†

Coming home

* If you are faced with a prolonged "therapeutic separation," discuss this with the director of the hospital. If it's private, you are agreeing to abide by the treatment philosophy when you choose to send your relative there and pay his bills, so be sure you know what it is. A public hospital, as we've seen, is an open institution. If you are forbidden to visit, or to withdraw your child when you think best, talk to other parents. (In union there is strength; see Chapter XIV.) Weigh carefully the advantages of the program. If you still want to protest, consult a civil liberties lawyer.

† According to a study made in Pennsylvania in the late sixties, about a third live with a spouse, 40 percent with other relatives. Max Silverstein, *Psychiatric Aftercare* (Philadelphia: University of Pennsylvania Press, 1968), p. 13.

No matter how complete your relative's recovery, there will be problems of adjustment when he leaves the predictable routine of the hospital. The world may still seem threatening and uncertain to him. She may be deeply doubtful of her ability to cope. You will need extra tact and patience during these weeks – or months – in treading that narrow line between expecting too much or too little. Barbara Benziger got well, yet she writes:

Advice on how to act

> During my recovery, I realized how very hard mental illness is on the people closest to the patient, who unknowingly makes demands that are, at times, almost impossible to fulfil. . . . A patient just released from a mental hospital feels, whether correctly or incorrectly, that he is being watched with some degree of doubt and suspicion and even with hostility. . . . He becomes so anxious to prove he is "normal" that he often does do and say strange things that make him appear "different."[47]

His illness and hospitalization has probably been a deeply significant experience for your relative. He will be trying hard to come to terms with it. Out of embarrassment and awkwardness, many relatives and friends make it hard for the ex-patient to talk out what has happened to him, although former patients often want to talk about their previously disturbed behavior. Try to make it easy, instead. Talking about it, *if your relative wants to,* should be a natural part of coming home. There's a lot of good advice on this period, not only (we hope) from your relative's doctor or social worker, but waiting for you in books.* Meetings of organizations such as Recovery, Inc., and Schizophrenics Anonymous can be helpful for both patients and families. (See Chapter XIV for descriptions.)

There will be practical problems as well as personal adjustment. Getting a job can be hard. Until recently, there has been a code number on military discharge papers which indicated discharge for psychiatric reasons; the code was only minimally secret, and employers have used it to discriminate against former patients. Don't be too discouraged; a survey of Washington state hospital patients a year after discharge found significantly more patients employed after hos-

Employment problems

* So we'll recommend, but not try to summarize, Edith Stern's and Dr. Cammer's brief but pithy suggestions, or Claire Burch's excellent chapter, which includes case histories with the feel of life and a sample "contract" for regulating the intercourse between a troubled teenager and his family. Excerpts: "John L. shall be responsible for obtaining food and cleaning his apartment at all times. . . . Mabel L. [mother] shall backstop John L. up until 8 p.m. on those nights when John L. is not scheduled to be at home. After 8 p.m. John L. shall avail himself of other agencies and persons for aid, comfort, and any other purpose whatever. John L. shall not telephone or otherwise attempt to contact Mabel L. from Saturday 8 a.m. to Sunday 10 a.m. thereby allowing Mabel L. one totally free day. . . . [While in Mabel L.'s home] John L. and any friends of his shall have their clothes on at all times. . . . No dirty laundry shall be brought by John L. John L. shall not act in an intentionally 'crazy' manner."[48]

pitalization than before.[49] But the better and more responsible the job, the greater the risk — as Senator Eagleton found out when it became known that he'd once been hospitalized for shock treatments. Your relative may not want to run for Vice-President — but he may still have to think carefully about whether he can be frank about his hospitalization. Dr. Richard Neiman of Dallas, Texas, instructs his patients that

> because of the stigma our culture associates with psychiatric illness and treatment, it is not very likely that they will be given unbiased consideration for a job. I go on to instruct them that once they have been working a while, if the employer should then learn of their previous illness, they are for the first time in a position of advantage rather than disadvantage. I point out that if their work has been satisfactory they may, in fact, be allowed to keep the job.[50]

Civil liberties lawyer Bruce Ennis has had clients who were barred from jobs as corrections officers, railroad clerks, cab drivers, sanitation men, trackmen. Even voluntary commitment can make a difference; one brilliant girl found her hospitalization barred her from medical school after medical school.[51] For a list of some of the state-licensed occupations that may be closed to mental patients, see Chapter X, pp. 297–298. Questions about former mental hospitalization are now against the law on Massachusetts job applications, where it's also illegal for an employer to refuse to hire or to fire any person who fails to furnish information about treatment for mental illness if he can produce a psychiatrist's certificate that he is mentally competent to do the job. You might ask about the situation in your state at the local Vocational Rehabilitation Office, which will also have knowledge of local job opportunities. The controversial Question 29 of the federal Civil Service application form ("Do you have, or have you had, heart disease, a nervous breakdown, epilepsy, tuberculosis, diabetes?") was removed in 1974. Federal policy is now to take into account a person's medical suitability only when he or she is actually under consideration for a particular position; the decision is to be made locally, after medical review, not at Civil Service headquarters in Washington.*

"After-care" as it should be

Must you and your relative put all this together for yourselves? Not necessarily. Some hospitals (usually general hospitals, VA hospitals, and state hospitals, but also a few fine private ones) have excellent "after-care" programs. You are not alone; the return home is prepared for with family counseling, home visits to see where problems lie (and strengths exist), specific training in daily living as well as help with

* *MH,* 58 (Summer 1974). *Psychiatric News* reported in the summer of 1974, however, that many local Civil Service officials were still unaware of the decision and were using old copies of application form 171 still containing the question.

emotional tensions. Some hospitals maintain their own partial hospitalization programs, halfway houses, and vocational programs; others are linked effectively with such services in mental health centers or other community programs.

This is the ideal — as usual, most likely to be found in teaching hospitals. It's nothing you can count on. In many hospitals, says Dr. John Mack, director of the psychiatric division of Cambridge (Massachusetts) City Hospital, "after-care" is a scheduled appointment for the patient, with no guidance for the family.[52] Outpatient care may be limited to adjusting medication. Then you're back in Chapter VI, doing your distracted best to locate and combine community resources to meet the needs of your particular family.

As it more often is

There is plenty of recognition of your problems — on paper. Expert after expert decries "the lack of integration between hospital staff and community agencies, which most of the time are not alerted to the plight of the patient's family or the plight of the discharged patient."* But paper recognition does no good if the problems aren't recognized in the community you live in. A 1974 news report warns what you can expect in many places, not only now but for the future. A Virginia state representative tells his state board of mental health to "be realistic" in its hopes for expanded after-care services:

An uncertain future

> Delegate A. R. Giesen, R. Staunton [the location of a major Virginia state hospital] told the board that many Virginia communities still look to the state hospitals as a primary source of help for the mentally ill, not local agencies. "Even knowledgeable people resist" spending the funds that would be required for an extensive counseling program to organize expatients' transition from the hospitals to the community.

"You've got a selling job to do to the citizenry," Giesen said.[53]

Mr. Giesen is thoroughly realistic. He knows his district, and he knows how many people there are who would prefer to see the mentally ill kept in hospitals, "where they belong." Mr. Giesen was addressing mental health professionals, but it's not only they who have to do a selling job. You do too. Professionals are more open to working with families than ever before. This should encourage us all to work together to make sure that the walls around the mental hospital remain a thing of the past.

* Eleanor Pavenstedt and Viola W. Bernard, eds., *Crises of Family Disorganization: Programs to Soften Their Impact on Children* (New York: Behavioral Publications, 1975). The problem envisaged is the effect on children when a psychotic parent returns from the hospital.

»» CHAPTER X ««

The Law and Your Relative

> For I blessed God in St. James's Park until I routed all the company. . . . For the officers of the peace are at variance with me, and the watchman smites me with his staff.
>
> CHRISTOPHER SMART, *Rejoice in the Lamb*

UP TO NOW, you may never have had to consider that there is such a thing as mental health law. Mentally ill people and their families have more than their share of problems, but these problems — like other people's — usually get handled in ways that don't involve the law. Most mentally ill people go through life without committing a crime, or even being suspected of one. And most hospitalizations begin, continue, and end routinely, in ways that patient and family don't too strenuously object to. In time of trouble, however, though the law is one of the most difficult (and expensive) ways of getting what you want or preventing what you don't want, it is one of the most effective. In case of need, this chapter will provide an overview of the kinds of laws that can affect the lives of the mentally ill and their families.

Laws vary

and change

Keep two things in mind as you read this chapter. Though we can make some broad generalizations, each state has different laws governing such matters as commitment for mental illness, responsibility for crime, guardianship, and the civil rights of persons judged to be mentally ill. Second, the laws concerning mental illness are changing fast. Laws on such things as guardianship and the management of property have kept relatively stable. But the ferment of the sixties, which made us so aware of the rights of prisoners and minority groups and how these are abridged, also focused attention on the mentally ill, that great minority group so many of whose members are also not free to live and move as they choose. The commitment process, accepted for so many years as a necessary protection for both the mentally ill person and the community, no longer escaped challenge. Even if most people didn't join Dr. Szasz in maintaining that those bearing the label of mental illness should be treated just the same as everybody else (jailed if they injured others, that is, and let alone if they didn't, the new sensitivity to unseen injustice made it possible to bring every hospitalization into question.

and must be reinterpreted

The series of court cases that began in the late sixties shows no sign of stopping. Rights of all sorts are being asserted and defended. Some are guaranteed already and need only to be noted and enforced. Other rights are just beginning to be asserted, like the right to treatment in decent conditions when a person is confined against his will. Establishing legal rights is a long process. Each case must be brought in an individual state, or, in some situations, a federal district, and can be appealed to a higher court if either party is dissatisfied with the decision. Similar cases can be decided in different ways by different courts in different places; the Supreme Court has only recently begun to consider the legal problems of the mentally ill and to apply national guidelines. Courts will enforce them differently; and so will communities, as the history of school desegregation shows.

and enforced by different agencies guaranteeing more local differences in practice.

We'll try to make this chapter as informative as we can. But there's no way it can be an authoritative guide to your legal problems. If you need to know about the law at all, you need to know about the laws of your state, or, if you're unlucky enough to feel responsible for a relative in another state, about the laws that apply to him there. You can find out a good deal from your state mental health association and from parents' organizations (see Chapter XIV, "The Lord Helps Those Who Help Themselves"), but if you really have a legal problem, you'll have to consult a lawyer. Some hints on how to find one, what to expect of him, and how to get the most out of his services will be found at the end of this chapter. If you can't afford a lawyer, however, and perhaps even if you can, some states run legal information services. The Mental Health Information Service of New York provides information and legal services for psychiatric patients throughout the state; Maryland, Minnesota, and West Virginia are among states providing similar services. Many public hospitals have legal divisions that are by no means simple arms of the hospital administration. (Some have even helped the patient sue the hospital.) There is a list of legal service agencies in Appendix B.

When in doubt, consult a lawyer.

AREAS OF CONFLICT

The law deals largely with conflicts. If there were no conflicts between what an individual thinks is good for him, what other individuals think, what the community thinks, there would be little need for laws. You and your relative may be in agreement, as when he's in the hospital and you are the person who gets the lawyer to get him out. (It's pretty hard locating a lawyer from a pay phone on the ward, and many wards have no phone.) But it's no good pretending you and your relative are a unit. His interests, as he sees them, may be in open conflict with yours. What you may want is not to get him out but to keep him in. (It's no good pretending all families are units either; mental illness is hardly a guarantee of family harmony. A husband may want to commit his wife while her parents oppose it, or it may work the other way.) We don't have to conjure up the image of Uncle

Conflicts between a mentally ill person and his family,

Leo at the back door with a gun; a checkbook, when a relative's in the grip of manic elation, may also seem a deadly weapon. There may be a conflict, too, between a manic or depressed or paranoid person's interests as he sees them, and his "best interests," as you, and perhaps a doctor, see them. In that case he may peg you as the enemy, and he, not you, may be the one to consult a lawyer.

between his interests and his "best interests."

If he does, what happens may suit him a lot better than it does you, for most of the current legal arguments, and many of the current court decisions, tend strongly in the direction of defending the patient's interests as he perceives them himself, whatever his family, or his doctor, or society in the person of the neighbors or the local police think about it. The courts take very seriously the liberty of the individual – as they should – and they are eloquent in its defense. But rarely do they make reference to the competing claims of members of an ill person's family. Yet conflict is sure to intensify as the back-to-the-community movement continues. "Distressing evidence does exist in some cases that the treatment of an ill person in the community succeeds for that person but contributes to the mental health problems of other family members."[1] Not to mention their physical health problems. In California, one released mental patient murdered his wife and three of his children before killing himself. His mother had opposed his release. A woman beheaded her baby daughter and young son. Her husband had tried unsuccessfully to commit her.[2]

These are sensational cases; only the hysterical would have nightmares because of them. But you know your relative. Because conflicts do exist, you should be aware of them, and let your awareness guide what you expect from a lawyer. Good lawyers are interested in reconciling conflicts, not just in winning cases, and they do a lot more mediating than they're given credit for. But the question remains. If you locate a lawyer and pay him to represent a relative who's in trouble, does that lawyer have two clients or one? You and your relative may disagree on what you want the lawyer to accomplish and how. You may feel you have a right to know the whole situation, including whatever your relative has told the lawyer. You should realize, however, that communications between a lawyer and his client – that's your relative, since the lawyer has been hired to work in his behalf – are "privileged" by law, protected by a confidentiality even more complete than between a patient and his doctor. Unless your relative is legally incompetent, you can expect a lawyer to tell you only what his client permits, and even if he or she is incompetent (or a minor), the lawyer will do as he thinks best. Your expectations concerning what he can do for your relative, and the part you play in the relationship between your relative and the lawyer, is something you should discuss at your very first meeting. (For more on what you should discuss at your first meeting, see p. 304.)

Your relative's lawyer and you

Attorney-client privilege

COMMITMENT: VOLUNTARY AND INVOLUNTARY

Voluntary commitment

In voluntary commitment (or hospitalization, or admission — recent statutes tend to replace the unpleasant older term) the patient signs himself into the hospital for a specified period.* It ranges between three and twenty days — two weeks is most usual. Legally, there are just two differences between voluntary and involuntary commitment. None of a patient's legal rights can be affected by the fact that he has been hospitalized voluntarily for mental illness. And a voluntary patient may sign himself out again. In some states he can leave as soon as he's changed his mind,† something that's pretty easy to do after a look at some hospitals. But in the vast majority he'll have to wait, a matter of hours in some states, in others as long as thirty days after written notice is given. One naive young woman, depressed and anticipating a bad weekend, packed her bag and signed herself into a state hospital one Friday. She signed something at the desk, but she didn't read it. When the books she had brought and her cosmetics and toothbrush were taken away and she received pills instead of psychotherapy, she wanted out, but it took real pressure from her parents (whom she managed to call from the nurses' room) to get her out before the statutory ten days were up. Those three days were ones she can't forget. "I asked to brush my teeth the morning of the second day and they said, 'What do you think we're running here, a hotel?' " Her parents told a reporter, "We finally got her out after having several people contact them. The young woman who spoke to us at the first floor desk . . . was very rude, very uncooperative and authoritarian. She said this girl did need to be there and as parents and laymen we couldn't understand so we should just go away and mind our own business."[3] As you can see, hospital staff are often uncomfortable with the idea of voluntary admission. They're in a bind sometimes; many voluntary patients really are in need of continuing care, whether or not they realize it, and many patients (like Clifford Beers) are glad later that they were kept in the hospital.

Legal rights are unaffected and a voluntary patient may leave after an interval and written notice.

Observation period

When someone is sick and doesn't know it, the waiting period serves a function; it allows an "observation period," and gives the hospital

* In a few states there is a kind of admission between voluntary and involuntary, "nonprotesting" admission, directed, in Judge Bazelon's words, "at the situation where an individual is unwilling for one reason or another to commit himself but is willing to submit when the initiative is taken by another." That might very well be you. The patient admitted as nonprotesting may leave within a specified time after he requests discharge, though in general the time limit is longer than that set for voluntary patients. (*In re John Ballay,* U.S. Court of Appeals, District of Columbia Circuit, 482 Federal Reporter 2d, 648 [1973].)

† Missouri and Georgia, in the early seventies — but note: statutes change, and many mental health codes have been recently revised. New York's Informal Admission (see Chapter IX, p. 247) also allows for prompt departure.

the opportunity to start the legal procedures necessary to keep a patient in the hospital – that is, to convert his status from voluntary to involuntary. (See below.) What you think of this depends, of course, on the situation and on you. It's seldom explained to entering voluntary patients that their status may be changed without their consent, and it's horrifying to think that that might have happened to the naive young woman. Her family got her out; if you and your relative both agree he should come home, the hospital is pretty sure to go along. Hospital doors open more easily than they used to. But if you don't agree?

Change to involuntary status

"Voluntary" commitment for minors

Unless your relative is of age he can't commit himself. And if he's under-age, in thirty-eight states his parents* (or guardian) have been able to commit him without his consent.

> An admission commenced by the parent or guardian of a minor . . . is considered voluntary; despite the state of mind of the minor . . . the legislature has determined that, for purposes of admission to a hospital the parent or guardian is legally empowered to act in behalf of the minor.†

The same is true of adult wards, people who have been adjudged incompetent to carry on their own affairs (see pp. 297–302).

"Voluntary" commitment for a minor or ward has actually been more stringent than involuntary commitment for an adult; it was the parent or guardian, not the patient, who gave consent for particular treatments such as ECT (though in some states the patient may refuse it, unless an incompetent), who applied for discharge, and who could waive the right to a hearing. In 1975, however, in a far-reaching decision, a three-judge district court in Philadelphia ordered new legal safeguards for the juvenile commitment process. In *Bartley* v. *Kremens*, a class action suit, the court held that parents can no longer waive the legal rights of their children. A need for institutionalization must be clearly proven; requirements ordered by the court include a prompt hearing at which the child has the right to be present, testify, and

Bartley *v.* Kremens

* Some children are no longer under the authority of their parents. Local juvenile or probate courts have jurisdiction over "neglected or delinquent" minors and retain custody until they're of age. Ralph Slovenko, *Psychiatry and Law* (Boston: Little, Brown, 1973), p. 212.

† Samuel J. Brakel and Ronald S. Rock, eds., *The Mentally Disabled and the Law* (revised ed.), American Bar Foundation Study (Chicago: University of Chicago Press, 1971). Although it is not completely up to date, this is the indispensable reference book you need when this chapter isn't enough. Its 487 large pages present in detail every subject we mention here, and many that we don't. Forty-one tables summarize the provisions of the statutes of all states on such things as voluntary and involuntary hospitalization, financial responsibility for relative's support in hospital, discharge procedures, patients' rights, marriage and divorce, insanity as a defense to crime, sterilization, transfer of patients within a state, and much, much else.

bring witnesses, and the right to legal counsel at all stages of the procedure. This decision should go far to discourage the use of hospitalization as a cure for adolescent rebelliousness.* The best safeguard, however, must still be that most parents aren't searching for ways to hospitalize their children but for ways to avoid it.

Involuntary commitment

The liberty of the individual is a precious right, and any abridgment of it requires careful justification. The freedom of people considered to be insane, however, has always been subject to limitation. By the common law of England, the traditional law which is the basis of United States law, people who were considered a danger to themselves or others could be put into asylums or otherwise treated; the basis for this process was the police power of the sovereign. Later another justification was added, the state's power of *parens patriae,* the power "to act to protect the well-being of its citizens when they cannot care for themselves."[4]

Common law

The beginning of medical commitment

The specific commitment procedures developed in the last 150 years were originally designed to protect the mentally ill against arbitrary power – we might as well call it arrest, since the end result was that the patient was held under confinement. In 1832 the French psychiatrist Esquirol after years of effort succeeded in bringing into being a law requiring that a physician must fill out forms, and a court must act upon them, if anyone was to be kept in an asylum. Similar legislation was developing in other countries, but then as now, opinions differed as to who ought to be in an asylum and who ought to decide the question. One of the early crusaders for the rights of mental patients was Mrs. E. P. W. Packard, an Illinois lady who in 1860 had been committed by her husband, a preacher who objected to her publicly disagreeing with him on religion, in accordance with a law which allowed husbands to petition for the commitment of their wives "without the evidence of insanity or distraction required in other cases."[5]

Women's lib and the rights of mental patients, 1860

Commitment isn't that easy today, but no one would claim that it is always just or fair when the legal procedures are followed, let alone when they aren't. Before we go on to describe commitment processes let's make clear for our relatives what we know for ourselves: that wrongful commitment is as terrible as wrongful imprisonment, if not worse, and that it is to the interest of everyone that strong legal safeguards should exist. Yet in states like Massachusetts, California, and New York, where "de-institutionalization" policies now encourage easy release, the results are making many people uneasy.

* For the case of a perfectly sane thirteen-year-old boy who spent four years in a state hospital because his father found him troublesome at home – and who, grown up and himself a father, found his employment threatened by that old stigma – see Bruce Ennis, *Prisoners of Psychiatry* (New York: Harcourt Brace Jovanovich, 1972).

> In the past five years commitment laws in many states have been rewritten to protect civil rights, but the laws will be only as effective as the vigilance of the community, the courts, and the physicians guarantee. There is, however, a nagging question . . . : Are we legislating a justification for indifference to human welfare? . . . When someone is grossly disturbed but refuses to seek help, what is our responsibility toward him? The law recognizes the legitimacy of intervention when the patient is suicidal or homicidal. Under what other circumstances is intervention warranted? That is a major issue for parents with a disturbed adolescent, for children with a disturbed parent and for friends helplessly watching a life being wasted. It may be that such casualties are the necessary price for the benefits of individual freedom, but the matter deserves more thought than it is being given.[6]

Criteria for involuntary commitment:

mental illness

need for care or supervision

mental illness with impaired social function

danger to self and others

risk because of impaired judgment

incapacity to make a responsible decision

Specific commitment laws reflect their basis, the state's police power to maintain public order and welfare, and the "parental" power to protect those who need it. Some states, like Delaware and Kentucky, have required only that a person be found to have a mental illness, defect, or disorder. Others, like Idaho, have required that a person be mentally ill and *also* in need of "supervision, treatment, care or restraint." Others, like Ohio, specify that the mental illness must impair self-control and judgment so as to hinder the conduct of the ill person's affairs.[7] Massachusetts's 1970 statute reaffirms the old common-law criterion: a person cannot be confined unless he is found to present a "substantial risk" of physical danger to himself or others, and this is a very common criterion. (Montana and New Jersey include danger to property.) Massachusetts also will commit if there is a "very substantial" physical risk to the person himself because of impaired judgment. Many states combine these criteria in one way or another: someone may be hospitalized if mentally ill *and* dangerous *or* in need of care and treatment. Twelve states require in addition that the mentally ill person lack the capacity to make a responsible decision regarding his own condition and treatment.

Right to liberty

In June, 1975, in a unanimous decision, the Supreme Court affirmed a constitutional "right to liberty" for mental patients. In *O'Connor* v. *Donaldson,* a case that we will discuss further on page 279, the Court held a finding of "mental illness" alone cannot justify a state's locking a person up against his will and keeping him indefinitely in simple custodial confinement. Assuming that that term can be given a reasonably precise content and that the "mentally ill" can be identified with reasonable accuracy, there is still no constitutional basis for confining such persons involuntarily if they are dangerous to no one and can live safely in freedom.[8] Though the decision still leaves many questions unanswered, it will give new impetus to the back-to-the-community movement.

Pages could be written about how to negotiate the commitment laws of a single state;* Ralph Slovenko, Professor of Law and Psychiatry at Wayne State University, writes that "civil commitment laws in most states are so complicated that they make criminal and tax laws appear simple in comparison."[9] For a crisp summary of the hospitalization laws of your state and forty-nine others, get *The Rights of Mental Patients,*† *An American Civil Liberties Union Handbook.* It will enable you to understand what your lawyer is talking about, and maybe, if he's new to the mental health game, give him a few pointers.

Abolish involuntary commitment?

The injustices Ennis and Siegel observed as director and associate director of the New York American Civil Liberties Union's Special Litigation Project on the Rights of Mental Patients made them convinced enemies of any kind of involuntary commitment, and they argue their case powerfully. Handle their book with care, therefore; if you believe your relative belongs in a hospital, it's not exactly what you'd choose to give him for Christmas.‡

Tough arguments and hard questions

The ACLU is suspicious of all the criteria for commitment and is doing all it can to challenge them in the courts. Some of their arguments are difficult to counter: "mental illness" is a vague concept by which to take away a person's liberty, and dangerousness, if you can't actually observe it in the present, is difficult or impossible to predict in the future.§ Others raise hard questions: have we a right to force

* And have been; from the Center for the Study of Legal Authority and Mental Patient Status (LAMP) in Berkeley, you can get a patients' guide to California mental health laws much longer than what you've read of this chapter. Dr. Jack Zusman and Professor William A. Carnahan have written an exhaustive two-volume guide to New York State law, *Mental Health: New York Law and Practice* (New York: Matthew Bender, 1975).

† Bruce Ennis and Loren Siegel (New York: Richard W. Baron, 1973; Avon, 1973). Partial table of contents: Emergency Hospitalization, Conditional Release; Periodic Review; Communication and Visitation; Notice of Rights . . . etc., etc. The state-by-state summary takes up over half the book. It's easier to carry around than Brakel and Rock, a bit more up to date, but far less comprehensive.

‡ For example, "What should you do if someone tries to take you against your will to a mental hospital?" "Because of the uncertainty about the laws governing the arrest of prospective mental patients, if a friend or relative or policeman attempts to take you against your will to a mental hospital, or to a judge, you should ask what statute or court decision gives him the right to infringe your liberty, pointing out that if the arrest is not authorized, he can be sued. And don't be put off by the response that you are not being 'arrested' but only transported to a hospital. *Any* substantial interference with your right to go or remain where you like is an arrest, whether the person arresting you calls it that or not." *ACLU Handbook,* p. 19.

§ "There is little reason to suspect that persons classified as 'mentally ill' tend to be more dangerous to society than others. A study of 5,000 patients discharged from New York State mental hospitals over a five and one-half year period showed that 'patients with no record of prior arrest have a strikingly low rate of arrest after release. . . . Their overall rate is less than 1/12 that of the general population, and the rate for each separate offence is also far lower, especially for more serious charges.'" *In re John Ballay,* U.S. Court of Appeals, District of Columbia Circuit, 482 Federal Reporter, 2d 648 (1973).

treatment on unwilling patients, especially in a hospital which gives bad treatment, or none? What is the standard of proof in an involuntary commitment proceeding? Should it be "according to the preponderance of the evidence," as in civil cases, or – as in criminal cases where the penalty is imprisonment – "beyond a reasonable doubt"?

John Ballay in Washington

A man showed up once at the Capitol, twice at the White House, claiming he was the Senator from Illinois, asking to see Tricia Nixon. Each time he was picked up and hospitalized; each time, when he was released, he did it again. Was he dangerous to others? To himself? Judge David Bazelon decided "not beyond a reasonable doubt," and ordered him released.[10] A nineteen-year-old Detroit woman began wandering the streets for days at a time just after she had her first baby; her grandmother asked for her commitment. "I cannot go crazy until 10 o'clock because they're going to the moon to play baseball," she said in court. "My brain isn't working." A few days before, a higher court had ruled that dangerousness must be the only criterion in Michigan, but Judge Ira Kaufman wrote a temporary detention order anyway. "The civil libertarians and the upper courts are just wrong about this," he told a reporter. "These people desperately need help and their desperateness doesn't necessarily go to the point of dangerousness."[11]

postpartum psychosis in Detroit

We have no answers. New cases are filed each year. They are decided in conflicting ways, sometimes for liberty, sometimes for protection. For mental patients (and their families) who seek to challenge commitment, the *ACLU Handbook* is a Bible. They (you?) will find a host of young lawyers on their side, some of them dedicated enough to work for free. And, at this writing (1975), the Mental Health Law Project in Washington, D.C., is compiling an up-to-the-minute list of such lawyers in every state. Families who, like the Detroit woman's grandmother, want to see their relative recovering in the hospital, will find most psychiatrists (and many lawyers) on their side.

Procedures for commitment:

There are two stages of involuntary commitment. The first is emergency hospitalization or temporary detention – what Judge Kaufman used to get the Detroit mother off the streets. Emergency hospitalization is usually for a limited time – five days or less in many states; fifteen in some; in a very few, thirty or more. Theoretically, it's for observation and diagnosis, not treatment, but even examination may be cursory. Usually there's not that much of an emergency; most involuntary hospitalizations (99 percent in New York City, according to Bruce Ennis) begin as emergency hospitalization. Procedures vary greatly. One state (Indiana) requires a hearing before a judge, even for emergency hospitalization. Some states, like Idaho and Texas, require a court order, though not a hearing. Most states require a petition, sometimes by a relative but in many states by any adult, sup-

Emergency hospitalization for a limited time

involving a petition,

ported by one (or two) doctors. In 1970, thirty-one states had a medical certification procedure. In a few of these (Connecticut is one) no complaint from a layman is required if one or more physicians certify they have personally examined someone and find him both mentally ill and dangerous.

judges, and/or doctors (medical certification).

Emergency hospitalization (like voluntary hospitalization) can readily be converted into nonemergency, or longer-term, hospitalization. Nonemergency hospitalization is usually for an indefinite period (until the hospital thinks the patient is ready to leave) or for a definite but renewable term. Since this is a very serious matter (it may be permanent), careful legal safeguards are provided. In most states such long-term commitment can only be by court order after a judicial hearing (in some states, with a jury). *Medical certification is thus subject to judicial review.*

Nonemergency hospitalization for an indefinite period (or anyway a long one) requires a hearing and a court order.

A few states authorize commitment on certification by two physicians and do not require a hearing. A hearing, however, will be granted if the patient requests it.

The "two-physician" rule

In fact, hearings are less common than you'd think. "In one year . . . Bellevue [Hospital, in New York City] admitted 15,000 involuntary patients, of whom only 531 requested judicial review."* Sometimes the patient waives, or gives up, his rights. Sometimes he never finds out about them, and since a hearing must be requested in writing, he's deemed to have waived his rights anyway. In some states (California is one) the law on patients' rights must be posted in wards, and is. But until recently, when mental health lawyers began to get after them, hospital staffs didn't break their backs making sure patients knew their rights. Recall the naive young lady. Staff are generally convinced that patients need hospitals; many psychiatrists feel that medical certification should be enough and that court proceedings upset vulnerable patients and make the tasks of recovery harder. Families too may find a hearing a painful experience if private lives are exposed in court. (Often, however, commitment procedures have taken place at the hospital, out of public view.)

To protect his interests during these procedures your relative has the right to a lawyer. And note this: you may not have a right to inspect your relative's hospital records, but his lawyer does. "Studies at Bellevue [Hospital, in New York City] . . . show that if you have a lawyer at your commitment hearing, the chances are about 300% greater that you will not be committed than if you don't have a lawyer."[12]

The right to legal counsel

* Bruce Ennis, *Prisoners of Psychiatry* (New York: Harcourt Brace Jovanovich, 1972), p. 197. Cf. p. 202: "[At Bellevue] to satisfy the requirement that patients be given notice of their rights it was common practice for hospital officials to slip the printed notice into the patient's hospital record and consider him notified, even though the patient did not have access to his record."

Free?

Everywhere in the United States, when a person accused of a crime can't pay a lawyer to defend him, the court must appoint one. But if your relative is threatened, not with jail, but with commitment, he may not be so lucky. A number of states do supply legal counsel for nonemergency commitment; the information is given, state by state, in the *ACLU Handbook*.

IN-HOSPITAL RIGHTS

Once he's committed, your relative still has rights, though in some states he hasn't many. Those he has can usually be restricted "for good cause." Put all the states together and you'll find a statutory right to every aspect of decent conditions and treatment surveyed in the last chapter. But your relative is hospitalized in only one state, so check its statutes. The *ACLU Handbook* specifies the relevant statutes by number. After checking it, you would do well to check again for the most recent information: ask your state or county mental health association and/or the state mental health department.* Some state legislatures (ask your state bar association about this) have "hotlines" for tracking bills once they are filed. In-hospital rights are listed in the *Handbook* under these headings: communication and visitation; civil rights; confidentiality of records; religious freedom; payment for work; notice of rights; control of personal property; restraints, shock therapy, sterilization, and surgery; and (maybe) right to treatment. (This last has been clarified in important ways since the handbook was published.) We won't summarize the ACLU's summaries, but some points need emphasis.

Communication and visitation

Many states have no provision at all regarding communication. If you care, check your state in the *Handbook*. In any case, be aware that in most state hospitals your relative's letters and yours can be opened and censored, although in practice they probably aren't.

Notice of rights

Notice of rights is obviously crucial, but many states have no statutory requirement that involuntary patients be notified, although in some of these it is done as a matter of policy. (On the other hand, it sometimes is *not* done in states where it's the law.) Check your state, if not for your relative's sake, for your own.

Control of personal property

Can your hospitalized relative wear his own clothes? Has he a legal right to hold on to his money, his watch, his Bible, his toothbrush? Not always; not even very often. North Carolina, Massachusetts, and Cali-

* Since statutes are implemented by detailed administrative regulations, in cases of doubt you (and your lawyer) should check these too. They should be available from your state Department of Mental Health, and doubtless there's a copy at the state hospital, too.

fornia are among the states safeguarding by statute a patient's right to keep his possessions (and have a place to keep them). Lots of others don't, so be aware; your relative may not have money for the canteen, even if he had money with him on admission. (Large sums will be under the control of the hospital, reasonably enough; a hospital ward is no place to keep money. But somebody ought to be able to give you an accounting. See Chapter XI.)

money, for instance

Will your relative work in the hospital? Probably not, if the 1973 court decision holds; if he does work, he must be paid the minimum wage, or a portion of it geared to his productivity.* A federal statute prohibits "peonage," as a form of involuntary servitude (ruled out under the Thirteenth Amendment to the Constitution). "That means the state may not compel any person to work in order to pay off a debt," including a debt to the hospital.† What this will mean in practice is doubtful. Vermont's statute, for instance, provides that a patient may be employed in the hospital with his consent, half of his earnings to be credited to his personal fund and the balance taken by the hospital. (Vermont is not a rich state, and they have a pretty good state hospital.) In Georgia, patients can keep all they earn. Most states make no provision. As we mentioned in Chapter IX, "work therapy" can be beneficial; as we mentioned in Chapter VIII, it is good for people to feel useful. The absolute prohibition against patients' labor unless paid according to the minimum wage may be due for revision. The courts may eventually rule that it is all right for patients to work if the task is suitable and planned to be therapeutic.

Payment for work

With the back-to-the-community movement, few new patients remain long enough in the hospital to be exploited, and long-time hospital work programs are being dismantled. Your relative is probably in more danger from boredom than from involuntary servitude. Nevertheless Edna Long, a bookkeeper with an IQ of 134, worked without pay eight hours a day in Harlem Valley State Hospital, in New York, for sixteen years, tending steam tables and scrubbing floors.‡ She was discharged at sixty-six with no compensation. The date was 1967, not so very long ago.

Edna Long

People need money when they're getting out, but though prisoners get a suit and some money when they are released from jail, in many states mental patients may be let out penniless. Alaska's good on this; a released patient must have clothes, a reasonable sum of money, and transportation to his home. California, Michigan, and Vermont have

Money on discharge?

* *Souder* v. *Brennan* (Peter Brennan, that is, then Secretary of Labor). In this class action suit, D.C. District Judge Aubrey Robinson directed the U.S. Department of Labor to apply the Fair Labor Standards Act to mental institutions.

† Ennis and Siegel in the *ACLU Handbook* give earlier legal citations on these points (p. 60).

‡ You can read about her case in Ennis's *Prisoners of Psychiatry,* Chapter 3.

good statutes. Many states make no provision. Many hospitals, of course, provide funds and clothing anyway. A chapter on law inevitably emphasizes dissatisfaction, but we shouldn't forget that people, and states, often behave better than the law requires.

Right to refuse treatment

Does a patient in a mental hospital have a right to refuse treatment, as a patient in a general hospital may? It depends. Voluntary patients fare better than involuntary, but primarily it depends on the kind of treatment. Psychosurgery? Yes – and so do his relatives – but psychosurgery is now a most uncommon treatment,* and one, moreover, which courts do not regard as a "regular surgical procedure." Sterilization, also rare, usually requires consent of the patient and relatives. In 1975 South Carolina and South Dakota still authorized involuntary sterilization of persons whose insanity is deemed "hereditary"; in Virginia a mental patient could be sterilized if the state board of hospitals found the patient "the probable parent of socially inadequate offspring." Under such statutes appeal and court review is provided. The operation is rarely performed on the mentally ill; practically, the provisions are likely to concern you only if your relative is also retarded.

Psychosurgery

Sterilization

ECT

Shock treatment, as we've seen, is virtually out of use in many state hospitals. In California and Massachusetts a statute allows patients specifically to refuse it, though the medical director can overrule. Massachusetts, Michigan, and New York are among the states which require consent of relatives,† but many don't mention it. You'd better discuss the matter when your relative enters the hospital.

Chemotherapy

As we've seen, the commonest treatment today for mental illnesses is with drugs. In few places (and no state codes) is it envisaged that a patient (or his family) has a right to refuse drugs except where religious principles conflict.[13] That would be to guarantee that a mentally ill patient could refuse what most doctors agree is the treatment of choice for the condition for which he was hospitalized.

But patients don't necessarily agree. N.A.P.A., the Network Against Psychiatric Assault (it also spells the name of the state hospital that serves California's Bay Area), was founded by psychiatrist Don Goldmacher and community mental health worker Wade Hudson. It opposes "involuntary treatments for unwilling subjects," and is pressing to insert a right to refuse chemotherapy in California's progressive

* Not only has the patient a right to refuse psychosurgery, but if an involuntary patient, he may not have the right to consent to it. "It was obvious from the record made in this case that the facts surrounding experimental brain surgery are profoundly uncertain, and the lack of knowledge on the subject makes a *knowledgeable consent*" [itals. ours] "to psychosurgery literally impossible." *Kaimowitz* v. *Dept. of Mental Health for the State of Michigan, et al.;* Mich. Cir. Ct. No. 73-19434-AW.

† By administrative regulations, not by statute.

mental health law. "No matter how wonderful the Miracle-Drug-of-the-Day, to force it into another's system is chemical rape, an unnatural and sacrilegious act, a violation of the constitutional protections of privacy and freedom of thought."[14] We can expect more and more cases on the right to refuse treatment.

Protection versus liberty – again and again the issue is joined. And let's be fair – when Thorazine is automatic for everybody, you can't call it protection. Remember the naive young lady. You might inquire whether drugs and dosages are individually prescribed; new right-to-treatment decisions are likely to require it.

Your relative may succeed in refusing drugs, and if you too refuse your consent the hospital probably won't insist. Consider, though, that treatment for any serious illness has its drawbacks. If he succeeds in refusing medication, your relative may escape the side effects of Thorazine. But there's a trade-off; he may have to undergo an extended (and expensive) stay in the hospital under less than ideal conditions.

Restraint: drugs

Drugs, today, are used not only for treatment but for restraint. Certainly we have all grown more enlightened with the years, but a major reason why the straitjackets and padded cells of Clifford Beers's day are rarely used today is that pills and injections work better. For people who are a danger to themselves and others may still be dangerous in the hospital, and when they are, their behavior has to be restrained in some way. The 1970 Massachusetts statute defines "restraint" as "bodily physical force, mechanical devices, chemicals, confinement in a place of seclusion other than the placement of an inpatient or resident in his room for the night, or any other means which unreasonably limits freedom of movement." It limits its use to emergencies and requires written authorization from the superintendent or his deputy, with review every eight hours. About half the states limit the use of restraints by law.[15] There may be more by the time you read this.

force, straitjackets, seclusion

Our interest in restraints may reflect who is being restrained. It may be your relative who is restrained against his will. But it may also be your relative who is injured by a violent patient, or who injures himself. Hospitals have been sued for this; usually they have escaped liability if they have been able to establish that the violent patient had never before shown dangerous or suicidal tendencies. Here too, liberty and protection clash.

Right to treatment?

Is there a right to treatment – to active treatment, by qualified personnel, in adequate numbers? Of those states whose laws seem to imply a right to treatment, only a few specify psychiatric, as opposed to general medical, care and treatment.

Active, qualified, adequate? You can read about snake pits in lots of other places. Here it's enough to quote District Judge Frank M. Johnson, Jr.'s ruling in the landmark case of *Wyatt* v. *Stickney:*

Wyatt *v.* Stickney

> To deprive any citizen of his or her liberty upon the altruistic theory that the confinement is for humane therapeutic purposes and then fail to provide adequate treatment violates the very fundamentals of due process.*

Bryce Hospital in Tuscaloosa, Alabama, where a patient named Ricky Wyatt was confined in terrible conditions, is now a better place than it was in 1970, and hospitals in other states are getting the message. The judge set detailed standards and Alabama is trying to reach them. But standards are met with money, and although Wyatt's lawyer, George Dean, created a stir by drawing attention to the appropriation for the Junior Miss Pageant when the state pleaded poor, in no state is money unlimited. Nor are other resources, and civil liberties lawyers know it. In 1972 there were only seventy-nine psychiatrists in the whole state of Alabama.† If the money could be found to entice, say, half of them to serve the four thousand patients at Bryce (1:100 – not impressive, but still higher than the court set), how would the three-and-a-half million other residents of Alabama meet their problems of living?

Bruce Ennis explains his interest in *Wyatt* v. *Stickney:*

> I became involved in the Alabama "right to treatment" case because we had some advance information that the judge would not only say there is something in the abstract called the "right to treatment," but that he would set standards so high that the State of Alabama would literally not be able to meet them. For example, he required that there be at least one Ph.D. psychologist for every sixty "mentally retarded" children in institutions. There simply were not enough psychologists in the State of Alabama to staff the institutions at that ratio with the then current resident populations. Using that ratio meant that instead of hiring more psychologists Alabama was going to have to discharge many of the residents. . . .[16]

In short, Ennis's purpose in pressing right-to-treatment was not primarily to improve mental hospitals, but to force the discharge of involuntary patients into the community. But money into institutions means money that's not spent for community programs,‡ and vice

* *Wyatt* v. *Stickney,* 325 F. Supp. 781, 334 F. Supp. 1341 (M.D. Ala. 1971), 344 F. Supp. 373, 387 (M.D. Ala. 1972), *aff'd in part sub nom. Wyatt* v. *Aderholt* 502 F. 2d 1305 (5th Cir., 1974). You can read about *Wyatt* v. *Stickney* and the conditions that gave rise to it – with pictures – in Walter Goodman, "The Constitution v. the Snakepit," *New York Times Magazine* (March 17, 1974), and in Ennis, *Prisoners,* Chapter 6. The full text of Judge Johnson's opinion is given in the *ACLU Handbook,* as well as the court-ordered "minimum constitutional standards for adequate treatment of the mentally ill."

† "Wyatt vs. [sic] Stickney, Revolutionary Standards," *Psychiatric News* (December 19, 1973). It's encouraging to note that Dr. Humphry Osmond, one of the most articulate of psychiatrists, has moved to Alabama to become a consultant at Bryce.

‡ See Honora A. Kaplan, "Institutions and Community Mental Health: The Paradox in *Wyatt* v. *Stickney,*" *Community Mental Health Journal,* 9, No. 1 (1973): 34–37.

versa – unless total mental health funding is substantially increased. Money is never unlimited, and citizens have to choose where they put it. A trade-off again. For many of us, sick and well, it's likely to be a cruel one.

O'Connor *v.* Donaldson

O'Connor v. *Donaldson* was also brought as a right-to-treatment case. But when in 1975 the Supreme Court unanimously affirmed the "right to liberty" for nondangerous mental patients, they held back from deciding whether the Constitution guarantees a right to treatment.*

O'Connor v. *Donaldson* is one of those indefinite-commitment stories which make you sick with outrage, but which (thanks to lawyers like Ennis) don't pose a likely problem for your relative today. On the initiative of infirm and elderly parents, Kenneth Donaldson was confined in Florida State Hospital fourteen years against his will, though he brought fifteen different legal petitions before state and federal courts and though a halfway house and a college classmate were ready to assume responsibility for him if he were released. (Hospital memoranda noted of the classmate that "this man must not be well himself to want to get involved with someone like this patient.") Donaldson was denied grounds privileges and access to occupational therapy,† and his contact with the psychiatrist in charge of his treatment averaged fourteen minutes a *year*. When another psychiatrist took over his case (and restored grounds privileges and began talking to him), things improved rapidly and Donaldson was released. (The increasing interest of civil liberties lawyers in his case doubtless also had something to do with it.)

A federal district court jury awarded Donaldson $38,000 in personal damages from two psychiatrists, including Dr. O'Connor,‡ the former superintendent of the hospital – not a high figure as malpractice awards go, especially since the jury found they had acted "maliciously or wantonly or oppressively" in withholding treatment and denying release. The Supreme Court, however, set aside the damages and sent the case back to the Court of Appeals, calling for further consideration of Dr. O'Connor's argument concerning his reliance on state law.

Though the American Psychiatric Association supports a right to treatment, it was sympathetic to the doctors' position. Dr. John Spiegel, A.P.A. president in 1974, fears that psychiatrists won't work in state hospitals if they become liable for personal damages.[17] Yet it would seem that psychiatrists who do work there will have little to

* Chief Justice Burger made clear that he, for one, was prepared to rule there was no such constitutional right.

† Those interested in the right to refuse treatment should note that he was able to refuse drug treatment on religious grounds, as a Christian Scientist. *Science News*, 106 (Sept. 28, 1974).

‡ The other doctor did not join in the appeal.

worry about should the award be upheld. The trial court judge told the jury that they could return a verdict against the doctors personally only if they found that Donaldson had not been dangerous to himself or others and had not been receiving treatment *and* that the doctors, knowing this, had obstructed his release anyway. Even after the Supreme Court's decision in *O'Connor* v. *Donaldson,* the law requires only that a doctor act in what the law describes as "the reasonable good faith belief" that his actions are consistent with the rights of his patient under state and constitutional law. This is the same standard to which schoolteachers, police personnel, and all other state employees are held.

Whether or not Donaldson collects for his fourteen lost years, hospital authorities from now on are on notice that they will be held liable for illegally confining nondangerous patients. We can be sure that right-to-treatment cases will continue to be brought, that they will now be focused on the right to treatment in the community as well as in the large mental institution, and that we will still be assessing the effects of *Donaldson* for years to come.[18]

DISCHARGE

These days it is pretty easy;

Discharge procedures vary from state to state and from hospital to hospital, but everywhere they are increasingly lenient. At least nine states have abolished indeterminate commitment; in these, all involuntary commitments expire at the end of fixed periods and patients must be recommitted (with the same right to judicial review as for the original commitment) or released. Today, when public hospitals vie with each other as to which can release more patients and private hospitals are considering whether insurance limits may not define the length of most hospital stays, Kenneth Donaldson's fourteen-year confinement seems almost inconceivable, and it's hard to believe that a doctor could have refused the request Edna Long's husband made for her release.* Your relative is not likely to be kept in the hospital if his family wants him to come out. But just in case, here's a description of habeas corpus, the oldest and simplest remedy available to every citizen as a protection against unjust imprisonment.† The judicial review procedures provided in most states are more complex; they may require a petition accompanied by medical certificates, notice to various parties, and one or more examinations. A habeas writ, however, will be

if not try habeas corpus.

* A doctor did, however, because she was "uncooperative" in her work assignments, and twice the court refused her petition for discharge. Ennis, *Prisoners,* p. 112.

† In some states (as at common law) the habeas petition can challenge only the initial confinement, not its continuation.

issued whenever the patient, or someone acting for him, addresses the judge in writing alleging that the detention is unlawful and stating the reasons why. Unless the allegations are clearly untrue, the court will issue a writ, and a hearing will be held. Your relative is likelier to get a writ if he has a lawyer. (See Chapter IX, p. 259.) In habeas petitions, the burden of proof is on the petitioner, however, whereas in judicial proceedings it is usually on the hospital. Localities vary in their use of habeas corpus. In some places it is virtually never used, but in the District of Columbia, patients have been known to submit as many as fifty petitions in five years. In fact, however, judicial proceedings (including habeas corpus) actually account for only a tiny proportion of all discharges. Most are granted by doctors, not judges.

Will somebody tell you when your relative is discharged?

Some thirteen states require that the guardian or a relative (sometimes a friend) be notified of a patient's discharge. That's a lot that don't. If this matters to you, make sure the hospital knows you expect notification, and that they have a current address and phone number.

Is getting out too easy?

Open wards are more and more common, and so they should be; the vast majority of patients are not dangerous.* Patients have grounds privileges; they have passes into town. Usually they come back, but not always. When they don't, their absence is more likely to be reported to the police than to you, but it may not be reported to anybody, from carelessness, or policy.

Going AWOL and worse

In 1974, when four patients transferred from Matteawan, New York's maximum security hospital for the criminally insane, to low-security Bronx State Hospital turned up missing, nobody at the hospital notified the police, although one of them was alleged to have shot three people. The absence of hundreds of nonviolent patients also went unreported.[19] In 1973, near Washington, a young man assaulted a fourteen-year-old girl, stripped her, and tied her to a tree where she died of exposure, on the wooded grounds of the same exclusive school where he had assaulted another fourteen-year-old two years before. Then, he had pleaded guilty; the judge, with touching faith in the powers of psychiatry, had given him a twenty-year suspended sentence on condition that he undergo intensive treatment in a psychiatric hospital, from which he would not be released without the judge's permission. The hospital was an expensive private facility, and after a year there his family's insurance ran out. (At that, it was the only insurance plan which does pay for such a long hospitalization – the one for federal government employees.) He became a day patient (with the judge's concurrence), and two months later the hospital discharged him, without notice to the judge (or the school, though they had expressly asked to be notified). Two

* At least three states "permit even dangerous persons to be administratively discharged in the event that they do not improve under treatment." Brakel and Rock, *op. cit.*, p. 137.

months after that, the girl was dead. The hospital refused to concede that the court had any interest in the discharge: "If we thought it was in the best interests of the patient to discharge him, the court had nothing to do with that decision."[20]

Keeping your relative in

It's not a typical story, but it can't be shrugged off. Cases like these threaten the humane aims of the back-to-the-community movement as nothing else could. Along with stories of suicides among recently released patients, it suggests that for some of us, the problem won't be getting our relative released but keeping him safe inside. You won't get any help from the civil liberties lawyers if that's what you want, and the growing number of patients' rights organizations will cast you as a villain. Nevertheless, if you fear for the safety of your relative or of others if he is discharged, discuss your reasons with the staff who know him best, and with the hospital director. Maybe you'll convince them, or maybe they'll convince you you needn't worry. If you still oppose the discharge, make clear to the director that if your relative is released against your recommendation, you will make sure that both the police and the court that originally committed him know about it. (The court ordered the hospital that released that young man to pay damages to the child's parents.) * If the hospital goes ahead anyway, your last resort — to be considered only after careful consultation with a doctor — is to petition for your relative to be committed again, according to the law of most states, which allows a relative (if not "any person") to ask for the commitment of someone who needs it. If you can't get a doctor to go along with you on this, you are probably wrong.

Criminal proceedings and the mentally ill

This is a poor introduction to this next section, for (we'll say it again) your relative is not more likely to commit a crime because he has been a mental patient.† In actual fact, mentally ill people commit fewer crimes than other members of the population; if your relative was harmless to start with he's likely to stay that way. In all probability you can safely skip this section. We can't leave it out, though. Mentally ill people do commit crimes, and they are accused of crimes probably more often than they commit them. If your relative is accused of a crime — stealing, dealing in narcotics, arson, assault, rape, murder — what happens then? Will he be tried and his guilt or innocence established like that of any other citizen? Will he be judged

More hard questions

* Washington *Star-News* (Oct. 18, 1974). They are giving the money for a scholarship to Yale, where she had hoped to go.

† Plenty of people think he is, of course. "That even the most intelligent persons may unwittingly harbor views associated with stigma is intimated by the following question posed to a witness by the Chief Counsel of [Senator Ervin's] Subcommittee [on Constitutional Rights]: 'But any person who is mentally ill has the potential for becoming dangerous, isn't that true?' " It isn't. (The quotation, and the comment, are taken from Judge Bazelon's opinion *In re John Ballay,* note 72.)

"not guilty by reason of insanity"? Will he escape trial altogether because of his mental state? Unless he's tried and acquitted, he'll get bars on his windows in any case, more likely than not in a state hospital for the criminally insane. Jail terms in most states are definite and cannot be increased; they can be decreased (by parole) only according to specified rules. Which will be better for him, jail, or an indefinite commitment in a hospital which is probably the grimmest in the state?* Which will be better for you, and for society?

Penalties for illness?

These are tricky questions, for indefinite commitment can work to your relative's disadvantage or advantage – if you can decide what *is* to his advantage (and yours) in such circumstances. It can be argued that he can get treatment in the hospital and stay out of trouble, and that the purpose of commitment is to treat him and not to punish him. But the hospital divisions for the criminally insane are not models of psychiatric treatment methods; in a well-run jail he will have more access to psychotherapy than in many state hospitals. Too, indefinite commitment can imprison a man longer, often much longer than the longest jail sentence for the crime he was accused of. People have spent years, sometimes lifetimes, in hospitals as a result of minor crimes. Seventeen-year-old Charles Rouse was picked up and sent to St. Elizabeths for carrying a loaded pistol, an offense for which he might have gotten perhaps a year in jail. He was over twenty-one when he got out. Theon Jackson, a twenty-seven-year-old retarded deaf-mute, spent three years in a hospital for an alleged robbery in which the total value of the items in question was less than $9. He would probably be there still but for the lawyers and organizations who appealed his case to the Supreme Court. Jackson had been judged incompetent to stand trial. So had Alfred Curt von Wolfersdorf, who spent his sixty-sixth to eighty-sixth years in Matteawan because he wasn't allowed to prove himself innocent of a murder for which another man was found guilty and electrocuted[21] soon after von Wolfersdorf was committed.

Heavy:

Rouse *v.* Cameron

Jackson *v.* Indiana

United States ex. rel. von Wolfersdorf *v.* Johnson

We can't, mustn't, won't minimize the injustices which Bruce Ennis reports in such gripping detail in his landmark book *Prisoners of Psychiatry,* a book everyone interested in this subject, or indeed in justice, should read. But there's another side to think about. Jackson and von Wolfersdorf never came to trial, but others do. Indefinite commitment can also be used to lighten a penalty. Ezra Pound's twelve-year stay in St. Elizabeths is often cited as a judicial and psychiatric outrage, and indeed he was certainly no crazier than many

And light:

Ezra Pound

* In many states, decisions about placement are made, not by judges, but by administrative boards within departments of correction. These are "invisible" decisions – nonpublic, nonappealable, intramural. To find out how they are made in your state, and by whom, try your state department of correction, the district attorney's office, and local projects for prison in-service and prisoners' rights.

another doctrinaire extremist. But he had broadcast for the enemy in wartime; his commitment was less a testimony to stupidity or malice than to the reluctance to execute a world-famous poet for treason. One well-educated gentleman blacked out and committed a brutal murder. He had been hospitalized more than once; his family had no difficulty getting psychiatric testimony. Tried, he was found not responsible and committed to the state hospital for the criminally insane. The institution was notorious for its conditions, but he did well there and was out in five years. He has gotten into no trouble since. Without the insanity defense, he would still be serving his sentence; twenty years earlier he would have been electrocuted.

An anonymous murderer

To help evaluate such possibilities a mentally ill person accused of a crime needs the best legal advice he can get. No matter what good books you read, an experienced criminal lawyer can evaluate far better than you or your relative whether a trial will be to your relative's advantage.

INCOMPETENCY AND THE INSANITY DEFENSE

If your relative's lawyer thinks his case can be defended like any other client's, he'll do just that, arranging bail, working for acquittal, plea bargaining (pleading guilty to a lesser charge), and using the other tactics you see on television. His approach will depend on many things – his impression of your relative, what he's accused of, whether he thinks he did it, what the circumstances were, what your relative wants him to do, maybe what you want. And it may also depend on whether the lawyer feels his client is able to appreciate the nature of the proceedings and assist adequately in his own defense. If not, he may ask for a mental examination and a finding that your relative is *incompetent to stand trial.* (The issue of incompetency can also be raised by the prosecution or the court itself.)

Incompetency to stand trial

It's important to realize that legally, competency to stand trial does not require full social or intellectual, or emotional, competence. Your relative may think his food is poisoned or his dentures are bugged and still function quite well enough for the purposes of his trial. If a defendant has the capacity to assist his counsel in preparing his defense and if he can understand the nature of the charges against him, he is a competent defendant. "The test is not whether he is of unsound mind or mentally ill, but whether he is rendered incompetent to make a rational defense thereby."[22]

is measured by the capacity to participate in a rational defense.

This is the legal standard. Unfortunately, it has not always been understood by psychiatrists testifying on competency in court. Often they've substituted the psychiatric criteria they're familiar with and assumed that if a person is psychotic he must be incompetent to stand trial, testifying accordingly. Too often judges, figuring they don't know anything about psychiatry, have gone along; as a result, many defendants who could have been tried and acquitted, or tried and served a limited sentence, have been indefinitely committed instead.

The Supreme Court's 1972 decision in *Jackson* v. *Indiana* clearly rules this out.

> . . . a person charged . . . with a criminal offense who is committed wholly on account of his incapacity to proceed to trial cannot be held more than the time necessary to determine whether there is a substantial probability that he will attain that capacity in the foreseeable future. If it is determined that this is not the case, then the state must either institute the customary civil commitment proceedings that would be required to commit indefinitely any other citizen, or release the defendant.[23]*

If an accused person is too confused, deteriorated, or out of touch to assist in his defense, a finding of incompetency may be a way to get him needed psychiatric and legal first aid at state expense. Noting that an accused cannot be held indefinitely in a hospital any more than in a prison, courts are beginning to assert the state has an obligation to provide the services necessary to bring a defendant to the point where he *can* take part in a rational defense. If it becomes clear that therapy and/or legal counseling cannot render him competent "in the foreseeable future," then his lawyer can argue that the *Jackson* standard should be applied, the criminal charges dropped, and the state deal with him in a way appropriate to his condition.

To read the civil liberties enthusiasts, you'd think that no defendant ever was incompetent; civil liberties lawyers seem to assume that it's always to the client's advantage to avoid commitment and stand trial. If only it were that simple. What of the chronic schizophrenic Dr. McGarry describes, who set a fire and turned himself in to the police, saying, "I can't make it on the outside. They won't admit me at the State Hospital. I've got to get away for a while. I'd like to get two to three years." Should he get what he asked for? And where?

* Nevertheless, it takes a long time for Supreme Court decisions to trickle into every court; the best guarantee against indefinite commitment on the basis of incompetency to stand trial is for you, your relative, and your lawyer to be aware of *Jackson* v. *Indiana.*

In the meantime, a team headed by Dr. A. Louis McGarry, Director of the Division of Legal Medicine of the Massachusetts Department of Mental Health, is trying to increase the understanding between law and psychiatry. Dr. McGarry has developed specific methods to guide psychiatrists, lawyers, and courts in assessing competency fairly and realistically. His *Competency to Stand Trial Assessment Instrument and Handbook* is available from the Laboratory of Community Psychiatry of Harvard Medical School. The work was supported by an NIMH grant—another example of the importance of federal support for mental health research.

The insanity defense

Volumes have been written on the insanity defense, and today many jurists would prefer, like Dr. Szasz, to abolish it.* We can't write volumes here, nor have we room to make the idea vivid by describing real cases.† Here, briefly and drily, are the current rules by which courts may weigh responsibility in 1975.

The M'Naghten Rule

The oldest of these is the M'Naghten Rule, named for a man who tried to assassinate the British Prime Minister Sir Robert Peel, under the paranoid delusion that the Tories were out to get him. (He shot the P.M.'s secretary instead.) As in every case in which the insanity defense is pleaded, the judge must make clear to the jury that "every man is presumed to be sane, and to possess a sufficient degree of reason to be responsible for his crimes, until the contrary is proved to their satisfaction." Under M'Naghten, the judge is required to instruct the jury that they must acquit the defendant if they find that he suffered from "such a defect of reason, from disease of the mind, as not to know the nature and quality of the act he was doing," or if he did know it, that he did not know it was wrong.[24] Dissatisfaction with this test crystallized early; in 1864 the Association of Medical Officers of Hospitals and Asylums pointed out that

> the power of distinguishing right and wrong exists very frequently among those who are undoubtedly insane, and is often associated with dangerous and uncontrollable delusions.[25]

A modern psychiatrist says much the same thing:

> Just about every defendant, no matter how mentally ill, no matter how advanced his psychosis, knows the difference between right and wrong in the literal sense. . . . [Thus the psychiatrist] becomes an expeditor to the gallows or the gas chamber.[26]

The "Irresistible Impulse" Rule

Because of criticisms like these, the M'Naghten Rule is usually‡ coupled with what is often called the "irresistible impulse" rule. Though the words may vary, the judge tells the jury, in effect, that even if the defendant did know right from wrong, he may not be legally responsible if they find that he could not choose between right and wrong, or could not control his actions or impulses.

The Durham Rule

Even looser is the Durham Rule, used in New Hampshire since

* This is the position taken by Professors Joseph Goldstein and Jay Katz of Yale Law School.

† To get the feel of an insanity defense case, you couldn't do better than read probation officer Dan Sakall's horrifying account of a nice guy who committed murder, was hospitalized, released in two years, and murdered again. Dan Sakall and Alan Harrington, *Love and Evil: From a Probation Officer's Casebook* (Boston: Little, Brown, 1974), Chapters 17 and 18. It's a nice balance to Ennis.

‡ In more than half the states and most federal courts. Brakel and Rock, *op. cit.*, p. 388.

1871 but given wider currency by Judge David Bazelon in 1954. In *Durham* v. *United States,* he held that "an accused is not criminally responsible if his unlawful act was the product of mental disease or mental defect."[27] Judge Bazelon hoped that the openness of the Durham rule would allow psychiatrists to help juries to understand more of a defendant's psychiatric background, and to introduce modern psychiatric ideas so that juries could be "guided by wider horizons of knowledge concerning mental life."[28] Though widely discussed, it was adopted only in the District of Columbia, Maine, and the Virgin Islands. In 1972, Judge Bazelon himself, discouraged with the quality of the years of psychiatric testimony he'd listened to since 1954 (his court, in Washington, D.C., hears a disproportionate number of cases involving mental illness), concurred in the shift from Durham to a fourth standard, the Model Penal Code Test of the American Law Institute.

American Law Institute Rule

This test states that a person is "not responsible for criminal conduct if at the time of such conduct as a result of mental disease or defect he lacks adequate capacity to appreciate the criminality of his conduct or to conform his conduct to the requirements of law."* As of 1971, this test had been adopted by ten states and some eight of the eleven federal circuits.

The criminal law tries to take account of the special problems of the mentally ill defendant. If your relative is accused of a crime, in fact, he may have a hard time keeping an option to be treated like anybody else, since the options of the insanity defense and incompetency to stand trial are meant to be invoked for his protection. In civil law the situation is less clear. In some areas of law he is treated like anybody else. In others he isn't. But first we'd better make clear that there are some differences between the scope of civil and criminal law.

Mental illness and civil law

There are certain kinds of behavior which society always has an interest in discouraging — stealing, assault, arson, rape, murder, perjury, treason are examples. The state, on behalf of its citizens — all of us and our relatives — forbids these kinds of behavior and calls them *crimes.* Crimes and how they're handled are, then, a public and not a private matter. When the government forbids its citizens to steal and murder, it is the government that assumes the power of enforcement. It's the state that prosecutes, then. If for some reason they don't, you can't. And you certainly don't settle the score privately. Crimes are to be dealt with by the criminal law.

Criminal law and civil law

Crimes concern everybody,

Civil law, in contrast, concerns private rights, though there are

* Model Penal Code Sect. 401. The tests make an exception for "an abnormality manifested only by repeated criminal or otherwise anti-social conduct" — what, in psychiatric terminology, would be called a character disorder.

overlaps. If someone comes onto your property to steal, the stealing is criminal, but you can sue him under civil law for trespass; if someone calls you obscene names and publicly accuses you untruthfully, he is in breach of the peace (criminal) and can be sued under civil law for slander and defamation of character.

torts don't.

Not crimes, generally, but torts, are offenses like the following: most damage to property; libel and slander; reckless acts or negligent ones (like leaving a hole unfenced); nuisance, and so on. (*Tort* means "wrong" in French.) The distinction between crimes and torts lies in the private nature of the injury. Injury has occurred, but whether to press for compensation is up to the injured party, provided the public safety is not affected. Society has no interest in whether you report that you have tripped on your neighbor's broken flooring; you do not *have* to sue for damages. It's a matter between you and your neighbor. If you do sue, however, the court that hears your opposing lawyers will be guided by the civil law. (Some acts, like assault and battery, certain kinds of damage to property, and reckless driving, are both crimes and torts, and can incur both criminal and civil liability.)

The law of torts is only one of the branches of civil law. Other important branches that may affect your relative and you are contract law, probate law, and the law of domestic relations. We'll treat these in order.

LIABILITY

One of the things families worry about is harm to persons or property caused by a relative they know to be mentally irresponsible. Is he liable for damages, and if he isn't, who is?

In torts according to Weaver *v.* Ward *(1617) your relative is liable for the harms he causes*

The common law tradition for 350 years has been that whoever was the cause of injury to another had to compensate for it. The special treatment the criminal law provides for the insane did not extend to torts. It did not – and apparently still does not – matter whether the wrongdoer (in law, tort-feasor) is, in the words of the earliest case, a "lunatick" who doesn't know what he is doing or can't control it; "If a lunatick hurt a man, he shall be answerable in trespass: and therefore no man shall be excused of a trespass . . . except it may be judged utterly without his fault."* The American Law Institute states some reasons the principle has survived:

* *Weaver* v. *Ward,* K.B. 1617, Hobart 134, 80 Engl. Reprint, 284, as cited in Harry Shulman and Fleming James, Jr., *Cases and Materials on the Law of Torts* (2nd ed., 1952), pp. 22–23. According to this case, however, "if a lunatick kill a man, it is no felony, because felony must be done animo felonico [with felonious intent]." Already in 1603 Lord Coke had explained that although a mentally incompetent person (*non compos mentis*) could perform acts that would bind him and his heirs

> . . . the feeling that if mental defectives are to live in the world they should pay for the damage they do, and that it is better that their wealth, if any, be used to compensate innocent victims than that it should remain in their hands. . . .

and

> the belief that their liability will mean that those who have charge of them or their estates will be stimulated to look after them, keep them in order, and see that they do not do harm.[29]

That certainly seems to mean us. But apparently it means that we should keep an eye on our relatives because we don't want *them* to have to pay damages, not because we ourselves are liable.* Although Ralph Slovenko, in *Psychiatry and Law,* raises "a question of liability of those responsible for [an insane person's] custody and supervision,"[30] he mentions not a single case. In actual fact, parents or guardians are very seldom held legally responsible for the wrongdoing of the mentally ill, even when they live together.

but you (probably) aren't.

As for the mentally ill person himself, he pays up if he can. He's wasting his time if he invokes the insanity defense; among many thousands of tort cases, Slovenko finds only forty-nine in which insanity was raised, and only once successfully.† It's a good idea, then, to make sure that an irresponsible and careless relative has good personal liability insurance, for his own protection and that of others (though no policy is likely to cover some areas within the law of torts we've been discussing).

Check his insurance

But not all harms can be compensated with money. The most common cause of serious injury, as we all know, is the operation of a motor vehicle. If you feel – or know – your relative is dangerous behind the wheel, can you prevent his driving?

Driving:

You can't. (After all, you can't do anything about your perfectly sane relatives who drive dangerously.) Almost all the states may restrict driving privileges of a released mental patient. A number of states‡ provide that a license may be refused, suspended, or revoked

restrictions on ex-patients

for life as far as his property was concerned, he should not lose his life for committing a felony, since felons are punished "so that by punishing a few, fear might come to many." The punishment of a man who is deprived of his reason and understanding, however, "cannot be an example to others." Judge Bazelon cites this opinion in *In re John Ballay,* note 38.

* In some states, however, relatives *are* liable for torts committed by their minor children.

† P. 281. It was in Louisiana, in 1934.

‡ They include Alabama, Alaska, Arizona, Arkansas, Colorado, Delaware, Florida, Massachusetts (if the patient has been adjudged incompetent), Michigan, North Carolina, Oklahoma (discretionary for those not adjudged incompetent), and South Dakota.

if the driver (or would-be driver) has been adjudged insane or legally incompetent. (See pp. 297–302.) These states provide for a hearing if the patient wants his license back, at which there must be introduced evidence of competency or hospital discharge, *sometimes* including the hospital's specific recommendation on whether he's fit to drive. If you have reason to worry, you could let the hearing officials know why.

in practice are mild or nonexistent.

In most other states, statutes prohibit "insane persons," "idiots," or those who are "mentally disabled" from driving, but there is no indication how their status is to be proved or disproved. In fact, there is no sign that such statutes are enforced, and it's hard to imagine how it could be done. Nobody wants to make things hard for people coming out of hospitals.

> Although it is important to prevent persons likely to endanger themselves or others from operating motor vehicles, it is equally important to see that persons are not unnecessarily deprived of this privilege. A discharged patient faces many problems in learning to live again in society. Opportunities for employment and recreation are essential to his rehabilitation and the operation of a motor vehicle is an important aid and factor in his convalescence.[31]

Guns?

If your relative is continuing drug therapy, discuss with his doctor whether there are any contraindications against driving. If you have real cause for concern, check your state law. You can at least ask the Bureau of Motor Vehicles what they think your responsibility is. (You're in much the same position if your relative gets a gun permit. Ask your local chief of police what he thinks.)

CONTRACTS

Invalidating circumstances

Suppose your relative has signed a contract, and wants — or you want him — to get out of it. He — or his guardian — has a reasonable chance of success. (Marriages are special kinds of contracts and will be treated later in this section.) Unlike the law of torts, the law of contracts recognizes "invalidating circumstances" — what in the criminal law are called excusing conditions. Duress and coercion are invalidating circumstances. (So are fraud and "infancy" — the state of being a minor.)

Insanity, for instance, may invalidate a contract

Contracts by their very nature are supposed to represent the free choice of the parties.* That's why they can be invalidated if it can be shown that one of the parties was forced to sign his name. Insanity has long been recognized as an invalidating circumstance for contracts.

* "In brief, the functions of these institutions of private law [contracts] is to render effective an individual's preferences in certain areas." H. L. A. Hart, *Punishment and Responsibility: Essays in the Philosophy of Law* (New York: Oxford University Press, 1968), pp. 33, 44–45.

A contract your relative signed when he was "insane," it can be argued, does not represent a genuine choice, and if your relative – or his family – takes it to court and can convince the court that he was mentally ill at the time of signing, the court may hold the contract invalid.

but very possibly won't.

You can't be sure. The other party to a contract has interests too, and he may be in trouble as a result of acting on what your relative has promised. After all, he thought he was dealing with a fully responsible person and acted accordingly. The modern view tries to balance both sides. "The right of avoiding obligations incurred while mentally disabled" is not absolute, but "is made dependent upon factors calculated to protect the interests of both the mentally disabled and the parties dealing with him."[32]

Things that may make a difference:

(1) whether the contract has had any effects

Some of the factors courts may take into account are: (1) whether the contract has been carried out, wholly or in part, or whether it has not yet been performed (is "executory"). If things have begun to happen under the contract, as when land has been transferred or money spent, then whether it's binding may be decided on the basis of whether the other party is able to return to his *status quo ante* – the condition he was in before. This is supposed to compensate for the fact that your relative can sue to set aside a contract on the grounds of his mental condition while the other party can't.

(2) if his impairment was known

(2) If your relative wants to get out of a contract it may matter whether the other party knew that he suffered from an impairment. If the terms of the contract are obviously unfair, for instance, the judge may conclude that a person "of weak understanding" has been deliberately taken advantage of.[33] Even if there's no notable unfairness, some courts have set aside contracts simply because it was shown that the other party knew he was contracting with a person lacking full capacity.

(3) if he contracted for necessaries

(3) If your relative has contracted to buy "necessaries" (food, clothing, drugs, medical or dental care) he can't avoid paying by claiming he was mentally ill. He can't, for instance, get out of paying his psychiatrist on the grounds that he was not himself and the psychiatrist knew it.

If your relative gets well, he must disavow a contract made during his illness within a "reasonable time," or a court may hold it has been ratified.

"Proving" insanity as an invalidating circumstance:

Your relative is presumed sane unless he can show otherwise by "a preponderance of the evidence" (not "beyond a reasonable doubt"). Expert medical testimony will probably be necessary, especially if he has never had psychiatric treatment. It must be shown that he was suffering from a mental defect or illness, but it must also be shown that because of the defect or illness he did not understand the nature of the contract and its consequences. Another possible ground of avoid-

mental illness plus *lack of understanding*

ing contractual obligations is the existence of an "insane delusion"—as in a case where a man made a promissory note believing that he'd be killed if he didn't, or another where a husband deeded his property to his son because he believed his wife was having an affair.[34]

An "insane delusion"?

Manic persons, however, have usually been held to their obligations, because they generally seem to know exactly what they're about; they "have the necessary cognitive ability required in law."[35] But even that depends on the court.

Manic-depressive psychosis?

Here's how it was for Mr. Faber, who sued to set aside a contract to buy some land on the grounds that he was not, at the time of purchase, "of sufficient mental competence." This is the way the judge described it.

Faber *v.* Sweet Style Manufacturing Corporation

> Though under care of Dr. Levine, a psychiatrist, beginning June 8th for his depression, he cancelled his August 8th appointment and refused to see the doctor further. Previously frugal and cautious, he became more expansive beginning in August, began to drive at high speeds, to take his wife out to dinner, to be sexually more active and to discuss his prowess with others. In a short period of time, he purchased three expensive cars for himself, his son and his daughter, began to discuss converting his Long Beach bathhouse and garage property into a twelve story cooperative and put up a sign to that effect, and to discuss the purchase of land in Brentwood for the erection of houses. In September, against the advice of his lawyer, he contracted for land at White Lake in the Catskills costing $11,500 and gave a $500 deposit on acreage, the price of which was $41,000 and talked about erecting a 400 room hotel with marina and golf course on the land. . . .
>
> On September 16, he discussed with Mr. Kass, defendant's president, the purchase of the property involved in this litigation for the operation of a discount drug store and merchandise mart.

On September 23 the contract was signed. In the next two weeks Mr. Faber erected an impressive sign, hired an architect, set laborers to digging, and drove to the state capital to get the necessary approval, all before the title was closed. He also went to Dr. Levine to tell him that his wife needed help because she was stopping him from doing what he wanted to. He was hospitalized on October 8, after buying a gun.

You couldn't find a better example of a manic-depressive psychosis, and that's what Mr. Faber's psychiatrists testified he had. The psychiatrist hired by the defendant agreed, but testified that his grasp of affairs showed that there was no abnormality in his thinking and that his judgment was intact. "In the great majority of cases," as the judge pointed out, "psychiatrists of equal qualifications and experience will reach diametrically opposed conclusions on the same behavioral evidence." The judge then proceeded to make up his own mind. He decided that Mr. Faber's plans for his business "fell short of establishing

Psychiatric testimony

on both sides

irrationality" and that the contract itself was not self-evidently abnormal, but that the speed with which he acted was. While taking account of earlier judgments that manic patients must be held competent since their ability to understand is not affected, he nevertheless declared the contract rescinded, as having been entered into "under the compulsion of plaintiff's psychosis," "but for which the contract would not have been made."[36] Sweet Style Manufacturing didn't suffer, since the digging had been minor and the site was quickly restored to the *status quo ante*.

The moral of this tale is that you never can tell. Get a first-class lawyer, and hope for an intelligent judge.

DOMESTIC LIFE: WILLS, MARRIAGE, DIVORCE, CUSTODY

Wills

Can your relative make a will? "I, being of sound mind . . ." — we all know the words from detective stories. In spite of them, your relative may very well be able to make a will that would withstand contest. Had Mr. Faber made a will on September 23, the same day he closed the sale, the will might well have been upheld. Even in the old-fashioned terms of the law, "lunatics" may have "lucid intervals,"* in which they may make valid wills. The provisions of the will itself are not likely to convince a court that the testator was crazy, though disappointed heirs may feel differently. As was said in a recent California case, "one has the right to make an unjust will, an unreasonable will, or even a cruel will."[37] Contesting a will in court is expensive, since it tends to involve a parade of witnesses, much circumstantial evidence, and many hours in the courtroom, so it's seldom done except for large estates. (Since of all the wills probated each year only some 3 percent are contested in court and fewer than one in six of these successfully,[38] your relative's will shouldn't be uppermost in your mind, and doubtless isn't.) The two most common conditions which have served as the basis for a judgment of testamentary incapacity have been cerebral arteriosclerosis, notably among the elderly, and delusions.

Marriage prohibitions

Marriage is a kind of contract, and as in other contracts insanity can be an "invalidating circumstance." "Possession of sufficient mental capacity to consent is a prerequisite for a valid marriage, and that implies sufficient ability to understand the duties and obligations involved."[39] As of 1971, in forty-one states "insane" persons were forbid-

* These words are from the Georgia statute, the only one that makes any attempt to define testamentary incapacity. What the statute grants with one hand, however, it takes away with the other: "An insane person generally may not make a will" but a "monomaniac may, if the will is in no way the result of his monomania." Georgia Code Annot., title 113, §§201, quoted in Slovenko, *op. cit.*, p. 338.

den to marry.[40]* In fact, says the American Bar Foundation study, the laws are not enforced, at least outside hospitals. It's hard to see how they could be. Nevertheless, the laws exist, and can be invoked by those who think they have reason. The marriage service contains the words "if any man can show just cause, why [these two persons] may not lawfully be joined together, let him speak now, or else hereafter forever hold his peace."† In fact, although these laws conceivably could be invoked by friends or relatives who wanted to prevent a marriage they feared would be disastrous, this is scarcely ever done. There is case law to the effect that an adjudged incompetent may still have sufficient capacity to contract a lawful marriage. The law is much more likely to be invoked by the other party to the marriage contract, either at the time of the marriage or later, to have it annulled. Marriage contracts thus differ from other contracts, in that (in most states) both the "sane" and the "insane" parties can put the mental condition at issue.‡ In actual fact, it's usually the sane person who takes the initiative to dissolve the marriage.

Annulment

In those forty-one states annulment means that the marriage will be declared void *ab initio* (treated as though it had never taken place.) In addition, the common law rule for *all* states is that if either party was, at the time of the marriage, suffering from "insanity" to the degree that he or she did not understand the rights and obligations being created (or, in some states, was "insane" in some other way—delusional, for instance), the marriage was never valid. For those married within the Catholic Church, where divorce is not permitted but annulment is, the Vatican is considerably more up-to-date on modern diagnostic categories. Within recent years marriages have been annulled on grounds of schizophrenia, paranoia, hysteria, obsessive neurosis, sexual monomania, drug addiction, alcoholism, and an excessive attachment to one's mother.[41] For non-Catholics (and Catholics who

* Some of the terms used in various states: "insane or imbecile" (Tennessee, 1955 Code); "idiots," "lunatics" (Utah, 1953 Code); "insane," "weak-minded" "persons of unsound mind," or "a person who is or has been a patient in an insane asylum" (Delaware, 1953 Code); a person "who because of insanity or idiocy lacks capacity of assenting to marriage" (Wisconsin, 1957 Code). As cited in Brakel and Rock, *op. cit.*, Table 7.1, pp. 240–243.

† Why so many states find an interest in preventing the marriage of the insane is suggested in the four state codes that make an exception if the woman is over forty-five, and the two states that allow marriage if one of the parties has been sterilized. Four states lift the prohibition in some cases, at the discretion of the commissioner of public welfare or the superintendent of the institution where one (or both) of the marriage partners was (or is) a patient.

‡ For a state-by-state summary of the laws on marriage and mental disability, including the exceptions to this statement, see Brakel and Rock, *op. cit.*, Table 7.1, pp. 240–243.

bypass the Church), annulments are granted by domestic relations courts. Considering the vagueness of the old terms, a lot is left up to the judge.

Divorce on grounds of postnuptial mental illness of long standing

Mental illness developing *after* marriage is a ground for divorce in thirty-one states. The condition has to have lasted a long time, five years in many states and nowhere (except Alaska) less than two. (In Alaska it's eighteen months.)[42] In many states there's no need for medical testimony, if the marriage partner has been confined in an institution for the necessary time. In others, however, the condition must be shown to be "incurable,"[43] and medical testimony is necessary. It's not obvious that this would be easy to get, at least from doctors involved in actual treatment of the spouse; they might well feel prevented from testifying by doctor-patient privilege. (See Chapter VII, p. 180.) Some judges, too, might not insist that medical personnel testify (let's not forget the nurses, psychologists, and social workers who don't yet have privilege), if impressed by their pleas that they should not undermine their patient's interests, as, for instance, when a divorce would cost a sick patient her right to be supported. In short, considering how long it takes to establish insanity as grounds for divorce and how unpleasant it is, there are easier ways.

Psychiatric testimony and confidentiality

Mental illness as a defense *to divorce*

In the nineteen states which do not recognize postnuptial mental illness as a ground for divorce, mental illness may be used as a defense to a divorce action. This occurs primarily where there has been "fault" on the part of the defendant, whose lawyer may then argue that his or her cruelty, desertion, or adultery, having taken place during a period of mental illness, was unintended, so that he or she was not responsible. If the defendant is successful, the plaintiff may go to another state and get a "migratory" divorce, tricky though this is to obtain. In states which provide "no-fault" grounds for divorce (today the vast majority), evidence concerning conduct during the marriage is not admitted.

Custody of children

In divorces where there are children, mental illness may be enough to reverse the usual tendency to award children to the mother.* (Visitation rights may also be denied.) Once custody has been awarded to one parent, it will be difficult for the other to get the children back, even though she (as it usually is) has recovered. The authoritative

* Most custody disputes arise out of divorces, but Ennis describes one painful case in which a woman hospitalized against her will lost custody of her three children to her sister. (*Prisoners,* pp. 179–185.) State agencies may sometimes also institute custody proceedings to remove children from the homes of mentally ill parents, if they are abused or neglected. Supposedly — and often actually — this is done in the children's best interests. (Cf. Chapter VIII, on children of psychotic parents, pp. 218–220.) It should never be done without careful assessment of the particular situation and the alternatives.

American Law Reports, Annotated cites case after case in which custody is taken from the mother at the time of divorce, or a later change of custody is denied her.*

When such cases come to court, the possibilities of pain and lasting hurt are at their greatest. Judges, anxious to be fair to all, will let in almost anything as evidence, from double or triple hearsay to a valentine scribbled years earlier. The child has no counsel, and each parent's advocate – lawyer, psychiatrist, friend – is more likely out to vindicate the interest of that parent than to seek the child's best interests, though that is the standard (first stated by Judge Benjamin Cardozo of the New York Court of Appeals) by which the judge will attempt to decide. The judge himself will do his best to figure out what nobody else has been able to untangle. He may interview the child alone, if he thinks it has attained the "age of reason" (and may end up awarding custody as the child sees fit at the moment, although a ten-year-old may not be the best person to assess his own best interests). Judges, being human, may have prejudices – against single parents, or people living with other people they're not married to, or people who go to psychiatrists. The proceeding will probably involve psychiatric testimony, and perhaps a court-ordered psychiatric examination by a court-appointed professional who might not be just the person you'd choose. Failure to cooperate invites the award of custody to the other parent. The psychiatrist can be called in by the other parent, especially since some states provide for custody cases a specific exception to the usual therapist-patient privilege. Then there's more unpleasantness. The whole proceeding may take months, during which no one knows which way it will go and everyone's upset. And judges don't hurry, hoping, perhaps, that the parties will resolve the situation themselves. Take it from our legal consultant, a mother as well as a lawyer:

In custody conflicts or any others

> It is extremely rare, in my experience, for a judge-made solution to improve upon the possibilities available through negotiation. The delays, prejudice, costliness, and disruption of therapeutic relationships involved in courtroom resolution of custody disputes more than outweigh, I would suggest, the not inconsiderable difficulties of arriving at private settlements.

don't rush to court.

In fact, we should broaden the scope of that advice. Nothing in this

* This sensible and humane decision unfortunately is *not* typical: "Under rule that mental illness of parent may not require deprivation of custody of his or her child when it appears that health, safety, and welfare of child will not be jeopardized by permitting it to remain with afflicted parent, mother was granted unsupervised visitation with her 11-year-old son where father had been granted custody and mother's health was not shown to be harmful to son." *Willey* v. *Willey* (Iowa), 115 N.W. 2d 833, as cited in 74 *American Law Reports 2d,* Later Case Service, pp. 127–128.

chapter should be taken to suggest that going to court is easy, let alone fun. In custody cases, or any others, the courtroom is an arena where adversaries meet. If you can find a way to stay out of it, do. The financial and emotional drain of extended legal proceedings, the exacerbation of conflicts produced by a winner-take-all atmosphere, should invite you and yours to give your most serious attention, at every point, to the commonsense compromises that can be arranged outside the courtroom.

"Substituted service"

One thing you should be aware of. It is legal in many states to provide only "substituted service" of process on people confined in institutions; that is, notice of custody, or divorce, or adoption, or any other legal proceedings may go to the superintendent of the institution, to a guardian, or to you instead of to your relative. It is painful to think of depriving a sick parent of notification of proceedings affecting child custody, support, and visitation, although doctors remind us that such news could make him or her sicker. Again, liberty and protection clash.

Adoption

In most states the children of mentally ill disabled parents may be adopted without their parents' consent. The criteria are, surprisingly, less strict than for divorce; only five demand the disability be "hopeless" or "incurable," only one specifies the period of disability, and only one requires the testimony of two physicians. Only eight states provide for notice to the ill parent. Such adoptions are seldom contested or appealed. Often, of course, this is because the mentally ill parent is satisfied with the adoption, too sick to be aware of it, or because it is a family affair and not like an adoption at all. But surely not always.

INCOMPETENCY AND GUARDIANSHIP

Incompetency and loss of civil rights

Loss of license to practice certain occupations

Incompetency proceedings are intended to safeguard a mentally ill person's interests when he can't do so himself. The status of incompetency is meant as a protection, but if he loses his freedom to manage (or mismanage) his own affairs, your relative will also forfeit important civil rights. Not only will he be prohibited from writing checks, selling property, making contracts, suing (or being sued), or entering into business, he will be unable to vote or serve on a jury. He may also be prohibited from practicing professions licensed by the state, such as nursing, dentistry, medicine, cabdriving.* (In many states people in-

* In various states, people judged incompetent (or involuntarily hospitalized for mental illness) may lose their licenses to practice as doctors, osteopaths, chiropodists, veterinarians, barbers, cosmetologists, physical therapists, chauffeurs, cabdrivers, pharmacists, architects, brokers, solicitors, insurance agents, and that's not nearly all. In one state they can't sell beer. (Brakel and Rock, *op. cit.*, Table 9.3, Statutory Provisions Regarding Engagement in Occupations, pp. 326–332.)

voluntarily hospitalized for mental illness also lose some or all of these rights, either by state law or by administrative regulations, whether they've been declared legally incompetent or not.)

Incompetency proceedings

The procedure for a legal determination of incompetency is similar to that for involuntary commitment. Though in a few states a friend or relative must petition the court, in most a petition can be presented by any "interested person," and a hearing will be held. Notice to the alleged incompetent is required in most states (but not all). About half the states also require notice to one or more relatives. In less than a fourth of the states must a medical certificate accompany the petition; some others require medical evidence at the hearing, or investigation by a committee of doctors. (It is not necessary that the person have been treated for psychiatric illness.) The allegedly incompetent person must usually be present at the hearing (not always), and if he wants to dispute the allegations against him he would do well to have a lawyer. In some states the court is required to appoint counsel or a guardian to represent the alleged incompetent at the proceedings.*

In at least two states (Ohio and Colorado) commitment proceedings have been themselves equivalent to a declaration of incompetency, so that a person involuntarily hospitalized there was automatically incompetent. In most, however, the two types of proceedings are quite separate, although the fact of hospitalization may be presented as *evidence* of incompetency.

Guardianship

Not all people declared mentally incompetent are under legal guardianship. Some are hospitalized, and the institution acts informally as guardian; others can take care of their personal needs and haven't enough property to need (or pay) somebody to take care of it. At common law, however, the courts have the obligation to see that the interests of incompetents (and minors) are protected, and a guardian — sometimes more than one — will usually be appointed. A *guardian of the person* sees that his ward has adequate living arrangements, clothing, medical care, and the like, and should be available in emergencies. It is the guardian who gives permission for medical treatments and for operations such as sterilization. A *guardian of the estate* (called in some places a *conservator* or *curator*) manages his ward's finances and property. Income from any source is payable only to him. Often a friend or relative is guardian of the person while someone else is guardian of the estate (often a lawyer or a bank). But it is quite possible for the same person to fulfill both functions. Some mentally ill people, of course, may need a conservator but no personal guardian. In some states (Wisconsin is one) *limited guardianships* allow the ward increased freedom. In a limited guardianship *of the person,* the

Guardian of the person

Guardian of the estate (conservator, curator)

Limited guardianship of person

* For a summary of these and other provisions, by state, see Brakel and Rock, *op. cit.,* Table 8.3, pp. 280–292.

court specifies which rights the disabled person is unable to exercise, and the guardian can only act in those areas. For someone who is substantially self-supporting, a limited guardianship *of property* allows him to receive and spend what he makes while the guardian manages his other property, including Social Security or veterans' benefits. In some states a guardian can apply for the "voluntary" hospitalization of his ward as if he were a minor, though in most this requires court approval.[44]

Of property

A guardian is responsible to the court which appointed him. A guardian of the estate must submit regular accounts and get the court's permission for certain activities, such as the sale of property.

Responsible to the court

How are guardians appointed? A friend or relative may volunteer, or be selected by the family, or be named as guardian in a will (see pp. 301–302); the court will usually appoint him. In addition, however, the court in all states may at its own discretion appoint a guardian *ad litem* ("for the case," in Latin), a "disinterested person" to oversee the activities of the other guardian (s) and report to the judge, so long as there is court action pending. That sounds like a lot of guardians, especially since the charges of the guardian *ad litem* are borne by the incompetent's estate. Often, of course, it's needed extra protection against a guardian who's dishonest or doesn't know what he's doing. But the practice deserves closer scrutiny than it has received. One canny lawyer warns that it can be a soft and steady job for one of the judge's courthouse cronies, who may do no better a job than a guardian selected by the family and may well do worse. For what you can do to head off this possibility see p. 302.

Guardian ad litem

If your relative is hospitalized in another state, a court in that state may appoint a "supplemental or substitute" guardian for him. If he already has a guardian in his own home state, the court that appointed that guardian must be notified of the new appointment and may end or restrict the original guardianship.

Guardianship and state lines

Not all guardians are private persons appointed by the court. Because any individual guardian may not live as long as his ward, agencies of various sorts can be guardians. Through a *trust,* a bank or trustee may act as property guardian (and be able to handle finances more flexibly than a guardian of the estate, who must get a time-consuming and costly court order before he can buy or sell). Most banks, however, don't handle estates of under $50,000; if they do, their charges will eat up a substantial part of the income.

Agencies as guardians

Banks

If you haven't got $50,000: a number of states have created public guardians in various state departments; Minnesota's system is outstanding. In Ohio the State Division of Mental Retardation may serve as guardian or trustee of retarded persons. An increasing number of states (New York and Wisconsin among them) permit nonprofit corpora-

Inquire about state agencies and associations for the handicapped.

tions such as the Association for Retarded Citizens to act as legal guardian.[45] What with veterans' benefits, pensions, insurance policies, annuities, and Social Security, there are relatively few people today who don't have some property interests that require management.

Restoration of competency

Unlike the retarded, most mentally ill people don't stay mentally ill permanently. They get better, and very often they get well. What happens when a legally incompetent recovers enough to want to take up his affairs again?

is automatic in some states,

In some states (Minnesota is one) competency is restored automatically when a hospitalized incompetent is discharged as recovered. The hospital is supposed to notify the probate court, which must then issue an order of restoration. The former patient need not take legal action or appear in court. Automatic processes don't always work, however.[46] And patients are in fact discharged often as "improved" (or "unimproved") rather than "recovered." Too, some lawyers argue that only the committing court can restore competency. Considering all the variations in law and in practice, Brakel and Rock consider that "the discharged patient's safest course of action . . . is the initiation of regular restoration proceedings."[47] When the incompetent has not been hospitalized but has been living in the community, court action is always necessary.

but even so, a formal proceeding is safer.

The restoration procedure will be similar to that which was gone through to declare incompetency. The incompetent himself may petition for a hearing, and in many states a relative or interested person may too. In a few states there are no specific restoration procedures; the court merely discharges the guardian if he is no longer needed.*

Incompetency and hospitalization

Many legally incompetent people are never hospitalized for mental illness, and many hospitalized people are not legally incompetent. (Fewer than 10 percent of the patients in New York state hospitals have been found incompetent.)[48] Indeed, they may be very competent, signing and endorsing checks, making out their tax returns, and looking after their property. One paranoid patient was convinced that his neighbors had conspired to fill his house with poison gas; yet his detailed grasp of the terms of his mortgage convinced the judge that he had no need for a guardian of his estate:

Illness and incapacity are not the same thing.

> The criterion [said the judge] is not the mental illness but rather the inability to manage property by reason of the mental illness. Unless the mental illness produces or results in such inability to manage property, the court is not warranted in appointing the guardian for the estate of a mentally ill person.[49]

But nobody made such a careful distinction between incapacity

* The details of restoration procedures vary a great deal from state to state. See Brakel and Rock, *op. cit.*, Table 8.4, pp. 293–302.

Edna Long again

and illness for Edna Long, the lady with the high IQ who worked so long and hard at Harlem Valley State Hospital. Her story is a good reminder to take nothing for granted, least of all that a system works when nobody's interested, or that courts and guardians always function to protect our relatives.

Mrs. Long managed her own affairs for the first eleven years of her hospitalization, using the U.S. mails, and she managed them very well. Her savings grew to almost $9,000, and when her husband died, she drew his railway retirement pension as well. However, at the end of this time, the director of the hospital, as one of the "interested persons," petitioned a court to declare her incompetent and put her estate under guardianship so that the proceeds could be applied to her maintenance. (This seemed particularly unjust, since she had been kept hospitalized contrary to her own and her husband's wishes.) She received no notification, and no hearing was held. The director's petition was routine, and the judge considered that for such a long-term patient, hospitalization itself was evidence enough. (Years later, under cross-examination by civil liberties lawyers, the director admitted he had never personally examined Mrs. Long, and was not certain he had even read through her record.)

The lawyer the judge appointed as guardian of her estate really *was* incompetent. He transferred her assets from a savings to a checking account and forfeited the interest, he failed to file the required annual report so that the Railway Retirement Board stopped sending the pension. He didn't forget to deduct his fee, however — $730. He did such a poor job that the court replaced him, but the next one wasn't much better. While under guardianship, Mrs. Long's savings shrank to $2,000.*

Quis custodiet ipsos custodes?

As a result of Edna Long's case, brought before a federal court by Ennis and two other lawyers, New York State got a new incompetency statute. And elsewhere? The statutes are varied and tricky, courts can be perfunctory, guardians lazy and careless. The institution of guardianship goes back to Roman times, and the Romans had a proverb: Who shall guard the guardians?

Planning for the future

Who indeed? If you can't watch over your relative's estate yourself, you and your family will want to have some say in who does. While you are alive, you can communicate your desires to the court; your opinion should certainly influence the court's appointment, unless the judge has good reason to distrust your choice. (After all, it is possible to set the fox to guard the chickens; he must be satisfied that the guardian will not administer the estate to his own advantage.) Many of us, however, must plan for our relative's future after we are dead — above all, of course, when we are parents of mentally ill children.

Making your will

You can designate a guardian in your will, or you can split the func-

* This whole account is based on Ennis, *Prisoners,* Chapter 3.

tions and designate one for person and one for property. Your will should be carefully drafted by a capable lawyer; the language and intent should be too clear to be argued over. You will want to name at least one *successor guardian,* especially if your relative is young. Loving aunts and uncles may not live much longer than you do. If you are lucky enough to have choices among your child's sisters, brothers, cousins, or friends, *specify them.** (Be sure they are willing and understand clearly what will be expected of them.) If you choose to name a lawyer, get good advice, and designate a successor there too. Remember, your relative may outlive you by fifty years.

Successor guardians should be specified.

If you have chosen well there should be no need for the additional expense of a guardian *ad litem,* useful as this court's representative may be when a guardian fails to do his job. (A guardian *ad litem* might have safeguarded the estate of Edna Long.) If a guardian *ad litem* should be required by law and you do not want the judge to appoint his own choice, you can specify this in your will. It's worth a try, though you can't bind the judge, but unless there's some special reason, your wishes should have some effect.†

Do not take these few paragraphs as an authoritative guide to the complex and highly individual problems of guardianship and estate planning. The State Bar of Wisconsin publishes an excellent booklet, *Planning for Their Future;*‡ though it emphasizes Wisconsin law, it will give you a good idea of some of the alternatives to discuss with your lawyer. Your own state bar association and Association for Retarded Citizens are additional resources.

CONSULTING A LAWYER

What kind of lawyer you want, of course, depends on what you want him for. An experienced local lawyer knows his area and how to be effective in it. He knows the police, the courts, the probation officers, the judges, and the ways their personalities and ways of operating affect what happens to his clients. He knows how long things take and how to move them along; he knows what judges are sympathetic, and

* A useful sample clause: "If A shall fail or cease to serve as guardian of the person or property of (name of relative), then B shall serve; if B shall fail or cease so to serve, then C shall serve . . . ," until you run out of names.

† Our canny lawyer suggests the following language:

"I request that so far as permitted by law no guardian *ad litem* shall be appointed to represent any person having an interest in my estate, whether or not ascertained; provided however that if such guardian for any reason is required to be appointed, I nominate and appoint to act in that capacity, such person as may then be acting or may be named herein to act as guardian of (or "of the person of") (name of relative)."

‡ Available from Special Committee on Legal Needs of the Mentally Retarded, 402 West Wilson, Madison, Wisc. 53703.

what they're sympathetic to. Most of his practice probably concerns such matters as divorces, wills, the care of property, and minor crimes and brushes with the law. A local lawyer is essential when local ordinances are in question – when, for instance, you must negotiate zoning regulations in order to set up a halfway house or group home. (See Chapter XIV, p. 418n.)

How to find the right lawyer

For a minor criminal matter or a small contract case, a local general practitioner is probably fine. Where to get him: word of mouth can be the best source. If an acquaintance was well-served in a similar matter, this is worth following up. If you don't have an acquaintance and you're within fifty miles of a law school, call whoever teaches family law there for suggestions about a domestic relations lawyer, their criminal law professor for someone good in that area, their estate planning person for a will or estate plan, and so on. (For some reason, contracts professors don't seem to be much help.) They may refer you to their school's clinical program for help (especially if you're low-income) or make further suggestions. For unusual or severe cases, you will probably want a specialist, whether local or not – if (again as in medicine) you can afford one. There are specialists in all branches of law – criminal law, domestic law, contract law, estates, trusts. (For those who can't afford the high fees, most cities where there are courts have Legal Aid Societies.)

For estate planning, you might do well to go first to a good firm of investment counselors (or the trust department of a bank that specializes in such matters) to review your own holdings before you have your will drawn. They will probably recommend their own lawyer for that job (he'll be good), and they may press you to name them as trustees or executors, as the fees can be substantial. This presumes that your estate will amount to $50,000 or more. If it doesn't, and you aren't "on the grapevine," go through mental health associations, call the probate court and ask an assistant register in the estates section what offices are active and well thought of (or an assistant in the divorce section), or try the local bar association. (And see Chapter XI, p. 327.)

If all else fails, a publication which every sizable law office and every large public library probably has is the Martindale-Hubbell Law Directory. This lists about every lawyer who practices in every state by the city in which he practices. It will list his specialties – at least, those he thinks he has – or those of his firm. For those in practice five years or longer, it will also list a *reasonably* reliable "rating," which is arrived at in some mysterious fashion involving informal polling of judges and other lawyers.

Mental health law

The landmark cases described in this chapter show the impact of a new legal specialty, mental health law. Crusading lawyers are doing more than most of us can to determine what rights all our relatives can count on, what services are available to them in and out of the hospital, even (by zoning cases) where and how they live. (See Chapter XII on the right of every child to a public education and Chapter XIV on class action suits and zoning and housing restrictions.) The American Bar Association has established an Interdisciplinary Commission on the Mentally Disabled, to spread information and press for reforms. If your relative needs a lawyer to stand up for his rights, your state bar association or Civil Liberties Union may be able to guide you to an expert. If not, the ABA Commission may help. Or you could call the Mental Health Law Project in Washington. (Its director, Paul Friedman, is the first lawyer to be accepted for training by the Baltimore–District of Columbia Institute for Psychoanalysis.) For addresses see Appendix B.

Fees:

ask.

Most lawyers charge by the hour, though some charge fixed fees – so much for a will, a contract, a title search, etc. Fees range from the neighborhood of $25 an hour up into the hundreds for legal stars; it depends on locality (towns are cheaper than cities), prosperity, experience, reputation. Since fees vary widely, you may shop around; a phoned inquiry as to the hourly fee is *not* poor etiquette. Lawyers charge more when a case is not routine; ten hours' research can easily cost you $500. It's quite fair to ask the lawyer for an estimate of the time he expects your problem will require. If your funds are limited, say so; he should inform you as the limit approaches.

Summarizing your problem in writing

Many of us, of course, go to a lawyer to put our problem completely into his hands, intending to sit back and trust the expert. But you can save time and money by doing some homework. Think over your problem and try to determine the important aspects. It's not a bad idea – as with a psychiatrist – to write down the history of the problem for your lawyer, with names, places and dates.

checking state laws

You can inform yourself of the relevant statutes of your state in the library of your county courthouse: the librarian should help you find what you want. The tables of state laws in the American Bar Foundation survey are a good guide to state statutes on the legal problems of mental illness, since they refer to them by number.* When you don't understand legal language, ask the librarian; she can certainly give you a law dictionary, and she may give you an explanation instead. (If you *really* don't understand, don't feel bad; many statutes are so badly drafted that lawyers and judges don't understand them either.)

important cases

If you want to keep up on what's happening in the important mental health cases, write the President's Committee on Mental Retardation of the U.S. Department of Health, Education and Welfare, asking to

* Again: that's S. J. Brakel and R. S. Rock, *The Mentally Disabled and the Law.* If it's not in the library, it ought to be. Or you can order it yourself from the American Bar Association, who are to be congratulated for producing a good, large, detailed book to sell for surprisingly little. Be sure you get the latest revised edition.

subscribe to their publication, *Mental Retardation and the Law, a Report on Status of Current Court Cases.** Virtually all the cases are significant for mentally ill people as well.

If you sense a certain haziness in your lawyer, an organization called The Research Group† will research any legal question he requests for less, generally, than his own hourly rate.

How you convey your new knowledge to your lawyer without insulting him is, of course, up to you. If he's good, he should be glad to discuss your case with you, and glad you understand what's at issue.

If you've gone to a lawyer and really feel you have reason to complain of how he served you, take it up with the Bar Association. Self-regulation among lawyers used to be a joke, but things are rapidly changing, says our source. The local association should have a grievance committee (but local lawyers will tend to stick together); the state association certainly has one.

Good luck!

Inform yourself, inform the person who's trying to help you, be frank, be tactful – where have you read that before? And this too may sound familiar: what you want in a lawyer is somebody you can talk to and somebody you can trust. The law too has its uses and abuses; it too is one of the great avenues toward helping people. It too is full of uncertainty and controversy, and it too is more an art than a science.

* Department MR-L, President's Committee on Mental Retardation, Washington, DC 20201.

† P.O. Box 139, Charlottesville, VA 22902 (telephone, 703-295-7109). They have several branches. Their services are available only to attorneys, but you can try persuading yours to use them.

»» CHAPTER XI ««

Money—A Very Unpleasant Chapter

A feast is made for laughter, and wine maketh merry, but money answereth all things. ECCLESIASTES

Treatment is expensive,

PSYCHOTHERAPEUTIC TREATMENT, like legal counsel, like all labor, skilled and unskilled, is a commodity, and it's bought and sold like other commodities. How much you can pay determines what you can buy and how much of it, and it has more bearing than we'd like on how good it is. And this is true whether *you* are buying it as an individual, or whether *we* buy it through insurance payments or as the taxpayers who ultimately support all public expenditures, including expenditures for mental hospitals, community facilities, health aid to the poor and the disabled, and subsidies for research and the training of physicians.

When *you* are paying, of course, the expenditures seem very high. When *we* are paying, the cost is spread between the well and the ill, and the impact on each particular family is lowered. The total cost, however, is no lower. In fact, it may be higher. If the items that go into the costs of treatment are left free to find their market value, uncontrolled economics will do its thing; the newly guaranteed supply of money will drive the price of treatment higher. Physicians who had been treating aged patients at reduced rates or free quite naturally sent bills when they knew that Medicare, not the patient, would be paying them. When payment is guaranteed by a third party, public or private, the cost of care generally rises.

however you slice it.

Doctors' fees are high. It costs a lot to go through medical school, but once they're established doctors can — and do — expect to make between $30,000 and $100,000 a year, and many make more. The median income in 1972, after business expenses were deducted, was $42,000 — half below and half above.* Psychiatrists make what other doctors make; if anything, they make a little less (though they have lower office expenses than most — no nurse, no equipment, usually no secretary). If it feels like more, that's because you pay more per visit, and there are so many more visits. But psychiatrists who are committed to the fifty-minute psychotherapeutic hour — and that's still most of them — make their income from many fewer patients than other doctors.

The (now old-fashioned) position of classical psychoanalysis, de-

* For incorporated doctors, the median is $62,500. Report on physicians' fees and incomes prepared by the Congressional Research Service of the Library of Congress, as reported by UPI, *Berkshire Eagle* (Oct. 30, 1974).

scribed, but not subscribed to, by Dr. Paul Chodoff, was that "the analyst must require sacrificial fees from his patients because they provide the patient with motivation, generate analytical material, and are beneficial to the countertransference."* "Sacrificial fees" feel somewhat less universally beneficial to the patient's family; most of us resonate when Louise Wilson speaks of "stunning, outrageous fees, out of the Arabian Nights."[1] Whatever we feel about doctor's fees, however, they are a fact of life, and therapy.

The compensation of other mental health professionals is roughly pegged to the going rate for psychiatrists. Like yours and mine, it follows the market. Under the American system, we've all felt entitled to as much as we can get, lawyers, farmers, businessmen, steelworkers, truckdrivers, teachers, sanitation men, and doctors — and we've been pretty much let alone to get it. So we can't be surprised that the care of illness is expensive and gets more so all the time.† Here we can't concern ourselves with the system, how well it works, for whom, what we'd lose and gain if we tried to change it, or whether it will change itself. This chapter is concerned with only one thing; how mental health services are paid for, out of our private or our public pockets.

INSURANCE, AND HOW COVERAGE AFFECTS YOUR CHOICES

Insurance coverage

Your first money question should be: Does my relative have health insurance?‡ Your second: Does the policy have psychiatric coverage? Your third: How much? Your fourth: How does the nature of the coverage limit the choices he and you can make?

isn't universal by a long shot.

More likely than not he has *some* coverage, but not so *much* more likely: in the early seventies, 63 percent of the civilian population had coverage for psychiatric care in a hospital, but only 38 percent had coverage for outpatient treatment.[2]§ The thrust of insurance

* Dr. Chodoff argues to his colleagues that "despite theoretical preconceptions . . . to the contrary, . . . psychoanalysis can proceed successfully in the absence of fees or with low fees." Patients, he maintains, can still make good use of visits paid for by insurance; "it appears that the fee is a more important source of motivation for the therapist than for the patient." "The Effect of Third-Party Payment on the Practice of Psychotherapy," *American Journal of Psychiatry,* 129 (Nov. 1972).

† How much more, you can judge for yourself by comparing the 1974–1975 prices cited throughout this book with the prices you encounter the year you read it.

‡ It will have to be your relative's insurance, not yours, unless you have a family policy and the troubled person is your spouse, or your child under nineteen. Some policies cover children as old as twenty-three or twenty-five if they're still in school; you may also be able to continue coverage for a mentally or physically handicapped child after the cutoff age. Your parents are not covered by your insurance, even if they live with you and you are their sole support.

§ A few states, Connecticut and Massachusetts among them, now *require* health insurance policies to provide coverage for mental illness.

If your relative is covered, expensive is cheaper, ridiculous as that may seem.

policies, thus, is to encourage the most expensive forms of treatment, to put people into hospitals, whether or not they could be treated as well or better as outpatients in their own communities. This is true of all present (1975) forms of health insurance, whether provided by a private insurance company, a nonprofit corporation (Blue Cross–Blue Shield), or government-funded Medicare. We'll talk about insurance in more detail later in this chapter. Here we just want to point out how having it, or not having it, can affect major decisions about the kind of care you or your relative can afford.

How insurance affects choices

Health insurance insures only against illness; its benefits are restricted to recognized medical conditions. If no doctor is ready to call it an illness, it can't be covered. Illnesses are traditionally treated by doctors and nurses, and in the last fifty years, severe or acute illnesses have more and more been treated in hospitals. If what health insurance pays for is medical services, this can limit choices as to who is to help your relative, where, and how.

Which mental health services are insured

QUESTIONS OF TREATMENT METHODS; HOSPITALIZATION VERSUS OUTPATIENT THERAPY; CONFIDENTIALITY; DRUGS

Which puts us right back where we started, as the bewildered insurance carriers try to cope with those questions on which there's so little agreement even among mental health professionals. Are mental illnesses really medical conditions, to be treated by medical doctors, using the purely medical means they have developed and that nobody else is qualified to prescribe – medical evaluations, drugs, ECT, and whatever else has been and will be developed as somatic treatments? If so there's no problem, for physical illness is what the policies are set up to cover. ECT poses no problem; neither do drugs if the policy covers outpatient prescriptions for physical illness. But what about psychotherapy or counseling: when are those to be considered medical treatments? And what about neuroses? Are those illnesses too, to be treated by doctors? Most policies imply that they'd better be, if they're to be covered, for it's asking a lot, in this imperfect world, to expect to be insured against problems of living. So it works out that, in Dr. David Viscott's words, "unless you have a very expensive insurance plan, the chances are that you will have to pay for most of your visits to a psychotherapist, but even the most basic insurance plans generally pay for ECT and often for outpatient ECT as well."[3]

as medical?

As Dr. Chodoff says, "Ultimately the third-party interest* raises

* That is, the interest of the insurance provider. Remember, there's the patient, the professional, and the third party who pays.

questions about the applicability of the medical model to psychotherapy."* But understandably, insurance companies haven't gone too deeply into our vexed psychiatric philosophies. They've found a simple way to decide these hard questions: they ask *Who?* and *Where?* Medical treatment, talking treatment, or whatever, if the person giving it is a licensed physician, it's reimbursable, subject to the limits set by the policy. If the treatment is being given in a hospital under a doctor's supervision, it's covered as part of the whole hospital package.† It may be individual psychotherapy or group therapy or behavior therapy or occupational therapy or rehabilitation therapy or family counseling. It may be given by a psychologist or nurse or social worker or occupational therapist or psychiatric aide;‡ if it takes place in a hospital, it fits the medical model, at least as far as the insurance carriers are concerned. But once outside the hospital, it's all different. If your relative is covered for outpatient treatment at all, it's usually from a doctor. Individual or group psychotherapy may keep him on an even keel or teach him to behave more adaptively; family counseling, sociotherapy, or vocational rehabilitation may improve his adjustment and enhance your family's ability to contribute to it, but that doesn't make them medical services — unless, of course, a doctor gives them. Services from physicians are more expensive, of course, but the best insurance programs pay enough so that to you it's cheaper. But some of these therapies aren't available from doctors; doctors in this country, for instance, don't concern themselves much with rehabilitation.§ Insurance companies are leery of the idea that services which don't look medical can be medically necessary.

It depends on who gives them and whether they work in a hospital.

Outside

many services won't be covered.

Obviously this will affect the choice of practitioner. As Dr. Chodoff says:

> If [the patient] is paying for the services out of his own pocket he can choose between the psychiatrist and the psychologist on the basis of what he knows about the kinds of services these two disciplines provide and

* *Op. cit.* Elsewhere Dr. Chodoff writes: "I am aware that the practice of attaching labels to complicated states of human distress is viewed in certain quarters with something close to contempt. However, if for no other reason than the recent increase in health insurance arrangements, psychiatrists who elect to receive their fees must act like doctors sufficiently to make medical-model diagnoses."[4]

† But insurance carriers are beginning to question this criterion; see p. 321.

‡ And it probably will be. You should be aware that in many hospitals personal consultation with a psychiatrist is not a routine part of treatment and costs extra.

§ Cf. Dr. George Gardos's remark: "In Eastern Europe . . . many different demands are placed on the psychiatrist, forcing him to fulfill a number of roles: physician, therapist, social worker, and rehabilitation counselor. Soviet psychiatrists, for example, plan and personally supervise work therapy for their hospitalized patients." "Three Paradoxes in American Psychiatry," *Psychiatric Opinion,* 11 (April 1974). If they did that here, patient work in the hospitals wouldn't be considered peonage.

his feeling about the particular individual. However, if the insurance carrier is paying a substantial portion of the fee, there will usually be an advantage in choosing the psychiatrist instead of the psychologist.[5]

Psychiatrist

Psychologist

Psychiatrist or psychologist: notice the choice. They're both called "Doctor," since the clinical psychologist generally has a Ph.D. And even the insurance carriers are beginning to think of psychologists as doctors, since what they do just isn't different enough from what most psychiatrists have been doing to support a distinction.* A number of companies (Aetna and Prudential among them) now cover clinical psychologists in some policies; others, like Massachusetts Mutual, will provide such coverage on request of the policyholder.[6] At this writing, the influential Blue Cross–Blue Shield covers services from clinical psychologists only if directly supervised by a doctor, but the American Psychological Association is pressing for equal coverage and sooner or later they'll get it, probably sooner. Even when they do, however, therapy from a psychologist without a Ph.D. wouldn't be covered, or from a nurse, or a social worker, or a paraprofessional.

Social worker? Nurse? Paraprofessional?

Tricky calculations

So check your policy and think about it. Help from a psychologist or social worker is actually cheaper, yet it may be more expensive for you and your relative. If you anticipate only a few sessions, however, it may still be cheaper. Most policies require that you pay for the first few outpatient treatment sessions yourself, under a set deductible allowance. In the Blue Cross–Blue Shield Master Medical, that's $100. Since the deductible might buy you four or five sessions with a psychologist or social worker (compared to two or three sessions with a psychiatrist), if those few sessions were enough you'd have got a good bargain. If they weren't, though, you'd regret your choice financially, for you'd have reached the dollar point where coverage with a psychiatrist would be just beginning and would last through many more sessions. That would be an even better bargain.

Insurance provisions discourage

What about partial hospitalization, community mental health centers, halfway houses, and all the fine things you've read about? How does the back-to-the-community movement fit into the insurance picture?

It doesn't. For all the talk, the insurance policies have quite a different message: *hospitalize.* Partial hospitalization *may* be covered if

* "Today, many of our regular Group Major Medical policies and all our small group Major Medical policies define 'physician' as a 'licensed practitioner of the healing arts acting within the scope of his practice.' Clinical psychologists are considered as coming within that definition." Richard J. Mellman, President, Group Insurance Department, Prudential Insurance of America, Newark, N.J., to Jack G. Wiggins, Ph.D., Chairman, Committee of Health Insurance of the American Psychological Association, January 11, 1972, as reproduced in "Health Insurance," a collection of documents available on inquiry from the American Psychological Association.

it's in a hospital ward with doctors around to keep things medical. Treatment in the hospital outpatient department, so important for discharged patients, may be covered if a psychiatrist gives or supervises it. But treatment in a mental health center, whether it's day hospitalization for really sick people or outpatient therapy for people who can make it in the community, is rarely covered, since mental health center treatment is given primarily by nonphysicians, who are seldom under close enough medical supervision to meet insurance requirements. (Some rural centers are hundreds of miles from the nearest psychiatrist.) Insurance payments have strengthened private hospitals and private psychiatric practice, but they have provided very little support* for community mental health centers, halfway houses, or other community services to the mentally ill.

less expensive modes of intervention.

Things are changing, however. Many private mental health units have managed to work out arrangements with insurance carriers to cover day hospitalization and outpatient therapy as well, administered by nurses, social workers, and aides as well as doctors. As general practitioners are becoming more sophisticated in psychological methods, we may hope that they will increasingly prescribe group therapy, care by paraprofessionals, nursing home placements, etc., as an aspect of general medical care. This would do a lot to clarify matters for the insurance carriers.

Third-party payment and confidentiality

Who pays for treatment can not only affect where it's given and by whom, it can affect one important aspect of the therapeutic relationship itself, its confidentiality. The insurance company who pays his claim requires certain information about your relative's diagnosis and treatment, just as they do if he has a heart attack. That's fine, of course — unless he's a professional pilot, he probably won't mind if his treatment for a heart condition is described in somebody's records. Or for gallstones, or diabetes, or cancer. But psychiatric diagnoses can stigmatize and this presents the treating psychiatrist with a problem.

Most psychiatrists feel that confidentiality is at the heart of the therapeutic alliance. Through their professional organizations, they have worked with insurance companies to keep the information required to a minimum. But you have to call a condition *something.*

> The use of insurance forms that require a therapist to state a diagnosis on a patient creates a sticky ethical problem. We have no assurances about the confidentiality of insurance records; and they do get lost or misplaced, or confused with other patients' records. . . . When it comes down to cases, most practitioners choose to protect their patients when possible. One rarely sees diagnoses such as schizophrenia, homosexuality,

* In the early seventies, only 15 percent of CMHC revenues came from third party payments, and half of that was from Medicare and Medicaid. *Behavior Today* (March 25, 1974).

> or anti-social personality. The nomenclature more commonly used includes such designations as anxiety neurosis, depressive neurosis, marital maladjustment, and other terms that are not as revealing.[7]

Not only are psychiatrists acutely sensitive to this question and to their patients' need for privacy, but some are able to make use of the problem for their patients' benefit.* But even though clinicians do their best to protect their patients, you and your relative should realize that under third party payment confidentiality cannot be complete. Most patients, says Dr. Robert Gibson of Baltimore's Sheppard Pratt Hospital, when they sign a blanket permission for the release of information for insurance purposes, have little idea of the amount of information that may be requested.† Insurance agencies are becoming interested in cost effectiveness: the idea of "accountability," already familiar in education and business, is becoming familiar in psychiatry too. As Dr. Chodoff observes, he who pays the piper can call the tune.

Accountability and cost effectiveness

> Insurance officials and their actuaries are going to want to know what they are paying for, whether patients are being treated under the proper indications [appropriately], and whether psychotherapeutic practices are being abused. They expect this kind of accountability from surgeons.[8]

In the long run, accountability should work to the advantage of the consumer. But if questions are going to be asked about individual cases, confidentiality for insured patients will be more limited in the future than it is today.‡

Saving money: a nice straightforward way

Paying (extra) for drugs

Drugs are a major expense for the mental patient§ outside the hospital. A study done in Pennsylvania in the sixties found the average cost for retail medications to released patients was $18 a *month.* (Fifty percent of the returned patients were living in families with yearly incomes of less than $4,000.)[9] According to Dr. Gertrude Gross of Baltimore's Psychiatric Day Care Center,

* "My practice," writes one psychiatrist, "has been to try to include this issue as part of a therapeutic alliance. A patient comes in with an insurance form, and I sit down with him and try to find some innocuous diagnosis he thinks acceptable. We did something like this when we were working with prisoners and had to make reports to the parole board—writing the report with the patient. It was an enormously useful therapeutic exercise."

† As reported in *Psychiatric News* (April 17, 1974). The application the policyholder (and his wife, too, if it's a family membership) signs usually contains a release. Here's a sample: "AUTHORIZATION TO PHYSICIANS OR PRACTITIONERS, HOSPITALS OR OTHER INSTITUTIONS: You are hereby authorized to give the —— Insurance Company any and all information you may have regarding my condition or the condition of any of my children when under observation or treatment by you including the history obtained, findings and diagnosis. . . ."

‡ See p. 324, on "PSRO" for Medicare and Medicaid.

§ Drugs account for 10 percent of the costs of *all* health care. "Drug Industry Regulation: Kennedy Hearings," Standish, Ayer and Wood, Inc., Investment Counsel, *Newsletter* (Boston, Oct. 1973).

> One of our main problems in referring our patients to private physicians for follow-up care is that these doctors too quickly reduce the dosage, or sometimes discontinue the medication altogether, usually at the patient's request, usually because of the financial burden.[10]

These patients, their families, or the welfare systems which support them are probably paying much more than they need to. Drug companies spend a lot of money on research, but they spend even more on the lavish advertising that is a major source of most physicians' information on drug therapy, and a major financial support of medical journals.* It pays; in 1972 the drug industry was second only to mining in return on sales.

Generic drugs by any other name cost more.

The name the companies use to advertise a drug is not the *generic* name of the drug — the chemical name that's the same all over the world and whatever company makes it — but the name the particular company christens it with. It costs a lot to persuade us that Kleenex is not just tissue, and it costs a lot to promote Thorazine when chlorpromazine is so much cheaper. In 1971, Serpasil sold for $49 per thousand; the same drug, under its generic name of reserpine, sold for $10 per thousand.[11]

All drugs sold in the United States must meet federal standards of quality and effectiveness. In late 1973, HEW Secretary Caspar Weinberger told Senator Kennedy's Health Subcommittee that "in terms of quality and therapeutic equivalence, no significant difference among chemically equivalent drugs has been shown." He was announcing plans to reimburse on a generic basis for drugs paid for with federal money under federal programs.

How can you save money the way the government does? The next time you go to the doctor — any doctor — ask him to let you look at his medical journals while you wait. You'll see handsome advertising spreads for psychoactive drugs; from them you can not only learn as much as most doctors know about drug side effects and contraindications, you can learn the generic names, which are also given in the chart on page 92 of this book.

Request generic drugs.

It should be easy to do — request the generic name and save. Unfortunately it isn't. There are doctors who don't know much about drugs but they know what they like, and they may not appreciate your advice. Ask just the same. The physician doesn't even have to *know* the generic name: he can write on his prescription, "Use generic drug." Habit is strong; even in states like Massachusetts that require doctors

* The *Physician's Desk Reference,* used by most doctors, is also prepared and paid for by the drug companies. Peter Ognibene, reviewing John Pekkanen's *The American Connection* (Chicago: Follett and Co., 1973) in the *New Republic* (Jan. 26, 1974).

to prescribe generic drugs for welfare cases, they don't do it.* Even when they do, it still may not work out in the drugstore. Pharmacists also know what they like. A Texas man persuaded his doctor to write him a generic prescription, only to find no local pharmacy in his town carried any but brand-name drugs. He called pharmacies in San Antonio, Houston, Dallas, and Austin and got a lot of wordage in favor of brand names, but no drugs. He now buys from a Washington mail service, which sells to members of cooperatives and credit unions.†

Dirty pool

A doctor who refers a patient to another professional should not take a proportion of the fee.

Saving money the obvious way

The most obvious way to save money is to buy cheaper services. You can save money at clinics and community mental health centers or by consulting psychologists, social workers, and psychiatrists just starting practice. What you pay will depend a great deal on where you live and the general level of prosperity. As a rule, where private psychiatrists' fees are high, other private professionals will follow, and agency and clinic fees will be high too. Where private treatment runs from $35 to $55 a session (and up) charges at mental health centers and clinics will run from $20 to $25. Partial hospitalization will be about the same – per day rather than per fifty-minute hour. But fees will be adjusted to your family's ability to pay, as measured by the usual things: income, number and age of children, educational and medical expenses, rent and mortgage payments, installment debt.

False economies

Don't ever try to save money initially, says one psychiatrist. At the beginning, you want the best advice you can get, even if you have to borrow. A first-class professional, he says (and he is one) should be able to refer you to a less expensive source of treatment if you can't pay his fee. Try for the best, at first, even if you have to take your relative to another city for consultation – and we'll hope some of the information in this book helps you determine what *is* the best for your family. For though money may determine access to the best, even money doesn't guarantee it.

Trade-offs

Extended hospitalization

When we start thinking about money we're besieged by trade-offs. The balancing of confidentiality against economy is only the beginning. Should you use up the family reserves on an extended stay in a good private hospital, or make use of the state hospital and hold back

* Dr. Richard Burack, former chairman of the Massachusetts Drug Formulary Commission, in his letter of resignation to Governor Michael Dukakis, stated that medical schools should be "obliged to teach their students more about medical economics" and called for "a frank and detailed discussion of the extent to which the drug industry has infiltrated the medical profession." A. A. Michelson, "Beacon Hill Weekly," *Berkshire Eagle* (Feb. 15, 1975). Dr. Burack's *New Handbook of Prescription Drugs* (New York: Pantheon, 1970) lists these drugs for the general reader.

† Lamar W. Hankins, Letter, *The New Republic* (June 23, 1973). The mail-order house is Direct Drug Service, 6905 4th St., N.W., Washington, DC 20012.

funds for prolonged office therapy when he comes out? Or suppose your relative is "medically indigent," as it's not hard to be, if you're a very young adult or an old adult or an adult who's never held a good job. In some states the family is liable for his hospital fees (see pp. 325–326) but in others, only his or her own resources are taken into consideration. In a big city, with established teaching hospitals, your relative may get very good care for nothing, when welfare pays his bill. If he has savings, however, he may have to turn over all but a minimum amount. In some places his house might be sold as a price of continued public aid.

versus outpatient therapy

Public assistance versus savings

The hospital business office and the hospital or mental health center social worker should be able to help you to think through hard choices such as these; how you can meet your bills is the business office's business, and the social worker's concerns cover how you and your family cope financially as well as emotionally.

Things to talk about with the hospital business office or social worker

As we said in Chapter VII, you can also discuss fees with a private professional. You should. Even if your relative is insured, coverage is sharply limited for outpatient psychotherapy. (See pp. 311, 321.) The therapist may be willing to adjust his fees. One reporter surveyed the scene in one of our psychotherapeutically most active cities:

with a private professional

> Everyone I spoke to said they had a sliding scale, but some of the scales slid a good deal farther and more easily than others. Some said that theoretically the scale went down to zero, or that they "never turned anyone away." Others said they sometimes accepted services in lieu of payment.[12]

The "average fee" we've spoken of is probably already outdated by inflation, but in fact, the only way to find out actual fees is by asking. Information on fees of specific physicians is rarely published. Most state laws on medical practice prohibit physicians from advertising or soliciting business except by simple listings in professional directories. In 1973 Ralph Nader's Health Research Group published the first consumer's guide to doctors (for Prince Georges County, Maryland). It listed fees, office hours, told where a doctor trained and whether he accepted Medicare patients. The second such guide, for Springfield, Illinois, prepared by Professor Ron Sakolsky of Sangamon State University and published in 1974, created a storm. "It was just like stirring up a hornet's nest; it was unbelievable," Professor Sakolsky told a reporter. Only fifty-four of Springfield's 215 doctors provided information; the medical society mailed out an "alert memo" warning that "it might be prudent NOT to approve the publication of information requested."[13] Professor Sakolsky plans to update the guide yearly (it's free) and believes more and more doctors will participate. According to Robert McGarrah, who headed the Nader project, a dozen more are in preparation around the country.

How to discuss payments

If this movement catches on, you may not need to ask, but in the meantime, don't be shy. Talking about money is an art in itself, but it's not a breach of etiquette. Next to sex, money is the most emotion-charged subject in our society, and for this very reason, your relative's therapist may hesitate to talk about fees when you first consult him. You may be feeling pretty upset when you walk in. His first object is to get to understand the immediate problems that have brought you to his door, and, if he can, to help you to deal with your anxieties so that you both can explore the situation lucidly. You may have to take the initiative in talking about money.

Since fee scales *do* slide, if you feel justified in asking for a reduced rate, do so at the start. It's much harder to later. You are asking him to see you and/or your relative for less than he could be seeing someone else, so prepare your case beforehand. The simplest thing would be to bring your latest income-tax form and a list of your fixed expenses. Don't, above all, be embarrassed. Almost all practitioners make reductions for some of their patients, and they simply want to find out what financial category you belong in. They don't want to contribute to your problems by creating an unbearable financial burden. If you can't afford his fees and he can't afford to reduce them for you, a good practitioner will try to help you make practical arrangements elsewhere.

You should be aware, though — as the therapist certainly is — that plenty of patients in psychotherapy (in psychoanalytic therapy, especially) are spending a third of their income for their treatment. As we said in an earlier chapter, the therapist's flair, personality, and experience matter more than his theories, and the best people don't come cheap. You may not need the best, either, after the initial evaluation. Some of the most bizarre conditions are relatively easy to treat. Don't suppose you are being fobbed off on a quack or a beginner if your eminent consultant refers you to a younger man or one not well-known. From a good doctor, you will get a good referral.

INSURANCE: DIFFERENT PLANS; FOR CHRONIC PATIENTS; FOR THE ELDERLY; FOR GOVERNMENT EMPLOYEES

Understanding insurance costs:

General questions are now behind us. The rest of this chapter will be about the specifics of the various programs, private and public, that help us bear the enormous* costs of mental illness.

* NIMH's 1975 report, "Research in the Service of Mental Health," estimates that mental illness conservatively represents a drain on the economy of $21 billion a year — "America's primary public health problem," affecting some 10 percent of the population. The report analyzes the $1 billion that has been spent for research — over the past twenty-five years. UPI report, *Berkshire Eagle* (July 31, 1975).

Premiums vary by regions.

What insurance costs you varies according to where you live. Daily hospital charges in a southern city may be half what they are in New England. Local hospital costs determine premiums.

If your family or your relative has insurance, either from a private company or Blue Cross–Blue Shield, root out the booklet that describes it. It will give you the broad outlines. If you can't find it, get another one from the employer or union through which your relative got the coverage and read it over. There's fine print in the policy that's not in the booklet, too. The employer or union has someone who specializes in health insurance claims, who will look over the fine print with you. Review *all* policies. In addition to health insurance, some people have disability insurance that provides a fixed sum per day or week of total disability; this can help meet costs too.

Getting coverage

Suppose you find your relative has no psychiatric coverage. He can't get it now; no new policy will insure a person who's sick for that illness. For the future, if he gets well again, he may be able to get coverage without difficulty, if he is able to join a large group program where risk is thinly spread. Under many such programs, coverage is granted without inquiring into the health history of the insured or his family. For smaller groups, and especially for the single policies that self-employed people must buy, it's harder. He may have had a psychiatric illness that got over and done with as completely as any physical illness. But psychiatric illnesses are full of uncertainties, and the insurance companies know it. Along with questions on previous physical illnesses, nongroup application forms contain such questions as "Has any person to be covered now or ever had: Epilepsy, mental disorder, nervous breakdown or other disease of the nervous system?" This doesn't mean the application will be rejected merely for that reason, but it certainly won't make it easier. If the policy is issued, certain benefits may be eliminated. (This is also true for preexistent physical illnesses.) In any case, be completely frank. Your answers will be thoroughly checked. The company would have to be convinced that your relative's illness is no more likely to recur than any other. A psychiatrist's assurance of full recovery from a depressive episode would certainly be relevant, but different companies will decide different cases differently. You might want to have your relative go back and see his doctor for a reevaluation.

Group or single

Nongroup application forms

Insurance provisions vary, like everything else, and so does the way they are applied by particular people in particular offices in particular companies. As we know so well, the terms the insurance companies have to use – terms like "mental illness" (or "disease" or "disorder" or "deficiency" or "disability"), "functional nervous disorder or reaction," "nervous breakdown," and the like – admit of many interpretations. The psychiatrist in charge of your relative's treatment will help when a claim is challenged, or when there's difficulty getting or keeping insurance coverage.

Continued coverage for mentally handicapped children

Look for a clause saying you may continue coverage for a mentally handicapped child after he reaches the age cutoff. Retardation is what's envisaged, but retardation and mental illness overlap. If you have such an option, take it up at once; otherwise a mentally disabled person may lose private insurance entirely, for physical conditions too. It's not easy, and may be impossible, for mentally disabled people to get health insurance on their own, let alone psychiatric coverage. (But see Medicare, Medicaid, pp. 323–324.) *You* must take the initiative in knowing when coverage may be continued and applying for it, with proof of disability. Some policies allow only a very brief period, after the child reaches the stated age, in which you can apply.

Supplementary insurance for the elderly

If your relative has his own insurance and is approaching sixty-five, make sure he takes up the option to continue some form of supplement to the government Medicare program, for unless he has ample private resources, that won't be enough.

Life insurance?

Insurance broker Benjamin Lipson, who specializes in high risk cases, finds a pattern of discrimination by life insurance companies against applicants under psychiatric care. He surveyed 250 Boston-area psychiatrists: many of them complained that companies ask about treatment but don't ask how the mere fact of treatment is relevant to the individual's life expectancy. Other psychiatrists noted that the word "depression" should be avoided in reports to insurance companies; it makes them think of suicide. Dr. Frank J. Kefferstan, senior medical director at the John Hancock Mutual Life Insurance Company, commented that certainly wasn't true of John Hancock. "We try to differentiate between different illnesses. Extenuating circumstances are very much considered."[14] Again, it all depends.

Limits on hospitalization

Let's assume you've found that there is psychiatric coverage and heaved a sigh of relief. Now check the limits set on the length of a hospital stay. The kind of hospital makes a difference. Time in a *mental* hospital will be limited, often to thirty days. Sixty days is a high benefit. Note, however, that most Major Medical plans do not set special time limits for mental illnesses if treated in a *general* hospital (see Chapter IX, pp. 226–228).

You can stay longer in a general hospital.

Working for the government

The federal government is the employer of choice for the mentally ill. Eight million people are covered by the Federal Employees Health Benefits Program (FEHBP), through Aetna Insurance and Blue Cross–Blue Shield. Their high-option plan provides for a full 365 days in a psychiatric hospital. Unlimited benefits, however, have brought rising costs and sharper supervision. Treatment philosophies too are changing. The full-year benefit seems on the way out. Claims once routinely allowed are now questioned. Dr. Robert Gibson, chairman of a special task force on federal employees' health insurance, notes the 1972 exclusion of milieu therapy from the federal program by Blue Cross–Blue Shield. Blue Cross–Blue Shield has defined milieu therapy as "confinement in an institution merely to control or change environment," says Dr. Gibson, and has refused to pay for it even though patients have been receiving drug therapy and psychotherapy at the same time. A bold-faced sentence in the federal employees' benefit pamphlet reads:

Milieu therapy?

> The fact that a physician may prescribe, order, recommend, or approve a service or supply does not, of itself, make it medically necessary or make the charge an allowable expense, even though it is not specifically listed as an exclusion.

Company nostalgia for the medical model

Even the traditional criterion, "medical" is what the doctor orders, is under question. So even if you're a federal employee, you may be in trouble, especially if your relative has had the treatment and his insurance hasn't paid the bill. As congressional staffer Don Terry says, "If the policy says 365 days and doesn't mean it, the insured would be better off if it said 30 days and meant it."[15]

Outpatient limits

If outpatient benefits are provided at all, they'll be only partly paid for. Note whether there's a deductible and its size. It will reapply for each person covered by the policy. Even with a deductible, office visits will be only partly covered; 80 percent is a high percentage, 50 percent more common. Most policies also limit either the dollar value of visits in a year, or the number of visits. Therapy for federal employees used to be unlimited, but in 1975 (January 1) Aetna cut back to twenty visits. Blue Cross–Blue Shield will probably have followed* before you read this.

MISCELLANEOUS CHARGES

Drugs? ECT?

Are prescription drugs covered? For psychiatric outpatients this may be a continuing expense. Is ECT covered (or partly covered) in a doctor's office, or does it require hospitalization?

Psychological testing?

Is there any provision for diagnostic psychological testing? (This is particularly important for children, if learning disabilities are implicated in their problems.) A thorough diagnostic workup runs upward

* Aetna's cutback was influenced by a study that showed they were spending about 12 percent of money paid in claims on 1 percent of subscribers. *Behavior Today* (Nov. 11, 1974). Under FEHBP, claims per thousand more than doubled from 1966 to 1972 and physicians' costs almost tripled; rate of claims increased much more for psychiatric conditions than for others. Louis H. Reed, "Utilization of Care for Mental Disorders under the Blue Cross and Blue Shield for Federal Employees, 1972," *American Journal of Psychiatry,* 131 (Sept. 1974).

from $100; Blue Cross–Blue Shield Master Medical provides for $45 in a two-year period.

Consultations?

We've talked pretty glibly about consultations (see Chapter VII, p. 190). These probably aren't provided for, but look. Even Blue Cross–Blue Shield Master Medical pays for consultations only "when necessary for proper diagnosis and treatment" *and* "requested by the attending physician." That's on his initiative, not yours, but he would probably not object to saying that he had requested the consultation even if you thought of it first.

Nursing?

What about the services of a private-duty nurse? Some policies pay up to 80 percent of the cost, if the need is certified by a physician. That might keep your relative at home. (Practical nursing or homemaker service is *not* covered, another example of the pressure to high-cost services.)

Hassles over payment:

And what about the actual process of paying for services? Does the doctor or hospital bill the insurance carrier directly, or must you pay first and wait for reimbursement? Well, it depends; hospitals and doctors vary. If you pay first, you may have a long, anxious wait. Be thankful if you have a strong organization to speak for you. Employers and unions put their own real money into group policies, and they want their money's worth. The single subscriber can have problems. The psychiatrist–social worker team of Butler and Lewis describe one woman's experience:

Mrs. K.

> We attempted to assist one of our patients who was having trouble collecting payments for psychotherapy. . . . Blue Cross–Blue Shield was refusing to pay for psychiatric services even though the insurance agent handling the policy assured us the woman was covered. . . . During . . . five months we were told twice by Blue Cross–Blue Shield that Mrs. K. was eligible for psychiatric services and three times that she was not. We were twice asked to resubmit *everything* (previous material had been lost, couldn't be transferred from one part of BC-BS to another, etc.). After five months of work on our part, Mrs. K still had not been paid. Like the carrot on a stick, there was a constant promise of payment — "in a month or six weeks." . . . BC-BS said they could not furnish her a list of covered services or allowable charges "because each case is considered separately."

"Each case is considered separately" — a joker or a protection?

In ten months, Mrs. K. was finally paid. Since you may not have a dedicated medical team to speak for your relative, be prepared to develop telephone persistence.

> It is difficult to reach the proper insurance official by phone. About half our calls never reached their target. Phone calls are not returned, nor are messages received. Conflicting information is given. Many health insurance employees do not know their own office procedures or the specifics of the programs they serve. Clients are shifted from one person to another

and tend to give up before they reach the "right" person. . . . Even though the insurance personnel seem to be pleasant and interested they give the impression of being "helpless" in straightening out problems efficiently.[16]

HMO'S; MEDICARE; MEDICAID

HMO's

In some areas, Health Maintenance Organizations provide another approach to meeting the costs of medical care. Subscribers pay a monthly premium, but instead of being used to pay fees of private doctors and hospitals chosen by the subscriber, the pooled premiums support a group of salaried doctors and health professionals paid by the HMO, who care for the subscribers' general health. Mental health, however, may be treated differently. Some HMO's do run their own mental health clinics, like the Health Insurance Plan of Greater New York, with salaried psychiatrists, psychologists, and social workers. Others contract with local psychiatric facilities for inpatient or outpatient care. Choice is still limited. Pressures for accountability and cost effectiveness are strong, and emphasis is on brief treatment and quick return to function. Some other well-known HMO's are Group Health Cooperative of Puget Sound, Kaiser of Southern California, Columbia Medical Plan, and Harvard Community Health Plan.

Medicare for Social Security beneficiaries;

Medicare, under the federal Social Security Administration, is a government program of medical insurance for anyone sixty-five or over who is entitled to Social Security (or Railway Retirement) benefits, and also for disabled people of any age. (For eligibility for the disabled, see Social Security, pp. 330–332.) Because of the difficulty of getting private health coverage, Medicare and Medicaid are very important for the mentally ill and their families, particularly for those of us who expect our relatives to outlive us.

Medicaid for the needy

Medicaid is also federally funded, but it is administered by state welfare departments, who sometimes add supplements of their own. It provides medical payments for old people and disabled people in need of public assistance, and for children whose families cannot afford medical care. You apply for Medicare at your local Social Security office; for Medicaid, at the local welfare office.

Medicare is no cure-all. "Ironically, the out-of-pocket costs of medical care have actually risen for older people since the introduction of Medicare, because of the increase in physicians' fees, hospital costs, and the general inflationary spiral."[17] It looks as if, in the absence of controls, all insurance drives up prices:

They reflect the general insurance scene.

It has been pointed out as a general trend in medicine that the existence of third-party payment provides "little incentive for efficiency. Instead, the trend is to use the higher cost facilities and services and to make as many of these available as possible."[18]

In the late sixties, general health service costs rose at a rate more than twice that of the Consumer Price Index; "the increased funding of Medicaid and Medicare gave major impetus to this inflationary trend."[19] Most of the problems in private health insurance are also problems in Medicare.

Hospitalization, outpatient services from a physician, some nursing and therapy at home, but no drugs

Like private health insurance, Medicare encourages hospitalization and discourages outpatient treatment. Treatment in mental hospitals has an 190-day lifetime limit (with an initial deductible). The first sixty days are covered; the next month is covered in part. Payment is for active treatment only; custodial care in a hospital is excluded. Still, for most illnesses, hospitalization is substantially covered. For outpatient treatment from a physician the patient must pay 50 percent and Medicare will not pay more than $250; outpatient treatment from social workers and psychologists is not covered. Some home nursing care is, however, as are medically ordered physical therapy and speech therapy – important services for the old and disabled. Drugs are not covered.

PEER REVIEW AMONG PROFESSIONALS

PSRO's

The need to review skyrocketing costs led in 1972 to the creation of a Professional Standards Review Organization for Medicare and Medicaid. Committees of local doctors are to review the treatment of individual cases to see "whether services provided . . . are necessary, whether they are delivered in the most appropriate setting, and whether they are consistent with locally agreed upon quality standards." Most doctors have accepted the idea reluctantly; some haven't accepted it at all. Confidentiality will be affected, as it already is by insurance company reviews; as Dr. Richard Dorsey notes in an article generally favorable to PSRO's, "in medicine as in many other spheres of life, complete privacy will become a luxury, available only to those with the means to pay for unreviewed care."[20]

Accountability again

versus confidentiality

Supplementary insurance

Supplementary insurance for the elderly may be had through the National Council of Senior Citizens and the American Association of Retired Persons as well as from Blue Cross–Blue Shield and commercial carriers. "One must be on the lookout for fly-by-night, fraudulent Medicare supplements that have been sold to old people."[21]

More hassles

If you have a relative who relies on Medicare, be prepared to spend more time on the phone. Mrs. K. had trouble with Medicare too. But hassles and all, those whose memories go back more than ten years can reflect how much better Medicare is than nothing used to be.

National health insurance

Some sort of national health insurance will probably be a reality, if not by the time you read this book, soon after, as it has been for years in most of Europe. It will spread the cost, but it looks as if it wouldn't change the system much. (The current bills even provide for the insurance itself to be handled by private companies.) Coverage for mental illness will still be limited. Proposed are thirty days in a hospital, or sixty days of partial hospitalization. Outpatient benefits would be limited too. The standard that has been proposed is the money equivalent of thirty visits, but the present weighting in favor of the private practitioner would be reversed. That is, patients who chose to spend their benefits in a community mental health center would get twice as much dollar value as those who consulted private practitioners. The emphasis, says Ron Klar, director of the Office of Health Insurance Policy Development in HEW, is on coverage of "acute care needs (including those resulting from chronic illness), not long-term care. Evidence and professional opinion suggest that almost all acute care requirements for the treatment of mental illness can be provided within the benefit limits specified."[22]

National health insurance as envisaged will not solve the problem of long term illness. As Representative Michael Harrington, a co-sponsor of the most liberal bill now under consideration, points out,

> those needing custodial care and home care are not even being *considered* for coverage under *any* of the national health insurance proposals. At this time, no federal funds go toward the maintenance of patients in institutions. States, suffering under crippling tax burdens, struggle to maintain a minimum level of care in most of their institutions. If our *Federal* dollars could be used to pay for the care and treatment of the disabled who require custodial care . . . the quality of their treatment could be considerably improved.[23]

Congressman Harrington suggests you write your representatives. (See Chapter XIV, on how to write a letter that will be read.)

If that long-term chronic care isn't in your home or in the community, it is likely to be in a state hospital. Who pays for that?

Who pays for your relative in a state hospital?

You do. We all pay as taxpayers, and in addition, in most states relatives of state hospital patients are liable for at least some part of the cost of their care.

The patient

State laws on this are extraordinarily varied. They agree on only one thing. Your relative (or the guardian of his estate) pays it as long as he can. If he or she draws a pension or Social Security these will be used (reserving a monthly sum for personal expenses). When patients

or "designated relatives"

can't pay, in almost all states "designated relatives" are liable for such charges as they can afford. Sometimes appeals procedures are provided. Only in Florida, New Mexico, Rhode Island, and Utah has the patient alone been liable; in Arizona, Indiana, and Montana liability is not clear. What relatives are designated may be left unclear, but usually they include spouse, parents, and adult children, not brothers and sisters.

The *American Civil Liberties Union Handbook*[24] surveys the statutes as of 1973. In Illinois, you were no longer liable if you'd paid for twelve years, in Ohio for fifteen. In Maryland if you'd paid in full for thirty months you needed to pay only twenty-five percent thereafter. In Rhode Island, local towns were liable. In Tennessee, Colorado, and New York, parents were not liable for children over twenty-one (in Massachusetts and Minnesota, over eighteen). In Georgia charges were limited to 10 percent of your previous year's income. Check your state in the *Handbook* and again in the county courthouse,* and talk it over with the hospital business office, making your financial situation clear. Some states (New York is one) provide for subpoena powers and citation for perjury. It sounds tough, but there's no way to run hospitals without somebody's money.

Your relative's money in a state hospital

What about the patient's money while he's in the hospital? Check the *Handbook*. In New Jersey, Oklahoma, Oregon, Texas, Massachusetts, Maine, Iowa, Idaho, money was to be placed in a special fund under the control of the hospital superintendent; in New York and Louisiana, the interest on it could be spent for the benefit of all patients; in Minnesota, the patient had his own personal deposit fund. In Pennsylvania, the Department of Revenue had control. A number of states designated an amount to be reserved for the patient's personal needs from any income he received. Other states operate under administrative regulations rather than by statute.

If your relative has income from any source, find out your state regulations, how much the state applies to maintenance, and who has charge of the rest. In many hospitals, a personal spending account is maintained for each patient, and small purchases made by or for him are applied against the balance of his account. If he wants something more expensive — a radio, for instance — he will probably need special permission from the hospital staff to buy it, or you could arrange to buy it for him. The hospital business office should provide an accounting. If you think there's something fishy, go to the hospital legal division with your figures.

in a nursing home

If your relative is in a private nursing home you should be no less watchful.

* Many states have recently revised their mental health codes.

> There are many reasons to believe, from studies made in Missouri and elsewhere, that public assistance payments and other small private funds patients have in nursing homes are not protected. They fall into the hands of the foster-care sponsor or nursing home owner, and unfortunately, are often not spent for the benefit of the patient.[25]

If your relative is in a state hospital or nursing home and receives Social Security payments (see pp. 330–332) there's somebody else who's interested in how that money is spent. The Social Security Administration is charged with the responsibility of seeing that payments are used for the benefit of the recipient. Charges for care and maintenance are subtracted, but your relative should get some spending money. Social Security staff are assigned to visit beneficiaries in institutional settings to make sure they are getting what they ought to. We can't look to the Social Security Administration as the all-purpose advocate for our relatives; their staffs are not trained evaluators of residential services, and they have many other duties. This on-site review takes place only every two years. But it's good to know that there'll be someone whose business it is to speak for our relatives when we're no longer able to.*

FINANCIAL PLANNING FOR THE FUTURE

Bequests and trusts

What more's to be said about money in that future so many of us have to plan for without being able to see into it? What can you leave, and how, to help your relative after you're gone?

No book can answer that. You need the best advice you can get, from people who know your state, its laws, and its customs, and its institutions too. Other families have had experiences that can guide you. Your state organization for the retarded should have suggestions, if there's no organization for families of the mentally ill.† What you *call* the condition will hardly matter much to how you plan. In some states you can designate such a group as guardian, with power to appoint a qualified person to oversee your relative's interests. You'll need a knowledgeable lawyer, yet with few exceptions, law schools do not train students to handle probates, trusts, and estate planning as they affect the disabled. Your state or local group may have lawyers they work with.

* See "Somebody Cares," *Oasis* (May 1971) — magazine for Social Security Administration employees.

† The New York State Association for Retarded Citizens has a publication, "Guardianship of Mentally Retarded Persons"; the Pennsylvania Association's *Legal Rights of the Mentally Retarded* also covers estate planning. There may be one for your state. See also the State Bar of Wisconsin's publication on guardianship.

What can happen

One father and mother denied themselves luxuries to leave a large trust fund for their daughter's care; they wanted her to stay in her own community, with familiar things around her. After their death, the trustee had her institutionalized. There she sat in the dayroom, doing nothing. Listening to music had been her only activity, and the institution had taken away her record player and her records. A friend of the family called the administering bank and accused it of not fulfilling the spirit of the trust. He was subsequently appointed guardian and is now trying to use the trust to establish a group home. The President's Committee on Mental Retardation has some advice (though dividing functions can cause problems):

Expert advice

> If parents desire a bank or corporate trustee, they may be encouraged to form a co-trusteeship. The individual trustee could have power to spend or not spend trust assets and to substitute another bank or corporate trustee. The bank, in turn, could invest, manage and account for trust assets and income. . . . Most lawyers advise against permitting a . . . person who cannot now manage money, property, or other affairs to inherit or own property. . . . Creditors, including government, will either claim most of the assets as reimbursement for costs of care or will deny government financial assistance and benefits until almost all of the assets have been expended.
>
> In many states a discretionary trust provides the best method to assure care. Under this plan, spendthrift provisions protect assets and income from creditors, including government. Trustees also have sole discretion in spending trust monies and income for items that are not basic costs of care or not covered by government benefits. These items might include a TV, radio, record player, vacation, trip to a baseball game, new dress or suit, and inspections and evaluations of social, work and living conditions.
>
> Trustees should be instructed to periodically check laws relating to government assistance and service, to survey programs of possible benefit . . . , to study work and living conditions . . . and to seek expert assistance to implement change where needed.[26]

Trust income, investment income, income from annuities, etc., does not affect Social Security benefits. (See pp. 330–332.)

If your problem is for life, think hard, and think now.

Leaving the medical model

Mental health is an all-inclusive concept; every good thing can be thought of as contributing to it. It's clear by now, though, that there's a limit to what can reasonably be expected of health insurance. It can help when our relative is sick, but it can't do much for his problems of living and surviving or for ours in living with him. For so many of those problems, any solution takes money, money for care in your relative's home, in yours; money for foster care, halfway houses, transportation; money for independent living. Sometimes the best thing the government can do is give us back some of our own money.

for support

What help can you expect from the government? More than ever before, and more, probably, than you are aware of. Tax deductions from the federal government may help you care for your relative. He or she may benefit from Social Security programs, Supplemental Social Security programs, veterans' programs. From the states: look in your own state capital for the programs administered by state health and welfare departments, and don't forget the departments of education and vocational rehabilitation. Government money: that's what the rest of this chapter is about.

for broader human services

Since almost all of us pay taxes, the simplest way the government helps those of us with extra burdens is to recognize them in the Internal Revenue Code. Medical expenses are deductible from your federal income tax return if they amount to more than three percent of your adjusted gross income. The Internal Revenue Service defines a medical expense as money paid for the cost of *preventing, treating,* and *alleviating* diseases or disabilities of a taxpayer and his dependents. That is a much broader standard of relevance than that set by any kind of health insurance, public or private. Psychotherapy is deductible, from both psychiatrists and psychologists.[27] For a mentally ill child, the full cost of a special school may be deducted if the principal purpose is to relieve his mental or emotional handicap. So is transportation to the school — for you too, if you must accompany him, and for visits, if seeing his family is part of his therapeutic care.* Special camps are deductible; so are sheltered workshops or group homes if a doctor considers them a therapeutic transition to normal living. Diagnostic tests and evaluations are deductible. So are prescribed drugs in excess of 1 percent of your total income. (Vitamins too, if prescribed by a physician.) So is special instruction, such as speech therapy. Half your medical insurance premium may be deducted (half what *you* pay; don't count your employer's contribution).

The IRS broadens the medical model:

psychotherapy

special schools

transportation

camps

tests, drugs

training

Keep a record, in diary form. All such expenses must be itemized, and documented with dated and signed notes from your relative's primary physician and whatever other specialists are involved. The nature of the disability should be explained, and the need for each kind of treatment should be made clear. You need not file the records with your return, but you should keep them four years, in case there is an audit.

carefully recorded, documented, and the record kept

If your relative is mentally disabled and lives with you, you may claim up to $400 a month for "child care," *if* the purpose of these expenses is to allow you *and* your spouse to hold jobs (or to allow you to work if the disabled person *is* your spouse). It is *not* necessary that the disabled person be a child. (The deduction will be reduced if your income exceeds a certain amount, or if your relative's income is over $750 a year.)

"Child care"

There are gray areas; for instance, the cost of attending a parents'

* A doctor or the school director must certify the necessity.

convention might be deductible, or the cost of your training in home therapy techniques. Tax provisions change, and they're complicated. Parents' magazines and newsletters usually publish up-to-date guides around tax time.* When in doubt, ask your local Internal Revenue Office.

PUBLIC MONEY AND MENTAL HEALTH

Social Security for the disabled too

If you think no one under sixty-five draws Social Security, go to your local Social Security office and read the free pamphlets. For many mentally and emotionally handicapped people, this program does more than any other to make it possible for them to remain in the community.

based on their own work

If your relative has worked for five of the past ten years but can work no longer, he is probably eligible for Social Security payments. He can get disability benefits if he is expected not to be able to work for a year or more, even if he will eventually recover. If he was disabled so early that he never built up the necessary Social Security credits, he is eligible for benefits based on his father's or mother's Social Security contributions, beginning when they reach sixty-five or at their death. (If he has lived with a grandparent, he may be eligible through a grandparent's work record; it depends.) A mother caring for a disabled son or daughter may also receive benefits. The criterion is "a severe physical or mental impairment which began before age 22 which keeps a person from doing any substantial gainful work."[28] Benefits continue as long as the disability lasts, which for those disabled in childhood is generally for life; *they do not stop when the insured parent dies.*† There's no age limit on filing an application; a disabled child may be in his forties when a parent dies. Stepchildren and adopted children are eligible too.

or their parents' on retirement (and maybe grandparents') if disabled before age 22 as long as the disability lasts.

These benefits go to people disabled in all sorts of ways. About one in ten is mentally ill.‡ A disabled person can receive coverage under Medicare when he or she has been drawing Social Security payments for two years.

In two years, Medicare

Social Security for the disabled has made it possible for thousands of us to keep our handicapped family members out of institutions, or to

Rx: money

* What's summarized here is given in detail in the tax guides in *The Exceptional Parent* (Jan.–Feb. 1974) and NSAC *Newsletter*, 5 (March 23, 1973).

† They do stop, however, if the person earns more than a token amount of money.

‡ Fifty-three and a half percent are mentally deficient; 6.8 percent suffer from schizophrenic disorders, 3.4 percent from "mental deterioration and certain other psychoses of unspecified etiology"; 7 percent from epilepsy; 2.7 percent from chronic brain syndrome. Tables on Childhood Disability Beneficiaries from *Social Security Disability Statistics 1967, Programs for the Handicapped* (HEW, Aug. 9, 1971).

bring them home. Because the money benefits continue after the parents' death (or begin with it, if the insured parent is under sixty-five), sisters and brothers and other kin who want to help can afford to take their relative in, and even have an incentive to do so. Money itself can be therapeutic, and that's no joke. In a world in which having money has so much to do with normal people's sense of themselves, is it any wonder that it is therapeutic for the mentally ill?

Supplemental Security Income

While you're in the office, find out about Supplemental Security Income for disabled adults (and, of course, old people) and for disabled children. Don't bother if you and your relative are comfortably off, though; these programs are only for those in need. Beginning in 1974, SSI replaced former public assistance programs administered by state welfare departments (with federal funding) — what used to be called Aid to the Totally Disabled. SSI is administered by the Social Security Administration now, but unlike Social Security benefits, which are financed from Social Security contributions, SSI benefits are funded from general federal revenues.

SSI replaces ATD.

You will receive payments for a disabled child under twenty-one only if you yourself are needy. Once a child reaches twenty-one, however, he is considered for SSI eligibility on the basis of his own income, not yours (in 1974, not more than about $1,500 a year). If you provide him room and board outside your home, that's considered part of his unearned income; if you support him in your home, however, that doesn't affect his income eligibility, but his SSI payment will be reduced by one third.[29]

Before 1974, in centers of the youth culture, "disabled" was often interpreted pretty liberally. The official phrase was "inability to work due to mental illness or psychological impairment." The young had a handier phrase, "crazy money." Two clinicians studied the clusters of mainland youth living on one of the lovelier Hawaiian islands and estimated that 10 to 15 percent of the young people lived on welfare, mostly crazy money.[30] That was ATD, locally administered. Now there are federal guidelines, and it looks as if some Social Security offices were overcorrecting; early reports have told of people being excluded from benefits because they had an IQ of over 49,[31] or found a job sweeping floors at $20 a week. This will serve to remind us once more that illness and disability are matters of interpretation, and that when benefits go to those who don't need them, the truly needy and their families are the ones who suffer in the end.

Differences between Social Security and SSI

There's an important difference between Social Security and Supplemental Security. Because Social Security benefits are based on payments made over a worker's lifetime, they are paid regardless of income; a worker may retire with a substantial income to which Social Security checks will simply be added. The only limit is on *earned* income. Make what sense of that you can; at any rate, it applies to a disabled relative too. Income from investments, annuities, or a trust will not affect his Social Security benefits. SSI benefits, however, will be reduced or eliminated if the recipient has significant income or property.* Another difference: the disabled under Social Security get Medicare coverage; those under SSI get Medicaid through state welfare departments. Your relative may benefit from these programs in combination, if Social Security alone is inadequate.

If this sounds complicated, it is. Don't depend on what you read here; regulations change, interpretations differ. Ask at your local Social Security office. If answers are confusing or inconsistent, you should be able to consult the *Social Security Manual,* a large and constantly changing document, at district (not local) SSA offices. (The portion of the *Manual* which applies to SSI is available from the National Senior Citizens Law Center, 1709 West Eighth Street, Suite 600, Los Angeles, CA 90017.) The *Social Security Handbook,* containing many of the rules and interpretations of the *Manual,* is available from the Superintendent of Documents, U.S. Government Printing Office, Washington, DC 20402. Or consult the national office of any organization that serves the handicapped. Staying on top of benefits is their business.

Money from the Defense Department

Members of the armed forces, of course, are treated free for all illness, physical and mental, during their service, and afterward for service-connected conditions. Under the Civilian Health and Medical Program of the Uniformed Services (CHAMPUS), the United States government provides for their families too what is probably the fullest protection against the costs of mental illness available to any citizen. From 1966 until 1974 there were no limits on hospital or outpatient treatment, and CHAMPUS paid the full costs of special schools for handicapped children (see Chapter XII), institutional care, rehabilitation training, and related services. Service families thus joined the very rich as essentially the only Americans who had access to the leisurely treatment available in the luxurious hospitals described in Chapter IX. In 1974, however, the Defense Department set a 120-day limit on hospitalization and scaled the outpatient benefit down to forty visits, citing "the rapid increase in the cost of the program, and psychotherapy as a specific cost factor."[32] The outpatient limit was later (August, 1974) raised to sixty visits. Though it's unlikely that unlimited benefits will return, CHAMPUS still covers the costs of psychiatric illness more completely than any other public or private program.

CHAMPUS

Confidentiality

Psychiatric help available through the military brings up the familiar problem of confidentiality. When the astronaut Colonel "Buzz"

* For what's significant, consult your local office.

Aldrin began to spend all his time in bed (see Chapter II), "every time I decided to get help I began to cry; the only help available was official Air Force treatment and the matter would go into my record."[33] For a time he paid his bills himself, seeing to it that they were for "family counseling" even though he got individual therapy. Things got worse; he was treated (and recovered) in a military hospital, but not, he thinks, without cost.

and Col. Aldrin

> My personal theory — confirmed by others who, like me, have spent over twenty years learning the military ropes — is that my chances for promotion ended when I asked for psychiatric help.[34]

Another trade-off — for he did get well.

Benefits after death

CHAMPUS is for the families of those on active duty. If you are a retired member of the armed forces, including the reserve, and entitled to retirement pay, the Survivor Benefit Plan (PL-92-425) enables you to plan for a disabled child or spouse after your death. Other family members can also be named as beneficiaries. Unlike CHAMPUS, participation in the plan is not automatic; you must apply through your individual service branch.*

Veterans' Administration helps, especially the elderly.

Eligibility for VA treatment was described in Chapter IX (p. 247). This is of particular importance to older people (for whom CHAMPUS offers virtually nothing). Veterans' Administration hospitals are leaders in the field of geriatric treatment. Not only may the veteran himself benefit, but through the VA, spouses *and parents* of veterans may also be eligible for assistance when needed. Veterans and their widows and children may receive pensions on the basis of need; the VA provides all or part of the income for more than 1.8 million people over sixty-five, income which is in addition to Social Security. The VA not only provides inpatient (and outpatient) treatment in centrally located hospitals, it may also pay for outpatient treatment from doctors where you live, or pay for supplemental insurance. If there's mental illness in the close family of a needy veteran, he or she should call the local veterans' representative or visit the nearest VA office and see what they can do.

Pensions

Medical treatment

Money from states and communities

State aid is for the disabled and needy, and for children in trouble. Of course the number and quality of services varies tremendously from state to state, from the almost Scandinavian comprehensiveness of Minnesota to — well, why particularize? Your own state probably provides more people with more help than you have any idea of. The Voca-

* At these addresses: Army Finance Agency, ATTN: Retired Pay Division, Indianapolis, IN 46249; Navy Finance Center, New Federal Office Building, Cleveland, OH 44199; AFMPC (DPNSAB), Randolph AFB, TX 78148 (Air Force); Commandant–U.S. Marine Corps., ATTN: Code DNC, Washington, DC 20380; Commandant (GFP-4/71) U.S. Coast Guard, 400 Seventh Street S.W., Washington DC 20590.

tional Rehabilitation Office, welfare, Aid to Families with Dependent Children (AFDC) may pay for therapy or education, for adults and children, which they could never afford for themselves. Disability payments make it possible to keep people out of institutions. Welfare may pay for homemaker or health aide service when you or your relative can't. In Massachusetts, local school committees, reimbursed by the state, pay the special educational costs for "children with special needs," in community public schools if possible, outside them if necessary. Connecticut pays for special schools too, and several states reimburse parents for part of the costs. In 1974 Massachusetts passed a subsidy to workers who make more than one-quarter of the minimum wage (and are thus ineligible for federal disability payments) but still cannot earn normally. Some big city welfare offices have mental health services right in the office, providing on-the-spot psychotherapy or evaluation for disability. Most of us know little about welfare, and we can't always rely on mental health professionals.* Most of us find it hard to contemplate a relative "on welfare," but consider: If money makes it possible for you to keep your relative in the community, and the lack of it would cost the state thousands for institutional treatment, "welfare" isn't charity, or even fair shares for the needy. It's payment for an essential public health service. Providing money to support your love and effort is the taxpayers' best bargain.

We can't tell you what your state does, and what are the agencies where help may be found. We can tell you you won't find everything in one place. How could you? For our sickest relatives – the ones who pass back and forth by that revolving door, or the ones who'll never be well at all, it's clear that no one system can do all that's needed – that many systems of social service must collaborate, from health to housing.

Coping with bureaucracies, public or private,

Who will guide you through the systems? It's hard enough to keep up with the requirements of modern life when we are in perfect health. When the problems of mental illness are added – well, let a British father describe a reality which is international.

> The great difficulty is that it is at the time when she needs help – medical or financial – that she is usually unable to cope with the normal procedures for seeking it. One result is that when, as on this last occasion, she gives up her job (because, perhaps, she is beginning to have delusions about her colleagues) she is unable to get unemployment assistance. . . .

* "Many private mental health practitioners and public mental health clinics with whom we dealt tended to be unaware of the workings of the welfare system. Often, for example, either in the name of protecting clients' confidentiality or under pressure of a large amount of paperwork, a disability report was submitted which was inadequate for disability determination. . . . Instead of protecting their clients, such practitioners unwittingly involve them in unnecessary red tape." Jay S. Flocks and David M. Paradise, "Mental Health Planning in Welfare Agencies," *Psychiatric Opinion* (Aug. 1974), pp. 31–37.

Confused with drugs and ECT, she comes out of the hospital. "It is then a great effort to take up the normal routine of shopping and generally fending for herself; any extra administrative complication of getting certificates, filling in forms, etc., is liable to be beyond her." And he quotes an official letter:

isn't the strong suit of the mentally ill.

> "I am afraid this benefit cannot be made payable to you or sent to your address unless I have your daughter's authorization in writing. . . . Perhaps when you see her you can discuss this with her." She was at the moment in another hospital, having taken an overdose of pills three days after leaving the first hospital.
>
> When they can work at all, mentally ill people may change jobs and addresses often. Each change jeopardizes carefully made arrangements. More difficult to get across to anyone who has not experienced it is the cumulative effect of trying to sort out the administrative tangles inevitably recurring month after month and year after year, explaining the position (as far as one knows it and is allowed to explain it without causing explosions) as patiently as possible to ever-changing officials.

The need for advocacy and continuity of care

He pleads for an advocate, and for a master record so that one bureaucratic hand knows what the other is doing. He tries to act as his daughter's advocate, to supply "this missing keystone" to insure what the social workers call "continuity of care." But the keystone

> constantly crumbles. The reasons for its crumbling are well known — the attitude of the medical authorities, and others, that a person's affairs are not the business of their parents; and the frequent attitude of the "patient" that their parents are about the last people who should be given information. What is the use of saying, "Perhaps you can discuss this with your daughter," when your daughter is accusing you of putting poison in her food or contaminating the water supply by some sort of action at a distance?[35]

Two hopeful projects

In some places, the initiative is coming from professionals. The Tufts–Columbia Point Health Center in Boston developed a group of medical ombudsmen, and some other comprehensive mental health centers are following suit. Most of their ombudsmen were community people, who were taught how to guide their clients around the system. In other places, concerned citizens have become do-it-yourself advocates. The Advocacy Project of the Mental Health Association of Alameda County (California) started as one of those informal services you read about in Chapter VI; in 1974 it got some revenue-sharing money, which we'll hope it's still getting by the time you read this. In the words of a long-time MHA activist, the mother of a mentally ill forty-year-old, "Advocates are volunteers who are trained to run around to all these agencies and get what's needed, whether it's medical service or housing, or welfare, or food stamps, or child care for the patient's children. Our project also helps relatives. It requires no psychiatric professionals, though we do need legal aid sometimes. *It could be done anywhere.*"

Let's hope it will be. In the meantime, the best advice is what Buddha told his disciples: "Be ye lamps unto yourselves." (See Chapter XIV.)

Three themes, then, emerge from this very unpleasant chapter: money is therapeutic, systems must work together, and it's probably up to you. Here's a true story which shows how money, finding out about it, and wisely spending it, transformed, not only the clinical symptoms of one human being, but two lives.

Jean

Do you remember the woman back in Chapter IX, the one who got transferred to the back ward because she would turn the lights on, and who stayed there four years? Jean was nearly thirty when she entered the state hospital. She had been ill – or seriously disturbed, or whatever you choose to call it – from babyhood. You can read about it, for she is a famous case; she has a chapter to herself in Erik Erikson's *Childhood and Society,*[36] a brilliant description of what a child whom experts a generation ago called schizophrenic (and now would probably call autistic) looked like to one of the most gifted therapists of our time. But the chapter stops when Jean's life had hardly started.

Jean was five when her desperate parents did what they were advised to do and sent her away from home, to the best therapeutic school the experts of that time could recommend. She lasted a year; home again, her mother taught her to read and write, but the search for "the right place" continued. Jean crossed the continent to one school; it gave up on her after nine months.

Jean was eleven when the good news came; a leading hospital in their own state was developing a program for schizophrenic children. Jean entered the fourth floor ward that year after year was to be her home. The work was supported by research funds; charges could be adjusted. They had to be; by the time Jean was seventeen, her parents had spent over fifty thousand pre-inflation dollars on her care, and their money had run out.

Jean had the finest psychoanalytic treatment – in those days when it was only beginning to be realized that a child could be what we call mentally ill. But she grew older, and with all the sympathy and dedication in the world, a grown woman cannot stay in a children's ward for life. When Jean was twenty-nine, she left the warm and personal atmosphere where for more than half her life she had been under treatment and was admitted to the state hospital. Four years later she was a typical chronic patient, rarely speaking, never smiling, drowsy with drugs at 9:30 in the morning. No one even knew that she could read.

What magic therapy enabled her to go home, this time to remain?

It was done with money. Jean's mother happened to hear that adults who were totally disabled could get money every month — those payments you've just read about, then called Aid to the Totally Disabled, now available through Social Security. "Mental health professionals . . . tended to be unaware of the workings of the welfare system." There were no advocates then; the information that changed the lives of Jean and her mother came entirely by chance.

Those disability payments brought Jean back home and kept her there. With them, her mother paid students from the local university community, at first to stay only for an hour or so. Later, as they won Jean's trust and she began again to smile and talk they taught her crafts, took her to movies and parties, helped her join the world she had seen so little of. They didn't know it, but they were acting as "paraprofessionals" — a word that was then just beginning to be heard in professional circles. Without the help of these young women Jean's mother could never have met the twenty-four-hour needs of this woman in her mid-thirties who had spent so little of her life outside an institution.

Jean is now in her forties. Her needs are not so all-demanding now. She rides the bus alone, she makes jewelry, she sews her own clothes. She takes no medication. She is under no psychiatric supervision. She attends an informal activity group run by volunteers in a local day program. She contributes to the household, making supper, cleaning the kitchen, tending the garden. She no longer needs continual supervision; she can spend an evening alone, and answer the phone and write down a message to give her mother when she returns. Sometimes she visits her friends for a few days, and her mother has a little time to herself. Jean is not "cured" — no money, no medicine, no therapy can yet do that. But she is living more fully, more humanly than she has ever done in her life. Money did that, money and the homely common sense and love we can all have access to. It wasn't very much money, really — a third, perhaps, of what it cost to keep her in an institution. How many thousands of dollars could the taxpayers have saved if that money, and the confidence to use it, had been available earlier, to buy the family a respite from the daily problems the deepest insight was unable to solve, to buy the homely services of other hands and heads, to buy a place in the community rather than a place on the ward?

PART THREE

Outrage—And How to Use It

CHAPTER XII

Children: The Need to Grow

> If the parents' potential for helping the child to develop his competence and master his handicap is mobilized, they will have more to give the child than any therapist can give, although expert intervention may occasionally be needed to supplement parental care or to remove some obstacle which prevents the child from accepting it.
>
> It is vital for the parents' own stability to be given a method for helping the child . . . and encouraged to use it and to enjoy some success.[1]
>
> ELIZABETH IRVINE

MANY PEOPLE DON'T REALIZE that children can be considered mentally ill. Yet children, like adults, can do such bewildering and frightening things that they are called psychotic. Children have problems in living, and children can begin early to grow into the kind of people professionals call character-disordered and newspapers and the law call delinquent.

PROBLEMS IN LIVING — AND LABELING

Diagnosis is even more difficult in children.

Children's disorders may be given the same names, and often are. Yet neurosis or depression or schizophrenia doesn't look the same in children. There are other diagnoses that aren't applied to adults at all. And diagnosis is difficult; the younger the child, the harder it is for even the most experienced professional to be sure what he's looking at. A child may be said to suffer from anxiety neurosis, or depression, or obsessive-compulsive neurosis, or a phobia, or even from a character disorder. But child psychiatrists have learned from Dr. Szasz; with children even more than with adults, we shouldn't be too quick to translate their problems into medical language and speak of "pathology" and "illness." As Dr. Henry Lennard of the University of California School of Medicine warns, "Once we define behavior as a medical problem, anything can become a deviance, an illness, a disease."[2] Children are so resilient, most of them; they change so fast. Even the mildest psychiatric term, *"transient situational neurosis,"* isn't a label you'd want to hang on a fifth grader, especially if you thought somebody else was going to see it. It's a pretty portentous way to say that somebody's troubled because of a particular situation and it'll pass. It may pass, however, and leave lasting traces, in the sense of constricted and limited behavior in adulthood; we certainly don't recommend complacency to any parent. Nevertheless, there's wisdom as well as reassurance in the familiar words, "he's just going through a phase."

Neuroses (again)

Transient situational neurosis

Yet how do we know what will clear up of itself and what needs professional help? According to a *New York Times* article,[3] "treatable problems which many parents might ignore as transient and insignificant include nail biting, thumb sucking, temper tantrums, and bedwetting." Children with such problems of living can get help from psychotherapists of various sorts, as adults do. But there's not much we can say about them here, nor about "seclusiveness, worrying, apathy, submissiveness, shame, guilt, fighting, cruelty, defiance of authority" – to name some of the other childhood problems for which the reporter suggests you might seek treatment. Such problems may be signs of real disturbance. Usually they're not. A child may begin to wet or soil again at the birth of a new sibling. He may resist going to school,* refuse food or overeat,† develop involuntary movements or tics in response to changes in family relationships, moves, deaths, etc. In most cases these are minor and self-limiting – they'll go away.

Danger signals?

Dr. Saul Kapel, a child psychiatrist whose sensible advice reaches millions, cites an NIMH study which listed fifty-five symptoms associated with some severe form of emotional disturbance. "The researchers discovered that most youngsters between five and eight had at least some symptoms and some had quite a few. Yet there was nothing seriously wrong with them."[4] Our children are stronger than we think. A recent study concludes that the majority of disturbed children not diagnosed psychotic improve without intervention.[5] As for what happens when they grow up, Professor Lawrence Kohlberg of Harvard's School of Education, summarizing many different studies, says they're as likely as anybody else to be normal. *Serious* learning problems and *continuing* antisocial behavior often do mark the childhood of the adult who becomes psychotic, or sociopathic, but these are very different from nail biting and bedwetting, or even seclusiveness, worrying, submissiveness, fighting, or defiance of authority. "Children who are referred to child guidance clinics for emotional problems without concurrent cognitive and antisocial behavior problems are almost as likely to be well adults as a random sample of the population."[6] Even of schizophrenia or criminal behavior, "childhood emotional-disturbance symptoms are not now useful predictors. Neither is adult neurotic emotional disturbance currently predictable from childhood symptoms."[7]

Don't be complacent, but save real worrying for serious trouble.

Dr. Kapel suggests that the nervous parent's "Is it normal?" be re-

* When a child is so anxious about school that he persistently refuses to go, it is called *school phobia*. It has been successfully treated in many ways, from psychoanalytic psychotherapy to behavior therapy to drugs. All therapists emphasize prompt intervention: getting the child back to school before the behavior gets rooted.

School phobia

† A *prolonged* refusal to eat leading to serious weight loss is called *anorexia nervosa;* in extreme cases it can end in death. Found most often in adolescent girls, it can be treated by individual, family, or behavior therapy.

Anorexia nervosa

placed by more precise questions: "Is it common, and does it indicate any kind of emotional disturbance?" "Usually the answer will be, "Yes, it is quite common; and no, it does not suggest a disturbance *unless the child shows other symptoms as well.*"[8] (Italics ours.)

It's the usual fine line we walk, between burdening children with the weight of our worries, and possibly ignoring real danger signals. One sturdy metropolitan six-year-old complacently told his astonished country cousins that he needed a psychiatrist (and had one) because "I've got *problems.*" So he did, and living in a psychologically over-sophisticated milieu was one of them. If you need advice on surmounting problems and minimizing unhappiness, this chapter will disappoint you. But Dr. Haim Ginott and Dr. Spock stand ready to help; Dr. Spock's *Raising Children in a Difficult Time* includes a good chapter on what you can overlook and when psychotherapy might be a good idea.* Don't overlook the possibility that you could make good use of counsel for yourself: advice on how to talk to a child who has been traumatized or molested, advice on how to "listen with the third ear" to a child too reserved to express his anxieties directly.

There are more serious, more sinister ways a child can be in trouble. Professor Kohlberg mentioned sociopathic or antisocial behavior as something that often does continue into adult life. What clinical meaning does the term "character disorder" (see Chapter III, pp. 40–41) have in children? Kids can do the same bad things that adults do; they lie, manipulate, steal, destroy; sometimes they kill. A few even show the cool, guilt-free personality of the classical adult psychopath.[9] Is it merely difficult, or just plain impossible, to distinguish when there's something "really" wrong (Dr. Harold Levy thinks Lee Harvey Oswald had a learning disability)[10] and when what's wrong is poverty, and a world in which destructiveness and violence are admired, rewarded, and merchandized†? If *that's* the illness, the remedy is outside the scope of this book.‡

"Character disorders?"

"Sociopathy?"

* Benjamin Spock, *Raising Children in a Difficult Time* (New York: W. W. Norton, 1974). Other commonsense guides: Haim Ginott, *Between Parent and Child* and *Between Parent and Teenager* (New York: Macmillan, 1965 and 1969); Gerald Patterson and M. Elizabeth Gullion, *Living with Children: New Methods for Parents and Teachers,* a good introduction to behavioral principles (Champaign, Ill.: Research Press, 1971); and T. Berry Brazelton's *Toddlers and Parents: A Declaration of Independence* (New York: Delacorte Press/Seymour Lawrence, 1974).

† Does anybody think that the young Claude Brown of *Manchild in the Promised Land* had a character disorder?

‡ Many, both within and outside the mental health professions, think that mental health professionals should go forth to war on poverty; Ralph Nader's group has bitterly criticized community mental health centers for sticking to a "medical model" and ignoring the conditions of the poor. It's a point of view we have given little space to, since the evidence on whether poverty does in fact breed mental illness is cloudy. But it certainly does breed "character disorders."

But you don't give up on a kid, and the mental health professions try to do what they can about "character disorders" – or very bad problems in living – which of course are not limited to the poor. They work with every technique of psychotherapy and reeducation they possess, in schools, mental health centers, sometimes private offices, to turn things round before the delinquent or predelinquent becomes the concern of the court, the probation officer, and whatever agencies the state provides for the "rehabilitation of youthful offenders." But it's not surprising that five hours of school and a weekly therapy hour often fail if what's needed is a restructuring of the child's whole environment. Group homes, residential schools, residential treatment centers of many kinds try to do this. Some are private, some are publicly supported. They don't always succeed in their hard task, but they succeed better than old-fashioned reform schools, whose major accomplishment is to teach the behavior they exist to reform. These new facilities, smaller, more community-based than the old, need more money, more recognition, more public support. That's talking politics, however. Delinquency, like crime, is finally a social, rather than a psychiatric, problem.

and society

So we'll leave society's business and return to our own, which is to describe the more serious psychiatric disorders of childhood. Like "character disorders" they aren't likely to go away by themselves. They too will grow worse with our neglect, and as yet we know no way to cure them. But far more surely than character disorders, they will respond to our skilled and persistent intervention.

DISABILITIES AND DYSFUNCTIONS

LD, MBD, HA

There are three terms that cluster in discussions of children who have trouble learning in school: *learning disabilities* (LD), *minimal brain dysfunction* (MBD) and *hyperactivity* (HA). They overlap; the hyperactive child usually (but not always) has learning disabilities, and learning disabilities and hyperactivity are both seen as the result of minimal brain dysfunction. But "minimal" shouldn't make you think "trivial"; the dysfunction is minimal only in comparison with the severe brain dysfunctions that cause cerebral palsy, retardation, epilepsy, and childhood psychoses.[11] MBD shows up in all sorts of specific learning disabilities, which may themselves be classified as mild, moderate, or severe. A child who gets called LD (or HA, or MBD) is *not* a generally "slow learner," and he may be very bright. The word "specific" is important; there are specific things that he can't do easily like other children. Here's the definition of the National Advisory Committee on the Handicapped:

Specific disabilities, not retardation

Children with specific learning disabilities exhibit a disorder in one or more of the basic psychological processes involved in understanding or in using spoken or written languages. These may be manifested in disorders of listening, thinking, talking, reading, writing, spelling or arithmetic. They include conditions which have been referred to as perceptual handicaps, brain injury, minimal brain dysfunction, dyslexia, developmental aphasia, etc.[12]*

A mixed bag of disabilities and terms

As you can see, educators' words and doctors' words are all mixed up together. *Aphasia* is severe difficulty in using language, and is almost always based on some neurological deficit. The aphasic child can't seem to get meaning from the sounds he hears; it's as if they come in scrambled. (This is called *receptive* aphasia.) Or he understands, but can't put his own words together to communicate (*executive* aphasia). *Dyslexia* and *dyscalculia* sound medical but aren't; as you've probably figured out by now, "dys" means "bad." Dyslexia is difficulty in reading; dyscalculia, difficulty with numbers. Reading, spelling, handwriting, arithmetic are the teacher's province; brain dysfunction (sometimes *damage* or injury) and *perceptual handicaps* are the doctors', along with other terms such as *neurological impairment* and *psychoneurological learning disorder*. Dr. Harold Levy of the Louisiana State University School of Medicine would like to see MBD called "central processing dysfunction": something is wrong in the brain, so that messages aren't received or transmitted properly, and eyes or hands or feet or subtle parts of the nervous system don't work as they should.

Dysgraphia is terrible handwriting; Dr. Levy asks his young patients to write him a note. If there's a real gap between what they can say and what they can write, further evaluation is needed. Don't confuse a learning disability with a *learning block*. A psychiatrist or psychologist uses that term if he thinks the problem is emotionally caused.

Learning block

visual and perceptual problems

A child with perceptual handicaps suffers even more. All these handicaps take their toll in frustration and a sense of failure, and invite emotional problems at home and at school. An invaluable parents' guide to learning disabilities of all sorts is Brutten, Richardson, and Mangel's *Something's Wrong with My Child*.[13]† In it educational psychologist Milton Brutten and pediatrician Sylvia Richardson quote

* The committee produced this definition in 1968 for the Office of Education in the U.S. Department of Health, Education and Welfare; it is used in the 1969 Elementary and Secondary Education Act Amendments.

† Whereas Dr. Levy takes a medical point of view, Brutten and Richardson show a bigger picture that includes a very important place for nonmedical professionals — and you.

In *Helping Children Overcome Learning Difficulties: A Step-by-Step Guide for Parents and Teachers* (New York: Walker Publishing Co., 1975), Dr. Jerome Rosner of the University of Pittsburgh shows parents how they can participate in both testing and teaching their children. Parental participation, he says, will be necessary until "school administrators and school boards . . . recognize that some children need not only good teachers but small classes and individualized instruction."

television writer-producer Jess Oppenheimer's account of "what seeing was like in my worst days":

> Describing the whole world as moving, or seeing double, is meaningless; because with the inner feelings of confusion, lack of equilibrium, nausea, strain and incompetence, a normal person can no more begin to sense it . . . than a congenitally blind person can begin to understand what the color red is. . . . The confusion [was] inside, with mental impressions all disoriented. The way I saw things was something like two still pictures out of register with each other, with this lack of register continually changing, but super-imposed on this was the lack of ability to . . . tell where up and down really were and whether you were going to fall over the next minute or not.[14]

The term "brain dysfunction" assumes an organic origin. Sometimes this can be clearly established. Often it can only be a guess – difficult pregnancies and complicated deliveries may lead to later problems. In other cases there may be no abnormal history and the problems may be ascribed to abnormally slow development, *developmental lag*. Learning problems run in families too, a strong indication that they are organically based. (Dr. Levy notes a frequency of over 80 percent;[15] maybe you can remember reading or spelling difficulties of your own. If so, it should help you not to blame your child, his teacher – or yourself.) His book, *Square Pegs, Round Holes,* gives a good physician's view of MBD, including diagrams of the brain.

developmental lag

HYPERACTIVITY

The commonest of these medical diagnoses is *hyperactivity* (or *hyperkinesis*), "the single most common behavioral disorder seen by the child psychiatrist," according to Dr. Paul Wender of Johns Hopkins Medical School.[16] "Hyper" means "too much" and "kinesis" means "movement," but hyperkinesis is *not* just a wiggly kid. What is called hyperactivity consists of a number of characteristics, no one of which should cause anxiety in itself, but which together signal trouble. The hyperactive child can't sit still, is in constant motion – but more important are his other problems. He's distractible; his attention span is short. Though his intelligence probably tests normal or better, his school performance doesn't show it. He's hard to live with, at home and at school. He demands more than his share of attention, he's impulsive, he's the child who can't wait for what he wants and acts before he thinks. He's usually a boy – in fact the serious disorders of childhood are all more common in boys than girls.

Hyperkinesis is more than perpetual motion.

The hyperactivity which causes so much trouble in elementary school tends to subside in adolescence. The other problems are likely to continue. Here is how one mother describes life with her hyperac-

Bill

tive son. Bill is sixteen now. He was born with difficulty and barely survived his first months. He's physically healthy now, but his doctor thinks his problems began during that hard delivery.

> Bill never knows why people are annoyed with him because he never can realize that he has done anything provocative, so the pattern repeats and repeats. There seems to be some short circuiting that seems effectively to prevent the connection between cause and effect. I have had some small success with infinitesimal matters when using various simple behavior modification approaches which are always explained fully to him. But it is not enough, and it tears me apart to see this basically sweet and generous child undercutting possible successes with people by behavior that they understandably respond to with extreme negativism. It is also a problem that one cannot get the attention of a hyperactive child unless one screams, over and over, and this raises the noise level to a point that most of us find unbearable, yet cannot stop or we lose contact with him. He becomes noisy too (after all, that is the model presented) and stomps and slams around. . . . Nobody so far as I know has done anything on the disruption that a hyperactive child can bring into a family. Aside from this effect, all hyperactive children are different. Yet I bet the families are significantly similar in their reactions. Unless one is saintly, one really can't help it. The failure comes when I am tired, preoccupied, trying to sleep, and he intrudes inescapably. So then I react, and feel guilty as all getout (which is not a bit rational). Yet this is a beautiful loving, bright, often unhappy, bewildered child. It does hurt when his brother says he doesn't like to come home because of Bill.*

Causes?

Dr. Wender belives that hyperactivity "is the result of an *inborn temperamental difference* in the child. How the child is treated and raised *can* affect the severity of his problem but it cannot cause the problem. Certain types of raising may make the problem worse, certain types of raising may make the problem better. No forms of raising can produce HA problems in a child who is not temperamentally predisposed to them."[17] This does not mean that hyperactive children are brain damaged. Some are, but most are not. Such temperamental differences run in families. In time, thinks Dr. Wender, they may be explained by the neurotransmitters of Chapter IV, but we can't say that yet.†

Hyperactivity and learning disabilities are one of the most controversial subjects in child psychiatry, because the symptoms shade so gradually into normal behavior and can be so easily confused with classroom rebelliousness or the results of social deprivation — and because the recommended therapy, thoroughly described by Wender and Levy — is drugs. Most commonly used are d-amphetamine (Dexedrine), methylphenidate (Ritalin), and thioridazine (Mellaril).

Drugs again

* Personal communication, January 13, 1974. Bill's mother is a professional psychologist.

† Dr. Wender's handbook for parents is short but thorough: five chapters, on characteristics, causes, development, treatment, and finding help (*The Hyperactive Child: A Handbook for Parents*. New York: Crown Publishers, 1973).

Amphetamines, of course, are the drugs illegally sold as "speed." Nevertheless, they don't speed up HA and MBD children; they calm them down. If they don't help, other drugs may, the major tranquilizers and antidepressants among them.*

Bill is on medication; it helps him, though it doesn't cure him. Dr. Wender and Dr. Levy agree that most of these children respond well to carefully administered drug therapy and that for some it clears up their problems altogether. There is "absolutely no danger" that they will become addicted.[18] Dr. Leon Eisenberg of Boston Children's Hospital agrees:

> These agents have the unique property of diminishing senseless motor activity and of enhancing attention span with the result of improving learning, all of this at the price of relatively minor side effects. . . .† None of these drugs produces a euphoric effect in the pre-adolescent child and thus there is no subjective experience that leads the patient to seek the drug deliberately.[19]

Nevertheless, many people fear that behavior troublesome to adults is being defined as illness and that powerful drugs are being used to control what another distinguished physician called "the natural exuberance of childhood."[20] Huck Finn always did have trouble fitting in. These opponents of drug therapy see the child's problems as originating not in himself, but in his home, his school, and in the society which puts so high a value on sitting still. The celebrated Bruno Bettelheim says, "There are no hyperactive children behind the Iron Curtain."[21] Carefully documenting their argument, Diane Divoky and Peter Schrag discuss *The Myth of the Hyperactive Child*.[22] They doubt the existence of learning disabilities, MBD, or hyperactivity, and question the validity of the studies which underlie claims of drug effectiveness. They point out that the research of proponents of drug therapy is frequently supported by drug companies, and they present drug therapy as simply another means of behavioral control.

Controversy over definitions,

over causes,

"The hyperkinetic syndrome needs reconsideration,"[23] writes Dr. Lester Grinspoon of Harvard Medical School in 1975. The organic causes of MBD are more often than not unproven. The side effects of amphetamine medication (which include insomnia, decreased appetite, and slowed-down growth) are not always minor, and its effectiveness, he believes, has been exaggerated. He fears that the drugs may

over side effects,

* Some physicians are trying megavitamin therapy; Dr. Wender considers this treatment so far unproven. For a claim of success with a diet free of chemical additives, see Chapter III, p. 106n. In *Can Your Child Read? Is He Hyperactive?* (Jackson, Tenn.: Pedicenter Press, 1975), Dr. William G. Crook documents a relationship between food allergies in children and behavior and learning problems. He recommends that before putting a child on drugs, physicians try a carefully planned elimination diet.

† The side effects include decrease in appetite and a slowing down of growth.

make a child "more attentive and manageable in the short run but in the long run leave him with a sense of failure and worthlessness, by giving him a false sense of well-being that prevents him from developing his own capacities for coping."[24] Dr. Wender sees an opposite danger: that needed medical treatment will be displaced by exclusively psychological therapies. He considers that while changes in environment can make the hyperactive child function better, without medical treatment "his basic problem will remain untouched, and unchanged."[25]

over treatment

Here are all the disagreements of psychiatry in miniature. Are we dealing with a real medical condition? If so, how should we treat it? Should we attempt to change children, parents, schools? Drugs can be toxic, socially as well as individually. So can psychotherapy, rejoins Dr. Eisenberg; it is "not necessarily benign: it can foster dependency, increase self-preoccupation, and induce feelings of futility and hopelessness when used to treat a condition for which it is not appropriate."[26]

Whom to believe?

Doctors disagree, but we can recognize one thing. What may be the treatment of choice in capable, experienced hands becomes dangerous when people use it as an easy solution for hard problems. In 1970 a scandal broke in Omaha, Nebraska; following the suggestions of school personnel, doctors had been prescribing drugs for schoolchildren freely enough that the kids had been swapping pills on the playgrounds. Estimates of children being medicated for hyperactivity ran to 10 percent.[27] (Dr. Wender's estimate of the incidence of the condition is up to 5 percent.) That figure appeared on investigation to be exaggerated, including such drugs as a diabetic child's insulin. Nevertheless, the danger of abuse cannot be shrugged away.

So?

So where does this leave you? In a doctor's office, probably, the best doctor you can find.* Let him know you're aware of the controversies and see what he says. (Ask him, says Dr. Wender, "if he uses medication in the treatment of children. If he is opposed *in principle,* he is not an open-minded student of child psychiatry.")[28] But don't be pressured by nonphysicians. Teachers and school psychologists can sense trouble, but they are not qualified to diagnose your child.† In too many school systems, parents have been told, "Put the child on drugs or we can't keep him in this school."[29] In some states parents have taken this mat-

Be cautious if the school is pressing you.

* Dr. Wender has a chapter on how to find one — including how to feel out a psychiatrist without making him mad. A good pediatrician or children's neurologist may also help you.

† One child, miserable and rebellious in a progressive private school, was labeled "borderline hyperkinetic" by school staff; her "hyperactivity" evaporated, along with her misery and rebellion, in a more traditional setting. (For a different child, a reverse switch might have done the trick.) A school can be wrong for a child, and wrong about a child. For parents who can afford private education, a change of schools may be the best therapy.

ter to court.* *If your child is troublesome at school but not at home,* be wary. And *never* accept the school's opinion without thorough medical and psychological evaluation by professionals *you* have chosen. Those the school recommends are likely to see things their way.

Helping your child at home

You have much more to contribute than a trip to the doctor and a bottle of pills. Children like this benefit from a home where they can be pretty sure what's going to happen next. A child who has difficulty adapting himself to the world around him has even more difficulty when expectations are always changing. Dr. Wender, like many others, stresses (in capitals) the importance of "a FIRM, CONSISTENT, EXPLICIT, PREDICTABLE home environment."[30] His twenty-five pages on this are worth careful study, not only by parents of HA, LD, and MBD children, but by parents whose children suffer from the even graver disabilities that will be described later in this chapter. He discusses the importance of establishing rules (make them clear and make them specific), rewards and punishments (make them predictable and make them specific), how to praise when you can and criticize if you must (specifically), while appreciating the child's feelings and helping him recognize that feelings and actions aren't the same.

in an environment where he knows what to expect

Be specific!

Behavior therapists may help you if FIRMNESS, CONSISTENCY, EXPLICITNESS, PREDICTABILITY aren't your family's natural style; that's their specialty. (Bill's mother wrote, "I guess I can make it about thirty percent of the time, with effort.") Be sure your child's teacher knows what you are doing at home and cooperate as closely with her as you can. For however the controversies over drugs are decided, these children need more than drugs to make real progress. "At least 90% of the treatment of learning-disabled children consists of remedial education, psychological guidance, and parent counseling." Though the doctor must diagnose and perhaps prescribe, "treatment itself doesn't take place in the physician's office. It occurs in the classroom, in the office of the remedial reading teacher, the perceptual training instructor, the speech therapist."[31] And at home.

PSYCHOLOGICAL EVALUATION

And if that's where treatment occurs, and if medical treatment isn't enough, then a medical examination isn't enough either. It is not the

* "Michigan legal services lawyers have asked the state to ban use of psychotropic drugs on school children without certification from the director of the public health department that medical need has been determined by a licensed psychiatrist. . . . Lawyers . . . asked that no school personnel be allowed to recommend that any parent consult a physician concerning a child's behavioral problems without first having provided the child with alternative classroom placement and educational services 'for a reasonable period of time.' School personnel also should not be permitted to initiate contact with a physician at any time." *Behavior Today* (Aug. 5, 1974).

neurologist or the child psychiatrist but the psychologist who is particularly skilled in evaluating the different aspects of a troubled child's psychological functioning. That means tests — first and foremost the famous IQ, which is supposed to measure how a child's intelligence compares with others' of the same age. It generally does this pretty well. It can make mistakes, though, and the mistakes make a lot of difference when it's your own child. No child should be labeled on the basis of the standardized IQ tests given with pencil and paper to a whole classroom, and though school psychologists are trained to give individual IQ tests to normal children, not all are experienced in winning the cooperation of children with special problems or interpreting unusual responses.

IQ tests

A caution: don't rush to get your child tested because of a couple of bad report cards, or this fall's problem of living, or because you're curious. The exact level of their child's IQ is information parents of normally developing children can do without. It's easy to use it wrong and hard to use it right. Knowing his IQ can transform a child who's been doing all right into an instant under- or overachiever — in his parents' or teachers' heads.

But the child whose behavior is seriously disturbed, or who has continued trouble learning, or who responds abnormally to normal situations and stresses, needs a thorough psychological assessment. IQ tests for children have both verbal and nonverbal parts. A child who cannot understand a question like "What do you wear on your feet?" or "Tell how a grapefruit and a pear are alike" may be able to group pictures of fruits together or copy a complex block structure. Assessing what a severely language-handicapped child can do takes very great skill and empathy. There are also tests to help determine the presence of social and emotional problems; others test perception and coordination.* There's a whole chapter in *Something's Wrong with My Child* about evaluations and who gives them (don't forget the audiologist, for ears, and the optometrist, for eyes). You can get the book from the Association for Children with Learning Disabilities, 5225 Grace Street, Pittsburgh, PA 15236, and if there's a question of learning disabilities in your family you need it.† Not only has ACLD books which can help you (ask for their list), but your state branch can guide you to a reliable psychological evaluation service. The ACLD's parents

and others

* Most common, for LD children, are the WISC (Wechsler Intelligence Test for Children), the Bender Visual Motor Gestalt Test, and the ITPA (Illinois Test of Psycholinguistic Abilities). Dr. Levy describes these in *Square Pegs, Round Holes.*

† Partial table of contents: How to Recognize the Learning Disabled Child; Where Can We Go For Help? The Physician; Other Professionals We'll Need; The School; The Child at Home; Adolescence; You're Not Out of the Woods Yet; Learning Disabilities and Juvenile Delinquency; Cause and Effect? Plus a list of university-affiliated facilities for the developmentally disabled, other sources of information, and a reading list.

have been there before you; they'll help you prove out what Dr. Brutten and Dr. Richardson say: "You, his parents, are your child's greatest resource."

AUTISM

Overlap

Diagnoses overlap, never more so than in children. Autism is classified as a psychosis; hyperactivity and learning disability are not. Yet many autistic children are hyperactive, and all have learning disabilities. In fact, older autistic children who are progressing well are hard to distinguish from many children with severe learning disabilities. They may very well be in a learning-disabilities class at school (just as hyperactive and learning-disabled children are often placed in classes for the emotionally disturbed). If an autistic child's IQ is very low, he may be in a class for the retarded. A few autistic children function well enough to be in regular classes.

Autism in early childhood

In infancy and early childhood, however, the autistic child was very different. It is in the very early years that the autistic syndrome is most striking, and it is sometimes detectable even in the early months. Dr. Leo Kanner, who first described the condition in 1943, called it early infantile autism;[32] you may also hear it referred to as childhood autism or Kanner's syndrome.* Some autistic children scream day and night; others are weirdly passive. Some rock for hours; some spin jar lids incessantly; some arrange objects in eerily neat rows that cannot be disturbed. What parents notice most, because it is so devastating in a baby, is the aloofness and self-absorption which give the condition its name. "Autistic" comes from the Greek word "autos," which means "self." The autistic two-year-old looks through people as if they were glass, uses their hands as tools to reach for a cookie or a toy, as if the human beings connected to them didn't exist. He pays no attention to what they say; often he's diagnosed as deaf, until somebody notices he hears the rustle of a candy wrapper a room away. If he speaks at all, it isn't to communicate; he may reel off lists of presidents or parrot radio commercials, yet be unable to call for Mommy or ask for a cookie. And these children are the ones for whom the prognosis is best; many autistic children will never learn to talk at all.†

* Autism, which has been called "the most overwhelmingly severe behavior disturbance of childhood,"[33] is rare; about as common as total deafness – perhaps one in three thousand – much more common than blindness.

† Occasionally a mentally normal child will speak in one situation and not in another; to his grandmother, for instance, but not at school. This is called *elective mutism;* it is generally a response to home or school tensions. The child in Virginia Axline's widely read *Dibs* (Boston: Houghton Mifflin, 1965) was mute in this way – by choice. Emotionally disturbed but not autistic, he was cured by psychoanalytic play therapy.

An autistic toddler's communication handicaps are similar to those of aphasic children but worse. For all his difficulty with language, the aphasic child understands gestures, and can use them to communicate even when he can't talk. The autistic child can't ask for a drink by putting an imaginary cup to his lips and pretending to swallow.[34] Nor does he understand the gestures of others. He can't imitate what other people do any more than what they say. Our "body language" is a mystery to him. Even those autistic children who eventually learn to talk fluently remain handicapped in communication. They "don't know what's going on" in social situations, because "they still have difficulty in recognizing exchanges of meanings between people."[35] It's not that they reject human relationships; the autistic aloofness that was so bewildering in the small child is the first symptom to subside, in good homes and schools. Autistic children do learn to respond to people and enjoy them, though their social relations remain naive and awkward. With help some learn to make their way well enough to hold jobs and function as normal, though somewhat eccentric, people. How well they do depends on treatment, but even more on the severity of the condition, for autism, like most medical conditions, comes in all degrees. Though IQ is particularly hard to measure in autistic children, experts have found no better indicator of adult adjustment than the child's IQ at five or six. And the prognosis for autistic children who have not made some start at talking by then is very discouraging.

And later

We have talked about overlaps with hyperactivity and learning disabilities. The question of IQ suggests another important overlap — with retardation. Autistic children appear retarded in many ways. Like some brain-injured and retarded children, they repeat the same stereotyped behavior over and over; they may rock their cribs until these must be nailed down, bang their heads against walls. The most terrible form of this behavior is self-mutilation, which is characteristic of many retarded and psychotic children in state hospitals, and some, even at home. "One can see children who tear with their teeth large amounts of tissue from their shoulders and arms, who chew off part of their fingers, hit their heads so violently against the wall that they detach their retinas. . . . Many of these children, although they may be only eight or nine years old, have spent most of their lives in restraints, being tied down both by their feet and arms."[36] These are the behaviors which therapists can extinguish rapidly with aversive conditioning (see p. 81), outraging the softhearted but not those who have seen the kind of life these children lead in state hospitals.

Retardation?

Though many children are autistic *and* retarded, there are important differences between the two conditions. Few retarded children show the social isolation or the peculiar speech disorders of autistic children. A mongoloid child may be friendly and communicative, with considerable social savoir faire, yet be quite unable to put together the complex puzzle the autistic child completes as fast as (or faster than) a normal child. For many autistic children, including some who appear severely retarded, have remarkable abilities – what the English psychiatrist Dr. Mildred Creak calls "islets of intelligence." Unlike children with perceptual difficulties, they may be adept with shapes and colors. (They can put that puzzle together blank side up; in fact, they probably don't notice the picture the normal child uses to guide him.) They may have remarkable gifts in mathematics or music, both of which require little comprehension of language. It used to be thought that *all* autistic children must have these abilities; parents were assured that their child was "really very bright," and it was implied, when it wasn't clearly stated, that what was blocking his development was the emotional problems caused by the way they handled him in the first years of life.* Parents were seen as cold and rejecting, "refrigerator parents," or as immature, smothering mothers whose overprotection created a "symbiotic psychosis"† in their babies. While some specialists still hold to a psychogenic etiology,[37] most psychiatrists who work with autistic children and their families now believe autistic symptoms are physically caused – though of course what parents do can make them worse (or better). Diseases like rubella (German measles) in the mother[38] or phenylketonuria in the baby can cause them;‡ it is likely that there are many other possible ways a baby's brain can be affected so that he becomes autistic. Understimulation, or rejection, or smothering attention, however, probably aren't among them. In 1974 testimony before a committee of the House of Representatives, Dr. Peter Tanguay of the U.C.L.A. Department of Psychiatry put it as strongly as he could:

"Islets of intelligence"

Refrigerator parents?

Biological causes

* See J. Louise Despert, *The Emotionally Disturbed Child: An Inquiry into Family Patterns* (New York: Doubleday Anchor Books, 1965); Bruno Bettelheim, *The Empty Fortress: Infantile Autism and the Birth of the Self* (New York: Free Press, 1967); Jules Henry, *Pathways to Madness* (New York: Random House, 1972); and many others. An up-to-date restatement of this point of view is to be found in *Clinical Studies in Childhood Psychoses,* S. A. Szurek and I. N. Berlin, eds. (New York: Brunner/Mazel, 1973).

† Tarlton Morrow and Earl Loomis describe "Symbiotic Aspects of a Seven-Year-Old Psychotic" in Gerald Caplan, ed., *Emotional Problems of Early Childhood* (New York: Basic Books, 1955). Billy was remembered by his parents as "not demanding" as a baby; "one may assume that this recollection reflects the likelihood that his demands were not appropriately met. By excessive anticipation of his needs, the parents denied him the right to demand." The authors speak of a "lack of differentiation of the self, the fusion of the mother-child unit," as characteristic of symbiotic psychosis.

‡ "Several weeks ago I saw a preschool aged girl with all the classical signs of childhood autism; social aloofness, developmental retardation, stereotypic behavior, emotional lability, and disturbed language functioning. Metabolic evaluation, however, revealed that this youngster was suffering from an entity for which practically every child in the United States is screened during the first week of life, phenylketonuria."[39]

> Ten years ago there may still have been room for doubt, but it is inconceivable that anyone who is thoroughly familiar with the literature on autism (literature which has appeared largely in the past five or six years) could conclude other than that autism is primarily an organic syndrome. I know of almost no expert in the field of autism today who thinks otherwise.[40]

Old theories take time to fade away, and it is quite possible that you may come across a professional who still adheres to a psychogenic explanation of autism. If he runs an unusually good program, or if it's the only game in town, you may decide to put up with the theory. But considering the probable emotional cost to you, you might be better off going to another city to consult with a professional who will help you piece together a program out of other local facilities and your own personal resources.

There is no cure for autism so far. Great claims have been made for the effectiveness of psychoanalytic milieu therapy,* but as in other psychoses — not to mention hyperactivity, learning disabilities, brain injury, or retardation — psychoanalytic therapy has not demonstrated itself to be particularly effective in autism,[41] though psychotherapy may help an older child who's progressed so well he knows he's different.

Parents as therapists

It is now established that parents can become effective therapists for their autistic children. (See Chapter VIII, p. 199.)

Dr. Cohen sums up the needs of the autistic child as he grows:

> Children with autism require professional care for many years, and, for most, throughout their lives. Such care requires the collaboration of a variety of specialists, including educators, speech therapists, psychologists, psychiatrists, neurologists, pediatricians, and experts in vocational rehabilitation. . . . For children during the preschool years, parental guidance and day programs emphasizing behavior modification may be required; during the schoolage years, more intensive special education is often required, and the use of medication, speech therapy, and psychotherapy may be important; during the adolescent years, vocational training must play a major role in the child's life.[42]†

* Bruno Bettelheim, *The Empty Fortress*. See, however, Szurek and Berlin, eds., *op. cit.*, pp. 348–371, for a report of far less encouraging outcomes to a similar treatment approach. For an impressive account of effective treatment combining psychoanalytic and behavioral approaches, see Uwe Stuecher, *Tommy: A Treatment Study of an Autistic Child* (Arlington, Va.: Council for Exceptional Children, n.d.).

† Far more controversial are megavitamin therapy (see Chapter IV, pp. 106–109) and the physical therapy techniques developed by Glenn Doman and Carl Delacato at the Institute for Human Potential in Philadelphia. For many years, though working with victims of brain injury and stroke, Doman and Delacato did not accept psychotic children for treatment. Recently they have come to consider autism as a result of brain injury. The Doman-Delacato techniques are designed to build brain functions as well as skills. Their success is a matter of dispute. Parents are the therapists, and treatment is a full-time job, for them and the child. Interested readers will find an account of the treatment of an autistic child in David Melton's

Like learning disabilities and hyperactivity (and most other biologically caused conditions), autism afflicts many more boys than girls. The best introduction is Dr. Lorna Wing's *Autistic Children: A Guide for Parents and Professionals,* a readable and authoritative survey full of the sense of real children. Parents should also contact the National Society for Autistic Children, 169 Tampa Avenue, Albany, NY 12208. (See Chapter XIV.) Among other services, they operate a bookstore from which you can order Dr. Wing's book and many other helpful publications.

OTHER PSYCHOSES

Childhood schizophrenia

If you remember how hard it is to agree on what "schizophrenia" means in adults, you won't expect it to be any easier in children. Some professionals still use the words *childhood schizophrenia* instead of "autism." (Now and then you may hear the term *atypical development.*) Most experts, however, follow Dr. Kanner in distinguishing autism from childhood schizophrenia, pointing out that autistic children do not hallucinate or have active fantasy lives, are not subject to delusions, and that their abnormalities of language are different from the schizophrenic's. Schizophrenic children too, as Dr. Kanner noted in his first descriptions, tend to have a more than average number of mentally ill relatives; the families of autistic children contain, if anything, less mental illness than average.

= autism?

When a professional uses the term *childhood schizophrenia,* try to find out whether he's using it to describe symptoms that others would call autistic. For there *are* children whose fears and fantasies are more like those of adult schizophrenia. Joey, the "mechanical boy" described by Bruno Bettelheim, considered himself a machine and devoted all his energies to maintaining an elaborate arrangement of wires and plugs which he believed kept him alive.* There is disagreement about whether childhood schizophrenia is a form of the adult illness or a different disorder altogether, and of course there are the usual disagree-

Or something more like schizophrenia?

When Children Need Help (New York: Crowell, 1972); Carl Delacato describes the institute's current thinking in *The Ultimate Stranger: The Autistic Child* (New York: Doubleday and Co., Inc., 1974). Peggy Napear describes the total dedication of a family to treatment of a brain-injured (not autistic) child in *Brain Child: A Mother's Diary* (New York: Harper and Row, 1974). Parents of autistic children will note many similarities.

---

* Bettelheim describes Joey's recovery under psychoanalytic milieu therapy in *The Empty Fortress;* M. A. Sèchehaye describes the successful analytic treatment of a schizophrenic young girl in *Symbolic Realization* (New York: International Universities Press, 1951). In general, however, those who have attempted the psychoanalytic psychotherapy of schizophrenic children have found the results discouraging.

ments on how to treat it. Childhood schizophrenics do not seem necessarily to grow up into adult schizophrenics, though they seldom become entirely normal.

Schizophrenia in adolescence

It is often in adolescence that the first insidious signs of adult schizophrenia are noticed. This is what it feels like to families:

> Families are emotionally involved, the victim often being a teenage son or daughter. At one level of this involvement there is nothing to be said about schizophrenia except that it is an obscenity, and that to talk of "living" with it, of having to watch someone one loves fragment, and to know that, although the pieces may never be put together in this world, nonetheless one must devise means for putting a bright, optimistic, forward-looking face on things is also an obscenity.
>
> The impact of schizophrenia on the most ordinary family can be as shattering as that of a natural cataclysm, and . . . many extreme reactions are probably normal and even to be expected. In the schizophrenias of slow onset particularly, families may be living with schizophrenia and making innumerable adaptations to it — good or bad, but all modifying any ordinary family pattern — before they or anybody else knows that they are, in fact, living with schizophrenia. It is difficult to imagine what this means. Suppose that one of your adolescent children begins to behave oddly. At first he just moons about. But many adolescents moon about. He or she becomes moody, bad tempered, slovenly, "difficult." But many adolescents daydream and are moody or difficult.
>
> To you, as a sensible parent, such behavior is well within the limits of the normal growing-up process and no attention is paid to it. He or she will "grow out of it," you say. But time goes on and he or she does not grow out of it. A crisis occurs when some wild display of aggression, truancy, or merely bizarre behavior, drives you to seek expert help.
>
> Blessed are you if, at this point, you get a firm diagnosis: twice blessed (one is almost tempted to say) if there is an acute and unmistakable schizophrenic episode and rapid hospitalization.[43]

For then, at least, you can know what you must deal with.

Recent years have seen an increasing number of adolescents hospitalized for acute schizophrenic reactions, often brought on or complicated by psychedelic drugs. The treatment of these adolescents is not essentially different from that given adults (see p. 90), and the prospects of recovery are good.

Depression?

Psychiatrists are doubtful that mania occurs in children, but some are beginning to feel that depression in children is too seldom recognized. Depression in children and adolescents usually grows out of a difficult situation, can be classed as neurotic, and is treated by relatively brief psychotherapy. Dr. Frank Ayd of Baltimore, however, believes that endogenous depressions, the kind that come from physical change within, occur in adolescents more often than is realized. Because physicians are inclined to view depression as an illness of adults, he feels adolescents with depression are often misleadingly tagged as suffering from anxiety neurosis, psychosomatic or psychophysiologic disorder, or behavior and adjustment reaction. "As a result, the endogenously depressed adolescent's suffering and disability are prolonged and the risk of suicide escalates."[44] There is, however, no general agreement on affective disorders in children.

TREATMENTS

Children and therapy

Children undergo the same range of therapies as adults, from psychoanalysis and its derivatives to behavior therapy to drugs and other somatic treatments.* These have already been described in Chapter IV. Yet no kind of therapy can be just the same for a child as for an adult; even chemicals work differently with children. So there's more to be said here too.

Play therapy

Play and learning are the activities through which a child develops, and play and teaching are the major avenues to the treatment of children. Of course play and learning and teaching can't be separated, since children learn through playing. Still, encouraging a child to express what's troubling him through play is different from teaching him skills for living, and the main approaches to the therapy of children tend to emphasize one of these or the other.

Psychoanalytic techniques

The therapists who developed psychoanalytic therapies for children had to modify the talking treatment. They developed ways of helping a child express unconscious conflicts through play. The way children play with clay, paints, water, blocks, cars, a dollhouse complete with doll parents, grandparents, brother and sister and baby, can reveal a great deal to a sensitive observer. In psychoanalytic play therapy, the child's play, ideally, is spontaneous and expressive, the equivalent of the adult's free association. The therapist, almost totally permissive, guides as little as he can, though he sets a few essential limits. When he believes he understands what is going on, he will make his interpretations, in terms that he hopes to make understandable to the child. Play therapy leads back to the talking treatment. It expects, not to teach new behaviors directly, but to influence indirectly, as psychodynamic psychotherapy does with adults. As with adults, it assumes at least normal intelligence. It's not much use for a child with a serious language disability, or for autistic children, one of whose problems is that they *cannot* play spontaneously.[45] There are a great many play techniques, ranging from nondirective, permissive therapy to carefully thought-out games with specific learning goals.†

Other methods

* ECT is rarely given to children; psychosurgery in children is rarer still.

† Virginia Axline's *Dibs: In Search of Self* (Boston: Houghton Mifflin, 1965) gives a very readable account of nondirective play therapy. Charles Schafer has edited a book of basic readings, *Therapeutic Use of Children's Play* (New York: Jason Aronson, 1974), which surveys all current methods, from analytic to behavioral approaches.

Psycho-education is crucial —

Whether or not it is combined with psychotherapy, appropriate education is crucial to helping severely troubled children. For mentally ill adults, education in school is not ordinarily a part of treatment. But school is a major part of a child's life. If you are responsible for a disturbed or mentally ill child who is in school, you should be in close contact with his teacher,* the school psychologist, the guidance counselor, perhaps the language therapist. If he's not in school, he ought to be. Good education — whether it is education in regular classrooms under a skilled and understanding teacher, or the kind of education called "special" because it is designed to compensate for handicaps — may make all the difference to the troubled child.†

professional

and non-professional,

And don't forget, either, those nonprofessionals concerned with children — all the people who coach teams, lead Scout troops, work at Boys' and Girls' Clubs and Y's, lead youth groups, and work and play with children in the parks, the streets, the vacant lots where they live and learn. It's fortunate that there are so many people besides mental health professionals who are concerned with children and adolescents, for otherwise many troubled young people would get no help at all. Forty-five percent of our population consists of children and adolescents,[46] but fewer than 10 percent of psychiatrists claim to be specialists in the treatment of children's psychological problems.[47] Though a psychiatrist may treat children without calling himself a child psychiatrist, those psychiatrists who do in fact tend to work mainly with adolescents. In 1970, fewer than 15 percent of psychiatrists treated children under twelve.[48] In community mental health centers too, adolescents are better served than children. Children under four have scarcely been served at all. A survey made in 1970 by the Joint

especially

because children are scandalously underserved.

* Among the "host of 'invisible' psychotherapists" described by William Schofield in *Psychotherapy: The Purchase of Friendship* (Englewood Cliffs, N.J.: Prentice Hall, 1960) the teacher is prominent: "The teacher occupies a strategic position as a potential source of emotional understanding, acceptance, and counsel for those younger members of our society who become frustrated, fearful, foolish, or frenetic. For many persons, it is the opportunity to function in this role which serves as a major attraction to a teaching career. It would be difficult to find a school faculty of any size in which there are not one or more teachers who have earned the respect and gratitude of students and staff alike for their special capacity and willingness to 'counsel,' to 'advise,' to give acceptance and understanding. These teachers would blush (or blanch?) to hear themselves described as psychotherapists. But a careful analysis of their conversations with students might very well reveal that they were neither different in form from or less effective than those of experts" (p. 139).

† A study by Victor Winston showed that while parents of autistic children typically recognized that special education was the preferred method of treatment for their children, this was not reflected in their choice of a professional on whose advice they would rely. Mr. Winston found that more than 70 percent of parents relied on the advice of physicians — either child psychiatrists, pediatricians, or neurologists. Less than 2 percent relied upon the advice of the specialist in special education, the teacher. Presented to the 48th Annual Meeting of the American Orthopsychiatric Association; reported in the *Newsletter* of the National Society for Autistic Children, 3 (Dec. 1971).

Information Service of the American Psychiatric Association and the National Association for Mental Health showed that over half the federally funded community mental health centers surveyed had no child psychiatrist, pediatrician, or neurologist on their staffs.[49]

Not that social workers and psychologists – like teachers – aren't important, and very important. But child psychiatrist Eveoleen Rexford warns of the seriousness of "turning away from the medical model." If we accept the idea of mental illness – in children or adults – we cannot do without doctors. Important as a child's environment, home and school are to his mental and emotional functioning, Dr. Rexford reminds us that "physical and mental health are difficult to separate out in a child," and "developmental and neurological dysfunctions make up a significant number of the problems that bring children to a mental health center."[50] Specialists are needed to assess developmental and neurological dysfunctions, things that just aren't working right as the child grows. It is just such developmental and neurological dysfunctions that can permanently cripple a child if left untended, and require the earliest and the most determined intervention on the part of specialists, educators, and family.

Don't give up on the medical model

Yet, as is generally true in the American mental health establishment, the less there is wrong with a child the easier it is to find him help. A South Carolina children's center especially singled out for praise by the Joint Information Service gives the picture for the early seventies. It took "mild and moderately disturbed only." The "severely disturbed" or psychotic, and "those with less-than-average intelligence or with moderate or severe brain damage were ineligible,"[51] and since the state hospital, usually the last resort in this region, would not accept such children either, the answer to parents seeking help for these sickest of children – in an unusually well served community – was a simple "No."*

unless

it gives up on you.

In 1975, Congress passed new legislation mandating federally funded mental health centers to provide specialized services for children. We'll hope that in your area the paragraphs you've just read are now out of date.

With seriously ill children even more than with adults, families all over the United States are on their own to put together a therapeutic milieu as best they can. So it's back to Chapter VI. Check every community institution that deals with children. Is there a speech and hearing clinic† or nursery school for the handicapped? Is there a col-

Getting it together on your own.

* How it feels to be told this — and then to have marriage counseling recommended for your problems — is bitterly described in Josh Greenfeld's *A Child Called Noah* (New York: Holt, Rinehart and Winston, 1972).

† The American Speech and Hearing Association 1975 *Guide to Clinical Services* lists association members in full-time private practice and all facilities that provide accredited speech and hearing services. Available for $5 from the American Speech and Hearing Association, 9030 Old Georgetown Road, Washington, DC 20014.

lege or university with a special education department which treats certain children as a part of its training? If not, maybe there's a psychologist or social worker or speech therapist nearby who knows something about children like yours or is interested in learning. Maybe there's a gifted teacher who's retired or at home and looking for part-time work. Maybe there's a specialist who can't treat your child but will help advise and coordinate what other people are doing.

More likely, however, you'll have to travel if you want an experienced consultant, and keep in touch by phone. Josh Greenfeld traveled across the country to learn from psychologist Ivar Lovaas how he could help his son Noah;[52] Professor Ogden Lindsley of the University of Kansas conducts phone sessions with groups of parents of seriously disturbed children; Lois Blackwell's Judevine Center in St. Louis admits parents and children together for training. There are other such programs, more every year. Yet there are still few parents of mentally ill children who are in reach of a center where they can be taught the psychoeducational techniques which their children need to help them learn and grow.*

A directory

Of immense assistance to parents seeking help is the 448-page directory of *U.S. Facilities and Programs for Children with Severe Mental Illnesses,* compiled for NIMH by the National Society for Autistic Children and published in 1974.† School and hospital programs, day and residential, are described and listed by state. Each listing specifies whether the program offers training to parents; an astonishing number do.

If you can find no services near home labeled "for seriously disturbed children," if you can't disrupt your family by traveling long distances, or can't afford it, you should be outraged — but you need not give up. You still have the family and the home, those major factors in a child's growth. And in more and more places you've got the local school. Many severely disturbed children have made good progress with no more.‡ Lucky as you'll be to get a skilled psychiatrist on your

* Under the 1973 Massachusetts special education law, Chapter 766, the local school evaluation team (which includes parents) may recommend parent training as part of the child's school program.

† DHEW Publication No. (ADM) 74–47; available from Supt. of Documents, U.S. Government Printing Office, Washington, DC, or (more quickly) from the National Society for Autistic Children, 169 Tampa Avenue, Albany, NY 12208. Since new programs are constantly appearing, however, check your area with NSAC's Ruth Sullivan, Director of NSAC Information and Referral Service, 306 31st St., Huntington, WV 25702. Tel. (304) 697–2638.

‡ Accounts of autistic children who made good progress in their homes with little or no assistance from professionals are James Copeland's *For the Love of Ann* (New York: Ballantine Books, 1974) and C. C. Park's *The Siege: The First Eight Years of an Autistic Child* (Boston: Atlantic–Little, Brown, 1973). Remarkable home therapy with children with severe learning disabilities and emotional disturbance, supervised by professionals, is described in two books by mothers that are virtually handbooks

team, psychiatry as yet knows so little about the causes and cure of severe disorders of childhood that for years it's offered little beyond sympathy – and not always that. A child who's surrounded by a loving family willing to act steadfastly to further his development, who can be placed early in one of the therapeutic nursery schools which many states now are beginning to offer for the retarded and the handicapped, and who can move into a good school program, public or private, may still progress without any professional therapy, whether psychological or medical. For the child, good education *is* therapy, as Carl Fenichel, founder of the League School, maintains, and good teachers *are* therapists.[53] Consequently there is much therapy that escapes professional notice, and the statistics on mental health services for children aren't as horrifying as they look. Not quite.

Of course there ought to be more child psychiatrists and psychologists and neurologists, especially those experienced in the diagnosis and treatment of severe conditions. They ought to be more thinly spread. There ought to be more knowledgeable pediatricians – again and again we hear parents tell of the doctor who told them not to worry when the child didn't talk, or rocked in his crib and spun metal objects hour after hour, because "he'll outgrow it." The statistics on the lack of mental health services for children are scandalous. They should arouse indignation, but not the desperation that comes if you assume that if your child can't be treated by a certified mental health professional he will get *no* help. Medical advances may be around the corner; it may in time be possible to understand the causes of these bewildering and heartbreaking conditions, and perhaps to treat them by medical means specific to the condition. In case your child's disorder can already be so treated, it is essential to get as careful a psychiatric and neurological examination, and as reliable a medical diagnosis, as can be had. But it may be just as important to get an *educational* diagnosis from an experienced educational psychologist, perhaps a language specialist. Organizations like the Association for Children with Learning Disabilities and the National Society for Autistic Children will try to help in locating psychoeducational specialists in your area.

Use your anger: never despair.

When the examinations are done – remember that the business of

of educational techniques: Barbara Trace and Shulamith Kastein, *The Birth of Language* (Springfield, Ill.: Charles C. Thomas, 1966) and Jane Hart and Beverley Jones, *Where's Hannah? A Handbook for Children with Learning Disorders* (New York: Hart Publishing Co., 1968). Another excellent guide is Rosalind Oppenheim's *Effective Teaching Methods for Autistic Children* (Springfield, Ill.: Charles C. Thomas, 1974); Mrs. Oppenheim's techniques were developed first with her own son, and later in the school she founded and directs. In *Benhaven's Way* (New Haven, Conn.: Benhaven School, 1972), Amy Lettick, another educator who began as a parent, describes the psychoeducational program of the school she founded for older autistic children.

childhood is learning, and see what can be accomplished by education. And even if your child doesn't speak, doesn't feed himself — however long the list of things he doesn't do — let your local school administration know early that he's there and will soon be old enough for school, so they can be thinking about it. Invisible children don't get services.

THE RIGHT TO EDUCATION AND OTHER LEGAL RIGHTS OF CHILDREN

Getting educational services for your child, in your district, may not be easy. In some places parents have fought your battles for you, and there already exists a school program that can help your child grow and learn.* In others laws guaranteeing appropriate education are already on the books, but the programs don't yet exist. Getting them means establishing the need and pushing for them community by community. In other places there are no laws at all. But there are schools and teachers everywhere, and every one of us pays taxes to support them. Until recently, more often than not, it has been possible for school administrators to tell us that our children are too handicapped — whether emotionally, or physically, or mentally, or in combination — for their schools to teach. If they say that to you — and it's still very likely they may — you can quote Dr. Frank Hewett, Professor of Education and Psychiatry at the University of California at Los Angeles. Tell them that "every child is ready to learn *something*," and that it's the school's business to find out what and how. But since 1972, you have had more than words behind you. You have had law.

NO CHILD IS INEDUCABLE!

In 1971 a federal court for the first time explicitly recognized the right of handicapped children to equal access to educational opportunity, in *PARC* v. *Commonwealth of Pennsylvania.* You might as well know the legal citation, for you may need it. PARC stands for Pennsylvania Association for Retarded Children, and you can learn something from that. When improvement in educational or mental health services is achieved for handicapped children, there's usually a citizens' organization behind it, and that organization is usually powered by those most concerned, those children's parents. Mental health professionals will do what they can, but they can't match the dedication of parents,† to whom the development of their child is not a job but a life. Besides, as Dr. Schopler said when good organization and steady

Parent power

* Eleanor Craig gives a sensitive and touching account of therapeutic teaching of seriously disturbed children in a public-school special class in *P.S. Your Not Listening* (New York: Richard Baron, Inc., 1972).

† Except now and then, when they *are* parents, like Dr. Bernard Rimland, who founded the National Association for Autistic Children.

parent pressure induced the North Carolina legislature to extend his program to the public schools of the whole state, "Parents have more clout." There are a lot more parents than M.D.'s, Ph.D.'s, and M.S.W.'s; and parents, together or separately, are the people who are responsible for the successful suits which established a right to education.

PARC *v.* Pennsylvania

The landmark case of *PARC* v. *Pennsylvania* challenged the whole weight of law and tradition that denied education to children whom school administrators deemed "ineducable" or "unable to profit from school," or too old, or too young for educational programs. The testimony, from a galaxy of nationally known specialists, was so impressive that the state didn't fight it; in the consent decree, Pennsylvania made history by acknowledging its responsibility to provide free public education and training to *all* children. (Were you thinking, "But my child is emotionally disturbed, not retarded?" Think again.) *PARC* v. *Pennsylvania* was followed the next year by *Mills* v. *Board of Education of the District of Columbia,* a "class action suit" brought in behalf of the whole class of children excluded from publicly supported education. Basing its decision not on local statutes but squarely on the due process and equal protection sections of the United States Constitution, the court ordered, in words you may find handy, that "the District of Columbia shall provide to each child of school age a free and suitable publicly-supported education regardless of the degree of the child's mental or emotional disability or impairment." They can't plead money either: "Furthermore, defendants shall not exclude any child resident in the District of Columbia from such publicly supported education on the basis of a claim of insufficient resources."[54]

Mills *v.* Board of Education

These cases are having their effect, state by state. By 1975, thirty-seven states recognized a legal responsibility to educate every child. But it's a long way from the courtroom and the capitol to your public school classroom. How to convert law into reality? The United States Bureau of Education for the Handicapped suggests you start by asking yourself some questions:

From law to reality;

Does your state law guarantee education for all? Does your school system exclude children who are considered "ineducable," or whose IQ's are below a certain number, either by law or in practice? (Don't think that this concerns only the families of the retarded—many mentally ill children have measured IQ's as low as any retarded child; often they cannot be tested at all.) Are children with behavior problems excluded? Are children placed on waiting lists because the classrooms they require are already filled or the programs without funds? Are there appropriate programs not only for young children, but in junior and senior high schools as well? Do you know how to request a

survey your situation.

Due process under Mills: *notice of placement right to a hearing with a lawyer right to relevant information*

diagnosis by the school if you suspect your child has a disability? Do you know who will test your child, and will you be fully informed of the results? (*Mills* detailed your rights under due process: right to advance notice of placement and the reasons for it; right to a hearing by an independent hearing officer or other advocate; right to inspect your child's records so you know where he and you are at. In the Family Educational Rights and Privacy Act of 1974, Congress gave parents of children in schools receiving any federal support the right to inspect, challenge, and protect the privacy of all official school records concerning their children.) * If no program is provided in your community, will your child be placed in a suitable program elsewhere in your region, and will transportation be provided? Will tuition aid be given if private schooling is necessary, and if so, will it be adequate?†

Your local school principal can answer many of these questions. If you can't find out from him what you need to know, write your State Director of Special Education (or Bureau for the Handicapped) at your state Department of Education. What will happen then depends on the answers, your resources, your persistence, and your strength. If you're lucky, your child may go right into a program. If there are no programs, or no suitable ones, combined action with other parents might be your next step.‡

Consulting a lawyer

If the worse comes to the worst and your child is excluded (or put in a program you think you can show to be unsuitable), you can con-

* Massachusetts law now guarantees this right to the *child,* when he is over 18. This right, however, is a double-edged sword. Knowing that his words may be read by those whom they intimately concern, a consultant is likely to be guarded, and information in the record may be limited to the results of medical and psychological testing, and school reports.

† The publication from whose Spring 1974 issue these questions are taken may be a major resource for you. *Closer Look: National Special Education Information Center* is put out by the Bureau of Education for the Handicapped, Office of Education, U.S. Department of Health, Education and Welfare. It's an information service for parents of children with emotional, physical, and mental handicaps, giving instructions on how to proceed when searching for services, names of local organizations, agencies, schools, and individuals who may be able to help, and state listings of organizations concerned with children with special needs. The publication — and the information – is free on request from SEIC, Box 1492, Washington, DC 20013, and don't say the government never did anything for you. The center will send you their *Guide to State Laws for Education of Handicapped Children;* all states have them, but some are not due to be implemented until 1977. Some forty states allow the use of public money to educate handicapped children in private schools if no public programs are available. *Insight,* Council for Exceptional Children, March 1973.

‡ Battle plans: Parent Dorothy Miller's *How to Obtain Educational Services for Your Child in the Public School System* (from the National Society for Autistic Children) and Ellen Lurie's *How to Change the Schools: A Parents' Action Handbook on How to Fight the System* (from the Association for Children with Learning Disabilities).

sult a lawyer. Not just any lawyer, though. Before you choose him, make sure he's up on this fast-evolving area of law; the Council for Exceptional Children has several useful publications, among them *Legal Change for the Handicapped through Litigation* and *A Continuing Summary of Pending and Completed Litigation Regarding the Education of Handicapped Children.** NAMH or one of the parents' organizations may be able to help you locate a knowledgeable lawyer. For years, parents had to beg for what they got. The road still isn't easy — but now you are in a position to demand.

SPECIAL TERMS FOR CHILDREN'S PROBLEMS

The words we use:

You may have noticed that somewhere along the way we switched adjectives — from "mentally ill" to "handicapped" and "disabled." Mental illness is certainly a handicap, and continuing emotional disturbance is certainly disabling. The fact that the mentally ill share these adjectives with the deaf and blind, the crippled and retarded, makes little difference when what is at issue is the right of all handicapped children to education (or the government's obligation to disabled adults). The schools use another set of terms in working out their special services, and since many mentally ill (or handicapped, or disabled) children end up in one special class or another, you need to get them straight.

Government terms

Special education terms

retarded, educable, trainable

Parents of the retarded were a generation ahead of parents of the emotionally disturbed in organizing services, and almost all school systems now offer classes for retarded children. For educational purposes, retarded children are not classified by medical diagnosis, but as *educable* and *trainable.*† To be classified educable, a child's IQ must be between 50 and 70 to 80 (it varies among school systems). Most school systems have educable classes; trainable classes are harder to find.‡ *Emotionally disturbed* is a term educational administrators have

Emotionally disturbed —

* Write the Governmental Relations Unit, CEC, 1920 Association Drive, Reston, VA 22091. They also publish *State Law and Education of Handicapped Children: Issues and Recommendations,* which includes a draft of a model law, in case your state doesn't have one.

† Children, the normal ones, have their own terms — the special class children are "retards" or "mentals."

‡ Large school systems have more of everything, including handicapped kids and special classes, but they may lack the flexibility of the good small school. One seven-year-old whom a fine private school program had brought to the point of recognizing letters and a few words, when "graduated" to a large city special education program was put in a class where no reading would be taught — because he was mongoloid, and by the rules of that school system mongoloid children were automatically classified "trainable" and not "educable"!

mild, moderate, severe

picked up from mental health people. Its main recommendation is its vagueness — by the time you divide it three ways, into "mild," "moderate," and "severe" disturbance, you have the whole range of trouble, from passing discomfort ("transient situational neurosis") to the continuing disability of autism and childhood schizophrenia — and without having used any of those frightening medical terms. Educators are right to leave it vague; precise diagnoses don't help in teaching (though precise description of the child's handicap does). And if diagnoses get between the child and the teacher — and they can — they can even hinder. The latest in educational classification, "learning disabilities," is similarly broad. There's nothing like seeing a class of real mentally or emotionally handicapped children to make you take classifications with a grain of salt. These kids are Elly and Noah and Hannah and Don, not a collection of walking categories. They can be emotionally disturbed and intellectually normal, they are often emotionally disturbed and learning-disabled, they are sometimes emotionally disturbed and retarded. Depending on the child, the circumstances, the teacher, they may manage as well under one category as another. The important thing is that the categories be used to serve children, not to exclude them from services. Many a parent who once welcomed a diagnosis of "emotionally disturbed" rather than "retarded" has lived to regret it when he found that label barring his child from the only existing school program. Some states — Texas and Massachusetts among them — are discarding labeling in special education altogether; Massachusetts's new law speaks of "children with special needs." Perhaps the best term is "exceptional"; it's broad enough to cover every kind of handicap — as well as the child who's exceptionally bright! It's certainly the nicest.*

Mixing categories

The "exceptional child"

School is no cure-all.

Have we made it sound as if getting your child in school will be a panacea? *There is no panacea.* With a seriously disturbed child almost anything is better than nothing, if only because it gives you and yours a respite. Yet your child needs not just a place to go, but a suitable program.

How suitable? You can't tell by the educational label. If the teacher is resourceful and flexible and the class is small, a mentally ill child may progress in a class for the retarded. If she isn't, he may spend his days sifting marbles into a coffee can.

Schools are much more willing to undertake work with a difficult child if they have the backup of mental health professionals. Consulta-

* The magazine *The Exceptional Parent* was started in 1970, under a board of well-known professionals, to provide practical guidance to parents of exceptional children, to recognize their contributions to their children's progress, and to support them in their efforts. Subscribe: you'll find $10 was never better spent. (Address: Psy-Ed Corporation, 264 Beacon Street, Boston, MA 02116.)

tion with schools is one of the essential services of the comprehensive community mental health center (see Chapter VI). Private practitioners are less used to consulting with schools, but your child's therapist, or the specialist who has evaluated his functioning, should be willing to consult with your child's teacher if you pay for the consultation.

BEING YOUR CHILD'S OMBUDSMAN — AT SCHOOL AND ELSEWHERE

Consultation

Don't assume that consultation will take place automatically — that therapist, clinic, school, and maybe even the probation officer will simply do what we think is their job and get together. If it *doesn't* happen automatically, you may have to make it happen.

Written reports?

That's why new laws guarantee your access to your child's school records. You provide the continuity between your child's past, present, and future. As an ombudsman, you need to know as much as you can about the problem if the search for the solution is your responsibility. But since social workers change jobs and psychiatrists relocate, and because the transmission of important information may depend on your memory of what somebody's told you, many parents would go further, and argue that parents have a right to a full, frank, written report from *any* professional they have consulted.*

Don't assume communication.

An ombudsman is friendly and expects the best; he doesn't get mad unless he must. So assume what's usually true, that all these people are genuinely concerned with children and would be in some other line of work if they weren't. But be realistic too. Assume goodwill, but don't assume that your child's teacher, the school principal, and the school psychologist discuss your child's problems over lunch. Yet everybody may be perfectly ready for a powwow if you take the initiative.

A suitable program?

What will the emotionally disturbed child learn in school? What he needs, we hope — from how to tie his shoes to calculus. "Every child is ready to learn something." One child is ready to learn to control his tantrums, another is ready to learn to look at the teacher, another is ready to complete a simple task with another child. One school teaches children how to listen to a secret and whisper it in another child's ear; that's normal social behavior for a six-year-old, but a suitable item on the curriculum of an autistic child who doesn't know what a secret is. There are no skills too basic to be taught in school. Representative

* If you want to do battle, see Beatrice Munsey's "Parents' Right to Read," *The Exceptional Parent* (May/June 1973), and Donald Anderson, "Parents' Right to Read, Continued" (May/June 1974). Mrs. Munsey is responsible for her daughter Carolyn, whose various records show diagnoses of deafness, retardation, autism, aphasia, and learning disability; Dr. Anderson's son has spina bifida.

Clair Burgener of California gives a perspective you might want to cite to a balky school board:

Important learning

> I remember an interesting debate I had with a fellow senator of mine in California. We were debating special education classes, and he said, "Oh, you spend all this money on these kids and you work with them two years and all they learn is how to go to the toilet." He is a good man. He is not evil. He just did not know. I said, "Senator, if I had to choose to learn one of two skills in my life, and one was reading and one was toilet training, I would take toilet training. That is very, very important learning."[55]

Private education

We've emphasized the right to public education because most of us haven't got the money for anything else. But good private education, if you can afford it, may make a great difference. Some private schools specialize in the education of the mentally and emotionally deviant; others don't, but because they're small and flexible will sometimes make room for a deviant child, especially if you're willing to push a bit, pledge your cooperation, and can back up your application with recommendations from responsible professionals. A letter from a respected psychiatrist may change a school director's idea of what's possible when he hesitates because "we've never taken a child like this before." Some children will flourish in the protected atmosphere of a good private school, especially when the alternative is a tough public school where vulnerable children are tormented in unsupervised buses and hallways. And some private schools lead the nation in developing educational techniques for special children. If you're near one of these, visit it, and if it looks right, investigate every possibility, including state tuition grants, of getting your child into it.

Day schools

More and more of the best special schools are day schools, mostly in large cities, and mostly fairly new. If there's one near you, you're very, very lucky. As many parents can testify, the weight of professional opinion until recently was that families and their severely deviant children were better apart, whether to spare the family, as with mongoloid children, whose parents were commonly advised to institutionalize them while still babies,[56] or to spare the child, as with psychotic children, whose condition was assumed to be the result of parental rejection or incompetence. (In the most famous school for emotionally disturbed children in the country, parents who enroll their child are told they cannot see him for a year, and then only in the presence of a staff member.) Experts are no longer so sure of either of these ideas as they once were, and most schools encourage parental visits. But the effects outlast the theory. The best-known schools for mentally and emotionally handicapped children are residential, and few parents will be able to find one near enough for frequent visits. Even so, it may be

Residential schools

that the best educational opportunity for your child may involve sending him or her away from home.* The director of one such school believes it is unrealistic to expect to be able to help all children in their own communities:

> Many of these children need a "total treatment environment" rather than the fragmented services provided, if provided at all, through community services. They cannot honestly be served in public schools and community mental health centers, even if such service were of a highly professional quality – which is often not the case – while in many instances, no service can be provided at all, even in nominally prescribed "special education programs." . . . [When] equivalent services are simply not available . . . residential placement has not only saved the child, but often, saved the family as well.[57]

The best special schools have years of experience and large staffs which provide a remarkable degree of personal attention to each child. Many are adept at moving an adolescent back into the community. Some have sheltered villages attached to which a child can move when he is a child no longer, and thus solve the problem of "what will happen to him after we're gone?" They are expensive, naturally – regard under $10,000 a year as a bargain. Fees reflect the ratio of staff to children, the quality of the services offered, and the severity of the disorders treated.

There are more residential schools for learning disordered, antisocial or poorly motivated adolescents than for mentally ill children. (Many of these schools advertise in the Sunday *New York Times Magazine.*)

Residential alternatives:

Residential schools are for the rich, the military (see p. 332), or for those lucky families whose states contribute largely to private school tuition. There are some options for the less affluent if separation from home seems advisable (as of course it sometimes is, particularly for older children and adolescents). *Residential treatment centers* for disturbed children are run by various agencies, usually private, but often with public funds, so costs to families are much lower. Most provide psychotherapy for the child and often work with the family too. Children do not usually remain in treatment centers more than a year or two, usually less. The centers are not primarily schools, though education is generally provided, either in the center or in community schools. Local social workers should be aware of treatment centers in your region. They serve mainly troubled and delinquent children;

lower cost

* The directory *U.S. Facilities and Programs for Children with Severe Mental Illnesses* describes hundreds of school programs, day and residential, specifying cost, types of condition accepted, visiting restrictions if any, types of therapy available (psychotherapy, individual, family, and group, behavior modification, chemotherapy, vitamin therapy, etc.). It also specifies programs which require parents to accept psychotherapy for themselves, a good indicator of a psychogenic orientation.

many of them exclude psychotic and autistic children. Children may also be placed in foster homes or group homes, usually supported by the state.[58]

There are some terrible schools, and terrible treatment centers. You can't run a good special facility on the cheap. "Bargain" prices are no bargain if they mean incompetent staff, unimaginative or obsolete programs, or neglect. But if you can locate the right school, if it offers more than you can get together in your community, if you can afford it, if the child is old enough to manage the separation and profit from it, if he — or the rest of you — *needs* the separation, residential placement may be the answer.

lots of if's

Both the Association for Children with Learning Disabilities and the National Association for Autistic Children provide information on the many schools for "exceptional" children. They don't make recommendations, but they will put you in touch with other parents who already have children in the school you're considering. (This will cut down on expensive trips to check out facilities.) To get a full picture, try to talk with more than one family. For problems of living that do not involve mental illness or learning disabilities, there are many more choices, since most good private boarding schools take at least a few troubled children.

A difficult choice

Few families can make this decision without pain, and the feeling that whatever we decide, it's wrong. If a child is unhappy at home or misplaced in his present school it's easier. But if he isn't unhappy, a change may still be in order. The rest of the family have their needs, too. The child will probably suffer less from the separation than you think. A good school, after all, is good because it provides experiences a child wouldn't have otherwise. One autistic twelve-year-old, lonely at home when her sisters went off to college, asked her mother if there was "a kind of school with beds in it." For the severely deviant child, a residential school may be the only way for him to experience the companionship of other children. And children grow; what might have been traumatic at six may be a valuable next step at ten, and a new start away from family and community may be the best thing for a troubled adolescent and everybody around him.

Hospitalization

If it hurts to send our troubled children away to school, what can we say about the decision that psychiatric hospitalization is necessary? Nothing. What *can* be said, and what good would it do? It will help if we are able to think of the hospital as another, more intensive educational experience, in which resourceful practitioners combine various kinds of therapies to meet needs even a special school can't meet. There are fine hospital programs, both public and private, of which this is true. (The NIMH directory describes many of these; additional information on hospital-based programs is available from NSAC.) In a good hospital program children go home when possible and return to the hospital when needed.* Visiting is generally welcomed, and there is close liaison with the family on treatment, whether psychological, somatic, or educational. Educational services are essential in any good program for children, in a hospital or out of it.

Liaison with home

There may be good hospital programs for children in your state. But a 1972 survey showed only 151 county and state hospitals with inpatient units exclusively for adolescents and/or children.[59] As for private hospitals, only a few have a children's service, though some serve adolescents. In 1971–1972, eleven states had *no* mental hospital, public or private, with a children's unit.[60] In 1974, Dr. Harold Visotsky of Northwestern University told his colleagues in the American Psychiatric Association that "the number of children in state and county hospitals, now 55,000, has doubled since 1963," but he also told them that "children's services are practically nonexistent."[61]

This means that in most hospitals children are admitted to adult hospital wards if they are admitted at all.† (I have vivid in my mind the sight of a fifteen-year-old autistic girl – almost the age of my own daughter – rocking aimlessly with ten old women in a locked third-floor ward, while the bright sun shone outside. There was no game, book, or magazine in the ward; the television set was shelved six feet up, for these patients, I was told, could be violent. Some of the old women were muttering unintelligibly, some were silent. Beth was silent too, except when she whined or screamed – not often, because of the drugs. She had not learned to communicate and certainly would never learn here. But she had once known how to dress herself; here the nurse put on her socks for her. She had once known how to embroider, but nobody here knew that. She had once lived where she could go outside in the sun. The ward was spotless, the nurse was amiable. That is what good custodial care is. Bad custodial care doesn't bear thinking about. C. C. P.)

Beth

Here's what Congressman Richard Ottinger found when he visited one children's unit in the rich state of New York:

> In the area of health care, I confirmed: that [the children] are getting less physical health care than the law mandates for children in public schools, that many . . . have never been given a full physical examination by a pediatrician, and that their last physical checkup was on ad-

* For example, the New York state hospital program directed by Dr. Mary B. Hagamen at Sagamore Children's Center includes weekend and holiday hospitalization to give respite to families.

† NIMH reported that the number of children under inpatient psychiatric care jumped by more than 30 percent between 1969 and 1971, although the number for other age groups dropped. Half these children were treated in adult facilities.

> mission to the hospital by a person trained in adult psychiatry; that many . . . have never been examined by professional audial or visual testers.
>
> In the area of education, I confirmed: that children were not receiving a full day's school program, geared to their capabilities, as mandated by the 1968 amendment to the New York State Mental Hygiene Law: that the ratio of students to teachers . . . was 27:1, more than three times higher than the 8:1 ratio officially approved by the State Department of Education. . . .[62]

As this shows, the laws of the most advanced states recognize that the right to education means the right to education even in the state hospital. It also shows how far even the most advanced states can be from making right into reality. Education and therapy may not be quite synonymous for a child, but it's rare indeed to find therapy where there's no education.

Investigate before you hospitalize a child. You may be comforted and reassured. Nothing could be better for a child in that severest degree of need than some of our best hospital programs. But the greatest need of a child is to grow. If that need isn't met, as it cannot be met by custodial care, nothing – *nothing* – can be worse. For the parents of thousands of children like Beth there is no reassurance, and the only comfort can be to forget they ever had a child – as so many professionals once told parents to do.

The decisions that put Beth where she is were made a long time ago. Things have changed; today most professionals agree with parents that hospitalization for a child is the last resort, that it should never be equated with institutionalization, that it should be thought of as temporary as long as there is any way to make that possible. Many professionals are ready to work with you to help you keep your child where most parents want their children, at home.

Search for allies and you will find them.

CHAPTER XIII

When Your Relative Is Old

Though leaves are many, the root is one;
Through all the lying days of my youth
I swayed my leaves and flowers in the sun;
Now I may wither into the truth.
WILLIAM BUTLER YEATS

TAKE EVERYTHING IN THIS BOOK that has made you angry and sick at heart. You can triple it if your relative is old. Getting old in America isn't so bad if you're comfortably off and in full possession of your faculties. If you're a Supreme Court justice or a congressman, you can expect to enjoy a respected and satisfying old age. But the elderly person who is none of these things, and has a psychiatric problem besides, is at the bottom of society's priority list. Remember the YAVIS syndrome that summarized the characteristics of that ideal patient that mental health professionals love to treat? The Y, you'll recall, stood for Young.

Old people

If Americans must be angered by the unavailability of mental health services for our children, we at least know that people are worried about it, writing about it, outraged by it, doing something about it. There may not be many child psychiatrists, but there is a whole profession — teaching — concerned with the nurturing of the young. There are whole libraries of books about the psychological problems of children, for the professional and the layman too, and every year more pour off the presses. But if you — or your doctor — should feel the need to read up on the psychological problems that people encounter as they get old, you could do it fast. People don't write about old people much, they don't read about them much,* they don't get outraged about them much, and they certainly don't do much about them.

Hundreds of papers are presented at a typical meeting of the American Psychiatric Association; if one or two are concerned with *geriatric psychiatry* — the psychiatry of the aging — that's a lot. "At one discussion on the aged," writes Dr. Paul Poinsard, "only ten doctors showed up out of the 7000 attending the convention."[1] Psychiatrists who serve the aging are angry, dedicated, and few. Writes one of them, Dr. Eric Pfeiffer of Duke University Medical School, "while it might be reasonable to assume that the care of the emotionally distressed, disturbed, or disturbing aged should be primarily the responsibility of psychiatri-

* If you — or your doctor — would like to, you couldn't do better than to get *Aging and Mental Health: Positive Psychosocial Approaches,* by psychiatrist Robert N. Butler and social worker Myrna Lewis (St. Louis: C. V. Mosby, 1973), to which this chapter is much indebted. It's a book that speaks to the heart as well as the mind.

cally trained physicians, the actual facts are quite otherwise."[2] The actual facts, another tells us, are that medical students refer to elderly patients as old crocks and raw young interns address them by their first names, and that mental health professionals who choose to work with old people do so in the face of "the often heard professional opinion that an interest in aging represents a morbid preoccupation with decline and death."[3] As we've seen, doctors like to cure people. Chronic patients are never popular, and old age is the most chronic of conditions. Psychiatrists also note the problem of "counter-transference," when mental health professionals transfer to their patients responses more appropriate to relationships out of their own personal lives. In Dr. Poinsard's word, "The physician's (and not only the physician's) security may be threatened by hostile feelings against his own parents, by the reminder of death in the aged, and by feelings of helplessness."*

make us uncomfortable.

A TIME OF STRESS

Yet in America the stage of life when people are expected to be getting "old and set in their ways" is just the stage when they undergo a series of changes that might well threaten anyone's emotional stability. Income drops, neighborhoods change, homes are sold, major moves are undertaken. Health declines; jobs and activities must be given up; friends, spouses, and children die. American society offers to few of its old people the respected, traditional roles that would partially compensate for these losses. Old people today are not often consulted for their wisdom. Instead they are expected to retire and to accept that a lifetime spent acquiring skills and experience has no relevance in the world of the young. It's small wonder that the American Psychological Association in 1971 estimated that at least 15 percent of the elderly — some three million people — were in need of mental health services.

They don't get what they need, though, from professionals in private practice or community facilities. Old people have more than their share of problems of living, and there is more severe mental illness among older people than in any other age group.† Yet old people

* Cf. Martin A. Berezin, "Psychodynamic Considerations of Aging and the Aged," *American Journal of Psychiatry,* 128 (June 1972): "Sometimes a hostile defensive attitude on the part of the therapist is managed by reaction formation and oversolicitude. Since countertransference attitudes are determined by the therapist's early and often unresolved experiences in reacting to his own parents and authority figures, an attempt to treat an older person may bring about some degree of regression in the therapist."

† The rate of psychosis is more than ten times higher for those over sixty-five than it is for those fifteen to thirty-four, the age group best served by mental health professionals. Benjamin Pasamanick, "A Survey of Mental Disease in an Urban Population," *Mental Hygiene,* 46 (1962), 567–572, cited by Erdman Palmore, in Busse and Pfeiffer, *op. cit.,* p. 46. Dr. Busse himself thinks the figure should be higher (p. 95).

make up only 4 to 5 percent of community mental health center clientèle, only 2 percent of clinic patients.[4] Old people are rarely taken into direct therapy. Over half of psychiatrists see no patients over sixty-five,[5] and only 2 percent of private psychiatric time is spent with older patients.[6] Another study found that whereas two-thirds of patients aged fifteen to twenty-nine in a private psychiatric hospital received psychotherapy, and about a third of those between thirty and thirty-nine, of those oldsters who'd passed forty less than one-sixth were considered "suitable."[7] This is only one reflection of our national accent on youth; Americans have been more successful in segregating our old people than any other society. Out of sight, out of mind — it's not surprising that until 1974, the only branch of the National Institutes of Health that dealt with aging was to be found under the National Institute of *Child* Health! A new National Institute on Aging was created in 1974; in 1975 NIMH established a Center for Studies of the Mental Health of the Aging. With proper support, these may prove to be important resources for your relative — and you. Dr. Pfeiffer of Duke University writes, "It is only within the last decade and a half that a substantial body of knowledge regarding the aging process and the treatment of the diseases of old age has been accumulated."[8]

Facts

The problems of age are our own problems: getting old is something most of us will do. In 1900 only 4 percent of Americans were sixty-five or older. Ten percent of us are today, and that percentage will increase. In 1972 there were 20,000,000 elderly people in the United States, half of them over seventy-three. They weren't bedridden old crocks in nursing homes. Eighty-one percent of the elderly get about on their own legs, and only 5 percent are in institutions.* Wherever they are, their need for mental health services does not decrease as they get older.

and myths

It isn't their families who give up on their older members. That's a myth. Four out of five elderly people have living children, and "when there are children in the family (sometimes in childless couples it may be nieces and nephews) it is rare when the children are not deeply involved."[9]

> Four out of every ten older unmarried people with children live in the same household with at least one child and an additional three of every ten are ten minutes or less distant from their nearest child. In all, 82% of all unmarried old persons in the U.S. who have children are less than 30 minutes distant from one of those children."[10]

Only about 1 percent have no relatives. "Only about 2% of the elderly in a national survey lived alone, had had no visitors the previous week and no human contact the day before their interviews." Those visitors usually were relatives.[11]

* Two percent of those sixty-five to seventy-four, 7 percent of those over seventy-five.

More facts

There are many more old women than old men. From birth to old age, males have a higher mortality than females. Between the ages of sixty-five and seventy-four there are 130 old women for every 100 old men; over seventy-five there are close to 160. This leads to another fact heavy with emotional and practical significance. Butler and Lewis put it succinctly, "Most elderly men are married; most elderly women are widows."*

Typically, we're not young ourselves when we take on responsibility for our older relatives. Already in 8 percent of United States families, three generations live together under one roof.[12] Herman Brotman of the United States Administration on Aging sees a future in which "the presence of several generations of retired persons in the same family will become increasingly common, each member struggling to live on a retirement income which is a fraction of pre-retirement income levels and all looking to each other for financial and psychological support in emergency situations."[13]

Most old people aren't crazy or disturbed – let's make that clear. They are able to use their years of experience to manage the stresses of living as well as (or better than) younger people. But for others, their special problems of living may push them close to the edge. Just as a child can balance on a fence if he knows you are there to catch him, so many old people are kept from despair by the reliable, noninterfering presence of devoted families, as in this social worker's letter about an elderly parent:

Mrs. Smith

> My mother is 75, but looks older. She is a woman who has been somewhat on the depressive side most of her life, a highly organized person, who has a graduate degree and did have a satisfying administrative job. She has been on the edge of a clinical depression ever since my father died fifteen years ago. She has lived alone by choice and continued to work. When she retired she got a part time job at a private school in town. She's very devoted to kids, likes to be around them, and keeps fairly busy there but finds she gets tired and really can't work a full week. However, her energy seems to revive when she gets involved with her grandchildren and her great-grandchildren – a kind of therapeutic miracle. She's preoccupied about her health, which is good, and has a physician whom she trusts, whom she sees periodically, essentially for reassurance. She has trouble sleeping and handles that by a big glass of whiskey before she goes to bed, which usually knocks her out for a good part of the night. One of the things that was most reassuring to her was to find out that she really didn't have to have more than 5½ hours of sleep a night and that she wouldn't fall apart. She manages to rest a bit during the day when

* "Old men, if they survive, have greater options maritally. Chances are their wives are younger and will outlive them. But if not, the man can quite freely find a second wife. . . . There are many women to choose from. It is socially acceptable for a man to find a wife in either his own age group or any of the younger age groups. An older woman, however, is looked upon with disdain if she marries someone much younger. Each year some 35,000 older men marry, while for women the comparable figure is only 16,000, even though women in the age group outnumber men by 3 million." *Op cit.*, p. 7.

she's tired and her preoccupation with getting a good night's sleep seems to have diminished recently. We don't hover over her and she takes the initiative with us in visiting. I think if she didn't, we would. She's somewhat shy and had to have some pressure from us to join a retired persons group so that she could do some occasional traveling which she was *very* afraid of. She's a little phobic about airplanes but with some coaxing, we've gotten her to go on short trips with some retired persons' groups where she has met some interesting friends. She lives frugally on her retirement income, I think too frugally, and refuses to take any kind of help, unless it's heavily disguised, from her children, who are more than willing to help her in any way she wants.

Reversibility

It's easy to assume that when an older person becomes depressed, or irresponsible, or confused, or continually upset, that it's "just old age" and that nothing can be done about it. Of course this is sometimes true. Very often, though, it isn't; the condition can be treated, is reversible — although if nothing *is* done it may very well become permanent. (When that happens, it's all too likely to be what we — and the doctor — expected to happen anyway, confirming our conviction that there really *was* nothing to be done.)

in spite of therapeutic pessimism

One married man in his seventies, living at home, began to get forgetful and confused and burst out angrily against his wife. His worried family learned that he was getting substantial bank loans and had rented an apartment in a nearby city; he said he was writing "the great American novel." They got him to the hospital, where he told the doctors he felt better than he had in years. Treated — as a younger manic patient would have been — with group therapy and medication, he was ready to go home in two weeks — to the surprise of the staff, and doubtless his family too.* Dr. Robert Gibson, Medical Director of the well-known Sheppard Pratt mental hospital, describes the "therapeutic pessimism" that hinders psychiatric treatment of the elderly and confirms that elderly patients respond well to treatment.[14] In his own fine hospital, a review of the records of 138 patients over sixty-five showed that the prognosis had been considered "poor" in 80 percent of the cases, though some 60 percent improved significantly within ninety days and went home. Psychiatrists were far more hopeful about younger patients, although in fact they did no better. Another Sheppard Pratt study of forty-three consecutive admissions of people over sixty-five found that three-fourths of those suffering primarily from depression were discharged as improved, "and even of those whose problem was primarily related to brain damage, more than a quarter improved sufficiently so that they could return to their homes."[15] A woman who is already sixty-five can expect to live sixteen years more; a man, thirteen. Even at seventy-five, a man can expect eight more years; a woman, ten.[16] So it's fortunate for us all that Dr. Eric Pfeiffer is telling his col-

* Described, with other cases of reversible psychotic conditions, by Robert J. Nathan, "The Psychiatric Treatment of the Geriatric Patient," *American Journal of Psychiatry,* 130 (June 1973).

leagues that "elderly patients do respond remarkably well to treatment."[17]

There are lots of reasons why old people get depressed, or confused, or suspicious, or forgetful. There is often plenty to be depressed or suspicious about. Many old people have lived to see familiar neighborhoods turn alien and dangerous. Losses, loneliness, the feeling of uselessness bring on depression. (The suicide rate is higher among the elderly than in any other age group.)

Social and physical factors

Social factors affect emotional and physical health together. "More than one out of every four older people live below the poverty line";[18] many more must practice strict economy. Services that once were taken for granted, like public transportation, foodstore delivery, doctors' house calls, no longer exist. What effect does this have on the mental health of an old lady who can't carry heavy shopping bags and can't afford taxis, or even, perhaps, a telephone? Dr. Busse points out the close relation between physical conditions common among the elderly and psychiatric disorders. It's easy to get confused (or depressed) when you're old and sick and isolated; one study found that when elderly people were hospitalized for "acute confusional states" the most common causes were malnutrition, heart failure, and alcoholism.[19]

WHICH CONDITIONS ARE REVERSIBLE?

To treat such problems they must be carefully diagnosed. Diagnosis is particularly difficult in the elderly, since there are many possible causes for the same symptoms. It's hard – sometimes impossible – even for a doctor to know whether mental and emotional symptoms come from a reversible condition or are the signs of a progressive brain impairment.* But most physicians – and families – are quicker to think of arteriosclerosis ("hardening of the arteries") or organic brain syndrome ("softening of the brain") than the many conditions for which treatment offers hope of reversibility. "Actual treatment," write Butler and Lewis, "is the only reliable way to judge the reversibility of symptoms."[20]

Giving their due

This has practical meaning for families. Because mental and physical illness are even more closely intertwined in old age than they are generally, it is crucial that an elderly person with psychiatric symptoms be seen by a doctor who will be alert to signals from both mind and body. And seen *early;* "once a disorder becomes chronic, improvement is slow and often requires a much greater effort."[21]

* One hale old gentleman of eighty-two was terrified and depressed by a year-long series of what his local doctor diagnosed as minor strokes. When his children, insisting on a more sophisticated consultation, sought out a neurologist, the "strokes" were found to be episodes of petit mal, a minor form of epilepsy easily controlled by medication.

Dr. Butler is particularly concerned about the sad or suspicious or confused or anxious old people whose distress is dismissed as natural for their age, or as the inevitable result of organic deterioration, when sensitive psychotherapy or sympathetic attention to living conditions could help as effectively as they could for a young patient. Dr. John Nowlin of Duke University's Center for the Study of the Aging is concerned that psychological symptoms of physical disease are often overlooked, pointing out that the aging process alters the way diseases show themselves. In the older person, changes in mood, alertness, and comprehension often come *before* typical symptoms of physical illness. Heart disease, diabetes, thyroid conditions, anemia, liver trouble can all cause mental and emotional symptoms. One possible, though not common, cause of senile symptoms is *hydrocephalus,* or "water on the brain." It has recently been recognized that this can afflict older people as well as children, though, since they do not show the characteristic hydrocephalic enlargement of the head, diagnosis is more difficult. Surgery to install a shunt to drain the excess fluid can reverse the senile symptoms.*

to mind and body

Studies of elderly patients hospitalized in medical and psychiatric units found 16 percent misassigned. More often than not they ended up in the psychiatric unit when their primary problem was medical.[22] Dr. David Viscott describes the case of an old lady hospitalized in the psychiatric ward in which he did his residency, depressed and complaining of continual pain. The staff had no difficulty explaining her symptoms as an attempt to get from other doctors the attention her doctor husband denied her; it was some days (during which she was encouraged to walk) before a nurse convinced them to order X-rays. They revealed a broken hip.[23] Dr. Viscott is a psychiatrist who is also a popular writer; he tells a good horror story. The results of a sober study by the distinguished British geriatric physician Agate back him up; in a review of one hundred consecutive admissions of older people to a psychiatric unit, he found fifty-two with significant, unrecognized medical problems.[24] And it works both ways: many other old people have been rendered trouble-free, to others if not to themselves, with drugs or ECT, without any attempt to treat their disturbance with understanding psychotherapy.

Mrs. Jones

So in hopes that her symptoms are treatable, do your best to obtain an examination that will do justice to your elderly relative's emotions, mind, and body. A good beginning would be to read Butler's and Lewis's Chapter 9 on what a good evaluation should be. But if there's

* Hydrocephalus and the shunt operation are described in Lawrence Galton's *Don't Give Up on an Aging Parent.* He also describes some still experimental treatments of senility with (1) anticoagulants, and (2) hydergine, a preparation to increase the blood flow to the brain (New York: Crown Publishers, 1975), pp. 39–50.

nowhere to get such an evaluation in your neighborhood, don't be surprised.

> Thorough diagnosis requires a comprehensive evaluation and treatment center. At present the elderly are not likely to receive such care in the U.S. As disreputable as state hospitals can be, it is still more likely that an older person will get an appropriate work-up there than at a general hospital or a community mental health center.[25]

Here, as in other things, the elderly come last.

Mental disorders of the elderly

As the story of the manic elderly gentleman shows, old people may suffer from the same mental and emotional disorders as young people, and respond to the same kinds of treatment.* However, it is rare for schizophrenia to develop for the first time in later life, and the schizophrenic who has grown old is usually less trouble to himself and others than when he was young.† Paranoid symptoms are more likely to develop in old age. An old lady thinks a neighbor pounds on her ceiling on purpose, or listens in via the wires in her toaster; an old gentleman thinks his daughter-in-law is plotting to put him away.‡ Isolation breeds suspicion, and people who are naturally suspicious won't get less so as they get older. But we shouldn't forget that "paranoia" is often justified; for one old person with delusions of persecution, says Dr. Butler, there are ten who really are persecuted. Deafness contributes to paranoia. Thirty percent of older people have some hearing loss (more men than women), and some become suspicious as they misinterpret what they can hardly hear. A hearing examination should be part of any comprehensive evaluation, since infections and even diseases like cancer and diabetes can cause ear problems.§ Consult an ear, nose, and throat specialist — an otolaryngologist. Dr. Butler cautions against the tests done by hearing-aid salesmen.

Paranoia

Deafness

Hypochondria, anxiety states

Hypochondria is common — which is one reason why so many genuine symptoms get discounted by families, and doctors. So are anxiety states.|| By far the most common psychiatric disorder of old

* One study of 222 hospitalized patients showed 13 percent with predominantly manic symptoms. Pfeiffer and Busse, "Affective Disorders," *op. cit.*, p. 122.

† Some personality types, too, adapt well to aging. "A so-called schizoid or introspective personality may function somewhat better in old age. Such an individual tends to be insulated against the experiences of life and therefore may feel relatively more comfortable in the loneliness and difficulties of old age. . . . Obsessive compulsiveness can become useful in taking care of oneself and keeping busy with many details; in fact this type of individual can create a whole life for himself by 'taking care' of things." Butler and Lewis, *op. cit.*, p. 58.

‡ Paranoid states are somewhat more common in old women than old men. Butler and Lewis, *op. cit.*, p. 52.

§ *Op. cit.*, pp. 97–98, a section well worth reading if your relative is getting deaf.

|| For these, see Butler, *op. cit.*, pp. 54, 57–58. You will probably want to read the chapters on "Functional Disorders" and "Organic Brain Disorders" in full. Busse and Pfeiffer have a particularly good discussion of hypochondria and its treatment, *op. cit.*, pp. 130–135.

Depression

age, however, is depression. NIMH Director Bertram Brown estimates that half the hospitalized elderly over sixty have a treatable depressive illness, which is usually not recognized for what it is.[26]

There's no point in belaboring the obvious; old people have a lot to be depressed about. But – as in young people – depressions may be deeper or longer than circumstances seem to warrant. As in younger people, they may be without apparent physical cause ("functional"). But they also accompany many organic conditions, whether because the condition physically causes the depression, or because it's depressing to be old and sick.* A psychiatric episode is particularly distressing for an older person. Even if it's successfully treated and fully reversed, it can (understandably) bring anxiety and depression in its wake. When this is so, these can be treated, by the methods you've already read about.

Organic brain syndrome

reversible or "acute"

It is estimated that about 60 to 70 percent of mental illness among the elderly is organic in origin. This is not as discouraging as it sounds, for up to half of these organic brain syndromes may be "acute" or reversible. ("Acute" loses its suggestion of suddenness when applied to brain syndromes of the elderly.) † The symptoms of organic brain syndromes are both mental and emotional. They include impairment of orientation for time, place, and person. Memory, problem solving, learning are affected. Emotions seem close to the surface and may be extreme or inappropriate. Of course some of these symptoms occur in many old people from time to time. When Grandma is hospitalized, or even just visiting, and wakes up in the new bedroom, it takes a little time for her to know where she is, and Dad sometimes calls little Mary by the name of the daughter who died. An elderly person who is depressed is even more likely to "turn off"‡ than a young one,

* "There appears to be a particularly intimate relationship between the existence of significant physical illness and depressive reactions in old age. . . . Studies . . . indicate that the older person can tolerate the loss of love objects and of prestige better than he can a decline in physical health." Pfeiffer and Busse, "Affective Disorders," *op. cit.*, p. 117.

† "The term 'acute' is not restricted in its use to a sudden onset of the disease but is meant to imply reversibility." Busse, "Organic Brain Syndromes," *op. cit.*, p. 92.

‡ "Some elder patients in depression may show cognitive deficits which, though transitory or reversible, may not be distinguishable from those commonly observed in brain impairment." H. Shan Wang, "Special Diagnostic Procedures – The Evaluation of Brain Impairment," in Busse and Pfeiffer, *op. cit.*, p. 79.

"When darkness came she entered a shadowy world, a world seen only by her. In hospitals they call it 'sundowning' and it is a common thing with old people when they are removed from a familiar environment and placed in the hospital. The darkness, the lack of familiar things around them, the strange sounds from the corridors cause a sort of sensory confusion which brings on hallucinations. Usually the simple act of turning on a night light will chase away the shadows, and the old people will sleep." Sharon R. Curtin, *Nobody Ever Died of Old Age* (Boston: Atlantic–Little, Brown, 1972), p. 135.

especially if he is getting deaf. Take Dr. Busse's caution to heart and don't jump to conclusions:

> None of these signs and symptoms is restricted to organic brain syndromes; hence, the mental status examination must be carefully done. Evidence of the existence of virtually all of these factors should be present in making the diagnosis of organic brain syndrome.[27]

Your observations may help discover a cause. Heart conditions, malnutrition

A confused and forgetful patient cannot tell the doctor what he needs to find out. Your careful observations may be crucial in helping the physician recognize a reversible brain syndrome. Besides heart failure and malnutrition, including specific vitamin lacks (avitaminosis),* the physician will have to consider other possible causes. Has your relative been sick? Infections may lead to exhaustion and dehydration (loss of body fluids) and affect the brain. The blood supply to the brain may be temporarily reduced (ischemic attack). The effects of stroke on mind and emotions are well known; so-called little strokes probably occur more often than we realize.[28] Has your mother fallen recently? Could she have hit her head? Old people are easily injured, even in minor accidents. Can you give the doctor a complete list of the drugs your father is taking? Reactions to prescription drugs are an important cause of reversible brain disorders, which become irreversible if the dosage is not stopped. Before you talk to the doctor, review all the information you have that might be relevant. Major illnesses? Continuing health problems? Recent losses? Most doctors will welcome your participation.

Cerebrovascular insufficiency or accident

Falls

Drug effects

IRREVERSIBLE CONDITIONS

Senile dementia or psychosis

There is no point in pretending; we all know that some old people are not going to get better. The early signs of what the doctor calls *senile dementia* or *senile psychosis,* and the layman calls senility or second childhood, are much the same as for the reversible brain syndromes. That's what makes diagnosis so difficult. Men are more likely to become senile than women. As the condition worsens, speech becomes rambling or incoherent; the old person may have difficulty finding the right word, particularly nouns. He or she may be restless, depressed, irritable, and anxious, sleepless; neglect personal appearance; wander away from home. Cerebral arteriosclerosis causes about one case in six.† The walls of the arteries supplying blood to the brain

caused by arteriosclerosis

* Often even the affluent don't eat as they should. Old-fashioned pellagra is by no means unknown among the elderly.

† In about an equal number of cases it is present but not causal. Robert Terry and Henry K. Wisniewski of the Pathology Department of the Albert Einstein College of Medicine, quoted in *Behavior Today* (March 25, 1974).

harden and thicken, so that it receives insufficient oxygen and nutrients.

Other causes?

Little is known as yet about other causes of senility,* but pathological examinations (done after death) show that the senile brain may actually lose 15 to 30 percent of its weight. But there's hope in current work; researchers Robert Terry and Henry Wisniewski feel that "is it not unreasonable to expect that biologic research on the tissue might, in the not too distant future, yield methods for the prevention of the lesions which give rise to this terrible disorder."[29]

Human factors

The amount of deterioration isn't neatly related to the amount of brain damage. Some people function relatively well with significant damage. Others deteriorate markedly, showing once more that personality and environment have a lot to do with how people meet even the results of organic conditions. Let's remind ourselves of what we know perfectly well, however: *most old people never become senile.*

TREATMENT — INCLUDING PSYCHOTHERAPY

Mr. Brown

Mr. Brown was a successful executive who retired at sixty-five expecting to live only a few more years. But (in the words of his physician) "you can't count on dying; one day he woke up and was seventy-eight years old and found himself having run out of anything to do." He went into a severe depression, staying in bed all day, upsetting his wife by compulsively reciting rhymes out of his childhood. When admitted to a psychiatric hospital, careful examination found nothing wrong with how his mind worked, although he was anxious and obsessive and, of course, depressed. When sensitive attention was given to helping him plan what he might do with the rest of his life he improved rapidly. He returned home, learned to type, and began work on an autobiography which turned out to be a fascinating record of life in three states around the turn of the century.

But his psychiatric history wasn't over. Some months later, after a mild heart attack, he was put on the usual heart regimen of digitalis, diuretics, no exercise, and a low salt diet. Depressed again, and hating the diet, he virtually stopped eating. He kept on taking the diuretics, though. His body depleted of fluids and nourishment, he again became lethargic, but this time he was also dizzy and confused. Back in the

* *Op. cit.*, p. 81. Two of the conditions under study are neurofibrillary tangle and senile plaque. Tangles, found also in punch-drunk boxers, mongoloid adults, and patients with postencephalitic Parkinson's disease, are twisted abnormal fibers of protein; plaque is made up of clusters of abnormal brain cells (neurites and enlarged synaptic endings). Terry and Wisniewski, *loc. cit.* Remembering the first of the organic brain syndromes to be understood, general paresis (Chapter III, p. 47), once a major cause of mental illness and death in old people, it's worth noting that Dr. Butler thinks that with the current increase in syphilis, "we can expect to see much more of this disorder in the future."

hospital, he was put on a regular diet, his medication was adjusted, and he was encouraged to exercise in moderation. Within a week his depression lifted, and he returned home.[30]

Dr. Pfeiffer tells this story – and we retell it – to show how difficult it is to separate physical and psychological problems in the elderly. Good treatment, if you can get it, takes account of both.

Treatments

The psychological problems of old age, when they can be separated from physical problems and even when they can't, are treatable by the same methods you've read about already in Chapters IV and IX: individual and group psychotherapy, family therapy, milieu therapy, behavior therapy, and the various somatic therapies, sensitively modified to meet the needs of older people. Even in the irreversible organic syndromes, treatment can make a difference to patient and family; here milieu therapy and behavior therapy make special contributions.

Individual psychotherapy

Most families – and mental health professionals – don't think of psychotherapy in connection with the elderly (and many of the elderly wouldn't feel comfortable with the idea themselves). When you do think about it, however, the talking-listening treatment is naturally suited to the needs of old people, who get fewer opportunities than the rest of us to talk and be listened to. We probably overestimate what psychotherapy can do for the young; we certainly underestimate what it can do for the elderly.* Goals can be limited or broad. The therapist can help an old lady adjust to widowhood or accept that she can no longer live independently. An imaginative therapist can find ways to reinvolve an old person in satisfying activity, as was done with Mr. Brown. "All forms of psychotherapy – 'uncovering' to 'supportive' and Freudian to Jungian to Rogerian – can contribute. . . . Psychoanalytic concepts, Skinner's ideas regarding conditioning and the extinction of dysfunctional patterns of behavior, and Jung's stages of development† all apply to the elderly condition."

> Freud and the vast majority of his colleagues ruled out psychoanalysis for the aged without ever testing its usefulness. Freud was preoccupied with death and pessimistic about old age. His work reflects his avoidance of the issues of later life and his decision to explain the human personality only in terms of the early years.[31]

Yet if Freud himself had died before the age of forty, remarks Dr. Butler, we would never have heard of him.

* On individual therapy, see Butler and Lewis's full and imaginative treatment (*op. cit.*, chapters 3 and 12) and Pfeiffer's sensible guidelines, "Interacting with Older Patients," in Busse and Pfeiffer, *op. cit.*

† Dr. Butler's own note points out that two-thirds of Jung's practice was made up of middle-aged and older persons, whereas Freud's patients were usually younger people. "These differences may help to account for variations in theoretical emphases with Freud's therapy concentrating on youth and sex while Jung emphasized individuation and creativity."

An increasing number of psychoanalysts are interesting themselves in the last stage of life. Dr. James Toolan, a Bennington, Vermont, psychoanalyst who is also medical director of the community mental health center, finds older people make particularly good use of psychoanalytic psychotherapy. More than the young are, they are ready to reflect, to search the past, to remember. Reminiscence, believes Dr. Butler, is a natural, healthy part of the last stage of life, a kind of spontaneous psychotherapy. Mr. Brown's depression lifted as he wrote his autobiography. Mental health professionals could assist this process; instead — like families — they are often bored and inattentive.

The "life review"

Old people "often exhibit a strong drive to resolve problems, put their lives in order — to review their lives, to seek meaning."[32] "Set in order thine house," says the Bible, and adds, "for thou must perish." Old people know this, and it is a lonely business for them when we pretend we don't. The sensitive therapist can encourage this process, the last stage of human growth, and, says Dr. Butler, he can grow himself while doing so.

> Psychotherapy in old age is a psychotherapy of atonement as well as of restitution. One cannot deny cruel and thoughtless acts, falsely reassuring that all is irrational Freudian guilt. Facing genuine guilt as well as the attrition of the person's physical and emotional world is what makes psychotherapy with the aged an intellectually and emotionally powerful experience.

For all that, the elderly are rarely referred for psychoanalytic psychotherapy — Dr. Toolan recalls "maybe two or three in ten years." A loss, perhaps, to psychotherapists as well as to potential patients.

Rigidity?

The mental health professionals concerned with the elderly are full of exhortations to their colleagues to forget their stereotypes and work with older patients. Dr. Martin Berezin tells psychiatrists not to assume "rigidity" in the old, that a flexible young man will be flexible in age, and the rigid old lady has probably been rigid all her life.[33] Dr. Elliott Feigenbaum alludes to therapists who "seem to expect that their interaction with older persons will bring them in contact with persons terribly disfigured both physically and psychologically," and to "the clinician who has enough demand for his services to keep busy in any field he chooses, and merely wants to promote for himself a practice with maximal pleasurable interactions."[34] In the meantime, older people themselves aren't clamoring for attention from psychiatrists, although they readily consult ordinary doctors — many of whom do a good deal of psychotherapy by the way. Many older people will prefer talking informally with clergymen, social workers, or paraprofessionals (read "neighbors") to something carrying the formal label of psychotherapy. Old people who are unhappy don't usually define their disturbance as psychological, or seek therapy for it. They grew up, after all, when psychiatry was still mainly concerned with crazy people. Old people

Psychotherapy from whom?

also tend to believe that "pain, lethargy, and unhappiness ought to be expected in their own and others' lives," whereas "for many younger people this is not true."[35]

Considering the importance of physical illness, it's important that we be sure physical factors have been ruled out, or are being treated. Once that's been done, psychotherapy is where you find it. Group therapy is somewhat more common. Involvement in groups — all kinds of groups* — may not only help an elderly person understand his own and others' problems and feelings. It can give him a ready-made circle of friends at a time when new friends are hard to come by.† Family therapy‡ is of obvious usefulness, especially when tensions arise between the generations, often living together again after years of independence. As you don't need a book to tell you, the problems are not small. Butler and Lewis summarize the observations of Margaret Blenkner:

Group therapy

Family therapy

> The adult in his forties and fifties experiences a *filial crisis* when it becomes evident that his parents are aging and that he will be called upon to provide the support and comfort which they need. This may contrast with his childhood visions of his parents as powerful and nurturing individuals who assist and support their offspring rather than vice versa. In view of the vicissitudes of early parent-child relationships, there is often unfinished developmental work to be done in freeing middle-aged adults from hostile, ambivalent, or immature parental ties. . . . "It is often necessary to assist the child to complete his unfinished emancipation . . . *in order that he may then be more free to help his parent.*" Neurotic guilt toward parents must be differentiated from the real guilt of failure to assume filial responsibility.[36]

"filial crisis"

You may, in short, be able to use some wise counseling yourself.

The physical treatments used for the elderly are the same ones you read about in Chapter IV, and accomplish the same things. No miracle

Somatic therapies —

* "The American Psychiatric Assn. presented a Gold Award for outstanding and innovative achievement . . . at its annual Institute of Hospital and Community Psychiatry meeting in Denver last week [to the] Veterans Administration Hospital, St. Cloud, Minn.: The hospital uses sixth-grade students, working under supervision, as 'remotivational therapists' for aged patients. The children meet with patients for 45 minutes twice a week in the wards and hospital dining room. They participate in groups of about 15, each working individually with one particular patient in sessions which focus on socialization, self-appreciation, shared experiences, community and current events, and travel — all part of the remotivation approach. The hospital reports that the program has stimulated renewed interest and fostered initiative and independence among the old people, and has helped give the children more respect and understanding for the aged. A manual describing the program is available free from William Bridges, Administrative Assistant, Chief of Staff, VAH. St. Cloud Minn. 56301." *Behavior Today* (Oct. 7, 1974).

† See Pfeiffer and Busse, "Affective Disorders," *op. cit.*, p. 107. The article by Nathan, already mentioned, describes an innovative approach to group therapy in an intensive private program, with discussion by Dr. Jacob Friedman of what can be done in a state hospital setting. See also "Psychogeriatric Group Approaches," by Milton M. Berger and Lynne F. Berger, in Sager and Kaplan, *Progress in Group and Family Therapy* (New York: Brunner/Mazel, 1972).

‡ On family therapy, see Geraldine Spark and Elaine Brody, "The Aged are Family Members," Sager and Kaplan, *op. cit.*

treatment to restore brain function has yet been found, although Dr. Bernard Stotsky considers the task of finding ways to retard intellectual deterioration "one of the greatest challenges to psychiatry."* It's much easier to alter mood. The minor and major tranquilizers, the antidepressants, lithium, and ECT are the staples of psychiatric treatment of the elderly, as of other psychiatric patients.

handle with care.

Old people are physically more vulnerable than younger patients. The effects of all drugs should be carefully watched. Drs. Busse and Pfeiffer warn that the central nervous system of the elderly is far more sensitive to psychoactive drugs.[37] Useful as they sometimes are, they can "reinforce . . . the slowing observed in old people, aggravate a sense of aging and depression, and can contribute to or cause acute and chronic brain syndromes."[38]

Psychoactive drugs

Mrs. Green

Dr. Butler tells of a woman whose opthalmologist quite properly prescribed a tranquilizer when she was hospitalized, tense and nervous, for a cataract operation. She woke up confused and in the dark. Her confusion was diagnosed as due to senile brain disease and she was sent to a nursing home. "She did not improve until, having occasion to see her during a consultation, I took her off Mellaril and in a short time she was a perked-up young seventy-year-old."[39]

Perhaps here's the place to mention that discount drugs can be obtained through the National Council of Senior Citizens, 1911 K St., N.W., Room 202, Washington, DC 20005 and the American Association of Retired Persons, 1225 Connecticut Ave., N.W., Washington, DC 20004. For a list of other helpful services, consult p. 429.

Other drugs

It's not only psychoactive drugs we need to watch out for. Old people take lots of medicine, and *all* drugs should be used with caution. "Perhaps the physician's prescription pad is the most insidious cause of mental aberration in the older person."[40] Dosage must be carefully monitored; "often, effective dosage levels of a drug prove to be very close to toxicity levels." The common medications for high blood pressure, heart conditions, kidney conditions, arthritis can all affect your relative's mental and emotional responses.

Insist on full information

Your relative's physician should explain to her the possible side effects of any medication.

for your relative

> Doctors remain all too secretive about preparing patients for drug effects, partly because they fear the development of symptoms in suggestible persons. Many also simply do not wish to take the time. It is archaic to assume that "what the patient doesn't know won't hurt him," because often it does. One must help patients overcome fears of medication while simultaneously encouraging them to respect effects and dangers.[41]

* Stotsky reviews some experimental treatments; others are described by Busse (*op. cit.,* pp. 101–103). Characteristically, hopeful first reports are followed by attempts to replicate, with doubtful results.

Your relative has a right to understand what is going on in his body. If he's taking a drug and feels weak or logy, or faint, he may assume it's just old age and say nothing about it, even though he's frightened and depressed. Important symptoms will then go unnoticed.

For yourself

If you don't think your relative will understand or remember the possible side effects (both the annoying minor symptoms like dry mouth and dangerous symptoms like low blood pressure, fainting, and tremors) * expect the doctor to tell *you* what to watch for. Ask him to tell the druggist to put the name of the medication and its proper dosage on the label. It's a good reminder for the vague and forgetful, and for you to have this information may prevent irreversible damage. It's polite to think, "Of course the doctor won't need *me* to tell him about Mom's medication," but it's too humble. The doctor may know well enough the effects of his own prescriptions. (He also may not.) But older people are often under the care of more than one physician, or are taking medication first prescribed many years before. It is extremely important for older people to have one doctor who knows them over a period of time, if at all possible. Remember Mrs. Green.

Things it won't hurt to know

If your relative becomes more agitated, not calmer, after he's taken a sedative, it helps to know that barbiturates sometimes cause agitation. Phenothiazines can too. Tranquilizers can cause depression. So can reserpine, no longer used in schizophrenia but now a common medication for high blood pressure. Diuretics can cause weakness and emotional changes. Patients taking monoamine oxidase inhibitors for depression (Chapter IV, pp. 96–97) must watch their diet. The drug affects the metabolism of certain foods; ask the doctor for a list. And many drugs do funny things when combined with alcohol.

Electro-convulsive treatment

Because depression is so common in the elderly, ECT is an important treatment when psychotherapy and antidepressants fail, or when a person is suicidal and there's no time to wait for them to work. (See Chapter IV, pp. 99–102.) You will worry, but carefully administered electroshock has no special dangers for the elderly, and improvement is often dramatic. Confusion and loss of memory are to be expected, but these are no greater or longer lasting than in younger patients.[42] If a doctor you trust recommends ECT, stand behind him and reassure your relative.

Paying for care for the elderly

Let's be realistic. Most of the elderly depend on Medicare and Medicaid for medical expenses. Yet the two programs cover only 45 percent of the medical expenses of elderly persons. The rest must be paid out of pocket. And "nowhere has medical care coverage been so inadequate as in the coverage of psychiatric care for the elderly."[43] For practical details see Chapter XI, "Money." For further details, consult your local Social Security office, a hospital business office, or a social worker in a

* "Extrapyramidal symptoms," Parkinsonism — see Chapter IV, p. 93.

community agency. Even when your relative does seem to be covered, you will probably find yourself agreeing that "the stress and frustration older people must go through to collect Medicare and private insurance must be experienced to be believed,"[44] as records are lost, phone calls multiply, and the voices at the end of the wire give conflicting information or none at all. We will thus change the subject to what you can do for your relative at home. Chapter VIII was about that, and a good deal of it applies to the elderly too. Old people, though, do have some special needs, and some special problems.

AT HOME, DAY BY DAY

Living with old age

Slow pace

Courtesy

If your elderly relative lives with you (or comes to visit), there's one basic prescription for everybody's comfort: Slow Down. We can learn from what Dr. Pfeiffer tells his colleagues: "Older people respond best if they are presented with one stimulus at a time, and if they are given sufficient time to respond to that one stimulus."[45] We used to call it courtesy; at any rate, it's a good therapeutic principle. In a room where too much is going on at once, the elderly person will withdraw. We then conclude she doesn't want to participate – unless we remember how we feel when we're sick or very tired, and try to imagine that confusion of voices demanding attention from all directions. Old people like talking, but the young talk fast, they slur their words, they speak from across the room. Our good-natured teenagers can learn to sit down and talk clearly, to listen and wait, and we too needn't be in such a hurry. It used to be called "respecting your elders," and everybody was supposed to do it. And why not?

Predictability

Old people with mental and emotional problems, however, need more than courtesy and respect. When our relative is "beginning to fail," there are still things we can do to make life go better for him, and for us too. Order, predictability, simplification – these are the watchwords for brains of any age that aren't working right. It's hard for an old lady to get her own breakfast when nothing in the refrigerator seems to be in the same place two days running, even if she's the one who tucked the juice away and then blamed you for it. It might save irritation to give her a shelf to herself, readably labeled for old eyes or marked with her own color. Of course it's quicker to make her breakfast yourself. But she'll feel even more helpless and useless, and soon she'll stop trying.

Some old people are wakeful and wander about the house at night. They nap by day, reassured by the sounds of daily life. If sleep patterns are becoming reversed, try to provide daytime stimulation to cut down on naps. And provide some reassurance in the silent dark. Dr. Daniel

Peak suggests a night-light, a fan, a radio turned low. It may help to move an old person from an isolated bedroom to one nearer the center of household life.[46]

In *Up from Depression* Dr. Leonard Cammer writes of "directive therapy."

> With older or partly senile patients who are unable to organize their own care and activity the entire day may have to be planned in detail. Their freedom from depression may depend on the extent to which they are kept busy, routinized, and entertained. However, take note that the activity itself puts the mind and body to work: it stimulates blood circulation, muscles, brain cells, and so on, all of which impel the person into further activity on his own initiative. Directives toward that end, with a resultant energizing force, often induce an improvement which cannot be duplicated by drugs or any other form of treatment.[47]

Though this is one of the few places in his book where old age is mentioned, anybody who's lived with the very old will be amazed to find how much of what Dr. Cammer says about depression in general describes the person they know. His chapters on "General Symptoms and What You Do about Them" and "Slowed-Down Symptoms and What You Do about Them" are resourceful guides to helping the elderly as well as the depressed, including coaxing someone to eat, wash, change clothes, even helping with memory troubles. (Tactfully, respectfully: don't make him feel stupid, "reacquaint him with the facts.")[48]

Reality orientation

You can also learn from a commonsense kind of milieu therapy recently developed in some progressive geriatric hospital programs. Its purpose is to rehabilitate chronic mental patients and return them to the community – people who were psychotic once, but who are now not grossly disturbed, just old and not used to looking out for themselves. Lars Peterson of the VA hospital in Tuscaloosa, Alabama, describes how treatment emphasizes orientation to the surrounding environment.[49] Staff call the patient by name whenever they meet him, mention where he's going, who he's going to be with, what he's going to be doing. Conspicuous "reality boards" show place, time, month, season, with pictures, and large readable calendars and clocks. Catawba Hospital in Virginia takes only patients over sixty from other state hospitals, the kind everybody used to give up on. Dr. Graham Bourhill directs an intensive program of psychosocial rehabilitation. Among other things, color is used to improve orientation (and affect mood); bathroom doors are black, the patients' own doors are painted in individual vivid colors, the hall to the dining room is painted the same color as the dining room itself. In Minnesota's Rochester State Hospital, behavior therapists developed a program to toilet train patients who regularly wet and soiled themselves. The six-week program reduced toilet accidents by half in the men and almost eliminated them in the women, although some of the group had been incontinent for twenty-five years. Even more remarkable than this achievement, however, were the methods which brought it about. Color again – bathroom doors bright yellow, readily identifiable. Posters of Joe Namath and Raquel Welch gazed approvingly down from the walls of the women's and men's bathrooms. Using the toilet was praised and immediately rewarded from a cart located in the bathroom and supplied with reinforcers to suit all tastes, including snacks, cold beer, and wine.[50]

Plan for as much independent function as possible.

What's possible in a hospital may not be practical in your relative's home, or yours. But the principle shines through, and you can think up your own applications: don't resign yourself to the pace of your relative's deterioration, but do your best to keep him or her functioning as fully as possible for as long as you can. Consultation with a rehabilitation specialist or social worker experienced in working with the aged can help show the way; if there's none such at your local community agencies, scream loud, for there ought to be. And remember the willingness of behavior therapists to consult on problems of daily living.

Community help

And do you have to do it all? Are there any rehabilitation programs outside of hospitals? There are some. Some cities have day hospital programs for the elderly, sometimes in community mental health centers, sometimes independently organized.

Some day programs give active treatment. Some are merely a place to sit. (Even so they give a needed respite.) Arthur Waldman, a Philadelphia consultant in gerontology, wants to see a Family Life Education Program "to encourage families to bring their parents for [rehabilitation] treatment at the earliest possible moment rather than wait for the crisis."[51] Good advice – when there's some way to follow it. Maybe there'll be more facilities by the time you read this, if state and federal governments find the money. And if you raise your voice loud and often. See Chapter XIV.

Living (and dying) at home

Old people want to live at home, and die there too. It's we, not they, who are uncomfortable with the word death. "Afraid to die?" said one old lady. "No, I welcome it. When people ask me, I say, 'Don't you know I have my ticket and I'm just waiting to be called?' To be old, doctor, to be sick, to be a burden. There is no way to understand, to reason, to think about it. Afraid to die? Ha!"[52]

What they are afraid of is that they will be forced* to move into nursing homes or hospitals that will maintain life longer than they

* "Almost all older people view the move to the home for the aged or to a nursing home with fear and hostility." Ethel Shanas, *The Health of Older People: A Social Survey* (Cambridge, Mass.: Harvard University Press, 1962), quoted in Butler and Lewis, *op. cit.*, p. 210.

have any use for it, eat up everything they've got, and leave them nothing to pass on to the future.* Even with Social Security, Medicare, Medicaid, that happens. State laws vary. Vermont, for instance, allows an old person publicly supported in a nursing home or hospital to keep his house and up to $1,500 in savings, though the home may have to be sold if the placement goes on for years. Not all states are so generous. Community social workers will advise you on regulations. In many welfare codes there is a "responsible relative" provision that requires relatives to use up their own resources before a parent, a wife or husband, brother or sister can get public assistance.[53] The spouses of long-term patients may lose the accumulated resources of a lifetime and end up on welfare themselves. If you can't keep your relative at home, or pay nursing home charges, the community will have to take over anyway. Sooner is better than later, and cheaper. You can quote Dr. Butler; even with senile psychosis, "many persons would be able to remain in their own homes throughout most of the course of the disease if adequate services and assistance were available."† An increasing number of states (Massachusetts is one) have Councils on Aging and Departments of Elder Affairs, good places to inquire. Fine plans are in the making; in some places they may be reality before you read this. When they are, they will save millions of dollars in hospitalization costs.‡ Frederick Whitham, Director of Berkshire Home Care, a state-funded agency in Pittsfield, Mass., is developing services ranging from daily telephone reassurance§ through assistance with shopping and home maintenance and repairs to daily home care, all directed toward keeping old people out of institutions and functioning independently as long as they can. Under the Older Americans Act, the federal government is organizing the "Triple A," the Area-wide Agency on Aging, to cover the whole country, coordinating and en-

Home help for your relative

* Dr. Robert Felix, former director of NIMH, remarks that putting old people in psychiatric institutions "reflects other people's solutions to their problems and in such cases often is both expensive and inhuman." "Revamped Aged Care Asked," *U.S. Medicine* (April 9, 1972). " 'Inappropriate hospitalization for mental problems is the undesirable and frequent fate of the aged.' Markson felt that 75 percent of geriatric patients in the two mental hospitals he studied did not require hospitalization. Furthermore, a survey of patients in the hospital in contrast to those receiving care at home showed 72.8 percent of hospital patients with chronic neglect as compared to 40.3 percent of those receiving home care." E. Markson, A. Kivoh, J. Cumming, and E. Cumming, "Alternatives to Hospitalization for Psychiatrically Ill and Geriatric Patients," *American Journal of Psychiatry,* 127 (1971):1055–1072, as cited by Robert J. Taylor and E. Fuller Torrey, "Mental Health Coverage Under a National Health Insurance Plan," *World Journal of Psychosynthesis,* 6 (1974): 22–27.

† Butler and Lewis, *op. cit.,* p. 78. Erdman Palmore notes that even among the psychotic elderly, more live at home than in institutions ("Social Factors in Mental Illness of the Aged," in Busse and Pfeiffer, *op. cit.,* p. 49).

‡ For dollars-and-cents examples, see Senator Charles Percy's *Growing Old in the Country of the Young* (New York: McGraw-Hill, 1974).

§ Some "Help" lines will also do this.

couraging necessary programs. In 1975 Congress for the first time mandated comprehensive community mental health centers to provide specialized services for the elderly. So inquire at your mental health center, or contact Family Service or the Visiting Nurses to see what's up where your elderly relative lives. (Don't expect services to be free unless you are really poor.)

and for you

When your relative lives with you, you still have needs. In most places, "respite services" are still in the talking stage. It might make all the difference to your emotional balance if Grandma could spend a week in the mental health center inpatient unit. Barring that, however, community agencies, churches, and service organizations may help you find a reliable sitter. Mother may accuse you of leaving her with a stranger, but the best thing you can do for the whole family may be to be firm and go to the movies without guilt.

AWAY FROM HOME

Homes for the aged

Homes for the aged are not the same as nursing homes, though some of these offer nursing services. To enter, the old person has to be in reasonably good physical and mental health. Most are selective, unless they are run, as some good ones are, by cities and counties. Some of the best are under the auspices of religious denominations, labor unions, or fraternal organizations. Your relative's social allegiances may help him in his old age.

Veterans' hospitals

For some families, the veterans' hospital is an option. (See Chapter XI, p. 246.) Dr. Paul Haber of the Veterans' Administration states that it "has the most comprehensive program for continued treatment and followup of the aging patient to be found anywhere in the free world."[54] State hospitals, as we've seen, are increasingly refusing geriatric patients and discharging the elderly, to live on their own if they can manage it, to foster homes and nursing homes if they can't.* Ironically, the less progressive your state is, the more likely that the state hospital admits old people.

State hospitals

When you just can't do it any longer

Dear Abby:

You printed a letter from a woman who felt guilty because she had put her senile, incontinent father in a nursing home. Her guilt was rein-

* More could be discharged if they had some place to go. Even Dr. Bourhill's rehabilitated patients don't all find satisfactory placements. He touches on a problem that is becoming more and more important: What can be done to assist the family of the returned patient? "It is our intention," he writes, "when we can spare the time and the personnel, to develop group counseling for relatives of patients. We feel that this would help to allay at least some of the fear felt by relatives whose only clear recollection of our patient is when he went berserk 20 or 30 years ago, prior to being rushed off to the mental hospital." (Personal communication, September 10, 1974.)

forced when she was reminded how her father had diapered her and put up with her childish babbling. . . . A child can be diapered in public. . . . An elderly person cannot. A child can be left in a playpen. An elderly person cannot. A child learns and matures in time. An older person becomes worse. The old person who can get around thinks he is capable of "cooking" and using matches and has to be watched every moment.

It's easy to get a baby sitter. Try to get someone to sit with an old person. Relatives won't even help.

"Princess" and her father

So, after eight years when I couldn't take any more, I found the nicest, cleanest nursing home I could afford and I took my elderly father there. I said goodbye with tears in my eyes to someone who didn't even know me. Then I went home and started to be a wife and mother again. I looked at my husband with grateful eyes for his willingness to pay for the care of my father in a nursing home. . . . Then the letters started to come from my brothers and sisters who had never offered to keep Dad for one day. They said, "YOU put Dad in a nursing home. How could you?"

I'll sign myself what my father always called me,

"Princess"[55]

Princess found a good home her family could afford. Will you? The United States is one of the few countries where the care of the sick elderly has become big business, run primarily for financial gain.[56] We may be able to accept that 90 percent of nursing homes are profit-making. It is a bit macabre, however, to learn that in 1969 Wall Street considered nursing homes a glamour industry. And rightly; they were a no-lose proposition for investors, their operation and expansion kept profitable by Social Security, Medicare, and government loans.[57] Nevertheless, many nursing homes give sympathetic care, and some provide active and resourceful programs. Many, many others don't. There's much worse to be said, but this is no place for one more exposé. You can read all about it in Adelaide Mendelson's *Tender, Loving Greed*.[58] But unless you are ready to make use of your anger (see the last chapter), save your energy for investigating what's available for your relative.

*"A place with few nurses and none of the characteristics of home"?**

Choosing a nursing home

Community agencies are good places to ask for advice, but other people's impressions are no substitute for your own. Senator Charles Percy's *Growing Old in the Country of the Young* is a useful guide to benefits and resources for the elderly; he devotes a whole section to choosing a nursing home. Watch out for unlicensed facilities and administrators (talk to the administrator); visit at midday so you can talk to the residents (and see what they have for lunch); don't spend less than an hour; see every floor. The senator gives a list of questions

* Butler and Lewis (p. 131) note this bitter definition. Moreover, "Doctors in nursing homes frequently tell patients and their families, 'Don't call me directly. I'll deal with your problems through the nurse.' The premium prices paid for care do not guarantee personal contact with the physician" (p. 134).

to ask; these, and more, are contained in *Nursing Home Care,* available for forty cents from your federal government.*

Community mental health centers should be providing outreach services to patients in nursing homes, but you can't count on it, "though hundreds of thousands of identified psychiatric patients now reside in such facilities."[59] You can't count on much. But since nursing homes are open institutions, you can visit, check conditions,† keep on visiting. Many mental health centers provide outreach services to nursing and foster homes.

Everybody's problem

Community mental health services should be for the elderly and their families; they are for everybody. There should be no age discrimination. The whole range of services should be available to all who need it, from psychotherapy and counseling, to rehabilitation and occupational therapy, to day treatment. Dr. Toolan considers the plight of old people, now and in years to come, America's most important mental health problem. The elderly already comprise 10 percent of our people. With failing health, steady inflation, and America's merciless accent on youth, they have much more than 10 percent of the trouble. Nobody expects much for them, and they don't expect much for themselves. What can you do? Voice your needs, and your parents'; you're not alone. This isn't just your problem. It's not going to go away, as the elderly live longer and there are more and more of them. Of us, that is.

* Write the Superintendent of Documents, U.S. Government Printing Office, Washington, DC 20402.

† Report complaints to your Social Security District (not local) Office, which will investigate. Each district office maintains a file of deficiencies in district nursing homes and hospitals; you can visit the office and ask to see it. In Idaho, Massachusetts, Michigan, Oregon, Pennsylvania, South Carolina, and Wisconsin, information and help are available from Nursing Home Ombudsman Projects.

»» CHAPTER XIV ««

The Lord Helps Those Who Help Themselves

The hand that helps best is the one at the end of your own arm.

S. CLARENCE GRIFFITH

late president of the National Society for Autistic Children

VOICE YOUR NEEDS. But you don't have to be told that one voice doesn't carry very far. This final chapter is about what people like ourselves have been able to accomplish together, making time when there isn't any, finding energy where there's no energy left. Cynics stop here, for this chapter is about hope and faith and communion, which rival the sun and the atom as energy resources. It's a mixture of inspiration and information, it's a pep talk, and it's all true.

There are times, we know it, when you're not ready for any pep talk, when all you want to do is crawl into your misery like a wounded animal, when encouragement seems like assault. We don't know anybody who hasn't felt like that. But it passes, because it has to. A mother who'd been trying for years to get help for her child explained why she'd missed a meeting with the school superintendent. "I just didn't have the strength," she said, "to hear 'no' again." The people who built the organizations described in this chapter heard "no" many times for every time they heard "yes." If you've gotten this far, you don't have to be told that you have to keep going, and why.

GETTING TOGETHER: CONSUMER ORGANIZATION THERAPY

Acorns

How does it happen that where there was nothing there comes to be something? People begin. That's the only way. It's February, 1974. A mother calls the information and referral service of a national organization, one of the organizations you're going to read about in this chapter. She's looking for a boarding school for her five-year-old son, because she's been told that's the best place for him. It's the only place for him, as far as she knows. The parent at the other end of the wire tells her about some residential schools, for she has a list, and some even take five-year-olds. But she also tells her about public school programs for children like hers and sends her the organization's information packet on how to go about getting them where they don't exist. With her information sheets and documents, the mother gets to work on her school board, her state representative, her state superintendent of schools. The plight of her child and of others like him makes headlines when she travels to the state capital and pickets on the statehouse steps. Within two months her state representative is writing the same parents' organization for model state legislation to guarantee a right to education. The director of special education, glad of public pressure for what he'd like to do anyway, pledges classes for September and gets on the wire to the parents' organization to find out about training programs for teachers. Public events — but there have also been private ones. That mother is no longer beaten, hopeless, miserable. She's someone who gets things done, someone to be consulted, someone who has influence. She feels different about herself, her child, her family's future. Shall we call it consumer organization therapy?

The number of pieces of mail handled by that information and referral office in that particular six months was 7,217 — half in, half out. After six years, money's been found to pay the mother of seven (the fourth is the sick one) who answers those inquiries. But she still runs it out of a room in her home, as she did in the days when it was hard to find the money even for stamps and the phone company.

That organization had begun only eight years before, with a group of distressed and angry parents sitting in a living room, not sure of what to do but sure that something had to be done and that nobody else was going to do it. Today it influences national legislation, helps get local services, and has transformed thousands of lives — not least, the lives of its founders.

into oaks

Seeds are small; everything living has small beginnings. That's what organizations grow from, schools,* workshops and activity centers, group homes. The first psychosocial rehabilitation center in the country, New York's Fountain House, was started by patients and volunteers who met on the steps of the New York Public Library. Today it has a $6 million building and serves three hundred people daily.[1] The typical history of local facilities for the mentally ill is that they got started on faith and hope and the hard, unpaid labor of love and *then* attracted community and governmental support. The Lord helps those who help themselves, and our neighbors do the same. We cannot depend on enlightened public policy; it is what we do, locally and in na-

* The League School grew out of one mother's phoning another; it started with their two children. Today it serves over one hundred and is an international model of therapeutic education. The physician Jacques May and his wife started the Parents' School (now the May Institute) when they could find no help for their twin autistic sons. Benhaven in New Haven and the Rimland School in Chicago were started by mothers who made of their private agony a public contribution. Their books have been noted in earlier chapters, for your encouragement and profit. The public school program for communication-disordered children in Pittsfield, Mass., is a paradigm of the development of community service. Started in borrowed quarters by two teachers, for children excluded from school, sustained by the hard work of parents, it was able to go out of business four years later when the public schools took over the program. The state of Massachusetts now guarantees education to all handicapped children, including, of course, the mentally ill. Private, volunteer effort can't meet the full need, but it can show the way.

tional organizations, that enlightens public policy and makes it responsive to our needs. What those of us who have lived these stories have discovered abolishes cynicism, for it's simply this: however it goes in the "normal" world, we cannot help our relatives or ourselves without helping others. Their personal needs for understanding and growth, their public needs for social services and research into causes and treatment, our needs for respite, support, and self-respect can be answered only by coming together with other people who know trouble from the inside.

Phone calls

We're inviting you to join a world of meetings, phone calls, letters, copies of letters, follow-up calls, follow-up visits, more letters, more phone calls, more visits. Not a very enticing prospect, when you're bruised and tired already. You'll get tireder. But it's a different kind of tiredness, and the bruises will pretty well disappear. Besides, you meet the most interesting people. First, those other families, your invisible neighbors, who understand your kind of trouble because they share it. But it's not to weep and commiserate and swap horror stories that you'll come together. You'll do some of that, and it will do you good, but you'll find it won't turn soggy and self-indulgent. Emotions don't when they're to be used as the motive power for action.

and new friends,

some of them

You'll also meet some fascinating professionals. You'll learn from them and they from you, for once there's no longer a desk between you you'll find you have a lot in common. What have you got to offer them? Plenty. It's exactly those people who are working on the most innovative programs, the most promising research, who care the most, who are most on the lookout for allies. "Parents," as Dr. Schopler said after a parents' campaign extended his program statewide, "have more clout." Don't be afraid; you'll find that these professionals treat you differently from what you're used to. A working alliance for public goals feels very different from a "therapeutic alliance," for both parties.*

pretty important

people

You'll meet people in government too, in your state and city (that's much easier than you think), maybe even in the nation. Every city has people who'd do something if they knew what to do (and a newspaper looking for human interest). Every state has dedicated officials — call them bureaucrats if you like — who have ideas on what to do and are looking for more ideas and for citizen support. And every state has legislators with a passionate concern for human needs, and others who are open to conviction, and others who are trying to get reelected and like to have citizens behind them. (Forget your usual politics in this; human needs make strange bedfellows.)

* I'm lucky enough to be friends with some of the distinguished professionals I've quoted in this book. I didn't meet them in therapy, or as a writer seeking information. I met them as a parent, through my organization. C. C. P.

Important people? Sure. But most of them have feelings and convictions,* and they all have telephones. You're important too, more important than you think. It feels very different when you call as the representative of an organization from what it did when you were "just a parent." Your very voice will show it, and so will the voice at the other end.

Consumer clout

Calls, visits, letters, more calls, more visits — for all you've heard about impersonal bureaucracies, they're made up of persons, and this, not magic, is what gets things done. It's amazing how quickly ordinary citizens can become influential. In any state the number of persistent, active citizens is small enough so that they get noticed. Before they know it, they find themselves on committees.

through personal interaction

If you don't like up-front work, there's plenty behind the scenes. Nobody helps more than those who stuff envelopes or scrounge for money. You can expect to spend more time thinking about money than mental illness, as even the most successful programs have a hard time attracting stable funding. You'll learn to move from cake sales to applications for government grants. It's all these things, along with faith, that move mountains.† That's a heady discovery, that mountains are movable. You could call it therapeutic.

They also serve who only bake for cake sales.

HOW TO WRITE A LETTER

In Washington, Congressman Michael Harrington of Massachusetts is one of those who are passionately concerned. Letters, he says, helped make him that way; they "opened my eyes to the extent of the problem." His advice can't be bettered:

What makes people listen:

> Your most effective tool in influencing legislators is your own experience. Let them know both the emotional and financial difficulties you face. Many Congressmen will be shocked at the actual cost and hardship you endure. . . . In a Congressional office most of the correspondence is bureaucratic, boring, statistical and intellectualized. But the letters from the parents showed me the human side of the problem. . . . Such letters do not allow your representatives to hide the reality of the situation by burying themselves in numbers.

advice from a Congressman.

Of course, you don't just pour out a tale of woe. Know what you want, and say it.

> The best action is collective. Letters by Presidents or Directors of groups are fine, but their effectiveness is increased by additional letters from

* You can bet that some of them have mentally ill relatives, too.

† See the excellent, detailed suggestions in *How to Organize an Effective Parent Group and Move Bureaucracies,* available from the Coordinating Council for Handicapped Children, Room 950, 407 S. Dearborn Street, Chicago, IL 60605.

Tell

members of your organization. Tell your Congressman and Senators the needs. . . . Offer proposals. You know better than he does what needs to be done. . . . The proposals do not have to be in the best prose, nor need they be in legal form. Your representatives have staffs skilled in writing legislation. Their biggest problem is in knowng what kind of legislation is needed. I also suggest that letters be brief and to the point. Congressmen and Senators receive a large amount of correspondence daily.

Encourage professionals to write too.

Many Congressmen have no idea of the types of treatment involved. . . . Some have no knowledge of what the diseases are or their effects. Parents and professionals make a powerful combination.

Talk to your representatives; all of them have offices in the district they represent.

and show.

Invite your representative to see the facilities available to your children. If the representative cannot go, ask one of his staff. They will never forget the experience.

But always be polite:

You may be faced with abysmal ignorance of your problems, but by losing your temper you lose the battle. By quietly and forcefully presenting your views you may not prevail the first time, but you will gain a lot of respect and will be well received the next time.[2]

CLASS ACTIONS

Going to law

Writing and talking to our representatives is a simple thing. Not simple at all is forcing the issue by recourse to law. That's hard, long, and expensive, and you almost need an organization behind you. But it may be what it takes to get things moving.

A class action suit is a suit which is brought in the name of a whole class of plaintiffs, as *Wyatt* v. *Stickney* was brought in the name of Ricky Wyatt "and all others similarly situated." Class actions are powerful tools, because they go beyond individual to collective injustice. Ricky Wyatt might have been discharged next day, or provided with individual treatment (as sometimes happens when administrators are threatened with lawsuits), and the case would have gone forward just the same. Class actions are perhaps the most powerful levers we have for moving mountains.* For this reason, organizations support class

* Up-to-date information on current court cases, including class action suits, can be had from *Mental Retardation and the Law,* published several times a year by the President's Committee on Mental Retardation, Office of the Assistant Secretary for Human Development, U.S. Department of Health, Education and Welfare, Washington, DC 20201.

actions, as the National Association for Mental Health did in *Wyatt,* and initiate them when they can, as in *PARC* v. *Pennsylvania.* Affirmations of a right to treatment and a right to education (see Chapter XII) may bring an expansion of rights into other areas. Attorney Frank Laski of the National Center for Law and the Handicapped feels that "something akin to a right to rehabilitation may emerge full blown from the convergence of right to education and right to treatment." Such a right would be of overwhelming importance.

A 1974 Supreme Court decision made class actions more difficult by requiring the plaintiff to notify all members of the class by mail at his own expense. Money is important, as we don't have to tell you. Even though members of public interest law firms often give their time, they can't always work for nothing, and there are many other costs. Peter Sitkin and Anthony Kline, attorneys for San Francisco's Public Advocates, Inc., suggest the use of court-awarded attorneys' fees to finance public interest litigation by public interest lawyers and law firms. Court-awarded fees would make a great difference to mental health law. "Vindication of important legal rights," say Kline and Sitkin, "should not depend upon the beneficence of private philanthropy or be subject to the whims of government."[3] And they cite a judicial opinion:

> If successful plaintiffs were routinely forced to bear their own attorney's fees, few aggrieved parties would be in a position to advance the public interest by invoking the injunctive powers of the federal courts.[4]

Society itself has an interest in the class action, wrote Supreme Court Justice Douglas.

> A class action serves not only the convenience of the parties but also prompt, efficient judicial administration. . . . There are bound to be innumerable people in common disasters, calamities, or ventures who would go begging for justice without the class action. . . . The class action is one of the few legal remedies the small claimant has against those who command the status quo. I would strengthen his hand with the view of creating a system of law that dispenses justice to the lowly as well as those liberally endowed with power and wealth.[5]

A sense of proportion

As consumer clout takes a lot of time and energy, there may be those to remind you that there can be something unhealthy about burying yourself in The Problem, to caution you "not to lose your sense of proportion," "to find other interests," "think about other things." And so you should, and so you will, when your concentration begins to pay off. The result of your efforts, after all, should be that your relative has some services and you have some time for yourself. But don't let anyone tell you that concerning yourself with what so deeply concerns you is unhealthy in itself. Will your close, intense focus on trouble distort your perceptions? Change your life? Do you know anyone who's lived close with mental illness who can ever see things in the same way again? Our lives are changed already. To work together to control those changes instead of being at their mercy is the way of growth, for us and our relative.

Not all of the organizations that can help you were started by relatives. Some were started by doctors; some, like the National Association for Mental Health, were started by former patients. The ultimate consumers of mental health services, after all, are the mentally ill themselves. Today more and more recovered mental patients are challenging the stigma of mental illness and taking an active part in pressing for needed services and enlightened policies. But those are the *ex*-patients. Those most in need are silent; the sickest cannot speak for themselves. In every organization that speaks for them, those who learned the problems of mental illness in their own families must play a leading part.

*National Association for Mental Health**

We'll start with NAMH,* the first and strongest of the consumer organizations. (Don't confuse it with NIMH, the National Institute of Mental Health, which is an agency of the federal government.) Founded by ex-patient Clifford Beers as the Connecticut Society for Mental Hygiene in 1908, it is now the primary mental health lobby in the United States. You've probably seen the bell that is its symbol, once a year at any rate when it's time to raise money. Four feet high and heavy bronze, it stands in the lobby of a handsome headquarters across the Potomac from the nation's capital. It was cast from the metal of chains and shackles once used to restrain the mentally ill.

NAMH is a good example of how attitudes have changed. The professionals who were once "ambivalent about whether they really wanted laymen getting into the act"[6] now gladly accept NAMH's influence. NAMH works for better programs, more research funding, for more community mental health centers, better hospitals, for the rights of patients, for increased understanding and an end to stigma, for just about everything you can think of. Its information service can locate any statistic you want on mental health and illness; its authoritative books, published in collaboration with the American Psychiatric Association, and its inexpensive booklets and leaflets are a valuable resource. See Chapter VI, p. 142, for what state and local chapters may be able to do for your personal problem.

What they can do depends, of course, on how hard the people in them work and how many there are. NAMH is the only organization that speaks for all the mentally ill. Joining it is a way to affect the state and national policies that affect you. It is a way to insure that the

* 1800 North Kent Street, Rosslyn, VA 22209. Tel. (703) 528-6405.

community facilities, like community mental health centers and clinics, which some are encouraging to spread their attention over all the problems of society, do not forget their commitment to serve the mentally ill and their families.

The National Association for Retarded Citizens

There are two organizations that aren't concerned with mental illness, but that no account of those who help themselves can overlook. The National Association for Retarded Citizens (formerly Retarded Children) was the first of the parents' organizations, and it now has chapters almost everywhere. Dorothy Murray, in *This Is Stevie's Story,** recalls those early days of hard work; it's hard to believe that in 1949, when she received a diagnosis of "mental retardation" for her son, it was a term she'd never even heard. Parents' organizations for the retarded led the way in pressing for decent facilities, for education (remember *PARC* v. *Pennsylvania*), for human rights (NARC was a "friend of the court" in *Jackson* v. *Indiana* and *Wyatt* v. *Stickney;* NAMH joined them in *Wyatt*). They were the first to show what wonders parents can accomplish.

and parent power

> Most, if not all, of the credit for the successful initiation and development of activity centers . . . belongs to the parents of the retarded. . . . The parents made the major breakthrough for diagnostic, education, sheltered workshops and employment programs for the retarded.[7]

Not mental health professionals, not educators, but families got the retarded out of society's back room. You can see the moral.

Alcoholics Anonymous

Alcoholics Anonymous is the foster-parent of all self-help groups; the World Health Organization has called it "the greatest therapeutic organization in the world."[8] We won't describe AA; everybody knows about it. For families of the mentally ill, AA is a model of how ordinary people, unpaid and untrained, can build a world organization to change the lives of millions. But it is more than an example. It's a major resource for you if your relative's problems of living include alcohol. AA recognized early the overlap between alcoholism and mental illness — in the early fifties volunteers from the community were already starting groups inside mental hospitals. Then professionals were at best indifferent; today AA groups operate in most hospitals with full professional support. For families, Alanon and Alateen (for teenagers) offer the expertise and support of those who know the problem. We've neglected alcoholism in this book. But don't forget AA (or its offspring, the other "Anonymous" organizations for narcotics, child abuse, etc.) † if your problems won't stay in the box with the easy-to-read label.

Alanon and Alateen

* (Revised and enlarged ed., New York: Abingdon Press, 1967.) "Stevie" illustrates the overlap between retardation and mental illness; he could equally well have been called autistic or schizophrenic.

† For addresses, see Appendix B.

Recovery, Inc., the Association of Former Nervous and Mental Patients

There's a self-help organization for mental patients too. Dr. Karl Menninger tells about it:

> Many years ago when Bob Knight [the psychoanalyst Robert Knight] and I used to go to Chicago from Topeka every two weeks for two hard days' work at the Institute, we used to see a kindly, quiet-voiced, short-statured man who was polite and friendly but, we thought, rather persistently obsessed with starting an organization for persons who had formerly been patients in state hospitals. It seemed a good enough thing, but not very exciting and I'm ashamed to say not very interesting to us. Dr. Abraham Low was a member of our psychoanalytic society, of the American Psychiatric Association, and of the Psychiatric Institute of the University of Illinois – of which he was Director. But he and his project were pretty largely ignored, except, of course, by the people who are legion whose lives were saved or fulfilled by it. Dr. Low published a textbook in 1950 (*Mental Health Through Will-Training*)[9] which numerous publishers had declined: it never received a review. But it is now in its 15th printing! His biography . . . is receiving shining reviews.[10] It is about the organization Recovery, which he founded.[11]

Dr. Low started Recovery* in 1937; he died in 1954, still ignored by his colleagues. Between 1952 and 1968 the organization grew from a dozen groups to 650 in forty-one states. But although these were years of mounting interest in group therapy, no article on Recovery appeared in any professional journal until 1971. When a psychiatrist did at length publish a brief report in the *American Journal of Psychiatry*, he praised with gingerly caution. He had, he said, referred two hundred patients to Recovery in twenty years and believed they showed "better progress than those who did not participate," but he still felt it necessary to list fourteen separate disadvantages in presenting the organization to his colleagues.†

Not surprisingly, there was no great rush to recommend Recovery, or even to investigate it. It's hard for doctors to trust patients to help themselves.

"Some are even self-referred."

> The ideal referral to Recovery should come from a physician or a psychiatrist [about 20 percent of referrals in fact do] with the patient remaining under his doctor's care. . . . The fact of the matter is that such ideals are not enforceable. . . . Patients are accepted from many sources, lay and professional, and some are even self-referred. . . . Therefore it follows that Recovery, though often serving an important need, is not an unmixed blessing.[13]

* 116 South Michigan Avenue, Chicago, IL 60603. Tel. (312) 263-2292.

† He reported "more rapid symptomatic improvement; less self-consciousness and embarrassment; a greater sense of pride, accomplishment, and degree of commitment; better coping behavior; accelerated social rehabilitation; and less tendency to decompensate under stress." Among the disadvantages: "frequent disregard of the admonition to follow the physician's authority; danger of delaying adequate professional care in serious cases; risk of bungling by inept amateurs"; and, "there is an antitherapeutic suppression of ambivalence and hostility."[12]

Unmixed blessings are as rare in psychiatry as in anything else, but thirty years of professional neglect came close to being one, for it allowed Recovery to become and remain a completely self-help organization. In 1952 Dr. Low turned it over to its members, and it has been entirely led by laymen ever since. Though groups are open and professionals are as welcome as anybody else, they are specifically barred from leading discussions.

If your relative goes to Recovery he'll soon meet Dr. Low. Readings from his works open every meeting; his heavily accented voice, preserved on records,* sounds like the psychiatrist of your dreams. Dr. Low is Aesculapian authority personified.

> Getting well is a business. It is emphatically not a game, certainly not a wild gamble. Unfortunately, my patients have the tendency to play and gamble with their health. They give unthinking and wanton precedence to the stirrings of their "human nature" to the detriment of their only legitimate goal: to get well.[14]

"Averageness"

Don't romanticize your illness, patients are told; don't intellectualize. Your symptoms and your distress are not exceptional but common. Recognize this. Train yourself to cope with the ordinary stresses you encounter daily; exceptional stresses are exceptional. Reduce your expectations; if you insist on being more than average, you expect too much. Exceptionality is for people who are well. Recovery is work:

> It is understandable and natural to hate the discomfort of laborious and untiring practice, to want to give way to temper, to play for attention, to crave sympathy and to indulge in self-pity, to complain and work oneself up. But all this is gambling with the business of getting well. . . . The business calls, first and foremost, for labor and exertion and self-control.[15]

Don't diagnose yourself. Trust your doctor, whoever he is, and do what he tells you. Recovery deals with symptoms, not diagnoses.

Not will power but will training

The "moral treatment" lives. The business of life is "to create and maintain values," the values of family, community, education, sociability. Duty, effort, will are key words. Recovery members encourage each other in a process Dr. Low called "will training." They expect each other to practice a set of very specific techniques for controlling temper, nipping self-pity in the bud, and pulling their socks up. The method must be continually practiced; it is a "modern fallacy to believe that understanding a method means acquiring it."[16] Buttressed by Dr. Low's Aesculapian authority, rhythmic formulas make the principles easy to remember. "Feelings are not facts." Symptoms are "dis-

* For instance, "There Is No Hopeless Case," "The Fear of Life Ebbing Away," "The Obsession of Being Contaminated," "The Obsessive Fear of Dirt and Germs," all available from Recovery, Inc.

tressing but not dangerous," "phasic but not basic" (that is, they'll go away if you let them). Above all, "command your muscles." Insomnia, for instance, is distressing but not dangerous; you will get adequate rest if you command your muscles to lie quietly. Are you obsessed with jealousy? Command your muscles not to rummage through your husband's pockets or open your wife's mail and let the idea die from lack of nourishment, "as ideas commonly do."[17] Are you too exhausted to get up? Swing your legs over the side of the bed. Are you working yourself into a panic? Palpitations, numbness, dizziness, difficulty of concentration, dimness of vision, nausea, headaches do not herald the return of mental illness; remind yourself firmly that they are phasic but not basic.

"Command your muscles."

Does all this sound too simple? Dr. Low has heard that before. "I like to think of myself as a lost soul," said one of his patients. He was one of the kind who

Too simple for lost souls?

> resent simple methods . . . as an insult to their intelligence. The procedure is likely to appear insulting and, indeed, humiliating because if excruciating tortures of years' duration can be disposed of with such simple means, why . . . the years of wailing, temper tantrums, neglect of duty, and financial sacrifice? Recovery [counters] with the alternative question: Is the fact that you suffered needlessly in the past sufficient excuse to continue the suffering into the future just because the mode of treatment fails to impress you as intricate or dignified?[18]

After this it will scarcely surprise you to learn that Recovery meetings are highly structured and that they do not encourage either "confrontation" or "insight." Nobody talks about how they got that way; instead they recount the successes of the method. The method is relentlessly practical. Facts are emphasized, interpretations discouraged.

> Be certain to describe, not to give opinions and interpretations. . . . Description mentions what was done, said, or felt. Interpretation deals with what was thought. . . . Don't say, "I was uncooperative at home." Instead, describe as follows: "Whenever my mother told me to do something I did the reverse. I yelled when somebody refused to give me what I wanted." It is permissible, however, to mention an interpretation and immediately supply the description. ["Pessimism" is an interpretation, but] you can say: "I was so pessimistic, I felt an emptiness in the stomach, my muscles were heavy, I had little desire to act or move."[19]

Evidently, Dr. Low knew about behavior therapy long before the behavior therapists did.* Recovery is simple, clear, unambiguous, structured, practical, external. Dr. Low had much to say about "romanto-

* Miriam Siegler and Dr. Humphry Osmond point out that behavior therapy is a modern example of a "moral model" of treatment, quite compatible with the medical model. Recovery, Inc., shows the combination with particular force. *Models of Madness, Models of Medicine* (New York: Macmillan, 1974), pp. 28, 41, 176, 190.

intellectual" patients, and if your relative is one, Recovery probably won't appeal. Many people drop out of Recovery. But it works for many others, some of whom have been very sick. The earlier career of Phil Crane, Recovery's leadership director since 1952, was cut short by paranoid schizophrenia;[20] he was hospitalized three times with over ninety shock treatments before he could be persuaded to go to Recovery. About half of Recovery members have been hospitalized at least once. The majority of members are what most psychiatrists would call neurotics; Dr. Low called them "nervous patients." Recovery does *not* admit openly disturbed people to meetings. Recall that in Dr. Low's day hospital doors had not yet begun to revolve, and really disturbed people were not likely to be released. Recovery is what its name implies — a group of people who are partly well already, a cheap ($7.50 a year) and for many people effective supplement to professional therapy or substitute for it. Like so many other programs, it excludes the sickest, and the sickest aren't likely to be up to it.

So don't think you've found the answer for your schizophrenic relative — as if you could. If he's stabilized, however, and acting pretty normal, Recovery meetings may be a good support. As Dr. Stanley Dean says, it can "serve an important 'caretaker' function in those cases where psychiatric treatment is not available for one reason or another, such as lack of funds or resistance on the part of a patient or his family to psychotherapy."[21] "The best prospects," according to Dr. Hanus Grosz, professor of Psychiatry at the Indiana School of Medicine, "seem to be patients with chronic recurrent symptoms, particularly of anxiety or phobia, depression, and obsessive compulsive neurosis."[22] And there are certainly a lot of those.

It's easy to poke fun at Recovery methods, especially for us romanto-intellectuals with a taste for the mysterious and complex and an intolerance for catchwords. For Recovery, however, we might coin one of our own: "Simple but not stupid."

Simple but not stupid

Recovery now has seven thousand members, with ten thousand people attending weekly meetings (which are free). In 1974 there were 1,025 chapters, in every state, Canada, and Puerto Rico. Relatives are welcome to attend; Dr. Low placed great emphasis on ordinary domestic transactions.*

We've devoted so much space to Recovery because it's the only self-help organization (besides AA) that is likely to have a group anywhere near you. A Schizophrenics Anonymous exists, with ongoing chapters in some cities,† but it has not been as successful as AA and Recovery.

Schizophrenics Anonymous

* Dr. Low has a book to help you reinforce the method, and to avoid being meddlesome and overprotective: *Lectures to Relatives of Former Patients* (Boston: Christopher Publishing House, 1943).

† Addresses from the Huxley Institute, p. 415.

Groups tend to peter out unless nonpatients keep them going. The sociologist Miriam Siegler, who has devoted a lot of effort to SA, points out that one of the things about schizophrenics is that they don't form groups.* Nevertheless, with a lot of help from nonpatients, including AA, Schizophrenics Anonymous is slowly spreading. Like Recovery (and AA) it subscribes to a medical model, buttressed by moral expectations. The schizophrenic patient must realize he has a physical illness, like tuberculosis or diabetes, for which neither he nor anybody else is to blame. It is his duty to follow doctor's orders to get well. Doctors who work with SA prescribe such old-fashioned remedies as rest, routine, and proper nourishment (Dr. Diet and Dr. Quiet, they were called a hundred years ago); they add modern somatic treatments, megavitamins, and psychotherapy in an atmosphere of confident optimism. As patients become physically healthy, they have the duty to work to "divest themselves of unsuitable and destructive behavior patterns acquired when ill."[23] SA and Recovery go well together, and some patients attend both.

A medical model

Mental Patients' Liberation

At the opposite pole are the patients' liberation groups. They stress, not moral bootstrapping (still less, medical treatments), but political action. Originating in New York in 1971, the ideas of the Mental Patients Liberation Project† have spread, and groups with similar names (Mental Patients' Liberation Front, Mental Patients' Resistance, Insane Liberation, etc.) have started up in Baltimore, Boston, Philadelphia, Oregon, Michigan, Minnesota, Kansas, and elsewhere. Goals are to help former hospital patients find jobs and housing and regain self-confidence, and to "fight the abuses of the existing mental health system," which "serves the interests of those in power in this society who desire to keep people who are 'different' out of sight, out of mind, and under control."[24] "We believe that we have 'gone crazy' because we live in a society that puts wealth, property, and power above the basic needs of human beings."[25] Szasz and Laing are heroes in the fight for "freedom from the oppression of institutional psychiatry."[26] Liberation groups deserve some of the credit if legislatures and hospitals today are more careful of patients' rights than they used to be.‡ If it will do your relative good to fight for his rights (and nourish a vivid sense of injustice) you can help him find his way to one of these groups. They

Political action

Self-help

* "Quite unlike all other deviants, mental patients do *not* combine or form a subculture based on their common deviance. There are no riots in mental hospitals, however abysmal the conditions." Schizophrenia is "a solvent which destroys the social glue of human relationships." *Op. cit.*, pp. 68, 183.

† 56 E. 4th Street, New York, NY 10003. Tel. (212) 475-9305. The radical therapist magazine *Rough Times*, reachable at Box 89, W. Somerville, MA 02144, maintains a current list of these organizations.

‡ Free to patients, MPLF in Massachusetts publishes a detailed insider's guide to state laws and practices affecting mental patients. Similar guides are available in some other states.

share some of SA's problems; David Kane, a New York member called "the can opener" for his success in getting patients out of hospitals, reports that very few of the patients he's helped ever join.

and no medical model

Unlike Recovery, liberation groups do *not* exhort their members to trust their physician.

Other liberation groups:

There are other groups who have reason to feel aggrieved at society's unfairness. Though they don't concern themselves specifically with mental illness, they do address themselves to the special mental health needs of the groups they serve. Women, homosexuals, ex-prisoners all have good reason for objecting to the attitudes they have observed in many mental health professionals – attitudes that, of course, aren't unique to them but reflect the values of society. These groups, which may be national or local, formal or informal, organized or (sometimes) disorganized, take as one of their functions to provide guidance to members – and nonmembers – in finding the kind of therapy they feel they can profitably use.

Women

City chapters of the National Organization for Women can advise on area therapists sympathetic to their aims. Where there's no chapter, there may well be a locally organized women's group, or an informal "consciousness-raising" group. For example, the Boston Women's Collective* publishes a yearly *Women's Yellow Pages* ("the original source book for women"), containing six closely printed pages on "Shopping for a Therapist," "How to Make Therapy Work for You," etc., with a list of agencies and clinics. The Women's Liberation Center and The Therapy Rights Committee of New Haven† publish a pamphlet, *Your Rights as a Woman in Therapy*. Other local women's organizations publish similar material.

Homosexuals

Local "gay" organizations will also advise on the problems of therapy and therapists. A newsletter, *Gay People and Mental Health,* is published from time to time (Suite 3b, 490 West End Avenue, New York, NY 10024).

Prisoners and ex-prisoners

The Fortune Society, run by ex-prisoners, publishes a newspaper and is a valuable resource for dealing with the problems of people coming out of jail, including their mental health problems. Address: 29 East 22nd Street, New York, NY 10010; tel. (213) 677-4600.

In places where there are no large organizations of this kind, you may be able to get in touch with local groups by inquiring at local colleges, health and birth control clinics, and from liberal church groups.

Some group organizations specialize in a particular disorder or group of disorders.

Epilepsy Foundation of America

The Epilepsy Foundation of America‡ serves the nation's four mil-

* 490 Beacon Street, Boston, MA 02115. Tel. (617) 261–1561.
† 215 Park Street, New Haven, CT 06511. Tel. (203) 436-0272.
‡ 1828 L. Street, N.W., Suite 406, Washington, DC 20036. Tel. (202) 293-2930.

lion epileptics and their families. Epilepsy has always been recognized as a medical condition. Doctors founded the organizations out of which today's EFA grew, and doctors (mostly neurologists) play a greater part in its administration than they do in the other organizations we've described. In 1974 EFA had 170 chapters nationwide. There may well be a chapter in your city; it will be listed in the telephone book under "E." Locally and nationally, the EFA is your quickest source of information on the types of epilepsy, on research and treatment, on where to find help and what kinds of help there are. Robin White received no such briefing after his son's first seizure, although the boy was treated in a major teaching hospital.

Like most of these organizations EFA has a professional-advisory board of distinguished specialists. The foundation grants training fellowships and supports research. An information and referral service operates on both the local and national levels. There is a directory of clinic facilities and of diagnostic and evaluation services. Some local chapters sponsor clinics. Local chapters provide counseling for patients and families. They give financial assistance with the costs of medication. They concern themselves with vocational rehabilitation and employment and with transportation – important, since most states bar epileptics from driving. They work with schools and teachers. They press for the repeal of discriminatory laws. The national office publishes a monthly newspaper, and offers genetic counseling. If your phone book yields no local number, the national office will tell you the location of the nearest chapter; if it's too far away, they'll send information on how to organize one. In some areas, epilepsy programs are maintained by the National Society for Crippled Children and Adults.*

Schizophrenia Fellowship in Britain

Schizophrenia, unlike epilepsy (or heart disease, or cancer, or other major illnesses) as yet has no representative national organization. This is not surprising, since there is as yet no common approach to the disease, or even common agreement that it *is* a disease. Providing information is one of the most important functions of a consumers' organization, but it's hard to imagine what information an organization on schizophrenia could give out that would not rouse an important section of professional opinion to fevered disagreement, or how it could decide where to refer an inquirer. Schizophrenia is the mirror of American psychiatry. In England the National Schizophrenia Fellow-

* On the national level, EFA is not consumer-run, but a highly professionalized organization. In 1974 hearings on charitable organizations, Senator Walter Mondale's Subcommittee on Children and Youth heard testimony that a disproportionate amount of money raised goes into administration and fund-raising, rather than services and research. Mondale, "The Truth in Contributions Act," *The Exceptional Parent,* 5 (March–April 1975).

ship, composed of relatives and professionals, has bypassed such conflicts by concerning itself specifically with the problems of living with schizophrenia. Much of their work is to press for recognition of "the fact that relatives are the real primary care agents,"[27] in these days of back-to-the-community, and for more guidance in the techniques of daily living and fuller support services, such as activity centers and permanent hostels. Schizophrenia Fellowship as yet has no American offspring. Fellowship can reach across the sea, however; their publications, *Schizophrenia at Home,* by social worker Clare Creer and the internationally known specialist in schizophrenia John Wing, and *Living with Schizophrenia,* described with simple eloquence as "By the Relatives," are well worth ordering from abroad.*

The Huxley Institute for Biosocial Research

The Huxley Institute for Biosocial Research,† named for the writer Aldous Huxley and his brother Julian, the British biochemist, concentrates on schizophrenia, but its interests include hyperactivity, learning disabilities, and aging, as well as alcohol and drug abuse. It was formerly the American Schizophrenia Foundation, and local chapters — about forty nationwide — still keep the word "schizophrenia" in their titles. The institute espouses a biological approach, emphasizing the controversial orthomolecular, or megavitamin, treatment (see Chapter IV, pp. 106–109). The New York Schizophrenia Foundation operates an orthomolecular clinic, and the institute sponsors medical training in orthomolecular methods, serving as a national education and referral center for physicians as well as schizophrenics and families.

Institute staff are sympathetic listeners, for each has had personal or family experience. Convinced advocates of the role of nutrition in curing mental illness, they will put you in touch with local chapters and refer you to doctors in your region who are experienced in orthomolecular methods — if there are any, for demand outstrips supply. The institute maintains a library and a list of publications and puts out a quarterly newsletter. The foundation maintains a friendly association with Schizophrenics Anonymous.

National Society for Autistic Children

Founded in 1965 by a professional who was also a parent (and author of a basic text on his child's disorder),[28] the National Society for Autistic Children‡ is "dedicated to the education and welfare of all children with severe disorders of communication and behavior,"

* *Schizophrenia at Home* is a detailed report of the different problems of living experienced by a representative group of the families of chronic schizophrenics. *Living with Schizophrenia* is a collection of extracts from members' letters; $7.50 to National Schizophrenia Fellowship, 29 Victoria Road, Surbiton, Surrey KT 4JT, England, should cover both, plus postage.

† 1114 First Avenue, New York, NY 10021. Tel. (212) 759-9554.

‡ 169 Tampa Avenue, Albany, NY 12208. Tel. (518) 489-7375.

"Severe disorders of communication and behavior"

whether they've been labeled autistic, aphasic, schizophrenic, psychotic, brain-injured, or retarded.* NSAC lobbies in Washington for the interests of such children, and the adults they grow into, including more and better educational programs, hospital facilities, community facilities, and research. If you'd heard the word "autistic" before you read Chapter XII, it was probably because of NSAC. A newsletter reports on successful psychoeducational programs, current research, legislation, and the development of individual children. A yearly conference brings together parents, medical and psychological specialists, teachers, mental health professionals to share ideas with unprecedented ease and freedom. For three years running autistic young people themselves have addressed the convention, describing their own unique experience and hard-won progress. NSAC's information and referral service† gives the usual information on diagnostic and evaluation centers, schools, and hospitals, and will put you in touch with parents with experience of a particular facility. It can connect you with other parents in your area with problems like your own.‡ It can furnish information on federal and state laws and important court rulings.

NSAC provides no direct services; although a few local chapters have founded or support private schools, NSAC's main push is to open the public schools and provide community facilities for mentally ill children. There are some ninety chapters in thirty states. Many chapters have their own collections of helpful books, and the national office operates a mail-order service for both popular and specialized books on childhood mental illness. Most of the books on children mentioned in Chapter XII are available by mail from NSAC or the Association for Children with Learning Disabilities (next section).

State organizations for emotionally disturbed children

NSAC is the only national organization for mentally ill children,§ but there are independent organizations in several states for children variously defined as mentally ill or emotionally disturbed. The Michigan Association for Emotionally Disturbed Children has thirteen local chapters. There is a similar association in California. In Milwaukee, Wisconsin, Parent Advocates for Children Today (ACT) has an active

* "The term 'Autistic Children' as used by the National Society for Autistic Children shall include persons regardless of age with severe disorders of communication and behavior whose disability became manifest during the early developmental stages of childhood. 'Autistic Children' includes but is not limited to: those afflicted with infantile autism (Kanner's syndrome), childhood psychosis, childhood schizophrenia or any other condition characterized by severe deficits in language ability (such as profound aphasia) and behavior and by a failure to relate appropriately to others." Revised definition, 1975.

† 306 31st Street, Huntington, WV 25702. Tel. (304) 697-2638.

‡ It can supply lists of parents with musically talented autistic children, autistic twins, adopted autistic children, blind autistic children, deaf autistic children.

§ The Association for Mentally Ill Children in Boston, Massachusetts, maintains a loose association with NSAC.

program. "Emotionally disturbed" is a deliberately vague term, and these groups serve all sorts of children. In general, however, they do not show the marked abnormalities of communication and behavior associated with a diagnosis of psychosis; they are likely to seem like "normal kids" who nevertheless have severe difficulty in coping with their world. If there is such a group in your area, your state mental health association will know.

Association for Children with Learning Disabilities

The Association for Children with Learning Disabilities,* like NSAC, is a parent-founded organization where parents and professionals work together. Its services to members are similar to NSAC's; it too assembles distinguished professionals for annual meetings, distributes useful books and articles, publishes directories,† serves as an information clearinghouse, puts you in touch with people who understand your problem. The parents of ACLD, like the parents of NSAC, have transformed the possibilities for their children. Two specialists, Professor Charles Brutten and Dr. Sylvia Richardson, put it succinctly:

> The Association for Children with Learning Disabilities has been primarily responsible for the gains made for learning-disabled children in this nation. It is a parent's biggest ally. Join it.[29]

and some affiliates

There are ACLD affiliates in forty-seven states, Puerto Rico, and the Virgin Islands. Parents of "exceptional children" can get first aid and encouragement from either of these organizations, and either will refer you to the other. A few ACLD affiliates have names that don't mention learning disabilities. One is the extremely active CANHC (California Association for Neurologically Handicapped Children – rhymes with "panic"). The New York Association for Brain-Injured Children is another. The Massachusetts group is called Massachusetts Child, Inc. Addresses of all affiliates are available from the national office.

All these groups offer sympathy and the shrewd, tough voice of experience at the other end of a telephone wire. All will advise you on how to form a new chapter. Yearly membership fees are ridiculously low, especially when you consider the price of information and support in the professional marketplace. In fact, we should have put these organizations in the chapter on money. They're a best buy.

The following paragraph could have been written about any of these organizations.

> It was a tremendous relief to me and my husband as parents of an autistic son to learn there was such an organization as yours. . . . In the course of our many visits to psychiatrists, neurologists, social workers,

* 5225 Grace Street, Pittsburgh, PA 15236. Tel. (412) 881-1191.

† Particularly useful is a list of state directors of special education and vocational rehabilitation.

> etc., we were often told to "get together" with other parents of autistic children as a therapeutic measure. However, no professional in this field ever told us of the National Society for Autistic Children. It was only by chance that I picked up a copy of *The Exceptional Parent* and thereby found mention of the NSAC. I find it truly appalling that these agencies do not refer a parent immediately to your organization and that, in our case, the professionals seemed to know so little about it.[30]

Appalling is a pretty strong word. But it certainly is too bad. You can help. Get the mental health professional you deal with a supply of leaflets for his office.

Not just children

Don't think we've forgotten about adults in our enthusiasm for organizations with "children" in their names. The parents who got these organizations going had young children once. But The Exceptional Child Grows Up, as the title of a very good book has it,[31] and organizations grow along with him, and her. The "C" of "Children" eventually comes to stand for "Citizen," as it has in NARC, which blazed the trail. Any of the parents' organizations will help you if your problem is with an adult suffering from the disorders they're concerned with. They are the best guide to vocational possibilities, counseling and support services, semi-independent and sheltered housing arrangements,* workshops, and activity centers when they exist. But here is the yawning gap, in services, in support, in understanding. Everybody likes children; public interest in children is easy to arouse; yet we are

* Restrictive zoning ordinances often stand in the way of group homes and halfway houses, requiring that a building be occupied only by a single family. Sometimes they specify that a family means those related by blood or adoption, sometimes they accept nonrelated persons as a single housekeeping unit. The organizers of a group home must first try to dissolve neighborhood fear and misunderstanding by visiting and talking. (Getting the support of the local newspaper helps.) Neighbors have a right to guarantees that homes will be properly supervised and maintained, so we all have an interest in well-drawn state licensing regulations. We should also press for legislation like California's, which declares that for zoning purposes, group homes for the handicapped are a single-family *residential* use of property. (If they are considered a business use they are forced to compete for space in commercial districts with higher land values and property taxes; if medical supervision is required, they will be limited to zones where hospitals and nursing homes are permitted.)

"If you don't convince the neighborhood of the value of a group home, and the city planning commission won't grant you a zoning permit, then you have to go to court, but that's the last resort. Avoid litigation if you can. It's cumbersome, costly, and creates hostile atmosphere. But if you must use it, it's very important to have your soldiers lined up when you start."[32] For fifty cents, the Center on Human Policy of Syracuse University will send you a basic guidebook full of useful advice: *Group Homes — One Alternative,* by Robert A. Goodfellow, Jr. (Write the Center at 216 Ostrom Ave., Syracuse, NY 13210.) Your state organizations for the retarded and the mentally ill can advise on the situation in your state, and your congressman can get you a copy of the forward-looking PL 93–383, the Housing and Community Development Act of 1974. *Coming Home,* a sensitive film that might help encourage community acceptance in your town, may be rented for $25 from Stanford House, 900 Euclid Ave., Santa Monica, CA 90403.

only beginning to get adequate services for children. Mentally and emotionally handicapped young people and adults are less appealing, and there's much, much more to be done. Here, where diagnoses have at length lost their importance, families of all the mentally ill can get together to voice our needs.

COMING OUT OF THE CLOSET

Leaving guilt behind

The time is ripe for families of *all* the mentally ill to join the families of mentally ill children, to put the legacy of medieval shame and modern guilt behind us and come out of the closet. Mrs. Harriet Mandelbaum, the only vice-president of the Joint Commission on the Mental Health of Children who was also the parent of a mentally ill child (and whose son, whom she was told to institutionalize at four, passed his Civil Service examinations last year), remembers the founding days of the League for Emotionally Disturbed Children — the first league of any sort of families of the mentally ill — and the sense of liberation when a man rose at a public meeting to say aloud, "I am the father of a schizophrenic son!"* It was hard to come out of the closet in those days, when psychogenic theories of mental illness appeared as hopeful new solutions to the age-old agony of families, who added to the age-old burdens of mental illness a new load of guilt.

It is easier today, if not easy. The work of those first parents helped make it possible to say what we must say: that we are the families of mentally ill children, of mentally ill parents, grandparents, sisters, brothers, and that we demand for them and ourselves the help we used to beg. Is it any wonder that we have been so much slower to voice our needs than families of the retarded,† that we have not rushed to lay public claim to the coldness, selfishness, cruelty, irrationality, stupidity, insensitivity, indifference that in their kaleidoscopic combinations have been attributed to us in the name of scientific detachment and thera-

* Even then, Mrs. Mandelbaum tells us, they were not alone. From the beginning parents found sympathetic allies among professionals — among them Dr. Marianne Kris and Dr. Lauretta Bender, two psychiatrists with very different orientations who both were early supporters of the league's work. The League School, directed by the psychologist and teacher Dr. Carl Fenichel, was the first to demonstrate that mentally ill children need not leave their homes to find a therapeutic education.

† "The psychogenic theory may . . . be implicated in social and political processes which appear to go against the best interests of the autistic child. In the U.S. various diseases and disorders like polio and mental retardation receive funds, attention, and care in proportion to the pressure groups that can be mobilized to affect legislation. It is extremely difficult to mobilize public sentiment in favor of a childhood disorder thought to have been caused by parents." E. Schopler and R. Reichler, "Developmental Therapy by Parents with Their Own Autistic Child," in M. Rutter, ed., *Infantile Autism: Concepts, Characteristics, and Treatment* (London: Churchill and Livingston, 1971).

peutic compassion? If the experts had established the truth of their indictment we would have tried to accept it and change our ways. Many of us did anyway. But it hasn't been established, and other possible causes of our relatives' mental illnesses should have been investigated long ago. It seems, not merely cruel, but foolishly wasteful, that so many professionals have regarded us as guilty until proven innocent, and thus failed of their opportunity to guide our energy and our love.

In 1973 Erwin Friedman, Director of the National Children's Center, chose for his retiring address as President of the American Psychological Association to review the work in childhood schizophrenia of the twenty-five years past. Medicine has a term, "iatrogenic," to be used when the healer, the *iatros,* causes damage and injury where he hoped to heal. Here are Dr. Friedman's rueful words:

> We created a host of guilt-ridden parents suffering unnecessarily from the notion that it was in their power to create these unresponsive monsters. [The Dutch psychiatrist] Van Krevelen called this iatrogenic guilt, and I called it psychogenic guilt in an earlier paper. *This guilt has no origin other than that induced by physicians and psychologists.* [Italics Dr. Friedman's.] Our ignorance in etiology and our impotence in treatment were projected to the parents: it is they who created these children and continue to fail them, and because of this we cannot use our great healing powers on them![33]

Dr. Friedman speaks of mentally ill children; for mentally ill adults too, respected voices are now raised on behalf of families. When an article on "The Mistreatment of Patients' Families by Psychiatrists" can appear in the *American Journal of Psychiatry,*[34] the future is bright for a new kind of alliance to bring hope to the mentally ill and their families.

LOOKING AHEAD

There is much to be done. As Dr. Seymour Kety told the National Association for Mental Health, on receiving a $10,000 award for research into the genetic basis of schizophrenia:

> For none of the major mental illnesses do we yet know the cause or understand the pathogenesis, nor can we cite specific prophylactic or therapeutic measures.[35]

The need for research

Yet every year of research brings us closer to understanding those intricate chemical events that accompany the mysterious changes in thought and emotion we call mental illness. We know many ways to affect them, and though we know no sure cures, we know some treatments that cure sometimes and others that ease the symptoms. We know that known treatment and rehabilitation methods, backed with the support of an enlightened community, already make it possible for most of our relatives to live in the same world we and our neighbors do. We can take heart for the future.

We stand on a threshold, and we are not alone. Today you need only look; you will find allies. Our immediate job, in fact, having memorialized our iatrogenic injuries, must be to forget them, and to rid ourselves of the defensiveness and mistrust that can only hinder our efforts as we work with psychiatrists, psychologists, nurses, social workers on our common task. We don't tell you to discard your armor totally — news travels slowly, and from time to time you may still need it. Or to forget your anger, although you should be ready to transfer it when old targets grow inappropriate. Anger is to be used. Controlled and directed, it is a renewable energy resource, like steam, like faith and hope, like love. Let's use them all for the work to be done.

and for common action

But there's something to add. Do you remember Beth?

Not three months have passed since Chapter XII was written, but something has changed. Somebody is experimenting with Beth's medication. Somebody else is thinking about what she could learn and what it might take to teach her. A new law in her state, the result of months, years — shall we say a generation? — of work by parents, professionals, citizens affirms that mentally ill children up to twenty-one — and handicapped children of all kinds — have the same right to education as other children, that their educational programs must be regularly reconsidered and adjusted, *that their parents have a right to participate in their individual educational plan.* That principle affects even Beth's medication, since that affects her learning, as Beth's mother, who once could hardly bear to visit the hospital, now calls the director to discuss drugs and educational therapy. It reaches even into that back ward, to proclaim that Beth isn't to be forgotten, to recognize that administrators are busy and doctors are hard-pressed and everyone overlooks those they can't see, but that families know where their children are and are their natural advocates. If the money is found to implement that law, if the public backs it, if the public *understands* it, it looks, it really looks, as if Beth mightn't be spending the next fifty years in that blank third-floor ward with the locked door.

Beth again, three months later

Is some miracle in preparation? No. Only the small miracles we already know how to perform, the kind that are bought with observation, and thought, and labor. There are no sheets on Beth's bed, for she tears them off. What would it take to teach her to keep the sheets on, to put her own socks on, to make her bed? If she learned these things, could she learn more? Where might she learn — in a different part of the hospital, in a school, a workshop, a sheltered village, a home in the community? Who can say? But people are asking the questions. Something living is stirring in Beth's future.*

Work

People of all sorts worked together to bring that law into being. People of all sorts must keep working if its hope is not to become a cruel illusion. To obtain change and secure it, dedicated professionals, passionately concerned legislators, and public-spirited citizens must join forces with us whose stake is personal, as they did in 1908 with Clifford Beers and his father and his brother to found the first consumers' organization on behalf of the mentally ill. The changes now taking place reflect the steady persistence of the families of the retarded over a generation, and the years of expanding effort by parents of mentally ill children, to make invisible needs visible.

and hope

For the sick children and the adults in our families, those whom treatment can restore and those who will need help always, have been invisible too long. Unless we speak out and tell what only families can know, they will return to the hospitals and back bedrooms from which they are beginning to emerge. For the ancient fears still linger beneath the lighted surface. All the good words, good will, good work, all the hopeful movement toward deinstitutionalization and community responsibility, can still go for nothing if we cannot convince our neighbors that it is a responsibility they must help us to assume. We can say it's more human, and we can say it's cheaper, and that makes people listen. But what will save money in twenty years will cost money today, and it's we and our neighbors, not posterity, who will make the decisions out of our pocketbooks. Your work and ours is needed to show our neighbors what can be done. Your voices and ours are needed to let them know what their money must buy, and to counter those other neighbors who will say, "Not on my block."

and money

The money is there. In prosperity or in depression, this is still the richest country in the world, incredible in its public and private wealth, incredibly misspent on highways and bubble gum and Tridents and MIRV's. The unreal billions fill the newspapers — unreal until we start to calculate what one missile costs in day treatment centers, or basic research into the causes of brain dysfunction, or some fresh air in Beth's future. Who votes the money? Our representatives, who represent the taxpayers — all of them good people, as that representative said, "They are not evil, they just don't know." How would they know? We've been too bruised and too burdened to tell them. But if we don't tell them, who else can?

*** Still later bulletin: Spurred by the concern of her mother and local school officials, the hospital has arranged for Beth to leave the ward daily for a treatment center in a neighboring town. Her violent impulses are diminishing. Last week she put together a puzzle and, looking at the picture, said, "Cake."**

Appendix A: Some Helpful Reading

SHORT: BOOKLETS AND ARTICLES

Mental Illness: A Guide for the Family, by Edith Stern. National Association for Mental Health, revised edition, 1968. A useful guide, especially to hospitalization. Available from NAMH or state chapters.

When a Parent Is Mentally Ill: What to Say to Your Child, by Helene S. Arnstein. New York: Child Study Association of America, 1960, 1974. Available from Child Study Association of America-Well-Met, Inc., 50 Madison Ave., New York, NY 10010.

Let Our Children Go: An Organizing Manual for Advocates and Parents, Center on Human Policy of Syracuse University. Available from Center on Human Policy, Syracuse University Division of Special Education and Rehabilitation, Syracuse, NY 13210.

Practical Advice for Parents: A Guide to Finding Help for Handicapped Children and Youth. Available from Closer Look, Box 1492, Washington, DC 20013.

A Bright Future: Your Guide to Work (1974), by Dick Flanagan. Practical tips on finding a job after mental illness. Free from NAMH or the President's Committee on Employment of the Handicapped, 1111 20th Street N.W., Washington, DC 20210.

Helping a Mental Patient at Home (1964). Brief but useful. Available from NAMH.

An American Problem (Aging) and *Mental Health in Nursing Homes.* Advice for those with elderly parents. Both free from Publications Division, Hogg Foundation, Box 7998, University Station, Austin, TX 78712.

Group Homes — One Alternative, by Robert A. Goodfellow, Jr. Includes checklists and specific suggestions on getting financial backing, choosing a site, overcoming opposition and winning friends in the neighborhood, choosing staff, planning budgets, etc. Center on Human Policy, Syracuse University Division of Special Education and Rehabilitation, Syracuse, NY 13210. Fifty cents.

Developing Community Mental Health Programs: A Resource Manual. For professionals and citizens concerned with the adult mentally ill. $4, from Mailing Office, United Community Planning Corp., 14 Somerset Street, Boston, MA 02108.

Schizophrenia — Is There an Answer? HEW Publication No. (HSM) 72-9070. Free from Public Inquiries, National Institute of Mental Health, Room 9C-05, 5600 Fishers Lane, Rockville, MD 20852. Up-to-date Fact Sheets also available on Autism, Adolescence, College Mental Health, Depressive Illness, Mental Health of Children, Group Therapy, etc.

Schizophrenia at Home, by Claire Creer and J. K. Wing, M.D. London: Institute of Psychiatry, 1974. Authoritative survey of problems of family living.

Living with Schizophrenia, by the Relatives. Both available from National Schizophrenia Fellowship, 29 Victoria Road, Surbiton, Surrey KT6 4JT, England. 50 pp.

"Shapers at Work," by Kenneth Goodall. *Psychology Today,* November 1972.

"This Little Girl Won't Interact with People and She Crawls around a Lot," by Kenneth Goodall. *Psychology Today,* June 1973. Together, these articles are an excellent introduction to behavior therapy and behavior therapists.

Basic Rights of the Mentally Handicapped. Available from Mental Health Law Project, 1751 N Street N.W., Washington, DC 20036. $1.25.

Planning for Their Future: Personal and Estate Planning for the Mentally Retarded of Wisconsin. Even though it's for Wisconsin, a good introduction for you (or your lawyer). Available from Wisconsin Bar Association, Special Committee on Legal Needs of the Mentally Retarded, 402 W. Wilson, Madison, WI 53703.

BOOKS

General

A Psychiatric Glossary, 4th edition. Washington, D.C.: American Psychiatric Association, 1969. About 1,000 terms, clearly defined. If your library has an earlier edition, tell them to get a new one. Available in paper from the American Psychiatric Association, 1700 18th Street N.W., Washington, DC 20009.

A Mind That Found Itself, by Clifford Beers. Garden City, N.Y.: Doubleday and Co., 1908, and still in print. A classic.

The Inner World of Mental Illness: A Series of First-Person Accounts of What It Was Like, edited by Bert Kaplan. New York: Harper and Row, 1964. In paperback.

Stranger in the Family: A Guide to Living with the Emotionally Disturbed, by Claire Burch. New York: Bobbs-Merrill, 1972. In paperback.

In a Darkness, by James A. Wechsler, with Nancy F. Wechsler and Holly W. Karpf. A heartrending and (fortunately) very influential book. New York: Norton, 1972. In paperback (Ace Books).

Madness and the Brain, by Solomon H. Snyder, M.D. New York: McGraw-Hill, 1973. The biology of mental illness and the drugs that combat it; interesting and readable.

The Death of Psychiatry, by E. Fuller Torrey, M.D. New York: Chilton, 1974. Making a sharp distinction between mental illness and problems in living, Dr. Torrey recommends that doctors treat the former, while "tutors" help us with the latter. In paperback (Penguin Books).

Models of Madness, Models of Medicine, by Miriam Siegler and Humphry Osmond. New York: Macmillan, 1974. A readable (and controversial) analysis of the confusions of psychiatry, with fascinating excursions into the history of medicine.

Speaking Out: Therapists and Patients—How They Cure and Cope with Mental Illness Today, by Barbara Field Benziger. New York: Walker, 1976. Interviews with practitioners and patients. Useful especially in New York area.

Psychotherapy

Shrinks, Etc.: A Consumer's Guide to Psychotherapies, by Thomas Kiernan. New York: Dial Press, 1974. If it was around in 1974, it's in this, from Adler to Rolfing.

A Practical Guide to Psychotherapy, by Daniel L. Wiener, Ph.D. New York: Harper and Row, 1968. A clinical psychologist's commonsense advice on finding psychotherapy. Good descriptions of four major kinds: psychoanalytic, non-directive, eclectic, and behavioral.

Free to Feel: Self-Healing through the New Therapies, by Jerome Liss, M.D. New York: Praeger, 1974. A psychiatrist's guide to the therapeutic left.

Inside Psychotherapy: Nine Clinicians Tell How and What They Are Trying to Accomplish, by Adelaide Bry. Frommian, Gestalt, Group, Family Therapies, etc. New York: Basic Books, 1972. In paperback (NAL; Signet).

Learning Psychotherapy, by Hilde Bruch, M.D. Cambridge: Harvard University Press, 1974. A master analyst's primer for beginning psychotherapists teaches the general reader a great deal about good (and poor) psychotherapy.

I Never Promised You a Rose Garden, by "Hannah Green." New York: Holt, Rinehart and Winston, 1964. Inspired and inspiring psychoanalytic treatment of a young girl's psychosis in the pre-phenothiazine days. Fiction. In paperback.

The Book of Family Therapy, edited by Andrew Ferber and Marilyn Mendelsohn. New York: Aronson, 1973. By family therapists for family therapists, it should give you a good idea of whether family therapy will suit your problem. In paperback.

Psychology Is about People, by H. J. Eysenck, Ph.D. New York: Library Press, 1972. A trenchant summary of the case against psychoanalytic psychotherapy.

The Victim Is Always the Same, by I. S. Cooper, M.D. New York: Harper and Row, 1973. An eminent neurosurgeon's account of two of his cases shows that psychotherapy can be as dangerous as any somatic treatment.

Psychotherapy: The Hazardous Cure, by Dorothy Tennov. New York: Abelard-Schuman, 1975. A clinical psychologist criticizes psychodynamic psychotherapy from a feminist point of view.

Through the Mental Health Maze: A Consumer's Guide to Finding a Psychotherapist. Includes a sample consumer/therapist contract. $2.50. With catalogue of Washington-area psychologists, psychiatric social workers, psychiatrists, $4.00. From Health Research Group (associated with Nader's Public Citizen, Inc.), 2000 P Street, N.W., Washington, DC 20036.

Specific Conditions

Aging

Aging and Mental Health: Positive Psychosocial Approaches, by Robert N. Butler, M.D., and Myrna I. Lewis. St. Louis: C. V. Mosby, 1973. Paperback only.

Nobody Ever Died of Old Age, by Sharon Curtin. Boston: Atlantic–Little, Brown, 1972. In praise, as the jacket says, of old people, and in outrage at how they're treated. In paperback (Atlantic–Little, Brown).

Growing Old in the Country of the Young, by Charles H. Percy. New York: McGraw-Hill, 1974. With a guide to government programs and resources.

Independent Living for the Handicapped and the Elderly, by Elizabeth E. May, Neva R. Waggoner, and Eleanor B. Hotte. Boston: Houghton Mifflin, 1974. Suggestions for rehabilitation, home management, recreation, etc.

Disorders of Children

Son Rise, by Barry Kaufman. New York: Harper & Row, 1976. Autism, and a family's 75-hour-a-week program of psycho-education. The earliest intervention (17 months) and most hopeful outcome yet reported.

The Siege: The First Eight Years of an Autistic Child, by C. C. Park. New York: Harcourt Brace, 1967. In paperback: Boston: Atlantic–Little, Brown, 1973.

I Can't See What You're Saying, by Elizabeth Browning. New York: Coward, McCann & Geohegan, 1973. A mother of an aphasic son with severe learning disabilities tells how he and his family built his independence.

P. S. Your Not Listening, by Eleanor Craig. New York: Richard Baron, 1972. A gifted teacher shows it's possible to teach severely disturbed children in the public schools. In paperback (NAL).

The above books give a great deal of information about particular disorders while telling a readable, personal story. For parents' guides, too numerous to list here, consult the appropriate parents' organization.

Psychological Testing of Children — A Consumer's Guide, by Stanley D. Klein, Ph.D. Boston: The Exceptional Parent, 1975. Special emphasis on the assessment of children with disabilities. Available from The Exceptional Parent Bookstore, P.O. Box 902, Manchester, NH 03105.

The Exceptional Parent magazine; information and guidance for parents of exceptional children. Subscription: $10. Psy-Ed Corp., 264 Beacon Street, Boston, MA 02116.

Depression

Why there are so many books on depression for the general reader (and so few on schizophrenia) is a mystery. Here are three of many:

Up from Depression, by Leo Cammer, M.D. New York: Simon & Schuster, 1968. A psychiatrist tells how the family can help recovery. In paperback.

From Sad to Glad: Kline on Depression, by Nathan S. Kline, M.D. New York: Putnam, 1974. A readable survey by one of the world's leading experts.

A Season in Hell, by Percy Knauth. New York: Harper and Row, 1974. Depression from the inside.

Schizophrenia

The Schizophrenias, Yours and Mine, by Carl C. Pfeiffer, M.D., *et. al.* New York: Pyramid Books, 1972. The Professional Committee of the Schizophrenia Foundation of New Jersey give a strictly biological view of schizophrenia; describing (and recommending) a combination of somatic treatments. Megavitamins figure, but not prominently. Paperback only.

Sanity, Madness, and the Family, by R. D. Laing, M.D., and Abraham Esterson, M.D. New York: Basic Books, 1971. Second edition. The schizophrenic as the victim of a sick family. Tapes of actual family interviews. In paperback (Penguin; Pelican).

Both these books present views most psychiatrists regard as extremes. Books for the general reader representing a middle ground? We haven't found any. (But see under "Booklets.")

The Eden Express, by Mark Vonnegut. New York: Praeger, 1975. Subtitled "A Personal Account of Schizophrenia," it tells what it's like to be schizophrenic and recover when you're young, sensitive, decent, poetic, and very smart.

Stroke

Episode: A Report on the Accident inside My Skull, by Eric Hodgins. New York: Atheneum, 1964. In paperback (S & S; Fireside Series). Stroke, depression, psychiatric hospitalization, rehabilitation, from the inside. A remarkable and informative narrative.

Law

The Rights of Mental Patients: An American Civil Liberties Union Handbook, by Bruce Ennis and Loren Siegel. New York: Richard Baron, 1973. In paperback (Avon). Essential if you fear your relative's rights are in jeopardy; brief but packed.

The Mentally Disabled and the Law, by Samuel J. Brakel and Ronald S. Rock, revised edition. Chicago: University of Chicago Press, 1971. The definitive work.

The Truth about Medical Malpractice: The Patient's Rights, The Doctor's Rights, by Ronald E. Gots. New York: Stein and Day, 1975.

Homosexuality and Mental Health

Monthly newsletter, *Gay People and Mental Health,* gives information on books, organizations, films, counseling, and other pertinent services. Subscription: $6 ($12 for libraries). Suite 3b, 490 West End Avenue, New York, NY 10024. NOTE: If you write, no sexist salutation. Editors insist on Dear Friends, Gentlepeople, etc., or your letter will come back unanswered.

Books for Children

Many teenaged readers will, of course, be able to use the preceding list. Books for younger readers are few; ask your children's librarian to watch for new ones.

Simon and the Game of Chance, by Robert Burch. New York: Viking, 1970. Among the many pressures on Simon is the illness of his mother.

Please Don't Say Hello, by Phyllis Gold. New York: Behavioral Publications, 1975. Eddie is nine, he's new in the neighborhood, and he's autistic. Informative as well as moving. Prefaces for adults by parent Ruth Sullivan and Dr. Mary Stewart Goodwin.

Next Door, by Ruth Harnden. Boston: Houghton Mifflin, 1970. The boy next door has a secret; his mother's in a mental hospital. She's getting better, though, and will be home for Christmas. Junior-high-school age.

The Boy Who Spoke Chinese, by Jessica Krasilovsky. New York: Doubleday, 1972. A little boy acts funny and can't talk; his embarrassed sister makes up stories to explain it. A picture book for younger children which older children can profit from discussing.

The Summer Before, by Patricia Windsor. New York: Harper and Row, 1975. Seventeen-year-old Sandy is back from the hospital, her self-confidence shaken and still grieving as she recovers from the psychotic episode brought on by what happened "the summer before." Sensitively and skillfully the author lets us discover what that was and draws us into the recovery process. High school age, and grown-ups too could learn from it.

Lisa, Bright and Dark, by John Neufield. New York: S. G. Phillips, 1969. A well-written story of a high-school girl's developing psychosis. Knowledgeable, sympathetic presentation of psychotic behavior in its early stages, though the stereotypes of Lisa's parents ("first-rate villains," according to the teenaged narrator) might give you pause. High-school age.

Headsparks, by Robert Coles, M.D. Boston: Atlantic–Little, Brown, 1975. Cathy's mind starts playing scary tricks on her. Supplying her with some typical teenage worries, Dr. Coles makes it sound perfectly natural, but not everybody will be reassured by the implication that it could happen to anybody. Junior-high-school age.

Dark Dreams, by C. L. Rinaldo. New York: Harper and Row, 1974. A boy tries to save his friend from life in an institution. The man is brain-damaged, not mentally ill, but the question is the same: has the community a place for the deviant? Junior-high-school age.

Stranger in the House, by Zoa Sherburne. New York: William Morrow, 1963. No one knows just how to act when Kathy's mother comes home from the mental hospital. A perceptive story for junior-high-school age.

The Hundred Penny Box, by Sharon Bell Mathis. New York: Viking, 1975. Aunt Dew comes to live with her grand-nephew's family; a brief and touching story of the alliance between a little boy and an old, old lady who is, as we say, "beginning to fail." Ages 8–11.

Skeezer: Dog with a Mission, by Elizabeth Yates. Irvington-on-Hudson, N.Y.: Harvey House, 1973. True story of a dog trained to work as a co-therapist in a psychiatric children's ward. Junior high and older.

Epilepsy, by Dr. Alan Silverstein and Virginia Silverstein. New York: Lippincott, 1975. Clearly explained for the adolescent reader.

Feminists may wish to speculate on the reasons why, in children's fiction, mental illness seems to be an exclusively feminine affliction.

Directories

U.S. Facilities and Programs for Children with Severe Mental Illnesses — A Directory. Compiled by the National Association for Autistic Children. National Institute of Mental Health, 1974. DHEW Publication No. (ADM) 74–47.

A.C.L.D. Directory. Association for Children with Learning Disabilities, 5225 Grace St., Pittsburgh, PA 15235.

Directory for Exceptional Children, seventh edition. Porter Sargent, 11 Beacon St., Boston, MA 02108. 1972.

Directory of Catholic Special Facilities in the U.S. for Handicapped Children and Adults. National Catholic Education Association, 1785 Massachusetts Ave. N.W., Washington, DC 20036.

Directory of Facilities for the Learning-Disabled and Handicapped. By Careth Ellingson and James Cass. Harper and Row, 10 East 53 St., New York, NY 10022.

Directory of Services for Emotionally Disturbed and Neurologically Handicapped Children and Adolescents. Mental Health Association, 1572 Los Padres Blvd., Santa Clara, CA 95050. 1973.

Early Identification and Intervention Programs for Infants with Developmental Delays and Their Families — A Summary and Directory. Easter Seal Society, 2023 West Ogden Ave., Chicago, IL 60612. 1973.

Easter Seal Directory of Resident Camps for Persons with Special Health Needs. Easter Seal Society, 2023 West Ogden Ave., Chicago, IL 60612.

Easter Seal Guide for Programs for the Developmentally Handicapped Preschool Child. Easter Seal Society, 2023 West Ogden Ave., Chicago, IL 60612.

Guide to Clinical Services, 1975. American Speech and Hearing Association, 9030 Old Georgetown Road, Washington, DC 20014. $5.00. Includes directory of association members in full-time private practice.

Registry of Private Schools for Children with Special Educational Needs. National Education Consultants, Inc., 711 Paul St., Baltimore, MD 21202.

Biographical Directory of the American Psychiatric Association. Sixth edition. New York: R. R. Bowker, 1973. Members listed geographically; board-certification noted.

Directory of the American Psychological Association. Washington, D.C.: American Psychological Association. Published every other year, with annual address list.

Directory of Professional Social Workers. New York: National Association of Social Workers. Published occasionally.

Appendix B

1. Useful Addresses

National Association for Mental Health, 1800 North Kent Street, Rosslyn, VA 22209. Tel. (703) 528-6405. There is a chapter in your state capital and probably in the nearest big city.

National Institute of Mental Health, Public Inquiries, Room 9C-05, 5600 Fishers Lane, Rockville, MD 20852. Your tax money buys information as well as research.

ADDICTION: ALCOHOLISM AND NARCOTICS

Alcoholism Advisory Council and Information Center, 401 Seventh Ave., New York, NY. Tel. (212) 279–2727.

Families of Alcoholics, 200 Central Park South, New York, NY. Tel. (212) 254–7230.

Alcoholics Anonymous (plus Alanon and Alateen for families) General Service Board, 468 Park Ave. South, New York, NY. Tel. (212) 686–1100. Or consult the phone book of the nearest city.

Synanon Foundation, 2240 24th St., San Francisco, CA 94107.

In any large city, more than one agency concerned with drug abuse will be listed in the phone book under "Narcotics."

AGING

National Senior Citizens Law Center, 1709 West Eighth St., Suite 600, Los Angeles, CA 90017. Tel. (213) 483–3990.

National Council of Senior Citizens, 1911 K St. N.W., Washington, DC 20005.

American Association of Homes for the Aging, 529 14th St. N.W., Washington, DC 20004. Represents nonprofit homes of all kinds.

American Association of Retired Persons, 1225 Connecticut Ave., N.W., Washington, DC 20004.

American Nursing Home Association, 1025 Connecticut Ave. N.W., Washington, DC 20036. Represents the nursing home industry.

Names and addresses of government programs for the elderly, as well as many more organizations, are listed in the Appendices of Butler and Lewis, *Aging and Mental Health*.

ASSORTED PROBLEMS

National Society for Autistic Children, 169 Tampa Ave., Albany, NY 12208. Tel. (518) 489–7375.

NSAC Information and Referral Service for Autistic and Autistic-like Persons, 306 31st St., Huntington, WV 25702. Tel. (304) 697–2638.

Association for Children with Learning Disabilities, 5225 Grace St., Pittsburgh, PA 15236. Tel. (412) 881–1191.

Council for Exceptional Children, 1920 Association Drive, Reston, VA 22091.

Closer Look: National Information Center for the Handicapped. Box 1492, Washington, DC 20013.

Epilepsy Foundation of America, 1828 L St. N.W., Suite 406, Washington, DC 20036. Tel. (202) 293–2930.

Huxley Institute/American Schizophrenia Foundation, 1114 First Ave., New York, NY 10021. Tel. (212) 759–9554.

LAW

American Civil Liberties Union, 22 East 40th St., New York, NY 10016. Tel. (212) 725–1222.

Mental Health Law Project, 1751 N St. N.W., Washington, DC 20036. Tel. (202) 872–0670.

National Center for Law and the Handicapped, 1235 North Eddy St., South Bend, IN 46617. Tel. (219) 288–4751.

National Juvenile Law Center, 3642 Lindell Blvd., St. Louis, MO 63108. Tel. (314) 533–8868.

Youth Law Center, 795 Turk St., San Francisco, CA 94102. Tel. (415) 474–5865.

American Bar Association, Commission on the Mentally Disabled, Director, Herbert Silverberg, Esq. 1705 De Sales Street, Washington, DC 20036. Tel. (202) 872–0670.

LIBERATION

Mental Patients' Liberation Front, Box 156, W. Somerville, MA 02144.

Mental Patients' Liberation Project, 56 East 4th St., New York, NY 10003. Tel. (212) 475–9305.

PROFESSIONAL ORGANIZATIONS

Family Service Association of America, 44 East 23rd St., New York, NY 10010. Tel. (212) 674–6100.

National Council for Homemaker-Health Aide Services, Inc., 67 Irving Place, New York, NY 10003. Tel. (212) 674–4990.

National Association of Private Psychiatric Hospitals, 353 Broad Ave., Leonia, NJ 07605.

American Medical Association Council on Mental Health, 535 North Dearborn St., Chicago, IL 60610.

American Academy of Neurology, 4005 West 65th Street, Minneapolis, MN 55902. Tel. (612) 920–3636.

American Psychiatric Association, 1700 18th St. N.W., Washington, DC 20009. Inquiries may also be addressed to the Committee on Therapy.

American Psychological Association, 1200 17th St. N.W., Washington, DC 20009.

American Speech and Hearing Association, 9030 Old Georgetown Road, Washington, DC 20014.

American Rehabilitation Counselors Association, 431 Erickson Hall, Michigan State University, East Lansing, MI 48823.

National Association of Sheltered Workshops and Homebound Programs, 1522 K St. N.W., Washington, DC 20005.

National Association of Social Workers, 600 Southern Bldg., 15th and H Sts. N.W., Washington, DC 20005.

Association of Black Social Workers, 2008 Madison Ave., New York, NY 10035. Tel. (212) 348-0035.

National Association of State Mental Health Program Directors; State Mental Health Representatives for Children and Youth. Both at Bellevue Hotel, 15th St. N.W., Washington, DC 20001. Tel. (202) 638-2383.

SELF-HELP ORGANIZATIONS

The Fortune Society (ex-prisoners), 29 East 22nd St., New York, NY 10010. Tel. (212) 677-4600.

Gamblers Anonymous, P.O. Box 17173, Los Angeles, CA 90017. Tel. (213) 386-8789; P.O. Box 1404, New York, NY 10001.

Narcotics Anonymous, 2335 Crenshaw Blvd., Los Angeles, CA 90016. Tel. (213) 463-3123.

Parents Anonymous (child abuse), 250 West 57th St., New York, NY 10019. Tel. (212) 765-2336. 2930 West Imperial Highway, Inglewood, CA 90303. Tel. (213) 379-0111.

Recovery, Inc., 116 South Michigan Ave., Chicago, IL 60603. Tel. (312) 263-2292.

Schizophrenics Anonymous. Inquire from Huxley Institute, 1114 First Ave., New York, NY 10021.

WOMEN

National Organization for Women, 5 South Wabash, Suite 1615, Chicago, IL 60603. Tel. (312) 332-1954.

2. Guide to Locating Types of Therapy

PSYCHODYNAMIC PSYCHOTHERAPY

The American Psychoanalytic Association (address below) will provide names of local practitioners from their roster. Ask for copies of the pages covering your region. (If you live near a state line, request the list for the adjoining area too.) Specify that you want the pages including members of local institutes, as many fully trained members of local societies don't join the national association. There are more than twenty-five psychoanalytic societies in the United States. Most are in the Northeast and on the West Coast, but there are societies in Chicago, Detroit, Cleveland, St. Louis, Cincinnati, Topeka, Denver, New Orleans, Florida. All refer within their region, and some (notably the New York and Boston societies) will give names of psychiatrists in other regions as well. The membership of the American Psychoanalytic Association is confined to M.D.'s. The same is true of the American Academy of Psychoanalysis, which represents a slightly less orthodox orientation; they also have a roster and will respond to inquiries.

The William Alanson White Institute of Psychiatry, Psychoanalysis, and Psychology and the Washington School of Psychiatry train analysts in the interpersonal approach. They will refer you to a trained therapist in your region (if there is one); he or she may or may not be an M.D. The other groups listed below will also refer you to therapists trained in their orientation.

Alfred Adler Institute, Alfred Adler Mental Hygiene Clinic, 333 Central Park West, New York, NY 10025. Tel. (212) MO3–7980.

The American Psychoanalytic Association, 1 East 57th St., New York, NY 10022. Tel. (212) PL2–0450.

The American Academy of Psychoanalysis, 40 Gramercy Park, New York, NY. 10003. Tel. (212) 477–4250.

Gestalt Therapy Institute of New York, 7 West 96th St., New York, NY 10025. Tel. (212) 850–5080.

Gestalt Center for Psychotherapy and Training, 1040 Park Ave., New York, NY 10028. Tel. (212) 752–1932.

The Karen Horney Clinic, 392 East 62nd St., New York, NY 10021. Tel. (212) TE8–4333.

The C. G. Jung Foundation, 28 East 39th St., New York, NY 10016. Tel. (212) 697–6430. There are also Jungian training institutes in New York, Los Angeles, San Francisco, London, and Zurich.

Washington School of Psychiatry, 1610 New Hampshire Ave., N.W., Washington, DC 20009. Tel. (202) NO7–3008.

William Alanson White Institute of Psychiatry, Psychoanalysis, and Psychology, 20 West 74th St., New York, NY 10021. Tel. (212) 873–0725.

Existential Therapy

Inquire from one of the psychoanalytic institutes above.

Family Therapy

Any of the following will be glad to refer you to practitioners in their area:

Nathan W. Ackerman Family Institute, 149 East 78th St., New York, NY 10021.

The Family Institute of Chicago, 6957 W. North Ave., Oak Park, IL 60302.

The Family Institute, 2600 Euclid Ave., Cincinnati, OH 45219.

Family Therapy Institute, 790 So. Cleveland Ave., Suite 208, St. Paul, MN 55116.

Boston Family Institute, 55 Williston Rd., Brookline, MA 02146.

Philadelphia Child Guidance Center, 1700 Bainbridge St., Philadelphia, PA 19146.

The Family Therapy Institute of Marin, 1353 Lincoln Ave., San Rafael, CA 94901.

Center for Human Communication, 120 Oak Meadow Drive, Los Gatos, CA 95030.

Group Therapy

Information on group therapists and programs in your area may be available from community mental health organizations, or from

The American Group Psychotherapy Association, 1865 Broadway, New York, NY 10023. Tel. (212) 245–7732.

The American Psychiatric Association Committee on Therapy (and the American Psychological Association (see *Professional Organizations,* above) also answer inquiries. There are some pretty chancy groups around these days; check if you're in doubt.

Non-directive Therapy

Most likely to be found around universities; practitioners are more likely to be psychologists than psychiatrists. The University of Chicago Counseling Center is the major training center and can give names of therapists.

Radical Therapy

Most likely to be found around universities and in sophisticated urban areas. So-called underground newspapers, and some that aren't so underground, like the *Village Voice* (New York), the *Boston Phoenix,* the *Berkeley Barb,* tend to have knowledgeable reporters who have researched local mental health facilities and are friendly to radical therapy. A phone call to one of these should turn up some names. You may inquire also from the radical therapist magazine, *Rough Times,* reachable at Box 89, W. Somerville, MA 02144. and from *Madness Network News,* 2150 Market St., San Francisco, CA 94114. Tel. (415) 863–4488.

Other

International Transactional Analysis Association, 3155 College Ave., Berkeley, CA 94705.

Institute for Reality Therapy, Brentwood, Los Angeles, CA.

BEHAVIORAL THERAPY

Most easily found in research settings — universities, public clinics, and public hospitals, particularly in the Midwest, West, and South. (See Kenneth Goodall's "Shapers at Work," Appendix A, for a guide to major centers of behavior modification research.) Both the organizations listed below will supply names of trained therapists. Mental health centers and psychology departments of colleges and universities may also help.

Center for Behavior Modification, 3001 University Ave. SE, Minneapolis, MN 55414. Tel. (612) 331–3998.

Behavior Therapy and Research Society, Eastern Pennsylvania Psychiatric Institute, Henry Ave., Philadelphia, PA 19129. A roster of Clinical Fellows of the Society will be sent on request.

SOMATIC THERAPY

Though all psychiatrists can prescribe somatic treatments, and most do, psychiatrists committed to a predominantly biological approach to mental illness are not easy to find. A Society for Biological Psychiatry exists and has its own journal, but it is primarily a research organization. (Dr. Leonard Cammer, author of *Up from Depression,* is chairman of its Committee on Public Relations.) Dr. E. Fuller Torrey of NIMH suggests you call the department of *neurology* of the nearest medical school and ask them to refer you to a psychiatrist; they should know those whose orientation is biological. Failing that, he suggests you ask a good G.P.

For psychiatrists committed to a nutritional as well as a primarily biological approach (orthomolecular psychiatry), inquire from

The Huxley Institute for Biosocial Research, 1114 First Ave., New York, NY 10021. Tel. (212) 759–9554.

Notes

CHAPTER I

1. George Vaillant, "Why Men Seek Psychotherapy: I. Results of a Survey of College Graduates," *American Journal of Psychiatry,* 129 (December, 1972).
2. Salzman, review of *New Horizons for Psychotherapy,* R. R. Holt, ed., in *American Journal of Psychiatry,* 129 (December, 1972); see also W. E. Henry, J. H. Sims, and S. L. Spray, *The Fifth Profession: Becoming a Psychotherapist* (San Francisco: Jossey-Bass, 1971).
3. Frank, *Persuasion and Healing* (Baltimore: Johns Hopkins Press, 1961).
4. Szasz, "The Myth of Mental Illness," *American Psychologist,* 15 (February, 1960); reprinted in *Behavior Disorders,* Ohmer Milton, ed. (New York: Lippincott, 1965).
5. Parris, Letter, *Psychology Today* (September, 1972).

CHAPTER II

1. Harrington, *Fragments of the Century* (New York: Saturday Review Press, 1973), pp. 168–169.
2. Leonard, *The Locomotive-God* (New York: The Century Co., 1927), p. 388.
3. Knauth, *NAMH Reporter,* 22 (Winter, 1973).
4. Knauth, "A Season in Hell," *Life,* June 9, 1972; expanded and published by Harper & Row, 1975.
5. Aldrin, *Return to Earth* (New York: Random House, 1973).
6. L. Pierce Clark, "A Psychological Study of Abraham Lincoln," *Psa. Review* (1921), pp. 1–21; quoted in Menninger, *The Vital Balance* (New York: Viking Press, 1963), p. 406.
7. Tolstoy, *My Confession* (New York: Crowell, 1887); excerpt in *The Inner World of Mental Illness,* Bert Kaplan, ed. (New York: Harper & Row, 1964).
8. Bunney, *New York Times,* June 25, 1973.
9. Woolf, *Mrs. Dalloway* (New York: Modern Library, 1928), pp. 31–32.
10. Jan Hulsker, ed., *Van Gogh's "Diary": The Artist's Life in His Own Words and Art* (New York: William Morrow, 1971), pp. 126–27.
11. Woolf, *op. cit.,* p. 137.
12. Barbara Field Benziger, *The Prison of My Mind* (New York: Walker, 1969; Pocket Books, 1970), p. 35.
13. Seymour Krim, "The Insanity Bit," *Views of a Farsighted Cannoneer* (New York: Excelsior Press, 1961), excerpt in Kaplan, *op. cit.*
14. Leighton, Discussion, in A. V. S. DeRueck and R. Porter, eds., *Transcultural Psychiatry* (Boston: Little, Brown, 1965); quoted in E. Fuller Torrey, *The Mind Game: Witchdoctors and Psychiatrists* (New York: Emerson Hall, 1972), p. 172.
15. Mark Vonnegut, "Why I Want to Bite R. D. Laing," *Harper's* (April, 1974).

CHAPTER III

1. See Theodore R. Sarbin, "On the Futility of the Proposition that Some People Be Labeled Mentally Ill," *Journal of Consulting Psychology,* 31 (1967) :447–453.
2. See the full issue of *Psychiatric Annals,* 3 (November, 1973) , devoted to "Psychiatry Under Siege."
3. B. Gurland, J. L. Fleiss, *et al.,* "The Mislabeling of Depressed Patients in New York State," in *Disorders of Mood,* J. Zubin, ed. (Baltimore: Johns Hopkins Press, 1972) .
4. American Psychiatric Association, *Diagnostic and Statistical Manual: Mental Disorders* (DSM II) (Washington, D.C., 1968) .
5. Leland E. Hinsie and Robert Jean Campbell, *Psychiatric Dictionary,* 4th edition (New York: Oxford University Press, 1970) .
6. Redlich and Freedman, *The Theory and Practice of Psychiatry* (New York: Basic Books, 1966) , p. 350.
7. *Op. cit.,* p. 38.
8. Max Jacobs, "An Holistic Approach to Behavior Therapy," in *Clinical Behavior Therapy,* Arnold Lazarus, ed. (New York: Brunner/Mazel, 1972) , p. 107.
9. Redlich and Freedman, *op. cit.,* p. 372.
10. Leston Havens, *Approaches to the Mind* (Boston: Little, Brown, 1973) .
11. O. Malamud, "The Psychoneuroses," in *Personality and the Behavior Disorders,* vol. 2, J. McV. Hand, ed. (New York: Ronald Press, 1944) , pp. 833–860.
12. Redlich and Freedman, *op. cit.,* p. 403.
13. Joseph L. Novello, "Psychiatric Referrals Made Easy," *Medical Times,* 101 (May, 1973) .
14. Gerald Adler and Leon N. Shapiro, "Psychotherapy with Prisoners," in *Current Psychiatric Therapies,* vol. IX (New York: Grune & Stratton, Inc., 1969) .
15. L. Mosher and John Gunderson, with Sherry Buchsbaum, "Special Report: Schizophrenia, 1972," NIMH, *Schizophrenia Bulletin,* 7 (Winter, 1973) .
16. Reported in *MH,* 58 (Summer, 1974) .
17. Mosher and Gunderson, *op. cit.*
18. Redlich and Freedman, *op. cit.,* p. 460.
19. J. K. Wing, personal communication, April, 1975.
20. See Dr. Nathan S. Kline, *From Sad to Glad: Kline on Depression* (New York: Putnam, 1974) . A more technical discussion can be found in Dr. Joseph J. Schildkraut's *Neuropharmacology and the Affective Disorders* (Boston: Little, Brown, 1970) .
21. Morton Kramer, Earl S. Pollack, Richard W. Redich and Ben Z. Locke, *Mental Disorders/Suicide* (Cambridge, Mass.: Harvard University Press, 1972) , p. 39.
22. "The Persuasive Problem of Mental Depression," *Medical World News* (April 20, 1973) .
23. Mosher and Gunderson, *op. cit.,* p. 17.
24. John Wing, Julian Leff, and Steven Hirsch, "Preventive Treatment of Schizophrenia: Some Theoretical and Methodological Issues," in *Psychopathology and Psychopharmacology,* J. O. Cole, A. M. Freedman, and A. J. Friedhoff, eds. (Baltimore, Johns Hopkins Press, 1973) .

25. Cancro, "The Treatment of Schizophrenia: Illusion or Elusion?" *American Journal of Psychiatry,* 130 (June, 1973).
26. American Psychiatric Association, *op. cit.,* p. 5.
27. Altschule, "Disease Entity, Syndrome, State of Mind, or Figment?" in *The Schizophrenic Reactions: A Critique of the Concept, Hospital Treatment, and Current Research,* Robert Cancro, ed. (New York: Brunner/Mazel, 1970).
28. Dr. D. Steinberg of Maudsley Hospital, London, in *Roche Medical Reports* (October 15, 1972).
29. See Irving S. Cooper, *The Victim is Always the Same* (New York: Harper and Row, 1973).

CHAPTER IV

1. Menninger, *The Vital Balance* (New York: Viking Press, 1963), p. 152.
2. Romano, interview, "Has Psychiatry Resigned from Medicine?" *Medical Opinion* (January, 1973).
3. Menninger, *op. cit.,* p. 272.
4. Farber, in *R. D. Laing and Anti-Psychiatry,* Robert Boyers and Robert Orrill, eds. (New York: Harper and Row, 1971), p. 215.
5. AP report of 1972 meeting of the American Psychiatric Association, Dallas, Texas; see also Scott H. Nelson and E. Fuller Torrey, "The Religious Functions of Psychiatry," *American Journal of Orthopsychiatry,* 43 (April, 1973).
6. Brown, NIMH Director's Report (July, 1974).
7. Bettelheim, "Milieu Therapy," pamphlet in series *Major Contributors to Modern Psychotherapy* (Roche Laboratories, n.d.).
8. Eileen Walkenstein, *Beyond the Couch* (New York: Crown Publishers, 1972).
9. Jarl E. Dyrud and P. S. Holzman, "The Psychotherapy of Schizophrenia: Does It Work?" *American Journal of Psychiatry,* 130 (June, 1973).
10. Havens, *Approaches to the Mind: Movement of the Psychiatric Schools from Sects toward Science* (Boston: Little, Brown, 1973), p. 181.
11. *Ibid.,* p. 194.
12. *Ibid.,* p. 169.
13. Dr. Donald Bloch, Director, Nathan W. Ackerman Family Institute, personal communication, April 20, 1973.
14. Quoted in Havens, *op. cit.,* p. 3.
15. Wiener, *A Practical Guide to Psychotherapy* (New York: Harper and Row, 1968), p. 77.
16. Havens, *op. cit.,* p. 393.
17. Grotjahn, in *Psychiatric News* (January 3, 1973).
18. "Encounter: The Leader Makes the Difference," *Psychology Today* (March, 1973); excerpted from *Encounter Groups: First Facts* (New York: Basic Books, 1973).
19. Berne, *Games People Play: The Psychology of Human Relationships* (New York: Grove Press, 1964).
20. Glasser, *Reality Therapy* (New York: Harper and Row, 1965).
21. I Samuel 16:16–23.
22. Jerome D. Frank, *Persuasion and Healing: A Comparative Study of Psychotherapy* (Baltimore: Johns Hopkins Press, 1961), p. 246. Studies re-

ferred to are R. W. Heine, "A Comparison of Patients' Reports on Psychotherapeutic Experience with Psychoanalytic, Nondirective and Adlerian Therapists," *American Journal of Psychotherapy,* 7 (1953) :16–23; F. E. Fiedler, "A Comparison of Therapeutic Relationships in Psychoanalytic, Nondirective and Adlerian Therapy," *J. Consult. Psycho.,* 14: 436–445.
23. Redlich and Freedman, *Principles of Psychiatry,* p. 363.
24. Wiener, *op. cit.,* p. 82.
25. *Behavior Modification: Principles and Clinical Applications* (Boston: Little, Brown, 1973), p. 8.
26. Wiener, *op. cit.,* p. 53.
27. As paraphrased in Wiener, *op. cit.,* p. 82.
28. Wiener, *op. cit.,* p. 84.
29. *Ibid.*
30. Wiener, *op. cit.,* p. 34.
31. William Schofield, *Psychotherapy: The Purchase of Friendship* (Englewood Cliffs, N.J.: Prentice-Hall, 1960).
32. Hewett, "The Autistic Child as Teacher and Learner," in *Research and Education: Proceedings of the Second Annual Meeting and Conference of the National Society for Autistic Children,* C. C. Park, ed. (NIMH Publication No. 2164, 1971).
33. Agras, *Behavior Modification: Principles and Clinical Applications* (Boston: Little, Brown, 1972).
34. Account based on K. Eileen Allen and Florence R. Harris, "Elimination of a Child's Excessive Scratching by Training the Mother in Reinforcement Procedures," *Behavior Research and Therapy,* 4 (1966).
35. See James A. Wechsler, with Nancy F. Wechsler and Holly W. Karpf, *In a Darkness* (New York: W. W. Norton, 1972).
36. See Jacques May, *A Physician Looks at Psychiatry* (New York: John Day, 1958), and Louise Wilson, *This Stranger, My Son* (New York: Putnam, 1968).
37. John Marquis, "An Expedient Model for Behavior Therapy," in *Clinical Behavior Therapy,* Arnold A. Lazarus, ed. (New York: Brunner/Mazel, 1972), pp. 49–50.
38. David Barlow, "Aversive Procedures," in Agras, *op. cit.;* Lee Birk, William Huddleston, Elizabeth Miller, and Bertram Cohler, "Avoidance Conditioning for Homosexuality," in *Annual Review of Behavior Therapy: Theory and Practice, 1973,* Cyril M. Franks and G. Terence Wilson, eds. (New York: Brunner/Mazel, 1973).
39. Barlow, in Agras, *op. cit.,* p. 119.
40. *Ibid.,* p. 88.
41. M. Serber and P. Nelson, "The Ineffectiveness of Systematic Desensitization and Assertive Training in Hospitalized Schizophrenics," *Journal of Behavior Therapy and Experimental Psychiatry,* 2 (1971) :107–109.
42. Isaac M. Marks, "Flooding (Implosion) and Allied Treatments," in Agras, *op. cit.,* p. 155.
43. Quoted in Agras, *op. cit.,* p. 177.
44. Agras, *op. cit.,* p. 21.
45. Robert D. O'Connor, "Relative Efficiency of Modeling, Shaping, and the Combined Procedures for the Modification of Social Withdrawal," in Franks and Wilson, *op. cit.*
46. Richard M. McFall and Diane Bridges Lillesand, "Behavioral Rehearsal with Modeling and Coaching in Assertive Training," in Franks and Wilson, *op. cit.*

47. McFall and Lillesand, *op. cit.*, p. 176.
48. Josh Greenfeld, *A Child Called Noah* (New York: Holt, Rinehart and Winston, 1972).
49. Bettelheim, "Milieu Therapy," *loc. cit.*
50. *Ibid.*
51. Marmor, "The Future of Psychoanalytic Therapy," *American Journal of Psychiatry,* 130 (November, 1973).
52. Pete Hamill, "Memoirs of a Drinking Life," *New York* (January 13, 1975).
53. A. E. Bergin, "The Effects of Psychotherapy: Negative Results Revisited," *Journal of Counseling Psychology,* 10 (1963):244; summarized in Agras, *op. cit.*, p. 5.
54. Leonard Horwitz, *Clinical Prediction in Psychotherapy* (New York: Jason Aronson, 1974).
55. "Behavior Therapy and Clinical Problems," *Annual Review of Behavior Therapy* (New York: Brunner/Mazel, 1973), p. 25.
56. C. B. Truax and R. R. Carkhuff, *Towards Effective Counseling and Psychotherapy* (Chicago: Aldine, 1967).
57. Arnold Lazarus, "Behavior Therapy and Clinical Problems: A Critical Overview," in Franks and Wilson, *op. cit.*, p. 31.
58. Redlich and Freedman, *op. cit.*, p. 176.
59. *Ibid.*, p. 359.
60. *Ibid.*, p. 364.
61. John Romano, in Lester Grinspoon, Jack R. Ewalt, and Richard I. Shader, *Schizophrenia: Psychotherapy and Pharmacotherapy* (Baltimore: Williams and Williams, 1972).
62. Study by Dr. Paul D. Stolley of Johns Hopkins and others. Reported in Rodale's *Health Bulletin* (May 27, 1972).
63. In "Recent Advances in Psychotherapeutic Drugs and Their Side Effects: A Symposium," *Psychiatric Annals,* 3 (July, 1973).
64. Snyder, *Madness and the Brain* (New York: McGraw-Hill, 1973); see also Richard I. Shader, ed., *Manual of Psychiatric Therapeutics: Practical Psychopharmacology and Psychiatry* (Boston: Little, Brown, 1975.)
65. David M. Engelhardt and Reuben A. Margolis, "Hospitalization of Schizophrenic Patients: Prediction and Prevention," in T. Rothman, ed., *Changing Patterns in Psychiatric Care* (New York: Crown, 1970), p. 124.
66. Milton Greenblatt and M. H. Sharaff, "Psychopharmacology in the Large Mental Hospital," in Rothman, *op. cit.*, pp. 58–59.
67. *Ibid.*
68. Kety, personal interview.
69. Brown, quoted in *Newsweek* (January 8, 1973).
70. Lothar Kalinowsky and Hanns Hippius, *Pharmacological, Convulsive, and Other Somatic Treatments in Psychiatry* (New York: Grune and Stratton, 1969), p. 122.
71. Kalinowsky and Hippius, *op. cit.*, pp. 139–140.
72. Percy Knauth, "A Season in Hell," *Life* (June 9, 1972).
73. Malitz, in "Recent Advances," *loc. cit.*
74. Antoinette Gatozzi, *Lithium in the Treatment of Mood Disorder* (Washington, D.C.: National Institute of Mental Health, 1970).
75. R. F. Prien, Eugene M. Caffey, Jr., and C. J. Klett, *Lithium Carbonate in Psychiatry* (Washington, D.C.: American Psychiatric Association, n.d.).
76. *Ibid.*
77. *Facts about Electroshock Therapy,* DHEW Pub. No. (HSM) 72–9152 (Washington, D.C.: NIMH, 1972).

78. Kalinowsky and Hippius, *op. cit.*, pp. 236–242.
79. Thomas N. Rusk and Randolph A. Read, San Diego, California, letter to California Assemblyman John Vasconcellos, author of 1974 law restricting use of ECT, reprinted in *Madness Network News,* 3 (April, 1975).
80. "200 Shock Treatments: The Wiswall Story," *Boston Phoenix* (November 14, 1972).
81. Dr. Leo Alexander, Letter, *New England Journal of Medicine,* 269 (August, 1973).
82. Case reported in *Science News,* 102 (May 12, 1973), and *Richmond Times-Dispatch* (April 12, 1973).
83. *Behavior Today* (June 25, 1973).
84. Pribram, "Autism: A Deficiency in Context-Dependent Processes?" in *Research and Education: Proceedings of the Second Annual Meeting and Conference of the National Society for Autistic Children,* C. C. Park, ed. (Washington, D.C.: NIMH: Public Service Publication No. 2164, 1971).
85. Dr. Orlando Andy, reported in the *New York Times* (March 12, 1973) and *Time* (April 3, 1973).
86. Stone, interviewed in *Harvard Today* (Fall, 1974).
87. Cases described by Dr. Kalinowsky in a personal interview in 1973.
88. Kalinowsky and Hippius, *op. cit.*, pp. 323–324, 330–331.
89. Cousins, "Commentary: Medical Prisoner, Family Have Scars," *Richmond Times-Dispatch* (December 14, 1972).
90. F. C. Dohan and J. C. Grasberger, "Relapsed Schizophrenics and Earlier Discharge from the Hospital After Cereal-Free, Milk-Free Diet," *American Journal of Psychiatry,* 130 (June, 1973).
91. Humphry Osmond and Abram Hoffer, "Massive Niacin Treatment in Schizophrenia: Review of a Nine-Year Study," *The Lancet* (February 10, 1962), pp. 316–320.
92. Reported in *Psychiatric News* (July 18, 1973).
93. *Ibid.*
94. Thomas A. Ban, S. Gershon, F. J. Kane, Jr., "The Present State of Nicotinic Acid Therapy in Treatment of Schizophrenia," presented at the annual meeting of the American Psychiatric Association, Dallas, Texas, May 1–5, 1972.
95. Toll, letter, *Schizophrenia Bulletin* 4 (Fall, 1971), and telephone interview, October, 1973.
96. Arieti, *Interpretation of Schizophrenia,* 2nd ed. (New York: Basic Books, 1974), p. 664; quoting H. E. Lehmann, "Physical Therapies of Schizophrenia," in *American Handbook of Psychiatry,* vol. III.
97. *Behavior Therapy in Psychiatry,* Task Force Report No. 5 (Washington, D.C.: American Psychiatric Association, 1973).
98. Lazarus, "Behavioral Therapy and Clinical Problems: A Clinical Overview," in Franks and Wilson, *op. cit.*, p. 31.
99. Akhter Ahsen and Arnold Lazarus, "Eidetics: An Internal Behavior Approach," in *Clinical Behavior Therapy* (New York: Brunner/Mazel, 1972), p. 87.
100. Lee Birk, "Avoidance Conditioning for Homosexuality," in Franks and Wilson, *op. cit.*
101. "Eidetics," *loc. cit.*
102. Michael Harrington, *Fragments of the Century* (New York: Saturday Review Press, 1973).
103. Tourney, in *Changing Patterns of Psychiatric Care,* Theodore Rothman, ed. (New York: Crown Publishers, 1970), p. 17.

104. W. E. Henry, John H. Sims, S. Lee Spray, *The Fifth Profession* and *Public and Private Lives of Psychotherapists* (San Francisco: Jossey Bass, 1971 and 1973).
105. Cammer, *Up from Depression* (New York: Simon and Schuster, 1966), p. 176.
106. Philip J. Hilts, *Behavior Mod* (New York: Harper's Magazine Press, 1974), p. 169.
107. *Behavior Today,* August 5, 1974.
108. Vaillant, "Why Men Seek Psychotherapy: I. Results of a Survey of College Graduates," *American Journal of Psychiatry,* 129 (December, 1972).

CHAPTER V

1. Lothar Kalinowsky and Hanns Hippius, *Pharmacological, Convulsive, and Other Somatic Treatments in Psychiatry* (New York: Grune and Stratton, 1969), p. 367.
2. Freud, quoted by Theodore Rothman, ed., in *Changing Patterns of Psychiatric Care: An Anthology of Evolving Scientific Psychiatry in Medicine* (New York: Crown Publishers, 1970), p. 229.
3. Don D. Jackson, *The Etiology of Schizophrenia* (New York: Basic Books, 1960).
4. S. S. Kety, David Rosenthal, Paul Wender, and Fini Schulsinger, "The Types and Prevalence of Mental Illness in the Biological and Adoptive Families of Adopted Schizophrenics," in *The Transmission of Schizophrenia,* D. Rosenthal and S. S. Kety, eds. (Oxford: Pergamon Press, 1968); S. S. Kety, "Genetic-Environmental Interactions in the Schizophrenic Syndrome," in *The Schizophrenic Reactions: A Critique of the Concept, Hospital Treatment, and Current Research,* R. Cancro, ed. (New York: Brunner/Mazel, 1970).
5. Mednick, Symposium, "Schizophrenia: Fact or Fiction?" November, 1973, reported in *Psychiatric News* (January 2, 1974).
6. J. L. Karlsson, "Genealogic Studies of Schizophrenia"; L. L. Heston and D. Denney, "Interactions Between Early Life Experiences and Biological Factors in Schizophrenia," in D. Rosenthal and S. Kety, eds., *The Transmission of Schizophrenia, loc. cit.*
7. Bleuler, "The Offspring of Schizophrenics," *Schizophrenia Bulletin,* 8 (Spring, 1974), a chapter from *On Schizophrenia,* translated by Siegfried Clemens (New Haven: Yale University Press, pub. date, 1977).
8. E. Slater, "A Review of Earlier Evidence on Genetic Factors in Schizophrenia," *Journal of Psychiatric Research,* 6 (Suppl. 1) (1968):15, cited in Lyman C. Wynne, "Family Research on the Pathogenesis of Schizophrenia," in *Progress in Group and Family Therapy,* C. J. Sager and H. J. Kaplan, eds. (New York: Brunner/Mazel, 1972).
9. Bleuler, *op. cit.*
10. Havens, *Approaches to the Mind* (Boston: Little, Brown, 1973), p. 248.
11. E. James Anthony, "A Clinical Evaluation of Children with Psychotic Parents," *American Journal of Psychiatry,* 126 (August, 1969). See also Snyder, *op. cit.,* pp. 99–100.
12. Sarnoff A. Mednick and Fini Schulsinger, "Factors Related to Breakdown in Children at High Risk for Schizophrenia," in *Life History Research in Psychopathology,* M. Roff and D. Ricks, eds. (Minneapolis: University of Minnesota Press, 1970.)

13. W. Pollin, J. R. Stabenau, and J. Tupin, "Family Studies in Identical Twins Discordant for Schizophrenia," *Psychiatry,* 28 (1965) : 119–132.
14. Hawkins, "The Orthomolecular Approach to the Diagnosis of Schizophrenia," in *Orthomolecular Psychiatry,* p. 601.
15. Rimland, "Psychogenesis vs. Biogenesis" in *Changing Perspectives in Mental Illness,* S. C. Plog and R. B. Edgerton, eds. (New York: Holt, Rinehart and Winston, 1969).
16. Brenner, *Mental Illness and the Economy* (Cambridge, Mass.: Harvard University Press, 1973).
17. F. C. Dohan, *American Journal of Psychiatry,* 130 (December, 1973) :1401.
18. Kety, "Genetic and Environmental Interactions in the Schizophrenic Syndrome," in Cancro, *op. cit.*
19. Kety, "Psychiatric Research — A Commitment for Mental Health," Annual Meeting of the National Association for Mental Health, Detroit, November 14, 1972.
20. Arnold J. Mandell, David S. Segal, Ronald T. Kuczenski, and Suzanne Knapp, "The Search for the Schizococcus," *Psychology Today* (October, 1972).
21. Jerry Higgins, "It Comes in Two Kinds," *Psychology Today* (October, 1972).
22. Fromm-Reichman, "Notes on the Development of Treatment of Schizophrenics by Psychoanalytic Psychotherapy," *Psychiatry,* 11 (1948) :263–273.
23. Theodore Lidz, "The Influence of Family Studies on the Treatment of Schizophrenia," in C. J. Sager and H. S. Kaplan, eds., *Progress in Group and Family Therapy* (New York: Brunner/Mazel, 1972), p. 629.
24. Bruno Bettelheim, *The Empty Fortress: Infantile Autism and the Birth of the Self* (New York: Free Press, 1967), p. 125.
25. Joel Kovel, in a review of Mary Barnes and Joseph Berke, *Mary Barnes: Two Accounts of a Journey Through Madness, New York Times Book Review* (July 2, 1972).
26. "An Interview with Theodore Lidz," in *R. D. Laing and Anti-Psychiatry,* Robert Boyers and Robert Orrill, eds. (New York: Harper and Row, 1971; Perennial Library Edition), p. 166.
27. Joseph Berke in Boyers and Orrill, eds., *op. cit.,* p. 275.
28. Ross Speck and Carolyn Attneave, *Family Networks* (New York: Pantheon Press, 1973), p. 10.
29. "Family Therapy," interview with Dr. Ross Speck in Adelaide Bry, *Inside Psychotherapy* (New York: Basic Books, Inc., 1972), p. 99.
30. W. W. Meissner, "Thinking About the Family: Psychiatric Aspects," *Journal of Family Process,* 3 (March, 1964).
31. Arieti, "An Overview of Schizophrenia from a Predominantly Psychological Approach," *American Journal of Psychiatry,* 131 (March, 1974) :241.
32. Bettelheim, *op. cit.,* p. 403.
33. Lidz, "The Influence of Family Studies on the Treatment of Schizophrenia," *op. cit.,* p. 633.
34. Jay Haley, "Whither Family Therapy?" *Journal of Family Process,* 1, no. 1 (March, 1962).
35. Y. O. Alanen, "The Mothers of Schizophrenic Patients," *Acta Psychiatrica et Neurologica Scandinavica,* Supplement no. 124 (1958).
36. M. Singer and L. Wynne, "Thought Disorders and Family Relations of Schizophrenics," *Archives of General Psychiatry,* 12 (February, 1965); Theodore Lidz, A. Cornelison, D. Terry, and S. Fleck: "Interfamilial Environment of the Schizophrenic Patient: VI. The Transmission of Irra-

tionality," *Archives of Neurological Psychiatry,* 79 (March, 1958), and three papers on "Thought Disorder and Family Relations of Schizophrenics," in *Archives of General Psychiatry,* 9 (1963) :199, and 12 (1965) : 187, 201.
37. D. L. Rosenhan, "On Being Sane in Insane Places," *Science,* 179 (January, 1973).
38. Arieti, *Interpretation of Schizophrenia,* 2nd ed. (New York: Basic Books, 1974), pp. 81–82.
39. Scheflen, *Communicational Structure: Analysis of a Psychotherapy Transaction* (Bloomington, Ind.: Indiana University Press, 1973), pp. 2–3.
40. Theodore Lidz, Y. O. Alanen, A. Cornelison, "Schizophrenic Patients and their Siblings," *Psychiatry,* 26 (1963) :1–18.
41. Harold Renaud and Floyd Estes, "Life History Interviews with 100 Normal American Males: "Pathogenicity of Childhood?" reprinted from *American Journal of Orthopsychiatry,* 31 (1961) :786–802; in *Perspectives in Psychopathology,* J. O. Palmer and J. J. Goldstein, eds. (New York: Oxford University Press, 1966), p. 78.
42. Howells, "Family Pathology and Schizophrenia," in *Modern Perspectives in World Psychiatry,* J. G. Howells, ed. (New York: Brunner/Mazel, 1972), pp. 407, 413.
43. Hirsch and Leff, "Parental Abnormalities of Verbal Communication in the Transmission of Schizophrenia," *Psychological Medicine,* 1 (1971): 118–127.
44. Joan Huser Liem, "Effects of Verbal Communications of Parents and Children: A Comparison of Normal and Schizophrenic Families," *Journal of Consulting and Clinical Psychology,* 42 (1974) :438–450.
45. Schopler and Loftin, "Thought Disorders in Parents of Psychotic Children — A Function of Test Anxiety," *Archives of General Psychiatry,* 20 (1969): 174–181.
46. Arieti, *Interpretation of Schizophrenia,* pp. 81–82.
47. Redlich and Freedman, *The Theory and Practice of Psychiatry,* p. 429.
48. Abrahamsen, interview in *Los Angeles Times* (July 17, 1973).
49. Lidz, "The Influence of Family Studies on the Treatment of Schizophrenia," *op. cit.,* p. 620.
50. Levenson, *The Fallacy of Understanding* (New York: Basic Books, Inc., 1972), pp. 72–73.
51. Eisenberg, "Psychiatric Intervention," *Scientific American* (September, 1973).
52. Romano, interview in *Medical Opinion* (June, 1973).
53. Havens, *op. cit.,* pp. 7, 248, 251.
54. Silvano Arieti, "The Concept of Schizophrenia," in Robert Cancro, ed., *The Schizophrenic Reactions: A Critique of the Concept Hospital Treatment, and Current Research* (New York: Brunner/Mazel, 1970), p. 28.
55. Roy S. Grinker, Sr., "Changing Styles in Psychoses and Borderline States," *American Journal of Psychiatry,* 130 (February, 1973).
56. Howells, "Family Pathology and Schizophrenia," *op. cit.,* p. 393.
57. Leon Eisenberg, *op. cit.,* p. 229.
58. Robert Cancro, reviewing Theodore Lidz, *The Origin and Treatment of Schizophrenic Disorders,* for Behavioral Science Book Service (1974).
59. Daniel X. Freedman and Robert P. Gordon, "Psychiatry Under Siege: Attacks from Without," *Psychiatric Annals,* 3 (November, 1973).
60. Kety, Address to the National Association for Mental Health, November 14, 1972.

CHAPTER VI

1. Seymour Halleck, "Future Trends in the Mental Health Professions," *Psychiatric Opinion,* 11 (April, 1974).
2. Leo Srole and Thomas Langner, *Mental Health in the Metropolis: The Midtown Manhattan Study* (New York: McGraw-Hill, 1962).
3. W. Robert Curtis, "Community Human Service Networks: New Roles for Mental Health Workers," *Psychiatric Annals,* 3 (July, 1973).
4. Quoted by Harvey M. Freed, *et al.,* "Community Mental Health – Second-Class Treatment?" *MH,* 56 (Summer, 1972).
5. David C. Bolin and Laurence Kivens, "Evaluation in a Community Mental Health Center: Huntsville, Alabama," *Evaluation,* 2, no. 1 (1974).
6. Daniel Wiener, *A Practical Guide to Psychotherapy* (New York: Harper and Row, 1968), pp. 162–163.
7. See the report by Ralph Nader's study group; Franklin Chu and Sharland Trotter, *The Mental Health Complex: Part I, Community Mental Health Centers* (Washington, D.C.: Center for the Study of Responsive Law, 1972).
8. "San Francisco Westside: A Community Mental Health Center Serves the People," NIMH *Mental Health Program Reports,* 5 (Washington, D.C.: DHEW Publication No. [HSM] 72–9042).
9. Chu and Trotter, *op. cit.*
10. Walter M. Beattie, Jr., Director of the All-University Gerontology Center, Syracuse University, in *Mental Health; Principles and Training Techniques in Nursing Home Care* (Washington, D.C.: NIMH, DHEW Publication No. 73–9046, 1072), p. 5.
11. See Raymond M. Glasscote, Michael E. Fishman, Meyer Sonis, *Children and Mental Health Centers* (Washington, D.C.: Joint Information Service of the American Psychiatric Association and the National Association for Mental Health, 1972.)
12. Mrs. Jack Robbins, Chairperson, NAMH Task Force on National Health Insurance, *News and Thoughts,* Young Adult Institute Newsletter (Winter, 1972).
13. Chu and Trotter, *op. cit.*
14. Wiener, *op. cit.,* p. 121.
15. *Ibid.*
16. Nat Hentoff, "The Privacy Shredders," *The Village Voice* (September 13, 1973).
17. Lazarus, *How to Get Your Money's Worth Out of Psychiatry* (Los Angeles: Sherbourne Press, 1973), p. 144.
18. John E. Nardini, "Careers in General Practice of Psychiatry," *Career Directions,* 5 (Sandoz Pharmaceuticals, 1973).
19. Harold E. Resteiner, Judge of Probate, County of Genessee, Flint, Michigan, personal communication, October 31, 1972.
20. Donald A. Schwartz *et al.,* "Community Psychiatry and Emergency Service," *American Journal of Psychiatry* (December, 1972).
21. Ching-Pao Chien and Jonathan Cole, "Landlord Supervised Apartments for Community-Based Treatment," *American Journal of Psychiatry,* 130 (February, 1973).
22. *HEW News,* press release (July 11, 1973).
23. Quoted in Raymond M. Glasscote, Jon E. Gudeman, Richard Elpers, *et al., Halfway Houses for the Mentally Ill* (Washington, D.C.: Joint

Information Service of the American Psychiatric Association and the National Association for Mental Health, 1971), pp. 56–57.

24. "Soteria House: The People Next Door," *San Francisco Chronicle* (March 1, 1972); personal interview with Mr. Goveia, May, 1973.
25. Doyle Casey, regional coordinator of Virginia's Service Integration for Deinstitutionalization Research and Demonstration Project, quoted in *Richmond Times-Dispatch* (September 22, 1974).
26. Interview with Mr. Goveia.
27. See Raymond M. Glasscote, Elaine Cumming, Irwin D. Rutman, James N. Sussex, Sidney M. Glassman, *Rehabilitating the Mentally Ill in the Community: A Study of Psychosocial Information Centers* (Washington, D.C.: Joint Information Service, APA and NAMH, 1971).
28. Reich and Siegel, "The Chronically Mentally Ill Shuffle Off to Oblivion," *Psychiatric Annals,* 3 (November, 1973).
29. "Major Disabling Conditions of Clients of State Vocational Rehabilitation Agencies Rehabilitated and Not Rehabilitated During the Fiscal Year of 1969," *Statistical Notes,* 27 (June, 1971), HEW Social and Rehabilitation Services.
30. Massachusetts Rehabilitation Commission, *Annual Report* (1972).
31. "For the Disabled: Help Through Rehabilitation," HEW SRS Pub. No. 152 (August, 1970).
32. Rehabilitation Amendments of 1973 (P.L. 93–112), summarized in "Programs for the Handicapped," Office for the Handicapped, HEW (November 22, 1974).
33. Frank Laski, "Civil Rights Victories for the Handicapped – II," HEW, *Social and Rehabilitation Record,* 1 (June, 1974).
34. "What Can the Commonwealth of Massachusetts Do for You If You Are Disabled?" (Boston: MRC Pub. 1-30 M-71-050686).
35. "Services Offered the Emotionally Handicapped by the Mental Health Program, Massachusetts Rehabilitation Commission" (Boston: MRC, M-1-20M-11-71).
36. Michael Dolnick, "How the Disabled Break into the Economy," HEW, *Human Services* (February, 1973).
37. *Ibid.*
38. Arthur E. Rubin, Director of 4-H Youth Program, Los Angeles County, formerly Director of Planning, United Community Services of Elmira, N.Y. Personal interview, January, 1974.
39. Robin White, *Be Not Afraid* (New York: Dial Press, 1972).

CHAPTER VII

1. Wiener, *A Practical Guide to Psychotherapy* (New York: Harper and Row, 1968), p. 156.
2. Bandura, *Principles of Behavior Modification* (New York: Holt, Rinehart, and Winston, 1969), p. 9.
3. Harvey M. Freed, Jonathan F. Borus, José A. Gonzales, Jerry D. Grant, Orlando B. Lightfoot, and Victor M. Uribe, "Community Mental Health – Second Class Treatment?" *MH,* 56 (Summer, 1972).
4. John R. Whittier, Audrey Heimler, and Charles Koremyi, "The Psychiatrist and Huntington's Disease (Chorea)," *American Journal of Psychiatry,* 128 (June, 1972).
5. White, *Be Not Afraid, op. cit.*

6. Leonard Cammer, *Up from Depression* (New York: Simon and Schuster, 1969), p. 187.
7. Millie Mills, "You in Partnership with Your Client," *Breakthrough,* Newsletter of the Autistic Children's Society of New South Wales, 20 (October-November-December, 1973).
8. Rappaport, in Harvey Ruben, Jonas Rappaport, Thomas Szasz, and Richard Allen, "Silence Is Golden – or Is It?" *MH,* 57 (Winter, 1973).
9. Szasz, *ibid.*
10. Richard L. Jenkins in a review of J. E. Meeks, *The Fragile Alliance, American Journal of Psychiatry,* 128 (February, 1972).
11. Lazarus, *How to Get Your Money's Worth out of Psychiatry* (Los Angeles: Sherbourne Press, 1973), p. 101.
12. *Ibid.,* pp. 102–106.
13. Ann A. Burgess and Aaron Lazare, *Psychiatric Nursing in the Hospital and the Community* (Englewood Cliffs, N.J.: Prentice-Hall, 1973), p. 90.
14. *Ibid.,* p. 71.
15. Robert Coles, *The South Goes North* (Boston: Atlantic–Little, Brown, 1971), pp. 377, 385.
16. Daniel E. deSole, Philip Singer, and Jacob Roseman, "Community Psychiatry and the Syndrome of Psychiatric Culture Shock – The Emergence of a New Functional Disorder," *Social Science and Medicine,* 1 (1968): 401–418.
17. "Learning to Laugh Together," in *Breakthrough,* 16 (October-November-December, 1972).
18. Wiener, *op. cit.,* pp. 143–146, 160.
19. "Patient and His Physician; Quandary for Medical Profession," *New York Times* (January 16, 1973).
20. Wechsler, *In a Darkness* (New York: Norton, 1972), p. 85.
21. See Martin Shepard, *The Love Treatment: Sexual Intimacy between Patients and Psychotherapists* (New York: Paperback Library, 1972) (pro), and Phyllis Chesler, *Women and Madness* (Garden City: Doubleday and Co., 1972) (anti).
22. Robert Coles, "The Case of Michael Wechsler," *New York Review of Books* (May 18, 1972).
23. Robert L. Bergman, "A School for Medicine Men," *American Journal of Psychiatry,* 130 (June, 1973).
24. James P. Comer, "The Need is Now: A Case for the Development of More Minority Group Professionals," *MH,* 57 (Winter, 1973).
25. W. E. Henry, J. H. Sims, and S. L. Spray, *The Fifth Profession: Becoming a Psychotherapist* (San Francisco: Jossey-Bass, 1971).

CHAPTER VIII

1. Burch, *Stranger in the Family* (New York: Bobbs-Merrill, 1972), p. 208.
2. Clare Creer and J. K. Wing, *Schizophrenia At Home* (London: Institute of Psychiatry, 1974), p. 74.
3. Ruth I. Knee, Discussion of "The Family as a Potential Resource in Rehabilitation," by A. S. Evans, D. M. Bullard, Jr., and M. H. Solomon, *American Journal of Psychiatry,* 117 (June, 1961).
4. Schopler and Reichler, "Parents as Co-Therapists in the Treatment of Psychotic Children," *Journal of Autism and Childhood Schizophrenia,* 1 (January-March, 1971).

5. Seymour Furman and Anne Feighner, "Video Feedback in Treating Hyperkinetic Children," *American Journal of Psychiatry,* 130 (July, 1973).
6. Sturm, telephone interview, May 15, 1974.
7. *Science News* (April 21, 1973).
8. See Robert Paul Liberman, "Behavioral Approaches to Family and Couple Therapy," in C. J. Sager and H. S. Kaplan, *Progress in Group and Family Therapy* (New York: Brunner/Mazel, 1972).
9. Speck and Attneave, *Family Networks* (New York; Pantheon Books, 1973).
10. J. E. Barrett, Jr., Judith Kuriansky, and Barry Gurland, "Community Tenure Following Emergency Discharge," *American Journal of Psychiatry,* 128 (February, 1972).
11. J. K. Wing, Julian Leff, and Steven Hirsch, "Preventive Treatment of Schizophrenia: Some Theoretical and Methodological Issues," in *Psychopathology and Psychopharmacology,* J. O. Cole, A. M. Freedman, and A. J. Friedhoff, eds. (Baltimore: Johns Hopkins University Press, 1973).
12. G. W. Brown, J. L. T. Birley, and J. K. Wing, "Influence of Family Life on the Course of Schizophrenic Disorders: A Replication," *British Journal of Psychiatry,* 121 (1972):241–248; also in Robert Cancro, ed., *Annual Review of the Schizophrenic Syndrome, 1973* (New York: Brunner/Mazel, 1974).
13. *Ibid.*
14. *Ibid.*
15. Wing, Leff, and Hirsch, "Preventive Treatment of Schizophrenia," *op. cit.*
16. "Hannah Green," *I Never Promised You a Rose Garden* (New York: Holt, Rinehart, and Winston, 1964), pp. 209–212.
17. H. Peter Laqueur, "Multiple Family Therapy and General Systems Theory," in *International Psychiatry Clinics,* vol. 7, no. 4 (Boston: Little, Brown, 1970), p. 105.
18. Laing and Esterson, *Sanity, Madness, and the Family,* 2nd ed. (New York: Basic Books, 1971), p. ix.
19. Kalinowsky and Hippius, *Pharmacological, Convulsive, and Other Somatic Treatments in Psychiatry* (New York: Grune and Stratton, 1969), p. 122.
20. Leonard Woolf, *Beginning Again* (New York: Harcourt, Brace and World, 1964), pp. 149, 166.
21. Leonard Cammer, *Up from Depression* (New York: Simon and Schuster, 1969), p. 194.
22. Farber, "Schizophrenia and the Mad Psychotherapist," in *R. D. Laing and Anti-Psychiatry,* ed. Robert Boyers and Robert Orrill (New York: Perennial Library, Harper and Row, 1971), p. 90; reprinted from *The Ways of the Will* (New York: Basic Books, 1966).
23. Farber, in "An R. D. Laing Symposium," in Boyers and Orrill, *op. cit.,* pp. 226, 227.
24. Brown, quoted in Creer and Wing, *Schizophrenia at Home* (London: Institute of Psychiatry, 1974), p. 69.
25. Anthony, "The Contagious Subculture of Psychosis," in C. L. Sager and H. S. Kaplan, *Progress in Group and Family Therapy* (New York: Brunner/Mazel, 1972), p. 636.
26. Anthony, *op. cit.,* p. 641.
27. Leonard Woolf, *op. cit.,* p. 161.
28. Farber, in "Symposium," *op. cit.,* p. 227.
29. From "Schizophrenia: The Family Burden," National Schizophrenia Fellowship (Surbiton, Surrey [England], 1973; reissued 1974).
30. Deykin, "The Reintegration of the Chronic Schizophrenic Patient Dis-

charged to his Family and Community as Perceived by the Family," *Mental Hygiene,* 45 (1961) :235–246.

31. Garmezy, "Children at Risk: The Search for the Antecedents of Schizophrenia," Part 1, *Schizophrenia Bulletin,* 8 (Spring, 1974) :58.
32. Lazarus, *op. cit.,* p. 103.
33. Anthony, *op. cit.,* in Sager and Kaplan, *Progress in Group and Family Therapy.*
34. Anthony, NIMH Study, "The Influence of Parental Psychosis on the Development of the Child," reported in Loren R. Mosher and David Feinsilver, *Special Report: Schizophrenia* (Washington, D.C.: NIMH, Pub. No. [HSM] 72–9042, 1971) , pp. 20–21.
35. Maggie Scarf, "Which Child Gets Scarred?" *New York Times* (December 3, 1972) .
36. Michael Rutter, *Children of Sick Parents: An Environmental and Psychiatric Study* (London: Maudsley Hospital Monograph No. 16, 1966) ; Dr. Anthony comes to a similar conclusion.
37. Bleuler, "The Offspring of Schizophrenics," *Schizophrenia Bulletin,* 8 (Spring, 1974) , a chapter from *On Schizophrenia,* translated by Siegfried Clemens (New Haven: Yale University Press, pub. date 1977) .
38. Burgess and Lazare, *Psychiatric Nursing in the Hospital and the Community* (Englewood Cliffs, N.J.: Prentice-Hall, 1973) , p. 31.

CHAPTER IX

1. Rosenhan, "On Being Sane in Insane Places," *Science,* 179 (April 27, 1973) .
2. Study by Walter Gove and Terry Fain of Vanderbilt University, reported in *Psychiatric News* (July 18, 1973) .
3. Burch, *Stranger in the Family* (New York: Bobbs-Merrill, 1972) , p. 25.
4. Dr. Otto Will, Medical Director, Austen Riggs Center, "What Riggs Is All About," *Berkshire Eagle* (April 15, 1972) .
5. Lynn, personal interview, May, 1973.
6. Dr. Francis de Marneffe, quoted in *Boston Phoenix–Boston After Dark* (November 14, 1972) .
7. Elliott A. Krause, *Factors Related to Length of Mental Hospital Stay: A Review of the Literature* (C.M.H. Monograph series, Massachusetts Department of Mental Health, n.d.) .
8. Cooperman, personal interview, May, 1974.
9. Alexander, quoted in *Boston Phoenix* (November 14, 1972) .
10. Benziger, *The Prison of My Mind* (New York: Walker, 1969) .
11. Brenner, *Saturday Review,* July 1, 1972.
12. Edwin Robbins and Lillian Robbins, "Charge to the Community: Some Early Effects of a State Hospital System's Change of Policy," *American Journal of Psychiatry,* 131 (June, 1974) .
13. Robert Paul Liberman, "Behavior Modification of Schizophrenia, a Review," *Schizophrenia Bulletin,* 6 (Fall, 1972) .
14. *Ibid.*
15. The phrase is Laura Godber's; she runs the Neighborhood Action Program in Laurelton, Queens, New York.
16. Braginski and Braginski, "Mental Hospitals as Resorts," *Psychology Today* (March, 1973) . They worked at Connecticut State and at a Veterans' Administration hospital nearby.

17. *Ibid.*
18. Reported in *Berkshire Eagle* (June 21, 1974).
19. Nardini, "Careers in General Practice of Psychiatry," *Career Directions,* 3, no. 5 (Sandoz Pharmaceuticals, 1973).
20. Pinsker, letter, *Science,* 180 (April 27, 1973).
21. Braginski and Braginski, *op. cit.*, p. 87.
22. Greenblatt, in Lester Grinspoon, Jack R. Ewalt, and Richard I. Shader, *Schizophrenia: Psychotherapy and Pharmacotherapy* (Baltimore: Williams and Wilkins, 1972), p. xi.
23. See Redlich and Freedman, *The Theory and Practice of Psychiatry* (New York: Basic Books, 1966), p. 68.
24. Teodoro Ayllon and J. Michael, "The Psychiatric Nurse as a Behavioral Engineer," in James O. Palmer and Michael Goldstein, eds., *Perspectives in Psychopathology* (New York: Oxford University Press, 1966). The date of the Ayllon and Michael paper is 1959.
25. See Michael Hersen, R. M. Eisler, Buren S. Smith, and W. Stewart Agras, "A Token Reinforcement Ward for Young Psychotic Patients," *American Journal of Psychiatry,* 129 (August, 1972).
26. Lee Birk *et al., Behavior Therapy in Psychiatry: A Report of the APA Task Force on Behavior Therapy* (Washington; D.C.: American Psychiatric Association, 1973).
27. T. Ayllon and Michael D. Roberts, "The Token Economy: Now," in *Behavior Modification: Principles and Clinical Applications,* W. Stewart Agras, ed. (Boston: Little, Brown, 1972), p. 83.
28. President's Committee on Mental Retardation, *Silent Minority* (DHEW pub. No. [OHD] 74–21002).
29. *Souder* v. *Brennan,* 367 F. Supp. 808 (1973).
30. Bruce Ennis, *Prisoners of Psychiatry: Mental Patients, Psychiatrists, and the Law* (New York: Harcourt Brace Jovanovich, 1972).
31. Erving Goffman, *Asylums* (Garden City, N.Y.: Anchor Books, Doubleday and Co., 1961), p. 148.
32. Karlins, personal interview, May, 1973.
33. Residential Environment Survey, 1973, Department of Public Welfare, State of Minnesota. The wording of some questions has been condensed.
34. Scott H. Nelson and Henry Grunebaum, "A Follow-up Study of Wrist-Slashers," *American Journal of Psychiatry,* 127 (April, 1971).
35. Egon Bittner, "Police Discretion in Emergency Apprehension of Mentally Ill Persons," in Richard H. Price and Bruce Denner, eds., *The Making of a Mental Patient* (New York: Holt, Rinehart and Winston, 1973), p. 53.
36. David Hawkins, in *Orthomolecular Psychiatry* (San Francisco: W. H. Freeman, 1972), p. 575.
37. Mary Barnes and Joseph Berke, *Mary Barnes: Two Accounts of a Journey Through Madness* (New York: Harcourt Brace Jovanovich, 1971).
38. Sylvia Plath, *The Bell Jar* (New York: Harper and Row, 1971).
39. Barbara Field Benziger, *op. cit.*, p. 21.
40. Leonard Cammer, *Up from Depression* (New York: Simon and Schuster, 1969), p. 221.
41. *Ibid.*, p. 223.
42. Association of Hospital and Institutional Libraries, *Bibliotherapy: Methods and Materials* (Chicago: American Library Association, 1971); Jack J. Leedy, *Poetry Therapy: The Use of Poetry in the Treatment of Emotional Disorders* (Philadelphia: Lippincott, 1969).
43. *The Boston Phoenix* (February 20, 1973).
44. Burch, *op. cit.*, p. 112.

45. Edith Stern, *Mental Illness: A Guide for the Family* (New York: Commonwealth Fund, 1944, rev. ed., 1968).
46. *Ibid.*
47. Benziger, *op. cit.*, p. 141.
48. Burch, *Stranger in the Family* (New York: Bobbs-Merrill, 1972), p. 112.
49. Study by Walter R. Gove and Terry Fain, reported in *Psychiatric News*, (July 18, 1973).
50. Neiman, letter, *Psychiatric News* (November 3, 1971).
51. Ennis, *op. cit.*, Chapters 9 and 10.
52. Mack, telephone interview, May 28, 1974.
53. *Richmond Times-Dispatch* (May 23, 1974).

CHAPTER X

1. David L. Chambers, "Alternatives to Civil Commitment of the Mentally Ill: Practical Guides and Constitutional Imperatives," 70 *Michigan Law Review* 1133 (1972).
2. Carole Wade Offir, "Field Report," *Psychology Today* (October, 1974).
3. Carol McCabe, "Stories from the Madhouse," *Providence Sunday Journal* (April 1, 1973).
4. "Developments in the Law—Civil Commitment of the Mentally Ill," Note, 87 *Harvard Law Review* 1190, 1254 (1974).
5. Cited in Ralph Slovenko, *Psychiatry and Law* (Boston: Little, Brown, 1973), p. 202.
6. Leon Eisenberg, "Psychiatric Intervention," *Scientific American*, 229 (September, 1973).
7. These statutes, including the citation from the Idaho statute, are noted in *Harvard Law Review*, *op. cit.*, pp. 1202–1203.
8. Language of decision, as quoted in *Washington Post* (June 27, 1975).
9. Slovenko, *op. cit.*, p. 221.
10. *In re John Ballay*, 482 F. 2d 648 (1973).
11. *Detroit Free Press* (May 6, 1974).
12. "Interview with Bruce Ennis," *Madness Network News*, 2 (February, 1974).
13. *Winters* v. *Miller*, 446 F. 2d 65 (1971). See also p. 000.
14. Wade Hudson, "NAPA Notes," *Madness Network News*, 2 (September, 1974).
15. Samuel J. Brakel and Ronald S. Rock, eds., *The Mentally Disabled and the Law*, rev. ed., American Bar Foundation Study (Chicago: University of Chicago Press, 1971), pp. 159, 180–181.
16. "Interview with Bruce Ennis," *Madness Network News*, *op. cit.*
17. *Behavior Today* (October 14, 1974).
18. Account of *Donaldson* based on report in *Psychiatric News* (July 3, 1974), Ennis, *Prisoners*, Chapter 5, and Washington *Post* (June 27, 1975).
19. Murray Schumach, "Hospital Escape Inquiry Opens," *New York Times* (August 17, 1974).
20. Jack Durrell, Medical Director, Psychiatric Institute of Washington, quoted in *Washington Star-News* (November 3, 1973).
21. Ennis, *op. cit.*, Chapter 3.
22. *Ex parte Hodges*, 166 Tex. Crim. Rep. 433, 437; 314 S. W. 2d 581, 584 (1958), cited in Brakel and Rock, *op. cit.*, p. 409.

23. *Jackson* v. *Indiana*, 406 U.S. 715 (1972), 730, 737–738.
24. *Daniel M'Naghten's case*, 10 Cl. and F. 200, 8 Eng. Rep. 718 (Hil. 1843).
25. Lloyd Weinreb, *Criminal Law: Cases, Comment, Questions* (Mineola, N.Y.: Foundation Press, 1969), p. 304.
26. Bernard L. Diamond, as cited in Brakel and Rock, *op. cit.*, p. 387.
27. *Durham* v. *U.S.*, 214 F.2d 862, 874–876 (1954).
28. *Ibid.*
29. American Law Institute, *Restatement of the Law, Second, Torts 2d* (St. Paul, Minn.: American Law Institute, 1965).
30. Slovenko, *op. cit.*, p. 283.
31. Brakel and Rock, *op. cit.*, p. 308.
32. *Ibid.*, p. 304.
33. *Walker* v. *McCoy*, 40 Tenn. 103, 105 (1859), cited in C. Henry Freas, "Mental Illness and Contract Law," 29 *Tenn. Law Review* 274, 274–275 (1962).
34. Slovenko, *op. cit.*, pp. 317–318.
35. *Ibid.*, p. 323.
36. *Faber* v. *Sweet Style Manufacturing Corporation*, 242 N.Y.S. 2d 763 (1963).
37. *In re Estate of Willits*, 175 Cal. 173 (1917), quoted in Slovenko, *op. cit.*, 336.
38. Brakel and Rock, *op. cit.*, p. 226; Slovenko, *op. cit.*
39. Slovenko, *op. cit.*, pp. 240–243.
40. *Ibid.*
41. Slovenko, *op. cit.*, p. 353.
42. Brakel and Rock, *op. cit.*, p. 230.
43. *Ibid.*, p. 248.
44. Brakel and Rock, *op. cit.*, p. 260.
45. Elizabeth Ogg, "Securing the Legal Rights of Retarded Persons," Public Affairs Pamphlet No. 492 (New York: Public Affairs Committee, 381 Park Avenue South, New York 10016, 1973).
46. Brakel and Rock, *op. cit.*, p. 262.
47. *Ibid.*, p. 263.
48. Ennis, *Prisoners*, *op. cit.*, p. 122.
49. *Streda Estate*, 137 *Legal Intell.* No. 97 at 8, col. z (Delaware Cty., Orphans Ct., Nov. 6, 1957). Cited in Brakel and Rock, *op. cit.*, p. 254.

CHAPTER XI

1. Wilson, *This Stranger, My Son* (New York: New American Library, 1968).
2. Louis Reed, Evelyn S. Myers, and Patricia N. Scheidemandel, *Health Insurance and Psychiatric Care* (Washington, D.C.: American Psychiatric Association, 1972).
3. Viscott, *The Making of a Psychiatrist* (New York: Arbor House, 1972), p. 352.
4. Chodoff, "Changing Styles in the Neuroses," *American Journal of Psychiatry*, 130 (February, 1973).
5. Chodoff, "The Effect of Third-Party Payment on the Practice of Psychotherapy," *American Journal of Psychiatry*, 129 (November, 1972).
6. C. G. Hill, Vice-President, Massachusetts Mutual Life Insurance Co.,

Springfield, Mass., to Rogers H. Wright of the American Psychological Association, December 1, 1971, in "Health Insurance," collection of documents from American Psychological Association.

7. Robert N. Butler and Myrna I. Lewis, *Aging and Mental Health: Positive Psychosocial Approaches* (St. Louis, Mo.: C. V. Mosby Co., 1973), p. 49.
8. Chodoff, "Third-Party Payment."
9. Max Silverstein, *Psychiatric Aftercare* (Philadelphia: University of Pennsylvania Press, 1968), p. 33.
10. Gross, quoted in Glasscote *et al., Partial Hospitalization for the Mentally Ill* (Washington, D.C.: Joint Information Service, American Psychiatric Association/National Association for Mental Health, 1969), p. 88.
11. Butler and Lewis, *op. cit.,* p. 254.
12. Steve Waugh, "How to Choose Your Psychotherapist," *The Boston Phoenix* (October 3, 1972).
13. AP report in North Adams (Mass.) *Transcript* (October, 1974).
14. AP report, North Adams (Mass.) *Transcript* (June 5, 1974).
15. "Blue Cross Claim Denials Spur Opposition, Probe," *Psychiatric News* (April 17, 1974).
16. Butler and Lewis, *op. cit.,* pp. 131–132.
17. *Ibid.,* p. 130.
18. Chodoff, "Third-Party Payment," quoting W. Bevan, "The Topsy-turvey World of Health Care Delivery," *Science,* 173 (September 10, 1971).
19. Robert W. Gibson, "Insurance Coverage for Treatment of Mental Illness in Later Life," in Ewald W. Busse and Eric Pfeiffer, eds., *Mental Illness in Later Life* (Washington, D.C.: American Psychiatric Association, 1973), p. 188.
20. Dorsey, "PSRO's: Salvation or Suicide for Psychiatry?" *Psychiatric News,* 11 (October, 1974).
21. Butler and Lewis, *op. cit.,* p. 171.
22. *Behavior Today* (March 25, 1974).
23. Harrington, "National Health Insurance Ignores Your Children," *The Exceptional Parent,* 1 (February-March, 1972).
24. Bruce Ennis and Loren Siegel, *The Rights of Mental Patients* (New York: Richard W. Baron, 1973).
25. Robert N. Butler, "Concerning Decent Institutional Care," in *Mental Health: Principles and Training Techniques in Nursing Home Care* (Washington, D.C.: NIMH, 1972), DHEW Publication No. (HSM) 73–9046.
26. *Silent Minority* (Washington, D.C., 1974), DHEW Publication No. (OHD) 74–21002.
27. Daniel Wiener, *A Practical Guide to Psychotherapy* (New York: Harper & Row, 1968), p. 118; *The Exceptional Parent* (January-February, 1974).
28. *Social Security Benefits for People Disabled before Age 22* (DHEW Publication No. [SSA] 73–10012), free from your local Social Security office.
29. NSAC *Newsletter,* 6 (April, 1974).
30. Karen Monsour and Beth Stone, "The Hawaii Trip: A Study of a Segment of American Youth," *Psychiatric Annals,* 4 (June, 1974).
31. *PCMR Message,* 38 (August, 1974), published by President's Committee on Mental Retardation, HEW; see also *Right to Appeal Supplemental Security Income,* DHEW Publication No. (SSA) 74–10281.
32. *Psychiatric News* (August 7, 1974).
33. Aldrin, *Return to Earth* (New York: Random House, 1973), p. 287.
34. Ibid., p. 327.

35. *Living with Schizophrenia – By the Relatives* (Surbiton, Surrey: National Schizophrenia Fellowship, 1974), pp. 22–23.
36. Erik Erikson, *Childhood and Society* (New York: W. W. Norton, 1950).

CHAPTER XII

1. Irvine, "The Risks of the Register, or the Management of Expectation," in *The Child in His Family: Children at Psychiatric Risk,* III, E. James Anthony and Cyrille Koupernik, eds. (New York: John Wiley and Sons, 1974), pp. 189–190.
2. Lennard, quoted by Diane Divoky, "Toward a Nation of Sedated Children," *Learning, The Magazine for Creative Teaching* (March, 1973).
3. "Child Psychotherapy Is Increasing Rapidly," *New York Times* (July 30, 1973).
4. Saul Kapel, "Parents and Children: Those 'Symptoms' are Normal Growth," *New York Daily News* (January 1, 1974).
5. J. Glavin and H. C. Quay, "Behavior Disorders," *Review of Educational Research,* 39 (1969):83–102; cited by Jack Bardon and Virginia Bennett, "Helping the Child in School," in *Manual of Child Psychopathology,* B. B. Wolman, ed. (New York: McGraw-Hill, 1972), pp. 1063–1064.
6. Kohlberg, "The Predictability of Adult Mental Health from Childhood Behavior," in *Manual of Child Psychopathology, op. cit.,* p. 1243.
7. *Ibid.*
8. Kapel, *loc. cit.*
9. See Gitta Sereny, *The Case of Mary Bell: A Portrait of a Child Who Murdered* (New York: McGraw-Hill, 1973).
10. Harold Levy, *Square Pegs, Round Holes* (Boston: Little, Brown, 1973), pp. 89–90.
11. Levy, *op. cit.,* p. 21.
12. Formulated in the First Annual Report of the National Advisory Commission on Handicapped Children, 1968, and now very widely used.
13. Milton Brutten, Sylvia O. Richardson, and Charles Mangel, *Something's Wrong with My Child: A Parents' Book about Children with Learning Disabilities* (New York: Harcourt Brace Jovanovich, 1973).
14. *Op. cit.,* p. 32; from "All About Me," *Journal of Learning Disabilities* (January, 1968).
15. Levy, *op. cit.,* p. 202.
16. Wender, *The Hyperactive Child: A Handbook for Parents* (New York: Crown Publishers, 1973), p. 3.
17. *Ibid.,* p. 31.
18. *Ibid.,* p. 62.
19. Leon Eisenberg, "Principles of Drug Therapy in Child Psychiatry with Special Reference to Stimulant Drugs," *Annual Progress in Child Psychiatry and Child Development,* S. Chess and A. Thomas, eds. (New York: Brunner/Mazel, 1972).
20. C. Hollister, quoted by Eisenberg, *op. cit.*
21. Bettelheim, Remarks at the Eighth International Conference on Child Psychiatry and Allied Professions, August 1, 1974.
22. Divoky and Schrag, *The Myth of the Hyperactive Child* (New York: Pantheon, 1975).
23. Lester Grinspoon and Peter Hedblom, *The Speed Culture: Amphetamine*

Use and Abuse in America (Cambridge, Mass.: Harvard University Press, 1975), p. 249.
24. *Ibid.*, p. 256.
25. Wender, *op. cit.*, p. 55.
26. Eisenberg, *op. cit.*, p. 631.
27. Washington *Post* (June 29, 1970); *New York Times* (June 30, 1970).
28. Wender, *op. cit.*, p. 113.
29. Divoky and Schrag, *op. cit.*, pp. 73–77. Nat Hentoff, "The Official Drug Scene," *The Village Voice* (September 27, 1973).
30. Wender, *op. cit.*, p. 78.
31. Brutten, Richardson and Mangel, *op. cit.*, pp. 57, 65.
32. Kanner's papers on autism are collected in *Childhood Psychosis: Initial Studies and New Insights* (Washington, D.C.: Winston-Wiley, 1973).
33. Donald Cohen, Professor of Pediatrics and Psychiatry at Yale Medical School, in testimony before the Subcommittee on Public Health and Environment of the House of Representatives, *Congressional Record,* 120, February 21, 1974.
34. Lorna Wing, *Autistic Children: A Guide for Parents and Professionals* (New York: Brunner/Mazel, 1972), p. 21.
35. Margaret A. Dewey, parent of an autistic child and chairman of Adult Programs, National Society for Autistic Children, personal communication; see also M. Dewey and Margaret Everard, "The Near-Normal Autistic Adolescent," *Journal of Autism and Childhood Schizophrenia,* 4 (December, 1974).
36. O. Ivar Lovaas, Laura Schreibman, and Robert L. Koegel, "A Behavior Modification Approach to the Treatment of Autistic Children," *Journal of Autism and Childhood Schizophrenia,* 4 (November, 1974).
37. Cf. S. A. Szurek and I. N. Berlin, eds., *Clinical Studies in Childhood Psychosis* (New York: Brunner/Mazel, 1973). The words "schizophrenogenic" and even "autistogenic" are used of families by L. H. Crabtree, Jr., James A. Brecht, and John C. Sonne, in "Monadic Orientation: A Contribution to the Structure of Families with Autistic Children," *Journal of Family Process,* 11 (September, 1972).
38. Stella Chess, "Autism in Children with Congenital Rubella," in *Annual Progress in Child Psychiatry and Child Development* (1972).
39. Donald J. Cohen, *Congressional Record,* 120, *loc. cit.*
40. Tanguay, *Congressional Record,* 120 (February 21, 1974).
41. Wing, *op. cit.*, p. 53.
42. Cohen, *Congressional Record,* 120, *loc. cit.*
43. From "Schizophrenia: The Family Burden," National Schizophrenia Fellowship (Surbiton, Surrey: 1973, reissued 1974).
44. Ayd, in *Psychiatric News* (December 19, 1973).
45. Wing, *op. cit.*, p. 28.
46. *Psychiatric News* (February 6, 1974).
47. William E. Henry, John H. Sims, and S. Lee Spray, *Public and Private Lives of Psychotherapists* (San Francisco: Jossey-Bass Publishers, 1973), p. 94.
48. American Psychiatric Association Manpower Survey, 1970, as reported in *Psychiatric News* (August 15, 1972).
49. Raymond M. Glasscote, Michael E. Fishman, Meyer Sonis, *Children and Mental Health Centers: Programs, Problems, Prospects* (Washington, D.C.: Joint Information Service of the American Psychiatric Association and the National Association for Mental Health, 1972).

50. Rexford, review of Glasscote *et al., op. cit., American Journal of Psychiatry,* 130 (July, 1973).
51. Glasscote *et al., op. cit.,* p. 201.
52. Greenfeld, *A Child Called Noah* (New York: Holt, Rinehart and Winston, 1972).
53. Carl Fenichel, "Special Education as the Basic Therapeutic Tool in Treatment of Severely Disturbed Children," *Journal of Autism and Childhood Schizophrenia,* 4 (June, 1974).
54. *Pennsylvania Association for Retarded Children* v. *Comm. of Pa.,* 334 F. Supp. 1257 (1971). *Mills* v. *Board of Education of the District of Columbia,* 348 F. Supp. 866 (1972).
55. Burgener, quoted in President's Committee on Mental Retardation, *Silent Minority* (DHEW Publication No. [OHD] 74–21002, 1974).
56. See Janet M. Bennett, "The Proof of the Pudding," *The Exceptional Parent* (May-June, 1974).
57. Leonard Zneimer, Director, the Rhinebeck County School, Rhinebeck, New York, "Disappearing in the Community," *The Exceptional Parent,* 4 (May-June, 1974).
58. National Institute of Mental Health, *Residential Psychiatric Facilities for Children and Adolescents, United States 1971–72* (DHEW Publication No. ADM 74–78, 1974).
59. National Institute of Mental Health, *Hospital Inpatient Treatment Units for Emotionally Disturbed Children: United States, 1971–72* (DHEW Publication No. ADM 74–82, 1972), p. 5.
60. *Ibid.,* pp. 29–30.
61. *Psychiatric News* (February 6, 1974).
62. *Newsletter* of the Metropolitan New York Chapter of the National Society for Autistic Children, 4 (October, 1970).

CHAPTER XIII

1. Paul Poinsard, "Society Shuns the Aged," *Pennsylvania Mental Health Bulletin,* 1 (April, 1973).
2. *Mental Illness in Later Life,* Ewald W. Busse and Eric Pfeiffer, eds., (Washington, D.C.: American Psychiatric Association, 1973), p. 9.
3. Robert N. Butler and Myrna I. Lewis, *Aging and Mental Health: Positive Psychosocial Approaches* (St. Louis, Mo.: C. V. Mosby Co., 1973).
4. *Ibid.,* pp. 46, 202.
5. 1970 Report of the American Psychiatric Association, reported in *Psychiatric News* (August 15, 1973).
6. Butler and Lewis, *op. cit.,* p. 47.
7. E. G. Gallagher, M. R. Sharaff, and D. J. Levinson, "The Influence of Patient and Therapist in Determining the Use of Psychotherapy in a Psychiatric Hospital," *Psychiatry,* 28 (1965):297–310.
8. Busse and Pfeiffer, *op. cit.,* p. 8.
9. Martin A. Berezin, "Psychodynamic Considerations of Aging and the Aged," *American Journal of Psychiatry,* 128 (June, 1972).
10. Ethel Shanas, "The Unmarried Old Person in the U.S.: Living Arrangements and Care in Illness, Myth and Fact," paper prepared for the International Social Science and Research Seminar in Gerontology, Markaryd, Sweden, August, 1963.

11. Shanas, cited in Busse and Pfeiffer, *op. cit.,* pp. 275–276.
12. Butler and Lewis, *op. cit.,* p. 108.
13. "Who Are the Aging?" in Busse and Pfeiffer, *op. cit.,* p. 27.
14. Robert Gibson, "Insurance Coverage for Treatment of Mental Illness in Later Life," in Busse and Pfeiffer, *op. cit.,* pp. 182–183.
15. Robert J. Nathan, "The Psychiatric Treatment of the Geriatric Patient," *American Journal of Psychiatry,* 130 (June, 1973).
16. Eric Pfeiffer in Busse and Pfeiffer, *op. cit.,* p. 8.
17. *Ibid.*
18. Butler and Lewis, *op. cit.,* p. 10.
19. Busse, "Organic Brain Syndromes," in Busse and Pfeiffer, *op. cit.,* p. 95.
20. Butler and Lewis, *op. cit.,* p. 71.
21. Bernard A. Stotsky, "Social and Clinical Issues in Geriatric Psychiatry," *American Journal of Psychiatry,* 129 (August, 1972).
22. John Nowlin, "Physical Changes in Later Life and Their Relationships to Mental Functioning," in Busse and Pfeiffer, *op. cit.,* pp. 147–150.
23. Viscott, *The Making of a Psychiatrist* (New York: Arbor House, 1973), pp. 189–192.
24. Agate, cited by Nowlin, *op. cit.,* p. 148.
25. Butler and Lewis, *op. cit.,* p. 256.
26. Brown, in *Psychiatric News* (July 3, 1974).
27. Busse, *op. cit.,* p. 91.
28. Butler and Lewis, *op. cit.,* p. 72.
29. Quoted in *Behavior Today* (March 25, 1974).
30. Eric Pfeiffer, "Interacting with Older Patients," in Busse and Pfeiffer, *op. cit.,* pp. 13–15.
31. Butler and Lewis, *op. cit.,* pp. 232–233.
32. *Ibid.*
33. Berezin, *op. cit*
34. Feigenbaum, "Ambulatory Treatment of the Elderly," in Busse and Pfeiffer, *op. cit.,* p. 165.
35. *Ibid.*
36. Butler and Lewis, *op. cit.,* p. 117, quoting Blenkner, "Social Work and Family Relationships in Later Life with Some Thought on Filial Maturity," in *Social Structure and the Family: Generational Relations* (Englewood Cliffs, N.J.: Prentice-Hall, Inc., 1965).
37. Busse and Pfeiffer, *op. cit.,* p. 122.
38. Butler and Lewis, *op. cit.,* p. 247.
39. Robert N. Butler, "Concerning Decent Institutional Care," in *Mental Health: Principles and Training Techniques in Nursing Home Care* (Washington, D.C.: NIMH, DHEW Publication No. [NSM] 73-9046, 1973).
40. Nowlin, in Busse and Pfeiffer, *op. cit.,* p. 151.
41. Butler and Lewis, *op. cit.,* p. 252.
42. Feigenbaum, in Busse and Pfeiffer, *op. cit.,* p. 160.
43. Pfeiffer, "Interacting with Older Patients," *op. cit.,* p. 8.
44. Butler and Lewis, *op. cit.,* pp. 131–132.
45. Busse and Pfeiffer, *op. cit.,* p. 11.
46. Peak, in Busse and Pfeiffer, *op. cit.,* pp. 253–254.
47. Cammer, *Up from Depression* (New York: Simon and Schuster, 1969), p. 182.
48. *Ibid.,* p. 99.
49. Peterson, quoted in "Reality Orientation," *Science News,* 102 (December 23, 1972).

50. Also candy, trinkets, and magazines. Nancy Bohac Flood and Margaret L. DuVall, "Geriatric Incontinence: A Successful Operant Treatment," *Center for Behavior Modification Newsletter,* 2 (Minneapolis: July, 1974).
51. In Busse and Pfeiffer, *op. cit.,* p. 253.
52. Quoted by Eric J. Cassell, "Caring for the Dying," distributed by The Institute of Society, Ethics, and the Life Sciences (Hastings-on-Hudson, N.Y., 1971).
53. Butler and Lewis, *op. cit.,* pp. 109, 131.
54. Haber, quoted in Butler and Lewis, *op. cit.,* p. 212.
55. "Princess," letter to "Dear Abby," *Chicago Tribune*–N.Y. News Syndicate, Inc. (April 5, 1973).
56. Butler and Lewis, *op. cit.,* p. 214.
57. William Fitch, Director of the National Council on the Aging, quoted in Butler and Lewis, *op. cit.,* pp. 215–216.
58. Mendelson, *Tender, Loving Greed* (New York: Alfred A. Knopf, 1974). For an authoritative overview, see Bernard Stotsky, *The Nursing Home and the Aged Psychiatric Patient* (New York: Appleton-Century-Crofts–Meredith Publishing Co., 1970).
59. Bernard Stotsky, "Social and Clinical Issues in Geriatric Psychiatry," *American Journal of Psychiatry,* 129 (August, 1972).

CHAPTER XIV

1. Raymond M. Glasscote *et al., Rehabilitating the Mentally Ill in the Community: A Study of Psychosocial Rehabilitation Centers* (Washington, D.C.: Joint Information Service of the American Psychiatric Association and the National Association for Mental Health, 1971), Chapter 6.
2. Harrington, "National Health Insurance Ignores Your Children," *The Exceptional Parent* (February/March, 1972).
3. J. Anthony Kline and Peter E. Sitkin, "Financing Public Interest Litigation," 13 *Arizona Law Review,* 823 (1971).
4. *Newman* v. *Piggie Park Enterprises,* 390 U.S. 400 (1968); as cited in Kline and Sitkin, *op. cit.*
5. Supplementary comments to the Supreme Court decision in *Eisen* v. *Carlisle and Jacquelin, et al.,* 417 U.S. 156, 94 S.Ct. 2140 (1974).
6. Perry London, "Morals and Mental Health," in Stanley C. Plog and R. B. Edgerton, *Changing Perspectives in Mental Illness* (New York: Holt, Rinehart and Winston, 1969), p. 47.
7. Cortazzo, *Activity Centers for Retarded Adults* (President's Committee on Mental Retardation: June, 1972), DHEW Publication No. (OS) 72-43.
8. *St. Elizabeths Reporter* (Summer, 1972).
9. Low, *Mental Health Through Will-Training: A System of Self-Help as Practiced by Recovery, Inc.* (Boston: Christopher Publishing House, 1950).
10. Neil and Margaret Rau, *My Dear Ones* (Englewood Clffs, N.J.: Prentice-Hall, 1971).
11. Menninger, "Reading Notes," *Psychiatric News* (March 7, 1973).
12. Stanley R. Dean, "The Role of Self-Conducted Group Therapy in Psychorehabilitation: A Look at Recovery, Inc.," *American Journal of Psychiatry,* 127 (January, 1971).
13. *Ibid.*
14. Low, *op. cit.,* p. 208.

15. *Ibid.*
16. *Ibid.*, p. 140.
17. *Ibid.*, p. 68.
18. *Ibid.*, p. 310.
19. "How a Panel Example Should Be Constructed," instructions for use in Recovery meetings.
20. "Mental Self-Help," *Time* (July 31, 1972).
21. Dean, *op. cit.*
22. Grosz, "Recovery, Inc. Survey: A Preliminary Report," distributed by Recovery, Inc., n.d.
23. Miriam Siegler and Humphry Osmond, *Models of Madness, Models of Medicine* (New York: Macmillan, 1974), p. 176.
24. 1974 form letter from Mental Patients' Liberation Front, Box 156, W. Somerville, MA 02144.
25. Statement of the Mental Patients' Liberation Front, n.d.
26. Kane, quoted in "Loony Liberation," *Boston Phoenix* (August 22, 1972).
27. Clare Creer and J. K. Wing, *Schizophrenia at Home* (London: Institute of Psychiatry, 1974).
28. Bernard Rimland, *Infantile Autism: The Syndrome and Its Implications for a Neural Theory of Behavior* (New York: Appleton-Century-Crofts, 1964).
29. *Something's Wrong with My Child* (New York: Harcourt Brace Jovanovich, 1973), p. 227.
30. Rosemary Lapertosa, Hinsdale, Ill., letter in *The Exceptional Parent* (July/August, 1973).
31. Ernest Siegel, *The Exceptional Child Grows Up: Guidelines for Understanding and Helping the Brain-Injured Adolescent and Young Adult* (New York: E. P. Dutton, 1974).
32. Jo Ann Chandler, Esquire, Public Advocates, Inc., quoted in President's Commission on Mental Retardation, DHEW Publication No. (OHD) 74-21002.
33. "Early Infantile Autism Revisited," *Journal of Clinical Child Psychology*, 3 (Winter–Spring, 1974).
34. William Appleton, *American Journal of Psychiatry*, 131 (June, 1974). The article was given unusual coverage in *Psychiatric News*, the psychiatrists' newspaper, as well.
35. "Psychiatric Research – A Commitment for Mental Health," Address to the Annual Meeting of the National Association for Mental Health, November 14, 1972.

Bibliography

I: General

Abroms, Gene M.; Fellner, Carl H.; and Whitaker, Carl A. "The Family Enters the Hospital," *American Journal of Psychiatry,* 127 (April 1971).

Adler, Gerald, and Shapiro, Leon N. "Psychotherapy with Prisoners," in *Current Psychiatric Therapies,* vol. IX. New York: Grune and Stratton, 1969.

Agras, W. Stewart, ed. *Behavior Modification: Principles and Clinical Applications.* Boston: Little, Brown, 1972.

Ahsen, Akhter, and Lazarus, Arnold. "Eidetics: An Internal Behavior Approach," in A. Lazarus, ed., *Clinical Behavior Therapy.* New York: Brunner/Mazel, 1972.

Alanen, Yrjo O. "The Mothers of Schizophrenic Patients," *Acta Psychiatrica et Neurologica Scandinavica,* Supplement no. 124, 1968.

Aldrin, Edwin E., with Wayne Warga. *Return to Earth.* New York: Random House, 1973.

Alexander, Leo. Letter to *New England Journal of Medicine,* 269 (August 1973).

Allen, K. Eileen, and Harris, Florence R. "Elimination of a Child's Excessive Scratching by Training the Mother in Reinforcement Procedures," in *Behavior Research and Therapy,* 4 (1966):79–84.

Altschule, Mark D. "Disease Entity, Syndrome, State of Mind, or Figment?" in Robert Cancro, ed., *The Schizophrenic Reactions: A Critique of the Concept, Hospital Treatment, and Current Research.* New York: Brunner/Mazel, 1970.

American Law Institute. *Restatement of the Law, Second, Torts 2d.* St. Paul, Minn.: American Law Institute, 1965.

American Law Reports 2d, Later Case Service. Rochester, N.Y.: Lawyers Co-operative Publishing Co., 1975.

American Psychiatric Association. *Diagnostic and Statistical Manual: Mental Disorders.* DSM II. Washington, D.C.: American Psychiatric Association, 1968.

———. *A Psychiatric Glossary: The Meaning of Terms Frequently Used in Psychiatry.* 4th ed. Washington, D.C.: American Psychiatric Association, 1975.

American Psychological Association, Committee on Health Insurance. "Psychology and Health Insurance." 1973 (unpublished: available on request).

Anderson, Donald. "Parents' Right to Read, Continued," *The Exceptional Parent* (May/June 1974).

Anthony, E. James. "A Clinical Evaluation of Children with Psychotic Parents," *American Journal of Psychiatry,* 126 (August 1969).

———. "The Contagious Sub-Culture of Psychosis," in C. L. Sager, and H. S. Kaplan, *Progress in Group and Family Therapy.* New York: Brunner/Mazel, 1972.

Anthony, E. James, and Koupernik, Cyrille, eds. *The Child in His Family: Children at Psychiatric Risk,* vol. III. New York: John Wiley and Sons, 1974.

Appleton, William S. "The Importance of Psychiatrists' Telling Patients the Truth," *American Journal of Psychiatry,* 129 (December 1972).

———. "Mistreatment of Patients' Families by Psychiatrists," *American Journal of Psychiatry,* 131 (June 1974).

Arehart-Treichel, Joan. "The Great Medical Debate Over Low Blood Sugar," *Science News,* 103 (March 17, 1973).

Arieti, Silvano. "The Concept of Schizophrenia," in Robert Cancro, ed. *The Schizophrenic Reactions: A Critique of the Concept, Hospital Treatment, and Current Research.* New York: Brunner/Mazel, 1970.

———. *Interpretation of Schizophrenia.* 2nd ed. New York: Basic Books, 1974.

———. "An Overview of Schizophrenia from a Predominantly Psychological Approach." *American Journal of Psychiatry,* 131 (March 1974).

Arieti, Silvano, ed. *American Handbook of Psychiatry,* vol. III. 2nd ed. New York: Basic Books, 1974.

Arnstein, Helene. *When a Parent is Mentally Ill: What to Say to Your Child.* New York: Child-Study Association, 1960. Revised ed., 1974.

Association of Hospital and Institutional Libraries. *Bibliotherapy: Methods and Materials.* Chicago: American Library Association, 1971.

Axline, Virginia. *Dibs: In Search of Self.* Boston: Houghton Mifflin, 1965.

Ayllon, Teodoro, and Azrin, Nathan. *The Token Economy: A Motivational System for Therapy and Rehabilitation.* New York: Appleton-Century-Crofts, 1968.

Ayllon, Teodoro, and Michael, J. "The Psychiatric Nurse as a Behavioral Engineer," in J. O. Palmer and M. Goldstein, *Perspectives in Psychopathology.* New York: Oxford University Press, 1966.

Ayllon, Teodoro, and Roberts, Michael D. "The Token Economy Now," in W. Stewart Agras, *Behavior Modification: Principles and Clinical Applications.* Boston: Little, Brown, 1972.

Ban, Thomas A. "Nicotinic Acid and Psychiatry," *Canadian Psychiatric Association Journal,* 16 (1971):413–431.

Ban, Thomas A.; Gershon, S.; and Kane, F. J. "The Present State of Nicotinic Acid Therapy in Treatment of Schizophrenia." Presented at the Annual Meeting of the American Psychiatric Association, Dallas, Texas, May 1–5, 1972.

Bandura, Albert. *Principles of Behavior Modification.* New York: Holt, Rinehart and Winston, 1969.

Bardon, Jane, and Bennett, Virginia. "Helping the Child in School," in B. B. Wolman, ed., *Manual of Child Psychopathology.* New York: McGraw-Hill, 1972, pp. 1063–1064.

Barlow, David. "Aversive Procedures," in W. Stewart Agras, ed., *Behavior Modification: Principles and Clinical Applications.* Boston: Little, Brown, 1972.

Barnes, Mary, and Berke, Joseph. *Mary Barnes: Two Accounts of a Journey through Madness.* New York: Harcourt Brace Jovanovich, 1971.

Barrett, J. E., Jr.; Kuriansky, Judith; and Gurland, Barry. "Community Tenure Following Emergency Discharge," *American Journal of Psychiatry,* 128 (February 1972).

Bateson, Gregory; Jackson, Don D.; Haley, J.; and Weakland, J. H. "Toward a Theory of Schizophrenia," *Behavioral Science,* 1 (1956):251–264.

Beers, Clifford. *A Mind That Found Itself.* New York: Longmans, Green, 1908.

Begelman, D. A. "Misnaming, Metaphors, the Medical Model, and Some Muddles," *Psychiatry,* 34 (February 1971).

Beisser, A. D.; Glasser, N.; and Grant, M. "Psychosocial Adjustment in Children of Schizophrenic Mothers," *Journal of Nervous and Mental Disease,* 145 (1967):429–440.

Bennett, Janet M. "The Proof of the Pudding," *The Exceptional Parent* (May–June, 1974).

Benziger, Barbara Field. *The Prison of My Mind.* New York: Walker, 1969; Pocket Books, 1970.
———. *Speaking Out: Therapists and Patients—How They Cure and Cope with Mental Illness.* New York: Walker, 1976.
Berezin, Martin A. "Psychodynamic Considerations of Aging and the Aged," *American Journal of Psychiatry,* 128 (June 1972).
Berger, Milton M., and Berger, Lynne F. "Psychogeriatric Group Approaches," in C. J. Sager and H. S. Kaplan, *Progress in Group and Family Therapy.* New York: Brunner/Mazel, 1972.
Bergin, A. E. "The Effects of Psychotherapy: Negative Results Revisited," *Journal of Counseling Psychology,* 10 (1963):244.
Bergman, Robert L. "A School for Medicine Men," *American Journal of Psychiatry,* 130 (June 1973).
Berne, Eric. *Games People Play: The Psychology of Human Relationships.* New York: Grove Press, 1964.
Bettelheim, Bruno. *The Empty Fortress: Infantile Autism and the Birth of the Self.* New York: Free Press, 1967.
———. "Milieu Therapy." Pamphlet in series, *Major Contributors to Modern Psychotherapy.* Nutley, New Jersey: Roche Laboratories, n.d.
Bittner, Egon. "Police Discretion in Emergency Apprehension of Mentally Ill Persons," in Richard H. Price and Bruce Denner, eds. *The Making of a Mental Patient.* New York: Holt, Rinehart & Winston, 1973.
Bleuler, Manfred. "The Offspring of Schizophrenics," *Schizophrenia Bulletin,* 8 (Spring 1974), a chapter in *Schizophrenic Disorders in the Light of Long-term Patient Observation* (New Haven: Yale University Press, 1977).
Birk, Lee, *et al. Behavior Therapy in Psychiatry: A Report of the APA Task Force on Behavior Therapy.* Washington, D.C.: American Psychiatric Association, 1973.
Birk, Lee; Huddleston, William; Miller, Elizabeth; and Cohler, Bertram. "Avoidance Conditioning for Homosexuality," in Cyril M. Franks and G. Terence Wilson, eds., *Annual Review of Behavior Therapy: Theory and Practice, 1973.* New York: Brunner/Mazel, 1973.
Bolin, David C., and Kivens, Laurence. "Evaluation in a Community Mental Health Center: Huntsville, Alabama," *Evaluation,* 2, no. 1 (1974).
Boston Women's Health Book Collective. *Our Bodies, Ourselves: A Book by and for Women.* New York: Simon and Schuster, 1971.
Boyers, Robert, and Orrill, Robert, eds. *R. D. Laing and Anti-Psychiatry.* New York: Harper and Row, 1971; Perennial Library Edition.
Boyle, John. "A Learning Experience in Helping Parents Get What They Want," *Children,* 17 (July–August 1970).
Braginski, Dorothea, and Braginski, Benjamin. "Mental Hospitals as Resorts," *Psychology Today* (March 1973).
Brakel, Samuel J., and Rock, Ronald S., eds. *The Mentally Disabled and the Law,* American Bar Foundation Study. Chicago: University of Chicago Press. Revised ed., 1971.
Brandt, Anthony. *Reality Police.* New York: William Morrow, 1975.
Brazelton, T. Berry. *Toddlers and Parents: A Declaration of Independence.* Boston: Delacorte Press/Seymour Lawrence, 1974.
Breggin, Peter. *The Crazy from the Sane.* New York: Lyle Stuart, 1971.
———. *After the Good War.* New York: Stein and Day, 1972.
———. "The Second Wave," *MH* (Winter 1973).
Brenner, M. Harvey. *Mental Illness and the Economy.* Cambridge, Mass.: Harvard University Press, 1973.
Brenner, Joseph. Review of James Wechsler, *In a Darkness. Saturday Review* (July 1, 1972).
Brown, Bertram S. "NIMH Director's Report." July 1974 (unpublished).

Brown, George W. "Measuring the Impact of Mental Illness on the Family," *Proceedings of the Royal Society of Medicine,* 59 (1966) : 18–20.

Brown, George W.; Birley, J. L. T.; and Wing, J. K. "Influence of Family Life on the Course of Schizophrenic Disorders: A Replication," *British Journal of Psychiatry,* 121 (1972) : 241–248. Also in Robert Cancro, ed. *Annual Review of the Schizophrenic Syndrome, 1973.* New York: Brunner/Mazel, 1974.

Bruch, Hilde. *Learning Psychotherapy.* Cambridge, Mass.: Harvard University Press, 1974.

Brutten, Milton; Richardson, Sylvia O.; and Mangel, Charles. *Something's Wrong with My Child: A Parents' Book about Children with Learning Disabilities.* New York: Harcourt Brace Jovanovich, 1973.

Bry, Adelaide. *Inside Psychotherapy.* New York: Basic Books, Inc., 1972.

Burack, Richard. *Handbook of Prescription Drugs.* New York: Pantheon, 1967, reprinted 1970.

Burch, Claire. *Stranger in the Family: A Guide to Living with the Emotionally Disturbed.* New York: Bobbs-Merrill, 1972.

Burgess, Ann C., and Lazare, Aaron. *Psychiatric Nursing in the Hospital and the Community.* Englewood Cliffs, N.J.: Prentice-Hall, Inc., 1973.

Busse, Ewald. "Organic Brain Syndromes," in Ewald W. Busse and Eric Pfeiffer, eds., *Mental Illness in Later Life.* Washington, D.C.: American Psychiatric Association, 1973.

Busse, Ewald W., and Pfeiffer, Eric, eds. *Mental Illness in Later Life.* Washington, D.C.: American Psychiatric Association, 1973.

Butler, Robert N. "Concerning Decent Institutional Care," in *Mental Health: Principles and Training Techniques in Nursing Home Care.* Washington, D.C.: NIMH, DHEW Publication No. (HSM) 73-9046, 1972.

Butler, Robert N., and Lewis, Myrna I. *Aging and Mental Health: Positive Psycho-social Approaches.* St. Louis: C. V. Mosby Co., 1973.

Cammer, Leonard. *Up from Depression.* New York: Simon and Schuster, 1969.

Cancro, Robert, ed. *Annual Review of the Schizophrenic Syndrome, 1973.* New York: Brunner/Mazel, 1974.

———. *The Schizophrenic Reactions: A Critique of the Concept, Hospital Treatment, and Current Research.* New York: Brunner/Mazel, 1970.

Cancro, Robert. Review of Theodore Lidz, *The Origin and Treatment of Schizophrenic Disorders,* for Behavioral Science Book Service, n.d. [1974].

———. "The Treatment of Schizophrenia: Illusion or Elusion?" *American Journal of Psychiatry,* 130 (June 1973).

Caplan, Gerald, ed. *Emotional Problems of Early Childhood.* New York: Basic Books, 1955.

Cassell, Eric J. "Caring for the Dying." Institute of Society, Ethics, and the Life Sciences, Hastings-on-Hudson, N.Y., 1971. Mimeographed.

Chambers, David L. "Alternatives to Civil Commitment of the Mentally Ill: Practical Guides and Constitutional Imperatives," 70 *Michigan Law Review* 1107, 1133 (1972).

Chesler, Phyllis. *Women and Madness.* Garden City, N.Y.: Doubleday and Co., 1972.

Chess, Stella. "Autism in Children with Congenital Rubella," in Stella Chess and Alexander Thomas, eds., *Annual Progress in Child Psychiatry, 1972.* New York: Brunner/Mazel, 1972.

Chess, Stella, and Thomas, Alexander, eds. *Annual Progress in Child Psychiatry and Child Development, 1972.* New York: Brunner/Mazel, 1972.

Chien, Ching Piao, and Appleton, William S. "The Need for Extensive Reform in Psychiatric Teaching," in Theodore Rothman, ed., *Changing Pat-*

terns in Psychiatric Care. Los Angeles: Rush Research Foundation; New York: Crown Publishers, 1970.

Chien, Ching-Piao, and Cole, Jonathan. "Landlord-Supervised Cooperative Apartments for Community-Based Treatment," *American Journal of Psychiatry,* 130 (February 1973).

Chodoff, Paul. "Changing Styles in the Neuroses," *American Journal of Psychiatry,* 130 (February 1973).

———. "The Effect of Third-Party Payment on the Practice of Psychotherapy," *American Journal of Psychiatry,* 129 (November 1972).

Chouinard, Edward. "Family Homes for Adults," *Social and Rehabilitation Record* (HEW), 2 (February/March 1975).

Chu, Franklin, and Trotter, Sharland. *The Mental Health Complex; Part I: Community Mental Health Centers.* Washington, D.C.: Center for the Study of Responsive Law, 1972.

Cole, Jonathan O.; Freedman, A. M.; and Friedhoff, A. J., eds. *Psychopathology and Psychopharmacology.* Baltimore: Johns Hopkins University Press, 1973.

Coleman, James. "Surviving Psychotherapy," *Motive,* 32, no. 2 (1972).

Coles, Robert. "The Case of Michael Wechsler," *New York Review of Books* (May 18, 1972). Collected in Robert Coles, *The Mind's Fate.* Boston: Atlantic–Little, Brown, 1975.

———. *The Middle Americans: Proud and Uncertain.* Boston: Atlantic–Little, Brown, 1971.

———. *The South Goes North.* Boston: Atlantic–Little, Brown, 1971.

Comer, James P. "The Need Is Now: A Case for the Development of More Minority Group Professionals," *MH,* 57 (Winter 1973).

Cooper, Irving S. *The Victim Is Always the Same.* New York: Harper and Row, 1973.

Coordinating Council for Handicapped Children. *How to Organize an Effective Parent Group and Move Bureaucracies.* Chicago, Illinois.

Copeland, James, based on a diary by Jack Hodges. *For the Love of Ann.* New York: Ballantine Books, 1974.

Cortazzo, Arnold. *Activity Centers for Retarded Adults.* President's Committee on Mental Retardation: June, 1972. DHEW Publication No. (OS) 72-43.

Council for Exceptional Children. *Legal Change for the Handicapped Through Litigation.* CEC, Reston, Va.

———. *A Continuing Summary of Pending and Completed Litigation Regarding the Education of Handicapped Children.* CEC, Reston, Va.

———. *State Law and Education of Handicapped Children: Issues and Recommendations.* CEC, Reston, Va.

Cousins, Norman. "Commentary: Medical Prisoner, Family Have Scars," Los Angeles Times Syndicate, Richmond, Va. *Times Dispatch* (October 14, 1972).

Crabtree, L. H., Jr.; Brecht, James A.; and Sonne, John C. "Monadic Orientation: A Contribution to the Structure of Families with Autistic Children," *Journal of Family Process,* 11 (September 1972).

Craig, Eleanor. *P.S. Your Not Listening.* New York: Richard Baron, Inc., 1972. New American Library, 1973.

Creer, Clare, and Wing, J. K. *Schizophrenia at Home.* London: Institute of Psychiatry, 1974.

Cronin, Robert E.; Kiel, O. Frederick; and Molitor, Rosemary C. "Agoraphobia Treatment Program," *Center for Behavior Modification Newsletter,* 2 (January 1975).

Crook, William G. *Can Your Child Read? Is He Hyperactive?* Jackson, Tenn.: Pedicenter Press, 1975.

Curtin, Sharon R. *Nobody Ever Died of Old Age.* Boston: Atlantic–Little, Brown, 1973; paperback, 1974.
Curtis, W. Robert. "Community Human Service Networks: New Roles for Mental Health Workers," *Psychiatric Annals,* 3 (July 1973).

Davidson, Henry A. "The Semantics of Psychotherapy," *American Journal of Psychiatry,* 115 (November 1958).
Dean, Stanley R. "The Role of Self-Conducted Group Therapy in Psychorehabilitation: A Look at Recovery, Inc.," *American Journal of Psychiatry,* 127 (January 1971).
Delacato, Carl. *The Ultimate Stranger: The Autistic Child.* Garden City, N.Y.: Doubleday and Co., Inc., 1974.
DesLauriers, A. M., and Carlson, Carole. *Your Child Is Asleep.* Homewood, Ill.: Dorsey Press, 1969.
de Sole, Daniel E.; Singer, Philip; and Roseman, Jacob. "Community Psychiatry and the Syndrome of Psychiatric Culture Shock – The Emergence of a New Functional Disorder," *Social Science and Medicine,* 1 (1968):401–418.
Despert, J. Louise. *The Emotionally Disturbed Child: An Inquiry Into Family Patterns.* Garden City, N.Y.: Doubleday Anchor Books, 1970.
"Developments in the Law – Civil Commitment of the Mentally Ill," note, 87 *Harvard Law Review* 1190, 1254 (1974).
Dewey, Margaret, and Everard, Margaret. "The Near-Normal Autistic Adolescent," *Journal of Autism and Childhood Schizophrenia,* 4 (December 1974).
Deykin, Eva. "The Reintegration of the Chronic Schizophrenic Patient Discharged to His Family and Community as Perceived by the Family," *MH,* 45 (1961):235–246.
DiScipio, William J., ed. *The Behavioral Treatment of Psychotic Illness.* New York: Behavioral Publications, 1974.
Divoky, Diane. "Toward a Nation of Sedated Children," *Learning, The Magazine for Creative Teaching* (March 1973).
Divoky, Diane, and Schrag, Peter. *The Myth of the Hyperactive Child.* New York: Pantheon, 1975.
Doernberg, Nanette; Rosen, Bernard; and Walker, Tomannie. *A Home Training Program for Young Mentally Ill Children.* New York: League School, 1968.
Dohan, F. C. Letter in *American Journal of Psychiatry,* 130 (December 1973): 1401.
Dohan, F. C., and Grassberger, J. C. "Relapsed Schizophrenics and Earlier Discharge from the Hospital after Cereal-Free, Milk-free Diet," *American Journal of Psychiatry,* 130 (June 1973).
Dolnick, Michael. "How the Disabled Break into the Community," *Human Services* (HEW) (February 1973).
Dorsey, Richard. "PSROs: Salvation or Suicide for Psychiatry?" *Psychiatric News,* 11 (October 1974).
Dyrud, Jarl E., and Holzman, P. S. "The Psychotherapy of Schizophrenia: Does It Work?" *American Journal of Psychiatry,* 130 (June 1973).

Eberhardy, Frances. "The View from the Couch," *Journal of Child Psychology and Psychiatry,* 8 (1967):257–263.
Ehrenburg, Otto, and Ehrenburg, Miriam. "How, When, and Why to Fire Your Shrink," *New York* (May 12, 1975).
Eisenberg, Leon. "Principles of Drug Therapy with Special Reference to Stimulant Drugs," in Stella Chess and Alexander Thomas, eds., *Annual*

Progress in Child Psychiatry and Child Development, 1972. New York: Brunner/Mazel, 1972.

———. "Psychiatric Intervention," *Scientific American*, 229 (September 1973).

Engelhardt, David M., and Margolis, Reuben A. "Hospitalization of Schizophrenic Patients: Prediction and Prevention," in Theodore Rothman, ed., *Changing Patterns of Psychiatric Care: An Anthology of Evolving Scientific Psychiatry in Medicine*. New York: Crown Publishers, 1970.

Ennis, Bruce. Interviewed in *Madness Network News*, 2 (February 1974).

———. *Prisoners of Psychiatry: Mental Patients, Psychiatrists, and the Law*. New York: Harcourt Brace Jovanovich, 1972.

Ennis, Bruce, and Siegel, Loren. *The Rights of Mental Patients*. An American Civil Liberties Union handbook. New York: Richard W. Baron, 1973.

Erikson, Erik H. *Childhood and Society*. New York: Norton, 1950.

Evans, A. S.; Bullard, D. M., Jr.; and Solomon, M. H. "The Family as a Potential Resource in Rehabilitation," *American Journal of Psychiatry*, 117 (June 1961).

Eysenck, H. E. *Psychology Is about People*. New York: Library Press, 1972.

Farber, Leslie. "Schizophrenia and the Mad Psychotherapist," in Boyers and Orrill, eds., *R. D. Laing and Anti-Psychiatry*, New York: Harper and Row, 1971. Reprinted from Leslie Farber, *The Ways of the Will*, New York: Basic Books, 1966.

Feigenbaum, Elliott. "Ambulatory Treatment of the Elderly," in E. W. Busse and E. Pfeiffer, eds., *Mental Illness in Later Life*. Washington, D.C.: American Psychiatric Association, 1973.

Feingold, Ben F. *Why Your Child Is Hyperactive*. New York: Random House, 1975.

Feinsilver, David, and Gunderson, John. "Psychotherapy for Schizophrenics," *Schizophrenia Bulletin* 6 (Fall 1972).

Fenichel, Carl. "Special Education as the Basic Therapeutic Tool in Treatment of Severely Disturbed Children," *Journal of Autism and Childhood Schizophrenia*, 4 (March 1974).

Ferber, Andrew, and Planz, Jules. "How to Succeed in Family Therapy: Set Reachable Goals – Give Workable Tasks," in C. J. Sager and H. S. Kaplan, eds., *Progress in Group and Family Therapy*. New York: Brunner/Mazel, 1972.

Finn, Molly. "The Unhelpful Social Worker," *Mental Hygiene*, 51 (April 1967).

Flocks, Jay S., and Paradise, David M. "Mental Health Planning in Welfare Agencies," *Psychiatric Opinion* (August 1974).

Flood, Nancy Bohac, and Du Vall, Margaret L. "Geriatric Incontinence: A Successful Operant Treatment," *Center for Behavior Modification Newsletter*, 2 (Minneapolis: July 1974).

Fodor, Iris. "The Parent as a Therapist," *Mental Hygiene* (Spring 1972).

"For the Disabled: Help Through Rehabilitation." U.S. Department of Health, Education, and Welfare, SRS Pub. No. 152 (August 1970).

Foudraine, Jan. *Not Made of Wood: A Psychiatrist Discovers His Profession*. New York: Macmillan, 1974.

Foy, Jessie Gray. *Gone Is Shadow's Child: Therapy for a Schizophrenic Child*. Plainfield, N.J.: Logos, 1970.

Frank, Jerome D. *Persuasion and Healing: A Comparative Study of Psychotherapy*. Baltimore: Johns Hopkins Press, 1961.

Franks, Cyril M., and Wilson, G. Terence, eds. *Annual Review of Behavior Therapy 1973*. New York: Brunner/Mazel, 1973.

Freas, C. Henry. "Mental Illness and Contract Law," 29 *Tenn. Law Review* (1962).
Freed, Harvey M.; Borus, Jonathan F.; Gonzalez, José A.; Grant, Jerry D.; Lightfoot, Orlando B.; Uribe, Victor M. "Community Mental Health—Second-Class Treatment?" *MH,* 56 (Summer 1972).
Freedman, Daniel X., and Gordon, Robert P. "Psychiatry under Siege: Attacks from Without," *Psychiatric Annals,* 3 (November 1973).
Friedman, Erwin. "Early Infantile Autism Revisited," *Journal of Clinical Child Psychology,* 3 (Winter–Spring 1974).
Fromm-Reichmann, Frieda. "Notes on the Development of Treatment of Schizophrenics by Psychoanalytic Psychotherapy," *Psychiatry,* 11 (1948): 263–273.
Furman, Seymour, and Feighner, Anne. "Video Feedback in Treating Hyperkinetic Children," *American Journal of Psychiatry,* 130 (July 1973).

Gallagher, E. G., Sharaff, M. H., and Levinson, D. J. "The Influence of Patient and Therapist in Determining the Use of Psychotherapy in a Psychiatric Hospital," *Psychiatry,* 28 (1965):297–310.
Galton, Lawrence. *Don't Give Up on an Aging Parent.* New York: Crown Publishers, 1974.
Gardner, Richard W. "Requiem for Agnews State," *Madness Network News,* 1 (May 1973).
Gardos, George. "Three Paradoxes in American Psychiatry," *Psychiatric Opinion,* 11 (April 1974).
Garmezy, Norman, with Sandra Streitman. "Children at Risk: The Search for the Antecedents of Schizophrenia, Part I. Conceptual Models and Research Methods," *Schizophrenia Bulletin,* 8 (Spring 1974).
Gatozzi, Antoinette A. *Lithium in the Treatment of Mood Disorders.* Washington, D.C.: National Institute of Mental Health, 1970.
———. "San Francisco Westside: A Community Mental Health Center Serves the People," in Julius Segal, ed., *NIMH Mental Health Program Reports 5.* DHEW Publication No. (MS) 72-9042, 1971.
Gibson, Robert W. "Insurance Coverage for Treatment of Illness in Later Life," in Ewald W. Busse and Eric Pfeiffer, eds., *Mental Illness in Later Life.* Washington, D.C.: American Psychiatric Association, 1973.
Ginnott, Haim. *Between Parent and Child.* New York: Macmillan, 1965.
———. *Between Parent and Teenager.* New York: Macmillan, 1969.
Glasscote, Raymond M.; Fishman, Michael E.; and Sonis, Meyer. *Children and Mental Health Centers: Programs, Problems, Prospects.* Washington, D.C.: Joint Information Service of the American Psychiatric Association and the National Association for Mental Health, 1972.
Glasscote, Raymond M.; Gudeman, Jon E.; Elpers, Richard; *et al. Halfway Houses for the Mentally Ill.* Washington, D.C.: Joint Information Service of the American Psychiatric Association and the National Association for Mental Health, 1971.
Glasscote, Raymond M. *et al. Partial Hospitalization for the Mentally Ill.* Washington, D.C.: Joint Information Service, American Psychiatric Association and the National Association for Mental Health, 1969.
———. *Rehabilitating the Mentally Ill in the Community: A Study of Psychosocial Rehabilitation Centers.* Washington, D.C.: Joint Information Service of the American Psychiatric Association and the National Association for Mental Health, 1971.
Glasser, William. *Reality Therapy.* New York: Harper and Row, 1965.
Goffman, Erving. *Asylums: Essays on the Social Situation of Mental Patients and Other Inmates.* Garden City, N.Y.: Doubleday Anchor Books, 1961.
Goldberg, Harold. "Home Treatment," *Psychiatric Annals,* 3 (June 1973).

Goodall, Kenneth. "Shapers at Work," *Psychology Today* (November 1972).

Goodman, Walter. "The Constitution v. the Snakepit," *New York Times Magazine* (March 17, 1974).

Greden, John. "Anxiety or Caffeinism: A Diagnostic Dilemma." Presented to the Spring, 1974, meeting of the American Psychiatric Association.

"Green, Hannah" (pseud.). *I Never Promised You a Rose Garden.* New York: Holt, Rinehart, and Winston, 1964.

Greenblatt, Milton. Interviewed in "Has Psychiatry Resigned from Medicine?" *Medical Opinion* (January 1973).

Greenblatt, Milton, and Sharaff, M. H. "Psychotherapy in the Large Mental Hospital," in Theodore Rothman, ed. *Changing Patterns of Psychiatric Care: An Anthology of Evolving Scientific Psychiatry in Medicine.* New York: Crown Publishers, 1970.

Greenfeld, Josh. *A Child Called Noah.* New York: Holt, Rinehart and Winston, 1972.

Grinker, Roy S., Sr. "Changing Styles in Psychoses and Borderline States," *American Journal of Psychiatry,* 130 (February 1973).

Grinspoon, Lester; Ewalt, Jack R.; and Shader, Richard I. *Schizophrenia: Pharmacotherapy and Psychotherapy.* Baltimore: Williams & Wilkins, 1972.

Grinspoon, Lester, and Hedblom, Peter. *The Speed Culture: Amphetamine Use and Abuse in America.* Cambridge, Mass.: Harvard University Press, 1975.

Grosz, Hanus. "Recovery, Inc. Survey: A Preliminary Report." Distributed by Recovery, Inc. Chicago, Illinois: n.d.

Gunderson, John. "Controversies about the Psychotherapy of Schizophrenia," *American Journal of Psychiatry,* 130 (June 1973).

Gurland, B.; Fleiss, J. L.; *et al.* "The Mislabeling of Depressed Patients in New York State," in J. Zubin, ed., *Disorders of Mood.* Baltimore: Johns Hopkins Press, 1972.

Haley, Jay. "Whither Family Therapy?" *Journal of Family Process,* 1 (March 1962).

Halleck, Seymour. "Future Trends in the Mental Health Professions," *Psychiatric Opinion,* 11 (April 1974).

Hamill, Pete. "Memoirs of a Drinking Life," *New York* (January 13, 1975).

Hand, J. McV., ed. *Personality and the Behavior Disorders.* Vol. II. New York: Ronald Press, 1944.

Hankins, Lamar W. Letter to *The New Republic* (June 23, 1973).

Harrington, Michael. *Fragments of the Century.* New York: Saturday Review Press, 1973.

Harrington, Hon. Michael. "National Health Insurance Ignores Your Children," *The Exceptional Parent,* 1 (February–March 1972).

Hart, H. L. A. *Punishment and Responsibility: Essays in the Philosophy of Law.* New York: Oxford University Press, 1968.

Hart, Jane, and Jones, Beverley. *Where's Hannah? A Handbook for Children with Learning Disorders.* New York: Hart Publishing Co., 1968.

Havens, Leston. *Approaches to the Mind: Movement of the Psychiatric Schools from Sects toward Science.* Boston: Little, Brown, 1973.

Hawkins, David. "The Orthomolecular Approach to the Diagnosis of Schizophrenia," in David Hawkins and Linus Pauling, eds., *Orthomolecular Psychiatry.* San Francisco: W. H. Freeman and Co., 1973.

Hawkins, David, and Pauling, Linus, eds. *Orthomolecular Psychiatry.* San Francisco: W. H. Freeman and Co., 1973.

Henry, Jules. *Pathways to Madness.* New York: Random House, 1972.

Henry, William E.; Sims, John H.; and Spray, S. Lee. *The Fifth Profession: Becoming a Psychotherapist.* San Francisco: Jossey-Bass, 1971.

———. *Public and Private Lives of Psychotherapists.* San Francisco: Jossey-Bass, 1973.
Hentoff, Nat. "The Official Drug Scene," *The Village Voice* (September 27, 1973).
———. "The Privacy Shredders," *The Village Voice* (September 13, 1973).
Hersen, Michel; Eisler, Richard M.; Smith, Buren S.; and Agras, W. Stewart. "A Token Reinforcement Ward for Young Psychotic Patients," *American Journal of Psychiatry,* 129 (August 1972).
Hertzman, Marc. "The Tale of a Pseudo-Neurotic: Or, A Little Knowledge May Be a Good Thing," *Psychiatric Opinion,* 11 (August 1974).
Heston, L. L., and Denney, D. "Interactions between Early Life Experiences and Biological Factors in Schizophrenia," in David Rosenthal and Seymour Kety, eds., *The Transmission of Schizophrenia.* Oxford: Pergamon Press, 1968.
Hewett, Frank. "The Autistic Child as Teacher and Learner," in C. C. Park, ed., *Research and Education: Proceedings of the Second Annual Meeting and Conference of the National Society for Autistic Children. June 1970.* NIMH Public Service Publication No. 2164, 1971.
Higgins, Jerry. "It Comes in Two Kinds," *Psychology Today* (October, 1972).
Hilts, Philip. *Behavior Mod.* New York: Harper's Magazine Press, 1974.
Hinsie, Leland E., and Campbell, Robert Jean. *A Psychiatric Dictionary.* New York: Oxford University Press, 4th ed., 1970.
Hirsch, Steven, and Leff, Julian. "Parental Abnormalities of Verbal Communication in the Transmission of Schizophrenia," *Psychological Medicine,* 1 (1971):118–127.
Hodgins, Eric. *Episode: A Report on the Accident Inside My Skull.* New York: Atheneum, 1964; paperback, Simon and Schuster, 1971.
Hoffer, A. "Megavitamin B-3 Therapy for Schizophrenia," *Canadian Psychiatric Association Journal,* 16 (1971):499–504.
Hogarty, Gerald, and Goldberg, Solomon. "Drug and Sociotherapy in the Aftercare of Schizophrenic Patients: One-year Relapse Rates," *Archives of General Psychiatry,* 28 (January 1973).
Hollingshead, August B., and Redlich, Fredrick. *Social Class and Mental Illness.* New York: John Wiley and Sons, 1958.
Horwitz, Leonard. *Clinical Prediction in Psychotherapy.* New York: Jason Aronson, 1974.
Howells, J. G. "Family Pathology and Schizophrenia," in J. G. Howells, ed., *Modern Perspectives in World Psychiatry.* New York: Brunner/Mazel, 1972.
Howells, J. G., ed. *Modern Perspectives in World Psychiatry.* New York: Brunner/Mazel, 1972.
Hudson, Wade. "NAPA Notes," *Madness Network News,* 2 (September 1974).
Hulsker, Jan, ed. *Van Gogh's "Diary": The Artist's Life in His Own Words.* New York: William Morrow, 1971.

"Income Tax Guide," *The Exceptional Parent* (January–February 1974).
Irvine, Elizabeth E. "The Risks of the Register: Or the Management of Expectation," in E. James Anthony and Cyrille Koupernik, eds., *The Child in His Family: Children at Psychiatric Risk,* vol. III. New York: John Wiley & Sons, 1974.

Jacobs, Max. "An Holistic Approach to Behavior Therapy," in A. Lazarus, ed., *Clinical Behavior Therapy.* New York: Brunner/Mazel, 1972.
Jackson, Don D. *The Etiology of Schizophrenia.* New York: Basic Books, 1960.

Jenkins, Richard L. Review of J. E. Meeks, *The Fragile Alliance, American Journal of Psychiatry,* 128 (February 1972).

Kadushin, Charles. *Why People Go to Psychiatrists.* New York: Atherton Press, 1969.

Kalinowsky, Lothar, and Hippius, Hanns. *Pharmacological, Convulsive and Other Somatic Treatments in Psychiatry.* New York: Grune and Stratton, 1969.

Kanner, Leo. *Childhood Psychosis: Initial Studies and New Insights.* New York: John Wiley & Sons, 1973.

Kapel, Saul. "Parents and Children: Those 'Symptoms' Are Normal Growth," New York *Daily News* (January 1, 1974).

Kaplan, Bert, ed. *The Inner World of Mental Illness.* New York: Harper & Row, 1964.

Kaplan, Honora A. "Institutions and Community Mental Health: The Paradox in *Wyatt* v. *Stickney,*" *Community Mental Health Journal,* 9 (1973):1.

Karlsson, J. L. "Genealogic Studies of Schizophrenia," in D. Rosenthal and S. Kety, eds., *The Transmission of Schizophrenia.* Oxford: Pergamon Press, 1968.

Kersch, Barbara A., and Negreto, Vida Francis. "Doctor-Patient Communication," *Scientific American* (August 1972).

Kesey, Ken. *One Flew Over the Cuckoo's Nest.* New York: Viking Press, 1962.

Kety, Seymour S. "Genetic-Environmental Interactions in the Schizophrenic Syndrome," in Robert Cancro, ed., *The Schizophrenic Reactions: A Critique of the Concept, Hospital Treatment, and Current Research.* New York: Brunner/Mazel, 1970.

———. "Psychiatric Research – A Commitment for Mental Health," address to the Annual Meeting of the National Association for Mental Health, November 14, 1972.

Kety, Seymour S.; Rosenthal, David; Wender, Paul; and Schulsinger, Fini. "The Types and Prevalence of Mental Illness in the Biological and Adoptive Families of Adopted Schizophrenics," in D. Rosenthal and S. S. Kety, eds., *The Transmission of Schizophrenia.* Oxford: Pergamon Press, 1968.

Kindwall, Josef A., and Kinder, Elaine F. "Postscript on a Benign Psychosis," *Psychiatry,* 3 (1940):527–534; reprinted in B. Kaplan, ed., *The Inner World of Mental Illness.* New York: Harper and Row, 1964.

Kline, Anthony, and Sitkin, Peter. "Financing Public Interest Litigation," *Arizona Law Review,* 13 (1971):823.

Kline, Nathan S. *From Sad to Glad: Kline on Depression.* New York: Putnam, 1974.

Knauth, Percy. "A Season in Hell," *Life* (June 9, 1972).

Knee, Ruth I. Discussion of A. S. Evans, D. M. Bullard, Jr., and M. H. Solomon, "The Family as a Potential Resource in Rehabilitation," *American Journal of Psychiatry,* 117 (June 1961).

Knight, Ward, Jr. *My Church Was a Mental Hospital.* Philadelphia: United Church Press, 1974.

Kohlberg, Lawrence. "The Predictability of Adult Mental Health from Childhood Behavior," in B. B. Wolman, ed., *Manual of Child Psychopathology.* New York: McGraw-Hill, 1972.

Kovel, Joel. Review of Mary Barnes and Joseph Berke, *Mary Barnes: Two Accounts of a Journey Through Madness, New York Times Book Review* (July 2, 1972).

Kramer, Morton; Pollack, Earl S.; Redick, Richard W.; and Locke, Ben Z. *Mental Disorders/Suicide.* Cambridge, Mass.: Harvard University Press, 1972.

Krause, Elliott A. *Factors Related to Length of Mental Hospital Stay: A Review of the Literature.* C.M.H. Monograph Series, Massachusetts Department of Mental Health, n.d.

Krim, Seymour. "The Insanity Bit," in B. Kaplan, *The Inner World of Mental Illness.* New York: Harper and Row, 1964.

Kyzar, John. "The Two Camps in Child Psychiatry: A Report from a Psychiatrist Father of an Autistic and Retarded Child," *American Journal of Psychiatry,* 125 (July 1968).

Laing, R. D., and Esterson, Abraham. *Sanity, Madness, and the Family.* New York: Basic Books, 1964.

Lapertosa, Rosemary. Letter in *The Exceptional Parent* (July/August 1973).

Laqueur, H. Peter. "Multiple Family Therapy and General Systems Theory," in *International Psychiatry Clinics,* vol. 7, no. 4. Boston: Little, Brown, 1970. Also in Sager, C. J., and Kaplan, H. S., eds., *Progress in Group and Family Therapy.* New York: Brunner/Mazel, 1972.

Laski, Frank. "Civil Rights Victories for the Handicapped – II," *Social and Rehabilitation Record,* 1 (June 1974), Department of Health, Education, and Welfare.

Lazarus, Arnold. "Behavior Therapy and Clinical Problems, A Critical Overview," in C. M. Franks and G. T. Wilson, eds., *Annual Review of Behavior Therapy 1973.* New York: Brunner/Mazel, 1973.

Lazarus, Arnold, ed. *Clinical Behavior Therapy.* New York: Brunner/Mazel, 1972.

Lazarus, Herbert. *How to Get Your Money's Worth Out of Psychiatry.* Los Angeles: Sherbourne Press, 1973.

"Learning to Laugh Together," *Breakthrough,* Newsletter of the Autistic Children's Association of New South Wales, no. 16 (October-November-December 1972).

Leedy, Jack J. *Poetry Therapy: The Use of Poetry in the Treatment of Emotional Disorders.* Philadelphia: Lippincott, 1969.

Lennard, Henry L.; Epstein, L. J., *et al. Mystification and Drug Misuse: Hazards in Using Psychoactive Drugs.* New York: Harper & Row, 1971.

Leonard, William Ellery. *The Locomotive-God.* New York: The Century Co., 1927.

Lettick, Amy. *Benhaven's Way.* New Haven, Conn.: Benhaven School, 1972.

Levenson, Edgar. *The Fallacy of Understanding.* New York: Basic Books, Inc., 1972.

Levy, Harold. *Square Pegs, Round Holes.* Boston: Little, Brown, 1973.

Liberman, Robert Paul. "Behavioral Approaches in Family and Couple Therapy," in C. J. Sager and H. S. Kaplan, eds., *Progress in Group and Family Therapy.* New York: Brunner/Mazel, 1972.

———. "Behavior Modification of Schizophrenia, a Review," *Schizophrenia Bulletin,* no. 6 (Fall 1972).

Lidz, Theodore. Interview, in Robert Boyers and Robert Orrill, eds., *R. D. Laing and Anti-Psychiatry.* New York: Harper and Row, 1971. Perennial Library Edition.

———. "The Influence of Family Studies on the Treatment of Schizophrenia," in C. J. Sager and H. S. Kaplan, eds., *Progress in Group and Family Therapy.* New York: Brunner/Mazel, 1972.

Lidz, Theodore; Cornelison, Alice; Terry, D.; and Fleck, S. "Intrafamilial Environment of the Schizophrenic Patient: VI. The Transmission of Irrationality," *Archives of Neurological Psychiatry,* 79 (March 1958).

———. "Thought Disorder and Family Relations of Schizophrenics," I, II, and III, *Archives of General Psychiatry,* 9 (1963):199; 12 (1965):187; 12 (1965):201.

Lidz, T.; Alanen, Yrjo O.; and Cornelison, A. "Schizophrenic Patients and Their Siblings," *Psychiatry,* 26 (1963) :1–18.

Lieberman, Morton; Miles, Matthew; and Yalom, Irvin. "Encounter: The Leader Makes the Difference," *Psychology Today* (March 1973). Excerpted from *Encounter Groups: First Facts.* New York: Basic Books, 1975.

Liem, Joan Huser. "Effects of Verbal Communications of Parents and Children: A Comparison of Normal and Schizophrenic Families," *Journal of Consulting and Clinical Psychology,* 42 (1974) :438–450.

Lipowski, Z. J. "Consultation-Liaison Psychiatry: An Overview," *American Journal of Psychiatry,* 131 (June 1974).

London, Perry. "Morals and Mental Health," in S. C. Plog and R. B. Edgerton, eds., *Changing Perspectives in Mental Illness.* New York: Holt, Rinehart and Winston, 1969.

Lorenz, Sarah E. *Our Son Ken.* New York: Dell, 1969. (Originally published 1963 as *And Always Tomorrow.*)

Lovaas, O. Ivar. "Strengths and Weaknesses of Operant Conditioning Techniques in the Treatment of Autism," in Clara Claiborne Park, ed., *Research and Education: Proceedings of the Second Annual Meeting and Conference of the National Society for Autistic Children.* Washington, D.C.: NIMH, Public Health Service Publication No. 2164, 1971.

———. Interviewed by Paul Chance. *Psychology Today.* January 1974.

Lovaas, O. Ivar; Schreibman, Laura; and Koegel, Robert L. "A Behavior Modification Approach to the Treatment of Autistic Children," *Journal of Autism and Childhood Schizophrenia,* 4 (March 1974).

Low, Abraham. *Lectures to Relatives of Former Patients.* Boston: Christopher Publishing House, 1943.

———. *Mental Health through Will Training: A System of Self-Help as Practiced by Recovery, Inc.* Boston: Christopher Publishing House, 1950.

Lurie, Ellen. *How to Change the Schools: A Parents' Action Handbook on How to Fight the System.* (Association for Children with Learning Disabilities.)

McCabe, Carol. "Stories from the Madhouse," *Providence Sunday Journal* (April 1, 1973).

McFall, Richard M., and Lillesand, Diane Bridges. "Behavior Rehearsal with Modeling and Coaching in Assertion Training," in Cyril M. Franks and G. Terence Wilson, eds., *Annual Review of Behavior Therapy 1973.* New York: Brunner/Mazel, 1973.

McGarry, A. Louis. *Competency to Stand Trial Assessment Instrument and Handbook.* Available from the Laboratory of Community Psychiatry of Harvard Medical School, Boston, Mass.

Maddi, Salvatore R. "The Victimization of Dora," *Psychology Today* (September 1974).

"Major Disabling Conditions of Clients of State Vocational Rehabilitating Agencies Rehabilitated and Not Rehabilitated During the Fiscal Year of 1969," *Statistical Notes,* 27 (June 1971). U.S. Department of Health, Education and Welfare: Social and Rehabilitation Services.

Malamud, W. "The Psychoneuroses," in J. McV. Hand, ed., *Personality and the Behavior Disorders,* vol. II. New York: Ronald Press, 1944.

Mandell, Arnold J.; Segal, David; Kuczenski, Ronald T.; and Knapp, Suzanne. "The Search for the Schizococcus," *Psychology Today* (October 1972).

Marks, Isaac M. "Flooding and Allied Treatments," in Stewart Agras, ed., *Behavior Modification: Principles and Clinical Application.* Boston: Little, Brown, 1972.

Markson, E.; Kivoh, A.; Cumming, J.; and Cumming, E. "Alternatives to

Hospitalization for Psychiatrically Ill and Geriatric Patients," *American Journal of Psychiatry,* 127 (1971):1055–1072.
Marmor, Judd. "The Future of Psychoanalytic Therapy," *American Journal of Psychiatry,* 130 (November 1973).
Marquis, John. "An Expedient Model for Behavior Therapy," in Arnold A. Lazarus, ed., *Clinical Behavior Therapy.* New York: Brunner/Mazel, 1972.
Martindale-Hubbell Law Directory. Summit, N.J.: Martindale-Hubbell, Inc., published annually.
May, Jacques. *A Physician Looks at Psychiatry.* New York: John Day, 1958.
May, P. R. A. "Changing Perspectives in Research and the Treatment of the Psychiatric Patient," in Theodore Rothman, ed., *Changing Patterns in Psychiatric Care: An Anthology of Evolving Scientific Psychiatry in Medicine.* New York: Crown Publishers, 1970.
———. "Psychotherapy Research in Schizophrenia: Another View of Present Reality," *Schizophrenia Bulletin,* 9 (Summer 1974).
Mazer, Milton. "Two Ways of Expressing Psychiatric Disorder." *American Journal of Psychiatry,* 128 (February 1972).
Medical Research Council. "The Functional Psychoses: A Review," *Annual Report, 1973–74.* London: Her Majesty's Stationery Office, 1974.
Mednick, Sarnoff A., and Schulsinger, Fini. "Factors Related to Breakdown in Children at High Risk for Schizophrenia," in Merrill Roff and David Ricks, eds., *Life History Research in Psychopathology.* Minneapolis: University of Minnesota Press, 1970.
Meissner, W. W. "Thinking About the Family – Psychiatric Aspects," *Journal of Family Process,* 3 (March 1964).
Melton, David. *When Children Need Help.* New York: Crowell, 1972.
Mendelson, Adelaide. *Tender, Loving Greed.* New York: Knopf, 1974.
Menninger, Karl. *The Vital Balance.* New York: Viking, 1963.
———. "Reading Notes," *Psychiatric News* (March 7, 1973).
Miller, Dorothy. "How to Obtain Educational Services for Your Child in the Public School System." Available from National Society for Autistic Children.
Mills, Millie. "You in Partnership with Your Client," *Breakthrough:* Newsletter of the Autistic Children's Society of New South Wales, 20 (October-November-December 1973.)
Minnesota Department of Public Welfare. Residential Environment Survey (unpublished).
Minuchin, Salvador, and Barcai, Avner. "Therapeutically Induced Family Crisis," in C. J. Sager and H. S. Kaplan, eds., *Progress in Group and Family Therapy.* New York: Brunner/Mazel, 1972.
Mondale, Walter. "The Truth in Contributions Act," *The Exceptional Parent,* 5 (March/April 1975).
Monsour, Karen, and Stone, Beth. "The Hawaii Trip: A Study of a Segment of American Youth," *Psychiatric Annals,* 4 (June 1974).
Morrow, Tarlton, and Loomis, Earl. "Symbiotic Aspects of a Seven-Year-Old Psychotic," in Gerald Caplan, ed., *Emotional Problems of Early Childhood.* New York: Basic Books, 1955.
Mosher, Loren R., and Feinsilver, David. *Special Report: Schizophrenia.* Washington, D.C.: NIMH, Publication No. (HSM) 72-9042, 1971.
Mosher, Loren, Goveia, Leonard, and Menn, Alma. "The Treatment of Schizophrenia as a Developmental Crisis." Paper presented to the Detroit meeting of the American Orthopsychiatric Association, April 1972.
Mosher, Loren R., and Gunderson, John G., with Sherry Buchsbaum. "Special Report: Schizophrenia, 1972," *Schizophrenia Bulletin,* 7 (Winter 1973).
Munsey, Beatrice. "Parent's Right to Read," *The Exceptional Parent* (May/June 1973).

Murray, Dorothy G. *This Is Stevie's Story*. New York: Abingdon Press, rev. ed., 1967.

Napear, Peggy. *Brain Child: A Mother's Diary*. New York: Harper and Row, 1974.

Nardini, John. "Careers in General Practice of Psychiatry," *Career Directions,* 3, No. 5, Sandor Pharmaceuticals, 1973.

Nathan, Robert J. "The Psychiatric Treatment of the Geriatric Patient," *American Journal of Psychiatry,* 130 (June 1973).

National Institute of Mental Health. *Facts about Electroshock Therapy*. DHEW Publication No. (HSM) 72-9152, 1972.

———. *Mental Health: Principles and Training Techniques in Nursing Home Care, Material Developed for a National Conference of the Gerontological Society, May 14–16, 1972*. Washington, D.C.: NIMH, DHEW Publication No. 73-9046, 1972.

———. *Research and Education: Proceedings of the Second Annual Meeting and Conference of the National Society for Autistic Children, June 1970,* Clara Claiborne Park, ed. Public Service Publication No. 2164, 1971.

———. *Schizophrenia: Is There an Answer?* DHEW Publication No. (HSM) 72-9070, 1972.

———. *NIMH Mental Health Program Reports — 5,* Julius Segal, ed. DHEW Publication No. (HMS) 72-9042 (1971).

———. *Staffing of Mental Health Facilities in the United States, 1972*. Series B, no. 6. HEW Publication No. (ADM) 74-28 (1974).

———, prepared by Michael J. Witkin. *Hospital Inpatient Treatment Units for Emotionally Disturbed Children: United States, 1971–72*. Mental Health Facility Reports Series A, No. 15, DHEW Publication No. (ADM) 74-82, 1974.

———, prepared by Michael J. Witkin. *Residential Psychiatric Facilities for Children and Adolescents: United States, 1971–72*. Mental Health Facility Reports, Series A, No. 14, DHEW Publication No. (ADM) 74-78, 1974.

National Schizophrenia Fellowship. *Living with Schizophrenia — By the Relatives*. Surbiton, Surrey: 1974.

———. "Schizophrenia: The Family Burden." Surbiton, Surrey: 1973, re-issued 1974.

National Society for Autistic Children. *U.S. Facilities and Programs for Children with Severe Mental Illnesses — A Directory*. NIMH, DHEW Publication No. (ADM) 74-47.

Neiman, Richard. Letter, *Psychiatric News* (November 3, 1971).

Nelson, Scott H., and Grunebaum, Henry. "A Follow-up Study of Wrist-Slashers," *American Journal of Psychiatry,* 127 (April 1971).

Nelson, Scott H., and Torrey, E. Fuller. "The Religious Functions of Psychiatry," *American Journal of Orthopsychiatry,* 43 (April 1973).

Novello, Joseph D. "Psychiatric Referrals Made Easy," *Medical Times,* 101 (May 1973).

Nowlin, John. "Physical Changes in Later Life and Their Relationships to Mental Functioning," in E. W. Busse and E. Pfeiffer, eds., *Mental Illness in Later Life*. Washington, D.C.: American Psychiatric Association, 1973.

O'Connor, Robert D. "Relative Efficacy of Modeling, Shaping, and the Combined Procedures for Modification of Social Withdrawal," in Cyril M. Franks and G. Terence Wilson, eds., *Annual Review of Behavior Therapy 1973*. New York: Brunner/Mazel, 1973.

Offir, Carole Wade. "Field Report," *Psychology Today* (October 1974).

Ogg, Elizabeth. "Securing the Legal Rights of Retarded Persons." Public Affairs Pamphlet No. 492. New York: Public Affairs Committee, 381 Park Ave. South, New York 10016, 1973.

Ognibene, Peter. Review of John Pekkanen, *The American Connection,* in *The New Republic* (January 26, 1974).

Oppenheim, Rosalind. *Effective Teaching Methods for Autistic Children.* Springfield, Ill.: Charles C. Thomas Publishing Co., 1974.

Osmond, Humphry. "Psychiatry under Siege: The Crisis Within," *Psychiatric Annals,* 3 (November 1973).

Osmond, Humphry, and Hoffer, Abram. "Massive Niacin Treatment in Schizophrenia: Review of a Nine-Year Study," *The Lancet* (February 10, 1972):316–320.

Palmer, James O., and Goldstein, Michael, eds. *Perspectives in Psychopathology.* New York: Oxford University Press, 1966.

Palmore, Erdman. "Social Factors in Mental Illness of the Aged," in Ewald W. Busse and Eric Pfeiffer, eds., *Mental Illness in Later Life.* Washington, D.C.: American Psychiatric Association, 1973.

Park, Clara Claiborne. *The Siege: The First Eight Years of an Autistic Child.* New York: Harcourt, Brace and World, 1967; paperback, Boston: Atlantic–Little, Brown, 1973.

Park, Clara Claiborne, ed. *Research and Education: Proceedings of the Second Annual Meeting and Conference of the National Society for Autistic Children, June 1970.* NIMH Public Service Publication No. 2164, 1971.

Park, David, and Youderian, Philip. "Light and Number: Ordering Principles in the World of an Autistic Child," *Journal of Autism and Childhood Schizophrenia,* 4 (December 1974).

Patterson, Gerald, and Gullion, M. Elizabeth. *Living with Children: New Methods for Parents and Teachers.* Champaign, Illinois: Research Press, 1971.

Pavenstedt, Eleanor, and Bernard, Viola W., eds. *Crises of Family Disorganization: Programs to Soften Their Impact on Children.* New York: Behavioral Publications, 1971.

Percy, Charles. *Growing Old in the Country of the Young.* New York: McGraw-Hill, 1974.

"The Pervasive Problem of Mental Depression: Four Psychiatrists Discuss Its Recognition and Treatment by the Nonpsychiatrist Physician," *Medical World News* (April 20, 1973).

Pfeiffer, Carl; Ward, Jack; El-Meligi, Moneim; and Cott, Allan. *The Schizophrenias: Yours and Mine.* New York: Pyramid Books, 1972.

Pfeiffer, Eric. "Interacting with Older Patients," in Ewald W. Busse and Eric Pfeiffer, eds., *Mental Illness in Later Life.* Washington, D.C.: American Psychiatric Association, 1973.

Pfeiffer, Eric, and Busse, Ewald. "Affective Disorders; Paranoid, Neurotic, and Situational Reactions," in Ewald W. Busse and Eric Pfeiffer, eds., *Mental Illness in Later Life.* Washington, D.C.: American Psychiatric Association, 1973.

Pinsker, Henry. Letter in *Science,* 180 (April 27, 1973).

Pirsig, Robert. *Zen and the Art of Motorcycle Maintenance.* New York: William Morrow, 1974.

Plath, Sylvia. *The Bell Jar.* London: Faber, 1966; New York: Harper & Row, 1971; Bantam, 1972.

Plog, Stanley C., and Edgerton, R. B. *Changing Perspectives in Mental Illness.* New York: Holt, Rinehart and Winston, 1969.

Poinsard, Paul. "Society Shuns the Aged." *Pennsylvania Mental Health Bulletin,* 1 (April 1973).

Pollin, W.; Stabenau, J. R.; and Tupin, J. "Family Studies in Identical Twins Discordant for Schizophrenia," *Psychiatry,* 28 (1965): 119-132.

President's Committee on Mental Retardation. *PCMR Message,* 38 (August 1974).

———. *Silent Minority.* DHEW Publication No. (OHD) 74-21002, 1974.

Pribram, Karl. "Autism: A Deficiency in Context-Dependent Processes?" in Clara Claiborne Park, ed., *Research and Education: Proceedings of the Second Annual Meeting and Conference of the National Society for Autistic Children.* Washington, D.C.: NIMH, 1971. Public Service Publication No. 2164.

Pribram, Karl, ed. *Brain and Behavior.* 4 vols. Harmondsworth, Middlesex: Penguin Books, 1969.

Price, Richard H., and Denner, Bruce, eds. *The Making of a Mental Patient.* New York: Holt, Rinehart and Winston, 1973.

Prien, R. F.; Caffey, Eugene M., Jr.; and Klett, C. J. *Lithium Carbonate in Psychiatry.* Washington, D.C.: American Psychiatric Association, n.d.

"Princess." Letter in *Dear Abby, Chicago Tribune*–New York News Syndicate (April 5, 1973).

"Programs for the Handicapped." Office for the Handicapped. Department of Health, Education and Welfare. November 22, 1974.

Rau, Neil, and Rau, Margaret. *My Dear Ones.* New York: Prentice-Hall, 1971.

"Recent Advances in Psychotherapeutic Drugs and Their Side Effects: A Symposium," *Psychiatric Annals,* 3 (July 1973).

Redlich, Frederick, and Freedman, Daniel X. *The Theory and Practice of Psychiatry.* New York: Basic Books, 1966.

Reed, Louis S. "Utilization of Care for Mental Disorders Under the Blue Cross and Blue Shield for Federal Employees, 1972," *American Journal of Psychiatry,* 131 (September 1974).

Reed, Louis S.; Myers, Evelyn S.; and Scheidemandel, Patricia. *Health Insurance and Psychiatric Care: Utilization and Cost.* Washington, D.C.: American Psychiatric Association, 1972.

Reich, Robert, and Siegel, Lloyd. "The Chronically Mentally Ill Shuffle Off to Oblivion," *Psychiatric Annals,* 3 (November 1973).

Renaud, Harold, and Estes, Floyd. "Life History Interviews with 100 Normal American Males: 'Pathogenicity of Childhood,'" in J. O. Palmer and M. J. Goldstein, eds., *Perspectives in Psychopathology.* New York: Oxford University Press, 1966.

Rexford, Eveoleen. Review of Glasscote *et al., Children and Mental Health Centers,* in *American Journal of Psychiatry,* 130 (July 1973).

Rimland, Bernard. *Infantile Autism: The Syndrome and Its Implications for a Neural Theory of Behavior.* New York: Appleton-Century-Crofts, 1964.

———. "Psychogenesis vs. Biogenesis," in Stanley C. Plog and R. B. Edgerton, eds., *Changing Perspectives in Mental Illness.* New York: Holt, Rinehart and Winston, 1969.

Robbins, Edwin, and Robbins, Lillian. "Charge to the Community: Some Early Effects of a State Hospital System's Change of Policy," *American Journal of Psychiatry,* 131 (June 1974).

Romano, John. Interviewed in "Has Psychiatry Resigned from Medicine?" *Medical Opinion* (January 1973).

Rosenhan, D. L. "On Being Sane in Insane Places," *Science,* 179 (April 27, 1973).

Rosenthal, David, and Kety, Seymour S., eds. *The Transmission of Schizophrenia.* Oxford: Pergamon Press, 1968.

Rosenthal, Robert. *Experimenter Effects in Behavioral Research.* New York: Appleton-Century-Crofts, 1966.

Rosenthal, Robert, and Jacobson, Lenore. *Pygmalion in the Classroom: Teacher Expectation and Pupils' Intellectual Development*. New York: Holt, Rinehart and Winston, 1968.

Rosner, Jerome. *Helping Children Overcome Learning Difficulties: A Step-by-Step Guide for Parents and Teachers*. New York: Walker, 1975.

Rothman, Theodore, ed. *Changing Patterns of Psychiatric Care: An Anthology of Evolving Scientific Psychiatry in Medicine*. New York: Crown Publishers, 1970.

Roueché, Berton. "As Empty as Eve," *The New Yorker* (September 9, 1974).

Ruben, Harvey; Rappaport, Jonas; Szasz, Thomas; and Allen, Richard. "Silence Is Golden – Or Is It?" *MH*, 57 (Winter 1973).

Ruitenbeck, Hendrik A., ed. *Going Crazy: The Radical Therapy of R. D. Laing and Others*. New York: Bantam Books, 1972.

Rusk, Thomas N., and Read, Randolph A. Letter to California Assemblyman John Vasconcellos, reprinted in *Madness Network News*, 3 (April 1975).

Rutter, Michael. *Children of Sick Parents: An Environmental and Psychiatric Study*. London: Maudsley Hospital Monograph No. 16, 1966.

Rutter, M., ed. *Infantile Autism: Concepts, Characteristics and Treatment*. London: Churchill and Livingston, 1971.

Sager, C. J., and Kaplan, H. S. *Progress in Group and Family Therapy*. New York: Brunner/Mazel, 1972.

Sakall, Dan, and Harrington, Alan. *Love and Evil: From a Probation Officer's Casebook*. Boston: Little, Brown, 1974.

Salzman, Leon. Review of R. R. Holt, ed., *New Horizons for Psychotherapy*, in *American Journal of Psychiatry*, 129 (December 1972).

Sampson, H., ed. *Approaches, Contexts, and Problems of Social Psychology*. Englewood Cliffs, N.J.: Prentice-Hall, 1965.

Sampson, H., Messinger, S. L., and Towne, R. D. "Family Processes and Becoming a Mental Patient," in H. Sampson, ed., *Approaches, Contexts, and Problems of Social Psychology*. Englewood Cliffs, N.J.: Prentice-Hall, 1965.

Sarbin, Theodore R. "On the Futility of the Proposition that Some People Be Labeled 'Mentally Ill,'" *Journal of Consulting Psychology*, 31 (1967): 447-453.

Scarf, Maggie. "Which Child Gets Scarred?" *New York Times* (December 3, 1972).

Schafer, Charles, ed. *Therapeutic Use of Children's Play*. New York: Jason Aronson, 1974.

Scheflen, Alfred. *Communicational Structure: Analysis of a Psychotherapy Transaction*. Bloomington, Ind.: Indiana University Press, 1973.

Schildkraut, Joseph J. *Neuropharmacology and the Affective Disorders*. Boston: Little, Brown, 1970.

Schofield, William. *Psychotherapy: The Purchase of Friendship*. Englewood Cliffs, N.J.: Prentice-Hall, 1960.

Schopler, Eric. "Parents of Psychotic Children as Scapegoats," *Journal of Contemporary Psychotherapy*, 4 (1972):1.

Schopler, Eric, and Loftin, J. "Thought Disorders in Parents of Psychotic Children: A Function of Test Anxiety," *Archives of General Psychiatry*, 20 (1969):174-181.

Schopler, Eric, and Reichler, Robert. "Developmental Therapy by Parents with Their Own Autistic Child," in M. Rutter, ed., *Infantile Autism: Concepts, Characteristics, and Treatment*. London: Churchill and Livingston, 1971.

———. "Parents as Co-Therapists in the Treatment of Psychotic Children," *Journal of Autism and Childhood Schizophrenia,* 1 (1971) :87–102.

Schumach, Murray. "Hospital Escape Inquiry Opens," *New York Times* (August 17, 1974) .

Schwartz, Donald A., *et al.* "Community Psychiatry and Emergency Service," *American Journal of Psychiatry,* 129 (December 1972) .

Scott, Robert A., and Houts, Peter. "What Will Therapy Do for Me? or If You Don't Know Where You're Going You'll Never Get There." Pamphlet. Hershey, Pa.: Pennsylvania State University College of Medicine, n.d.

Sèchehaye, M. S. *Symbolic Realization: A New Method of Psychotherapy Applied to a Case of Schizophrenia.* New York: International Universities Press, 1951.

Serban, George, and Thomas, Alexander. "Attitudes and Behaviors of Acute and Chronic Schizophrenic Patients Regarding Ambulatory Treatment," *American Journal of Psychiatry,* 131 (September 1974) .

Serber, M., and Nelson, P. "The Ineffectiveness of Systematic Desensitization and Assertive Training in Hospitalized Schizophrenics," *Journal of Behavior Therapy and Experimental Psychiatry,* 2 (1971) :107-109.

Sereny, Gitta. *The Case of Mary Bell: A Portrait of a Child Who Murdered.* New York: McGraw-Hill, 1973.

"Services Offered the Emotionally Handicapped by the Mental Health Program, Massachusetts Rehabilitation Commission." Boston: MRC M-1-20 M-11-71.

Shader, Richard I., ed. *Manual of Psychiatric Therapeutics: Practical Psychopharmacology and Psychiatry.* Boston: Little, Brown, 1975.

Shanas, Ethel. "The Unmarried Old Person in the U.S.: Living Arrangements and Care in Illness, Myth and Fact." Paper prepared for the International Social Science and Research Seminar in Gerontology, Markaryd, Sweden, August 1963.

Shapiro, L. N. "The Influence of Psychiatry in Medical Education," *Seminars in Psychiatry,* vol. 2, no. 2 (May 1970) .

Shepard, Martin. *The Love Treatment: Sexual Intimacy between Patients and Psychotherapists.* New York: Paperback Library, 1972.

Shulman, Harry, and James, Fleming, Jr. *Cases and Materials on the Law of Torts.* Brooklyn: The Foundation Press. 2nd ed., 1952.

Siegel, Ernest. *The Exceptional Child Grows Up: Guidelines for Understanding and Helping the Brain-Injured Adolescent and Young Adult.* New York: E. P. Dutton, 1974.

Siegler, Miriam, and Osmond, Humphry. *Models of Madness, Models of Medicine.* New York: Macmillan, 1974.

Silverstein, Max. *Psychiatric Aftercare.* Philadelphia: University of Pennsylvania Press, 1968.

Singer, M., and Wynne, Lyman. "Thought Disorder and Family Relations of Schizophrenics." *Archives of General Psychiatry,* 12 (February 1965) .

Sitkin, Peter E., and Kline, J. Anthony. "Financing Public Interest Litigation," 13 *Arizona Law Review* 823 (1971) .

Slovenko, Ralph. *Psychiatry and Law.* Boston: Little, Brown, 1973.

Snyder, Solomon H. *Madness and the Brain.* New York: McGraw-Hill, 1973.

Social Security Administration. *Right to Appeal Supplemental Security Income.* DHEW Publication No. (SSA) 74-10281, November 1973.

———. *Social Security Benefits for People Disabled before Age 22.* DHEW Publication No. (SSA) 73-10012, April 1973.

———. *Social Security Disability Statistics 1967, Programs for the Handicapped.* HEW, August 9, 1971.

"Somebody Cares," *Oasis: A Magazine for Employees of the Social Security Administration* (May 1971).

Spark, Geraldine, and Brody, Elaine. "The Aged Are Family Members," in C. J. Sager and H. S. Kaplan, eds., *Progress in Group and Family Therapy*. New York: Brunner/Mazel, 1972.

Speck, Ross, and Attneave, Carolyn. *Family Networks*. New York: Pantheon Books, 1973.

Spiegel, Don, and Younger, Jenny B. "Life Outside the Hospital: A View from the Patients and Relatives," *Mental Hygiene* (Spring 1972).

Spock, Benjamin. *Raising Children in a Difficult Time*. New York: Norton, 1974.

Srole, Leo, and Langner, Thomas. *Mental Health in the Metropolis: The Midtown Manhattan Study*. New York: McGraw-Hill, 1962.

Stefan, Gregor. *In Search of Sanity*. Hyde Park, N.Y.: University Books, n.d.

Stern, Edith. *Mental Illness: A Guide for the Family*. New York: Commonwealth Fund, 1944; revised edition, 1968.

Stotsky, Bernard. *The Nursing Home and the Aged Psychiatric Patient*. New York: Appleton-Century-Crofts–Meredith Publishing Company, 1970.

Stotsky, Bernard A. "Social and Clinical Issues in Geriatric Psychiatry." *American Journal of Psychiatry,* 129 (August 1972).

Stuecher, Uwe. *Tommy: A Treatment Study of an Autistic Child*. Arlington, Va.: Council for Exceptional Children, n.d.

Szasz, Thomas. "The Myth of Mental Illness," *American Psychologist,* 15 (February 1960).

———. Reply to Letter, *American Journal of Psychiatry* (June 1972):128.

Szurek, S. A., and Berlin, I. N., eds. *Clinical Studies in Childhood Psychoses*. New York: Brunner/Mazel, 1973.

Szurek, S. A., and Berlin, I. N. "The Problem of Blame in Therapy with Parents and Children," in S. A. Szurek and I. N. Berlin, eds., *Clinical Studies in Childhood Psychoses*. New York: Brunner/Mazel, 1973.

Taylor, Robert L., and Torrey, E. Fuller. "Mental Health Coverage Under a National Insurance Plan," *World Journal of Psychosynthesis,* 6 (1974): 22-27.

Thompson, Travis. "Behavior Therapy in Treating Acute Major Psychoses," *Center for Behavior Modification Newsletter,* 1 (May 1974).

Toll, Nina. Letter, *Schizophrenia Bulletin,* 4 (Fall 1971).

Tolstoy, Leo. *My Confession*. New York: Crowell, 1887; excerpt in B. Kaplan, ed., *The Inner World of Mental Illness*. New York: Harper and Row, 1964.

Torrey, E. Fuller. *The Death of Psychiatry*. Radnor, Pa.: Chilton, 1974.

———. *The Mind Game: Witchdoctors and Psychiatrists*. New York: Emerson Hall, 1972.

Tourney, Garfield. "Psychiatric Therapies, 1800–1968," in Theodore Rothman, ed., *Changing Patterns in Psychiatric Care*. New York: Crown Publishers, 1970.

Trace, Barbara, and Kastein, Shulamith. *The Birth of Language*. Springfield, Ill.: Charles C. Thomas Publishing Co., 1966.

Truax, C. B., and Carkhuff, R. R. *Towards Effective Counseling and Psychotherapy*. Chicago: Aldine, 1973.

Unger, Sanford M. "Mescaline, LSD, Psilocybin and Personality Change," in James O. Palmer and Michael Goldstein, eds., *Perspectives in Psychopathology*. New York: Oxford University Press, 1966.

Vaillant, George. "Why Men Seek Psychotherapy: I. Results of a Survey of College Graduates," *American Journal of Psychiatry,* 129 (December 1972).

Viscott, David. *The Making of a Psychiatrist.* New York: Arbor House, 1972.

Vonnegut, Mark. *The Eden Express: A Personal Account of Schizophrenia.* New York: Praeger, 1975.

———. "Why I Want to Bite R. D. Laing," *Harpers* (April 1974).

Waugh, Steve. "How to Choose Your Psychotherapist," *The Boston Phoenix* (October 3, 1972).

Walkenstein, Eilen. *Beyond the Couch.* New York: Crown, 1972.

Wang, H. Shan. "Special Diagnostic Procedures – The Evaluation of Brain Impairment," in E. W. Busse and E. Pfeiffer, *Mental Illness in Later Life.* Washington, D.C.: American Psychiatric Association, 1973.

Wechsler, James A., with Wechsler, Nancy F., and Karpf, Holly W. *In a Darkness.* New York: W. W. Norton, 1972.

Weed, Lawrence. *The POMR Patient Book: Problem Oriented Medical Record, a Key to Better Health Care.* Greene, 1974.

Weinreb, Lloyd. *Criminal Law, Cases, Comment, Questions.* Mineola, N.Y.: The Foundation Press, 1969.

Weiss, Robert J.; Kleinman, Joel C.; Brandt, Ursula C.; Feldman, Jacob J.; and McGuinness, Aims C. "Foreign Medical Graduates and the Medical Underground," *New England Journal of Medicine,* 290 (June 20, 1974).

Wender, Paul. *The Hyperactive Child: A Handbook for Parents.* New York: Crown Publishers, 1973.

West, Paul. *Words for a Deaf Daughter.* New York: Harper and Row, 1970.

Wexler, David B. "Token and Taboo: Behavior Modification, Token Economies, and the Law," 61 *California Law Review* 81–109 (1973).

"What Can the Commonwealth of Massachusetts Do for You If You Are Disabled?" Boston: MRC Pub. 1-30 M-71-050686.

Wheelis, Allen. *How People Change.* New York: Harper and Row, 1973.

White, Robin. *Be Not Afraid.* New York: Dial Press, 1972.

Whittier, John R.; Heimler, Audrey; and Korenyi, Charles. "The Psychiatrist and Huntington's Disease (Chorea)," *American Journal of Psychiatry,* 128 (June 1972).

Wiener, Daniel. *A Practical Guide to Psychotherapy.* New York: Harper and Row, 1968.

Will, Otto. "What Riggs Is All About," *Berkshire Eagle* (April 15, 1972).

Wilson, Louise. *This Stranger, My Son: A Mother's Story.* New York: Putnam, 1968; NAL, 1968.

Wing, J. K.; Leff, Julian; and Hirsch, Steven. "Preventive Treatment of Schizophrenia: Some Theoretical and Methodological Issues," in J. O. Cole, A. M. Freedman, and A. J. Friedhoff, eds., *Psychopathology and Psychopharmacology.* Baltimore: Johns Hopkins University Press, 1973.

Wing, J. K., and Nixon, Janice. "Discriminating Symptoms in Schizophrenia: A Report from the International Pilot Study of Schizophrenia." Manuscript [1975] accepted for *Archives of General Psychiatry.*

Wing, Lorna. *Autistic Children, A Guide for Parents and Professionals.* New York: Brunner/Mazel, 1972.

———. "The Handicaps of Autistic Children," in *Autism: Proceedings of the Fourth Annual Meeting of the National Society for Autistic Children, June 1972.* Washington, D.C.: DHEW Publication No. (ADM) 74-2.

Wisconsin, State Bar of, Special Committee on the Legal Needs of the Mentally Retarded. *Planning for Their Future.* Madison, Wisconsin: n.d.

Wolberg, Lewis R. *The Technique of Psychotherapy*. New York: Grune and Stratton. 2nd ed., 1967.

Wolfe, Mary Ellen. *Aftershock: The Story of a Psychotic Episode*. New York: Putnam, 1969.

Wolman, B. B., ed. *Manual of Child Psychopathology*. New York: McGraw-Hill, 1972.

Woolf, Leonard. *Beginning Again*. New York: Harcourt, Brace and World, 1964.

Woolf, Virginia. *Mrs. Dalloway*. New York: Modern Library, 1928.

Wynne, Lyman C. "Family Research on the Pathogenesis of Schizophrenia," in C. J. Sager and H. S. Kaplan, eds., *Progress in Group and Family Therapy*. New York: Brunner/Mazel, 1972.

Zneimer, Leonard. "Disappearing in the Community." *The Exceptional Parent*, 4 (May/June 1974).

Zubin, J., ed. *Disorders of Mood*. Baltimore: Johns Hopkins Press, 1972.

Zusman, Jack, and Carnahan, William. *Mental Health: New York Law and Practice*. 2 vols. New York: Matthew Bender, 1975.

II: Law Cases

In re John Ballay, 482 F.2d 648 (1973).

Bartley et al. v. Kremens et al., Civil Action No. 72-272, U.S. D. Ct., E.D., Pa. (1975).

Durham v. U.S., 214 F.2d 862 (D.C. Cir. 1954).

Eisen v. Carlisle and Jacquelin, et al., 417 U.S. 156, 94 S. Ct. 2140 (1974).

Faber v. Sweet Style Manufacturing Corporation, 242 N.Y.S. 2d 763 (1963).

Ex parte Hodges, 166 Tex. Crim. Rep. 433; 314 S.W.: 2d 581, 584 (1958).

Jackson v. Indiana, 406 U.S. 715 (1972), 730, 737-8.

Kaimowitz v. Department of Mental Health for the State of Michigan, et al., Circuit Court, Wayne County, Michigan, No. 73-19434-AW.

Daniel M'Naghten's Case, 10 Cl. and F. 200, 8 Eng. Rep. 718 (Hil. 1843).

Mills v. Board of Education of the District of Columbia, 348 F. Supp. 866 (1972).

Newman v. Piggie Park Enterprises, 390 U.S. 400 (1968).

O'Connor v. Donaldson, 95 S. Ct. 2486 (1975).

Pennsylvania Association for Retarded Children v. Comm. of Pa., 334 F. Supp. 1257 (1971).

People ex. rel. Simpkins v. Director of Pilgrim State Hospital, 22 AD 2d 699.

Souder v. Brennan, 367 F. Supp. 808 (1973).

Streda Estate, 137 *Legal Intell.* No. 97 at 1, Col. 3 (Delaware Cty. Orphans Ct., Nov. 6, 1957).

Walker v. McCoy, 40 Tenn. 103, 105 (1859).

Weaver v. Ward, K.B. 1617, Hobart 134, 80 Engl. Reprint, 284.

Willey v. Willey (Iowa), 115 N.W., 2d 833.

In re Estate of Willits, 175 Cal. 173 (1917).

Winters v. Miller, 446 F.2d 65, 1971.

Wyatt vs. Stickney, 325 F. Supp. 781, 334 F. Supp. 1341 (M.D. Ala. 1971), 344 F. Supp. 373 & 387 (M.D. Ala. 1972), *aff'd in part subnom. Wyatt v. Aderholt*, 502 F. 2d 1305 (5th Cir., 1974).

Index

For the explanation of a term, turn to the page indicated in boldface.

Index of Names

Names found only in backnotes or appendices are not listed; for these, see Bibliography or Reading List.